C

Turkish Dictionary

Türkçe–İngilizce
İngilizce-Türkçe

HarperCollins Publishers
Westerhill Road
Bishopbriggs
Glasgow
G64 2QT
Great Britain

First Edition 2010

10 9 8 7 6

ISBN 978-0-00-732471-2

www.collinslanguage.com

A catalogue record for this book is available from the British Library

Typesetting by Lingea s.r.o.
Printed in China by South China Printing Company Ltd.

Acknowledgements
We would like to thank those authors and publishers who kindly gave permission for copyright material to be used in the Collins Word Web. We would also like to thank Times Newspapers Ltd for providing valuable data.

Series Editor
Rob Scriven

Managing Editor
Gaëlle Amiot-Cadey

Editor
Rachel Smith

Contributor
Joyce Littlejohn

İÇİNDEKİLER

CONTENTS

GİRİŞ

Bu Türkçe sözlüğü almaya karar verdiğiniz için teşekkür ederiz, umarız bu sözlüğü evde, tatilde ya da iş yerinizde kullanmaktan keyif alır ve faydalanırsınız.

INTRODUCTION

We are delighted that you have decided to buy this Turkish dictionary and hope you will enjoy and benefit from using it at home, on holiday or at work.

KISALTMALAR

ABBREVIATIONS

sıfat	*adj*	adjective
zarf	*adv*	adverb
ünlem	*excl*	exclamation
konuşma dili (!argo)	*inf (!)*	colloquial (! offensive)
edat	*prep*	preposition
zarf	*pron*	pronoun
isim	*n*	noun
dişil	*f*	feminine
eril	*m*	masculine
cinssiz	*nt*	neuter
çoğul	*pl*	plural
fiil	*v*	verb

TURKISH PRONUNCIATION

VOWELS

a	[a]	*kapı*	like *a* in *car*
e	[e]	*gelir*	like *e* in *pet*
ı	[ə]	*kapı*	like *e* in *open*
i	[i]	*iki*	like *i* in *machine*
o	[o]	*mor*	like *o* in *more*
ö	[ø]	*öğrenci*	like *u* in *burn*
u	[u]	*uyku*	like *u* in *rude*
ü	[y]	*üzgün*	like *u* in *cube*

CONSONANTS

c	[j]	cam	like *j* in *john*
ç	[tʃ]	çağdaş	like *ch* in *chain* or *c* in *cello*
ğ	[:]	ağaç	silent letter, which doubles the length of the previous vowel
j	[ʒ]	ajans	like *s* in *measure*
ş	[ʃ]	şeftali	like *sh* in *share* or *s* in *sugar*

b, d, g, h, k, l, m, n, p, r, s, t, v, y, and z are pronounced as in English.

STRESS
The rules of stress in Turkish are as follows:

(a) The main stress usually occurs on the last syllable of a word:
ara'ba (car), ka'dın (woman), or'tak (partner)

(b) For proper names, the stress occurs on the penultimate syllable, unless the penultimate syllable is light and the antepenultimate syllable is heavy:
Penultimate:
An'talya, O'regon, İs'tanbul
Antepenultimate:
'Ankara

(c) The regular stress pattern occurs on words where suffixes are added to stems. The stress shifts away from the stem as suffixes are concatenated:
el'ma (apple)
elma'lar (apples)
elmalar'ım (my apples)

In the phonetic transcription, the symbol ['] precedes the syllable on which the stress falls.

İNGILIZCE TELAFFUZ

	İngilizce Örnek	*Açıklamalar*
[ɑ:]	**fa**ther	Türkçede karşılığı tam olarak bulunmaz. Uzatılmış *a* sesinin sonuna *ğ* eklenmiş halidir.
[ʌ]	b**u**t, c**o**me	Türkçedeki *a* sesidir. Örnek olarak *kapı* verilebilir
[æ]	m**a**n, c**a**t	Türkçede tam olarak karşılığı bulunmaz. *a* ile *e* sesleri arasındaki bir sese benzer.
[ə]	fath**er**, **a**go	Türkçede tam olarak karşılığı bulunmaz. *a* ile *ı* sesleri arasındaki bir sese benzer.
[ə]	b**i**rd, h**ea**rd	Köprü, Göz gibi sözcüklerdeki *ö* sesinin biraz daha uzatılmış halidir.
[ɛ]	g**e**t, b**e**d	Türkçedeki *e* sesinin tam karşılığıdır. Örnek olarak *Eylül* verilebilir.
[i]	**i**t, b**i**g	Türkçedeki *i* sesinin tam karşılığıdır. Örnek olarak *Simit* verilebilir.
[i]	**tea**, **see**	Türkçedeki *i* sesinin uzatılmış halidir.
[ɔ]	h**o**t, w**a**sh	Türkçede tam olarak karşılığı bulunmaz. Yine de *o* sesine çok benzer. Tam olarak *o* sesinin sonuna hafif bir *a* eklenmiş hali denilebilir.
[ɔ]	s**aw**, **a**ll	Türkçede tam olarak karşılığı bulunmaz. Uzunca söylenen *oğ* sesine benzer.
[u]	p**u**t, b**oo**k	Türkçedeki *u* sesinin karşılığıdır. Örnek olarak *dokuz* verilebilir.
[u]	**too**, **you**	Türkçede tam olarak karşılığı bulunmaz. Uzunca söylenen *ıu* sesine benzer.

[ai]	fl**y**, h**i**gh	Hızlıca *ai* sesinin çıkarılmasına benzer.
[au]	h**ow**, h**ou**se	Hızlıca *au* sesinin çıkarılmasına benzer.
[ɛə]	th**ere**, b**ear**	Hızlıca *eı* sesinin çıkarılmasına benzer.
[ei]	d**ay**, ob**ey**	Hızlıca *ei* sesinin çıkarılmasına benzer.
[iə]	h**ere**, h**ear**	Hızlıca *iı* sesinin çıkarılmasına benzer.
[əu]	g**o**, n**o**te	Hızlıca *ıu* sesinin çıkarılmasına benzer. Fakat buradaki *ı* sesi, *ı* ile *a* arası bir sestir.
[ɔi]	b**oy**, **oi**l	Hızlıca *oi* sesinin çıkarılmasına benzer.
[uə]	p**oo**r, s**ure**	Hızlıca *ıuı* sesinin çıkarılmasına benzer. Buradaki ikinci *ı* sesi yine *ı* ile *a* arası bir sestir.

[ʤ]	**g**in, ju**dg**e	Türkçedeki *c* sesinin tam karşılığıdır. Örnek olarak Cuma verilebilir.
[ŋ]	si**ng**	Türkçede tam olarak karşılığı bulunmaz. *ng* sesinin çıkartılmasına benzer fakat sondaki *g* sesi tam olarak söylenmez, böylelikle uzatılmış bir *n* sesine benzer bir ses elde edilir.
[k]	**c**ome, mo**ck**	Türkçedeki *k* sesinin tam karşılığıdır. Örnek olarak *k*apı verilebilir.
[z]	ro**s**e, **z**ebra	Türkçedeki *z* sesinin tam karşılığıdır. Örnek olarak *z*or verilebilir.
[ʃ]	**sh**e, ma**ch**ine	Türkçedeki *ş* sesinin tam karşılığıdır. Örnek olarak *ş*eref verilebilir.

[tʃ]	**ch**in, ri**ch**	Türkçedeki *ç* sesinin tam karşılığıdır. Örnek olarak çocuk verilebilir.
[w]	**w**ater, **wh**ich	Türkçede tam olarak karşılığı bulunmaz. *v* sesinden önce *u* sesi varmış gibi okunur fakat u sesinin yalnızca son kısmı söylenir.
[ʒ]	vi**s**ion	Türkçedeki *j* sesinin tam karşılığıdır. Örnek olarak ajanda verilebilir.
[θ]	**th**ink, my**th**	Türkçede tam olarak karşılığı bulunmaz. *t* ile s sesleri arasındaki bir sese benzer. Bu sesi çıkartmak için dil dişler arasında sıkıştırılarak sert bir şekilde *t* sesi çıkartılmaya çalışılır.
[ð]	**th**is, **th**e	Türkçede tam olarak karşılığı bulunmaz. *d* ile s sesleri arasındaki bir sese benzer. Bu sesi çıkartmak için dil dişler arasında sıkıştırılarak sert bir şekilde *d* sesi çıkartılmaya çalışılır.

Fonetik çevriyazıda, [ʳ] simgesi, İngiliz İngilizcesinde ardından gelen sözcük sesli harf ile başlıyorsa çok hafif şekilde telaffuz edilen sözcük sonundaki 'r' harfini temsil eder. Fonetik çevriyazıda, [ˈ] simgesi vurgunun olduğu heceden önce kullanılır.

SAYILAR		NUMBERS
sıfır	0	zero
bir	1	one
iki	2	two
üç	3	three
dört	4	four
beş	5	five
altı	6	six
yedi	7	seven
sekiz	8	eight
dokuz	9	nine
on	10	ten
on bir	11	eleven
on iki	12	twelve
on üç	13	thirteen
on dört	14	fourteen
on beş	15	fifteen
on altı	16	sixteen
on yedi	17	seventeen
on sekiz	18	eighteen
on dokuz	19	nineteen
yirmi	20	twenty

yirmi bir	21	twenty-one
yirmi iki	22	twenty-two
yirmi üç	23	twenty-three
otuz	30	thirty
otuz bir	31	thirty-one
kırk	40	fourty
elli	50	fifty
altmış	60	sixty
yetmiş	70	seventy
seksen	80	eighty
doksan	90	ninety
yüz	100	one hundred
yüz on	110	one hundered and ten
iki yüz	200	two hundred
iki yüz elli	250	two hundred and fifty
bin	1,000	one thousand
bir milyon	1,000,000	one million

HAFTANIN GÜNLERİ	DAYS OF THE WEEK
Pazartesi	Monday
Salı	Tuesday
Çarşamba	Wednesday
Perşembe	Thursday
Cuma	Friday
Cumartesi	Saturday
Pazar	Sunday

MESES	MONTHS
Ocak	January
Şubat	February
Mart	March
Nisan	April
Mayıs	May
Haziran	June
Temmuz	July
Ağustos	August
Eylül	September
Ekim	October
Kasım	November
Aralık	December

TURKISH–ENGLISH
TÜRKÇE–İNGILIZCE

a

AB [ap] *abbr* EU
abajur [abaʒur] *n* lampshade
abartı [abartə] *n* exaggeration
abartmak [abartmak] *v* exaggerate
ABD [abd] *n* USA
abonelik [abonelik] *n* subscription
abonman [abonman] *n* **abonman kartı** *n* season ticket; **tren abonmanı** *n* railcard
abseiling [abseiling] *n* **Abseiling yapmak isterdim** I'd like to go abseiling
Abu Dabi [abudabi] *n* Abu Dhabi
acaip [adʒaip] *adj* odd, weird
acele [adʒele] *n* hurry ▷ *v* **acele etmek** *v* hurry, hurry up; **Acelem var** I'm in a hurry
acemi [adʒemi] *adj* green *(inexperienced)*
acemice [adʒemidʒe] *adj* poorly
acenta [adʒenta] *n* **seyahat acentası** *n* travel agency, travel agent's, *(kişi)* travel agent
acı [adʒə] *adj (tat)* bitter ▷ *n* pain, *(biber)* chilli; **acı çekmek** *v* suffer; **sıla acısı çeken** *adj* homesick; **Burası acıyor** I have a pain here
acık [adʒək] *n* **acıklı bir şekilde** *adv* sadly
acılı [adʒələ] *adj* painful, spicy
acıma [adʒəma] *n (duygu)* pity
acımak [adʒəmak] *v* pity
acımasız [adʒəmasəz] *adj* ruthless
acınası [adʒənasə] *adj* pathetic
acil [adʒil] *adj* immediate; **acil çıkış kapısı** *n* emergency exit; **acil durum** *n* emergency; **acil iniş** *n* emergency landing; **kaza & acil servis** *n* accident & emergency department
acre [adʒre] *n* acre
aç [atʃ] *adj (karın)* hungry; **kurt gibi aç** *adj* ravenous; **Aç değilim** I'm not hungry
açacak [atʃadʒak] *n* **kalem açacağı** *n* pencil sharpener; **kutu açacağı** *n* can-opener, tin-opener; **şişe açacağı** *n* bottle-opener
açgözlü [atʃgøzly] *adj* greedy
açı [atʃə] *n* angle; **bakış açısı** *n* aspect; **dik açı** *n* right angle
açığa çıkarmak *v* bare
açık [atʃək] *adj (hava vb)* clear, *(kapı, pencere vb)* open, *(kavram)* obvious, *(renk)* light *(not dark)* ▷ *adv* on ▷ *n (finans)* deficit; **açık arttırma** *n* auction; **açık çek** *n* blank cheque; **açık büfe** *n* buffet; **açık fikirli** *adj* broad-minded; **açık görüşlü** *adj* liberal; **açık hava** *adj* outdoor; **açık havada** *adv*

out-of-doors, outdoors; **açık iş** *n* vacancy; **açık renk** *(ten/saç) adj* fair *(light colour)*; **açık saçık** *adj* obscene; **açık sözlü** *adj* outspoken, straightforward; **açıkça fikrini söylemek** *v* speak up; **açıklık kazandırmak** *v* clarify; **mali açıklık** *n* shortfall; **rüzgara açık** *adj* bleak; **rekabete açık** *adj* competitive; **Açık mısınız?** Are you open?; **Banka bugün açık mı?** Is the bank open today?; **Bugün açık mı?** Is it open today?; **Müze ne zaman açık?** When is the museum open?; **Saray ne zaman açık?** When is the palace open?; **Tapınak ne zaman açık?** When is the temple open?; **Yarın açık mı?** Is it open tomorrow?

açıkça [atʃəktʃa] *adv* apparently, clearly

açıkçası [atʃəktʃasə] *adv* obviously

açıklama [atʃəklama] *n (beyan)* statement, *(izah)* explanation

açıklamak [atʃəklamak] *vi* explain; **kamuoyuna açıklamak** *v* issue

açıklık [atʃəklək] *n (aralık)* aperture

açılır [atʃələr] *adj* **üstü açılır araba** *n* convertible

açılış [atʃələʃ] *n* **açılış saatleri** *npl* opening hours; **açılış sayfası** *n* home page

açlık [atʃlək] *n* hunger; **açlık çekmek** *v* starve; **Açım** I'm hungry

açmak [atʃmak] *v* turn on, *(paket)* unwrap, *(paket, fermuar vb)* undo, *(rulo/sargı)* unroll ▷ *vt (kapı vb)* open, *(sargı)* unwind; **çiçek açmak** *v* blossom, flower; **fermuarı açmak** *v* unzip; **şalter açmak** *v* switch on; **oturum açmak** *v* log in, log on; **yol açmak** *v* cause

ad [ad] *n (gramer)* noun, *(kişi)* name; **adın baş harfleri** *n* initials; **adının ön harflerini yazmak** *v* initial; **ön ad** *n* first name; **ön adı** *n* Christian name; **diğer adıyla** *prep* alias; **takma ad** *n* alias, nickname, pseudonym; **... adına yer ayırtmıştım** I booked a room in the name of...; **Adınız ne?** What's your name?; **Benim adım...** My name is...

ada [ada] *n* island; **ıssız ada** *n* desert island; **Mauritius Adası** *n* Mauritius

Ada [ada] *n* **Bahama Adaları** *n* Bahamas; **Batı Hint Adaları** *npl* West Indian, West Indies; **Faroe Adaları** *npl* Faroe Islands; **Kanarya Adaları** *n* Canaries; **Polonezya Adaları** *n* Polynesia

adalet [adalet] *n* justice

adaletsizlik [adaletsizlik] *n* injustice

adam [adam] *n* guy; **bilim adamı** *n* scientist; **iş adamı** *n* businessman; **kardan adam** *n* snowman

adanmış [adanməʃ] *adj* dedicated

adaptör [adaptør] *n* adaptor

aday [adaj] *n* candidate; **aday göstermek** *v* nominate

adaylık [adajlək] *n* nomination

adet [adet] *n (gelenek)* custom

adım [adəm] *n* footstep, pace, step; **adım adım** *adv* gradually;

uygun adım yürümek *v* march; **uygun adım yürümek** *v* keep up with
adımlamak [adəmlamak] *v* tread
adil [adil] *adj* fair *(reasonable)*
adres [adres] *n* address *(location)*; **adres defteri** *n* address book; **adres listesi** *n* mailing list; **e-posta adresi** *n* email address; **ev adresi** *n* home address; **internet adresi** *n* web address; **Adresi yazar mısınız lütfen?** Will you write down the address, please?; **İnternet adresi...** The website address is...; **Mektuplarımı şu adrese gönderin lütfen** Please send my mail on to this address
Adriyatik [adrijatik] *adj* Adriatic
Adriyatik Denizi [adrijatikdenizi] *n* Adriatic Sea
adsız [adsəz] *adj* anonymous
aerobik [aerobik] *npl* aerobics
aerosol [aerosol] *n* aerosol
aferin [aferin] *excl* well done!
affedersiniz [affedersiniz] excuse me, sorry
Afgan [afgan] *adj* Afghan ▷ *n* Afghan
Afganistan [afganistan] *n* Afghanistan
afiyet [afijet] *n* appetite; **Afiyet olsun!** Enjoy your meal!
afiyette [afijette] *adj* well
Afrika [afrika] *n* Africa; **Güney Afrika** *adj* South Africa, South African; **Kuzey Afrika** *adj* North Africa, North African; **Orta Afrika Cumhuriyeti** *n* Central African Republic
Afrikaanca [afrikaandʒa] *n* Afrikaans
Afrikalı [afrikalə] *adj* African ▷ *n* African; **Güney Afrikalı** *n* South African; **Kuzey Afrikalı** *n* North African
Afrikaner [afrikaner] *n* Afrikaner
ağ [aː] *n* web, *(bilişim)* network; **örümcek ağı** *n* cobweb
ağac [aːadʒ] *n* **köknar ağacı** *n* fir (tree)
ağaç [aːatʃ] *n* tree ▷ *adj* wooden; **ağaç üflemeli** *(çalgı) n* woodwind; **ağaç gövdesi** *n* trunk; **ağaç işleri** *n* woodwork; **huş ağacı** *n* birch; **kayın ağacı** *n* beech (tree); **Noel ağacı** *n* Christmas tree; **porsuk ağacı** *n* yew; **zeytin ağacı** *n* olive tree
ağartıcı [aːartədʒə] *n* bleach
ağartılmış [aːartəlməʃ] *adj* bleached
ağır [aːər] *adj* heavy; **ağır bir şekilde** *adv* heavily; **ağır yük taşıma aracı** *n* HGV; **Bu çok ağır** This is too heavy
ağırlık [aːərlək] *n* weight; **ağırlık kaldırma** *n* weightlifting; **kağıt ağırlığı** *n* paperweight
ağız [aːəz] *n* mouth, *(çaydanlık vb)* rim; **ağız dalaşı** *v* squabble; **dört yol ağzı** *n* crossroads; **kol ağzı** *n* sleeve
ağlamak [aːlamak] *n* cry ▷ *v* cry, weep; **hıçkırarak ağlamak** *v* sob
ağrı [aːrə] *n* ache; **ağrı kesici** *n* painkiller; **baş ağrısı** *n* headache; **diş ağrısı** *n* toothache; **kulak ağrısı** *n* earache; **mide ağrısı** *n* stomachache; **sırt ağrısı** *n* back

pain, backache; **Ağrıyor** It's sore
ağrılı [a:rələ] *adj* sore
ağrımak [a:rəmak] *v* ache
Ağustos [a:ustos] *n* August
ahbap [ahbap] *n* mate
ahçı [ahtʃə] *n* cook
ahır [ahər] *n* stable
ahlak [ahlak] *n* **ahlak dışı** *adj* immoral; **ahlak kuralları** *npl* morals
ahlaki [ahlaki] *adj* ethical, moral
ahmak [ahmak] *n* fool
ahpap [ahpap] *n* chap
ahtapot [ahtapot] *n* octopus
ahududu [ahududu] *n* raspberry
AIDS [aids] *n* AIDS
aile [aile] *n* family; **aile oyunları** *n* board game; **eşinin ailesi** *npl* in-laws; **koruyucu aile bakımındaki çocuk** *n* foster child; **koruyucu aile olmak** *v* foster; **Aile odası ayırtmak istiyorum** I want to reserve a family room; **Aile odası istiyorum** I'd like to book a family room; **Ailemle geldim** I'm here with my family
ait [ait] *n* **ait olmak** *v* belong, belong to; **Georgia'ya ait** *adj* Georgian; **Hollanda'ya ait** *n* Dutch; **Lübnan'a ait** *n* Lebanese; **Meksika'ya ait** *n* Mexican
ajans [aʒans] *n* agency
ak [ak] *n* **yumurta akı** *n* egg white
akademi [akademi] *n* academy; **akademik yıl** *n* academic year
akademik [akademik] *adj* academic
akbaba [akbaba] *n* vulture
akciğer [akdʒjier] *n* lung
akçaağaç [aktʃaa:atʃ] *n* maple
Akdeniz [akdeniz] *adj* Mediterranean ▷ *n* Mediterranean
akdiken [akdiken] *n* hawthorn
akıcı [akədʒə] *adj* fluent
akıl [akəl] *adj* mental; **akıl hastanesi** *n* mental hospital; **akıllı dokunuş** *n* touchpad; **akıllı telefon** *n* smart phone; **akıllıca olmayan** *adj* unwise
akıllı [akəllə] *adj* brainy, wise
akıllıca [akəllədʒa] *adj* advisable, rational
akım [akəm] *n* current *(electricity)*; **moda akımı** *n* trend
akın [akən] *n* **akın etmek** *v* invade
akıntı [akəntə] *n (nezle)* catarrh
akış [akəʃ] *n* current *(flow)*
akmak [akmak] *v* flow ▷ *vt* pour
akne [akne] *n* spot *(blemish)*
akordiyon [akordijon] *n* accordion
akraba [akraba] *adj* related; **en yakın akraba** *n* next-of-kin
akrep [akrep] *n* scorpion
Akrep [akrep] *n* **Akrep burcu** *n* Scorpio
akrobat [akrobat] *n* acrobat
aksesuar [aksesuar] *n* accessory
aksi [aksi] *prep* **saatin aksi yönünde** *adv* anticlockwise; **ya da aksine** *adv* vice versa
akşam [akʃam] *n* evening, in the evening; **akşam okulu** *n* evening class; **akşam yemeği** *n* dinner; **akşamdan kalma** *n* hangover; **hafif akşam yemeği** *n* supper; **kahvaltı ve akşam yemeği dahil** *n* half board; **İyi akşamlar** Good evening; **Bu akşam ne yapıyorsunuz?** What are you

doing this evening?; **Burada akşamları yapılabilecek ne var?** What is there to do in the evenings?; **Masa bu akşam saat dokuz için rezerve edildi** The table is booked for nine o'clock this evening
aktarım [aktarəm] *n (doku/organ)* transplant; **kan aktarımı** *n* transfusion
aktif [aktif] *adj* active
aktivite [aktivite] *n* **aktivite tatili** *n* activity holiday
aktör [aktør] *n* actor
akupunktur [akupuŋtur] *n* acupuncture
akustik [akustik] *adj* acoustic
akü [aky] *n* **Akü çalışmıyor** The battery is flat; **Yeni bir akü gerekiyor** I need a new battery
akvaryum [akvarjum] *n* aquarium
alabalık [alabalək] *n* trout
alabora [alabora] *v* **alabora olmak** *v* capsize
alacakaranlık [aladʒakaranlək] *n* dusk
alakasız [alakasəz] *adj* irrelevant
alan [alan] *n (ölçü birimi)* area, *(yer)* site; **alan kodu** *n* postcode; **çalışma alanı** *n* workspace; **çöp döküm alanı** *n* rubbish dump; **çim alan** *n* lawn; **fuar alanı** *n* fairground; **inşaat alanı** *n* building site; **kapalı alan** *adj* indoor; **konaklama alanı** *n* service area; **koruma alanı** *n* reserve *(land)*; **oyun alanı** *n* playground, playing field; **paten alanı** *n* rink, skating rink
alarm [alarm] *n* alarm; **duman alarmı** *n* smoke alarm; **hırsız alarmı** *n* burglar alarm; **yangın alarmı** *n* fire alarm; **yanlış alarm** *n* false alarm
alay [alaj] *n (askeri)* regiment, *(tören/gelin)* procession; **alay etmek** *v* mock; **alay etmek** *v* scoff; **ince alay** *n* irony; **tören alayı** *n* parade
alaycı [alajdʒə] *adj* ironic, sarcastic
albay [albaj] *n* colonel
albüm [albym] *n (müzik, fotoğraf)* album; **fotoğraf albümü** *n* photo album
alçak [altʃak] *adj* lousy; **alçak gönüllü** *adj* humble, modest
aldırmak [aldərmak] *vi* mind
alerji [alerʒi] *n* allergy; **buğday alerjisi** *n* wheat intolerance; **fıstık alerjisi** *n* nut allergy, peanut allergy
alerjik [alerʒik] *adj* allergic
alet [alet] *n* instrument; **kayıt aleti** *n* recorder *(scribe)*; **şarj aleti** *n* charger; **müzik aleti** *n* musical instrument
alev [alev] *n* flame; **parlak alev** *n* blaze
alfabe [alfabe] *n* alphabet
alıcı [alədʒə] *n* buyer, receiver *(electronic)*, *(kişi)* recipient
alım [aləm] *n* **bagaj alım** *n* baggage reclaim
alın [alən] *n* forehead
alınmış [alənməʃ] *adj* **satın alınmış** *adj* bought
alıntı [aləntə] *n* quotation, quote ▷ *v* **alıntı yapmak** *v* quote
alışılagelmiş [aləʃəlagelmiʃ] *adj*

usual
alışılmadık [aləʃəlmadək] *adj* unusual
alışkanlık [aləʃkanlək] *n* habit
alışveriş [aləʃveriʃ] *n* shopping; **alışveriş çantası** *n* shopping bag; **alışveriş merkezi** *n* shopping centre; **alışveriş torbası** *n* carrier bag
alkış [alkəʃ] *n* applause
alkışlamak [alkəʃlamak] *v* applaud
alkışlanmak [alkəʃlanmak] *vi* clap
alkol [alkol] *n* alcohol; **alkollü içki** *npl* spirits; **düşük alkollü** *adj* low-alcohol; **Bunda alkol var mı?** Does that contain alcohol?
alkolik [alkolik] *n* alcoholic
alkollü [alkolly] *adj* alcoholic
alkolsüz [alkolsyz] *adj* alcohol-free
Allah [allah] *n* Allah
allık [allək] *n* blusher
alma [alma] *n* **eleman alma** *n* recruitment
almak [almak] *v* get, get *(to a place)*, receive ▷ *vt* take, take *(time)*; **askıya alma** *n* suspension; **askıya almak** *v* suspend; **ödünç almak** *v* borrow; **garantiye almak** *v* ensure; **gözaltına alma** *n* detention; **geri almak** *v* take back; **hafife almak** *v* underestimate; **içeri almak** *v* admit *(allow in)*; **içeriye almak** *v* let in; **ileriye almak** *v* put forward; **işe alma** *n* employment; **işe almak** *v* employ; **miras almak** *v* inherit; **nefes alma** *n* breathing; **nefes almak** *v* breathe, breathe in; **not almak** *v* jot down, note down; **risk almak** *v* risk; **satın alma** *(şirket) n* buyout; **satın almak** *v* buy, purchase; **sıkı tedbirler almak** *v* crack down on; **toz almak** *vt* dust; **yönetimi ele almak** *v* take over; **yeniden ele almak** *vt* reconsider; **yerden almak** *v* pick up; **yerini alma** *n* replacement; **yerini almak** *v* replace
Alman [alman] *adj* German ▷ *n* German *(person)*
Almanca [almandʒa] *n (dil)* German *(language)*
Almanya [almanja] *n* Germany
Alpler [alpler] *npl* Alps
alt [alt] *n* **alt geçit** *n* underpass; **alt kat** *adj* downstairs; **alt katta** *adv* downstairs; **altını çizmek** *v* underline; **el altında** *adj* handy; **en alt** *adj* bottom; **yerin altında** *adv* underground
alternatif [alternatif] *adj* alternative
altgeçit [altgetʃit] *n* subway
altı [altə] *number* six
altın [altən] *adj (metal)* golden ▷ *n (metal)* gold; **altın kaplama** *n* gold-plated
altıncı [altəndʒə] *adj* sixth
altında [altənda] *adv* below, underneath ▷ *prep* below, beneath, under, underneath
altmış [altməʃ] *number* sixty
altyapı [altjapə] *n* infrastructure
altyazı [altjazə] *npl* subtitles
altyazılı [altjazələ] *adj* subtitled
alüminyum [alyminjum] *n*

aluminium
Alzheimer [alsheimer] *n*
Alzheimer hastalığı *n* Alzheimer's disease
amaç [amatʃ] *n* cause *(ideals)*, objective
amaçsız [amatʃsəz] *adj* senseless
amatör [amatør] *n* amateur
ambulans [ambulans] *n*
Ambulans çağırın Call an ambulance
amca [amdʒa] *n* uncle
ameliyat [amelijat] *n* surgery *(operation)*, *(tıp)* operation *(surgery)*; **ameliyat etmek** *v* operate *(to perform surgery)*; **ameliyat odası** *n* operating theatre
Amerika [amerika] *n* America; **Güney Amerika** *adj* South America, South American; **Kuzey Amerika** *adj* North America, North American; **Latin Amerika** *adj* Latin America, Latin American; **Orta Amerika** *n* Central America
Amerikalı [amerikalə] *n* American; **Güney Amerikalı** *n* South American; **Kuzey Amerikalı** *n* North American
Amerikan [amerikan] *adj* American; **Amerikan futbolu** *n* American football
amir [amir] *n (iş)* supervisor
amper [amper] *n* amp
ampul [ampul] *n* light bulb, *(elektrik)* bulb *(electricity)*
an [an] *n* moment; **aynı anda** *adv* simultaneously; **aynı anda olan** *adj* simultaneous; **bir anlık** *adj* momentary; **şu an** *n* present *(time being)*; **şu anda** *adv* currently, presently
ana [ana] *n* base, lead *(position)*; **ana okulu** *n* infant school; **ana yemek** *n* main course; **deniz anası** *n* jellyfish
anadil [anadil] *n* mother tongue; **anadilini konuşan** *n* native speaker
anafikir [anafikir] *n* basis
anahtar [anahtar] *n (kilit)* key *(for lock)*; **araba anahtarları** *npl* car keys; **İngiliz anahtarı** *n* spanner; **Anahtar alabilir miyim?** Can I have a key?; **Anahtar lütfen** The key, please; **Anahtar uymuyor** The key doesn't work; **Anahtarı nereden alacağız?** Where do we get the key...?; **Anahtarım çalışmıyor** My key doesn't work; **Anahtarımı unuttum** I've forgotten the key; **Anahtarla sorunum var** I'm having trouble with the key; **Anahtarları arabada bıraktım** I left the keys in the car; **Ayrılırken anahtarı nereye bırakacağız?** Where do we hand in the key when we're leaving?; **Bu anahtar nerenin?** What's this key for?; **Bu kapının anahtarı hangisi?** Which is the key for this door?; **Hangisi ön kapının anahtarı?** Which is the key for the front door?; **Hangisi garaj anahtarı?** Which is the key for the garage?; **Yedek bir anahtar istiyoruz** We need a second key
anahtarlık [anahtarlək] *n* keyring
anakara [anakara] *n* mainland

analiz [analiz] *n* **sistem analizcisi** *n* systems analyst
ananas [ananas] *n* pineapple
anason [anason] *n* aniseed
anavatan [anavatan] *n* homeland
anayol [anajol] *n* main road
ancak [a:ndʒak] *adv* however
ançuez [antʃuez] *n* anchovy
And Dağları [andda:larə] *npl* Andes
Andora [andora] *n* Andorra
anestetik [anestetik] *n* anaesthetic
anestezi [anestezi] *n* **genel anestezi** *n* general anaesthetic; **lokal anestezi** *n* local anaesthetic
Angola [angola] *adj* Angolan ▷ *n* Angola
Angolalı [angolalə] *n* Angolan
anında [anənda] *adv* immediately
anıt [anət] *n* memorial, monument
ani [ani] *adj* abrupt, sudden; **ani rüzgar** *n* gust; **ani yükselme** *n* surge
aniden [aniden] *adv* abruptly, suddenly
anjin [anʒin] *n* angina
ankesör [aŋesør] *n* **ankesörlü telefon** *n* payphone
anket [aŋet] *n* questionnaire
anlam [anlam] *n* meaning; **anlamına gelmek** *v* stand for
anlama [anlama] *n* comprehension
anlamak [anlamak] *v* understand; **halden anlama** *n* sympathy; **halden anlamak** *v* sympathize; **yanlış anlama** *n* misunderstanding; **yanlış anlamak** *v* misunderstand;
Anladım I understand
anlamsız [anlamsəz] *adj* pointless
anlaşılır [anlaʃələr] *adj* understandable
anlaşma [anlaʃma] *n* agreement, deal, *(tarih)* treaty
anlaşmazlık [anlaʃmazlək] *n* disagreement
anlatıcı [anlatədʒə] *n* teller
anlatım [anlatəm] *n* expression
anlatmak [anlatmak] *vt* tell
anlayış [anlajəʃ] *adj* understanding
anlayışlı [anlajəʃlə] *adj* sympathetic
anlık [anlək] *adj* **bir anlığına** *adv* momentarily
anma [anma] *n* **anma yazısı** *(ölünün ardından) n* obituary
anmalık [anmalək] *n* souvenir
anne [anne] *n* mother, mum; **üvey anne** *n* stepmother; **isim annesi** *n* godmother; **ninenin annesi** *n* great-grandmother; **taşıyıcı anne** *n* surrogate mother
annecim [annedʒim] *n* mummy *(mother)*
annelik [annelik] *n* maternal
anons [anons] *n* **anons etmek** *v* page
anorak [anorak] *n* anorak
anoreksi [anoreksi] *n* anorexia
anoreksik [anoreksik] *adj* anorexic
anormal [anormal] *adj* abnormal
ansiklopedi [ansiklopedi] *n* encyclopaedia
Antarktik [antarktik] *n* Antarctic
anten [anten] *n* aerial
antibiyotik [antibijotik] *n*

antibiotic
antidepresan [antidepresan] *n* antidepressant
antifriz [antifriz] *n* antifreeze
antihistamin [antihistamin] *n* antihistamine
antika [antika] *n* antique; **antikacı dükkanı** *n* antique shop
antikor [antikor] *n* antibody
antilop [antilop] *n* antelope
antiseptik [antiseptik] *n* antiseptic
antivirüs [antivirys] *n* antivirus
antre [antre] *n* hallway
antreman [antreman] *n* **antreman giysisi** *n* tracksuit
apaçık [apatʃək] *adj* blatant
apandisit [apandisit] *n* appendicitis
apartman [apartman] *n* **apartman dairesi** *n* apartment, flat;**... adına bir apartman dairesi ayırtmıştık** We've booked an apartment in the name of...; **Bir apartman dairesi bakıyorduk** We're looking for an apartment
aperatif [aperatif] *n* **Aperatif almak istiyoruz** We'd like an aperitif
apse [apse] *n* abscess; **Burası apse yaptı** I have an abscess
aptal [aptal] *adj* stupid
aptalca [aptaldʒa] *adj* silly
ara [ara] *n (konser, tiyatro)* interval; **bir ara** *adv* sometime; **bu arada** *adv* meantime; **devre arası** *n* half-time; **reklam arası** *n* commercial break; **tavan arası** *n* loft
araba [araba] *n* car; **araba anahtarları** *npl* car keys; **araba kazası** *n* crash; **araba kiralama** *n* car hire; **araba sigortası** *n* car insurance; **araba tutması** *n* travel sickness; **arabalı feribot** *n* car-ferry; **arabayı çekmek** *v* tow away; **at arabası** *n* buggy, cart; **üstü açılır araba** *n* convertible; **bebek arabası** *n* pram; **birini arabayla evine bırakma** *n* lift *(free ride)*; **devriye arabası** *n* patrol car; **el arabası** *n* wheelbarrow; **içkili araba kullanma** *n* drink-driving; **kiralık araba** *n* hire car, hired car, rental car; **şirket arabası** *n* company car; **market arabası** *n* shopping trolley; **sedan araba** *n* saloon car; **yarış arabası** *n* racing car; **yük arabası** *n* lorry; **Araba çalışmıyor** The car won't start; **Araba güvertesine nasıl gidebilirim?** How do I get to the car deck?; **Araba kaydı** The car skidded; **Araba kiralamak istiyorum** I want to hire a car; **Araba ne zaman hazır olur?** When will the car be ready?; **Arabada stereo var mı?** Is there a stereo in the car?; **Arabam bozuldu** My car has broken down; **Arabamı çarptım** I've crashed my car; **Arabamı nereye park edebilirim?** Where can I park the car?; **Arabamı soydular** My car has been broken into; **Arabanın garantisi var** The car is still under warranty; **Arabanızı çeker misiniz lütfen?** Could you move your car, please?;

Arabayı buraya mı geri getirmem gerekiyor Do I have to return the car here?; **Arabayı yıkamak istiyorum** I would like to wash the car; **Beş günlüğüne bir araba kiralamak istiyorum** I want to hire a car for five days; **Beni arabayla alabilir misiniz?** Can you take me by car?; **Birisine araba çarptı** Someone has been knocked down by a car; **Hafta sonu için bir araba kiralamak istiyorum** I want to hire a car for the weekend

aracılık [aradʒələk] *n* **hakem aracılığıyla çözümleme** *n* arbitration

araç [aratʃ] *n* device, *(mekanik)* tool, *(otomobil)* vehicle; **ağır yük taşıma aracı** *n* HGV; **üstü kapalı yük aracı** *n* van; **kar temizleme aracı** *n* snowplough; **karşılıklı sefer yapan araç** *n* shuttle; **kurtarma aracı** *n* breakdown van; **uzay aracı** *n* spacecraft

Aralık [aralək] *n (ay)* December; **Otuz bir Aralık Cuma günü** on Friday the thirty first of December

arama [arama] *n* search; **arama ekibi** *n* search party; **arama motoru** *n* search engine

aramak [aramak] *v* ask for, look for, look up, search, seek ▹ *vt* call; **geri aramak** *v* call back, phone back, ring back; **telefonla aramak** *v* ring up;**... ı arıyoruz** We're looking for...; **Dışarıyı aramak istiyorum, hat bağlar mısınız?** I want to make an outside call, can I have a line?

Arap [arap] *adj* Arab, Arabic ▹ *n* Arab; **Birleşik Arap Emirlikleri** *npl* United Arab Emirates

Arapça [araptʃa] *n* Arabic *(language)*

arasında [arasənda] *prep* among, between

arasıra [arasəra] *adj* occasional

araştırma [araʃtərma] *n* enquiry, research; **pazar araştırması** *n* market research

araştırmak [araʃtərmak] *v* enquire, explore

arazi [arazi] *n* **bina ve etrafındaki arazi** *npl* premises

arazide [arazide] *n* cross-country

ardıç [ardətʃ] *n* **ardıç kuşu** *n* thrush

ardıl [ardəl] *adj* successive

arduvaz [arduvaz] *n* slate

argo [argo] *n* slang

arı [arə] *n* bee; **hezen arısı** *n* bumblebee

arındırmak [arəndərmak] *v* **önyargılardan arındırma** *n* liberation

arıza [arəza] *n* breakdown; **Arızalı** It's faulty

arife [arife] *n* eve; **büyük perhizin arife günü** *n* Shrove Tuesday; **Noel arifesi** *n* Christmas Eve

Arjantin [arʒantin] *adj* Argentinian ▹ *n* Argentina

Arjantinli [arʒantinli] *n (kişi)* Argentinian *(person)*

arka [arka] *adj* back, rear ▹ *n* behind, rear; **arka ayna** *n* rear-view mirror; **arka plan** *n* background; **arkaya dönmek** *v* turn round, turn around; **Hangisi**

arka kapının anahtarı? Which is the key for the back door?
Arka [arka] *abr* **Lütfen Arka Sayfaya Bakınız** *abbr* PTO
arkada [arkada] *adv* back ▷ *prep* behind
arkadaş [arkadaʃ] *n* friend; **erkek arkadaş** *n* boyfriend; **iş arkadaşı** *n* associate; **kalem arkadaşı** *n* penfriend; **kız arkadaş** *n* girlfriend; **oda arkadaşı** *n* roommate; **sınıf arkadaşı** *n* classmate; **Arkadaşlarımla geldim** I'm here with my friends; **Buraya arkadaşlarımı görmeye geldim** I'm here visiting friends
arkasında [arkasənda] *adv* behind
arkeolog [arkeolog] *n* archaeologist
arkeoloji [arkeoloʒi] *n* archaeology
armağan [arma:an] *n* gift, present *(gift)*; **birine ufak bir armağan alma** *n* treat; **Bir çocuk için armağan almak istiyordum** I'm looking for a present for a child; **Bu armağan sizin için** This is a gift for you; **Eşime bir armağan almak istiyordum** I'm looking for a present for my husband, I'm looking for a present for my wife
armonika [armonika] *n* mouth organ
armut [armut] *n* pear
Arnavut [arnavut] *adj* Albanian ▷ *n (kişi)* Albanian *(person)*
Arnavutça [arnavuttʃa] *n (dil)* Albanian *(language)*
Arnavutluk [arnavutluk] *n* Albania
aromaterapi [aromaterapi] *n* aromatherapy
arpa [arpa] *n* barley
arsa [arsa] *n* plot *(piece of land)*
arsız [arsəz] *adj* cheeky
arşiv [arʃiv] *n* archive
art arda [artarda] *adj* **ardı ardına** *adj* consecutive
artık [artək] *adv* yet *(interrogative)*; **artık yıl** *n* leap year; **artık yemek** *npl* leftovers
artış [artəʃ] *n* increase
artmak [artmak] *v* increase; **gitgide artarak** *adv* increasingly
artrit [artrit] *n* **Artrit hastasıyım** I suffer from arthritis
arttırmak [arttərmak] *v* **açık arttırma** *n* auction
arzu [arzu] *n* desire ▷ *v* **arzu etmek** *v* desire
as [as] *n* ace; **as solist** *n* lead singer
asansör [asansør] *n* **Asansör nerede?** Where is the lift?; **Asansör var mı?** Is there a lift?; **Binada asansör var mı?** Is there a lift in the building?; **Tekerlekli sandalyeler için asansör var mı?** Do you have a lift for wheelchairs?
asfalt [asfalt] *n* tarmac
asık [asək] *adj* **suratı asık** *adj* sulky
asılmak [asəlmak] *vi* hang
asi [asi] *adj* disobedient
asistan [asistan] *n* assistant; **kişisel asistan** *n* personal assistant, PA
asit [asit] *n* acid; **asit yağmuru** *n* acid rain
asker [asker] *n* soldier; **asker traşı** *n* crew cut; **askeri öğrenci** *n* cadet

askeri [askeri] *adj* military
askı [askə] *n* hanger; **askıya alma** *n* suspension; **askıya almak** *v* suspend; **elbise askısı** *n* coathanger; **kol askısı** *(sağlık) n* sling; **pantolon askıları** *npl* braces
askılık [askələk] *n* rack
asla [asla] *adv* never
aslan [aslan] *n* lion, *(dişi)* lioness
Aslan [aslan] *n* **Aslan burcu** *n* Leo
aslında [asləndа] *adv* actually, basically
asma [asma] *n (bitki)* vine; **asma köprü** *n* suspension bridge; **asma kilit** *n* padlock
asmak [asmak] *vt* hang; **suratını asmak** *v* sulk
aspirin [aspirin] *n* aspirin; **Aspirin alamıyorum** I can't take aspirin; **Aspirin rica ediyorum** I'd like some aspirin
ast [ast] *n* inferior
astar [astar] *n (kumaş)* lining
astım [astəm] *n* asthma; **Astımım var** I suffer from asthma
astroloji [astroloʒi] *n* astrology
astronomi [astronomi] *n* astronomy
astronot [astronot] *n* astronaut
Asya [asja] *adj* Asian ▷ *n* Asia
Asyalı [asjalə] *adj* Asiatic ▷ *n* Asian
aşağı [aʃa:ə] *adj (durum)* inferior, *(konum)* low ▷ *adv (konum)* low; **aşağıya inmek** *v* come down; **baş aşağı** *adv* upside down; **daha aşağı** *adj* lower
aşağıda [aʃa:əda] *adv* down
aşçı [aʃtʃə] *n* **Aşçının özel tercihi nedir?** What is the chef's speciality?
aşçıbaşı [aʃtʃəbaʃə] *n* chef
aşçılık [aʃtʃələk] *n* cookery
aşı [aʃə] *n (tıp)* jab, *(tıp)* vaccination; **Aşı yaptırmam gerek** I need a vaccination
aşık [aʃək] *n* lover
aşılamak [aʃəlamak] *v* vaccinate
aşırı [aʃərə] *adj* excessive, extreme; **aşırı derecede** *adv* extremely, terribly; **aşırı derecede korkmuş** *adj* terrified; **aşırı duygusal** *adj* soppy; **aşırı kilolu** *adj* overweight; **aşırı uçta** *n* extremist
aşırıcılık [aʃərədʒələk] *n* extremism
aşırma [aʃərma] *n (dükkanda)* shoplifting
aşina [aʃina] *adj* **aşina olmayan** *adj* unfamiliar
at [at] *n (hayvan)* horse; **at arabası** *n* buggy, cart; **at nalı** *n* horseshoe; **at yarışı** *n* horse racing; **ata binme** *n* riding; **sallanan at** *n* rocking horse; **yarış atı** *n* racehorse; **At yarışı görmek isterdim** I'd like to see a horse race; **Ata binebilir miyiz?** Can we go horse riding?; **Ata binmeye gidelim** Let's go horse riding
ata [ata] *n* ancestor
atamak [atamak] *v* appoint
atardamar [atardamar] *n* artery
atasözü [atasøzy] *n* proverb
ataş [ataʃ] *n* paperclip
ateş [ateʃ] *n* shot, *(sağlık)* fever; **ateş etme** *n* shooting; **ateş etmek** *vt* shoot; **ateşe dayanıklı** *adj* ovenproof; **şenlik ateşi** *n* bonfire; **Ateşi çok yüksek** He has a fever

ateşkes [ateʃkes] *n* ceasefire, truce
ateşleme [ateʃleme] *n* ignition
atık [atək] *v* **atık boşaltmak** *vt* drain ▷ *n* **atık borusu** *n* drain, drainpipe
atıştırma [atəʃtərma] *n* snack
atkı [atkə] *n (giysi)* muffler
atkuyruğu [atkujru:u] *n* ponytail
atlama [atlama] *n* **sırıkla atlama** *n* pole vault; **uzun atlama** *n* long jump; **yüksek atlama** *n* high jump
atlamak [atlamak] *vi* jump ▷ *vt* skip; **engel atlama** *n* show-jumping; **hızla atlamak** *v* plunge ▷ *n* **uzun atlama** *n* jump
Atlantik [atlantik] *n* Atlantic
atlas [atlas] *n* atlas
atlet [atlet] *n* athlete, vest
atletik [atletik] *adj* athletic
atletizm [atletizm] *npl* athletics
atlıkarınca [atləkarəndʒa] *n* merry-go-round
ATM [atm] *abr* **Buralarda ATM var mı?** Is there a cash machine here?; **En yakın ATM nerede?** Where is the nearest cash machine?
atma [atma] *n* **işten atma** *n* sack *(dismissal)*
atmak [atmak] *v* dump, scrap, throw away, throw out, toss ▷ *vt* throw; **çığlık atmak** *v* scream; **e-posta atmak** *v* email *(a person)*; **göz atmak** *vi* browse; **hapse atmak** *v* jail; **işten atmak** *v* sack; **şaplak atmak** *v* spank; **mesaj atmak** *v* text; **tehlikeye atmak** *v* endanger; **tokat atmak** *v* smack
atmosfer [atmosfer] *n* atmosphere
atom [atom] *n* atom; **atom bombası** *n* atom bomb
atölye [atølje] *n* workshop
au-pair [aupair] *n* au pair
av [av] *n* hunting; **balık avlamak** *n* fishing; **kaçak avlanmış** *adj* poached *(caught illegally)*
avanak [avanak] *n* twit
avara [avara] *v* **avara etmek** *v* bounce
avare [avare] *n* rambler
avcı [avdʒə] *n* hunter
avlamak [avlamak] *v* hunt; **balık avlamak** *n* fish
avlu [avlu] *n* courtyard, yard *(enclosure)*
avokado [avokado] **(avokadolar)** *n* avocado
avro [avro] *n* euro
Avrupa [avrupa] *adj* European ▷ *n* Europe; **Avrupa Birliği** *n* European Union
Avrupalı [avrupalə] *n* European
avuçiçi [avutʃitʃi] *n* palm *(part of hand)*
avukat [avukat] *n* attorney, lawyer
Avustralasya [avustralasja] *n* Australasia
Avustralya [avustralja] *n* Australia
Avustralyalı [avustraljalə] *adj* Australian ▷ *n* Australian
Avusturya [avusturja] *adj* Austrian ▷ *n* Austria
Avusturyalı [avusturjalə] *n* Austrian
ay [aj] *n (uydu)* moon, *(zaman)* month; **bir ay önce** a month ago; **bir ay sonra** in a month's time;

Beş ay sonra doğuracağım I'm due in five months
ayak, ayaklar [ajak, ajaklar] *n* foot; **ayağını yere vurmak** *v* stamp; **ayak parmağı** *n* toe; **ayak uzmanı** *n* chiropodist; **ayaklarını sürüyerek yürümek** *v* shuffle; **ayaklı merdiven** *n* stepladder; **çıplak ayak** *adj* barefoot; **çıplak ayakla** *adv* barefoot; **karbon ayak izi** *n* carbon footprint; **yangılı ayak şişi** *n* bunion; **Ayaklarım ağrıyor** My feet are sore
ayak bileği [ajakbileji:] *n* ankle
ayakizi [ajakizi] *n* footprint
ayakkabı [ajakkabə] *n* shoe; **ayakkabı bağı** *n* shoelace; **ayakkabı cilası** *n* shoe polish; **lastik spor ayakkabısı** *npl* trainers; **spor ayakkabısı** *npl* sneakers; **Ayakkabılar hangi katta?** Which floor are shoes on?; **Ayakkabılarımın topuklarını değiştirebilir misiniz?** Can you re-heel these shoes?; **Ayakkabımda delik var** I have a hole in my shoe; **Bu ayakkabıları tamir edebilir misiniz?** Can you repair these shoes?
ayakkabıcı [ajakkabədʒə] *n* shoe shop
ayaklanma [ajaklanma] *n* outbreak, riot
ayaklar [ajaklar] *npl* feet
ayarlama [ajarlama] *n* adjustment, set
ayarlamak [ajarlamak] *v* adjust ▷ *vt* set
ayarlanabilir [ajarlanabilir] *adj* adjustable
ayartma [ajartma] *n* temptation
ayçiçeği [ajtʃitʃeji:] *n* sunflower
aygır [ajgər] *n* **deniz aygırı** *n* walrus
aygıt [ajgət] *n* apparatus
ayı [ajə] *n* bear; **kutup ayısı** *n* polar bear; **oyuncak ayı** *n* teddy bear
ayık [ajək] *adj* sober
ayırılmak [ajərəlmak] *v* part with
ayırım [ajərəm] *n* **cinsiyet ayrımcılığı yapan** *adj* sexist
ayırmak [ajərmak] *vt* separate, split
ayırt [ajərt] *n* **ayırt etmek** *v* distinguish
ayin [ajin] *n (kilise)* mass *(church)*, *(tören)* ritual; **Ayin ne zaman?** When is mass?
ayinsel [ajinsel] *adj* ritual
aylık [ajlək] *adj (zaman)* monthly
ayna [ajna] *n* mirror; **arka ayna** *n* rear-view mirror; **yan ayna** *n* wing mirror
aynasız [ajnasəz] *n* cop
aynı [ajnə] *adj* same; **aynı anda** *adv* simultaneously; **aynı anda olan** *adj* simultaneous; **aynı fikirde olmak** *v* agree; **Bana da aynısından** I'll have the same
ayraç [ajratʃ] *n* **kitap ayracı** *n* bookmark
ayrı [ajrə] *adj* separate ▷ *adv* apart; **ayrı olarak** *adv* separately ▷ *n* **sürüden ayrılmış** *n* stray; **Hesabı ayrı alalım** Separate bills, please; **sütü ayrı getirin** with the milk separate
ayrıca [ajrədʒa] *prep* plus
ayrıcalık [ajrədʒalək] *n* concession, privilege

ayrılış [ajrələʃ] *n* parting
ayrılma [ajrəlma] *n* separation
ayrılmak [ajrəlmak] *v* leave, split up; **biryerden ayrılmak** *v* leave; **Yarın sabah onda ayrılıyorum** I will be leaving tomorrow morning at ten a.m.
ayrılmış [ajrəlməʃ] *adj* reserved
ayrımcılık [ajrəmdʒələk] *n* discrimination
ayrıntı [ajrəntə] *n* detail
ayrıntılı [ajrəntələ] *adj* detailed
az [az] *adj* slight; **az görülür** *adj* rare *(uncommon)*; **az pişmiş** *adj* rare *(undercooked)*; **daha az** *pron* *(miktar olarak)* less, *(sayıca)* fewer; **en az** *adj* least, minimum; **en aza indirgemek** *v* minimize; **en azından** *adv* at least
az-yağlı [azja:lə] *adj* low-fat
azalma [azalma] *n* decrease
azalmak [azalmak] *v* decrease, go down
azaltma [azaltma] *n* cutback
azaltmak [azaltmak] *v* diminish, reduce
azap [azap] *n* **vicdan azabı** *n* remorse
azarlamak [azarlamak] *v* scold, tell off
Azerbaycan [azerbajdʒan] *adj* Azerbaijani ▷ *n* Azerbaijan
Azerbaycanlı [azerbajdʒanlə] *n* Azerbaijani
azgın [azgən] *adj* fierce
azıcık [azədʒək] *adv* slightly
azınlık [azənlək] *n* minority
aziz [aziz] *n* saint
azmetmek [azmetmek] *v* persevere

b

baba [baba] *n* dad, father, *(mafya)* godfather *(criminal leader)*; **üvey baba** *n* stepfather; **dedenin babası** *n* great-grandfather; **isim babası** *(vaftiz)* *n* godfather *(baptism)*
babacığım [babadʒəm] *n* daddy
babalık [babalək] *n* **babalık izni** *n* paternity leave
baca [badʒa] *n* chimney
bacak [badʒak] *n* leg; **Bacağım kaşınıyor** My leg itches; **Bacağıma kramp girdi** I've got cramp in my leg; **Bacağımı oynatamıyorum** I can't move my leg; **Bacağını incitti** She has hurt her leg; **Bacağını oynatamıyor** He can't move his leg
badana [badana] *n* plaster *(for wall)*; **yeniden badana yapmak** *v* redecorate
badanalamak [badanalamak] *v*

whitewash
badem [badem] *n* almond; **badem ezmesi** *n* marzipan
bademcik [bademdʒik] *n* **bademcik iltihabı** *n* tonsillitis
bademcikler [bademdʒikler] *npl* tonsils
badminton [badminton] *n* badminton; **badminton topu** *n* shuttlecock
bagaj [bagaʒ] *n* baggage, luggage; **bagaj alım** *n* baggage reclaim; **bagaj emanet dolabı** *n* left-luggage locker; **bagaj limiti** *n* baggage allowance; **bagaj trolleyi** *n* luggage trolley; **el bagajı** *n* hand luggage; **emanet bagaj** *n* left-luggage; **emanet bagaj bürosu** *n* left-luggage office; **fazla bagaj** *n* excess baggage; **port bagaj** *n* luggage rack, roof rack;**... uçağının bagajları nerede?** Where is the luggage for the flight from...?; **Bagaj limiti ne kadar?** What is the baggage allowance?; **Bagajım çıkmadı** My luggage hasn't arrived; **Bagajım hasar görmüş** My luggage has been damaged; **Bagajım kaybolmuş** My luggage has been lost; **Bagajımı sigorta ettirebilir miyim?** Can I insure my luggage?; **Bagajımız çıkmadı** Our luggage has not arrived; **Bagajlarımı nerede check-in yaptırabilirim** Where do I check in my luggage?
bağ [baː] *n* bond, *(üzüm)* vineyard; **ayakkabı bağı** *n* shoelace; **göz bağı** *n* blindfold; **isteğe bağlı** *adj* optional
bağdaşım [baːdaʃəm] *n* **gerçeklerle bağdaşmayan** *adj* unrealistic
bağımlı [baːəmlə] *adj* addicted ▷ *n* addict
bağımlılık [baːəmlələk] *n* **uyuşturucu bağımlısı** *n* drug addict
bağımsız [baːəmsəz] *adj* freelance, independent; **bağımsız olarak** *adv* freelance
bağımsızlık [baːəmsəzlək] *n* independence
bağırmak [baːərmak] *v* shout, yell
bağırsak [baːərsak] *n* gut
bağırsaklar [baːərsaklar] *npl* bowels
bağırtı [baːərtə] *n* shout
bağışıklık [baːəʃəklək] *n* **bağışıklık sistemi** *n* immune system
bağışlama [baːəʃlama] *n* pardon
bağışlamak [baːəʃlamak] *v* donate, forgive; **hayatını bağışlamak** *v* spare
bağlamak [baːlamak] *v* attach, tie, *(kablo)* connect, *(tekne)* moor; **birini bağlamak** *v* tie up; **gözlerini bağlamak** *v* blindfold
bağlanmak [baːlanmak] *v* **Minimum bağlanma süresi ne kadar?** What's the minimum amount of time?
bağlantı [baːlantə] *n* conjunction, connection, joint *(junction)*; **bağlantı yolu** *n* slip road; **Bağlantı çok yavaş** The connection seems very slow; **Bağlantı uçağımı kaçırdım** I've

missed my connection
Bahama [bahama] *n* **Bahama Adaları** *n* Bahamas
bahane [bahane] *n* pretext
bahar [bahar] *n* springtime; **bahar temizliği** *n* spring-cleaning
baharat [baharat] *n* spice; **köri baharatı** *n* curry powder; **tuzlu ve baharatlı** *adj* savoury
bahçe [bahtʃe] *n* garden; **bahçe kulübesi** *n* shed; **bahçe merkezi** *n* garden centre; **bahçe sulama bidonu** *n* watering can; **hayvanat bahçesi** *n* zoo; **meyve bahçesi** *n* orchard; **Bahçeleri gezebilir miyiz?** Can we visit the gardens?
bahçecilik [bahtʃedʒilik] *n* gardening
bahçıvan [bahtʃəvan] *n* gardener
bahis [bahis] *n* bet; **bahis bayii** *n* betting shop ▷ *v* **bahse girmek** *vi* bet
Bahreyn [bahrejn] *n* Bahrain
bahriyeli [bahrijeli] *n* sailor
bahsetmek [bahsetmek] *v* mention
bahşiş [bahʃiʃ] *n* tip *(reward)* ▷ *v* **bahşiş vermek** *vt* tip *(reward)*; **Bahşiş vermek adet midir?** Is it usual to give a tip?; **Ne kadar bahşiş vermem gerek?** How much should I give as a tip?
bakan [bakan] *n (hükümet)* minister *(government)*
bakanlık [bakanlək] *n* ministry *(government)*
bakıcı [bakədʒə] *n (apartman, ev)* caretaker; **çocuk bakıcısı** *n* childminder, nanny; **bebek bakıcısı** *n* babysitter
bakım [bakəm] *n (araba vb)* maintenance, *(hasta vb)* care; **çocuk bakımı** *n* childcare; **yüz bakımı** *n* facial; **yoğun bakım ünitesi** *n* intensive care unit
bakınmak [bakənmak] *v* look round
bakır [bakər] *n* copper
bakış [bakəʃ] *n* glance, look; **bakış açısı** *n* aspect; **bakış noktası** *n* standpoint, viewpoint; **yaşama bakış** *n* outlook
bakire [bakire] *n* virgin
bakiye [bakije] *n* bank balance
bakkal [bakkal] *n* grocer, shopkeeper, *(dükkan)* grocer's
bakla [bakla] *n (sebze)* broad bean
bakliyat [baklijat] *npl* pulses
bakmak [bakmak] *v* look after, *(hasta vb)* care, *(karşılıklı)* face; **öfkeyle bakmak** *v* glare; **bebek bakma** *n* babysitting; **bebek bakmak** *v* babysit; **boşluğa bakmak** *v* stare; **şaşı bakmak** *v* squint
bakteri [bakteri] *npl* bacteria
bal [bal] *n* honey
balayı [balajə] *n* honeymoon
bale [bale] *n* ballet; **bale patiği** *npl* ballet shoes; **Baleye nereden bilet alabilirim?** Where can I buy tickets for the ballet?
balerin [balerin] *n* ballerina
balet [balet] *n* ballet dancer
balığı [balɜə] *n* **yılan balığı** *n* eel
balık [balək] *n* fish; **balık avlamak** *n* fish, fishing; **Japon balığı** *n* goldfish; **kılıç balığı** *n* swordfish; **köpek balığı** *n* shark; **mezgit balığı** *n* haddock; **morina balığı** *n*

cod; **ringa balığı** *n* herring; **som balığı** *n* salmon; **tatlısu balığı** *n* freshwater fish; **ton balığı** *n* tuna; **tuzlanıp tütsülenmiş ringa balığı** *n* kipper; **İçinde balık olmayan bir yemek yapabilir misiniz?** Could you prepare a meal without fish?; **İçinde et / balık olmayan ne yemekleriniz var mı?** Which dishes have no meat / fish?; **Balık alayım** I'll have the fish; **Balık yemiyorum** I don't eat fish; **Balıklarınız taze mi, dondurulmuş mu?** Is the fish fresh or frozen?; **Balıklardan ne var?** What fish dishes do you have?; **Bu yemekte balık suyu var mı?** Is this cooked in fish stock?; **Burada balık avlanabilir mi?** Can we fish here?; **Burada balık avlayabilir miyim?** Am I allowed to fish here?; **Nerede balık tutabilirim?** Where can I go fishing?
Balık [balək] *n* **Balık burcu** *n* Pisces
balıkadam [balәkadam] *n* **balıkadam kıyafeti** *n* wetsuit
balıkçı [baləktʃə] **(balıkçılar)** *n* fisherman, *(dükkan)* fishmonger; **balıkçı teknesi** *n* fishing boat; **olta balıkçısı** *n* angler
balıkçıl [baləktʃəl] *n* **balıkçıl kuşu** *n* heron
balıkçılık [baləktʃələk] *n* **olta balıkçılığı** *n* angling
balina [balina] *n* whale
balkabağı [balkaba:ə] *n* pumpkin
Balkan [balkan] *adj* Balkan
balkon [balkon] *n* balcony; **Balkonlu odanız var mı?** Do you have a room with a balcony?
balmumu [balmumu] *n* wax
balo [balo] *n* ball *(dance)*; **balo kostümü** *n* fancy dress
balon [balon] *n* balloon; **balonlu çiklet** *n* bubble gum
balta [balta] *n* axe
bambu [bambu] *n* bamboo
banço [bantʃo] **(bançolar)** *n* banjo
band [band] *n* **elastik band** *n* rubber band
bandaj [bandaʒ] *n* bandage
bando [bando] *n* **bando takımı** *n* brass band
bank [baŋ] *n* bench
banka [baŋa] *n* bank *(finance)*; **banka ödeme emri** *n* standing order; **banka ücretleri** *npl* bank charges; **banka hesabı** *n* bank account; **banka kartı** *n* debit card; **ticaret bankası** *n* merchant bank; **Banka bugün açık mı?** Is the bank open today?; **Banka buraya ne kadar uzakta?** How far is the bank?; **Banka ne zaman açılıyor?** When does the bank open?; **Banka ne zaman kapanıyor?** When does the bank close?; **Bankamdan para transferi yapmak istiyorum** I would like to transfer some money from my bank in...; **Burada banka var mı?** Is there a bank here?; **Yakınlarda bir banka var mı?** Is there a bank nearby?
bankacı [baŋadʒə] *n* banker
bankamatik [baŋamatik] *n* cash dispenser

banknot [baŋnot] *n* banknote
banliyö [banlijø] *adj* suburban ▷ *n* suburb
bant [bant] *n* band *(strip)*; **cırt bant** *n* Velcro®; **geniş bant** *n* broadband; **lastik bant** *n* elastic band; **saç bandı** *n* hairband; **taşıyıcı bant** *n* conveyor belt; **yara bandı** *n* Elastoplast®, plaster *(for wound)*
banyo [banjo] *n* bath, bathroom; **banyo havlusu** *n* bath towel; **köpüklü banyo** *n* bubble bath; **Banyo taşıyor** The bathroom is flooded; **Banyoda tutunma rayı var mı?** Are there support railings in the bathroom?; **Odada banyo var mı?** Does the room have a private bathroom?
Baptist [baptist] *n* Baptist
bar [bar] *n* bar *(alcohol)*; **bar işletmecisi** *n* publican; **snack bar** *n* snack bar; **İyi bir bar biliyor musunuz?** Where is there a nice bar?; **Bar ne tarafta?** Where is the bar?
baraj [baraʒ] *n* dam
baraka [baraka] *n* hut
Barbados [barbados] *n* Barbados
barbar [barbar] *adj* barbaric
barbekü [barbeky] *n* barbecue; **Barbekü kısmı nerede?** Where is the barbecue area?
bardak [bardak] *n* **cam bardak** *n* glass *(vessel)*; **Bir bardak limonata lütfen** A glass of lemonade, please; **Bir bardak su** a glass of water; **Temiz bir bardak alabilir miyim lütfen?** Can I have a clean glass, please?
barınak [barənak] *n* shelter
barındırmak [barəndərmak] *v* accommodate
barış [barəʃ] *n* peace
barışçıl [barəʃtʃəl] *adj* peaceful
bariyer [barijer] *n* barrier
bariz [bariz] *adj* glaring
barmen [barmen] **(barmenler)** *n* barman, bartender; **kadın barmen** *n* barmaid
bas [bas] *n* bass; **bas davul** *n* bass drum
basın [basən] *n* **basın toplantısı** *n* press conference; **Basın büronuz var mı?** Do you have a press office?
basınç [basəntʃ] *n* pressure
basit [basit] *adj* simple
basitçe [basittʃe] *adv* simply
basitleştirmek [basitleʃtirmek] *v* simplify
Bask [bask] *adj* Basque ▷ *n* **Bask dili** *n* Basque *(language)*
basketbol [basketbol] *n* basketball
baskı [baskə] *n* *(gazete, dergi)* edition, *(matbaa)* print; **baskı hatası** *n* misprint; **baskı yapmak** *v* lean on, pressure; **ikinci baskı kitap** *n* paperback
baskın [baskən] *n* raid; **baskın yapmak** *v* raid
baskısı [baskəsə] *n* **deneme baskısı** *n* proof *(for checking)*
Basklı [basklə] *n* *(kişi)* Basque *(person)*
basmak [basmak] *v* *(matbaa)* print; **su basmak** *(vt)* *vi* flood
basmakalıp [basmakaləp] *n* stereotype
bastırmak [bastərmak] *v* press;

bastırarak söndürmek *v* stub out
baston [baston] *n* walking stick
basur [basur] *npl* piles
baş [baʃ] *adj* chief, *(tepede)* principal ▷ *n (vücut)* head *(body part)*, *(yönetim)* head *(principal)*; **adın baş harfleri** *n* initials; **baş ağrısı** *n* headache; **baş aşağı** *adv* upside down; **baş belası** *n* pest; **baş eğmek** *v* bow; **baş parmak** *n* thumb ▷ *v* **başı çekmek** *v* head; **başı dönmüş** *adj* dizzy; **başıyla onaylamak** *v* nod; **baştan başa** *prep* throughout; **merdiven başı** *n* landing; **saat başı** *adv* hourly
Başak [baʃak] *n* **Başak burcu** *n* Virgo
başarı [baʃarə] *n* achievement, success ▷ *v* **başarısız olmak** *vi* fail
başarılı [baʃarələ] *adj* successful
başarısız [baʃarəsəz] *adj* unsuccessful
başarısızlık [baʃarəsəzlək] *n* failure
başarıyla [baʃarəjla] *adv* successfully
başarmak [baʃarmak] *v* achieve, succeed
başbakan [baʃbakan] *n* prime minister
başına [baʃəna] *prep* per
başka [baʃka] *adj, adv* **başka bir yerde** *adv* elsewhere; **başka türlü** *adv* otherwise; **ilgisini başka yöne çekmek** *v* distract; **Başka bir oda istiyorum** I'd like another room; **Başka bir yol var mı?** Is there a diversion?; **Başka neyiniz var?** Have you anything else?; **Başka odanız var mı?** Do you have any others?; **Bunun başka rengi var mı?** Do you have this in another colour?
başkaldırmak [baʃkaldərmak] *v* riot
başkan [baʃkan] **(başkanlar)** *n* chairman, *(şirket)* president, *(okul)* prefect; **belediye başkanı** *n* mayor
başkent [baʃkent] *n* capital
başlama [baʃlama] *n* **başlama vuruşu** *n* kick-off; **başlama vuruşu yapmak** *v* kick off
başlamak [baʃlamak] *v* begin ▷ *vt* start
başlangıç [baʃlangətʃ] *adj (ilk)* initial ▷ *n* beginning, *(çıkış)* outset, *(iş, yarış vb)* start; **başlangıç olarak** *adv* originally
başlangıçta [baʃlangətʃta] *adv* initially
başlatmak [baʃlatmak] *vi* start ▷ *vt* launch
başlayan [baʃlajan] *adj* **yeni başlayan** *n* beginner
başlıca [baʃlədʒa] *adv* mainly, primarily
başlık [baʃlək] *n* caption, *(haber)* headline, *(kitap, albüm vb)* title; **duş başlığı** *n* shower cap
başpiskopos [baʃpiskopos] *n* archbishop
başrol [baʃrol] *n (oyun/film)* lead *(in play/film)*
baştanbaşa [baʃtanbaʃa] *adj* thorough
başucu [baʃudʒu] *n* **başucu lambası** *n* bedside lamp
başvurmak [baʃvurmak] *v* resort to

başvuru [baʃvuru] *n* application; **başvuru formu** *n* application form
başvurucu [baʃvurudʒu] *n* applicant
bataklık [bataklək] *n* bog, marsh, swamp
batı [batə] *adj* west, western ▷ *n* west; **batıya doğru** *adj* westbound
Batı [batə] *n* **Batı Hint Adaları** *npl* West Indian, West Indies
batıda [batəda] *adv* west
batıl [batəl] *adj* **batıl inançları olan** *adj* superstitious
batmak [batmak] *vi* sink
battal [battal] *adj* **battal boy yatak** *n* king-size bed
battaniye [battanije] *n* blanket; **elektrikli battaniye** *n* electric blanket; **Bana bir battaniye daha getirir misiniz lütfen?** Please bring me an extra blanket
Bay [baj] *n* Mr
bayağı [baja:ə] *adv (oldukça)* pretty
bayan [bajan] *n* **Bayanlar tuvaleti nerede?** Where is the ladies?; **Bir bayan doktorla konuşmak istiyorum** I'd like to speak to a female doctor; **Bir bayan polisle konuşmak istiyorum** I want to speak to a policewoman
Bayan [bajan] *n (evlenmemiş kadınlara hitap şekli)* Miss, *(evli olup olmadığını belirtmeyenler için)* Ms, *(hanım)* Mrs
bayat [bajat] *adj* stale
bayılmak [bajəlmak] *v* faint, pass out; **Bayıldı** She has fainted
bayii [bajii] *n* **bahis bayii** *n* betting shop; **gazete bayii** *n* newsagent
baykuş [bajkuʃ] *n* owl
bayrak [bajrak] *n* flag
Bayram [bajram] *n* **Musevilerin Fısıh Bayramı** *n* Passover
bazen [bazen] *adv* sometimes
bazı [bazə] *pron* some
bebe [bebe] *n* **bebe sandalyesi** *n* highchair
bebek [bebek] *n* baby; **ıslak bebek mendili** *n* baby wipe; **bebe bisküvisi** *n* rusk; **bebek arabası** *n* pram; **bebek bakıcısı** *n* babysitter; **bebek bakma** *n* babysitting; **bebek bakmak** *v* babysit; **bebek bezi** *n* nappy; **bebek karyolası** *n* cot; **bebek sütü** *n* baby milk; **oyuncak bebek** *n* doll; **Bebeği nerede emzirebilirim?** Where can I breast-feed the baby?; **Bebeğin altını nerede değiştirebilirim?** Where can I change the baby?; **Bebek sandalyeniz var mı?** Do you have a baby seat?; **Bebekli aileler için kolaylıklarınız var mı?** Are there facilities for parents with babies?
beceri [bedʒeri] *n* skill
becerikli [bedʒerikli] *adj* skilful, skilled
beceriksiz [bedʒeriksiz] *adj* awkward
becermek [bedʒermek] *v* manage
bedava [bedava] *adj* free *(no cost)*
bedbin [bedbin] *adj* moody
beden [beden] *n* body; **bedenine göre büyük** *adj* outsize

beğenmek [bejenmek] *n* **kendini beğenmiş** *adj* arrogant, bigheaded
bej [beʒ] *adj* beige
bekar [bekar] *n* bachelor; **bekarlığa veda partisi** *(erkek) n* stag night; **Bekarım** I'm single
bekçi [bektʃi] *n* warden
bekle [bekle] *n* **Lütfen beni bekleyin** Please wait for me
bekleme [bekleme] *adj* **beklemede bilet** *n* stand-by ticket
beklemek [beklemek] *v* wait for ▹ *vt* wait; **bekleme listesi** *n* waiting list; **bekleme odası** *n* waiting room; **olması beklenen** *adj* due; **uçuş bekleme salonu** *n* departure lounge; **yatmayıp beklemek** *v* wait up
beklenti [beklenti] *n* **gelecek beklentisi** *n* prospect
bekleyiş [beklejiʃ] *n* **kuşku ve gerilimli bekleyiş** *n* suspense
bektaşi [bektaʃi] *n* **bektaşi üzümü** *n* gooseberry
bel [bel] *n* waist; **bel çantası** *n* bum bag, money belt
bela [bela] *n* **baş belası** *n* pest
Belarus [belarus] *adj* Belarussian
Belarusca [belarusdʒa] *n* Belarussian *(language)*
Belaruslu [belaruslu] *n* Belarussian *(person)*
Belçika [beltʃika] *adj* Belgian ▹ *n* Belgium
Belçikalı [beltʃikalə] *n* Belgian
belediye [beledije] *n* **belediye başkanı** *n* mayor; **belediye binası** *n* town hall; **belediye meclis üyesi** *n* councillor
belge [belge] *n* document, *(döküm)* transcript; **hasta belgesi** *n* sick note; **sağlık belgesi** *n* medical certificate; **sigorta belgesi** *n* insurance certificate; **Bu belgenin fotokopisini çektirmek istiyorum** I want to copy this document
belgeleme [belgeleme] *n* documentation
belgeler [belgeler] *npl* documents
belgesel [belgesel] *n* documentary
belirgin [belirgin] *adj* distinctive
belirlemek [belirlemek] *v* **kimlik belirlemek** *v* identify
belirleyici [belirlejidʒi] *adj* decisive
belirsiz [belirsiz] *adj* uncertain, vague; **belli belirsiz** *adj* subtle
belirsizlik [belirsizlik] *n* uncertainty
belirteç [belirtetʃ] *n* adverb
belirti [belirti] *n* trace, *(hastalık)* symptom
belirtmek [belirtmek] *v* specify; **miktar belirtmek** *v* quantify
belkemiği [belkeməə] *n* spine
belki [be:lki] *adv* maybe, perhaps
bellek [bellek] *n* memory
belli [belli] *adj* **belli belirsiz** *adj* subtle; **ne yapacağı belli olmayan** *adj* unpredictable
ben [ben] *pron (kişi)* I, me; **... a geldiğimizde beni uyarır mısınız?** Please let me know whe we get to...; **Ben dondurma alayım** I'd like an ice cream; **Ben gelmiyorum** I'm not coming
bencil [bendʒil] *adj* self-centred,

selfish
bengaldeş [bengaldeʃ] *n* **Bengaldeş ile ilgili** *n* Bangladeshi
Bengaldeş [bengaldeʃ] *n* Bangladesh
Bengaldeşli [bengaldeʃli] *n* Bangladeshi
benim [benim] *adj* my ▷ *pron* mine; **Benim adım...** My name is...; **Pardon, orası benim yerim** Excuse me, that's my seat
bent [bent] *n* embankment
benzemek [benzemek] *v* take after
benzer [benzer] *adj* similar
benzerlik [benzerlik] *n* resemblance, similarity
benzetmek [benzetmek] *v* resemble
benzin [benzin] *n* petrol; **benzin deposu** *n* petrol tank; **benzin istasyonu** *n* petrol station, service station; **kurşunsuz benzin** *n* unleaded petrol; **Benzin bitti** The petrol has run out; **Benzinim bitti** I've run out of petrol; **Buraya en yakın benzin istasyonu nerede?** Is there a petrol station near here?; **Depo benzin sızdırıyor** The petrol tank is leaking
beraber [beraber] *adv* **beraber yaşamak** *v* live together
berabere [berabere] *n* **berabere kalmak** *vt* draw *(equal with)*
berbat [berbat] *adj* awful, nasty; **berbat etmek** *v* spoil, wreck; **berbat etmek** *v* mess up; **Hava çok berbat!** What awful weather!
berber [berber] *n* barber
bere [bere] *n (giyim)* beret, *(tıp)* bruise
beri [beri] *prep* **den beri** *prep* since; **o zamandan beri** *adv* since; **Dünden beri kusuyorum** I've been sick since yesterday
beslemek [beslemek] *vt* feed
beslenme [beslenme] *n* nutrition; **yetersiz beslenme** *n* malnutrition
besleyici [beslejidʒi] *adj* nutritious ▷ *n (gıda)* nutrient
beste [beste] *n* composition
besteci [bestedʒi] *n* composer
beş [beʃ] *number* five; **Beş ay sonra doğuracağım** I'm due in five months; **Beş günlüğüne bir araba kiralamak istiyorum** I want to hire a car for five days; **Beş numaralı kabin nerede?** Where is cabin number five?; **Beş yüz... rica ediyorum** I'd like five hundred...
beşik [beʃik] *n* cradle
beşinci [beʃindʒi] *adj* fifth
betimleme [betimleme] *n* description
betimlemek [betimlemek] *v* describe
beton [beton] *n* concrete
bey [bej] *n* master
beyan [bejan] *n* **özür beyan etmek** *v* excuse
beyaz [bejaz] *adj* white; **beyaz güvercin** *n* dove; **beyaz saçlı** *adj* grey-haired; **beyaz yazı tahtası** *n* whiteboard; **İyi bir beyaz şarap tavsiye edebilir misiniz?** Can you recommend a good white wine?; **Bir şişe beyaz şarap** a bottle of white wine; **Bir sürahi beyaz**

şarap a carafe of white wine; **Siyah beyaz** in black and white
beyin [bejin] *n* brain
beyzbol [bejzbol] *n* baseball; **beyzbol kepi** *n* baseball cap
bez [bez] *n* **bebek bezi** *n* nappy; **kurulama bezi** *n* dishcloth
beze [beze] *n* gland, *(tatlı)* meringue
bezelye [bezelje] *npl* peas
bıçak [bətʃak] *n* blade, knife; **çatal, bıçak, kaşık** *n* cutlery; **traş bıçağı** *n* razor, razor blade
bıçaklamak [bətʃaklamak] *v* stab
bıkmış [bəkməʃ] *adj* fed up
bıldırcın [bəldərdʒən] *n* quail
bırakmak [bərakmak] *vt* keep, quit, stop; **birini arabayla evine bırakma** *n* lift *(free ride)*; **serbest bırakma** *n* release ▷ *v* **serbest bırakmak** *v* release
bıyık [bəjək] *n* moustache, whiskers
biber [biber] *n* pepper; **kırmızı toz biber** *n* paprika
biberiye [biberije] *n* rosemary
biberlik [biberlik] *n* peppermill
biberon [biberon] *n* baby's bottle
biçim [bitʃim] *n* **dikdörtgen biçiminde** *adj* rectangular; **etkili bir biçimde** *adv* efficiently; **şalvar biçimi** *adj* baggy; **yaşam biçimi** *n* lifestyle
biçmek [bitʃmek] *v* mow; **çim biçme makinesi** *n* lawnmower, mower ▷ *v* **fiyat biçmek** *vt* charge *(price)*
bidon [bidon] *n* **bahçe sulama bidonu** *n* watering can
biftek [biftek] *n* rump steak, steak
bigudi [bigudi] *n* curler
bikini [bikini] *n* bikini
bilanço [bilantʃo] *n* balance sheet
bilardo [bilardo] *n* billiards
bildik [bildik] *adj* familiar
bildirim [bildirim] *n* **bildirimde bulunmak** *v* notify
bile [bile] *adv* even
bilek [bilek] *n* wrist
bileşen [bileʃen] *adj* component ▷ *n* component, element
bilet [bilet] *n* ticket; **beklemede bilet** *n* stand-by ticket; **bilet gişesi** *n* booking office, box office, ticket office; **bilet kontrolörü** *n* ticket inspector; **bilet otomatı** *n* ticket machine; **bilet turnikesi** *n* ticket barrier; **günlük bilet** *n* day return; **gidiş-dönüş bilet** *n* return ticket; **otobüs bileti** *n* bus ticket; **otopark bileti** *n* parking ticket; **tek gidiş bileti** *n* one-way ticket; **tek yön bilet** *n* single ticket; **... a gidiş dönüş iki bilet** two return tickets to...; **İki bilet, lütfen** I'd like two tickets, please; **Baleye nereden bilet alabilirim?** Where can I buy tickets for the ballet?; **Bilet almam gerekiyor mu?** Do I need to buy a car-parking ticket?; **Bilet makinası çalışmıyor** The ticket machine isn't working; **Bilet makinası nasıl çalışıyor?** How does the ticket machine work?; **Bilet makinası nerede?** Where is the ticket machine?; **Biletimi değiştirmek istiyorum** I want to change my ticket; **Biletimi kaybettim** I've lost my ticket; **Biletler ne kadar?** How

much are the tickets?; **Biletleri buradan alabilir miyim?** Can I buy the tickets here?; **Biletleri siz ayırtır mısınız lütfen?** Can you book the tickets for us?; **Bir çocuk bileti** a child's ticket; **Bir bilet, lütfen** A ticket, please; **Birkaç seyahati içeren bilet satıyor musunuz?** Do you have multi-journey tickets?; **Bu akşam için iki bilet almak istiyorum** I'd like two tickets for tonight; **Bu akşam için iki bilet lütfen** Two tickets for tonight, please; **Gidiş dönüş bilet ne kadar?** How much is a return ticket?; **Haftalık bir bilet lütfen** A book of tickets, please; **Konser biletlerini nereden alabilirim?** Where can I buy tickets for the concert?; **Nereden bilet alabilirim?** Where can I get tickets?, Where do I buy a ticket?; **Nereden bilet alabiliriz?** Where can we get tickets?; **Tek gidiş bilet ne kadar?** How much is a single ticket?

biletçi [bilettʃi] *n* bus conductor, ticket collector

bilgi [bilgi] *n* information, knowledge; **bilgi tazeleme eğitimi** *n* refresher course; **bilgi vermek** *v* inform; **bilgi yarışması** *n* quiz; **teknik bilgi** *n* know-how; **temel bilgiler** *npl* basics;**... hakkında bilgi istiyordum** I'd like some information about...

bilgiç [bilgitʃ] *n* know-all

bilgilendirici [bilgilendiridʒi] *adj* informative

bilgili [bilgili] *adj* knowledgeable

bilgisayar [bilgisajar] *n* computer; **bilgisayar çalışması** *n* computing; **bilgisayar bilimi** *n* computer science; **bilgisayar hafızası** hard disk; **bilgisayar oyunu** *n* computer game; **dizüstü bilgisayarı** *n* laptop; **Bilgisayar odası nerede?** Where is the computer room?; **Bilgisayarınızı kullanabilir miyim?** May I use your computer?; **Bu bilgisayarda CD yapabilir miyim?** Can I make CDs at this computer?

bilim [bilim] *n* science; **bilgisayar bilimi** *n* computer science; **bilim adamı** *n* scientist; **bilim kurgu** *n* science fiction; **din bilimi** *n* theology; **doğa bilimleri uzmanı** *n* naturalist; **elektronik bilimi** *npl* electronics; **genetik bilimi** *n* genetics; **insan bilimi** *n* anthropology

bilimsel [bilimsel] *adj* scientific

bilinçli [bilintʃli] *adj* conscious

bilinçlilik [bilintʃlilik] *n* consciousness

bilinçsiz [bilintʃsiz] *adj* unconscious

bilinen [bilinen] *adj* known

bilinmeyen [bilinmejen] *adj* **bilinmeyen numaralar** *npl* directory enquiries

bilinmez [bilinmez] *adj* unknown

bilmece [bilmedʒe] *n* puzzle

bilmek [bilmek] *v* know; **Bilmiyorum** I don't know

bin [bin] *number (sayı)* thousand

bina [bina] *n* **belediye binası** *n* town hall; **bina sorumlusu** *n* janitor; **bina ve etrafındaki arazi**

npl premises; **Binada asansör var mı?** Is there a lift in the building?
binici [binidʒi] *n* rider
binicilik [binidʒilik] *n* horse riding
bininci [binindʒi] *adj* thousandth ▹ *n* thousandth
biniş [biniʃ] *n* **biniş kartı** *n* boarding card, boarding pass; **Biniş kartım burada** Here is my boarding card
binmek [binmek] *v* get on ▹ *vt* *(hayvana)* ride; **ata binme** *n* riding; **bisiklete binme** *n* cycle *(bike)*, cycling; **Ata binebilir miyiz?** Can we go horse riding?; **Ata binmeye gidelim** Let's go horse riding
bir [birr] *art* a, an ▹ *pron* one; **... a bir bilet** a single to... ▹ *number* one; **ağır bir şekilde** *adv* heavily; **başka bir yerde** *adv* elsewhere; **bir anlığına** *adv* momentarily; **bir anlık** *adj* momentary; **bir ara** *adv* sometime; **bir araya gelmek** *v* get together; **bir kaşık dolusu** *n* spoonful; **bir şey** *pron* something; **bir seferinde** *adv* once; **bir seferlik** *n* one-off; **bir sonraki** *adv* next; **bir yerde** *adv* someplace, somewhere; **dokuzda bir** *n* ninth; **her bir** *pron* each; **herhangi bir şey** *pron* anything; **herhangi bir yer** *adv* anywhere; **kötü bir şekilde** *adv* badly; **Ayrıca bir ücret ödenmesi gerekiyor mu?** Is there a supplement to pay?; **bir ay önce** a month ago; **bir ay sonra** in a month's time; **bir hafta önce** a week ago; **bir hafta sonra** in a week's time; **Bana bir otelde yer ayırtabilir misiniz?** Can you book me into a hotel?; **Bir apartman dairesi bakıyorduk** We're looking for an apartment; **Bir araç ve dört kişi ne kadar?** How much is the crossing for a car and four people?; **Bir araç ve iki kişi ne kadar?** How much is it for a car with two people?; **Bir çay lütfen** A tea, please; **Bir çekme bira lütfen** A draught beer, please; **Bir çocuğum var** I have a child; **Bir büroda çalışıyorum** I work in an office; **Bir bilet, lütfen** A ticket, please; **Bir dakika lütfen** Just a moment, please; **Bir fabrikada çalışıyorum** I work in a factory; **Bir günlük kayak kartı almak istiyorum** I'd like a ski pass for a day; **Bir gece daha kalmak istiyorum** I want to stay an extra night; **Bir haftalığı ne kadar?** How much is it for a week?; **Bir kahve lütfen** A coffee, please; **Bir şey içmek ister misiniz?** Would you like a drink?; **Bir metro haritası lütfen** Could I have a map of the tube, please?; **Bir oda kiralamak istiyorum** I'd like to rent a room; **Bir otel arıyoruz** We're looking for a hotel; **Bir otel tavsiye edebilir misiniz?** Can you recommend a hotel?; **Bir saatlik internet bağlantısı kaça?** How much is it to log on for an hour?; **Bir tarife alabilir miyim, lütfen?** Can I have a timetable, please?; **Bir torba daha alabilir miyim lütfen?** Can I have an extra bag, please?; **Bir villa kiralamak**

istiyorum I'd like to rent a villa; **Hafta sonu için bir araba kiralamak istiyorum** I want to hire a car for the weekend; **Haftalık bir bilet lütfen** A book of tickets, please; **Size bir içki ısmarlayabilir miyim?** Can I get you a drink?; **Standart bir kabin bileti** a standard class cabin

bira [bira] *n* beer; **bira fabrikası** *n* brewery; **hafif bira** *n* lager; **Bir çekme bira lütfen** A draught beer, please; **Bir bira daha lütfen** Another beer, please

birader [birader] *n* **kayın birader** *n* brother-in-law

birahane [birahane] *n* pub

biraz [biraz] *pron* some; **Bana biraz borç verebilir misiniz?** Could you lend me some money?

birey [birej] *adj* individual

bireysel [birejsel] *adj* **Bireysel kaza sigortası yaptırmak istiyorum** I'd like to arrange personal accident insurance

biri [biri] *pron* either; **biri bizi gözetliyor** *n* reality TV; **birinin hesabına borç kaydetmek** *v* debit; **herhangi biri** *pron* anybody, anyone

birikim [birikim] *npl* savings

birikinti [birikinti] *n* drift; **su birikintisi** *n* puddle

birikmek [birikmek] *v* mount up

biriktirmek [biriktirmek] *v* put aside, save up

birinci [birindʒi] *num* **birinci sınıf** *adj* first-class;**... a birinci sınıf bir gidiş dönüş bilet** a first-class return to...; **Biletimi birinci sınıfa çevirmek istiyorum** I want to upgrade my ticket; **Birinci sınıf bir kabin** a first-class cabin; **Birinci sınıf seyahat etmek istiyorum** I would like to travel first-class

birisi [birisi] *pron* somebody, someone

birkaç [birkatʃ] *adj* few, several ▷ *pron* few, several

birleşik [birleʃik] *adj* united; **Birleşik Arap Emirlikleri** *npl* United Arab Emirates; **Birleşik Devletler** *n* US, *(Amerika)* United States; **Birleşik Krallık** *(İngiltere)* *n* UK, United Kingdom

birleşim [birleʃim] *n* **cinsel birleşim** *n* sexual intercourse

birleşme [birleʃme] *n* conjugation

birleştirme [birleʃtirme] *n* combination

birleştirmek [birleʃtirmek] *v* combine, *(kişileri)* unite, *(parçaları)* link (up) ▷ *vi* join

birlik [birlik] *n* union, *(dernek)* association; **Avrupa Birliği** *n* European Union; **oy birliği** *n* consensus

birlikler [birlikler] *npl (askeri)* troops

birlikte [birlikte] *adv* together; **birlikte yatmak** *v* sleep together; **bununla birlikte** *adv* nevertheless; **hep birlikte** *adv* altogether; **Hepsini birlikte yazın lütfen** All together, please

bisiklet [bisiklet] *n* bicycle, bike; **üç tekerlekli bisiklet** *n* tricycle; **bisiklet pompası** *n* bicycle pump ▷ *v* **bisiklet sürmek** *v* cycle;

bisiklet yolu *n* cycle path; **bisiklet yolu** *n* cycle lane; **bisiklete binme** *n* cycle *(bike)*, cycling; **dağ bisikleti** *n* mountain bike; **tandem bisiklet** *n* tandem; **Bisiklet kiralamak istiyorum** I want to hire a bike; **Bisiklet vitesli mi?** Does the bike have gears?; **Bisikleti ne zaman geri getirmem gerekiyor?** When is the bike due back?; **Bisikletimi buraya bırakabilir miyim?** Can I keep my bike here?; **Bisikletin frenleri var mı?** Does the bike have brakes?; **Bisikletin geri frenleri var mı?** Does the bike have back-pedal brakes?; **Bisikletin lambaları var mı?** Does the bike have lights?; **En yakın bisiklet tamircisi nerede?** Where is the nearest bike repair shop?; **Nereden bisiklet kiralayabilirim?** Where can I hire a bike?

bisikletçi [bisiklettʃi] *n* cyclist

bisküvi [biskyvi] *n* biscuit; **bebe bisküvisi** *n* rusk

bit [bit] *npl (saç)* lice

bitişiğinde [bitiʃəənde] *prep* near

bitişik [bitiʃik] *adj* adjacent; **bitişik nizam ev** *n* semi, semi-detached house

bitki [bitki] *n* plant; **bitki örtüsü** *n* vegetation; **bitki çayı** *n* herbal tea; **bitki yetiştirmek** *vi* grow; **Yerel bitkileri ve ağaçları görmek isterdik** We'd like to see local plants and trees

bitkin [bitkin] *adj* shaky

bitmek [bitmek] *v (tükenmek)* run out of ▹ *vt (son bulmak)* finish

bitmiş [bitmiʃ] *adj* over

bit pazarı [bitpazarə] *n* flea market

biyo-çözünür [bijotʃøzynyr] *adj* biodegradable

biyokimya [bijokimja] *n* biochemistry

biyoloji [bijoloʒi] *n* biology

biyolojik [bijoloʒik] *adj* biological

biyometrik [bijometrik] *adj* biometric

biz [biz] *pron* us, we, *(kendimiz)* ourselves; **Bizi davet ettiğiniz için çok teşekkürler** It's very kind of you to invite us

bizim [bizim] *adj* our

bizimki [bizimki] *pron* ours

BlackBerry [pladʒkberrj] *n* BlackBerry®

blazer [plazer] *n* blazer

blog [plog] *n* blog ▹ *v* **blog yazmak** *v* blog

blok [plok] *n* block *(solid piece)*, *(bina)* block *(buildings)*

bloke [ploke] *v* **bloke etmek** *v* block

blöf [pløf] *n* bluff ▹ *v* **blöf yapmak** *v* bluff

blucin [pludʒin] *npl* denims, jeans; **blucin kumaşı** *n* denim

bluz [pluz] *n* blouse

bodrum [bodrum] *n* basement

boğa [boa:] *n* bull

Boğa [boa:] *n* **Boğa burcu** *n* Taurus

boğaz [boa:z] *n* throat

boğazlamak [boa:zlamak] *v* strangle

boğmak [boɣmak] *v* suffocate

boğucu [bou:dʒu] *adj* stifling

boğulmak [bou:lmak] *v* **boğucu sıcak** *adj* sweltering; **suda boğulmak** *v* drown
boks [boks] *n* box, boxing
bokser [bokser] *n* **bokser şort** *npl* boxer shorts
boksör [boksør] *n* boxer
Bolivya [bolivja] *adj* Bolivian ▷ *n* Bolivia
Bolivyalı [bolivjalə] *n* Bolivian
bomba [bomba] *n* bomb; **atom bombası** *n* atom bomb; **gözyaşı bombası** *n* teargas; **saatli bomba** *n* time bomb
bombacı [bombadʒə] *n* **intihar bombacısı** *n* suicide bomber
bombalama [bombalama] *n* bombing
bombalamak [bombalamak] *vt* bomb
boncuk [bondʒuk] *n* bead
borazan [borazan] *n* trumpet
borç [bortʃ] *n* debt; **birinin hesabına borç kaydetmek** *v* debit; **borçlu olmak** *v* owe; **vadesi geçmiş borç** *npl* arrears
bornoz [bornoz] *n* bathrobe
borsa [borsa] *n* stock exchange, stock market
borsacı [borsadʒə] *n* stockbroker
boru [boru] *n* pipe; **atık borusu** *n* drain, drainpipe; **boru hattı** *n* pipeline; **egzos borusu** *n* exhaust pipe; **lağım borusu** *n* sewer
Bosna [bosna] *adj* Bosnian ▷ *n* Bosnia
Bosna-Hersek [bosnahersek] *n* Bosnia and Herzegovina
Bosnalı [bosnalə] *n (kişi)* Bosnian *(person)*
boş [boʃ] *adj (daire, ev, sandalye)* vacant, *(insan)* idle, *(kağıt, zihin)* blank, *(mekan)* empty; **boş durmak** *v* mess about; **boş vakit** *n* leisure; **boş zaman** *n* spare time
boşaltmak [boʃaltmak] *v* unpack, *(bina)* evacuate, *(yük)* unload ▷ *vt* empty; **atık boşaltmak** *vt* drain
boşanma [boʃanma] *n* divorce
boşanmış [boʃanməʃ] *adj* divorced; **Boşandım** I'm divorced
boşluk [boʃluk] *n (konum)* slot, *(mekan)* space, *(uzay, geometri)* void, *(yazı, zihin)* blank; **boşluğa bakmak** *v* stare; **boşluk payı** *(tavanda) n* headroom; **karın boşluğu ile ilgili** *adj* coeliac
bot [bot] *n* **Fiyata botlar da dahil mi?** Does the price include boots?; **Kayak botu kiralamak istiyorum** I want to hire boots
Botsvana [botsvana] *n* Botswana
bovling [bovling] *n* tenpin bowling
bowling [bovling] *n* bowling; **bowling salonu** *n* bowling alley
boy [boj] *n* **battal boy yatak** *n* king-size bed; **boy göstermek** *v* turn up; **orta boy** *adj* medium-sized; **uzun boylu** *adj* tall; **Boyunuz kaç?** How tall are you?
boya [boja] *n (giysi)* dye, *(yapı)* paint; **boya fırçası** *n* paintbrush; **mum boya** *n* crayon; **Dip boya yapar mısınız lütfen?** Can you dye my roots, please?; **Saçımı boyar mısınız lütfen?** Can you dye my hair, please?
boyalı [bojalə] *adj* tinted

boyama [bojama] *n* colouring
boyamak [bojamak] *v* dye ▷ *vt* paint
boylam [bojlam] *n* longitude
boynuz [bojnuz] *n* horn
boyun [bojun] *n* neck; **boyun eğmek** *v* obey
boyunca [bojundʒa] *prep* along
boyut [bojut] *n* extent, size; **üç boyutlu** *adj* three-dimensional
bozkır [bozkər] *n* moor
bozmak [bozmak] *v* break down; **kararı bozmak** *v* overrule; **sinir bozucu** *adj* annoying; **sinirini bozmak** *v* annoy
bozuk [bozuk] *adj* **Arabam bozuldu** My car has broken down; **Bana... lık bozuk para verebilir misiniz?** Could you give me change of...?; **Biraz bozuk para verebilir misiniz?** Can you give me some change, please?; **Bozuk param yok** I don't have anything smaller; **Bozuk paranız var mı?** Do you have any small change?; **Et bozulmuş** This meat is off; **Kusura bakmayın, hiç bozuk param yok** Sorry, I don't have any change; **Taksimetre bozuk** The meter is broken; **Telefon için bozuk para rica ediyorum** I'd like some coins for the phone, please
böbrek [bøbrek] *n* kidney
böbürlenmek [bøbyrlenmek] *v* boast
böcek [bødʒek] *n* beetle, bug, insect; **böcek ilacı** *n* insect repellent; **böcek zehiri** *n* pesticide; **cırcır böceği** *n* cricket *(insect)*; **hamam böceği** *n* cockroach; **uç uç böceği** *n* ladybird; **Böcek ilacınız var mı?** Do you have insect repellent?; **Odamda böcek var** There are bugs in my room
böğürtlen [bø:yrtlen] *n* blackberry
bölge [bølge] *n* district, region, *(arazi)* territory, *(kent)* precinct, *(savaş, kuraklık)* zone, *(seçim)* ward *(area)*; **kırsal bölge** *n* countryside; **kilisenin dini bölgesi** *n* parish; **seçmen bölgesi** *n* constituency, electorate; **yayalara özel bölge** *n* pedestrian precinct; **Bu bölgenin haritasını nereden alabilirim?** Where can I buy a map of the region?
bölgesel [bølgesel] *adj* regional
bölme [bølme] *n* division
bölmek [bølmek] *vt* divide
bölüm [bølym] *n (bina, konum)* section, *(dizi)* episode, *(idari)* department, *(kitap)* chapter
börek [børek] *n* pie
böyle [bøjle] *adj* such
böylesine [bøjlesine] *adv* such
brendi [brendi] *n* brandy; **Ben brendi alayım** I'll have a brandy
Brezilya [brezilja] *adj* Brazilian ▷ *n* Brazil
Brezilyalı [breziljalə] *n* Brazilian
brifing [brifing] *n* briefing
brokoli [brokoli] *n* broccoli
bronşit [bronʃit] *n* bronchitis
bronz [bronz] *n* bronze; **bronzlaşmış ten** *n* tan
bronzlaşma [bronzlaʃma] *n* suntan
bronzlaşmak [bronzlaʃmak] *n*

bronzlaşma losyonu *n* suntan lotion
broş [broʃ] *n* brooch
broşür [broʃyr] *n* brochure, leaflet, pamphlet; **tanıtma broşürü** *n* prospectus;**... hakkında broşürünüz var mı?** Do you have any leaflets about...?; **Broşürünüz var mı?** Do you have any leaflets?
Brüksel lahanası [bryksellahanasə] *n* Brussels sprouts
bu [bu] *adj* that, this ▷ *pron* this; **bu arada** *adv* meantime; **bu gece** *adv* tonight; **bununla birlikte** *adv* nevertheless; **ya o, ya bu** *conj* either (... or); **Bu akşam ne yapıyorsunuz?** What are you doing this evening?; **Bu anahtar nerenin?** What's this key for?; **Bu armağan sizin için** This is a gift for you; **Bu elbiseyi deneyebilir miyim?** Can I try on this dress?; **Bu eşim** This is my husband, This is my wife; **Bu ilacı kullanıyorum** I'm on this medication; **Bu kadar yeter, sağolun** That's enough, thank you; **Bu koltuk boş mu?** Is this seat free?; **Bu mektubu postalamak istiyorum** I'd like to send this letter; **Bu ne demek?** What does this mean?; **Bu otobüs... a gider mi?** Does this bus go to...?; **Bu pantalonu deneyebilir miyim?** Can I try on these trousers?; **Bu partnerim** This is my partner; **Bu sabahtan beri kusuyorum** I've been sick since this morning; **Bunu değiştirmek istiyorum** I'd like to exchange this; **Bunu kasaya koyun lütfen** Put that in the safe, please; **Bunun içinde ne var?** What is in this?
buçuk [butʃuk] *n* **Saat iki buçuk** It's half past two; **Saat neredeyse iki buçuk** It's almost half past two
Buda [buda] *n* Buddha
Budist [budist] *adj* Buddhist ▷ *n* Buddhist
Budizm [budizm] *n* Buddhism
bugün [bugyn] *adv* today; **Banka bugün açık mı?** Is the bank open today?; **Bugün açık mı?** Is it open today?; **Bugün deniz dalgalı mı?** Is the sea rough today?; **Bugün günlerden ne?** What day is it today?; **Bugün ne yapmak istersiniz?** What would you like to do today?; **Bugünün tarihi nedir?** What is today's date?
bugünlerde [bugynlerde] *adv* nowadays
buğday [bu:daj] *n* wheat; **buğday alerjisi** *n* wheat intolerance
buğu [bu:u] *n* condensation
buhar [buhar] *n* steam
buji [buʒi] *n* spark plug
buket [buket] *n* bouquet
bukle [bukle] *n (saç)* curl, *(saç)* lock *(hair)*
bulantı [bulantə] *n* nausea; **hamilelik bulantısı** *n* morning sickness
bulaşıcı [bulaʃədʒə] *adj* catching, contagious, infectious; **Bulaşıcı mı?** Is it infectious?
bulaşık [bulaʃək] *n* **bulaşık deterjanı** *n* washing-up liquid;

bulaşık makinesi *n* dishwasher; **bulaşık yıkama** *n* washing-up; **bulaşık yıkamak** *v* wash up

buldozer [buldozer] *n* bulldozer

Bulgar [bulgar] *adj* Bulgarian ▹ *n* *(kişi)* Bulgarian *(person)*

Bulgarca [bulgardʒa] *n* *(dil)* Bulgarian *(language)*

Bulgaristan [bulgaristan] *n* Bulgaria

bulgu [bulgu] *n* **bulgularla kanıtlamak** *v* demonstrate

bulimia [bulimia] *n* bulimia

bulma [bulma] *n* **iş bulma kurumu** *n* job centre

bulmaca [bulmadʒa] *n* crossword

bulmak [bulmak] *v* *(aradığı bir şeyi)* find, *(keşfetmek)* find out

bulunmak [bulunmak] *v* **bildirimde bulunmak** *v* notify; **katkıda bulunmak** *v* contribute; **tahminde bulunmak** *v* estimate; **varsayımda bulunmak** *v* speculate

buluşma [buluʃma] *n* meeting

buluşmak [buluʃmak] *v* meet up

bulut [bulut] *n* cloud

bulutlu [bulutlu] *adj* cloudy, overcast

bulvar [bulvar] *n* avenue

bulyon [buljon] *n* stock cube

bundan [bundan] *pron* **bundan dolayı** *adv* accordingly

bungalov [bungalov] *n* bungalow

bunje-jumping [bunʒeʒumping] *n* **Nerede bunje-jumping yapabilirim?** Where can I go bungee jumping?

bunlar [bunlar] *pron* these

bunların [bunlarən] *adj* these

bu oda [buoda] *n* **Bu oda çok gürültülü** The room is too noisy

burada [burada] *adv* here

burç [burtʃ] *n* **Akrep burcu** *n* Scorpio; **Aslan burcu** *n* Leo; **İkizler burcu** *n* Gemini; **burçlar kuşağı** *n* zodiac; **Balık burcu** *n* Pisces; **Başak burcu** *n* Virgo; **Boğa burcu** *n* Taurus; **Koç burcu** *n* Aries; **Kova burcu** *n* Aquarius; **Oğlak burcu** *n* Capricorn; **Terazi burcu** *n* Libra; **Yay burcu** *n* Sagittarius

Burç [burtʃ] *n* **Yengeç Burcu** *n* Cancer *(horoscope)*

burger [burger] *n* burger

burkmak [burkmak] *v* *(bilek)* sprain

burkulma [burkulma] *n* sprain

burma [burma] *n* wrench

Burma [burma] *adj* Burmese ▹ *n* Burma; **Burma dili** *(dil)* *n* Burmese *(language)*

burmak [burmak] *v* wrench

Burmalı [burmalə] *n* *(kişi)* Burmese *(person)*

burs [burs] *n* scholarship

burun [burun] *n* nose; **burnunu çekmek** *v* sniff; **burun deliği** *n* nostril; **burun kanaması** *n* nosebleed

but [but] *n* thigh

buyurgan [bujurgan] *adj* bossy

buz [buz] *n* ice; **çubuk buz** *n* ice lolly; **buz çözücü** *n* de-icer; **buz hokeyi** *n* ice hockey; **buz kutusu** *n* icebox; **buz pateni** *n* ice-skating; **buz pateni sahası** *n* ice rink; **gizli buz** *n* black ice; **küp buz** *n* ice cube; **buzlu lütfen** With

ice, please; **Buz pateni yapmak için nereye gidebiliriz?** Where can we go ice-skating?
buzdağı [buzda:ə] *n* iceberg
buzdolabı [buzdolabə] *n* fridge, refrigerator
buzlu [buzlu] *adj* frosty, icy
buzul [buzul] *n* glacier
Buzul [buzul] *n* **Kuzey Buzul Kuşağı** *n* Arctic Circle
büfe [byfe] *n (dükkan)* kiosk, *(mobilya)* sideboard; **açık büfe** *n* buffet
bükmek [bykmek] *vt* twist
bükülmüş [bykylmyʃ] *adj* bent *(not straight)*
büro [byro] *n* office; **danışma bürosu** *n* inquiries office; **döviz bürosu** *n* bureau de change; **emanet bagaj bürosu** *n* left-luggage office; **enformasyon bürosu** *n* information office; **turizm bürosu** *n* tourist office; **Basın büronuz var mı?** Do you have a press office?; **Büronuza nasıl gelebilirim?** How do I get to your office?; **Bir büroda çalışıyorum** I work in an office; **Turizm bürosu nerede?** Where is the tourist office?
bürokrasi [byrokrasi] *n* bureaucracy
büsbütün [bysbytyn] *adv* quite
bütçe [byttʃe] *n* budget
bütün [bytyn] *adj* complete, *(bölünmemiş)* intact, *(hepsi)* all, *(tamamı)* entire, *(tüm)* whole ▷ *n (tamamı)* whole; **Bütün gün hiç kimseyi değil, sadece kendimizi görmek isterdik!** We'd like to see nobody but us all day!
bütünleyici [bytynlejidʒi] *adj* complementary
bütünüyle [bytynyjle] *adv* entirely, quite
büyü [byjy] *n* magic, spell *(magic)*
büyücü [byjydʒy] *n* sorcerer
büyük [byjyk] *adj* big, *(iri)* large, *(müthiş)* great ▷ *n* major; **çok büyük** *adj* tremendous; **büyük çoğunluk** *n* majority; **büyük karides** *npl* scampi; **büyük mağaza** *n* department store; **büyük perhizin arife günü** *n* Shrove Tuesday; **büyük yolcu gemisi** *n* liner; **bedenine göre büyük** *adj* outsize; **daha büyük** *adj* bigger; **yaşça en büyük** *adj* eldest; **Çok büyük** It's too big; **Büyük beden var mı?** Do you have a large?; **Bunun bir büyük bedeni var mı?** Do you have this in a bigger size?; **Daha büyük bir odanız var mı?** Do you have a bigger one?; **Ekstra büyük beden var mı?** Do you have an extra large?; **Ev oldukça büyük** The house is quite big
Büyük [byjyk] *adj* **Büyük perhizin ilk Çarşambası** *n* Ash Wednesday
büyükanne [byjykanne] *n* grandmother; **büyükanne ve büyükbaba** *npl* grandparents
büyükbaba [byjykbaba] *n* grandfather; **büyükanne ve büyükbaba** *npl* grandparents
büyükelçi [byjykeltʃi] *n* ambassador
büyüleyici [byjylejidʒi] *adj* fascinating

büyülü [byjyly] *adj* magic
büyüme [byjyme] *n* growth
büyümek [byjymek] *v* grow up ▷ *vi* grow
büyüteç [byjytetʃ] *n* magnifying glass
büyütme [byjytme] *n* enlargement
büyütmek [byjytmek] *v* **gözünde büyütmek** *v* overestimate

cadde [dʒadde] *n* street
cadı [dʒadə] *n* witch
cafe [kafe] *n* café; **Internet cafe** *n* Internet café; **Buralarda Internet cafe var mı?** Are there any Internet cafés here?
cahil [dʒahil] *adj* ignorant
cam [dʒam] *n* glass; **ön cam** *n* windscreen; **çift cam** *n* double glazing; **cam bardak** *n* glass *(vessel)*; **cam kenarı koltuğu** *n* window seat; **cam sileceği** *n* windscreen wiper; **pencere camı** *n* window pane
cami [dʒami] *n* mosque; **Cami nerede var?** Where is there a mosque?
cam yünü [dʒamjyny] *n* fibreglass
can [dʒan] *v* **can kurtaran** *adj* life-saving; **can sıkıntısı** *n* boredom; **can sıkmak** *v* bore *(be dull)*; **canı sıkılmış** *adj* bored; **canı**

sıkkın *adj* depressed
canavar [dʒanavar] *n* monster
cankurtaran [dʒaŋurtaran] *n* *(sahil)* lifeguard, *(tıp)* ambulance; **cankurtaran sandalı** *n* lifeboat; **cankurtaran simidi** *n* lifebelt; **cankurtaran yeleği** *n* life jacket; **Cankurtaran çağırın!** Get the lifeguard!; **Cankurtaran var mı?** Is there a lifeguard?
canlandırmak [dʒanlandərmak] *v* revive; **gözünde canlandırmak** *v* visualize
canlı [dʒanlə] *adj* *(hayatta)* alive, *(parlak)* vivid, *(yaşayan)* live ▷ *n* *(yaşayan)* living; **Canlı müzik dinleyebileceğimiz bir yer var mı?** Where can we hear live music?
cari [dʒari] *adj* **cari hesap** *n* current account
casus [dʒasus] *n* spy ▷ *v* **casusluk etmek** *v* spy
casusluk [dʒasusluk] *n* espionage, spying
catering [dʒatering] *n* catering
caz [dʒaz] *n* jazz
cazibe [dʒazibe] *n* **cazibesine kapılmak** *v* fall for
CD [si:di:] *n* CD; **CD ne zaman hazır olur?** When will the CD be ready?
CD-ROM [si:di:rom] *n* CD-ROM
cehalet [dʒehalet] *n* ignorance
cehennem [dʒehennem] *n* hell
ceket [dʒeket] *n* jacket
cenaze [dʒenaze] *n* funeral; **cenaze kaldırıcısı** *n* undertaker; **cenazenin gömülmeye ya da yakılmaya hazırlandığı oda** *n* funeral parlour
cenin [dʒenin] *n* foetus
cennet [dʒennet] *n* heaven, paradise
centilmen [dʒentilmen] **(centilmenler)** *n* gentleman
CEO [dʒeo] *abbr* CEO
cep [dʒep] *n* pocket; **cep harçlığı** *n* pocket money; **cep hesap makinesi** *n* pocket calculator; **cep matarası** *n* flask; **cep numarası** *n* mobile number; **cep telefonu** *n* mobile phone
cephane [dʒephane] *n* ammunition
cephe [dʒephe] *n* frontier
cereyan [dʒerejan] *n* draught
cerrah [dʒerrah] *n* surgeon
cerrahi [dʒerrahi] *n* **kozmetik cerrahi** *n* cosmetic surgery; **plastik cerrahi** *n* plastic surgery
cesaret [dʒesaret] *n* bravery, courage; **cesaret verici** *adj* encouraging; **cesaretini kırmak** *v* discourage
ceset [dʒeset] *n* corpse
cesur [dʒesur] *adj* brave, daring
cetvel [dʒetvel] *n* ruler *(measure)*
ceviz [dʒeviz] *n* walnut; **Hindistan cevizi** *n* coconut; **küçük Hindistan cevizi** *n* nutmeg
ceza [dʒeza] *n* fine, punishment, sentence *(punishment)*; **dayak cezası** *n* corporal punishment; **idam cezası** *n* capital punishment; **Ceza ne kadar?** How much is the fine?; **Cezayı nereye yatıracağım?** Where do I pay the fine?
cezalandırmak [dʒezalandərmak] *v* penalize,

punish
Cezayir [dʒezajir] *adj* Algerian ▷ *n* Algeria
Cezayirli [dʒezajirli] *n* Algerian
cezve [dʒezve] *n* coffeepot
check-in [dʒhedʒkin] *v* **... uçağı için nerede check-in yaptırabilirim?** Where do I check in for the flight to...?; **Check-in yaptırmak istiyorum lütfen** I'd like to check in, please; **En son kaçta check-in yaptırmam gerekiyor?** When is the latest I can check in?; **Kaçta check-in yaptırmam gerekiyor?** When do I have to check in?
cımbız [dʒəmbəz] *npl* tweezers
cırcır [dʒərdʒər] *n* **cırcır böceği** *n* cricket *(insect)*
cırt [dʒərt] *n* **cırt bant** *n* Velcro®
cıva [dʒəva] *n* mercury
cıyaklamak [dʒəjaklamak] *v* squeak
ciddi [dʒiddi] *adj* serious; **Ciddi bir şey mi?** Is it serious?
ciddiyetle [dʒiddijetle] *adv* seriously
ciğer [dʒjier] *n* **Ciğer yiyemem** I can't eat liver
cihaz [dʒihaz] *n* appliance; **üfleme cihazı** *n* Breathalyser®; **çağrı cihazı** *n* bleeper, pager; **gizli dinleme cihazı yerleştirilmiş** *adj* bugged; **işitme cihazı** *n* hearing aid; **inhalasyon cihazı** *n* inhaler; **otopark ödeme cihazı** *n* parking meter; **ses kayıt cihazı** *n* recorder *(music)*, tape recorder; **yağmurlama cihazı** *n* sprinkler
cila [dʒila] *n* polish, *(vernik)* varnish; **ayakkabı cilası** *n* shoe polish; **tırnak cilası** *n* nail varnish
cilalamak [dʒilalamak] *v* polish, varnish
cilt [dʒilt] *n* skin
cimnastik [dʒimnastik] *n* **Cimnastik salonu nerede?** Where is the gym?
cin [dʒin] *n (alkol)* gin; **Ben bir cin tonik alayım lütfen** I'll have a gin and tonic, please
cinayet [dʒinajet] *n* murder
cins [dʒins] *adj* pedigree ▷ *n (hayvan)* breed
cinsel [dʒinsel] *adj* sexual; **cinsel birleşim** *n* sexual intercourse
cinsiyet [dʒinsijet] *n* gender, *(seks)* sex; **cinsiyet ayrımcılığı** *n* sexism; **cinsiyet ayrımcılığı yapan** *adj* sexist
cips [dʒips] *n* crisps
civar [dʒivar] *adv* **Civarda ilginç yürüyüş yerleri var mı?** Are there any interesting walks nearby?
civciv [dʒivdʒiv] *n* chick
coğrafya [dʒoɣrafja] *n* geography
conta [dʒonta] *n* gasket
coşku [dʒoʃku] *n* ecstasy
cömert [dʒømert] *adj* generous
cömertlik [dʒømertlik] *n* generosity
cross-country [dʒrossdʒountrj] *n* **Cross-country kayağı kiralamak istiyorum** I want to hire cross-country skis; **Cross-country kayağı yapmak mümkün mü?** Is it possible to go cross-country skiing?
Cuma [dʒuma] *n* Friday; **Kutsal Cuma** *n* Good Friday; **Cuma günü**

on Friday; **Cuma günü için iki bilet almak istiyorum** I'd like two tickets for next Friday

Cumartesi [dʒumartesi] *n* Saturday; **önümüzdeki Cumartesi** next Saturday; **bu Cumartesi** this Saturday; **Cumartesi günü** on Saturday; **Cumartesileri** on Saturdays; **geçen Cumartesi** last Saturday; **her Cumartesi** every Saturday; **Cumartesileri** on Saturdays

cumhuriyet [dʒumhurijet] *n* republic

Cumhuriyet [dʒumhurijet] *n* **Çek Cumhuriyeti** *n* Czech Republic; **Dominik Cumhuriyeti** *n* Dominican Republic; **Orta Afrika Cumhuriyeti** *n* Central African Republic

cüce [dʒydʒe] **(cüceler)** *n* dwarf

cümle [dʒymle] *n* sentence *(words)*

cüret [dʒyret] *n* nerve *(boldness)* ▷ *v* **cüret etmek** *v* dare

cüzdan [dʒyzdan] *n (erkek)* wallet, *(kadın)* purse; **evlilik cüzdanı** *n* marriage certificate; **nüfus cüzdanı** *n* birth certificate; **Cüzdanım çalındı** My wallet has been stolen; **Cüzdanımı kaybettim** I've lost my wallet

CV [si:vi:] *n* CV

çaba [tʃaba] *n* effort, try

çabalamak [tʃabalamak] *v* go after, try

çabucak [tʃabudʒak] *adv* promptly

çabuk [tʃabuk] *adj* prompt, quick; **çabuk kızan** *adj* irritable

çabukça [tʃabuktʃa] *adv* quickly

Çad [tʃad] *n* Chad

çadır [tʃadər] *n* tent; **çadır direği** *n* tent pole; **çadır kazığı** *n* tent peg; **Çadırımızı buraya kurabilir miyiz?** Can we pitch our tent here?; **Çadırın bir geceliği ne kadar?** How much is it per night for a tent?; **Çadırın bir haftalığı ne kadar?** How much is it per week for a tent?; **Bir çadır yeri istiyoruz** We'd like a site for a tent

Çağ [tʃa:] *n* **Orta Çağ** *n* Middle Ages

çağdaş [tʃa:daʃ] *adj* contemporary

çağlayan [tʃa:lajan] *n* cataract

(waterfall)
çağlayanlar [tʃa:lajanlar] *npl* rapids
çağrı [tʃa:rə] *n* call; **çağrı cihazı** *n* bleeper, pager; **çağrı merkezi** *n* call centre; **uyarı çağrısı** *n* alarm call
çakı [tʃakə] *n* penknife
çakıl [tʃakəl] *n* gravel; **çakıl taşı** *n* pebble
çakırkeyif [tʃakərkejif] *adj* tipsy
çakışmak [tʃakəʃmak] *v* coincide
çakmak [tʃakmak] *n* cigarette lighter, lighter
çalgıcı [tʃalgədʒə] *n* **sokak çalgıcısı** *n* busker
çalı [tʃalə] *n* bush, shrub; **çalı fasulyesi** *n* French beans, runner bean; **çalı meyvesi** *n* berry
çalıkuşu [tʃaləkuʃu] *n* wren
çalılık [tʃalələk] *n* bush *(thicket)*
çalışan [tʃaləʃan] *n* **serbest çalışan** *adj* self-employed
çalışma [tʃaləʃma] *n* **çalışma alanı** *n* workspace; **çalışma köşesi** *n* workstation; **yol yapım çalışması** *npl* roadworks
çalışmak [tʃaləʃmak] *v* study ▷ *vt* work; **çalışma izni** *n* work permit; **çalışma köşesi** *n* work station; **çalışma saatleri** *npl* office hours; **bilgisayar çalışması** *n* computing; **esnek çalışma saati** *n* flexitime; **köle gibi çalışmak** *v* slave;**... a çalışıyorum** I work for...; **Çalışıyorum** I work; **Nerede çalışıyorsunuz?** Where do you work?; **Sizinle çalışmak bir zevkti** It's been a pleasure working with you
çalkalamak [tʃalkalamak] *vt* shake
çalkalanmak [tʃalkalanmak] *vi* shake
çalkantı [tʃalkantə] *n* turbulence
çalma [tʃalma] *v* **çalma tonu** *n* ringtone
çalmak [tʃalmak] *v* steal, *(zil/çan)* ring ▷ *vt* play *(music)*; **ıslık çalmak** *v* whistle; **çalar saat** *n* alarm clock; **CD çalar** *n* CD player; **kapıyı çalmak** *v* knock *(on the door etc.)*
çam [tʃam] *n* pine
çamaşır [tʃamaʃər] *n* laundry, washing; **çamaşır ipi** *n* clothes line, washing line; **çamaşır kurutma makinesi** *n* spin dryer, tumble dryer; **çamaşır makinesi** *n* washing machine; **çamaşır mandalı** *n* clothes peg; **çamaşır odası** *n* utility room; **çamaşır tozu** *n* washing powder; **iç çamaşırı** *n* lingerie, underwear; **Çamaşır makineleri nerede?** Where are the washing machines?; **Çamaşır makinesi nasıl çalışıyor?** How does the washing machine work?; **Çamaşır servisi var mı?** Is there a laundry service?; **Çamaşır tozunuz var mı?** Do you have washing powder?; **Çamaşırlarımı nerede yıkayabilirim?** Where can I do some washing?
çamaşırhane [tʃamaʃərhane] *n* Launderette®
çamur [tʃamur] *n* mud; **sulu çamur** *n* slush
çamurlu [tʃamurlu] *adj* muddy

çamurluk [tʃamurluk] *n* mudguard
çan [tʃan] *n* **çan sesi** *n* toll
çanak [tʃanak] *n* **çanak çömlek** *n* pottery; **uydu çanak** *n* satellite dish
çanta [tʃanta] *n* handbag; **alışveriş çantası** *n* shopping bag; **bel çantası** *n* bum bag, money belt; **evrak çantası** *n* briefcase; **gecelik seyahat çantası** *n* overnight bag; **ilk yardım çantası** *n* first-aid kit; **okul çantası** *n* schoolbag; **omuz çantası** *n* satchel; **sırt çantası** *n* backpack, holdall, rucksack; **sırt çantasıyla dolaşan gezgin** backpacker; **sırt çantasıyla gezme** *n* backpacking; **tuvalet çantası** *n* sponge bag, toilet bag
çap [tʃap] *n* diameter
çapa [tʃapa] *n* anchor
çapkın [tʃapkən] *adj* **yalı çapkını** *n* kingfisher
çapraz [tʃapraz] *n* cross
çaput [tʃaput] *n* rag
çarkıfelek [tʃarkəfelek] *n* **çarkıfelek meyvası** *n* passion fruit
çarpıcı [tʃarpədʒə] *adj* striking
çarpışma [tʃarpəʃma] *n* collision
çarpışmak [tʃarpəʃmak] *v* collide ▷ *vi (araçla)* crash
çarpma [tʃarpma] *n* bump, hit; **elektrik çarpması** *n* electric shock; **güneş çarpması** *n* sunstroke
çarpmak [tʃarpmak] *v (matematik)* multiply; **çarparak kapatmak** *v* slam; **çarpma işlemi** *n* multiplication; **kazara çarpmak** *v* bump into; **vasıta ile çarpmak** *vi* crash
çarşaf [tʃarʃaf] *n* sheet; **yatak çarşafı** *n* bed linen; **Çarşaflar kirli** The sheets are dirty; **Çarşaflarım kirli** My sheets are dirty
Çarşamba [tʃarʃamba] *n* Wednesday; **Büyük perhizin ilk Çarşambası** *n* Ash Wednesday; **Çarşamba günü** on Wednesday
çatal [tʃatal] *n* fork; **çatal, bıçak, kaşık** *n* cutlery; **Temiz bir çatal alabilir miyim lütfen?** Could I have a clean fork please?
çatı [tʃatə] *n* roof; **Çatı akıyor** The roof leaks
çatışma [tʃatəʃma] *n* conflict
çatışmak [tʃatəʃmak] *vi* clash
çatlak [tʃatlak] *adj* cracked ▷ *n* crack *(fracture)*
çatlatmak [tʃatlatmak] *vi* crack
çatmak [tʃatmak] *n* **kaşlarını çatmak** *v* frown
çavdar [tʃavdar] *n* rye
çavuş [tʃavuʃ] *n* sergeant
çay [tʃaj] *n* tea; **çay fincanı** *n* teacup; **çay kaşığı** *n* teaspoon; **çay saati** *n* teatime; **bitki çayı** *n* herbal tea; **torba çay** *n* tea bag; **Bir çay daha alabilir miyiz?** Could we have another cup of tea, please?; **Bir çay lütfen** A tea, please
çaydanlık [tʃajdanlək] *n* kettle, teapot
çayır [tʃajər] *n* meadow
Çeçenistan [tʃetʃenistan] *n* Chechnya
çek [tʃek] *n* cheque; **açık çek** *n*

blank cheque; **çek defteri** *n* chequebook; **hediye çeki** *n* gift voucher; **seyahat çeki** *n* traveller's cheque; **Çek bozdurabilir miyim?** Can I cash a cheque?; **Çek bozdurmak istiyorum lütfen** I want to cash a cheque, please; **Çekle ödeme yapabilir miyim?** Can I pay by cheque?; **Bu seyahat çeklerini bozdurmak istiyorum** I want to change these traveller's cheques; **Seyahat çeki kabul ediyor musunuz?** Do you accept traveller's cheques?; **Seyahat çeklerimi burada bozdurabilir miyim?** Can I change my traveller's cheques here?

çek-yat [tʃekjat] *n* sofa bed

Çek [tʃek] *adj* Czech ▷ *n (kişi)* Czech *(person)*; **Çek Cumhuriyeti** *n* Czech Republic; **Çek dili** *(dil) n* Czech *(language)*

çekici [tʃekidʒi] *adj* attractive; **ilgi çekici** *adj* interesting; **Çok çekicisiniz** You are very attractive

çekiç [tʃekitʃ] *n* hammer

çekiliş [tʃekiliʃ] *n* draw *(tie)*, raffle

çekilmek [tʃekilmek] *v* opt out

çekim [tʃekim] *n* attraction, charm; **yeniden çekim** *n* remake

çekirdek [tʃekirdek] *n* pip; **çekirdekli kısım** *(meyve) n* core; **kahve çekirdeği** *n* coffee bean; **metal çekirdek** *n* pellet

çekirge [tʃekirge] *n* grasshopper; **sopa çekirgesi** *n* stick insect

çekme [tʃekme] *n* withdrawal

çekmece [tʃekmedʒe] *n* drawer; **Çekmece takılmış** The drawer is jammed

çekmek [tʃekmek] *v* attract, withdraw, *(ağırlık)* weigh ▷ *vt* pull; **açlık çekmek** *v* starve; **acı çekmek** *v* suffer; **arabayı çekmek** *v* tow away; **başı çekmek** *v* head; **burnunu çekmek** *v* sniff; **dikkatini çekmek** *v* point out; **fişten çekmek** *v* unplug; **fotoğrafını çekmek** *v* photograph; **fotokopisini çekmek** *v* photocopy; **halat çekme oyunu** *n* tug-of-war; **hesabından çekilen para** *n* debit; **iç çekme** *n* sigh; **ilgisini başka yöne çekmek** *v* distract; **kürek çekmek** *v* row *(in boat)*; **kenara çekmek** *v (araç)* pull out, *(araç)* pull up; **şınav çekmek** *n* press-up; **röntgenini çekmek** *v* X-ray

çelik [tʃelik] *n* steel; **paslanmaz çelik** *n* stainless steel

çelişki [tʃeliʃki] *n* contradiction

çelişmek [tʃeliʃmek] *v* contradict

çene [tʃene] *n* chin, jaw

çerçeve [tʃertʃeve] *n* frame; **resim çerçevesi** *n* picture frame

çeşit [tʃeʃit] *n* assortment, sort, variety; **çeşitlilik göstermek** *v* vary

çeşitli [tʃeʃitli] *adj* miscellaneous, varied, various

çeşitlilik [tʃeʃitlilik] *n* **çeşitlilik göstermek** *v* range

çeşme [tʃeʃme] *n* fountain

çeşni [tʃeʃni] *n* seasoning

çete [tʃete] *n* gang

çetin [tʃetin] *adj* **çetin sınav** *n* ordeal

çevirimiçi [tʃevirimitʃi] *adj* online

çevirme [tʃevirme] *n (trafik)* roadblock
çevirmek [tʃevirmek] *v* **elektrik düğmesini çevirmek** *v* switch; **geri çevirmek** *v* turn down
çevre [tʃevre] *n* environment, vicinity ▷ *npl* surroundings; **çevre dostu** *adj* ecofriendly, environmentally friendly; **çevre yolu** *n* bypass, ring road
çevrebilim [tʃevrebilim] *n* ecology
çevrelemek [tʃevrelemek] *v* surround
çevresel [tʃevresel] *adj* environmental
çeyrek [tʃejrek] *n* quarter; **çeyrek final** *n* quarter final; **Saat ikiyi çeyrek geçiyor** It's quarter past two
çığ [tʃəɣ] *n* avalanche; **Çığ tehlikesi var mı?** Is there a danger of avalanches?
çığlık [tʃəɣlək] *n* scream ▷ *v* **çığlık atmak** *v* scream
çıkarıcı [tʃəkarədʒə] *n* **oje çıkarıcı** *n* nail-polish remover
çıkarma [tʃəkarma] *n* **çıkarma işlemi** *v* subtract
çıkarmak [tʃəkarmak] *v* leave out, stick out, take away, *(matematik)* deduct; **üstünü çıkarmak** *v* take off; **diş çıkarmak** *v* teethe; **elden çıkarmak** *v* sell off; **işten çıkarma** *(ihtiyaç fazlası olarak) n* redundancy; **işten çıkarmak** *v* lay off
çıkartmak [tʃəkartmak] *v* **işten çıkarmak** *v* dismiss; **ortaya çıkarmak** *v* disclose
çıkış [tʃəkəʃ] *n* checkout, exit, way out ▷ *v* **çıkış yapmak** *v* check out; **yangın çıkışı** *n* fire escape; **... çıkışı nerede?** Which exit for...?; **Çıkış nerede?** Where is the exit?
çıkış, kapı [tʃəkəʃkapə] *n* **acil çıkış kapısı** *n* emergency exit
çıkmak [tʃəkmak] *v* come out, get out; **dışarı çıkmak** *n* go out, outing; **iki katına çıkmak** *vt* double; **karşı çıkmak** *v* oppose; **ortaya çıkmak** *v* show up; **sahip çıkmak** *v* own up; **sıradan çıkmak** *v* fall out; **tura çıkmak** *v* tour; **yürüyüşe çıkma** *n* hike; **yola çıkmak** *v* go away, start off; **zahmetli bir yürüyüşe çıkmak** *v* trek
çıkmaz [tʃəkmaz] *n* **çıkmaz sokak** *n* dead end
çıktı [tʃəktə] *n (bilgisayar)* printout
çıldırmak [tʃəldərmak] *n* **öfkeden çıldırmış** *adj* furious
çılgın [tʃəlgən] *adj* crazy, frantic, mad *(angry)*
çılgınca [tʃəlgəndʒa] *adv* madly
çılgınlık [tʃəlgənlək] *n* madness, mania
çıngırak [tʃəngərak] *n* rattle; **çıngıraklı yılan** *n* rattlesnake
çıplak [tʃəplak] *adj* bare, naked, nude ▷ *n* nude; **çıplak ayak** *adj* barefoot; **çıplak ayakla** *adv* barefoot ▷ *v* **sığ suda çıplak ayak yürümek** *v* paddle
çırak [tʃərak] *n* apprentice
çırpıcı [tʃərpədʒə] *n* whisk
çırpmak [tʃərpmak] *n* **kanat çırpmak** *v* flap
çiçek [tʃitʃek] *n* flower ▷ *v* **çiçek**

açmak *v* blossom, flower; **çiçek saksısı** *n* plant pot; **çiçek tozu** *n* pollen; **çuha çiçeği** *n* primrose; **düğün çiçeği** *n* buttercup; **inci çiçeği** *n* lily of the valley; **kadife çiçeği** *n* marigold; **saksı çiçeği** *n* pot plant
çiçekçi [tʃitʃektʃi] *n* florist
çift [tʃift] *adj* double ▷ *n* couple, pair; **çift cam** *n* double glazing; **çift kişilik yatak** *n* double bed; **çift odaklı gözlük** *npl* bifocals; **çift tırnak** *npl* quotation marks; **çift yatak** *npl* twin beds; **çift yataklı oda** *n* twin room, twin-bedded room; **çift-şeritli yol** *n* dual carriageway; **Çift yataklı bir oda rica ediyorum** I'd like a room with a double bed
çiftçi [tʃifttʃi] *n* farmer
çiftçilik [tʃifttʃilik] *n* farming
çiftlik [tʃiftlik] *n* farm; **çiftlik evi** *n* farmhouse
çiğ [tʃji] *adj (pişmemiş)* raw; **Çiğ yumurta yiyemiyorum** I can't eat raw eggs
çiğdem [tʃjidem] *n (çiçek)* crocus
çiğnemek [tʃjinemek] *v* chew
çiklet [tʃiklet] *n* chewing gum; **balonlu çiklet** *n* bubble gum
çikolata [tʃikolata] *n* chocolate; **sade çikolata** *n* plain chocolate; **sütlü çikolata** *n* milk chocolate
çile [tʃile] *n* **çileden çıkaran** *adj* infuriating
çilek [tʃilek] *n* strawberry
çilingir [tʃilingir] *n* locksmith
çiller [tʃiller] *npl* freckles
çim [tʃim] *n* **çim alan** *n* lawn; **çim biçme makinesi** *n* lawnmower, mower
çimdiklemek [tʃimdiklemek] *vt* pinch
çimento [tʃimento] *n* cement
Çin [tʃin] *adj* Chinese ▷ *n* China; **Çin çubuğu** *npl* chopsticks
Çince [tʃindʒe] *n (dil)* Chinese *(language)*
çingene [tʃingene] *n* gypsy
çinko [tʃiŋo] *n* zinc
Çinli [tʃinli] *n (kişi)* Chinese *(person)*
çip [tʃip] *n (elektronik)* chip *(electronic)*; **silikon çip** *n* silicon chip
çirkin [tʃirkin] *adj* ugly
çisenti [tʃisenti] *n* drizzle
çit [tʃit] *n (çalılık)* hedge, *(tahta, tel örgü)* fence
çivi [tʃivi] *n* nail
çizelge [tʃizelge] *n* **hesap çizelgesi** *n* spreadsheet
çizgi [tʃizgi] *n* line; **çizgi öykü** *n* comic strip; **eğik çizgi** *n* forward slash; **geriye yatık çizgi** *n* backslash; **taç çizgisi** *n* touchline
çizgili [tʃizgili] *adj* striped, stripy
çizim [tʃizim] *n* drawing
çizme [tʃizme] *n (ayakkabı)* boot, *(boyasını vb)* scratch; **lastik çizme** *npl* wellies; **lastik çizmeler** *npl* wellingtons
çizmek [tʃizmek] *v (arabanın boyasını vb)* scratch ▷ *vt (resim)* draw *(sketch)*; **altını çizmek** *v* underline
çoban [tʃoban] *n* shepherd; **İskoç çoban köpeği** *n* collie; **çoban köğeği** *n* sheepdog; **çoban püskülü** *n* holly

çocuk [tʃodʒuk] **(çocuklar)** *n* child, kid; **çocuk bakıcısı** *n* childminder, nanny; **çocuk bakımı** *n* childcare; **çocuk felci** *n* polio; **çocuk şarkıları** *n* nursery rhyme; **çocuk odası** *n* nursery; **çocuk oyun grubu** *n* playgroup; **çocuk tacizi** *n* child abuse; **koruyucu aile bakımındaki çocuk** *n* foster child; **oğlan çocuğu** *n* boy; **okul çocukları** *n* schoolchildren; **vaftiz çocuğu** *n* godchild; **yeni yürümeye başlayan çocuk** *n* toddler; **İki yaşında bir çocuk için çocuk koltuğu istiyorum** I'd like a child seat for a two-year-old child; **Çocuğum hasta** My child is ill; **Çocuğum kayıp** My child is missing; **Çocuğum yok** I don't have any children; **Çocuk bu pasaportta** The child is on this passport; **Çocuk havuzu var mı?** Is there a children's pool?; **Çocuk koltuğu var mı?** Do you have a child's seat?; **Çocuk menüsü var mı?** Do you have a children's menu?; **Çocuk porsiyonu yapıyor musunuz?** Do you have children's portions?; **Çocuklar bu pasaportta** The children are on this passport; **Çocuklar için etkinlikleriniz var mı?** Do you have activities for children?; **Çocuklar için güvenli mi?, Çocuklara verilebilir mi?** Is it safe for children?; **Çocuklar için kolaylıklarınız neler?** Do you have facilities for children?; **Çocuklar için neler var?** What is there for children to do?; **Çocuklar için yüzme havuzu var mı?** Is there a paddling pool for the children?; **Çocuklara indirim var mı?** Are there any reductions for children?; **Çocukları alıyor musunuz?** Is it okay to take children?; **Çocuklarım arabada** My children are in the car; **Üç çocuğum var** I have three children; **Bir çocuğum var** I have a child; **Bir çocuk bileti** a child's ticket; **Bir çocuk için armağan almak istiyordum** I'm looking for a present for a child; **Bu akşam çocuklara bakacak birine ihtiyacım var** I need someone to look after the children tonight

çocukça [tʃodʒuktʃa] *adj* childish

çocukluk [tʃodʒukluk] *n* childhood

çoğul [tʃou:l] *n* plural

çoğunluk [tʃou:nluk] *n* **büyük çoğunluk** *n* majority

çoğunlukla [tʃou:nlukla] *adv* mostly

çok [tʃok] *adj* many ▷ *adv* very ▷ *n* plenty ▷ *pron* many, most *(majority)*; **çok önemli** *adj* momentous; **çok büyük** *adj* tremendous; **çok güzel** *adj* gorgeous; **çok gizli** *adj* top-secret; **çok iyi** *n* fine; **çok komik** *adj* hilarious; **çok pişmiş** *adj* overdone; **çok sevinmiş** *adj* thrilled; **çok uluslu** *n* multinational; **çok yönlü** *n* versatile; **en çok** *adv* most, most *(superlative)*; **Çok az İngilizce konuşabiliyorum** I speak very little English; **Çok üzgünüm** I'm very sorry; **Çok çekicisiniz** You are very attractive; **Çok naziksiniz** That's very kind of you; **Çok sıcak** It's very hot; **Çok teşekkürler** Thank you very much; **Çok yakın** It's very near; **Beni davet ettiğiniz için çok teşekkürler** It's very kind of you to invite me; **Bu yemek çok yağlı** The food is very greasy; **Kar çok şiddetli** The snow is very heavy

çokça [tʃoktʃa] *adv* much

çoksatar [tʃoksatar] *n* bestseller

çorap [tʃorap] *n* sock; **külotlu çorap** *npl* tights; **naylon çorap** *n* stocking

çorba [tʃorba] *n* soup; **çorba kaşığı** *n* tablespoon; **et ya da sebze suyuna çorba** *n* broth; **Günün çorbası ne?** What is the soup of the day?

çökmek [tʃøkmek] *v* collapse; **diz çökmek** *v* kneel, kneel down

çöl [tʃøl] *n* desert; **çöl faresi** *n* gerbil

çömelmek [tʃømelmek] *v* crouch down

çömlek [tʃømlek] *n* **çanak çömlek** *n* pottery

çöp [tʃøp] *n* garbage, litter, rubbish, trash; **çöp döküm alanı** *n* rubbish dump; **çöp kutusu** *n* litter bin; **çöp sepeti** *n* dustbin, wastepaper basket; **çöp tenekesi** *n* bin; **Çöpü nereye bırakacağız?** Where do we leave the rubbish?

çöpçü [tʃøptʃy] **(çöpçüler)** *n* dustman

çöplük [tʃøplyk] *n* dump

çörek [tʃørek] *n* bun; **çörek ve kahve ya da çaydan oluşan kahvaltı** *n* continental breakfast

çözmek [tʃøzmek] *v* figure out, solve, work out, *(bağcık)* untie

çözücü [tʃøzydʒy] *n* solvent; **buz çözücü** *n* de-icer

çözüm [tʃøzym] *n* solution

çözümleme [tʃøzymleme] *n* analysis

çözümlemek [tʃøzymlemek] *v* analyse; **hakem aracılığıyla çözümleme** *n* arbitration

çözünür [tʃøzynyr] *adj* soluble

çubuk [tʃubuk] *n* bar *(strip)*, *(demir)* rod; **Çin çubuğu** *npl* chopsticks; **çubuk buz** *n* ice lolly; **kulak çubuğu** *n* cotton bud; **yağ çubuğu** *n* dipstick

çuha [tʃuha] *n* **çuha çiçeği** *n* primrose

çukur [tʃukur] *n* **foseptik çukuru** *n* septic tank; **yol çukuru** *n* pothole

çuval [tʃuval] *n* sack *(container)*

çünkü [tʃyŋy] *conj* because

çürük [tʃyryk] *n* **vişne çürüğü renginde** *adj* maroon

çürümek [tʃyrymek] *v* decay, rot

çürümüş [tʃyrymyʃ] *adj* rotten

d

da [da] *prep* on
dağ [da:] *n* mountain; **dağ bisikleti** *n* mountain bike; **Dağ manzaralı bir oda rica ediyorum** I'd like a room with a view of the mountains; **En yakın dağ kulübesi nerede?** Where is the nearest mountain hut?; **En yakın dağ kurtarma ekibi nerede?** Where is the nearest mountain rescue service post?
dağarcık [da:ardʒək] *n* **sözcük dağarcığı** *n* vocabulary
dağcı [da:dʒə] *n* mountaineer, *(tırmanıcı)* climber
dağcılık [da:dʒələk] *n* mountaineering, *(tırmanıcılık)* climbing
dağınık [da:ənək] *adj* untidy
dağınıklık [da:ənəklək] *n* mess
dağıtıcı [da:ətədʒə] *n* dispenser
dağıtım [da:ətəm] *n* **gazete dağıtım** *n* paper round
dağıtmak [da:ətmak] *v* distribute, *(vermek)* give out
dağlık [da:lək] *adj* mountainous
daha [daha] *adv* more; **daha aşağı** *adj* lower; **daha az** *pron* less, *(miktar olarak)* less, *(sayıca)* fewer; **daha önce** *adv* earlier; **daha önceden** *adv* beforehand, previously; **daha önceden olmamış** *adj* unprecedented; **daha önemsiz bir göreve kaydırmak** *v* relegate; **daha büyük** *adj* bigger; **daha erken** *adv* sooner; **daha fazla** *pron* more; **daha genç** *adj* younger; **daha ileri, daha ileriye** *adv* further; **daha iyi, daha iyisi** *adv* better; **daha kötü, daha kötüsü** *adv* worse; **daha sonra** *adv* later; **daha uzun** *adv* longer; **daha yaşlı** *adj* elder; **Biraz daha yavaş konuşabilir misiniz lütfen?** Could you speak more slowly, please?; **Daha fazla çarşafa ihtiyacımız var** We need more sheets; **Daha fazla battaniyeye ihtiyacımız var** We need more blankets; **Daha fazla tabak çanağa ihtiyacımız var** We need more crockery
dahi [dahi] *adv (o da)* also ▷ *n (zeki)* genius
dahil [dahil] *adj* included ▷ *prep* including; **dahil etmek** *v* include, involve; **Fiyata neler dahil?** What is included in the price?; **KDV dahil mi?** Is VAT included?; **Sebze de dahil mi?** Are the vegetables included?; **Servis dahil mi?** Is

service included?
dahili [dahili] *adj* **Dahili ht numara** extension
daimi [daimi] *adj* continual ▷ *adv* continually
daire [daire] *n* circle; **apartman dairesi** *n* flat; **evlendirme dairesi** *n* registry office; **stüdyo daire** *n* studio flat; **yarım daire** *n* semicircle
dairesel [dairesel] *adj* circular
dairesi [dairesi] *n* **apartman dairesi** *n* apartment
dakika [dakika] *n* minute; **Her yirmi dakikada bir otobüs var** The bus runs every twenty minutes; **On dakika geciktik** We are ten minutes late; **Tren on dakika rötarlı** The train is running ten minutes late
daktilo [daktilo] *n* typewriter
daktilograf [daktilograf] *n* typist
dal [dal] *n (ağaç vb)* branch
dalaş [dalaʃ] *n* **ağız dalaşı** *v* squabble
daldırmak [daldərmak] *vt* dip
dalga [dalga] *n* wave *v* **dalga geçmek** *v* kid
dalgaboyu [dalgaboju] *n* wavelength
dalgalı [dalgalə] *adj* wavy
dalgıç [dalgətʃ] *n* diver
dalgın [dalgən] *adj* absent-minded
dalış [daləʃ] *n* dive; **tüplü dalış** *n* scuba diving
dalma [dalma] *n (denize)* diving
dalmak [dalmak] *v (deniz vb)* dive; **Burada dalınacak en iyi yer neresi?** Where is the best place to dive?; **Dalmak istiyorum** I'd like to go diving
dama [dama] *n* **dama oyunu** *npl* draughts
damar [damar] *n* vein
damat [damat] **(damatlar)** *n (kızının kocası)* son-in-law, *(gelinin kocası)* bridegroom, groom
damga [damga] *n* stamp; **posta damgası** *n* postmark
damıtımevi [damətəmevi] *n* distillery
damla [damla] *n* drip, drop; **göz damlası** *npl* eye drops
damlalık [damlalək] *n* **damlalıklı eviye** *n* draining board
damlamak [damlamak] *v* drip
dan [dan] *conj* than ▷ *prep* from, off
dana [dana] **(danalar)** *n* calf; **dana eti** *n* veal
danışma [danəʃma] *n* inquiry desk; **danışma bürosu** *n* inquiries office
danışmak [danəʃmak] *v* consult
danışman [danəʃman] *n* consultant *(adviser)*; **hukuk danışmanı** *n* solicitor
Danimarka [danimarka] *adj* Danish ▷ *n* Denmark; **Danimarka dili** *(dil) n* Danish *(language)*
Danimarkalı [danimarkalə] *n* Dane
dans [dans] *n* dance *v* **dans etmek** *v* dance; **danslı toplantı** *n* dancing; **salon dansı** *n* ballroom dancing; **step dansı** *n* tap-dancing; **Dans etmek için nereye gidebiliriz?** Where can we go dancing?; **Dans etmek ister misiniz?** Would you like to dance?

Dans etmek istiyorum I feel like dancing; **Dans etmem pek** I don't really dance
dansçı [danstʃə] *n* dancer
dantel [dantel] *n* lace
dar [dar] *adj* narrow; **dar görüşlü** *adj* narrow-minded; **dar sokak** *n* alley; **dar yol** *n* lane
daracık [daradʒək] *adj* skin-tight
darbe [darbe] *n* bash *v* **darbe yemek** *vi* strike
darlık [darlək] *n* austerity
darphane [darphane] *n* mint *(coins)*
dart [dart] *n* **dart oku** *n* dart; **dart oyunu** *npl* darts
dava [dava] *npl* proceedings *v* **dava etmek** *v* sue
davalı [davalə] *n* defendant
davar [davar] *npl* cattle
davet [davet] *n* invitation; **davet etmek** *v* invite; **davetsiz misafir** *n* intruder
davranış [davranəʃ] *n* behaviour
davranmak [davranmak] *v (hareket)* act, *(muamele)* treat, *(tavır)* behave
davul [davul] *n* drum; **bas davul** *n* bass drum
davulcu [davuldʒu] *n* drummer
dayak [dajak] *v* **dayak cezası** *n* corporal punishment
dayanan [dajanan] *adj* based
dayanıklılık [dajanəklələk] *n* stamina
dayanılmaz [dajanəlmaz] *adj* unbearable
dayanmak [dajanmak] *v* bear up
dazlak [dazlak] *adj* bald; **dazlak kafa** *n* skinhead
de [de] *prep* on
de, da [deda] *prep* at
debriyaj [debrijaʒ] *n* clutch
dede [dede] *n* granddad, grandfather, grandpa; **dedenin babası** *n* great-grandfather
dedektif [dedektif] *n* detective
dedikodu [dedikodu] *n* gossip; **dedikodu yapmak** *v* gossip
defalarca [defalardʒa] *adv* repeatedly
define [define] *n* treasure
defne [defne] *n* **defne yaprağı** *n* bay leaf
defter [defter] *n* **adres defteri** *n* address book; **çek defteri** *n* chequebook; **digital not defteri** *n* e-book; **karalama defteri** *n* scrapbook; **not defteri** *n* jotter, notebook, notepad
değer [de:er] *n* value, worth; **dikkate değer** *adj* remarkable; **görülmeye değer** *adj* spectacular; **resmedilmeye değer** *adj* picturesque; **Tamir ettirmeye değer mi?** Is it worth repairing?
değerlendirmek [de:erlendirmek] *v* regard
değerli [de:erli] *adj* precious, valuable; **değerli eşyalar** *npl* valuables; **Değerli eşyalarımı kasaya koymak istiyorum** I'd like to put my valuables in the safe; **Değerli eşyalarımı nereye bırakabilirim?** Where can I leave my valuables?
değersiz [de:ersiz] *adj* worthless
değil [deji:l] *adv* not, no; **iyi değil** *adj* unwell; **net değil** *adj* unclear;

Aç değilim I'm not hungry; **Bir şey değil** You're welcome; **Bundan memnun değilim** I'm not satisfied with this; **Bunun tadı pek iyi değil** It doesn't taste very nice; **Sorun değil** No problem; **Uzak değil** It's not far

değirmen [deji:rmen] *n* mill, windmill

değişik [deji:ʃik] *adj* different; **değişiklik yapmak** *v* modify

değişiklik [deji:ʃiklik] *n* modification; **iklim değişikliği** *n* climate change

değişim [deji:ʃim] *n* change

değişken [deji:ʃken] *adj* variable

değişmemiş [deji:ʃmemiʃ] *adj* unchanged

değiştirilebilir [deji:ʃtirilebilir] *adj* changeable

değiştirmek [deji:ʃtirmek] *v* alter, swap ▷ *vi* change ▷ *vt* change, *(dönüştürmek)* convert; **güzergah değiştirme** *n* detour; **kılık değiştirmek** *v* disguise; **yer değiştirme** *n* shift*v* **yer değiştirmek** *v* shift

değnek [de:inek] *n* **koltuk değneği** *n* crutch

dehşet [dehʃet] *n* horror; **dehşet verici** *adj* horrifying, outrageous *v* **dehşete düşürmek** *v* terrify

deklare [deklare] *adj* **deklare etmek** *v* declare; **İzin verilen miktarda içki deklare etmek istiyorum** I have the allowed amount of alcohol to declare; **İzin verilen miktarda sigara deklare etmek istiyorum** I have the allowed amount of tobacco to declare

dekoratör [dekoratør] *n* decorator

dekore etmek *v* decorate

delege [delege] *n* delegate

deli [deli] *adj* insane

delici [delidʒi] *n* piercing

delik [delik] *adj (kulak vb)* pierced ▷ *n (çorap, duvar vb)* hole; **burun deliği** *n* nostril; **musluk deliği** *n* plughole

delikanlı [delikanlə] *n* lad

delil [delil] *n* clue

delmek [delmek] *v* bore *(drill)*, pierce, *(iğneyle)* prick ▷ *vt (matkapla)* drill

demet [demet] *n* bunch

demir [demir] *n* iron; **demir dövmek** *v* forge

demirci [demirdʒi] *n* **demirci dükkanı** *n* ironmonger's

demiryolu [demirjolu] *n* railway

demo [demo] *n* demo

demokrasi [demokrasi] *n* democracy

demokratik [demokratik] *adj* democratic

den [den] *conj* than ▷ *prep* from, off

deneme [deneme] *n* essay; **deneme baskısı** *n* proof *(for checking)*; **deneme sınavı** *adj* mock; **deneme süresi** *n* trial period

denemek [denemek] *v* rehearse, test, try out, *(giysi)* try on; **Deneyebilir miyim?** Can I try it on?

denetçi [denettʃi] *n* surveyor, *(maliye)* auditor, *(müfettiş)* inspector

denetim [denetim] *n* check; **hesap denetimi** *n* audit; **yazım denetimi** *n* spellchecker
denetlemek [denetlemek] *v* supervise, *(teftiş)* inspect ▷ *vt* *(kontrol)* check; **hesapları denetlemek** *v* audit
deney [denej] *n* experiment; **deney tüpü** *n* test tube
deneyim [denejim] *n* experience; **iş deneyimi** *n* work experience
deneyimli [denejimli] *adj* experienced
deneyimsiz [denejimsiz] *adj* inexperienced
denge [denge] *n (durum)* stability, *(fizik)* balance
dengede [dengede] *adj* stable
dengeli [dengeli] *adj* balanced
dengesiz [dengesiz] *adj* unstable
dengesizlik [dengesizlik] *n* instability
deniz [deniz] *adj (askeri)* naval ▷ *n (coğrafya)* sea; **deniz anası** *n* jellyfish; **deniz aygırı** *n* walrus; **deniz ürünü** *n* seafood; **deniz feneri** *n* lighthouse; **deniz kazası** *n* shipwreck; **deniz kazası geçirmiş** *adj* shipwrecked; **deniz kıyısı** *n* seaside, *(sahil)* seashore; **deniz kızı** *n* mermaid; **deniz motoru** *n* motorboat; **deniz seviyesi** *n* sea level; **deniz suyu** *n* sea water; **deniz tarağı** *n* scallop; **deniz tutmuş** *adj* seasick; **deniz yatağı** *n* Lilo®; **kabuklu deniz ürünü** *n* shellfish; **Karayip denizi** *n* Caribbean; **Bugün deniz dalgalı mı?** Is the sea rough today?; **Deniz manzaralı bir oda rica ediyorum** I'd like a room with a view of the sea
Deniz [deniz] *n* **Kızıl Deniz** *n* Red Sea; **Kuzey Denizi** *n* North Sea
denizaltı [denizaltə] *n* submarine
deniz anası [denizanasə] *n* **Burada deniz anası var mı?** Are there jellyfish here?
denizaşırı [denizaʃərə] *adv* overseas
denizci [denizdʒi] **(denizciler)** *n* seaman
denizcilik [denizdʒilik] *adj* **denizcilikle ilgili** *adj* maritime
denk [deŋ] *n (eşit)* equivalent, *(uygun)* match *(partnership)*
deodoran [deodoran] *n* deodorant
deodorant [deodorant] *n* **ter önleyici deodorant** *n* antiperspirant
depo [depo] *n* storage, store, warehouse; **benzin deposu** *n* petrol tank; **depoyu doldurmak** *v* stock up on; **su deposu** *n* reservoir
depolamak [depolamak] *v* store
depozito [depozito] *n* deposit
deprem [deprem] *n* earthquake
depresyon [depresjon] *n* depression
dere [dere] *n* stream
derece [deredʒe] *n (düzey)* grade, *(sıcaklık)* degree; **aşırı derecede** *adv* extremely, terribly; **aşırı derecede korkmuş** *adj* terrified; **derece derece** *adj* gradual; **Fahrenheit derece** *n* degree Fahrenheit; **lisans derecesi** *(edebiyat) abbr* BA; **son derece** *adv* awfully; **Santigrat derece** *n*

degree centigrade, degree Celsius
derecede [deredʒede] *adv* **dikkat çekecek derecede** *adv* remarkably
dergi [dergi] *n* magazine *(periodical)*; **mizah dergisi** *n* comic book; **Dergi nereden alabilirim?** Where can I buy a magazine?
derhal [derhal] *adj* instant ▷ *adv* instantly
deri [deri] *n (hayvan, giysi vb)* leather
derin [derin] *adj* deep
derinden [derinden] *adv* deeply
derinlemesine [derinlemesine] *adv* thoroughly
derinlik [derinlik] *n* depth
derlemek [derlemek] *v* **derleyip toplamak** *v* tidy up
derli toplu *adj* tidy ▷ *adv* neatly
dernek [dernek] *n* **yardım derneği** *n* charity; **yardım derneği dükkanı** *n* charity shop
ders [ders] *n* lecture, *(ahlaki)* moral, *(özel)* tutorial, *(sınıf)* lesson; **ders kitabı** *n* schoolbook, textbook ▷ *v* **ders vermek** *v* lecture; **direksiyon dersi** *n* driving lesson; **Ders alabilir miyiz?** Can we take lessons?; **Ders veriyor musunuz?** Do you give lessons?; **Kayak dersleri veriyor musunuz?** Do you organise skiing lessons?
destek [destek] *n (bağ, kuşak vb)* brace *(fastening)*, *(manevi)* support; **destek olmak** *v* back up; **mali destek** *n* sponsorship; **mali destek sağlamak** *v* subsidize
destekleme [destekleme] *n* backing
desteklemek [desteklemek] *v* support
deterjan [deterʒan] *n* detergent; **bulaşık deterjanı** *n* washing-up liquid
dev [dev] *n* giant ▷ *adj* **dev gibi** *adj* giant
devalüasyon [devalyasjon] *n* devaluation
devam [devam] **devam etmek** *v* carry on, continue, go on; **doldurmaya devam etmek** *v* refill
devamı [devamə] *n* sequel
devasa [devasa] *adj* gigantic, mammoth
deve [deve] *n* camel; **deve dikeni** *n* thistle
devekuşu [devekuʃu] *n* ostrich
devir [devir] *n* **sermaye devri** *n* turnover
devirmek [devirmek] *v* *(düşürmek)* knock down ▷ *vt* *(dökmek)* tip *(incline)*
devlet [devlet] *v* **devlet koleji** *n* public school
Devlet [devlet] *n* **Birleşik Devletler** *n* US, *(Amerika)* United States
devralma [devralma] *n* takeover
devre [devre] *n* circuit; **devre arası** *n* half-time; **devre mülk** *n* timeshare
Devre [devre] *n* **Kapalı Devre Televizyon Sistemi** *n* CCTV
devrim [devrim] *n* revolution
devrimci [devrimdʒi] *adj* revolutionary

devriye [devrije] *n* patrol; **devriye arabası** *n* patrol car
deyim [dejim] *n* saying
dezavantaj [dezavantaʒ] *n* disadvantage
dezenfektan [dezenfektan] *n* disinfectant
dırdır [dərdər] *n* **dırdır etmek** *v* nag
dış [dəʃ] *adj (harici)* external, *(iç karşıtı)* out, *(yapı vb)* exterior; **ahlak dışı** *adj* immoral; **dışa dönük** *adj* outgoing; **dışarı çıkmak** *n* outing; **gerçek dışı** *adj* unreal; **olasılık dışı** *adj* unlikely; **sezon dışı, on dışında** *adv* off-season
dışarı [dəʃarə] *adj* outside *v* **dışarda tutmak** *v* keep out; **Dışarıyı aramak istiyorum, hat bağlar mısınız?** I want to make an outside call, can I have a line?
dışarıda [dəʃarəda] *adv* out, outside; **Dışarıda** He's out
dışarısı [dəʃarəsə] *n* outside
dışında [dəʃənda] *n (haricinde)* exception ▷ *prep* outside, *(ondan ayrı olarak)* apart from, *(onu hariç tutarak)* excluding; **dışında tutmak** *v* exclude
digital [digital] *adj* **digital not defteri** *n* e-book
diğer [djier] *adj* another, other ▷ *adv* else; **diğer adıyla** *prep* alias
dijital [diʒital] *adj* digital; **dijital fotoğraf makinesi** *n* digital camera; **dijital radyo** *n* digital radio; **dijital saat** *n* digital watch; **dijital televizyon** *n* digital television; **Bu dijital kameraya hafıza kartı almak istiyorum lütfen** A memory card for this digital camera, please
dik [dik] *adj (yokuş vb)* steep ▷ *adv* upright; **dik açı** *n* right angle
dikdörtgen [dikdørtgen] *n* rectangle; **dikdörtgen biçiminde** *adj* rectangular; **dikdörtgen şeklinde** *adj* oblong
diken [diken] *n* thorn; **deve dikeni** *n* thistle; **diken diken olmuş tüyler** *mpl* goose pimples; **dikenli tel** *n* barbed wire
dikey [dikej] *adj* vertical
dikiş [dikiʃ] *n (eylem)* sewing, *(giysinin)* seam, *(tıp, nakış vb)* stitch; **dikiş makinesi** *n* sewing machine
dikkat [dikkat] *n* attention; **dikkat çekecek derecede** *adv* remarkably; **dikkat çeken** *adj* noticeable *v* **dikkat etmek** *v* watch out; **dikkat etmek** *v* spot; **dikkate değer** *adj* remarkable; **dikkatini çekmek** *v* point out
dikkatinize [dikkatinize] *abbr* NB *(notabene)*
dikkatli [dikkatli] *adj* careful ▷ *adv* carefully
dikkatsiz [dikkatsiz] *adj* careless
dikmek [dikmek] *v* put up, sew, *(bitki)* plant, *(onarmak)* sew up, *(tıp, nakış vb)* stitch; **gözünü dikmek** *v* gaze
diktatör [diktatør] *n* dictator
dikte [dikte] *n* dictation
dil [dil] *n (anatomi)* tongue, *(lisan)* language; **Çek dili** *(dil) n* Czech *(language)*; **Bask dili** *n* Basque *(language)*; **Burma dili** *(dil) n*

Burmese *(language)*; **dil laboratuvarı** *n* language laboratory; **dil okulu** *n* language school; **Danimarka dili** *(dil) n* Danish *(language)*; **Estonya dili** *(dil) n* Estonian *(language)*; **iki dilli** *adj* bilingual; **işaret dili** *n* sign language; **modern diller** *npl* modern languages; **Malta dili** *(dil) n* Maltese *(language)*; **Maori dili** *(dil) n* Maori *(language)*; **Hangi dilleri konuşabiliyorsunuz?** What languages do you speak?
dilbilim [dilbilim] *adj* linguistic
dilbilimci [dilbilimdʒi] *n* linguist
dilek [dilek] *n* wish
dilekçe [dilektʃe] *n* petition
dilemek [dilemek] *v* wish
dilenci [dilendʒi] *n* beggar
dilenmek [dilenmek] *v* beg
dilim [dilim] *n* slice; **dilimli grafik** *n* pie chart; **zaman dilimi** *n* time zone
dilimlemek [dilimlemek] *v* slice
dilsiz [dilsiz] *adj* dumb
din [din] *n* religion; **din bilimi** *n* theology; **kilisenin dini bölgesi** *n* parish
dinamik [dinamik] *adj* dynamic
dindirmek [dindirmek] *v (acı)* relieve
dingil [dingil] *n* axle
dini [dini] *adj* religious
dinlemek [dinlemek] *v* listen; **gizli dinleme cihazı yerleştirilmiş** *adj* bugged; **söz dinlemek** *v* listen to
dinlememek [dinlememek] *v* **söz dinlememek** *v* disobey
dinlendirici [dinlendiridʒi] *adj* restful
dinlenme [dinlenme] *n* rest, the rest; **dinlenme günü** *(Yahudiler için Cumartesi, Hristiyanlar için Pazar) n* Sabbath
dinlenmek [dinlenmek] *vi* rest
dinleyici [dinlejidʒi] *n* listener
dinleyiciler [dinlejidʒiler] *n* audience
dinozor [dinozor] *n* dinosaur
dip [dip] *n* bottom
diploma [diploma] *n* diploma
diplomat [diplomat] *n* diplomat
diplomatik [diplomatik] *adj* diplomatic
direk [direk] *n* pole, *(çit)* post *(stake)*, *(elektrik, telgraf)* pole, *(kale, gemi)* mast; **çadır direği** *n* tent pole; **elektrik direği** *n* pylon; **lamba direği** *n* lamppost
direksiyon [direksijon] *n* steering wheel; **direksiyon öğretmeni** *n* driving instructor; **direksiyon dersi** *n* driving lesson; **direksiyon sınavı** *n* driving test; **direksiyonu kırmak** *v* swerve
direktör [direktør] *n* director
direnme [direnme] *n* resistance
direnmek [direnmek] *v* resist
dirsek [dirsek] *n* elbow
disiplin [disiplin] *n* discipline
disk [disk] *n* disc, disk; **disk kayması** *n* slipped disc; **disk sürücü** *n* disk drive; **kompakt disk** *n* compact disc
disket [disket] *n* diskette, floppy disk
disk jokey [diskʒokej] *n* disc jockey
disko [disko] *n* disco

disleksi [disleksi] *n* dyslexia
disleksik [disleksik] *adj* dyslexic ▹ *n* dyslexic
distribütör [distribytør] *n* distributor
diş [diʃ] *adj* dental ▹ *n* tooth; **diş ağrısı** *n* toothache; **diş çıkarmak** *v* teethe; **diş fırçası** *n* toothbrush; **diş ipi** *n* dental floss; **diş macunu** *n* toothpaste; **takma dişler** *npl* dentures; **yirmi yaş dişi** *n* wisdom tooth; **Bu dişim ağrıyor** This tooth hurts; **Diş sigortam var mı bilmiyorum?** I don't know if I have dental insurance; **Diş sigortam yok** I don't have dental insurance; **Dişim kırıldı** I've broken a tooth
dişçi [diʃtʃi] *n* dentist; **Dişçiye ihtiyacım var** I need a dentist
dişli [diʃli] *n* gear *(mechanism)*
divan [divan] *n* settee
diyabetik [dijabetik] *adj* diabetic
diyagonal [dijagonal] *adj* diagonal
diyagram [dijagram] *n* diagram
diyalekt [dijalekt] *n* dialect
diyalog [dijalog] *n* dialogue
diyet [dijet] *n* diet *v* **diyet yapmak** *v* diet
diz [diz] *n* knee; **diz çökmek** *v* kneel, kneel down
dizayn [dizajn] *n* design
dizel [dizel] *n* diesel; **...lık dizel lütfen** ... worth of diesel, please
dizgin [dizgin] *npl (at)* reins
dizi [dizi] *n* sequence, series; **televizyon dizisi** *n* soap opera
dizin [dizin] *n (sayısal)* index *(numerical scale)*
dizkapağı [dizkapa:ə] *n* kneecap
dizüstü [dizysty] *n* **dizüstü bilgisayarı** *n* laptop; **Burada dizüstü bilgisayarımı kullanabilir miyim?** Can I use my own laptop here?
DJ [di:dʒej] *n* DJ
DNA [de:ena:] *n* DNA
doğa [doa:] *n* nature; **doğa bilimleri uzmanı** *n* naturalist; **vahşi doğa** *n* wildlife
doğal [doa:l] *adj* natural; **doğal gaz** *n* natural gas; **doğal kaynaklar** *npl* natural resources; **doğal olarak** *adv* naturally; **doğal yiyecek** *npl* wholefoods
doğan [doa:n] *adj* **yeni doğan** *adj* newborn
doğaüstü [doa:ysty] *adj* supernatural
doğmuş [doɣmuʃ] *adj* born
doğrama [doɣrama] *n* chop
doğramacı [doɣramadʒə] *n* joiner
doğramak [doɣramak] *v* hack, *(et, sebze)* chop
doğru [doɣru] *adj (çizgi)* straight, *(işlem, hareket)* correct, *(işlem, hareket)* right *(correct)*, *(söz, eylem, sonuç)* accurate; **batıya doğru** *adj* westbound; **doğru dürüst** *adv* proper, properly; **doğru olarak** *adv* accurately, correctly, right; **doğru olmayan** *adj* inaccurate; **...e doğru** *(yön) prep* towards; **geriye doğru** *adv* backwards; **kuzeye doğru** *adj* northbound; **yana doğru** *adv* sideways; **yukarıya doğru** *adv* upwards
doğrudan doğruya [doɣrudandoɣruja] *adv* directly

doğrulamak [doɣrulamak] *v* confirm
doğrulma [doɣrulma] *n* rise
doğrulmak [doɣrulmak] *v* rise
doğruluk [doɣruluk] *n* accuracy
doğu [dou:] *adj* east, eastern ▷ *n* east; **doğu yönünde** *adj* eastbound
Doğu [dou:] *n* Orient; **Orta Doğu** *n* Middle East; **Uzak Doğu** *n* Far East
doğum [dou:m] *n* birth; **doğum öncesi** *adj* antenatal; **doğum günü** *n* birthday; **doğum hastanesi** *n* maternity hospital; **doğum izni** *n* maternity leave; **doğum kontrol hapı** *n* contraceptive; **doğum kontrolü** *n* birth control, contraception; **doğum yeri** *n* birthplace, place of birth
doğurgan [dou:rgan] *adj* fertile
doğusunda [dou:sunda] *adv* east
doğuş [dou:ʃ] *n* birth; **gün doğuşu** *n* sunrise
dok [dok] *n* dock
doksan [doksan] *number* ninety
doktor [doktor] *n* doctor; **Bana bir doktor gerek** I need a doctor; **Bir bayan doktorla konuşmak istiyorum** I'd like to speak to a female doctor; **Bir doktor çağırın** Call a doctor!; **Doktordan randevu alabilir miyim?** Can I have an appointment with the doctor?; **Doktorla konuşmak istiyorum lütfen** I'd like to speak to a doctor; **Nöbetçi doktoru çağırın lütfen** Please call the emergency doctor
doktora [doktora] *n* PhD
dokunaklı [dokunaklə] *adj (konuşma)* touching, *(sahne, film)* moving
dokunmak [dokunmak] *v* touch; **akıllı dokunuş** *n* touchpad
dokuz [dokuz] *number* nine; **dokuzda bir** *n* ninth; **Masa bu akşam saat dokuz için rezerve edildi** The table is booked for nine o'clock this evening
dokuzuncu [dokuzundʒu] *adj* ninth
dolambaçlı [dolambatʃlə] *adj* tricky
dolandırıcı [dolandərədʒə] *n* cheat
dolandırıcılık [dolandərədʒələk] *n (hileli iş)* scam, *(sahte para vb)* fraud
dolandırmak [dolandərmak] *v* cheat
dolap [dolap] *n (hile)* trick, *(mobilya)* cupboard; **bagaj emanet dolabı** *n* left-luggage locker; **kilitli dolap** *n* locker; **mutfak dolabı** *n* dresser
dolar [dolar] *n* dollar; **Dolar kabul ediyor musunuz?** Do you take dollars?
dolaşım [dolaʃəm] *n* **kan dolaşım** *n* circulation
dolaşmak [dolaʃmak] *v* wander; **sırt çantasıyla dolaşan gezgin** backpacker
dolayı [dolajə] *prep* due to
dolaylı [dolajlə] *adj* indirect
doldurmak [doldurmak] *v* fill in, *(benzin deposu)* fill up ▷ *vt (içini)* fill; **depoyu doldurmak** *v* stock

up on; **doldurmaya devam etmek** *v* refill; **tıkabasa doldurmak** *vi* cram
dolgu [dolgu] *n* **Dolgum düştü** A filling has fallen out; **Geçici dolgu yapabilir misiniz?** Can you do a temporary filling?
dolmakalem [dolmakalem] *n* fountain pen
dolu [dolu] *adj* full ▷ *n (hava)* hail; **bir kaşık dolusu** *n* spoonful ▷ *v* **dolu yağmak** *v* hail; **enerji dolu** *adj* energetic; **tıkabasa dolu** *adj* crammed
dolunay [dolunaj] *n* full moon
domates [domates] **(domatesler)** *n* tomato; **domates sosu** *n* tomato sauce
Dominik [dominik] *n* **Dominik Cumhuriyeti** *n* Dominican Republic
domino [domino] *n* domino; **domino oyunu** *npl* dominoes
domuz [domuz] *n* pig; **domuz eti** *n* pork; **domuz pastırması** *n* bacon; **domuz pirzolası** *n* pork chop
don [don] *n (hava)* frost
donanım [donanəm] *n* equipment
donanımlı [donanəmlə] *adj* equipped
donanma [donanma] *n (deniz)* navy
dondurma [dondurma] *n* ice cream; **Ben dondurma alayım** I'd like an ice cream
dondurmak [dondurmak] *vi* freeze
dondurucu [dondurudʒu] *adj (çok soğuk)* freezing ▷ *n (derin)* freezer
donmuş [donmuʃ] *adj* frozen
donut® [donut] *n* doughnut
dosdoğru [dosdoɣru] *adv* straight on
dost [dost] *n* friend; **çevre dostu** *adj* ecofriendly, environmentally friendly; **kullanıcı dostu** *adj* user-friendly; **yakın dost** *n* pal
dostça [dosttʃa] *adj* friendly
dostluk [dostluk] *n* friendship
dosya [dosja] *n* file *(folder)*, folder
dosyalamak [dosjalamak] *v* file *(folder)*
doz [doz] *n* dose
dozda [dozda] *n* **yüksek dozda** *n* overdose
dökmek [døkmek] *vt* spill
döküm [døkym] *n* **çöp döküm alanı** *n* rubbish dump
dönem [dønem] *n* period, *(akademik dönem)* term *(division of year)*, *(belirli bir süre)* spell *(time)*; **40 günlük Paskalya dönemi** *n* Lent
dönemeç [dønemetʃ] *n* hard shoulder
döner [døner] *adj* turning; **döner kavşak** *n* roundabout
döngü [døngy] *n* cycle *(recurring period)*
dönme [dønme] *n* turn
dönmek [dønmek] *v* go back ▷ *vi* turn; **arkaya dönmek** *v* turn round, turn around; **başı dönmüş** *adj* dizzy; **eski haline dönmek** *n* relapse; **geri dönmek** *v* return, reverse, turn back
dönük [dønyk] *n* **dışa dönük** *adj* outgoing

dönüş [dønyʃ] *n* turning; **gidiş dönüş yolculuk** *n* round trip; **gidiş-dönüş bilet** *n* return ticket; **... a gidiş dönüş iki bilet** two return tickets to...; **Gidiş dönüş bilet ne kadar?** How much is a return ticket?
dönüştürmek [dønyʃtyrmek] *v* transform; **geri dönüştürmek** *n* recycle, recycling
dönüşüm [dønyʃym] *n* transformation; **şişe geri dönüşüm kutusu** *n* bottle bank
dördüncü [dørdyndʒy] *adj* fourth
dört [dørt] *number* four; **dört çekerli** *n* four-wheel drive; **Bu akşam saat sekiz için dört kişilik bir masa ayırtmak istiyordum** I'd like to book a table for four people for tonight at eight o'clock; **Bu dört kartpostal için pul alacaktım... a gidecek** Can I have stamps for four postcards to...; **Dört kişilik bir kamper ne kadar?** How much is it for a camper with four people?; **Dört kişilik bir masa lütfen** A table for four people, please
dört yol [dørtjol] *n* **dört yol ağzı** *n* crossroads
döviz [døviz] *n* **döviz bürosu** *n* bureau de change; **döviz kuru** *n* exchange rate, rate of exchange; **Burada döviz bürosu var mı?** Is there a bureau de change here?; **Döviz bürosu arıyorum** I need to find a bureau de change; **Döviz bürosu ne zaman açılıyor?** When is the bureau de change open?; **Döviz kuru ne kadar?** What's the exchange rate?; **Nereden döviz alabilirim?** Where can I change some money?
dövme [døvme] *n* tattoo
dövmek [døvmek] *v* beat *(strike)*
dövüş [døvyʃ] *n* fight; **hayvan dövüşleri** *n* blood sports
dövüşme [døvyʃme] *n* fighting
dram [dram] *n* drama
dramatik [dramatik] *adj* dramatic
dua [dua] *n* prayer; **dua etmek** *v* pray
dublör [duplør] **(dublörler)** *n* stuntman, stunt
dudak [dudak] *n* lip; **dudak kremi** *n* lip salve; **dudak okuma** *v* lip-read
dul [dul] *n (kocası/karısı ölmüş)* widow, widower
duman [duman] *mpl (pis kokulu)* fumes ▷ *n* smoke; **duman alarmı** *n* smoke alarm; **Odada duman kokusu var** My room smells of smoke
dur [dur] *interj* **Burada durun lütfen** Stop here, please; **Lütfen durun** Please stop the bus
durak [durak] *n* stop; **otobüs durağı** *n* bus stop;**... için hangi durakta inmem gerek?** Which stop is it for...?;**... a kaç durak var?** How many stops is it to...?; **Bir sonraki durak neresi?** What is the next stop?; **Otobüs durağı buraya ne kadar uzakta?** How far is the bus stop?; **Sonraki durak... mı?** Is the next stop...?; **Taksi durağı nerede?** Where is the taxi stand?
duraklama [duraklama] *n* pause

duraksama [duraksama] *n* halt
duraksamak [duraksamak] *v* hesitate
durdurma [durdurma] *n* stop
durdurmak [durdurmak] *vi* stop
durgun [durgun] *adj* still
durgunluk [durgunluk] *n (piyasa)* recession
durmak [durmak] *v* stop; **ayakta durmak** *v* stand
durulama [durulama] *n* rinse
durulamak [durulamak] *v* rinse
durum [durum] *n* situation, *(ruhsal)* state; **acil durum** *n* emergency; **ruh durumu** *n* mood
duruşma [duruʃma] *n* trial
duş [duʃ] *n* shower; **duş başlığı** *n* shower cap; **duş jeli** *n* shower gel; **Burada duş var mı?** Are there showers?; **Duş çalışmıyor** The shower doesn't work; **Duş kirli** The shower is dirty; **Duş soğuk akıyor** The showers are cold; **Duşlar nerede?** Where are the showers?
duty-free [dutjfree] *adj* duty-free ▷ *n* duty-free; **Duty-free nerede?** Where is the duty-free shopping?
duvar [duvar] *n* wall; **duvar kağıdı** *n* wallpaper; **güvenlik duvarı** *n* firewall
duvarcı [duvardʒə] *n* bricklayer
duvardan duvara halı [duvardanduvarahalə] *n* fitted carpet
duyarlı [dujarlə] *adj* sensitive, *(tensel)* sensuous
duyarsız [dujarsəz] *adj* insensitive
duygu [dujgu] *n* emotion; **mizah duygusu** *n* sense of humour
duygulanmış [dujgulanməʃ] *adj* touched
duygusal [dujgusal] *adj* emotional, sentimental; **aşırı duygusal** *adj* soppy
duymak [dujmak] *v* hear, feel; **gerek duymak** *v* need; **kuşku duymak** *v* doubt; **saygı duymak** *v* respect
duyu [duju] *n* sense
duyurmak [dujurmak] *v* announce
duyuru [dujuru] *n* announcement
düğme [dy:me] *n (giysi, elektrik)* button; **elektrik düğmesi** *n* switch *v* **elektrik düğmesini çevirmek** *v* switch; **kol düğmeleri** *npl* cufflinks; **Hangi düğmeye basacağım?** Which button do I press?
düğüm [dy:ym] *n* knot
düğün [dy:yn] *n* wedding; **düğün çiçeği** *n* buttercup; **Buraya bir düğüne geldik** We are here for a wedding
dükkan [dykkan] *n* shop; **antikacı dükkanı** *n* antique shop; **demirci dükkanı** *n* ironmonger's; **hediye dükkanı** *n* gift shop; **içki satan dükkan** *n* off-licence; **kuyumcu dükkanı** *n* jeweller's; **yardım derneği dükkanı** *n* charity shop; **Dükkanlar kaçta kapanıyor?** What time do the shops close?
dün [dyn] *adv* yesterday
dünya [dynja] *n* world; **Üçüncü Dünya** *n* Third World; **Dünya Kupası** *n* World Cup
dürbün [dyrbyn] *n* binoculars
dürtmek [dyrtmek] *v* poke

dürüst [dyryst] *adj* honest, truthful; **dürüst olmayan** *adj* dishonest; **doğru dürüst** *adv* proper, properly
dürüstçe [dyrysttʃe] *adv* honestly
dürüstlük [dyrystlyk] *n* fairness, honesty
düş [dyʃ] *n (rüya)* dream; **düş görmek** *v* dream; **düş kırıklığı** *n* disappointment
düşman [dyʃman] *n* enemy
düşmanca [dyʃmandʒa] *adj* hostile, unfriendly
düşmanlık [dyʃmanlək] *n* hostility; **düşmanlığını kazanmak** *v* antagonize
düşmek [dyʃmek] *v* fall down ▷ *vi* fall
düşük [dyʃyk] *adj* low; **düşük alkollü** *adj* low-alcohol; **düşük ücretli** *adj* underpaid; **düşük yapmak** *n* miscarriage; **en düşük** *adj* minimal
düşünce [dyʃyndʒe] *n* thought
düşünceli [dyʃyndʒeli] *adj* thoughtful, *(özenli)* considerate
düşüncesiz [dyʃyndʒesiz] *adj* thoughtless
düşünmek [dyʃynmek] *v* think
düşürmek [dyʃyrmek] *v* lower ▷ *vt* drop
düşüş [dyʃyʃ] *n* fall
düz [dyz] *adj (düzgün)* even, *(desensiz, süssüz)* plain, *(yassı)* flat; **düz ekran** *adj* flat-screen
düzelti [dyzelti] *n* correction
düzeltme [dyzeltme] *n* regulation
düzeltmek [dyzeltmek] *v (hata, yanlış)* correct, *(hatalı bir davranış)* rectify; **kesip düzeltmek** *v* trim
düzen [dyzen] *n* order; **düzenli olarak** *adv* regularly
düzenbaz [dyzenbaz] *n* crook, crook *(swindler)*
düzenleme [dyzenleme] *n (aranjman)* arrangement, *(masa vb)* layout
düzenlemek [dyzenlemek] *v (masa, eşya vb)* set out, *(toplantı)* arrange; **yeniden düzenlemek** *v* reorganize
düzenleyen [dyzenlejen] *v* **eğlence düzenleyen** *n* entertainer
düzenli [dyzenli] *adj* regular
düzensiz [dyzensiz] *adj* irregular
düzey [dyzej] *n* level
düzine [dyzine] *n* dozen
düzlem [dyzlem] *n* plane *(surface)*
düzmece [dyzmedʒe] *adj* false
DVD [dvd] *n* DVD; **DVD oynatıcı** *n* DVD player; **DVD yazıcı** *n* DVD burner

e

ebat [ebat] *n* dimension
ebe [ebe] **(ebeler)** *n* midwife
ebediyen [ebedijen] *adv* forever
ebeveyn [ebevejn] *n* parent; **yalnız ebeveyn** *n* single parent
ebeveynler [ebevejnler] *npl* parents
e-bilet [ebilet] *n* e-ticket
eczacı [edʒzadʒə] *n* chemist, pharmacist
eczane [edʒzane] *n* chemist('s), pharmacy; **En yakın eczane nerede?** Where is the nearest chemist?; **Hangi eczane nöbetçi?** Which pharmacy provides emergency service?
edebiyat [edebijat] *n* literature
eder [eder] *n* cost
editör [editør] *n* editor
efsane [efsane] *n* legend, myth
egzema [egzema] *n* eczema
egzersiz [egzersiz] *n* exercise
egzos [egzos] *adj* **egzos borusu** *n* exhaust pipe; **egzos gazı** *npl* exhaust fumes; **Egzos patladı** The exhaust is broken
egzotik [egzotik] *adj* exotic
eğe [e:e] *n* file *(tool)*
eğer [e:er] *conj* if
eğik [eji:k] *adj* **eğik çizgi** *n* forward slash
eğilim [eji:lim] *n* tendency; **eğilim göstermek** *v* tend
eğilmek [eji:lmek] *v (ayak uçlarına doğru)* bend over, *(kıvrılarak)* bend down
eğitilmiş [eji:tilmiʃ] *adj* trained
eğitim [eji:tim] *n (kurs)* training, *(okul)* education; **üniversite sonrası eğitim yapan öğrenci** *n* postgraduate; **bilgi tazeleme eğitimi** *n* refresher course; **eğitim kursu** *n* training course; **ileri eğitim** *n* further education; **yüksek eğitim** *n* higher education; **yetişkin eğitimi** *n* adult education
eğitimli [eji:timli] *adj* educated
eğitimsel [eji:timsel] *adj* educational
eğitmek [eji:tmek] *vt* train
eğitmen [eji:tmen] *n (spor vb)* trainer
eğlence [e:lendʒe] *n* fun; **eğlence düzenleyen** *n* entertainer; **eğlence merkezi** *n* leisure centre; **eğlence sanayii** *n* show business; **konulu eğlence parkı** *n* theme park
eğlendirici [e:lendiridʒi] *adj* entertaining, fun
eğlendirmek [e:lendirmek] *v*

entertain, *(şakayla)* amuse
eğmek [e:mek] *n* **baş eğmek** *v* bow; **boyun eğmek** *v* obey
eğrelti otu [e:reltiotu] *n* fern
ehliyet [ehlijet] *n* licence; **sürücü ehliyeti** *n* driving licence; **İşte ehliyetim** Here is my driving licence; **Ehliyet numaram...** My driving licence number is...; **Ehliyetim üzerimde değil** I don't have my driving licence on me
ejderha [eʒderha] *n* dragon
ek [ek] *adj* additional ▷ *n* attachment
Ekim [ekim] *n (ay)* October; **Üç Ekim Pazar** It's Sunday the third of October
ekip [ekip] *n* team; **arama ekibi** *n* search party
eklemek [eklemek] *v* add
ekli [ekli] *adj* attached
ekmek [ekmek] *n* bread; **ekmek kırıntısı** *n* breadcrumbs, crumb; **ekmek kızartma makinesi** *n* toaster; **ekmek kutusu** *n* bread bin; **esmer ekmek** *n* brown bread; **yuvarlak ekmek** *n* bread roll; **Biraz daha ekmek getirir misiniz?** Please bring more bread; **Biraz daha ekmek ister misiniz?** Would you like some bread?
ekmekçi [ekmektʃi] *n (fırın)* bakery
ekolojik [ekoloʒik] *adj* ecological
ekonomi [ekonomi] *adj* economic ▷ *n* economy ▷ *npl* economics; **ekonomi yapmak** *v* economize
ekonomik [ekonomik] *adj* economical
ekonomist [ekonomist] *n* economist
ekose [ekose] *adj* tartan
ekran [ekran] *n* screen; **düz ekran** *adj* flat-screen; **ekran koruyucusu** *n* screen-saver; **plazma ekran** *n* plasma screen
eksantrik [eksantrik] *adj* eccentric
eksi [eksi] *prep* minus
eksik [eksik] *adj* incomplete
eksiklik [eksiklik] *n* lack, shortcoming
ekskavatör [ekskavatør] *n* digger
ekstra [ekstra] *adj* **Ekstra büyük beden var mı?** Do you have an extra large?; **Yanında ekstra... istiyorum lütfen** I'd like it with extra..., please
ekşi [ekʃi] *adj* sour
ekşime [ekʃime] *n* **mide ekşimesi** *n* heartburn
Ekvador [ekvador] *n* Ecuador
ekvator [ekvator] *n* equator
Ekvator [ekvator] *n* **Ekvator Ginesi** *n* Equatorial Guinea
el [el] *n* hand; **el altında** *adj* handy; **el arabası** *n* wheelbarrow; **el bagajı** *n* hand luggage; **el feneri** *n* torch; **el freni** *n* handbrake; **el sallamak** *v* wave; **el yapımı** *adj* handmade; **el yazısı** *n* handwriting; **elden çıkarmak** *v* sell off; **eli sıkı** *adj* mean; **elle yapmak** *v* handle; **elle yoklamak** *v* grope; **ikinci el** *adj* secondhand; **sağ elini kullanan** *adj* right-handed; **yeniden ele almak** *vt* reconsider; **Ellerimi nerede yıkayabilirim?** Where can I wash my hands?

elastik [elastik] *adj* **elastik band** *n* rubber band
elbise [elbise] *n* clothes; **elbise askısı** *n* coathanger; **gece elbisesi** *n* evening dress; **takım elbise** *n* suit; **Bu elbiseyi deneyebilir miyim?** Can I try on this dress?
elçilik [eltʃilik] *n* embassy; **Elçiliğe telefon etmem gerek** I need to call my embassy; **Elçiliği aramak istiyorum** I'd like to phone my embassy
eldiven [eldiven] *n* glove; **fırın eldiveni** *n* oven glove; **lastik eldiven** *npl* rubber gloves; **parmaksız eldiven** *n* mitten
elek [elek] *n* sieve
elektrik [elektrik] *n* electricity; **elektriği kapamak** *v* switch off; **elektrik çarpması** *n* electric shock *v* **elektrik düğmesi** *n* switch; **elektrik düğmesini çevirmek** *v* switch; **elektrik direği** *n* pylon; **elektrik kesintisi** *n* power cut; **elektrik süpürgesi** *n* Hoover®, vacuum cleaner; **elektrikli battaniye** *n* electric blanket; **Elektrik ücrete dahil mi?** Is the cost of electricity included?; **Elektrik için ayrıca para ödememiz gerekiyor mu?** Do we have to pay extra for electricity?; **Elektrik sayacı nerede?** Where is the electricity meter?; **Elektrik yok** There is no electricity
elektrikçi [elektriktʃi] *n* electrician
elektrikli [elektrikli] *adj* electric, electrical
elektronik [elektronik] *adj* electronic; **elektronik bilimi** *npl* electronics
eleman [eleman] *n* staff *(workers)*; **eleman alma** *n* recruitment; **satış elemanı** *n* sales rep, shop assistant
eleme [eleme] *v* **ön eleme listesi** *n* shortlist
eleştiri [eleʃtiri] *n (kitap, film vb)* review
eleştirmek [eleʃtirmek] *v* criticize
eleştirmen [eleʃtirmen] *n* critic
elişi [eliʃi] *n* **elişiyle süslemek** *v* embroider
elkoymak [elkojmak] *v* confiscate
elli [elli] *number* fifty; **Elli yaşındayım** I'm fifty years old
elma [elma] *n* apple; **elma şarabı** *n* cider; **elmalı turta** *n* apple pie
elmacık [elmadʒək] *n* **elmacık kemiği** *n* cheekbone
elmas [elmas] *n* diamond
elti [elti] *n* sister-in-law
elveda [elveda] *excl* farewell!
elverişsiz [elveriʃsiz] *adj* unfavourable
elyazması [eljazmasə] *n* manuscript
e-mail [i:meil] *n* **istenmeyen e-mail** *n* spam
emanet [emanet] *v* **bagaj emanet dolabı** *n* left-luggage locker; **emanet bagaj** *n* left-luggage; **emanet bagaj bürosu** *n* left-luggage office
emaye [emaje] *n* enamel
emek [emek] *n* labour
emeklemek [emeklemek] *v* crawl

emekli [emekli] *adj* retired ▷ *n* old-age pensioner, pensioner; **emekli maaşı** *n* pension; **emekli olmak** *v* retire; **Emekliyim** I'm retired
emeklilik [emeklilik] *n* retirement
emektar [emektar] *adj* veteran ▷ *n* veteran
emin [emin] *adj* sure; **emin olmayan** *adj* unsure
emir [emir] *n* command, order; **banka ödeme emri** *n* standing order
emlakçı [emlaktʃə] *n* estate agent
emmek [emmek] *v* suck
emniyet [emnijet] *n* safety; **emniyet kemeri** *n* safety belt, seatbelt
emzirmek [emzirmek] *v* breast-feed
en [en] *n* **en alt** *adj* bottom; **en az** *adj* least, minimum; **en aza indirgemek** *v* minimize; **en azından** *adv* at least; **en çok** *adv* most, most *(superlative)*; **en düşük** *adj* minimal; **en fazla** *adj* maximum; **en genç** *adj* youngest; **en iyi** *adj* best; **en iyi şekilde** *adv* ideally; **en iyisi** *adv* best; **en kısa zamanda** *adv* asap *(as soon as possible)*; **en kötü** *adj* worst; **en yakın akraba** *n* next-of-kin; **eninde sonunda** *adv* ultimately; **yaşça en büyük** *adj* eldest; **Buraya en yakın metro istasyonu nerede?** Where is the nearest tube station?; **Buraya en yakın otobüs durağı nerede?** Where is the nearest bus stop?; **En geç ne zaman?** By what time?; **En sevdiğiniz içki hangisi?** What is your favourite drink?; **En son çıkış kaçta?** When is the last ascent?; **En ucuz bilet olsun lütfen** I'd like the cheapest option; **En yakın bisiklet tamircisi nerede?** Where is the nearest bike repair shop?; **En yakın gazete satan dükkan nerede?** Where is the nearest shop which sells newspapers?; **Umarım en kısa zamanda tekrar birlikte çalışabiliriz** I hope we can work together again soon
endişe [endiʃe] *n* anxiety; **endişe etmek** *vt* fret; **endişe verici** *adj* worrying
endişeli [endiʃeli] *adj* apprehensive, worried
Endonezya [endonezja] *adj* Indonesian ▷ *n* Indonesia
Endonezyalı [endonezjalə] *n* Indonesian *(person)*
endüstri [endystri] *n* industry
endüstriyel [endystrijel] *adj* industrial
enerji [enerʒi] *n* energy; **enerji dolu** *adj* energetic; **güneş enerjisi** *n* solar power
enerjik [enerʒik] *adj* lively
enfeksiyon [enfeksijon] *n* infection
enfes [enfes] *adj* delicious; **Enfesti** That was delicious; **Yemek enfesti** The dinner was delicious
enflasyon [enflasjon] *n* inflation
enformasyon [enformasjon] *n* **enformasyon bürosu** *n* information office
Enformasyon [enformasjon] *n* **Enformasyon Teknolojisi** *n* IT

engebe [engebe] *n* **engebeli yol** *n* track
engel [engel] *n* block *(obstruction)*, drawback, hurdle, obstacle, setback; **engel atlama** *n* show jumping
engellenmiş [engellenmiʃ] *adj* frustrated
enginar [enginar] *n* artichoke
enjeksiyon [enʒeksijon] *n* injection
enjekte [enʒekte] *n* **enjekte etmek** *v* inject
enkaz [eŋaz] *n* wreck, wreckage
enlem [enlem] *n* latitude
enstantane [enstantane] *n* snapshot
enstitü [enstity] *n* institute
ensülin [ensylin] *n* insulin
entellektüel [entellektyel] *adj* intellectual ▷ *n* intellectual
envanter [envanter] *n* inventory
E-posta [eposta] *n* **E-posta adresim...** My email address is...; **E-posta adresiniz nedir?** What is your email address?; **E-posta gönderebilir miyim?** Can I send an email?; **E-postamı aldınız mı?** Did you get my email?; **E-postanız var mı?** Do you have an email?
e-posta [eposta] *n* email; **e-posta adresi** *n* email address; **e-posta atmak** *v* email *(a person)*; **E-postanızı alabilir miyim?** Can I have your email?
ergen [ergen] *n* adolescent, teenager
ergenler [ergenler] *npl* teens
ergenlik [ergenlik] *n* adolescence
erik [erik] *n* plum; **kuru erik** *n* prune
erimek [erimek] *vt* dissolve
erişilebilir [eriʃilebilir] *adj* accessible
erişkin [eriʃkin] *n* grown-up
erişmek [eriʃmek] *v* access
eritmek [eritmek] *vi* melt
Eritre [eritre] *n* Eritrea
erkek [erkek] *adj* male ▷ *n* man, male; **erkek arkadaş** *n* boyfriend; **erkek öğrenci** *n* schoolboy; **erkek Fatma** *n* tomboy; **erkek kardeş** *n* brother; **erkek polis** *n* policeman; **erkek torun** *n* grandson; **erkekler tuvaleti** *n* gents'; **Fransız erkek** *n* Frenchman; **üvey erkek kardeş** *n* stepbrother
erkeksi [erkeksi] *adj* masculine
erken [erken] *adj* early, premature ▷ *adv* early; **daha erken** *adv* sooner; **Daha erken bir uçak tercih ederim** I would prefer an earlier flight; **Erken/ geç geldik** We arrived early/late
Ermeni [ermeni] *adj* Armenian ▷ *n* *(kişi)* Armenian *(person)*
Ermenice [ermenidʒe] *n* *(dil)* Armenian *(language)*
Ermenistan [ermenistan] *n* Armenia
eroin [eroin] *n* heroin
erotik [erotik] *adj* erotic
ertelemek [ertelemek] *v* postpone, put off
erzak [erzak] *npl* supplies
eser [eser] *n* **sanat eseri** *n* work of art
esinti [esinti] *n* blow
eski [eski] *adj* ancient, *(ölmüş)* late *(dead)*, *(önceki)* former; **eski**

grubun yerini alan yeni grup *n* relay; **eski haline dönmek** *n* relapse; **eski karı** *n* ex-wife; **eski koca** *n* ex-husband; **eski moda** *adj* old-fashioned; **eski püskü** *adj* shabby; **eski ve hoş** *adj* quaint
eskimiş [eskimiʃ] *adj* worn
esmek [esmek] *v (rüzgar)* wind *(coil around)*, *(rüzgar)* wind *(with a blow etc.)*
esmer [esmer] *adj* brown; **esmer ekmek** *n* brown bread; **esmer pirinç** *n* brown rice
esnek [esnek] *adj* flexible, *(materyal)* stretchy; **esnek çalışma saati** *n* flexitime; **esnek olmayan** *adj* inflexible
esnemek [esnemek] *v* yawn
esnetmek [esnetmek] *vi* stretch
esprili [esprili] *adj* witty
esrar [esrar] *n (bitki)* cannabis
Estonya [estonja] *adj* Estonian ▷ *n* Estonia; **Estonya dili** *(dil) n* Estonian *(language)*
Estonyalı [estonjalə] *n (kişi)* Estonian *(person)*
eş [eʃ] *n (karıkoca)* spouse; **eşinin ailesi** *npl* in-laws
eşarp [eʃarp] **(eşarplar)** *n* headscarf, scarf
eşek [eʃek] *n* donkey
eşekarısı [eʃekarəsə] *n* wasp
eşik [eʃik] *n* **kapı eşiği** *n* doorstep
eşit [eʃit] *adj* equal
eşitlemek [eʃitlemek] *v* equal, equalize
eşitlik [eʃitlik] *n (matematik)* equation, *(siyasi)* equality
eşkin [eʃkin] *n* **eşkin gitmek** *v* canter
eşkiya [eʃkija] *n* thug
eşlik [eʃlik] *n* **eşlik etmek** *v (refakat)* escort, *(yanında gitmek)* accompany
eşofman [eʃofman] *n* shell suit
eşsiz [eʃsiz] *adj* unique
eşya [eʃja] *npl* belongings; **değerli eşyalar** *npl* valuables; **indirimli fiyatla sunulan eşya** *n* special offer; **kayıp eşya bürosu** *n* lost-property office
et [et] *n (yiyecek)* meat; **dana eti** *n* veal; **domuz eti** *n* pork; **et sosu** *n* gravy; **et ya da sebze suyuna çorba** *n* broth; **geyik eti** *n* venison; **kırmızı et** *n* red meat; **kemikli et** *n* joint *(meat)*; **koyun eti** *n* mutton; **sığır eti** *n* beef; **Bu yemeğin içinde et suyu var mı?** Is this cooked in meat stock?; **Et bozulmuş** This meat is off; **Et sevmem** I don't like meat; **Et soğuk** The meat is cold; **Et yemiyorum** I don't eat meat; **Et yiyor musunuz?** Do you eat meat?; **Kırmızı et yemiyorum** I don't eat red meat
etek [etek] *n (giysi)* skirt; **mini etek** *n* miniskirt
eteklerinde [eteklerinde] *npl* outskirts
e-ticaret [etidʒaret] *n* e-commerce
etiket [etiket] *n (bilişim)* tag, *(defter vb)* sticker, *(fiyat vb)* label
etki [etki] *n* effect, *(nüfuz)* influence, *(sonuç)* impact; **etkili bir biçimde** *adv* efficiently; **etkili bir şekilde** *adv* effectively; **yan etki** *n* side effect

etkilemek [etkilemek] *v* influence, *(bir sonuç yaratarak)* affect, *(iz bırakmak)* impress
etkilenmiş [etkilenmiʃ] *adj* impressed
etkileyici [etkilejidʒi] *adj* impressive
etkili [etkili] *adj* effective
etkin [etkin] *adj (nüfuzlu)* efficient
etkinlik [etkinlik] *n* activity
etmek [etmek] *prep* **acele etmek** *v* hurry, hurry up; **akın etmek** *v* invade; **alay etmek** *v* mock; **ameliyat etmek** *v* operate *(to perform surgery)*; **anons etmek** *v* page; **arzu etmek** *v* desire; **ateş etmek** *vt* shoot; **ayırt etmek** *v* distinguish; **ısrar etmek** *v* insist; **özür beyan etmek** *v* excuse; **berbat etmek** *v* spoil, wreck; **casusluk etmek** *v* spy; **cüret etmek** *v* dare; **dahil etmek** *v* include, involve; **dans etmek** *v* dance; **dava etmek** *v* sue; **davet etmek** *v* invite; **dırdır etmek** *v* nag; **devam etmek** *v* carry on, continue, go on; **dikkat etmek** *v* watch out; **dua etmek** *v* pray; **eşlik etmek** *v (refakat)* escort, *(yanında gitmek)* accompany; **endişe etmek** *vt* fret; **enjekte etmek** *v* inject; **feda etmek** *n* sacrifice; **feryat etmek** *v* shriek; **finanse etmek** *v* finance, sponsor; **flört etmek** *v* flirt; **garanti etmek** *v* guarantee; **göç etmek** *v* emigrate; **gemiyle yolculuk etmek** *n* sail; **hak etmek** *v* deserve; **hizmet etmek** *v* serve, service; **ibadet etmek** *v* worship; **icat etmek** *v* invent; **idam etmek** *v* execute; **idare etmek** *v* go round, manipulate; **ifade etmek** *v* express, state; **ihanet etmek** *v* betray; **ihmal etmek** *v* neglect; **ihraç etmek** *v* export; **ikna etme** *v* persuade; **iltifat etmek** *v* compliment; **işaret etmek** *v* sign; **işkence etmek** *v* torture; **inkar etmek** *v* deny; **inşa etmek** *vt* build; **iptal etmek** *vt* call off, cancel; **israf etmek** *v* waste; **istifa etmek** *v* resign; **ithal etmek** *v* import; **itiraf etmek** *v* confess; **kabul etmek** *v* accept, *(itiraf)* admit *(confess)*; **kötü muamele etmek** *v* ill-treat; **şarj etmek** *(elektrik) v* charge *(electricity)*; **mahkum etmek** *v* sentence; **merak etmek** *v* wonder; **modernize etmek** *v* modernize; **nefret etmek** *v* hate; **organize etmek** *v* organize; **park etmek** *v* park; **pazarlık etmek** *v* haggle; **protesto etmek** *v* protest; **rahatsız etmek** *v* disturb; **restore etmek** *v* restore; **rezerve etmek** *v* book; **rica etmek** *v* appeal, request; **sırılsıklam etmek** *v* drench; **söz etmek** *v* refer; **seyahat etmek** *vi* travel; **sohbet etmek** *v* chat; **sterilize etmek** *v* sterilize; **tahrip etmek** *n* vandalize; **taklit etmek** *v* imitate; **talep etmek** *v* claim, demand; **tecavüz etmek** *v* rape; **tedavi etmek** *vt* cure; **tehdit etmek** *v* threaten; **teklif etmek** *v* offer; **telaffuz etmek** *v* pronounce, spell; **telafi etmek** *v*

compensate; **telaş etmek** *vi* rush; **telefon etmek** *v* phone; **teşekkür etmek** *v* thank; **temin etmek** *v* supply; **temsil etmek** *v* represent; **tercüme etmek** *v* translate; **teslim etmek** *vt* deliver; **umut etmek** *v* hope; **vekalet etmek** *v* substitute; **yardım etmek** *vt* help; **yok etmek** *v* destroy; **zahmet etmek** *v* bother; **ziyaret etmek** *v* visit; **zorbalık etmek** *v* bully; **Bunu iade etmek istiyorum** I'd like to return this; **Dans etmek ister misiniz?** Would you like to dance?

etnik [etnik] *adj* ethnic

etraf [etraf] *adv* **bina ve etrafındaki arazi** *npl* premises; **Bize etrafı gösterebilir misiniz?** Could you show us around?

etrafında [etrafənda] *prep* around

etrafını [etrafənə] *prep* round

Etyopya [etjopja] *adj* Ethiopian ▷ *n* Ethiopia

Etyopyalı [etjopjalə] *n* Ethiopian

ev [ev] *n* home, house; **çiftlik evi** *n* farmhouse; **birini arabayla evine bırakma** *n* lift *(free ride)*; **ev adresi** *n* home address; **ev ödevi** *n* homework; **ev hayvanı** *n* pet; **ev işi** *n* housework; **ev şarabı** *n* house wine; **ev sahibesi** *n* landlady; **ev sahibi** *n* host *(entertains)*, landlord; **ev yapımı** *adj* home-made; **evde kalmak** *v* stay in; **kişinin evinin önündeki özel yol** *n* driveway; **müstakil ev** *n* detached house; **sıra evler** *adj* terraced; **taşınabilir ev** *n* mobile home; **tatil evi** *n* holiday home; **Ayrılmadan önce evi temizlememiz gerekiyor mu?** Do we have to clean the house before we leave?; **Ev oldukça büyük** The house is quite big; **Eve gitmek istiyorum** I'd like to go home; **Eve ne zaman gideceksiniz?** When do you go home?; **Eve ne zaman isterseniz o zaman dönebilirsiniz** Come home whenever you like; **Evi aramak ister misiniz?** Would you like to phone home?; **Evi arayabilir miyim?** May I phone home?

evcil [evdʒil] *adj* tame

evde [evde] *adv* home; **Akşam saat on bire kadar evde olun lütfen** Please come home by 11p.m.

evet [evet] *excl* yes; **Evet, çok isterdim** Yes, I'd love to; **Evet, bekarım** Yes, I'm single

eviye [evije] *n* **damlalıklı eviye** *n* draining board

evkadını [evkadənə] **(ev kadınları)** *n* housewife

evlat [evlat] *n* **üvey kız evlat** *n* stepdaughter; **evlat edinilmiş** *adj* adopted; **kız evlat** *n* daughter

evlendirme [evlendirme] *n* **evlendirme dairesi** *n* registry office

evlenmek [evlenmek] *v* marry; **yeniden evlenmek** *v* remarry

evlenmemiş [evlenmemiʃ] *adj* unmarried

evli [evli] *adj* married

evlilik [evlilik] *n* marriage; **evlilik cüzdanı** *n* marriage certificate;

evlilik yıldönümü *n* wedding anniversary; **şirket evliliği** *n* merger; **Evliyim** I'm married

evrak [evrak] *n* documents, papers; **evrak çantası** *n* briefcase; **evrak işi** *n* paperwork; **Evraklarım burada** Here are my vehicle documents

evren [evren] *n* universe

evrim [evrim] *n* evolution

evsiz [evsiz] *adj* homeless

eylem [ejlem] *n* action

Eylül [ejlyl] *n* September

ezberlemek [ezberlemek] *v* memorize

ezme [ezme] *n* squash, *(yiyecek)* dip *(food, sauce)*; **badem ezmesi** *n* marzipan; **fıstık ezmesi** *n* peanut butter; **yulaf ezmesi** *n* oatmeal, porridge

ezmek [ezmek] *v* squash, *(arabayla)* run over, *(sıkıştırarak)* crush

f

fabrika [fabrika] *n* factory; **bira fabrikası** *n* brewery; **Bir fabrikada çalışıyorum** I work in a factory

fagot [fagot] *n* bassoon

fahişe [fahiʃe] *n* prostitute

Fahrenheit [fahrenheit] *n* **Fahrenheit derece** *n* degree Fahrenheit

faiz [faiz] *n* interest *(income)*; **faiz oranı** *n* interest rate

fakat [fakat] *conj* but

faks [faks] *n* fax; **Buradan faks çekebilir miyim?** Can I send a fax from here?; **Faks çekmek istiyorum** I want to send a fax; **Faks göndermek ne kadar?** How much is it to send a fax?; **Faks numarası nedir?** What is the fax number?; **Faksınız var mı?** Do you have a fax?; **Faksınızı bir daha gönderin** Please resend

your fax; **Faksınızda bir sorun var** There is a problem with your fax; **Kullanabileceğim bir faks makinesi var mı?** Is there a fax machine I can use?
fakslamak [fakslamak] *v* fax
fakülte [fakylte] *n* faculty; **hukuk fakültesi** *n* law school
fal [fal] *n* fortune; **yıldız falı** *n* horoscope
fanatik [fanatik] *n* fanatic
fanila [fanila] *n* flannel
far [far] *n* headlight; **göz farı** *n* eye shadow; **Farlar çalışmıyor** The headlights are not working
faraş [faraʃ] *n* dustpan
fare [fare] **(fareler)** *n* mouse; **çöl faresi** *n* gerbil; **fare pedi** *n* mouse mat; **kobay faresi** *n* guinea pig *(rodent)*
fark [fark] *n* difference; **fark gözetme** *n* distinction; **farkına varma** *n* notice *(note)*; **farkına varmak** *v* notice, realize; **Farketmez** It doesn't matter
farkında [farkənda] *adj* aware
farklı [farklə] *adj* different; **farklı olarak** *prep* unlike; **Farklı bir şey istiyordum** I would like something different
Faroe [faroe] *adj* **Faroe Adaları** *npl* Faroe Islands
farzetmek [farzetmek] *v* presume
Fas [fas] *adj* Moroccan ▹ *n* Morocco
Faslı [faslə] *n* Moroccan
fasulye [fasulje] *n* bean; **çalı fasulyesi** *n* French beans, runner bean; **fasulye filizi** *npl* beansprouts
fatura [fatura] *n* invoice; **telefon faturası** *n* phone bill
faturalamak [faturalamak] *v* invoice
faul [faul] *n* foul
fayans [fajans] *n* tile; **fayans döşeli** *adj* tiled
fazla [fazla] *adj* much, surplus ▹ *pron* more, much; **daha fazla** *pron* more; **en fazla** *adj* maximum; **fazla bagaj** *n* excess baggage; **fazla fiyat isteme** *n* surcharge; **fazla fiyat istemek** *v* overcharge; **fazla mesai** *n* overtime; **fazla para çekme** *n* overdraft; **hesabından fazla para çekmiş** *adj* overdrawn; **Çok fazla... koymuşsunuz** There's too much... in it; **Daha fazla çarşafa ihtiyacımız var** We need more sheets; **Daha fazla battaniyeye ihtiyacımız var** We need more blankets; **Daha fazla tabak çanağa ihtiyacımız var** We need more crockery; **Taksimetrenin gösterdiğinden daha fazla** It's more than on the meter
fazlalık [fazlalək] *n* surplus
feda [feda] *n* sacrifice ▹ *v* **feda etmek** *n* sacrifice
fedai [fedai] *n* bouncer
felaket [felaket] *n* disaster, *(doğal afet)* catastrophe
felç [feltʃ] *n* paralysis; **çocuk felci** *n* polio
felçli [feltʃli] *adj* paralysed
felsefe [felsefe] *n* philosophy
feminist [feminist] *n* feminist
fener [fener] *n* flashlight; **deniz feneri** *n* lighthouse; **el feneri** *n* torch

ferah [ferah] *adv (geniş)* wide; **iç ferahlatıcı** *adj* refreshing
ferahlamak [ferahlamak] *v* freshen up
feribot [feribot] *n* ferry; **arabalı feribot** *n* car ferry; **... feribotuna nereden binebiliriz?** Where do we catch the ferry to...?; **... a feribot var mı?** Is there a car ferry to...?
fermuar [fermuar] *n* zip; **fermuarı açmak** *v* unzip
fersiz [fersiz] *adj* dull
feryat [ferjat] *n* scream, cry ▷ *v* **feryat etmek** *v* shriek
feshetmek [feshetmek] *v* abolish
fesleğen [fesle:en] *n* basil
festival [festival] *n* festival
fıçı [fətʃə] *n* barrel
fındık [fəndək] *n* hazelnut; **fındık fıstık** *n* nut *(food)*
fırça [fərtʃa] *n* brush; **boya fırçası** *n* paintbrush; **diş fırçası** *n* toothbrush; **saç fırçası** *n* hairbrush; **tırnak fırçası** *n* nailbrush
fırçalamak [fərtʃalamak] *v* brush
fırın [fərən] *n* oven; **fırın eldiveni** *n* oven glove; **fırında pişirilmiş** *adj* baked; **fırında pişirme** *n* baking; **fırında pişirmek** *v* bake; **mikrodalga fırın** *n* microwave oven
fırıncı [fərəndʒə] *n* baker
fırlatmak [fərlatmak] *v* pitch
fırsat [fərsat] *n (durum)* occasion, *(olanak)* opportunity
fırtına [fərtəna] *n* storm; **gök gürültülü fırtına** *n* thunderstorm; **kar fırtınası** *n* blizzard, snowstorm; **Fırtına çıkabilir mi?** Do you think there will be a storm?
fırtınalı [fərtənalə] *adj* stormy
Fısıh [fəsəh] *n* **Musevilerin Fısıh Bayramı** *n* Passover
fısıldamak [fəsəldamak] *v* whisper
fıstık [fəstək] *n* **fındık fıstık** *n* nut *(food)*; **fıstık alerjisi** *n* nut allergy, peanut allergy; **fıstık ezmesi** *n* peanut butter; **Hint fıstığı** *n* cashew; **İçinde fındık fıstık olmayan bir yemek yapabilir misiniz?** Could you prepare a meal without nuts?; **Bunda fıstık var mı?** Does that contain peanuts?; **Fıstığa alerjim var** I'm allergic to peanuts
fıtık [fətək] *n* hernia
fibre [fibre] *n* fibre
fidye [fidje] *n* ransom
fiil [fiil] *n* verb
Fiji [fiʒi] *n* Fiji
fikir [fikir] *n (bir konuda)* opinion, *(düşünce)* idea; **açık fikirli** *adj* broad-minded; **açıkça fikrini söylemek** *v* speak up; **aynı fikirde olmak** *v* agree
fiks [fiks] *adj* **fiks mönü** *n* set menu; **Fiks menü alalım** We'll take the set menu; **Fiks menü ne kadar?** How much is the set menu?; **Fiks menünüz var mı?** Do you have a set-price menu?
fil [fil] *n* elephant
fildişi [fildiʃi] *n* ivory
fileto [fileto] *n* fillet ▷ *v* **fileto kesmek** *v* fillet
Filipinli [filipinli] **(Filipinler)** *adj*

Filipino ▷ *n* Filipino
Filistin [filistin] *adj* Palestinian ▷ *n* Palestine
Filistinli [filistinli] *n* Palestinian
filiz [filiz] *n* **fasulye filizi** *npl* beansprouts
film [film] *n (fotoğraf vb)* film, *(sinema)* movie; **film müziği** *n* soundtrack; **film yıldızı** *n* film star; **korku filmi** *n* horror film; **kovboy filmi** *n* western; **Bu filmi banyo edebilir misiniz lütfen?** Can you develop this film, please?; **Bu makine için renkli film istiyorum** I need a colour film for this camera; **Burada film çekebilir miyim?** Can I film here?; **Film görmek için nereye gidebiliriz?** Where can we go to see a film?; **Film kaçta başlıyor** When does the film start?; **Film takıldı** The film has jammed; **Renkli film istiyorum lütfen** A colour film, please; **Sinemada hangi film oynuyor?** Which film is on at the cinema?
filo [filo] *n* fleet
filtre [filtre] *n* filter
Fin [fin] *adj* Finnish ▷ *n* Finn
final [final] *n* final; **çeyrek final** *n* quarter final; **yarı final** *n* semifinal
finans [finans] *n* finance ▷ *v* **finanse etmek** *v* finance, sponsor
finansör [finansør] *n* sponsor
fincan [findʒan] *n* **çay fincanı** *n* teacup; **fincan tabağı** *n* saucer; **Bir fincan kahve daha alabilir miyiz?** Could we have another cup of coffee, please?
Finlandiya [finlandija] *n* Finland
Finli [finli] *n* Finnish
firma [firma] *m* firm
fiş [fiʃ] *n* receipt; **fişten çekmek** *v* unplug; **Fiş istiyorum lütfen** I need a receipt, please
fişek [fiʃek] *n (silah)* cartridge
fitil [fitil] *n* **fitilli kadife** *n* corduroy
fitted çarşaf [fittedtʃarʃaf] *n* fitted sheet
fiyasko [fijasko] *n* flop
fiyat [fijat] *n* price; **fazla fiyat isteme** *n* surcharge ▷ *v* **fazla fiyat istemek** *v* overcharge; **fiyat biçmek** *vt* charge *(price)*; **fiyat listesi** *n* price list; **fiyat vermek** *(açık arttırmada) vi* bid *(at auction)*; **indirimli fiyatla sunulan eşya** *n* special offer; **perakende fiyatı** *n* retail price; **satış fiyatı** *n* selling price; **yarı fiyatı** *adj* half-price; **yarı fiyatına** *adv* half-price; **Fiyata botlar da dahil mi?** Does the price include boots?; **Fiyata neler dahil?** What is included in the price?; **Fiyata sıcak su dahil mi?** Is hot water included in the price?; **Fiyata sopalar da dahil mi?** Does the price include poles?; **Fiyata tam kapsamlı sigorta dahil mi?** Is fully comprehensive insurance included in the price?; **Fiyatı yazar mısınız?** Please write down the price
fizik [fizik] *n (görünüş)* physical ▷ *npl* physics
fizikçi [fiziktʃi] *n* physicist
fiziksel [fiziksel] *adj* physical
fizyoterapi [fizjoterapi] *n*

physiotherapy
fizyoterapist [fizjoterapist] *n* physiotherapist
flamingo [flamingo] *n* flamingo
flaş [flaʃ] *n* flash; **Flaş çalışmıyor** The flash is not working
flora [flora] *n* flora
floresan [floresan] *adj* fluorescent
flört [flørt] *n* flirt ▷ *v* **flört etmek** *v* flirt
flüt [flyt] *n* flute
fobi [fobi] *n* phobia
fok [fok] *n* seal *(animal)*
folklor [folklor] *n* folklore
folyo [foljo] *n* foil
fon [fon] *n (destek)* grant, *(mali birikim)* pool *(resources)*
form [form] *n* form; **başvuru formu** *n* application form; **istek formu** *n* claim form; **sipariş formu** *n* order form
formalite [formalite] *n* formality
format [format] *n* format
formatlamak [formatlamak] *v* format
formül [formyl] *n* formula
foseptik [foseptik] *adj* **foseptik çukuru** *n* septic tank
fotoğraf [fotoɣraf] *n* photo, photograph; **dijital fotoğraf makinesi** *n* digital camera; **fotoğraf albümü** *n* photo album; **fotoğraf makinesi** *n* camera ▷ *v* **fotoğrafını çekmek** *v* photograph; **fotoğraflı telefon** *n* camera phone; **Bu fotoğrafları CD'ye yükleybilir misiniz lütfen?** Can you put these photos on CD, please?; **Fotoğraf inidirebilir miyim?** Can I download photos to here?; **Fotoğraflar kaça malolur?** How much do the photos cost?; **Fotoğraflar ne zaman hazır olur?** When will the photos be ready?; **Fotoğrafları mat kağıda basın lütfen** I'd like the photos matt; **Fotoğrafları parlak kağıda basın lütfen** I'd like the photos glossy
fotoğrafçı [fotoɣraftʃə] *n* photographer
fotoğrafçılık [fotoɣraftʃələk] *n* photography
fotokopi [fotokopi] *n* photocopy; **fotokopi makinesi** *n* photocopier ▷ *v* **fotokopisini çekmek** *v* photocopy; **Bunun fotokopisini istiyorum lütfen** I'd like a photocopy of this, please; **Bunun renkli fotokopisini istiyorum lütfen** I'd like a colour photocopy of this, please; **Nerede fotokopi çektirebilirim?** Where can I get some photocopying done?
fön [føn] *n* blow-dry; **Kesip fön çekin lütfen** A cut and blow-dry, please
Fransa [fransa] *n* France
Fransız [fransəz] *adj* French ▷ *n* French; **Fransız erkek** *n* Frenchman; **Fransız kadın** *n* Frenchwoman
fren [fren] *n* brake; **el freni** *n* handbrake; **fren lambası** *n* brake light; **Bisikletin frenleri var mı?** Does the bike have brakes?; **Bisikletin geri frenleri var mı?** Does the bike have back-pedal brakes?; **Frenler çalışmıyor** The

brakes are not working, The brakes don't work
Frenk [freŋ] **Frenk soğanı** *mpl* chives; **kırmızı Frenk üzümü** *n* redcurrant
frenlemek [frenlemek] *v* brake
frikik [frikik] *n* free kick
fuar [fuar] *n* fair; **fuar alanı** *n* fairground
full-board [fullboard] *n* **Full-board ne kadar?** How much is full board?
futbol [futbol] *n* football; **Amerikan futbolu** *n* American football; **futbol maçı** *n* football match; **Futbol maçı görmek isterdim** I'd like to see a football match; **Futbol oynayalım** Let's play football
futbolcu [futboldʒu] *n* football player, footballer
füze [fyze] *n* missile

g

Gabon [gabon] *n* Gabon
gaddar [gaddar] *adj* cruel
gaf [gaf] *n* blunder
gaga [gaga] *n* beak
Gal [gal] *adj* Welsh
gala [gala] *n* premiere
galeri [galeri] *n* gallery; **sanat galerisi** *n* art gallery
Galler [galler] *n* Wales
Galli [galli] *n* Welsh
Gambiya [gambija] *n* Gambia
Gana [gana] *adj* Ghanaian ▷ *n* Ghana
Ganalı [ganalə] *n* Ghanaian
gangster [gangster] *n* gangster
garaj [garaʒ] *n* garage; **Hangisi garaj anahtarı?** Which is the key for the garage?
garanti [garanti] *n* guarantee, warranty ▷ *v* **garanti etmek** *v* guarantee; **garantiye almak** *v* ensure; **Arabanın garantisi var**

The car is still under warranty; **Hala garantisi var** It's still under guarantee

gardrop [gardrop] *n* wardrobe

gargara [gargara] *n* mouthwash

garip [garip] *adj* strange

garson [garson] *n* waiter; **kadın garson** *n* waitress

gaspetmek [gaspetmek] *v* hijack

gayda [gajda] *npl* bagpipes

gaz [gaz] *n* gas; **doğal gaz** *n* natural gas; **egzos gazı** *npl* exhaust fumes; **gaz pedalı** *n* accelerator; **gazlı ocak** *n* gas cooker; **tüp gaz** *n* camping gas; **Gaz kokusu alıyorum** I can smell gas; **Gaz sayacı nerede?** Where is the gas meter?; **Gaz tüpümü doldurabilir misiniz?** Do you have a refill for my gas lighter?

gazete [gazete] *n* newspaper; **gazete bayii** *n* newsagent; **gazete dağıtım** *n* paper round; **gazete kesiği** *n* cutting; **En yakın gazete satan dükkan nerede?** Where is the nearest shop which sells newspapers?; **Gazete almak istiyorum** I would like a newspaper; **Gazete nereden alabilirim?** Where can I buy a newspaper?; **Gazete satıyor musunuz?** Do you have newspapers?

gazeteci [gazetedʒi] *n* journalist

gazetecilik [gazetedʒilik] *n* journalism

gazyağı [gazja:ə] *n* kerosene

gebe [gebe] *adj* pregnant

gebelik [gebelik] *n* pregnancy

gece [gedʒe] *n* at night, night; **bu gece** *adv* tonight; **dün gece** *n* last night; **gece elbisesi** *n* evening dress; **gece hayatı** *n* nightlife; **gece kulübü** *n* nightclub; **gece nöbeti** *n* nightshift; **gece okulu** *n* night school; **kına gecesi** *n* hen night; **İki gece kalmak istiyorum** I'd like to stay for two nights; **İyi geceler** Good night; **Çadırın bir geceliği ne kadar?** How much is it per night for a tent?; **Bir gece daha kalmak istiyorum** I want to stay an extra night; **Geceliği ne kadar?** How much is it per night?

gecekondu [gedʒekondu] *n* slum

gecelik [gedʒelik] *n* nightdress, nightie, *(hafif)* negligee; **gecelik seyahat çantası** *n* overnight bag

geceyarısı [gedʒejarəsə] *n* midnight, at midnight

gecikme [gedʒikme] *n* delay

gecikmek [gedʒikmek] *v* delay

gecikmeli [gedʒikmeli] *adj* delayed, late *(delayed)*

geç [getʃ] *adv* late; **geç saatlere kadar oturmak** *v* stay up; **Çok geç** It's too late

geçen [getʃen] *adj* past, last; **geçen hafta** last week

geçer [getʃer] *n (standartlara uygun)* pass *(meets standard)*

geçerli [getʃerli] *adj* valid

geçersiz [getʃersiz] *adj* void

geçici [getʃidʒi] *adj* temporary, *(bir süreliğine)* provisional; **geçici görevli** *n* temp; **yol kenarında geçici park yeri** *n* layby

geçilmek [getʃilmek] *vi* pass

geçim [getʃim] *n* **geçimini sağlamak** *v* provide for

geçinmek [getʃinmek] *v* live on
geçirmek [getʃirmek] *v* go through; **gözden geçirmek** *(yeniden) v* revise; **iç geçirmek** *n* sigh; **şok geçirmek** *v* shock
geçiş [getʃiʃ] *n* transition; **geçiş hakkı** *n* right of way
geçit [getʃit] *n* crossing, passage *(route)*, *(dağ)* pass *(in mountains)*; **alt geçit** *n* underpass; **ışıklı yaya geçidi** *n* pelican crossing; **hemzemin geçit** *n* level crossing; **şeritli yaya geçidi** *n* zebra crossing; **yaya geçidi** *n* pedestrian crossing
geçmek [getʃmek] *v* go by, *(deneyim/ameliyat)* undergo ▹ *vt* pass; **dalga geçmek** *v* kid; **karşıdan karşıya geçmek** *vt* cross; **yanından geçmek** *v* go past
geçmiş [getʃmiʃ] *adj* gone, past ▹ *n* past; **ödeme günü geçmiş** *adj* overdue; **günü geçmiş** *adj* out-of-date; **modası geçmiş** *adj* obsolete; **vadesi geçmiş borç** *npl* arrears
gedik [gedik] *n (yer)* gap
geğirme [geji:rme] *n* burp
geğirmek [geji:rmek] *vi* burp
gelebilirsiniz *v* **Gelebilirsiniz!** Come in!
gelecek [geledʒek] *adj* coming, future, next ▹ *n* future; **gelecek beklentisi** *n* prospect
gelen [gelen] **gelen kutusu** *n* inbox; **yeni gelen** *n* newcomer
gelenek [gelenek] *n* tradition
geleneksel [geleneksel] *adj (töre)* traditional
gelgit [gelgit] *n* tide
gelin [gelin] *n* daughter-in-law, *(damadın eşi)* bride; **gelin teli** *n* tinsel
gelincik [gelindʒik] *n (çiçek)* poppy, *(hayvan)* weasel
gelinlik [gelinlik] *n* wedding dress
gelir [gelir] *n (maaş)* income ▹ *npl (aylık kazanç)* earnings, *(toplanan para)* proceeds; **gelir vergisi** *n* income tax; **vergi geliri** *n* revenue
gelişigüzel [geliʃigyzel] *adv* casually ▹ *n* chance
gelişme [geliʃme] *n (büyüme)* development, *(iyileşme)* improvement
gelişmek [geliʃmek] *vt* develop; **gelişmekte olan ülke** *n* developing country
gelişmemiş [geliʃmemiʃ] *adj* immature
geliştirmek [geliʃtirmek] *v* improve ▹ *vi (büyüme)* develop; **vücut geliştirme** *n* bodybuilding
gelmek [gelmek] *v* come, come from; **anlamına gelmek** *v* stand for; **üstesinden gelmek** *v* master, overcome, tackle; **bir araya gelmek** *v* get together; **gündeme gelmek** *v* come up; **geri gelmek** *v* come back; **kendine gelmek** *v* come round, regain; **yeniden bir araya gelme** *n* reunion
gemi [gemi] *n* ship; **büyük yolcu gemisi** *n* liner; **gemi gezisi** *n* cruise; **gemi teknesi** *n* hull; **gemi yapımı** *n* shipbuilding ▹ *v* **gemiyle yolculuk etmek** *n* sail
gen [gen] *n* gene
genç [gentʃ] *adj* young; **daha genç**

adj younger; **en genç** *adj* youngest; **genç kız** *n* lass; **gençlerin kaldığı otel** *n* youth hostel
gençlik [gentʃlik] *n* youth; **gençlik klubü** *n* youth club
genel [genel] *adj* general ▷ *n* general; **genel anestezi** *n* general anaesthetic; **genel kültür** *n* general knowledge; **genel müdür** *n* managing director; **genel merkez** *n* HQ; **genel seçim** *n* general election
genellemek [genellemek] *v* generalize
genellikle [genellikle] *adv* generally, usually
genetik [genetik] *adj* genetic; **genetik bilimi** *n* genetics; **genetik olarak değiştirilmiş** *adj* genetically-modified
geniş [geniʃ] *adj (ferah, yaygın)* extensive, *(yayvan)* broad, *(yayvan)* wide; **geniş bant** *n* broadband
genişlik [geniʃlik] *n* width
Georgia [georgia] *n (Amerikan eyaleti)* Georgia *(US state)*; **Georgia'ya ait** *adj* Georgian
gerçek [gertʃek] *adj (durum)* real, *(mücevher)* genuine, *(söz)* true ▷ *n* actual, *(bilgi)* fact, *(doğruluk)* truth; **gerçek dışı** *adj* unreal; **gerçeklerle bağdaşmayan** *adj* unrealistic; **gerçek kahveniz var mı?** Have you got real coffee?
gerçekçi [gertʃektʃi] *adj* realistic
gerçekleştirmek [gertʃekleʃtirmek] *v* fulfil
gerçeklik [gertʃeklik] *n* reality; **sanal gerçeklik** *n* virtual reality
gerçekten [gertʃekten] *adv* indeed, really, truly
gerçi [gertʃi] *adv* though
gerek [gerek] *adj* necessary; **gerek duymak** *v* need; **Bana bir doktor gerek** I need a doctor; **Geri dönmeniz gerekiyor** You have to turn round; **Ne giymem gerekiyor?** What should I wear?; **Ne kadar almam gerekiyor?** How much should I take?
gerekli [gerekli] *adj* necessary
gereklilik [gereklilik] *n* necessity
gereksinim [gereksinim] *n* requirement
gereksiz [gereksiz] *adj* unnecessary
gerektirmek [gerektirmek] *v* require
gergin [gergin] *adj (huzursuz)* tense, *(sinirleri yay gibi)* uptight, *(sinirli)* edgy
gerginlik [gerginlik] *n* tension; **gerginlik yaratıcı** *adj* stressful
geri [geri] *adv* back; **geri almak** *v* take back; **geri aramak** *v* call back, phone back, ring back; **geri ödeme** *n* repayment; **geri ödemek** *v* pay back, repay; **geri çevirmek** *v* turn down; **geri dönüş** *n* return *(coming back)*; **geri dönüştürmek** *n* recycle, recycling; **geri döndürmek** *vi* return; **geri dönmek** *v* return, reverse, turn back; **geri göndermek** *v* send back; **geri gelmek** *v* come back; **geri getirmek** *v* bring back, get back; **geri gitmek** *v* move back; **geri kalmak** *v* back out; **geri**

koymak *v* put back; **geri sarmak** *v* rewind; **geri tepmek** *v* backfire; **geri vermek** *v* give back; **geride kalmak** *v* lag behind; **geriye yatık çizgi** *n* backslash; **Arabayı buraya mı geri getirmem gerekiyor** Do I have to return the car here?; **Bisikleti ne zaman geri getirmem gerekiyor?** When is the bike due back?; **Geri dönmeniz gerekiyor** You have to turn round; **Kaçta geri döneriz?** When do we get back?; **Lütfen beni geri arayın** Please call me back; **Paramı geri alabilir miyim?** Can I have a refund?, Can I have my money back?; **Paramı geri istiyorum** I want my money back

geribildirim [geribildirim] *n* feedback

gerilim [gerilim] *n* tension; **kuşku ve gerilimli bekleyiş** *n* suspense

gerilmiş [gerilmiʃ] *adj* stressed

geriye [gerije] *adv* **geriye doğru** *adv* backwards

germek [germek] *v* tighten, stretch; **psikolojik anlamda germek** *v* strain

getiri [getiri] *n* return *(yield)*

getirmek [getirmek] *v* bring ▷ *vt* fetch; **geri getirmek** *v* bring back, get back

gevelemek [gevelemek] *v* waffle

gevrek [gevrek] *adj* crispy, *(çıtır çıtır)* crisp; **mısır gevreği** *n* cornflakes; **tahıl gevreği** *n* cereal

gevşek [gevʃek] *adj (düğüm vb)* loose, *(sarkmış karın vb)* flabby, *(tavır)* slack

gevşeme [gevʃeme] *n* relaxation

gevşemek [gevʃemek] *vi* relax

gevşetici [gevʃetidʒi] *adj* relaxing

geyik [gejik] **(geyikler)** *n* deer; **geyik eti** *n* venison; **ren geyiği** *n* reindeer

gezegen [gezegen] *n* planet

gezgin [gezgin] *n* tourist, traveller; **sırt çantasıyla dolaşan gezgin** backpacker

gezi [gezi] *n* excursion, tour; **gemi gezisi** *n* cruise; **keşif gezisi** *n* expedition

gezinti [gezinti] *n (at/araba/bisiklet)* ride; **gezinti yeri** *n* promenade

gezmek [gezmek] *v* walk, go out, tour; **gezip görme** *n* sightseeing; **sırt çantasıyla gezme** *n* backpacking

gıda [gəda] *n* food; **gıda zehirlenmesi** *n* food poisoning

gıdıklamak [gədəklamak] *v* tickle

gibi [gibi] *adv* as ▷ *prep* like; **dev gibi** *adj* giant; **sırık gibi** *n* lanky

giden [giden] *adj* **güneye giden** *adj* southbound

gidermek [gidermek] *v* eliminate

gidiş [gidiʃ] *n* departure; **dörtnala gidiş** *n* gallop; **gidiş dönüş yolculuk** *n* round trip; **gidiş-dönüş bilet** *n* return ticket; **tek gidiş bileti** *n* one-way ticket;**... a gidiş dönüş iki bilet** two return tickets to...; **Gidiş dönüş bilet ne kadar?** How much is a return ticket?; **Tek gidiş bilet ne kadar?** How much is a single ticket?

gidon [gidon] *npl* handlebars

Gine [gine] *n* Guinea; **Ekvator**

Ginesi *n* Equatorial Guinea
giriş [giriʃ] *n* entry, *(geçiş)* access, *(havaalanı)* check-in, *(kapı)* entrance, *(yer, nokta)* way in; **giriş ücreti** *n* admission charge, entrance fee; **giriş hakkı** *n* admittance ▷ *v* **giriş yapmak** *v* check in; **Özürlüler için girişiniz var mı?** Do you provide access for the disabled?; **Giriş vizem var** I have an entry visa; **Tekerlekli sandalye girişi olan bir oda istiyorum** I need a room with wheelchair access
girişim [giriʃim] *n* attempt, *(inisiyatif)* initiative
girmek [girmek] *v* get into, *(içeriye)* come in, *(içeriye)* go in ▷ *vt (bir yere)* enter; **bahse girme** *n* betting; **bahse girmek** *vi* bet; **kuyruğa girmek** *v* queue; **mekana girmek** *v* get in; **yeniden sınava girmek** *v* resit
gişe [giʃe] *n* **bilet gişesi** *n* booking office, box office, ticket office
git [git] *v* **Gidin buradan!** Go away!
gitar [gitar] *n* guitar
gitmek [gitmek] *v* go; **önden gitmek** *v* go ahead; **geri gitmek** *v* move back; **ileri gitmek** *v* move forward; **tırıs gitmek** *v* trot; **uçup gitmek** *v* fly away; **... a gitmek istiyorduk** We'd like to go to...; **... a gitmek istiyorum** I'm going to...; **Eve gitmek istiyorum** I'd like to go home; **Gitme zamanı geldi mi?** Is it time to go?; **Sörf için nereye gitmek gerek?** Where can you go surfing?; **Tırmanmaya gitmek isterdim** I'd like to go climbing
giyim [gijim] *n* clothing
giyinik [gijinik] *adj* dressed
giyinmek [gijinmek] *vi* dress
giymek [gijmek] *vt* wear
giysi [gijsi] *n (elbise)* dress, *(kıyafet)* garment; **antreman giysisi** *n* tracksuit; **spor giysisi** *n* sportswear; **Giysi kuralı var mı?** Is there a dress-code?
giysiler [gijsiler] *n* clothes
giz [giz] *n* mystery; **çok gizli** *adj* top-secret
gizem [gizem] *n* mystery
gizemli [gizemli] *adj* mysterious
gizli [gizli] *adj* confidential, secret; **gizli buz** *n* black ice; **gizli dinleme cihazı yerleştirilmiş** *adj* bugged; **gizli plan** *v* plot *(conspire)*; **gizli servis** *n* secret service
gizlice [gizlidʒe] *adv* secretly
glükoz [glykoz] *n* glucose
glüten [glyten] *n* gluten
GM [gm] *abbr* GM
gofret [gofret] *n* wafer
gol [gol] *n* goal, *(Amerikan futbolunda)* touchdown
golf [golf] *n* golf; **golf klübü** *n* golf club *(society)*; **golf sahası** *n* golf course; **golf sopası** *n* golf club *(stick)*, tee; **Buraya yakın bir golf sahası var mı?** Is there a public golf course near here?; **Golf sopaları kiralıyorlar mı?** Do they hire out golf clubs?; **Nerede golf oynayabilirim?** Where can I play golf?
Google® [google] *v* Google®
goril [goril] *n* gorilla
göbek [gøbek] *n* belly, navel,

(deliği) belly button
göç [gøtʃ] *n* migration; **göç etmek** *v* emigrate
göçme [gøtʃme] *n* immigration
göçmen [gøtʃmen] *adj* migrant ▷ *n* immigrant, migrant
göçük [gøtʃyk] *n* dent
göçürmek [gøtʃyrmek] *v* dent
göğüs [gøːys] *n* breast, bust, chest; **Göğsümde bir ağrı var** I have a pain in my chest
gök [gøk] *n* sky; **gök gürültülü** *adj* thundery; **gök gürültülü fırtına** *n* thunderstorm; **gök gürültüsü** *n* thunder
gökdelen [gøkdelen] *n* high-rise, skyscraper
gökkuşağı [gøkkuʃaːə] *n* rainbow
göktaşı [gøktaʃə] *n* meteorite
göl [gøl] *n* lake
gölcük [gøldʒyk] *n* pond
gölge [gølge] *n (birinin ya da bir şeyin)* shadow, *(tente, ağaç altı)* shade
gömlek [gømlek] *n* shirt; **iç gömleği** *n* slip *(underwear)*; **polo gömlek** *n* polo shirt
gömmek [gømmek] *v* bury
gönderen [gønderen] *n* sender
gönderme [gønderme] *n (kaynak)* reference
göndermek [gøndermek] *v* send, send out; **geri göndermek** *v* send back
gönenç [gønentʃ] *n* prosperity
gönül [gjønylj] *n* heart, mind, affection; **alçak gönüllü** *adj* humble, modest; **gönüllü olarak** *adv* voluntarily; **gönüllü olmak** *n* volunteer
gönüllü [gønylly] *adj* voluntary; **gönüllü olmak** *n* volunteer
gönülsüz [gønylsyz] *adj* reluctant
gönülsüzce [gønylsyzdʒe] *adv* reluctantly
göre [gøre] *prep* according to; **bedenine göre büyük** *adj* outsize; **göreceli olarak** *adv* comparatively, relatively
göreceli [gøredʒeli] *n* relative
görenek [gørenek] *n* custom; **göreneklere uymayan** *adj* unconventional
görev [gørev] *n* duty, task, *(ödev vb)* assignment, *(pozisyon)* post *(position)*; **daha önemsiz bir göreve kaydırmak** *v* relegate
görevli [gørevli] *adj* assigned ▷ *n* official, employee; **görevli memur** *(polis/asker) n* officer; **güvenlik görevlisi** *n* security guard; **geçici görevli** *n* temp; **hapishane görevlisi** *n* prison officer; **hükümet görevlisi** *n* civil servant; **oda görevlisi** *n* chambermaid; **polis görevlisi** *n* police officer; **sahil koruma görevlisi** *n* coastguard; **sınav görevlisi** *n* examiner; **sosyal hizmetler görevlisi** *n* social worker; **Görevliyi gördünüz mü?** Have you seen the guard?
görgü [gørgy] *npl* manners
görkem [gørkem] *n* majesty
görkemli [gørkemli] *adj* glorious, splendid
görmek [gørmek] *vt* see; **düş görmek** *v* dream; **görme yetisi** *n* eyesight; **gezip görme** *n* sightseeing; **hor görme** *n*

contempt
görsel [gørsel] *adj* visual
görünmek [gørynmek] *v* appear, seem; **yapar gibi görünmek** *v* pretend
görünmez [gørynmez] *adj* invisible
görünür [gørynyr] *adj* apparent, visible
görünüş [gørynyʃ] *n* appearance
görüş [gøryʃ] *n* view, *(fikir)* remark, *(göz)* sight, *(göz)* visibility; **açık görüşlü** *adj* liberal; **dar görüşlü** *adj* narrow-minded; **görüşe katılmamak** *v* disagree; **ortak görüş** *n* communion; **Görüşürüz** See you later
görüşme [gøryʃme] *n* interview ▷ **görüşme yapmak** *v* interview; **telefon görüşmesi** *n* phonecall
görüşmeci [gøryʃmedʒi] *n* interviewer, negotiator
görüşmek [gøryʃmek] *v* discuss, negotiate
görüşmeler [gøryʃmeler] *npl* negotiations
gösterge [gøsterge] *n* indicator; **gösterge tablosu** *n* dashboard
gösteri [gøsteri] *n* *(eğlence)* show, *(politik)* demonstration; **havai fişek gösterileri** *npl* fireworks; **Gösteri için nereye gidebiliriz?** Where can we go to see a show?
gösterici [gøsteridʒi] *n* demonstrator
gösterim [gøsterim] *n* *(film vb)* showing; **yeniden gösterim** *n* replay
gösteriş [gøsteriʃ] *n* show-off; **gösteriş yapmak** *v* show off
gösterişli [gøsteriʃli] *adj* grand
göstermek [gøstermek] *v* show ▷ *vi* point; **aday göstermek** *v* nominate; **çeşitlilik göstermek** *v* range, vary; **boy göstermek** *v* turn up; **eğilim göstermek** *v* tend; **haklılığını göstermek** *v* justify; **kendini göstermek** *v* stand out; **tepki göstermek** *v* react; **yeniden göstermek** *v* replay; **yol göstermek** *vt* lead
gövde [gøvde] *n* **ağaç gövdesi** *n* trunk
göz [gøz] *n* eye; **göz atmak** *vi* browse; **göz önünde tutarak** *prep* considering; **göz bağı** *n* blindfold; **göz damlası** *npl* eye drops; **göz farı** *n* eye shadow; **göz kamaştırıcı** *adj* glamorous, stunning; **göz kapağı** *n* eyelid; **göz kırpmak** *v* wink; **göz kırpmak** *v* blink; **gözünü dikmek** *v* gaze; **gözünü dikmek** *v* look, look at; **gözünü korkutmak** *v* intimidate; **gözünde büyütmek** *v* overestimate; **gözünde canlandırmak** *v* visualize; **gözden geçirmek** *(yeniden)* *v* revise; **gözden kaybolma** *n* disappearance; **gözden kaybolmak** *v* disappear; **gözlerini bağlamak** *v* blindfold; **torpido gözü** *n* glove compartment; **Gözüme bir şey kaçtı** I have something in my eye; **Gözlerim yanıyor** My eyes are sore
gözaltı [gøzaltə] *n* **gözaltına alma** *n* detention
gözatmak [gøzatmak] *v* glance
gözbebeği [gøzbebeji:] *n* pupil

(eye)
gözcü [gøzdʒy] *n* monitor; **sınav gözcüsü** *n* invigilator
gözde [gøzde] *adj* favourite ▹ *n* favourite
gözden [gøzden] *n* **gözden kaçırmak** *v* overlook
gözetim [gøzetim] *n* oversight *(supervision)*
gözetlemek [gøzetlemek] *v* pry ▹ *vt* watch
gözetmek [gøzetmek] *v* protect, look after, consider, respect; **fark gözetme** *n* distinction
gözlemci [gøzlemdʒi] *adj* observant ▹ *n* observer
gözlemek [gøzlemek] *v* watch, observe; **kuş gözleme** *n* birdwatching
gözlemevi [gøzlemevi] *n* observatory
gözlemlemek [gøzlemlemek] *v* observe
gözlük [gøzlyk] *npl* glasses, spectacles; **çift odaklı gözlük** *npl* bifocals; **güneş gözlüğü** *npl* sunglasses; **koruma gözlüğü** *npl* goggles; **Gözlüklerimi tamir edebilir misiniz?** Can you repair my glasses?
gözlükçü [gøzlyktʃy] *n* optician
gözyaşı [gøzjaʃə] *n* tear *(from eye)*; **gözyaşı bombası** *n* teargas
GPS [dʒi:pi:es] *n* **GPS sistemi** *n* GPS; **GPS var mı?** Does it have GPS?
grafik [grafik] *n* graph ▹ *npl* graphics; **dilimli grafik** *n* pie chart
grafiti [grafiti] *n* graffiti
gram [gram] *n* gramme
gramatik [gramatik] *adj* grammatical
gramer [gramer] *n* grammar
granit [granit] *n* granite
grev [grev] *n* strike; **grev yapmak** *vi* strike *(suspend work)*; **grev vardı, o yüzden** because of a strike
grevci [grevdʒi] *n* striker
greyfurt [grejfurt] *n* grapefruit
gri [gri] *adj* grey
grip [grip] *n* flu, influenza; **kuş gribi** *n* bird flu; **Grip geçiriyorum** I've got flu; **Yakınlarda grip atlattım** I had flu recently
Grönland [grønland] *n* Greenland
grup [grup] *n* group; **çocuk oyun grubu** *n* playgroup; **eski grubun yerini alan yeni grup** *n* relay; **kan grubu** *n* blood group; **sözcük grubu** *n* phrase; **Grup indirimi var mı?** Are there any reductions for groups?; **Kan grubum O pozitif** My blood group is O positive
Guatemala [guatemala] *n* Guatemala
guguk [guguk] *n* **guguk kuşu** *n* cuckoo
gurur [gurur] *n* pride
gururlu [gururlu] *adj* proud
gübre [gybre] *n* fertilizer, manure
gücendirmek [gydʒendirmek] *v* offend
güç [gytʃ] *adj (zor)* difficult ▹ *n (erk)* power, *(kuvvet)* force, *(kuvvet)* strength; **gücü yetmek** *v* afford; **insan gücü** *n* manpower
güçlendirmek [gytʃlendirmek] *v* strengthen

güçlü [gytʃly] *adj* powerful, strong
güçlük [gytʃlyk] *n* difficulty, trouble; **güçlük çıkaran** *n* troublemaker
güçlükle [gytʃlykle] *adv* hardly
güfte [gyfte] *npl* lyrics
gül [gyl] *n* rose
gülmek [gylmek] *v* laugh; **kahkahayla gülmek** *v* laugh; **kıs kıs gülmek** *v* snigger
gülümseme [gylymseme] *n* smile
gülümsemek [gylymsemek] *v* smile
gülünç [gylyntʃ] *adj* ridiculous
gülüş [gylyʃ] *n* laugh
gümrük [gymryk] *n* customs, (customs) duty; **gümrük memuru** *n* customs officer; **gümrük tarifesi** *n* tariff; **Bunun için gümrük ödemem gerekiyor mu?** Do I have to pay duty on this?
gümüş [gymyʃ] *n* silver
gün [gyn] *n* day; **dinlenme günü** *(Yahudiler için Cumartesi, Hristiyanlar için Pazar)* *n* Sabbath; **doğum günü** *n* birthday; **gün ışığı** *n* sunlight, sunshine; **gün batımı** *n* sunset; **gün doğuşu** *n* sunrise; **günü geçmiş** *adj* out-of-date; **her gün** *adv* daily; **resmi tatil günü** *n* public holiday; **Sevgililer Günü** *n* Valentine's Day; **tam gün** *adv* full-time; **yarım gün** *adv* part-time; **ödeme günü geçmiş** *adj* overdue; **Beş günlüğüne bir araba kiralamak istiyorum** I want to hire a car for five days; **Bugün günlerden ne?** What day is it today?; **Günün çorbası ne?** What is the soup of the day?; **Günün yemeği ne?** What is the dish of the day?; **Harika bir gün!** What a lovely day!; **Müze her gün açık mı?** Is the museum open every day?; **öbür gün** the day after tomorrow
günah [gynah] *n* sin
güncel [gyndʒel] *adj* current, *(haber vb)* topical, *(yenilenmiş)* up-to-date; **güncel haberler** *npl* current affairs
güncellemek [gyndʒellemek] *v* update
gündem [gyndem] *n* agenda; **gündeme gelmek** *v* come up
gündüz [gyndyz] *n* daytime
güneş [gyneʃ] *adj* solar ▷ *n* sun; **güneş çarpması** *n* sunstroke; **güneş enerjisi** *n* solar power; **güneş gözlüğü** *npl* sunglasses; **güneş kremi** *n* suncream; **güneş sistemi** *n* solar system; **güneş sonrası krem** *n* after sun lotion; **güneş yağı** *n* suntan oil; **güneş yanığı** *adj* sunburn, sunburnt; **güneşte yanmak** *v* sunbathe; **güneşte yanmış** *adj* tanned; **güneşlenme yatağı** *n* sunbed; **koruyucu güneş kremi** *n* sunblock
güneşli [gyneʃli] *adj* sunny
güneşlik [gyneʃlik] *n* sunscreen
güney [gynej] *adj* south, southern ▷ *n* south; **güneye giden** *adj* southbound; **Güney Afrika** *adj* South Africa, South African; **Güney Afrikalı** *n* South African; **Güney Amerika** *adj* South America, South American; **Güney Amerikalı** *n* South American;

Güney Kore *n* South Korea; **Güney Kutbu** *n* South Pole, the Antarctic, Antarctica
güneybatı [gynejbatə] *n* southwest
güneyde [gynejde] *adv* south
güneydoğu [gynejdou:] *n* southeast
günlük [gynlyk] *adj* daily ▷ *n* diary; **günlük bilet** *n* day return; **günlük ifadeler sözlüğü** *n* phrasebook
Gürcistan [gyrdʒistan] *n* Georgia *(country)*
Gürcü [gyrdʒy] *n* Georgian *(inhabitant of Georgia)*
güreş [gyreʃ] *n* wrestling
güreşçi [gyreʃdʒi] *n* wrestler
gürültü [gyrylty] *n* noise; **gök gürültülü** *adj* thundery; **gök gürültülü fırtına** *n* thunderstorm; **gök gürültüsü** *n* thunder; **Gürültüden uyuyamıyorum** I can't sleep for the noise
gürültülü [gyryltyly] *adj* loud, noisy
gütmek [gytmek] *n* **kin gütmek** *v* spite
güve [gyve] *n* moth
güveç [gyvetʃ] *n* casserole, stew
güven [gyven] *n* confidence *(trust)*, trust; **güven verici** *adj* reassuring; **güven vermek** *v* reassure; **güvenine bağlı olmak** *v* depend; **kendine güvenen** *adj* confident, self-assured
güvence [gyvendʒe] *n* **güvence vermek** *v* assure
güvenen [gyvenen] *adj* trusting
güvenilir [gyvenilir] *adj* reliable
güvenilmez [gyvenilmez] *adj* unreliable
güvenli [gyvenli] *adj* safe, secure
güvenlik [gyvenlik] *n* safety, security; **güvenlik duvarı** *n* firewall; **güvenlik görevlisi** *n* security guard; **sosyal güvenlik** *n* social security
güvenmek [gyvenmek] *v* count on, rely on, trust
güvensiz [gyvensiz] *adj* insecure
güvercin [gyverdʒin] *n* pigeon; **beyaz güvercin** *n* dove
güverte [gyverte] *n* deck; **Araba güvertesine nasıl gidebilirim?** How do I get to the car deck?; **Güverteye çıkabilir miyiz?** Can we go out on deck?
Güyan [gyjan] *n* Guyana
güzel [gyzel] *adj* beautiful; **çok güzel** *adj* gorgeous; **güzel manzaralı yer** *n* beauty spot
güzellik [gyzellik] *n* beauty; **güzellik salonu** *n* beauty salon
güzergah [gyzergah] *n* itinerary, route; **güzergah değiştirme** *n* detour

h

ıaber [haber] *n* news, information, knowledge; **güncel haberler** *npl* current affairs; **haber sunucusu** *n* newsreader; **Gecikeceğiniz zaman lütfen bize haber verin** Please call us if you'll be late; **Haberler kaçta?** When is the news?; **Polise haber vermemiz gerekiyor** We will have to report it to the police

ıaberler [haberler] *npl* news

ıac [hadʒ] *n* pilgrimage

ıacı [hadʒə] *n* pilgrim

ıacim [hadʒim] *n* volume

ıacker [hadʒker] *n* hacker

ıafıza [hafəza] *n* memory; **bilgisayar hafızası** hard disk; **hafıza kartı** *n* memory card

ıafif [hafif] *adj* light *(not heavy)*; **hafif akşam yemeği** *n* supper; **hafif bira** *n* lager; **hafif rüzgar** *n* breeze; **hafif vuruş** *n* tap; **hafife almak** *v* underestimate

hafta [hafta] *n* week; **hafta içi** *n* weekday; **hafta sonu** *n* weekend; **iki hafta** *n* fortnight; **bir hafta önce** a week ago; **bir hafta sonra** in a week's time; **bundan bir hafta önce** the week before last; **Bir haftalığı ne kadar?** How much is it for a week?; **geçen hafta** last week; **gelecek hafta** next week; **Odanın haftalığı ne kadar?** How much is it per week?

haftalık [haftalək] *adj* weekly; **Haftalık bir bilet lütfen** A book of tickets, please; **Haftalık kart kaça?** How much is a pass per week?; **Haftalık kayak kartı rica ediyorum?** I'd like a ski pass for a week; **Haftalık tarifeniz nedir?** What are your rates per week?

haham [haham] *n* rabbi

hain [hain] *adj (cadı vb)* wicked ▷ *n (kötü)* villain

Haiti [haiti] *n* Haiti

hak [hak] *n* right; **özlük hakları** *n* civil rights; **geçiş hakkı** *n* right of way; **giriş hakkı** *n* admittance; **hak etmek** *v* deserve; **haklı olarak** *adv* rightly; **haklılığını göstermek** *v* justify; **insan hakları** *npl* human rights; **telif hakkı** *n* copyright; **Yol hakkı sizin değildi** It wasn't your right of way

hakaret [hakaret] *n* insult

hakaretamiz [hakaretamiz] *adj* abusive

hakem [hakem] *n* referee, umpire; **hakem aracılığıyla çözümleme** *n* arbitration

hakim [hakim] **sulh hakimi** *n*

magistrate
hakimiyet [hakimijet] *n* curb
hakkında [hakkənda] *prep* about
haksız [haksəz] *adj* unfair
hal [hal] *n* condition, state; **eski haline dönmek** *n* relapse; **halden anlama** *n* sympathy; **halden anlamak** *v* sympathize; **hali vakti yerinde** *adj* well-off; **medeni hal** *n* marital status; **ruh hali** *n* temper
hala [hala] *adv* still
halat [halat] *n* rope; **halat çekme oyunu** *n* tug-of-war
halef [halef] *n* successor
half-board [halfboard] *n* **Half-board ne kadar?** How much is half board?
halı [halə] *n* carpet; **küçük halı** *n* rug
halk [halk] *adj* public ▷ *n* public; **halk müziği** *n* folk music; **halkla ilişkiler** *npl* public relations; **hane halkı** *n* household; **Kale halka açık mı?** Is the castle open to the public?; **Manastır halka açık mı?** Is the monastery open to the public?; **Saray halka açık mı?** Is the palace open to the public?; **Tapınak halka açık mı?** Is the temple open to the public?
halka [halka] *n (çember)* round *(circle), (zincir)* link
halletmek [halletmek] *v* deal with, sort out
halterci [halterdʒi] *n* weightlifter
halükar [halykar] *adv* **her halükarda** *adv* anyhow
hamak [hamak] *n* hammock
hamal [hamal] *n* porter
hamam [hamam] *n* baths; **hamam böceği** *n* cockroach
hamburger [hamburger] *n* beefburger, hamburger
hamile [hamile] *adj* pregnant; **Hamileyim** I'm pregnant; **Hamile kalmamak için bir şey istiyorum** I need contraception
hamilelik [hamilelik] *n* pregnancy; **hamilelik bulantısı** *n* morning sickness
hamster [hamster] *n* hamster
hamur [hamur] *n* dough, pastry; **hamur yuvarı** *n* dumpling; **milföy hamuru** *n* puff pastry; **sulu hamur** *n* batter; **un kurabiyesi hamuru** *n* shortcrust pastry
han [han] *n* inn
handikap [handikap] *n* handicap; **Handikapım...** My handicap is...; **Handikapınız kaç?** What's your handicap?
handsfree [handsfree] *adj* hands-free; **handsfree set** *n* hands-free kit
hane [hane] *n* house; **hane halkı** *n* household
hang-gliding [hanggliding] *n* hang-gliding; **Hang-gliding yapmak isterdim** I'd like to go hang-gliding
hangi [hangi] *adj* which ▷ *pron* which; **Ayakkabılar hangi katta** Which floor are shoes on?; **Hangi düğmeye basacağım?** Which button do I press?; **Hangi eczane nöbetçi?** Which pharmacy provides emergency service?
hanım [hanəm] *n* Mrs, Miss;...

hanımla konuşabilir miyim lütfen? Can I speak to Ms..., please?
hanımeli [hanəmeli] *n* honeysuckle
hantal [hantal] *adj* gross *(income etc.)*
hap [hap] *n* pill, tablet; **doğum kontrol hapı** *n* contraceptive; **uyku hapı** *n* sleeping pill
hapis [hapis] *n* **hapse atmak** *v* jail
hapishane [hapishane] *n* jail, prison; **hapishane görevlisi** *n* prison officer
hapşırmak [hapʃərmak] *v* sneeze
hararet [hararet] *n* heat; **Motor hararet yapıyor** The engine is overheating
harcamak [hardʒamak] *v* spend, use up
harcamalar [hardʒamalar] *npl* expenditure
harç [hartʃ] *n* mortar *(plaster)*
harçlık [hartʃlək] *n* **cep harçlığı** *n* pocket money
hardal [hardal] *n* mustard; **hardal otu** *n* rape *(plant)*
harekat [harekat] *n* **yeraltı harekatı** *n* underground
hareket [hareket] *n* act, move, movement; **bir yerden hareket etmek** *v* depart
hareketsiz [hareketsiz] *adj* motionless
harf [harf] *n* letter *(a, b, c)*; **adın baş harfleri** *n* initials; **adının ön harflerini yazmak** *v* initial; **harfi harfine** *adv* literally
hariç [haritʃ] *prep* except; **liste harici** *adj* unlisted
harika [harika] *adj* fantastic, magnificent, marvellous, smashing, wonderful
harita [harita] *n* chart, map; **sokak haritası** *n* street map; **yol haritası** *n* road map;**... haritası var mı?** Have you got a map of...?;**... yol haritası istiyorum** I need a road map of...; **Ülkenin haritasını nereden alabilirim?** Where can I buy a map of the country?; **Bölgenin haritasını nereden alabilirim?** Where can I buy a map of the area?; **Bir metro haritası lütfen** Could I have a map of the tube, please?; **Bu bölgenin haritasını nereden alabilirim?** Where can I buy a map of the region?; **Harita alabilir miyim?** Can I have a map?; **Haritada yerini gösterebilir misiniz?** Can you show me where it is on the map?; **Kentin haritasını nereden alabilirim?** Where can I buy a map of the city?; **Kentin yol haritasını istiyorum** I want a street map of the city; **Metro haritası var mı?** Do you have a map of the tube?; **Nerede olduğumuzu haritada gösterebilir misiniz?** Can you show me where we are on the map?
harp [harp] *n (müzik)* harp
hasar [hasar] *n* damage; **Bagajım hasar görmüş** My luggage has been damaged; **Valizim hasar görmüş** My suitcase has arrived damaged
hasat [hasat] *n* harvest; **hasat**

kaldırmak *v* harvest
haset [haset] *n* envy
hasetlenmek [hasetlenmek] *v* envy
hasılat [hasəlat] *npl* takings
hassas [hassas] *adj* delicate, touchy
hasta [hasta] *adj* ill, sick ▷ *n* patient; **hasta belgesi** *n* sick note; **şeker hastası** *n* diabetic
hastalık [hastalək] *n* illness, sickness; **Alzheimer hastalığı** *n* Alzheimer's disease; **hastalık ödentisi** *n* sick pay; **hastalık izni** *n* sick leave; **şeker hastalığı** *n* diabetes
hastalıklı [hastaləklə] *adj* frail
hastane [hastane] *n* hospital; **akıl hastanesi** *n* mental hospital; **doğum hastanesi** *n* maternity hospital; **Hastane nerede?** Where is the hospital?; **Hastanede çalışıyorum** I work in a hospital; **Hastaneye götürmemiz gerek** We must get him to hospital; **Hastaneye gitmesi gerekiyor mu?** Will he have to go to hospital?, Will she have to go to hospital?; **Hastaneye nasıl gidebilirim?** How do I get to the hospital?
haşlama [haʃlama] *adj* boiled; **haşlanmış yumurta** *n* boiled egg
hat [hat] *n* line; **boru hattı** *n* pipeline; **yardım hattı** *n* helpline;**... için nerede hat değiştirmem gerek?** Where do I change for...?;**... a hangi hat gider?** Which line should I take for...?; **Hat kesildi** I've been cut off; **Hat meşgul** It's engaged; **Hattı düşüremiyorum** I can't get through
hata [hata] *n* fault *(defect)*, fault *(mistake)*, mistake, oversight, slip, slip-up; **baskı hatası** *n* misprint ▷ *v* **hata yapmak** *v* mistake, slip up; **Hata bende değildi** It wasn't my fault
hatalı [hatalə] *adj* faulty, mistaken
hatchback [hatdʒhbadʒk] *n* hatchback
hatıra [hatəra] *n* memento
hatırlamak [hatərlamak] *v* remember
hatırlatıcı [hatərlatədʒə] *n* reminder
hatırlatmak [hatərlatmak] *v* remind
hatta [hatta] *adv* even, *(bilgisayar)* online
hava [hava] *n* air, *(meteoroloji)* weather; **açık hava** *adj* outdoor; **açık havada** *adv* out-of-doors, outdoors; **hava sahası** *n* airspace **hava tahmini** *n* weather forecast **hava trafik kontrolörü** *n* air-traffic controller; **hava yastığı** *n* airbag; **havaya uçmak** *vi* blow; **Hava çok berbat!** What awful weather!; **Hava değişecek mi?** Is the weather going to change?; **Hava postası ile ne kadar zamanda gider?** How long will it take by air?; **Hava tahmini nasıl?** What's the weather forecast?; **Hava yarın nasıl olacak?** What will the weather be like tomorrow?; **Tekerleklerin havasını kontrol eder misiniz**

lütfen? Can you check the air, please?; **Umarım hava böyle kalır** I hope the weather stays like this; **Umarım hava düzelir** I hope the weather improves

Hava [hava] *n* **Hava Kuvvetleri** *n* Air Force

hava alanı [havaalanə] *n* airport; **hava alanı otobüsü** *n* airport bus

havaalanı [havaalanə] *n* airport; **Havaalanına nasıl gidebilirim?** How do I get to the airport?; **Havaalanına otobüs var mı?** Is there a bus to the airport?; **Havaalanına taksi ne kadar?** How much is the taxi to the airport?

havai fişek [havaifiʃek] *n* **havai fişek gösterileri** *npl* fireworks

havalandırma [havalandərma] *n* air conditioning, ventilation

havalandırmalı [havalandərmalə] *adj* air-conditioned

havale [havale] *n* **posta havalesi** *n* postal order

havalı [havalə] *adj* cool *(stylish)*

havan [havan] *n* **havan topu** *n* mortar *(military)*

havasız [havasəz] *adj* stuffy

havaya [havaja] *n* **havaya uçurmak** *v* blow up

havayolu [havajolu] *n* airline

havlamak [havlamak] *v* bark

havlu [havlu] *n* towel; **banyo havlusu** *n* bath towel; **kurulama havlusu** *n* dish towel; **mutfak havlusu** *n* tea towel; **yüz havlusu** *n* face cloth; **Bana bir havlu verebilir misiniz?** Could you lend me a towel?; **Birkaç tane daha havlu getirir misiniz lütfen?** Please bring me more towels; **Havlu kalmamış** The towels have run out

havuç [havutʃ] *n* carrot; **yabani havuç** *n* parsnip

havuz [havuz] *n* pool *(water)*; **kum havuzu** *n* sandpit; **sığ havuz** *n* paddling pool; **yüzme havuzu** *n* swimming pool; **Açık yüzme havuzu mu?** Is it an outdoor pool?; **Çocuk havuzu var mı?** Is there a children's pool?; **Havuz ısıtılmış mı?** Is the pool heated?; **Yüzme havuzu nerede?** Where is the public swimming pool?; **Yüzme havuzu var mı/Yüzme havuzunuz var mı?** Is there a swimming pool?

haya [haja] *n (anatomi)* testicle

hayal [hajal] *n* imagination; **hayal kırıklığına uğramış** *adj* disappointed; **hayal kırıklığına uğratmak** *v* disappoint, let down

hayalet [hajalet] *n* ghost

hayali [hajali] *adj* imaginary

hayat [hajat] *n* life; **gece hayatı** *n* nightlife; **hayat pahalılığı** *n* cost of living; **hayatını bağışlamak** *v* spare; **hayatta kalan** *n* survivor; **hayatta kalmak** *v* survive

hayıflanmak [hajəflanmak] *v* regret

hayır [hajər] no

hayranlık [hajranlək] *n* admiration; **hayranlık duymak** *v* admire

hayret [hajret] *n* amazement, surprise; **hayret verici** *adj*

amazing
haysiyet [hajsijet] *n* dignity
hayvan [hajvan] *n* animal; **ev hayvanı** *n* pet; **hayvan dövüşleri** *n* blood sports
hayvanat [hajvanat] *npl* fauna; **hayvanat bahçesi** *n* zoo
hayvanbilim [hajvanbilim] *n* zoology
haz [haz] *n* delight, zest *(excitement)*
hazımsızlık [hazəmsəzlək] *n* indigestion
hazır [hazər] *adj* finished, ready; **hazır bir şekilde** *adv* readily; **hazır mutfak** *n* fitted kitchen; **hazır yemek** *n* ready-cooked, takeaway; **Araba ne zaman hazır olur?** When will the car be ready?; **CD ne zaman hazır olur?** When will the CD be ready?; **Hazır değilim** I'm not ready; **Hazır mısınız?** Are you ready?; **Ne zaman hazır olur?** When will it be ready?
hazırlama [hazərlama] *v* prepare
hazırlanmış [hazərlanməʃ] *adj* prepared
hazırlık [hazərlək] *n* preparation
Haziran [haziran] *n* June; **bütün Haziran boyunca** for the whole of June; **Haziran başında** at the beginning of June; **Haziran sonunda** at the end of June; **On beş Haziran Pazartesi** It's Monday the fifteenth of June
hece [hedʒe] *n* syllable
heceleme [hedʒeleme] *n* spelling
hedef [hedef] *n* aim, target
hedeflemek [hedeflemek] *v* aim
hediye [hedije] *n* gift; **hediye çeki** *n* gift voucher; **hediye dükkanı** *n* gift shop; **Hediye paketi yapar mısınız?** Please can you gift-wrap it?; **Hediyelik eşya nereden alabilirim?** Where can I buy gifts?; **Hediyelik eşyanız var mı?** Do you have souvenirs?
hekim [hekim] *n* doctor; **pratisyen hekim** *n* GP
helal [helal] *adj* permissible; **Helal yemeğiniz var mı?** Do you have halal dishes?
helikopter [helikopter] *n* helicopter
helva [helva] *n* **pamuk helva** *n* candyfloss
hemen [hemen] *adv* nearly, immediately; **hemen hemen** *adv* nearly; **Hemen mi ödemem gerekiyor?** Do I have to pay it straightaway?; **Hemen yapabilir misiniz?** Can you do it straightaway?
hemoroid [hemoroid] *npl* haemorrhoids
hemşire [hemʃire] *n* nurse; **Hemşireyle konuşmak istiyorum** I'd like to speak to a nurse
hemzemin [hemzemin] *n* **hemzemin geçit** *n* level crossing
hendek [hendek] *n* ditch, moat
hentbol [hentbol] *n* handball
henüz [henyz] *adv* just, yet *(with negative)*
hep [hep] *adj* **hep birlikte** *adv* altogether
hepsi [hepsi] *pron* all; **hepsini satmak** *v* sell out; **Hepsi küçük**

harf all lower case; **Hepsini birlikte yazın lütfen** All together, please
her [her] *adj* any, every; **her bir** *pron* each; **her gün** *adv* daily; **her halükarda** *adv* anyhow; **her iki** *adj* both; **her ikisi de** *pron* both; **her ne kadar** *conj* though; **her yıl** *adv* annually, yearly; **her yerde** *adv* everywhere; **her zaman** *adv* always; **Müze her gün açık mı?** Is the museum open every day?
herhangi [herhangi] *adj* some ▷ *pron* any; **herhangi bir şey** *pron* anything; **herhangi bir yer** *adv* anywhere; **herhangi biri** *pron* anybody, anyone
herif [herif] *n* bloke
herkes [herkes] *pron* everybody, everyone
herşey [herʃej] *pron* everything
hesap [hesap] *n* bill *(account)*, *(banka)* account *(in bank)*; **banka hesabı** *n* bank account ▷ *v* **birinin hesabına borç kaydetmek** *v* debit; **cari hesap** *n* current account; **cep hesap makinesi** *n* pocket calculator; **hesaba katmak** *v* consider, reckon; **hesaba katmamak** *v* rule out ▷ *n* **hesabından çekilen para** *n* debit; **hesabından fazla para çekmiş** *adj* overdrawn; **hesap özeti** *n* bank statement; **hesap çizelgesi** *n* spreadsheet; **hesap denetimi** *n* audit; **hesap makinesi** *n* calculator; **hesap numarası** *n* account number; **hesap vermek** *v* account for ▷ *v* **hesapları denetlemek** *v* audit; **ortak hesap** *n* joint account; **Ayrıntılı hesap alabilir miyim?** Can I have an itemized bill?; **Hesabı alalım lütfen** Please bring the bill; **Hesabı ayrı alalım** Separate bills, please; **Hesabıma yazın** Put it on my bill; **Hesabımdan para transferi yapmak istiyorum** I would like to transfer some money from my account; **Hesapta bir yanlışlık var** The bill is wrong
hesaplama [hesaplama] *n* calculation
hesaplamak [hesaplamak] *v* calculate
heteroseksüel [heteroseksyel] *adj* heterosexual
heves [heves] *n* enthusiasm
hevesli [hevesli] *adj* enthusiastic
heybe [hejbe] *n* saddlebag
heyecan [hejedʒan] *n* thrill; **heyecan verici** *adj* exciting, thrilling
heyecanlı [hejedʒanlə] *adj* excited
heykel [hejkel] *n* sculpture, statue
heykeltraş [hejkeltraʃ] *n* sculptor
hıçkırık [hətʃkərək] *npl* hiccups
hıçkırmak [hətʃkərmak] *v* **hıçkırarak ağlamak** *v* sob
hırdavat [hərdavat] *n* hardware
hırka [hərka] *n* cardigan
hırlamak [hərlamak] *v* growl, snarl
hırs [hərs] *n* ambition
hırsız [hərsəz] *n* burglar, thief; **hırsız alarmı** *n* burglar alarm
hırsızlık [hərsəzlək] *n* break-in, burglary, theft; **kimlik hırsızlığı** *n* identity theft; **Bir hırsızlığı bildirmek istiyorum** I want to

report a theft
hırslı [hərslə] *adj* ambitious
Hırvat [hərvat] *adj* Croatian ▹ *n (kişi)* Croatian *(person)*
Hırvatça [hərvattʃa] *n (dil)* Croatian *(language)*
Hırvatistan [hərvatistan] *n* Croatia
hız [həz] *n* speed; **hız sınırı** *n* speed limit; **hız yapmak** *v* speeding ▹ *v* **hızla atlamak** *v* plunge; **hızla koşmak** *v* dash, sprint; **Bu yolda hız limiti nedir?** What is the speed limit on this road?
hızlanma [həzlanma] *n* acceleration
hızlanmak [həzlanmak] *v* accelerate, speed up
hızlı [həzlə] *adj* fast ▹ *adv* fast; **Çok hızlı gidiyordu** He was driving too fast; **Çok hızlı gidiyordunuz** You were driving too fast
hızölçer [həzøltʃer] *n* speedometer
hi-fi [hifi] *n* hifi
hiç [hitʃ] *adj* no ▹ *adv* ever; **hiç durmadan** *adv* non-stop; **hiç kimse** *pron* no one, nobody;**... a hiç gittiniz mi?** Have you ever been to...?; **Hiç param yok** I have no money
hiçbir [hitʃbir] *pron* neither; **hiçbir şey** *n* nothing; **hiçbir yerde** *adv* nowhere
hiçbiri [hitʃbiri] *pron* none ▹ *sfb* neither
hiddet [hiddet] *n* rage
hidrojen [hidroʒen] *n* hydrogen
hijyen [hiʒjen] *n* hygiene
hikaye [hikaje] *n* tale
hindi [hindi] *n* turkey
Hindistan [hindistan] *n* India; **Hindistan cevizi** *n* coconut; **küçük Hindistan cevizi** *n* nutmeg
Hindu [hindu] *adj* Hindu ▹ *n* Hindu
Hinduizm [hinduizm] *n* Hinduism
Hint [hint] *adj* Indian; **Batı Hint Adaları** *npl* West Indian, West Indies; **Hint fıstığı** *n* cashew; **Hint keneviri** *(yaprakları esrar olarak kullanılır) n* marijuana; **Hint Okyanusu** *n* Indian Ocean
Hintli [hintli] *n* Indian
hipermarket [hipermarket] *n* hypermarket
hipopotam [hipopotam] **(hipopotamlar)** *n* hippopotamus, hippo
hippi [hippi] *n* hippie
his [his] *n* feeling
hisar [hisar] *n* fort
hisse [hisse] *n* share; **hisse sahibi** *n* shareholder
hissedar [hissedar] *n* stockholder
hissetmek [hissetmek] *v* feel
hitap [hitap] *n* address *(speech)*
HIV [hiv] *n* **HIV'li olmayan** *adj* HIV-negative; **HIV'li** *adj* HIV-positive; **HIV'liyim** I am HIV positive
hizmet [hizmet] *n* service; **hizmet eden** *n* server *(person)*; **hizmet etmek** *v* serve, service; **hizmet sınıfı** *n* business class; **sosyal hizmetler** *npl* social services; **sosyal hizmetler görevlisi** *n* social worker
hizmetçi [hizmettʃi] *n* servant;

hizmetçi kadın *n* maid
hobi [hobi] *n* hobby
hokey [hokej] *n* hockey; **buz hokeyi** *n* ice hockey
hokkabaz [hokkabaz] *n* juggler
Hollanda [hollanda] *n* Holland ▷ *npl* Netherlands
Hollandalı [hollandalə] **(Hollandalı erkekler)** *n* Dutchman, Dutchwoman, Dutch
homeopati [homeopati] *n* homeopathy
homeopatik [homeopatik] *adj* homeopathic
Honduras [honduras] *n* Honduras
hoparlör [hoparlør] *n* loudspeaker
hor [hor] *adj* **hor görme** *n* contempt
hor görmek [horgørmek] *v* despise
horlamak [horlamak] *v* snore
hormon [hormon] *n* hormone
horoz [horoz] *n* cock, cockerel
hortum [hortum] *n* hose, hosepipe
hostes [hostes] *n* air hostess, steward; **uçuş hostesi** *n* flight attendant
hoş [hoʃ] *adj* lovely, nice, pleasant, pretty; **eski ve hoş** *adj* quaint; **hoş bir şekilde** *adv* prettily; **hoş olmayan** *adj* unpleasant
hoşça [hoʃtʃa] *adv* beautifully
hoşçakal [hoʃtʃakal] *excl* bye!, bye-bye!, goodbye!
hoşgeldiniz [hoʃgeldiniz] *excl* welcome!
hoşgörülü [hoʃgøryly] *adj* tolerant
hoşgörüsüz [hoʃgørysyz] *adj* intolerant
hoşlanmak [hoʃlanmak] *v* enjoy
hoşlanmamak [hoʃlanmamak] *v* dislike
hoşnut [hoʃnut] *adj* delighted
hoşnutsuz [hoʃnutsuz] *adj* dissatisfied
hoverkraft [hoverkraft] *n* hovercraft
Hristiyan [hristijan] *adj* Christian ▷ *n* Christian
Hristiyanlık [hristijanlək] *n* Christianity
hukuk [hukuk] *n* law; **hukuk danışmanı** *n* solicitor; **hukuk fakültesi** *n* law school
huni [huni] *n* funnel
hurra [hurra] *excl* hooray!
huş [huʃ] *n* **huş ağacı** *n* birch
huy [huj] *n* nature, temper; **iyi huylu** *adj* good-natured
huysuz [hujsuz] *adj* bad-tempered, grumpy
huzurevi [huzurevi] *n (yaşlılar için)* nursing home
huzursuz [huzursuz] *adj* restless
hücre [hydʒre] *n* cell
hüküm [hykym] *n* judgement; **yanlış hüküm vermek** *v* misjudge
hükümdar [hykymdar] *n* ruler *(commander)*
hükümet [hykymet] *n* government; **hükümet görevlisi** *n* civil servant
hükümlü [hykymly] *n* inmate ▷ *v* convict
hümanist [hymanist] *adj* humanitarian

I

ığğ [ələdʒa] *excl* ugh
İkizler [əkizler] *n* **İkizler burcu** *n* Gemini
ılıca [ələdʒa] *n* spa
ılık [ələk] *adj* lukewarm, warm
ılımlı [ələmlə] *adj* medium *(between extremes)*, mild, moderate
ılımlılık [ələmlələk] *n* moderation
İncil [əndʒil] *n* Bible
İngiliz [əngiliz] *adj* British, English ▷ *n* Englishman, British; **İngiliz anahtarı** *n* spanner; **İngiliz kadın** *n* Englishwoman
İngilizce [əngilizdʒe] *n* English
İngiltere [əngiltere] *n* Britain, Great Britain, England; **İngiltere'nin kodu kaç?** What is the dialling code for the UK?
İnternet [ənternet] *n* Net
İÖ [əø] *abbr* BC
İran [əran] *adj* Iranian ▷ *n* Iran
İranlı [əranlə] *adj* Persian ▷ *n (kişi)* Iranian *(person)*
ırk [ərk] *n* race *(origin)*; **ırkla ilgili** *adj* racial
ırkçı [ərktʃə] *adj* racist ▷ *n* racist
ırkçılık [ərktʃələk] *n* racism
İrlanda [ərlanda] *adj* Irish ▷ *n* Eire, Ireland; **Kuzey İrlanda** *n* Northern Ireland, Ulster
İrlandalı [ərlandalə] **(İrlandalı adamlar)** *n (erkek)* Irishman, *(kadın)* Irishwoman, Irish
ırmak [ərmak] *n* river; **ırmak kıyısı** *n* bank *(ridge)*
İsa [əsa] *n* Christ, Jesus
ısı [əsə] *n* heat
ısınma [əsənma] *n* **küresel ısınma** *n* global warming
ısırgan [əsərgan] *n* nettle
ısırıcı [əsərədʒə] *adj* stingy
ısırma [əsərma] *n* bite
ısırmak [əsərmak] *n* bite
ısıtıcı [əsətədʒə] *n* heater
ısıtma [əsətma] *n* heating; **Isıtma çalışmıyor** The heating doesn't work
ısıtmak [əsətmak] *v* heat, warm up; **merkezi ısıtma** *n* central heating
İskandinav [əskandinav] *adj* Scandinavian
İskandinavya [əskandinavja] *n* Scandinavia
İskoç [əskotʃ] *adj* Scots, Scottish ▷ *n* Scotswoman, *(erkek)* Scotsman, Scot; **İskoç çoban köpeği** *n* collie
İskoçya [əskotʃja] *n* Scotland
ıslak [əslak] *adj* moist, soaked, soggy, wet; **ıslak bebek mendili** *n*

baby wipe
İslami [əslami] *adj* Islamic
ıslatmak [əslatmak] *v* soak
ıslık [əslək] *n* whistle; **ıslık çalmak** *v* whistle
ısmarlamak [əsmarlamak] *v* order *(request)*
ıspanak [əspanak] *n* spinach
İspanya [əspanja] *n* Spain
İspanyol [əspanjol] *adj* Spanish ▷ *n* Spaniard, Spanish
İsrail [əsrail] *adj* Israeli ▷ *n* Israel
İsrailli [əsrailli] *n* Israeli
ısrar [əsrar] *n* insistence; **ısrar etmek** *v* insist
ısrarlı [əsrarlə] *adj* persistent
ıssız [əssəz] *n* **ıssız ada** *n* desert island
ıstaka [əstaka] *n* cue *(billiards)*
ıstırap [əstərap] *n* agony
İsveç [əsvetʃ] *adj* Swedish ▷ *n* Sweden
İsveçli [əsvetʃli] *n* Swede, Swedish
İsviçre [əsvitʃre] *adj* Swiss ▷ *n* Switzerland
İsviçreli [əsvitʃreli] *n* Swiss
ışık [əʃək] *n* light; **ışığı söndürmek** *v* turn out; **ışıklı yaya geçidi** *n* pelican crossing; **gün ışığı** *n* sunlight, sunshine; **projektör ışığı** *n* floodlight; **tehlike uyarı ışığı** *npl* hazard warning lights; **trafik ışıkları** *npl* traffic lights; **Işığı söndürebilir miyim?** Can I switch the light off?; **Işığı yakabilir miyim?** Can I switch the light on?; **Işık yanmıyor** The light doesn't work; **Işıkta bakabilir miyim?** May I take it over to the light?; **Yağ ikaz ışığı yanıyor** The oil warning light won't go off
ışıklandırma [əʃəklandərma] *n* lighting
ışın [əʃən] *n* beam
İtalya [ətalja] *n* Italy
İtalyan [ətaljan] *adj* Italian ▷ *n* *(kişi)* Italian *(person)*
İtalyanca [ətaljandʒa] *n* *(dil)* Italian *(language)*
ızgara [əzgara] *n* grid, grill ▷ *v* **ızgara yapmak** *v* grill
ızgarada [əzgarada] *adj* grilled
İzlanda [əzlanda] *adj* Icelandic ▷ *n* Iceland
İzlandalı [əzlandalə] *n* Icelandic

◆

İ

iade [iade] *n* returning, giving back; **iadeli taahhütlü** *n* recorded delivery; **para iadesi** *n* rebate, refund; **para iadesi yapmak** *v* refund; **vergi iadesi** *n* tax return; **İadeli taahhütlü ne kadar sürer?** How long will it take by registered post?; **Bunu iade etmek istiyorum** I'd like to return this
ibadet [ibadet] *v* **ibadet etmek** *v* worship
icap ettirmek [idʒapettirmek] *v* call for
icat [idʒat] *n* invention; **icat etmek** *v* invent
iç [itʃ] *adj* inner, *(organ vb)* internal ▹ *n* interior; **ülke içi** *adj* domestic; **hafta içi** *n* weekday; **iç çamaşırı** *n* lingerie, underwear; **iç çekme,iç geçirmek** *n* sigh; **iç ferahlatıcı** *adj* refreshing; **iç gömleği** *n* slip *(underwear)*; **iç lastik** *n* inner tube; **iç mimar** *n* interior designer; **iç rahatlığı** *n* relief; **iç savaş** *n* civil war; **içine kapanık** *adj* self-conscious
içecek [itʃedʒek] *n* drink, soft drink; **serinletici içecek** *npl* refreshments
içeri [itʃeri] *prep* into; **içeri almak** *v* admit *(allow in)*
içeride [itʃeride] *adv* indoors, inside ▹ *prep* inside; **İçeride** It's inside
içerik [itʃerik] *n* context
içerisi [itʃerisi] *n* inside
içerlemiş [itʃerlemiʃ] *adj* resentful
içermek [itʃermek] *v* contain
içgüdü [itʃgydy] *n* instinct
için [itʃin] *prep* for, owing to; **Özürlüler için kolaylıklarınız nelerdir?** What facilities do you have for disabled people?; **Özürlüler için tuvaletiniz var mı?** Are there any toilets for the disabled?
içinde [itʃinde] *prep* in, within *(space)*
içinden [itʃinden] *prep* through
içine [itʃine] *prep* within *(term)*
iç karartıcı *adj* depressing, dismal
içki [itʃki] *n* booze; **alkollü içki** *npl* spirits; **içki satan dükkan** *n* off-licence; **içkili araba kullanma** *n* drink-driving; **yemek öncesi içki** *n* aperitif
içmek [itʃmek] *vt* drink; **ölçüsüz içme** *n* binge drinking; **içme suyu** *n* drinking water ▹ *v* **sigara içmek** *v* smoke; **Bir şey içmek ister misiniz?** Would you like a drink?;

Ne içmek istersiniz? What would you like to drink?; **içmiyorum** I'm not drinking
içten [itʃten] *adj* sincere
içtenlikle [itʃtenlikle] *adv* frankly, sincerely
idam [idam] *n* execution; **idam cezası** *n* capital punishment; **idam etmek** *v* execute
idare [idare] *n* management, direction; **idare etmek** *v* go round, manipulate; **idare etmek** *v* control
idari [idari] *adj* administrative
iddia [iddia] *n* allegation; **iddia edilen** *adj* alleged
ideal [ideal] *adj* ideal
ideoloji [ideoloʒi] *n* ideology
idrar [idrar] *n* urine
ifade [ifade] *n* expression; **günlük ifadeler sözlüğü** *n* phrasebook; **ifade etmek** *v* express, state
ifşa [ifʃa] *n* **ifşa etmek** *v* reveal
iğne [jine] *n* needle; **kilitli iğne** *n* safety pin; **toplu iğne** *n* pin; **İğne ipliğiniz var mı?** Do you have a needle and thread?
iğrenç [jirentʃ] *adj* disgusting, filthy, obnoxious, repulsive, revolting
ihanet [ihanet] *n* **ihanet etmek** *v* betray
ihmal [ihmal] *n* neglect; **ihmal edilmiş** *adj* neglected ▹ *v* **ihmal etmek** *v* neglect
ihracat [ihradʒat] *n* export
ihraç [ihratʃ] *v* **ihraç etmek** *v* export
ihtiyaç [ihtijatʃ] *n* need; **ihtiyaca uyarlanmış** *adj* customized; **Ütüye ihtiyacım var** I need an iron; **Bir ihtiyacınız var mı?** Do you need anything?; **Yardıma ihtiyacım var** I need assistance
ikaz [ikaz] *n* warning; **Yağ ikaz ışığı yanıyor** The oil warning light won't go off
iken [iken] *conj* as, while
iki [iki] *num* two; **her iki/her ikisi de** *pron* both; **iki dilli** *adj* bilingual; **iki hafta** *n* fortnight; **iki katına çıkmak** *vt* double; **iki kere** *adv* twice; **iki kişilik oda** *n* double room; **iki nokta üst üste** *n* colon; **İki bilet, lütfen** I'd like two tickets, please; **İki gece kalmak istiyorum** I'd like to stay for two nights; **İki yaşında bir çocuk için çocuk koltuğu istiyorum** I'd like a child seat for a two-year-old child; **İki yüz... rica ediyorum** I'd like two hundred... ; **İki yüz iki numaralı odanın anahtarı lütfen** the key for room number two hundred and two; **Saat ikiye çeyrek var** It's quarter to two; **Saat yedi buçuğa iki kişilik bir rezervasyon yaptırmak istiyorum** I'd like to make a reservation for half past seven for two people; **Yarın akşam için iki kişilik bir masa ayırtmak istiyordum** I'd like to book a table for two people for tomorrow night; **Yolculuk iki saat sürüyor** The journey takes two hours
ikilem [ikilem] *n* dilemma
ikinci [ikindʒi] *n* second, *(yarışma)* runner-up; **ikinci baskı kitap** *n* paperback; **ikinci el** *adj*

secondhand; **ikinci kalite** *adj* second-rate; **ikinci olarak** *adv* secondly; **ikinci sınıf** *adj* economy class, second class, second-class; **Soldan ikinci sokağa dönün** Take the second turning on your left

ikiz [ikiz] *n* twin

iklim [iklim] *n* climate; **iklim değişikliği** *n* climate change

ikmal [ikmal] *n* **yakıt ikmali yapmak** *v* refuel

ikna [ikna] *n* persuasion; **ikna edici** *adj* persuasive; **ikna etme** *v* persuade

ikon [ikon] *n* icon

ikrar [ikrar] *n* acknowledgement

ilaç [ilatʃ] *n* drug, medicine, remedy; **böcek ilacı** *n* insect repellent; **ilaç yazmak** *v* prescribe; **Bu ilacı alıyorum zaten** I'm already taking this medicine

ilahi [ilahi] *n* hymn

ilan [ilan] *n* notice; **ilan tahtası** *n* bulletin board, notice board; **küçük ilanlar** *npl* small ads

ilave [ilave] *adj (fazladan)* extra ▷ *n (ek)* supplement

ilaveten [ilaveten] *adv* extra

ile [ile] *prep* with

ileri [ileri] *adj* advanced; **daha ileri/daha ileriye** *adv* further; **ileri eğitim** *n* further education; **ileri gitmek** *v* move forward; **ileriye almak** *v* put forward

ileriye [ilerije] *adv* forward

ilerleme [ilerleme] *n* advance, progress

ilerlemek [ilerlemek] *v* advance

iletişim [iletiʃim] *n* communication; **iletişim kurmak** *v* communicate

iletlemek [iletlemek] *v* forward

ilgi [ilgi] *n (merak)* interest *(curiosity)*; **ilgi çekici** *adj* interesting; **ilgisini başka yöne çekmek** *v* distract

ilgilenmek [ilgilenmek] *v* interest

ilgili [ilgili] *adj* concerned, interested ▷ *prep* concerning; **ırkla ilgili** *adj* racial; **Bengaldeş ile ilgili** *n* Bangladeshi; **denizcilikle ilgili** *adj* maritime; **ilgili olarak** *prep* regarding

ilginç [ilgintʃ] *adj* interesting; **Gidilecek ilginç yerler önerebilir misiniz?** Can you suggest somewhere interesting to go?

ilik [ilik] *n (anatomi)* marrow

ilişki [iliʃki] *n* relation, relationship; **halkla ilişkiler** *npl* public relations

ilişkin [iliʃkin] *adj* relevant

ilk [ilk] *adj* first, primary ▷ *n* first; **Büyük perhizin ilk Çarşambası** *n* Ash Wednesday; **ilk yardım** *n* first aid; **ilk yardım çantası** *n* first-aid kit;**... a ilk otobüs kaçta?** When is the first bus to...?;**... a ilk tren kaçta?** When is the first train to...?; **İlk teleferik kaçta?** When does the first chair-lift go?; **İlk vapur kaçta?** When is the first boat?; **Bu benim... a ilk gelişim** This is my first trip to...; **Sağdan ilk sokağa dönün** Take the first turning on your right

ilkbahar [ilkbahar] *n* spring *(season)*

ilke [ilke] *n* principle

ilkel [ilkel] *adj* primitive, uncivilized
ilkin [ilkin] *adv* first
ilkokul [ilkokul] *n* elementary school, primary school
illet [illet] *n* disease
illüzyonist [illyzjonist] *n* conjurer
iltifat [iltifat] *n* compliment; **iltifat etmek** *v* compliment
iltihap [iltihap] *n* inflammation; **bademcik iltihabı** *n* tonsillitis; **karaciğer iltihabı** *n* hepatitis; **mafsal iltihabı** *n* arthritis
im [im] *n* tick
ima [ima] *n* hint ▷ *v* **imada bulunmak** *v* hint
imdat [imdat] *excl* help!
imge [imge] *n* image
imha [imha] *n* destruction
imkansız [imkansəz] *adj* impossible
imleç [imletʃ] *n* cursor
imparator [imparator] **(imparatoriçe)** *n* emperor
imparatorluk [imparatorluk] *n* empire
imza [imza] *n* autograph, signature
inanç [inantʃ] *n* belief, faith; **batıl inançları olan** *adj* superstitious
inandırıcı [inandərədʒə] *adj* convincing, credible
inandırmak [inandərmak] *v* convince, rope in ▷ *vi* believe
inanılmaz [inanəlmaz] *adj* incredible, unbelievable ▷ *afj* fabulous
inanmak [inanmak] *vt* believe
inatçı [inattʃə] *adj* stubborn
ince [indʒe] *adj* thin, *(vücut vb)* slim; **ince alay** *n* irony
inceleme [indʒeleme] *n* survey
incelemek [indʒelemek] *v* examine
incelik [indʒelik] *n* tact
incelikli [indʒelikli] *adj* tactful
inci [indʒi] *n* pearl; **inci çiçeği** *n* lily of the valley
incil [indʒil] *n* gospel
incinmiş [indʒinmiʃ] *adj* hurt
incir [indʒir] *n* fig
incitmek [indʒitmek] *vt* hurt; **Acıyor** It hurts
inç [intʃ] *n* inch
indeks [indeks] *n* index *(list)*
indirgemek [indirgemek] *v* **en aza indirgemek** *v* minimize
indirim [indirim] *n* discount, reduction; **öğrenci indirimi** *n* student discount; **indirimli fiyatla sunulan eşya** *n* special offer; **Çocuklara indirim var mı?** Are there any reductions for children?; **Öğrenci indirimi var mı?** Are there any reductions for students?; **Özürlüler için indiriminiz var mı?** Is there a reduction for disabled people?; **Bu kartla indirim alabilir miyim?** Is there a reduction with this pass?; **Grup indirimi var mı?** Are there any reductions for groups?; **Yaşlılara indirim var mı?** Are there any reductions for senior citizens?
indirme [indirme] *n (bilgisayar)* download
indirmek [indirmek] *v (bilgisayar)* download; **denize indirmek** *v* launch; **yere indirmek** *v* ground

inek [inek] *n* cow
ineklemek [ineklemek] *v* swot
ingilizce [ingilizdʒe] *n* English *(language)*; **İngilizce bilen bir doktor var mı?** Is there a doctor who speaks English?; **İngilizce bilen biri var mı?** Does anyone speak English?; **İngilizce biliyor musunuz?** Do you speak English?; **İngilizce bilmiyorum** I don't speak English; **İngilizce broşürünüz var mı?** Do you have a leaflet in English?; **İngilizce film var mı?** Are there any films in English?; **İngilizce kılavuzunuz var mı?** Do you have a guide book in English?; **İngilizce konuşan bir rehber var mı?** Is there a guide who speaks English?; **İngilizce rehberli turunuz var mı?** Is there a guided tour in English?; **Çok az İngilizce konuşabiliyorum** I speak very little English
inhalasyon [inhalasjon] *n* **inhalasyon cihazı** *n* inhaler
iniş [iniʃ] *n* **acil iniş** *n* emergency landing; **iniş yapmak** *vi* land; **Bu iniş zor mu?** How difficult is this slope?; **Yokuş iniş kayağı kiralamak istiyorum** I want to hire downhill skis
inkar [iŋar] *n* denial; **inkar edilemez** *adj* undeniable; **inkar etmek** *v* deny
inlemek [inlemek] *v* groan, moan
inmek [inmek] *v* get off, *(alçalmak)* descend; **aşağıya inmek** *v* come down
insan [insan] *adj* human; **insan bilimi** *n* anthropology; **insan gücü** *n* manpower; **insan hakları** *npl* human rights
insanlar, kişi [insanlar, kiʃi] *npl* people
insanlık [insanlək] *n* mankind
insanoğlu [insanoɣlu] *n* human being
inşa [inʃa] *n* construction; **inşa etmek** *vt* build
inşaat [inʃaat] *n* **inşaat alanı** *n* building site
inşaatçı [inʃaattʃə] *n* builder
interkom [interkom] *n* intercom
Internet [internet] *n* Internet; **internet adresi** *n* web address; **Internet cafe** *n* Internet café; **internet kamerası** *n* webcam; **Internet kullanıcısı** *n* Internet user; **internet sitesi** *n* website; **internet suçu** *n* cybercrime; **internet tarayıcı** *n* web browser; **Buralarda Internet cafe var mı?** Are there any Internet cafés here?; **Odada Internet bağlantısı var mı?** Is there an Internet connection in the room?
intihar [intihar] *n* suicide; **intihar bombacısı** *n* suicide bomber
intikam [intikam] *n* revenge
ip [ip] *n* rope, string; **çamaşır ipi** *n* clothes line, washing line; **diş ipi** *n* dental floss
ipek [ipek] *n* silk
iplik [iplik] *n* thread; **İğne ipliğiniz var mı?** Do you have a needle and thread?
iPod® [ipod] *n* iPod®
iptal [iptal] *n* cancellation; **iptal etmek** *vt* call off, cancel; **İptal olan uçuş var mı?** Are there any

cancellations?

IQ [ajkju:] *abbr* IQ

irade [irade] *n* will *(motivation)*, willpower

Irak [irak] *adj* Iraqi ▷ *n* Iraq

Iraklı [iraklə] *n* Iraqi

iri [iri] *adj* large, big; **iri parça** *n* lump

iribaş [iribaʃ] *n* tadpole

irin [irin] *n* pus

iris [iris] *n* iris

irkilmek [irkilmek] *v* startle

ishal [ishal] *n* diarrhoea; **İshal oldum** I have diarrhoea

isim [isim] *n* name; **isim annesi** *n* godmother; **isim babası** *(vaftiz)* *n* godfather *(baptism)*

iskele [iskele] *n (deniz)* quay, *(inşaat)* scaffolding

iskelet [iskelet] *n* skeleton

ISP [isp] *abbr* ISP

israf [israf] *n* waste; **israf etmek** *v* waste

istakoz [istakoz] *n* lobster

istasyon [istasjon] *n* station; **benzin istasyonu** *n* petrol station, service station; **metro istasyonu** *n* metro station, tube station; **polis istasyonu** *n* police station; **radyo istasyonu** *n* radio station; **tren istasyonu** *n* railway station; **Buraya en yakın benzin istasyonu nerede?** Is there a petrol station near here?; **Tren istasyonuna en kolay nasıl gidebilirim?** What's the best way to get to the railway station?

istek [istek] *n* wish, request; **isteğe bağlı** *adj* optional; **istek formu** *n* claim form

istekli [istekli] *adj* keen, willing

istemek [istemek] *v* want; **fazla fiyat isteme** *n* surcharge

istenmeyen [istenmejen] *adj* **istenmeyen e-mail** *n* spam

istifa [istifa] *n* resignation; **istifa etmek** *v* resign

istridye [istridje] *n* oyster

isyankar [isjaŋar] *adj* rebellious

iş [iʃ] *n* job, work; **ağaç işleri** *n* woodwork; **açık iş** *n* vacancy; **ev işi** *n* housework; **evrak işi** *n* paperwork; **her gün işe trenle giden kimse** *n* commuter; **her gün işi ile evi arasında gidip gelmek** *v* commute; **iş adamı** *n* businessman; **iş arkadaşı** *n* associate; **iş bulma kurumu** *n* job centre; **iş kadını** *n* businesswoman; **iş saatleri dışında** *adv* off-peak; **iş seyahati** *n* business trip; **işe alma** *n* employment; **işe almak** *v* employ; **işten atma** *n* sack *(dismissal)*; **işten çıkarılmış** *(ihtiyaç fazlası olarak)* *adj* redundant; **işten çıkarma** *(ihtiyaç fazlası olarak)* *n* redundancy; **işten çıkarmak** *v* dismiss, lay off; **musluk işleri** *n* plumbing; **usta işi** *adj* ingenious; **yazlık iş** *n* holiday job; **Buraya iş için geldim** I'm here for work

işaret [iʃaret] *n* mark, sign, signal; **ünlem işareti** *n* exclamation mark; **işaret dili** *n* sign language; **işaret etmek** *v* sign; **işaret parmağı** *n* index finger; **sınır işareti** *n* landmark; **soru işareti** *n* question mark; **ters tırnak işareti** *npl* inverted commas;

trafik işareti *n* road sign; **at işaretini bulamıyorum** I can't find the 'at' sign
işaretlemek [iʃaretlemek] *v* indicate, mark *(make sign)*
işbirliği [iʃbirləə] *n* cooperation; **işbirliği yapmak** *v* collaborate
işçi [iʃtʃi] **(işçiler)** *n* workman, employee, labourer, worker; **işçi sınıfı** *adj* working-class
işgal [iʃgal] *n* occupation *(invasion)*
işgücü [iʃgydʒy] *n* workforce
işitme [iʃitme] *n* hearing; **işitme cihazı** *n* hearing aid; **İşitme aracı kullanıyorum** I have a hearing aid; **İşitme özürlüler için cihaz var mı?** Is there an induction loop?
işitmek [iʃitmek] *v* hear
işkence [iʃkendʒe] *n* torture ▹ *v* **işkence etmek** *v* torture
işlem [iʃlem] *n* process, transaction; **çarpma işlemi** *n* multiplication; **çıkarma işlemi** *v* subtract
işlemek [iʃlemek] *v* commit, operate *(to function)*
işletme [iʃletme] *n* **bar işletmecisi** *n* publican; **işletme masrafları** *npl* overheads
işsiz [issiz] *adj* unemployed
işsizlik [iʃsizlik] *n* unemployment
işşiz [iʃʃiz] *adj* jobless
iştah [iʃtah] *n* appetite
işveren [iʃveren] *n* employer
işyeri [iʃjeri] *n* workplace
itaatkar [itaatkar] *adj* obedient
itfaiye [itfaije] *n* fire brigade; **İtfaiyeyi çağırın** Please call the fire brigade
itfaiyeci [itfaijedʒi] **(itfaiyeciler)** *n* fireman
ithaf [ithaf] *n* dedication
ithal [ithal] *n* import ▹ *v* **ithal etmek** *v* import
itici [itidʒi] *adj* hideous, repellent
itimatname [itimatname] *n* credentials
itiraf [itiraf] *n* confession; **itiraf etmek** *v* confess
itiraz [itiraz] *n* objection, reservation
ittifak [ittifak] *n* alliance
ittirmek [ittirmek] *vt* push
ivedi [ivedi] *adj* urgent
ivedilik [ivedilik] *n* urgency
iyi [iji] *adj* good ▹ *adv* all right, well; **çok iyi** *n* fine; **daha iyi/daha iyisi** *adv* better; **en iyi/en iyisi** *adv* best; **en iyi şekilde** *adv* ideally; **iyi değil** *adj* unwell; **iyi huylu** *adj* good-natured; **iyi kalpli** *adj* kind; **iyi yüreklilik** *n* kindness; **iyi yetiştirilmiş** *adj* well-behaved; **İyi akşamlar** Good evening; **İyi bir beyaz şarap tavsiye edebilir misiniz?** Can you recommend a good white wine?; **İyi bir kırmızı şarap tavsiye edebilir misiniz?** Can you recommend a good red wine?; **İyi bir kulüp biliyor musunuz?** Where is there a good club?; **İyi bir şarap tavsiye edebilir misiniz?** Can you recommend a good wine?; **İyi bir restoran tavsiye edebilir misiniz?** Can you recommend a good restaurant?; **İyi günler** Good afternoon; **İyi geceler** Good night; **İyi konserler var mı?** Are there any good concerts on?; **İyi**

uyudunuz mu? Did you sleep well?; **İyi yolculuklar!** Have a good trip!; **Buralarda iyi bir plaj var mı?** Are there any good beaches near here?; **Gidilecek iyi bir yer biliyor musunuz?** Do you know a good place to go?; **Hiç iyi değil** He's not well
iyileşme [ijileʃme] *n* recovery
iyileşmek [ijileʃmek] *v* heal ▷ *vi* recover
iyilikle [ijilikle] *adv* kindly
iyimser [ijimser] *adj* optimistic ▷ *n* optimist
iyimserlik [ijimserlik] *n* optimism
iz [iz] *n* footprint, mark, trace; **iz sürmek** *v* retrace; **izini sürmek** *v* track down; **karbon ayak izi** *n* carbon footprint; **parmak izi** *n* fingerprint
izci [izdʒi] *n* scout
izin [izin] *n* permit, *(birine bir şey yapmak için verilen)* permission, *(işten alınan)* time off, *(işten izne ayrılmak)* leave; **çalışma izni** *n* work permit; **babalık izni** *n* paternity leave; **doğum izni** *n* maternity leave; **hastalık izni** *n* sick leave; **izin vermek** *n* allow, let, permit; **kayak izni** *n* ski pass; **Avlanma izin belgesi gerekiyor mu?** Do you need a fishing permit?
izlemek [izlemek] *vt* follow
izlenim [izlenim] *n* impression
izleyen [izlejen] *adj* following
izleyici [izlejidʒi] *n* onlooker, spectator, viewer
izmarit [izmarit] *n (sigara)* stub

J

jackpot [ʒdekpot] *n* jackpot
jaluzi [ʒaluzi] *n* blind, Venetian blind
Jamaika [ʒamaika] *adj* Jamaican
Jamaikalı [ʒamaikalə] *n* Jamaican
jambon [ʒambon] *n* ham
jant [ʒant] *n* **jant kapağı** *n* hubcap; **jant teli** *n* spoke
Japon [ʒapon] *adj* Japanese ▷ *n (kişi)* Japanese *(person)*; **Japon balığı** *n* goldfish
Japonca [ʒapondʒa] *n (dil)* Japanese *(language)*
Japonya [ʒaponja] *n* Japan
jartiyer [ʒartijer] *npl* suspenders
jel [ʒel] *n* **duş jeli** *n* shower gel
jeneratör [ʒeneratør] *n* generator
jeoloji [ʒeoloʒi] *n* geology
jest [ʒest] *n* gesture
jet [ʒet] *n* jet; **jumbo jet** *n* jumbo jet
jet-ski [ʒetski] *n* **Jet-ski nereden**

kiralayabilirim? Where can I hire a jet-ski?
jeton [ʒeton] *n* **jetonlu makine** *n* slot machine
jimnastik [ʒimnastik] *npl* gymnastics; **jimnastik salonu** *n* gym
jimnastikçi [ʒimnastiktʃi] *n* gymnast
jinekolog [ʒinekolog] *n* gynaecologist
jogging [ʒogging] *n* jogging ▷ *v* **jogging yapmak** *v* jog; **Nerede jogging yapabilirim?** Where can I go jogging?
jokey [ʒokej] *n* jockey
joystick [ʒojstik] *n* joystick
jöle [ʒøle] *n (saç)* gel, *(tatlı)* jelly; **saç jölesi** *n* hair gel
judo [ʒudo] *n* judo
jumbo [ʒumbo] *adj* **jumbo jet** *n* jumbo jet
jüpon [ʒypon] *n* underskirt
jüri [ʒyri] *n* jury; **jüri kararı** *n* verdict

K

kaba [kaba] *adj (aceleyle yapılmış)* rough, *(davranış)* rude, *(iş vb)* crude, *(insan)* vulgar, *(kumaş, sakal vb)* coarse; **kaba şaka** *n* prank
kabaca [kabadʒa] *adv* grossly, roughly
kabak [kabak] *n* courgette, zucchini
kabakulak [kabakulak] *n* mumps
kaban [kaban] *n* coat
kabara [kabara] *n* stud
kabarcık [kabardʒək] *n* bubble; **sulu kabarcık** *n* blister
kabartmak [kabartmak] *v* raise; **kabartma tozu** *n* baking powder
kabız [kabəz] *adj* constipated; **Kabızlık çekiyorum** I'm constipated
kabile [kabile] *n* tribe
kabin [kabin] *n* cabin; **kabin mürettebatı** *n* cabin crew; **Beş**

numaralı kabin nerede? Where is cabin number five?; **Standart bir kabin bileti** a standard class cabin

kabine [kabine] *n* cabinet

kablo [kaplo] *n* cable, flex; **kablolu yayın** *n* cable television; **takviye kablosu** *npl* jump leads; **uzatma kablosu** *n* extension cable

kablosuz [kaplosuz] *adj* **Odada kablosuz Internet bağlantısı var mı?** Does the room have wireless Internet access?

kabuk [kabuk] *n* shell; **kabuklu deniz ürünü** *n* shellfish; **kabuksuz sümüklüböcek** *n* slug; **limon kabuğu** *n* zest *(lemon-peel)*; **meyva kabuğu** *n* peel

kabul [kabul] *n* admission; **kabul edilebilir** *adj* acceptable; **kabul edilemez** *adj* unacceptable; **kabul etmek** *v* accept, *(itiraf)* admit *(confess)*

kabullenmek [kabullenmek] *n* **yenilgiyi kabullenmek** *v* give in

kaburga [kaburga] *n* rib

kabza [kabza] *n* hold, handle; **kısa kabzalı tabanca** *n* pistol

kaç [katʃ] *num* how many?, how much?;**... a kaç durak var?** How many stops is it to...?; **Boyunuz kaç?** How tall are you?; **Kaç yaşındasınız?** How old are you?; **Kaça olur?** How much will it be?; **Kaçıncı katta?** What floor is it on?; **Kaçta kapatıyorsunuz?** What time do you close?; **Sabah kaçta kalkıyorsunuz?** What time do you get up?; **Tren... a kaçta varıyor?** What time does the train arrive in...?; **Tren kaçta kalkacak?** What time does the train leave?

kaçak [katʃak] *n* **kaçak avlanmış** *adj* poached *(caught illegally)*

kaçakçı [katʃaktʃə] *n* smuggler; **kaçakçılık yapmak** *v* smuggle

kaçakçılık [katʃaktʃələk] *n* smuggling

kaçık [katʃək] *adj* mad *(insane)* ▷ *n* lunatic, nutter *(inf, pej)*; **keyfi kaçık** *adj* upset

kaçınılmaz [katʃənəlmaz] *adj* inevitable, unavoidable; **kaçınılmaz bir şekilde** *adv* necessarily

kaçırmak [katʃərmak] *v (adam)* kidnap, *(birini)* abduct ▷ *vt (treni, otobüsü)* miss; **gözden kaçırmak** *v* overlook; **keyfini kaçırmak** *v* upset

kaçış [katʃəʃ] *n* escape

kaçmak [katʃmak] *v* avoid, flee, *(uzaklara)* run away ▷ *vi* escape; **kenara kaçmak** *v* dodge; **okuldan kaçmak** *v* play truant

kadar [kadar] *conj (zaman, olay vb)* until ▷ *prep* as, *(yer)* until;**...'e kadar** *(zaman) prep* till;**...e kadar** *(yer) prep* till; **her ne kadar** *conj* though

kadeh [kadeh] *n* glass, cup; **kadeh kaldırmak** *n* toast *(tribute)*; **şarap kadehi** *n* wineglass

kader [kader] *n* destiny, fate

kadın [kadən] *adj* female ▷ *n* woman, female; **İngiliz kadın** *n* Englishwoman; **Fransız kadın** *n* Frenchwoman; **hizmetçi kadın** *n* maid; **iş kadını** *n* businesswoman;

kadın barmen *n* barmaid; **kadın garson** *n* waitress; **kadın kahraman** *n* heroine; **kadın oyuncu** *n* actress; **kadın polis** *n* policewoman; **kadın postacı** *n* postwoman; **kadın sporcu** *n* sportswoman; **kadınlar tuvaleti** *n* ladies'
kadınsı [kadənsə] *adj* feminine
kadife [kadife] *n* velvet; **fitilli kadife** *n* corduroy; **kadife çiçeği** *n* marigold
kadro [kadro] *n* **oyuncu kadrosu** *n* cast
kafa [kafa] *n* head; **dazlak kafa** *n* skinhead; **kafası karışık** *adj* confused; **kafası karışmış** *adj* puzzled; **kafasını takmış** *adj* preoccupied
kafatası [kafatasə] *n* skull
kafein [kafein] *n* caffeine
kafeinsiz [kafeinsiz] *adj* decaffeinated; **kafeinsiz kahve** *n* decaffeinated coffee
kafes [kafes] *n* cage
kafeterya [kafeterja] *n* cafeteria
Kafkas [kafkas] *n* Caucasus
kağıt [ka:ət] *n* paper; **aydınger kağıdı** *n* tracing paper; **duvar kağıdı** *n* wallpaper; **kağıt ağırlığı** *n* paperweight; **kağıt mendil** *n* tissue *(anatomy)*, tissue *(paper)*; **kağıt parçası** *n* slip *(paper)*; **kağıt peçete** *n* serviette; **karalama kağıdı** *n* scrap paper; **not kağıdı** *n* notepaper; **paket kağıdı** *n* wrapping paper; **tuvalet kağıdı** *n* toilet paper, toilet roll; **yazı kağıdı** *n* writing paper; **Tuvalet kağıdı yok** There is no toilet paper
kahkaha [kahkaha] *n* laughter ▷ *v* **kahkahayla gülmek** *v* laugh
kahkül [kahkyl] *n* fringe
kahraman [kahraman] *n* hero; **kadın kahraman** *n* heroine
kahvaltı [kahvaltə] *n* breakfast; **kahvaltı ve akşam yemeği dahil** *n* half board; **yatak ve kahvaltı** *n* bed and breakfast, B&B; **kahvaltı dahil** with breakfast; **kahvaltı hariç** without breakfast; **Kahvaltı dahil mi?** Is breakfast included?; **Kahvaltı kaçta?** What time is breakfast?; **Kahvaltı nerede veriliyor?** Where is breakfast served?; **Kahvaltıda ne yemek istersiniz?** What would you like for breakfast?; **Odamda kahvaltı edebilir miyim?** Can I have breakfast in my room?
kahve [kahve] *n* coffee; **kafeinsiz kahve** *n* decaffeinated coffee; **kahve çekirdeği** *n* coffee bean; **sütsüz kahve** *n* black coffee; **Bir fincan kahve daha alabilir miyiz?** Could we have another cup of coffee, please?; **Bir kahve lütfen** A coffee, please; **gerçek kahveniz var mı?** Have you got real coffee?; **Kahve lekesi** This stain is coffee; **Salonda kahve içebilir miyiz?** Could we have coffee in the lounge?; **Sütlü kahve lütfen** A white coffee, please; **Taze kahveniz var mı?** Have you got fresh coffee?
kahverengi [kahverengi] *adj* brown
kakao [kakao] *n* cocoa
kaktüs [kaktys] *n* cactus

kalabalık [kalabalək] *adj* crowded ▹ *n* crowd, host *(multitude)*
kalamar [kalamar] *n* squid
kalan [kalan] *adj* remaining; **hayatta kalan** *n* survivor
kalay [kalaj] *n* tin; **kalay yaldızı** *n* tinfoil
kalça [kaltʃa] *n* hip ▹ *npl* buttocks
kaldırım [kaldərəm] *n* pavement; **kaldırım taşı** *n* kerb
kaldırmak [kaldərmak] *v* hold up, remove, *(yukarıya)* lift; **ağırlık kaldırma** *n* weightlifting; **hasat kaldırmak** *v* harvest; **kadeh kaldırmak** *n* toast *(tribute)*; **yürürlükten kaldırma** *n* abolition
kale [kale] *n (şato vb)* castle; **kumdan kale** *n* sandcastle; **Kale halka açık mı?** Is the castle open to the public?; **Kaleyi görebilir miyiz?** Can we visit the castle?
kaleci [kaledʒi] *n* goalkeeper
kalem [kalem] *n* pen; **kalem açacağı** *n* pencil sharpener; **kalem arkadaşı** *n* penfriend; **keçe kalem** *n* felt-tip pen; **kurşun kalem** *n* pencil; **tükenmez kalem** *n* Biro®; **Tükenmez kalem** *n* ballpoint pen; **Kaleminiz var mı?** Do you have a pen I could borrow?
kalemlik [kalemlik] *n* pencil case
kalıcı [kalədʒə] *adj* permanent; **kalıcı bir şekilde** *adv* permanently
kalın [kalən] *adj* thick; **pamuklu kalın tişört** *n* sweatshirt
kalınlık [kalənlək] *n* thickness
kalıntı [kaləntə] *npl* remains
kalıp [kaləp] *n (dikiş)* pattern, *(pasta, jöle, briket vb)* mould *(shape)*
kalış [kaləʃ] *n* stay
kalıtsal [kalətsal] *adj* hereditary
kalite [kalite] *n* quality; **ikinci kalite** *adj* second-rate
kalkan [kalkan] *n* shield
kalkış [kalkəʃ] *n* departure, *(uçak)* takeoff
kalkışmak [kalkəʃmak] *v* attempt
kalkmak [kalkmak] *v* get up; **ayağa kalkmak** *v* stand up
kalma [kalma] *adj* remaining; **akşamdan kalma** *n* hangover
kalmak [kalmak] *v* remain, stay; **berabere kalmak** *vt* draw *(equal with)*; **geri kalmak** *v* back out; **geride kalmak** *v* lag behind; **hayatta kalmak** *v* survive; **kalacak yer** *n* accommodation; **kısılıp kalmak** *adj* stranded; **Otelde kalıyorum** I'm staying at a hotel
kalori [kalori] *n* calorie
kalorifer [kalorifer] *n* heating; **Kalorifer nasıl çalışıyor?** How does the heating work?; **Odada kalorifer var mı?** Does the room have heating?
kalp [kalp] *n* heart; **iyi kalpli** *adj* kind; **kalbi kırık** *adj* heartbroken; **kalp krizi** *n* heart attack; **kalp pili** *n* pacemaker; **Kalp hastasıyım** I have a heart condition
kalsiyum [kalsijum] *n* calcium
Kamboçya [kambotʃja] *adj* Cambodian ▹ *n* Cambodia
Kamboçyalı [kambotʃjalə] *n (kişi)* Cambodian *(person)*
kamera [kamera] *n* camera; **internet kamerası** *n* webcam; **video kamera** *n* camcorder;

video kamerası *n* video camera; **Bu dijital kameraya hafıza kartı almak istiyorum lütfen** A memory card for this digital camera, please; **Bu video kamera için teyp alabilir miyim?** Can I have a tape for this video camera, please?; **Kameram tutukluk yapıyor** My camera is sticking
kameraman [kameraman] **(kameramanlar)** *n* cameraman
Kamerun [kamerun] *n* Cameroon
kamış [kaməʃ] *n* reed
kamp [kamp] *n* camp ▷ *v* **kamp yapmak** *v* camp; **kamp yeri** *n* campsite; **karavan kampı** *n* caravan site
kampanya [kampanja] *n* campaign
kampçı [kamptʃə] *n* camper
kamping [kamping] *n* camping
kampüs [kampys] *n* campus
kamulaştırmak [kamulaʃtərmak] *v* nationalize
kamuoyu [kamuoju] *n* public opinion; **kamuoyu yoklaması** *n* opinion poll, poll; **kamuoyuna açıklamak** *v* issue
kamyon [kamjon] *n* truck; **kamyon şoförü** *n* lorry driver, truck driver; **taşınma kamyonu** *n* removal van
kan [kan] *n* blood; **kan aktarımı** *n* transfusion; **kan dolaşımı** *n* circulation; **kan grubu** *n* blood group; **kan kırmızısı** *adj* scarlet; **kan nakli** *n* blood transfusion; **kan testi** *n* blood test; **kan zehirlenmesi** *n* blood poisoning; **Kan grubum O pozitif** My blood group is O positive; **Kan lekesi** This stain is blood
Kanada [kanada] *adj* Canadian ▷ *n* Canada
Kanadalı [kanadalə] *n* Canadian
kanal [kanal] *n* canal, channel
kanama [kanama] *n* bleeding; **burun kanaması** *n* nosebleed
kanamak [kanamak] *vi* bleed
kanarya [kanarja] *n* canary
Kanarya [kanarja] *n* **Kanarya Adaları** *n* Canaries
kanat [kanat] *n* wing; **kanat çırpmak** *v* flap; **sağ kanat** *adj* right-wing
kanca [kandʒa] *n* hook, peg
kancık [kandʒək] *n* bitch
kandırmak [kandərmak] *v* fool, trick
kanepe [kanepe] *n* couch, *(koltuk)* sofa
kanguru [kanguru] *n* kangaroo
kanıt [kanət] *n* evidence, proof *(evidence)*
kanıtlamak [kanətlamak] *v* prove; **bulgularla kanıtlamak** *v* demonstrate
kaniş [kaniʃ] *n* poodle
kanlı [kanlə] *adj* bloody
kano [kano] *n* canoe; **kano sporu** *n* canoeing; **Kano sporu nerede yapabiliriz?** Where can we go canoeing?
kanser [kanser] *n (hastalık)* cancer *(illness)*
kansız [kansəz] *adj* anaemic
kantin [kantin] *n* canteen
kap [kap] *n* container; **yumurta kabı** *n* eggcup
kapa [kapa] *v* **Pencereyi**

kapatabilir miyim? May I close the window?
kapak [kapak] *n* lid; **göz kapağı** *n* eyelid; **jant kapağı** *n* hubcap; **motor kapağı** *n* bonnet *(car)*
kapalı [kapalə] *adj* closed ▷ *adv* off; **üstü kapalı yük aracı** *n* van; **kapalı alan** *adj* indoor; **kapalı yer korkusu olan** *adj* claustrophobic; **Kapalı Devre Televizyon Sistemi** *n* CCTV
kapamak [kapamak] *v* go off; **elektriği kapamak** *v* switch off
kapanık [kapanək] *adj* **içine kapanık** *adj* self-conscious
kapanış [kapanəʃ] *n* closure; **kapanış saati** *n* closing time
kaparo [kaparo] *n* deposit; **Kaparo ne kadar?** How much is the deposit?; **Kaparomı geri alabilir miyim?** Can I have my deposit back, please?
kapasite [kapasite] *n* capacity
kapatmak [kapatmak] *v* close, shut down, turn off ▷ *vt* shut, *(fermuar)* zip (up); **çarparak kapatmak** *v* slam; **oturum kapatmak** *v* log off, log out; **telefonu kapatmak** *v* hang up
kapı [kapə] *n* door, gate; **kapı eşiği** *n* doorstep; **kapı kolu** *n* door handle; **kapı telefonu** *n* entry phone; **kapı zili** *n* doorbell ▷ *v* **kapıyı çalmak** *v* knock *(on the door etc.)*;**... numaralı kapıya gidiniz** Please go to gate...; **Bu kapının anahtarı hangisi?** Which is the key for this door?; **Hangisi arka kapının anahtarı?** Which is the key for the back door?; **Hangisi ön kapının anahtarı?** Which is the key for the front door?; **Kapı açılmıyor** The door won't open; **Kapı kapanmıyor** The door won't close; **Kapı kilitlenmiyor** The door won't lock; **Kapının kolu çıktı** The door handle has come off; **Kapınızı kilitleyin** Keep the door locked
kapıcı [kapədʒə] **(kapıcılar)** *n* doorman
kapılmak [kapəlmak] *v* **cazibesine kapılmak** *v* fall for; **paniğe kapılmak** *v* panic
kapitalizm [kapitalizm] *n* capitalism
kapkaççı [kapkatʃtʃə] *n* mugger
kapkaççılık [kapkatʃtʃələk] *n* mugging
kaplama [kaplama] *n* coating; **altın kaplama** *n* gold-plated
kaplan [kaplan] *n* tiger
kaplumbağa [kaplumba:a] *n* tortoise; **su kaplumbağası** *n* turtle
kapmak [kapmak] *v* snatch
kapsamlı [kapsamlə] *adj* comprehensive, inclusive ▷ *adv* overall
kapsül [kapsyl] *n* capsule
kaptan [kaptan] *n* captain
kapüşon [kapyʃon] *n* hood
kar [kar] *n* snow; **kar fırtınası** *n* blizzard, snowstorm; **kar tanesi** *n* snowflake; **kar temizleme aracı** *n* snowplough; **kar topu** *n* snowball ▷ *v* **kar yağmak** *v* snow; **kardan adam** *n* snowman; **sulu kar** *n* sleet;**... yolunda kar var mı?** Is the road to... snowed up?;

Kar çok şiddetli The snow is very heavy; **Kar durumu nasıl?** What are the snow conditions?; **Kar nasıl?** What is the snow like?; **Kar yağacak mı dersiniz?** Do you think it will snow?; **Kar yağıyor** It's snowing; **Kar zinciri almam gerekiyor mu?** Do I need snow chains?
kara [kara] *n (coğrafya)* land; **kara kurbağa** *n* toad
karaağaç [karaa:atʃ] *n* elm
karabasan [karabasan] *n* nightmare
karaciğer [karadʒjier] *n* liver; **karaciğer iltihabı** *n* hepatitis
kara hindiba [karahindiba] *n* dandelion
karakol [karakol] *n* police station; **Polis karakolu nerede?** Where is the police station?; **Polis karakolunu arıyorum** I need to find a police station
karakter [karakter] *n* character
karakteristik [karakteristik] *n* characteristic
karalama [karalama] *n* sketch; **karalama defteri** *n* scrapbook; **karalama kağıdı** *n* scrap paper
karalamak [karalamak] *v* scribble; **karalama yapmak** *v* sketch
karamela [karamela] *n* toffee
karamelâ [karamela:] *n* caramel
karanfil [karanfil] *n (çiçek)* carnation, *(baharat)* clove
karanlık [karanlək] *adj* dark ▷ *n* dark, darkness; **Karanlık** It's dark
karantina [karantina] *n* quarantine
karaoke [karaoke] *n* karaoke
karar [karar] *n* decision; **jüri kararı** *n* verdict; **karar vermek** *v* decide; **kararı bozmak** *v* overrule
kararlı [kararlə] *adj* determined
kararlılık [kararlələk] *n* resolution
kararsız [kararsəz] *adj* indecisive, undecided
karartma [karartma] *n* blackout, curfew
karatahta [karatahta] *n* blackboard
karatavuk [karatavuk] *n* blackbird
karate [karate] *n* karate
karavan [karavan] *n* camper, caravan; **karavan kampı** *n* caravan site; **Karavanımızı buraya park edebilir miyiz?** Can we park our caravan here?; **Karavanımızla kamp edebileceğimiz bir yer arıyoruz** We'd like a site for a caravan
Karayip [karajip] *adj* Caribbean
karayolu [karajolu] *n* road; **Bu bölgenin karayolları haritası var mı?** Do you have a road map of this area?
karbon [karbon] *n* carbon; **karbon ayak izi** *n* carbon footprint
karbonat [karbonat] *n* bicarbonate of soda
karbonhidrat [karbonhidrat] *n* carbohydrate
karbüratör [karbyratør] *n* carburettor
kardeş [kardeʃ] *n* sibling; **erkek kardeş** *n* brother; **üvey erkek kardeş** *n* stepbrother
kardeşler [kardeʃler] *npl* siblings

kare [kare] *adj* square ▷ *n* square
kareli [kareli] *adj* checked
karga [karga] *n* crow
kargaşa [kargaʃa] *n* chaos, muddle
kargo [kargo] *n* cargo
karı [karə] **(karılar)** *n (eş)* wife; **eski karı** *n* ex-wife
karın [karən] *n* abdomen, tummy; **karın boşluğu ile ilgili** *adj* coeliac
karınca [karəndʒa] *n* ant
karışık [karəʃək] *adj* mixed ▷ *n (şeker/çiçek)* mix; **kafası karışık** *adj* confused; **karışık salata** *n* mixed salad
karışıklık [karəʃəklək] *m* confusion ▷ *n* mix-up
karışım [karəʃəm] *n* mixture
karıştırmak [karəʃtərmak] *v (fikir)* confuse, *(salata, baharat vb)* mix up ▷ *vt (çorba vb)* stir, *(nesne)* mix
karides [karides] *n* prawn; **büyük karides** *npl* scampi; **ufak karides** *n* shrimp
karikatür [karikatyr] *n* cartoon
kariyer [karijer] *n* career
karmakarışık [karmakarəʃək] *adj* chaotic
karnabahar [karnabahar] *n* cauliflower
karnaval [karnaval] *n* carnival
karne [karne] *n* report card
karpuz [karpuz] *n* watermelon
karşı [karʃə] *adj* opposed ▷ *prep* against, versus; **karşı çıkan** *adj* opposing; **karşı çıkmak** *v* oppose; **karşıdan karşıya geçmek** *vt* cross
karşılama [karʃəlama] *n* welcome
karşılamak [karʃəlamak] *v* welcome; **zararını karşılamak** *v* reimburse
karşılık [karʃələk] *n* **karşılıklı sefer yapan araç** *n* shuttle ▷ *v* **karşılıklı yapmak** *v* exchange
karşılıklı [karʃələklə] *adj* alternate, mutual ▷ *adv* opposite
karşın [karʃən] *prep* despite
karşısında [karʃəsənda] *prep* opposite
karşıt [karʃət] *adj* opposite ▷ *n* opponent
karşıtlık [karʃətlək] *n* contrast
karşıya [karʃəja] *prep* across
kart [kart] *n* card; **abonman kartı** *n* season ticket; **üyelik kartı** *n* membership card; **banka kartı** *n* debit card; **biniş kartı** *n* boarding card, boarding pass; **hafıza kartı** *n* memory card; **kartlı telefon** *n* cardphone; **kimlik kartı** *n* badge, identity card, ID card; **kredi kartı** *n* credit card; **kredi kartı şifresi** *npl* PIN; **Noel kartı** *n* Christmas card; **oyun kartı** *n* playing card; **tebrik kartı** *n* greetings card; **telefon kartı** *n* phonecard, top-up card; **Banka kartı alıyor musunuz?/Banka kartı kabul ediyor musunuz?** Do you take debit cards?; **Biniş kartım burada** Here is my boarding card; **Bu kartı bu makinede kullanabilir miyim?** Can I use my card with this cash machine?; **Bu kartları nereden postalayabilirim?** Where can I post these cards?; **Buyurun kartım** Here is my card; **Kartım çalındı** My card has been stolen; **Kartımı iptal ettirmek**

istiyorum I need to cancel my card; **Kartınız var mı?** Do you have a business card?; **Kartınızı alabilir miyim?** Can I have your card?; **Kredi kartı kabul ediyor musunuz?** Do you take credit cards?; **Kredi kartıma nakit ödeme alabilir miyim?** Can I get a cash advance with my credit card?; **Kredi kartıyla ödeme yapabilir miyim?** Can I pay by credit card?; **Makine kartımı yuttu** The cash machine swallowed my card; **Nakit almak için kartımı kullanabilir miyim?** Can I use my card to get cash?; **Nereden otobüs kartı alabilirim?** Where can I buy a bus card?; **Telefon kartı nereden alabilirim** Where can I buy a top-up card?; **Telefon kartı satıyor musunuz?** Do you sell phone cards?; **Uluslararası telefon kartı satıyor musunuz?** Do you sell international phone cards?; **Yirmibeş euroluk telefon kartı rica ediyorum** I'd like a twenty-five euro phone card

kartal [kartal] *n* eagle

karton [karton] *n* carbboard; **karton kutu** *n* carton

kartpostal [kartpostal] *n* postcard; **Bu dört kartpostal için pul alacaktım... a gidecek** Can I have stamps for four postcards to...; **Kartpostal bakıyordum** I'm looking for postcards; **Kartpostal satıyor musunuz?** Do you have any postcards?; **Nereden kartpostal alabilirim?** Where can I buy some postcards?

karyola [karjola] *n* bed; **bebek karyolası** *n* cot; **portatif karyola** *n* camp bed

kas [kas] *adj* muscular ▷ *n* muscle

kasa [kasa] *n* safe; **yazar kasa** *n* till; **Bunu kasaya koyun lütfen** Put that in the safe, please; **Kasada eşyalarım vardı** I have some things in the safe

kasap [kasap] *n* butcher, butcher's

kase [kase] *n* bowl

kaset [kaset] *n* cassette

Kasım [kasəm] *n (ay)* November

kasımpatı [kasəmpatə] *n* chrysanthemum

kasırga [kasərga] *n* hurricane, tornado

kasıt [kasət] *n* purpose, intention; **kasıtlı olarak** *adv* deliberately; **kasıtsız olarak** *adv* inadvertently

kasıtlı [kasətlə] *adj* deliberate, intentional

kasıtsız [kasətsəz] *adj* unintentional

kasiyer [kasijer] *n* cashier

kask [kask] *n (motosiklet)* helmet; **Kask alabilir miyim?** Can I have a helmet?

kastetmek [kastetmek] *v* mean

kasvetli [kasvetli] *adj* gloomy

kaş [kaʃ] *n* eyebrow; **kaşlarını çatmak** *v* frown

kaşer [kaʃer] *adj* kosher

kaşık [kaʃək] *n* spoon; **çay kaşığı** *n* teaspoon; **çorba kaşığı** *n* tablespoon; **bir kaşık dolusu** *n* spoonful; **tatlı kaşığı** *n* dessert spoon; **Temiz bir kaşık alabilir miyim lütfen?** Could I have a

clean spoon, please?
kaşınmak [kaʃənmak] *v* itch
kaşıntılı [kaʃəntələ] *adj* itchy
kaşif [kaʃif] *n* explorer
kaşmir [kaʃmir] *n* cashmere
kat [kat] *n (giysi, kağıt vb)* fold ▹ *adj* **alt kat** *adj* downstairs ▹ *adv* **alt katta** *adv* downstairs; **üç katı** *adj* treble, triple; **üst katta** *adv* upstairs; **iki katına çıkmak** *vt* double; **zemin kat** *n* ground floor
katalitik [katalitik] *adj* **katalitik konvertör** *n* catalytic converter
katalog [katalog] *n* catalogue; **Katalog istiyorum** I'd like a catalogue
Katar [katar] *n* Qatar
katarakt [katarakt] *n* cataract *(eye)*
katedral [katedral] *n* cathedral; **Katedral ne zaman açık?** When is the cathedral open?
kategori [kategori] *n* category
katı [katə] *adj (durum)* stark, *(kumaş vb)* stiff, *(kural vb)* strict, *(maddenin hali)* solid; **katı bir şekilde** *adv* strictly
katılım [katələm] *n* attendance
katılmak [katəlmak] *v* attend, participate ▹ *vi* join; **partiye katılmak** *v* party; **Size katılabilir miyim?** Can I join you?
katır [katər] *n* mule
katil [katil] *n* killer, murderer
katkı [katkə] *n* contribution; **katkı maddesi** *n* additive, preservative; **katkıda bulunmak** *v* contribute
katlamak [katlamak] *vt* fold
katlanır [katlanər] *adj* folding
katletmek [katletmek] *v* murder
katliam [katliam] *n* massacre
katman [katman] *n* layer
Katolik [katolik] *adj* Catholic ▹ *n* Catholic; **Roma Katoliği/Roma Katolik** *n* Roman Catholic
kavak [kavak] *n* poplar
kaval [kaval] *n* **kaval kemiği** *n* shin
kavanoz [kavanoz] *n* jar; **reçel kavanozu** *n* jam jar
kavga [kavga] *n* quarrel, scrap *(dispute)*; **yaşam kavgası** *n* survival
kavramak [kavramak] *v* grab, grasp; **sımsıkı kavramak** *v* grip
kavrulmuş [kavrulmuʃ] *adj* roast
kavşak [kavʃak] *n* junction; **döner kavşak** *n* roundabout;**... kavşağı nerede?** Which junction is it for...?; **Araba... numaralı kavşağa yakın** The car is near junction number...; **Bir sonraki kavşaktan sağa dönün** Go right at the next junction; **Bir sonraki kavşaktan sola dönün** Go left at the next junction
kavun [kavun] *n* melon
kaya [kaja] *n* rock
kayak [kajak] *n* ski; **kayak alıştırma pisti** *n* nursery slope; **kayak izni** *n* ski pass ▹ *v* **kayak yapmak** *v* ski; **su kayağı** *n* water-skiing; **Burada kayak kiralayabilir miyiz?** Can we hire skis here?; **Burada kayak okulu var mı?** Is there a ski school?; **Cross-country kayağı yapmak mümkün mü?** Is it possible to go cross-country skiing?; **Haftalık kayak kartı rica ediyorum?** I'd

like a ski pass for a week; **Kayak dersleri veriyor musunuz?** Do you organise skiing lessons?; **Kayak güzergahlarının haritası var mı?** Do you have a map of the ski runs?; **Kayak gereçlerini nereden kiralayabilirim?** Where can I hire skiing equipment?; **Kayak kartı ne kadar?** How much is a ski pass?; **Kayak kartı nereden alabilirim?** Where can I buy a ski pass?; **Kayak kiralamak istiyorum** I want to hire skis; **Kayak sopası kiralamak istiyorum** I want to hire ski poles; **Kayak yapmak istiyorum** I'd like to go skiing; **Yokuş iniş kayağı kiralamak istiyorum** I want to hire downhill skis

kayakçı [kajaktʃə] *n* skier

kayalık [kajalək] *n* cliff

kaybetmek [kajbetmek] *vt* lose

kaybolmak [kajbolmak] *vi* lose; **gözden kaybolma** *n* disappearance; **gözden kaybolmak** *v* disappear

kaydetmek [kajdetmek] *v* record, tape; **birinin hesabına borç kaydetmek** *v* debit

kaydolmak [kajdolmak] *v* sign on

kaygan [kajgan] *adj* slippery

kayın [kajən] *n* **kayın ağacı** *n* beech (tree); **kayın birader** *n* brother-in-law

kayınpeder [kajənpeder] **(kayınpederler)** *n* father-in-law

kayınvalide [kajənvalide] **(kayınvalideler)** *n* mother-in-law

kayıp [kajəp] *adj* lost, missing ▷ *n* loss; **kayıp eşya bürosu** *n* lost-property office; **kaybolup bulunmuş** *n* lost-and-found; **Çocuğum kayıp** My child is missing; **Bagajım kaybolmuş** My luggage has been lost; **Kızım kayıp** My daughter is missing; **Kızım kayboldu** My daughter is lost; **Oğlum kayıp** My son is missing; **Oğlum kayboldu** My son is lost

kayısı [kajəsə] *n* apricot

kayış [kajəʃ] *n* strap; **saat kayışı** *n* watch strap; **soğutucu kayışı** *n* fan belt

kayıt [kajət] *n* record, recording, register, registration; **kayıt aleti** *n* recorder *(scribe)* ▷ *v* **kayıt yaptırmak** *v* register; **ses kayıt cihazı** *n* recorder *(music)*, tape recorder

kayıtlı [kajətlə] *adj* registered

kayma [kajma] *n* slide; **toprak kayması** *n* landslide

kaymak [kajmak] *v* skid, slide ▷ *vi* slip; **disk kayması** *n* slipped disc; **kayma sporu** *n* skiing; **kızak kayma** *n* tobogganing; **kızak kaymak** *n* sledging; **patenle kaymak** *n* rollerskating

kaynak [kajnak] *adj (çıkış noktası)* origin ▷ *n (destek)* resource; **doğal kaynaklar** *npl* natural resources; **parasal kaynak** *npl* funds

kaynamış [kajnaməʃ] *adj* boiled

kaynar [kajnar] *adj* boiling

kaynaştırmak [kajnaʃtərmak] *v* merge

kaynatmak [kajnatmak] *vt* boil; **yavaş yavaş kaynatmak** *v*

simmer
kaypak [kajpak] *adj* shifty
kaytarmak [kajtarmak] *v* skive
kaz [kaz] **(kazlar)** *n* goose
kaza [kaza] *n* accident; **araba kazası** *n* crash; **deniz kazası** *n* shipwreck; **deniz kazası geçirmiş** *adj* shipwrecked; **kaza & acil servis** *n* accident & emergency department; **kaza sigortası** *n* accident insurance; **kaza sonucu** *adj* accidental; **Bir kaza oldu!** There's been an accident!; **Bireysel kaza sigortası yaptırmak istiyorum** I'd like to arrange personal accident insurance; **Kaza geçirdim** I've been in an accident, I've had an accident; **Kaza geçirirsem ne yapmam gerekiyor?** What do I do if I have an accident?
kazak [kazak] *n* jersey, jumper, pullover, sweater; **polo yakalı kazak** *n* polo-necked sweater
Kazakistan [kazakistan] *n* Kazakhstan
kazan [kazan] *n* boiler
kazanan [kazanan] *adj* winning
kazanç [kazantʃ] *n* gain, profit
kazançlı [kazantʃlə] *adj* lucrative, profitable
kazandırmak [kazandərmak] *v* **açıklık kazandırmak** *v* clarify
kazanma [kazanma] *n* winner
kazanmak [kazanmak] *v* earn, win ▷ *vt* gain; **düşmanlığını kazanmak** *v* antagonize
kazara [kazara] *adv* accidentally, by chance, by accident
kazık [kazək] *n (pahalı)* rip-off; **çadır kazığı** *n* tent peg
kazıklamak [kazəklamak] *v* rip off
kazımak [kazəmak] *v* engrave
kazma [kazma] *n* pick
kazmak [kazmak] *vt* dig
kâfi [ka:fi] *adj* enough ▷ *pron* enough
KDV [kdv] *abbr* VAT; **KDV dahil mi?** Is VAT included?
kebap [kebap] *n* kebab; **kebap şişi** *n* skewer
keçe [ketʃe] *n* felt; **keçe kalem** *n* felt-tip pen
keçi [ketʃi] *n* goat
keder [keder] *n* grief
kedi [kedi] *n* cat; **kedi yavrusu** *n* kitten
kefalet [kefalet] *n* bail
kehanet [kehanet] *n* premonition
kehribar [kehribar] *n* amber
kek [kek] *n* cake; **şekerli kek süsü** *n* frosting
kekelemek [kekelemek] *v* stammer, stutter
kekik [kekik] *n* thyme
keklik [keklik] *n* partridge
kel [kel] *adj* bald
kelebek [kelebek] *n (hayvan)* butterfly
kelepçe [keleptʃe] *npl* handcuffs
keler [keler] *n* **su keleri** *m* newt
keman [keman] *n* violin
kemancı [kemandʒə] *n* violinist
kemer [kemer] *n* arch, belt; **emniyet kemeri** *n* safety belt, seatbelt; **kemer tokası** *n* buckle
kemik [kemik] *n* bone; **elmacık kemiği** *n* cheekbone; **kaval kemiği** *n* shin; **köprücük kemiği**

n collarbone; **kürek kemiği** *n* shoulder blade; **kemikli et** *n* joint *(meat)*; **leğen kemiği** *n* pelvis
kemirgen [kemirgen] *n* rodent
kenar [kenar] *n* **cam kenarı koltuğu** *n* window seat; **kenara çekmek** *v (araç)* pull out, *(araç)* pull up; **kenara kaçmak** *v* dodge; **yol kenarında geçici park yeri** *n* layby
kendi [kendi] *adj* own; **kendinden memnun** *adj* smug; **kendine güvenen** *adj* self-assured; **kendine gelmek** *v* regain; **kendini beğenmiş** *adj* arrogant, bigheaded
kendileri [kendileri] *pron* themselves
kendiliğinden [kendiləənden] *adj* spontaneous
kendim [kendim] *pron* myself
kendin [kendin] *pron* yourself, yourself *(intensifier)*, yourself *(polite)*
kendine [kendine] *adv* **kendine gelmek** *v* come round
kendiniz [kendiniz] *pron* yourselves *(intensifier)*, yourselves *(polite)*, yourselves *(reflexive)*
kendin-yap [kendinjap] *n* DIY
kendisi [kendisi] *pron* itself, *(erkek)* himself, *(kadın)* herself
kenevir [kenevir] *n* **Hint keneviri** *(yaprakları esrar olarak kullanılır)* *n* marijuana
kent [kent] *n* city, town; **kent merkezi** *adv* city centre; **kent merkezinde** *adv* downtown; **Kent merkezine lütfen** Please take me to the city centre; **Kent turunuz var mı?** Are there any sightseeing tours of the town?; **Kente otobüs var mı?** Is there a bus to the city?; **Kente taksi ne kadar?** How much is the taxi fare into town?; **Kenti gezecek kadar zamanımız var mı?** Do we have time to visit the town?; **Kentin haritasını nereden alabilirim?** Where can I buy a map of the city?; **Kentin yol haritasını istiyorum** I want a street map of the city
Kenya [kenja] *adj* Kenyan ▷ *n* Kenya
Kenyalı [kenjalə] *n* Kenyan
kep [kep] *n* cap; **beyzbol kepi** *n* baseball cap
kepaze [kepaze] *adj* miserable
kepçe [keptʃe] *n (mutfak)* ladle
kepek [kepek] *n* bran, *(saç)* dandruff; **kepekli undan yapılmış** *adj* wholemeal
kepenk [kepeŋ] *n* shutters
kereste [kereste] *n* timber
kerevit [kerevit] *n* crayfish
kereviz [kereviz] *n* **kereviz sapı** *n* celery
kertenkele [kerteŋele] *n* lizard
keseye uygun [kesejeujgun] *adj* affordable
kesici [kesidʒi] *n* **ağrı kesici** *n* painkiller
kesilmek [kesilmek] *v (bağlantı)* disconnect
kesin [kesin] *adj* certain, definite
kesinlik [kesinlik] *n* certainty
kesinlikle [kesinlikle] *adv* absolutely, certainly, definitely
kesinti [kesinti] *n* deduction, interruption; **elektrik kesintisi** *n*

power cut
.esintisiz [kesintisiz] *adj* continuous
.eski [keski] *n* chisel
.eskin [keskin] *adj* sharp
.esme [kesme] *n* cut
.esme imi [kesmeimi] *n* apostrophe
.esmek [kesmek] *v* cut, cut down, cut off; **fileto kesmek** *v* fillet; **kesip düzeltmek** *v* trim; **sözünü kesmek** *v* interrupt
.estane [kestane] *n* chestnut
:estirme [kestirme] *adj* direct ▷ *n* *(uyku)* nap; **kestirme yol** *n* shortcut; **saç kestirme** *n* haircut
estirmek [kestirmek] *v* doze
.eşfetmek [keʃfetmek] *v* discover
:eşif [keʃif] *n* **keşif gezisi** *n* expedition
:eşiş [keʃiʃ] *n* monk
.etçap [kettʃap] *n* ketchup
:eten [keten] *n* *(kumaş)* linen
:etlenme [ketlenme] *n* inhibition
eyif [kejif] *n* pleasure, joy; **keyfi kaçık** *adj* upset; **keyfini kaçırmak** *v* upset; **keyif verici** *adj* delightful
.ıbrıs [kəbrəs] *n* Cyprus
:ıbrıs [kəbrəs] *adj* Cypriot
:ıbrıslı [kəbrəslə] *n* *(kişi)* Cypriot *(person)*
ıç [kətʃ] *n* backside, bum
.ıkırdamak [kəkərdamak] *v* giggle
ılavuz [kəlavuz] *n* guide; **kullanım kılavuzu** *n* manual; **... kılavuzunuz var mı?** Do you have a guide book in...?; **İngilizce kılavuzunuz var mı?** Do you have a guide book in English?
kılıç [kələtʃ] *n* sword; **kılıç balığı** *n* swordfish
kılıf [kələf] *n* cover, case; **yastık kılıfı** *n* pillowcase
kılık [kələk] *n* outfit; **kılık değiştirmek** *v* disguise
kıllı [kəllə] *adj* hairy
kımıldamak [kəməldamak] *vi* move; **Kımıldayamıyor** She can't move
kımıldatmak [kəməldatmak] *vt* move
kına [kəna] *n* **kına gecesi** *n* hen night
kınamak [kənamak] *v* condemn
kırat [kərat] *n* carat
kırbaç [kərbatʃ] *n* whip
Kırgızistan [kərgəzistan] *n* Kyrgyzstan
kırık [kərək] *adj* broken, broken down ▷ *n* break, fracture; **düş kırıklığı** *n* disappointment; **hayal kırıklığına uğramış** *adj* disappointed; **hayal kırıklığına uğratmak** *v* disappoint, let down; **kalbi kırık** *adj* heartbroken
kırılgan [kərəlgan] *adj* fragile
kırılmaz [kərəlmaz] *adj* unbreakable
kırıntı [kərəntə] *n* fragment, piece; **ekmek kırıntısı** *n* breadcrumbs, crumb
kırışık [kərəʃək] *adj* creased ▷ *n* wrinkle
kırışıklık [kərəʃəklək] *n* crease
kırışmış [kərəʃməʃ] *adj* wrinkled
kırk [kərk] *number* forty
kırmak [kərmak] *v* break up ▷ *vt* break; **cesaretini kırmak** *v* discourage; **direksiyonu kırmak**

v swerve; **onur kırmak** *v* insult
kırmızı [kərməzə] *adj* red; **kan kırmızısı** *adj* scarlet; **kırmızı et** *n* red meat; **kırmızı Frenk üzümü** *n* redcurrant; **kırmızı şarap** *n* red wine; **kırmızı toz biber** *n* paprika; **kırmızı turp** *n* radish; **kırmızı yaban mersini** *n* cranberry; **İyi bir kırmızı şarap tavsiye edebilir misiniz?** Can you recommend a good red wine?; **Bir şişe kırmızı şarap** a bottle of red wine; **Bir sürahi kırmızı şarap** a carafe of red wine; **Kırmızı et yemiyorum** I don't eat red meat
kırpmak [kərpmak] *v* **göz kırpmak** *v* wink; **göz kırpmak** *v* blink
kırsal [kərsal] *adj* rural; **kırsal bölge** *n* countryside
kırtasiye [kərtasije] *n* stationery
kırtasiyeci [kərtasiedʒi] *n* stationer's
kısa [kəsa] *adj* brief, short; **en kısa zamanda** *adv* asap *(as soon as possible)*; **kısa öykü** *n* short story; **kısa kabzalı tabanca** *n* pistol; **kısa kürek** *n* paddle; **kısa kollu** *adj* short-sleeved; **kısa menzilli silah** *n* shotgun; **kısa mesafe hız koşusu** *n* sprint; **kısa mesafe koşucusu** *n* sprinter; **kısa not** *n* memo; **kısa ve öz** *adj* concise; **kısa zamanda** *adv* shortly, soon
kısaca [kəsadʒa] *adv* briefly
kısalmak [kəsalmak] *v* shrink
kısalmış [kəsalməʃ] *adj* shrunk
kısaltma [kəsaltma] *n* abbreviation, acronym
kısım [kəsəm] *n* part, section; **çekirdekli kısım** *(meyve) n* core; **Bu kısım doğru dürüst çalışmıyor** This part doesn't work properly
kıskanç [kəskantʃ] *adj* envious, jealous
kısmen [kəsmen] *adv* partly
kısmi [kəsmi] *adj* partial
kısrak [kəsrak] *n* mare
kış [kəʃ] *n* winter; **kış sporları** *npl* winter sports
kışkırtmak [kəʃkərtmak] *v* tempt
kıt [kət] *adj* scarce
kıta [kəta] *n* continent
kıtlık [kətlək] *n* famine
kıvılcım [kəvəldʒəm] *n* spark
kıvırcık [kəvərdʒək] *adj* curly; **Saçım doğuştan kıvırcık** My hair is naturally curly
kıvrılmak [kəvrəlmak] *v* bend
kıvrım [kəvrəm] *n* turning
kıyafet [kəjafet] *n* dress, clothes; **balıkadam kıyafeti** *n* wetsuit
kıyaslama [kəjaslama] *n* comparison
kıyaslamak [kəjaslamak] *v* compare
kıyaslanabilir [kəjaslanabilir] *adj* comparable
kıyı [kəjə] *n* coast, shore; **ırmak kıyısı** *n* bank *(ridge)*; **deniz kıyısı** *n* seaside, *(sahil)* seashore
kıyma [kəjma] *n* mince
kıymık [kəjmək] *n* splinter
kız [kəz] *n* girl; **deniz kızı** *n* mermaid; **kız arkadaş** *n* girlfriend; **kız öğrenci** *n* schoolgirl; **kız evlat** *n* daughter; **kız kurusu** *n* spinster; **kız torun** *n* granddaughter; **vaftiz kızı** *n*

goddaughter; **üvey kız evlat** *n* stepdaughter
ızak [kəzak] *n* sledge, toboggan; **kızak kayma** *n* tobogganing; **kızak kaymak** *n* sledging; **Kızak kaymak için nereye gitmemiz gerek?** Where can we go sledging?
ızamık [kəzamək] *npl* measles; **Yakınlarda kızamık geçirdim** I had measles recently
ızamıkçık [kəzaməktʃək] *n* German measles
ızarıklık [kəzarəklək] *n* rash
ızarmak [kəzarmak] *v* blush; **yüz kızarması** *n* flush; **yüzü kızarmak** *v* flush
ızarmış [kəzarməʃ] *adj* fried
ızartma [kəzartma] *v* deep-fry; **ekmek kızartma makinesi** *n* toaster; **kızartma tavası** *n* frying pan; **patates kızartması** *npl* chips
ızartmak [kəzartmak] *v* fry
ızdırmak [kəzdərmak] *vt* tease
ızgın [kəzgən] *adj* angry, inflamed
ızıl [kəzəl] *adj* red; **Kızıl Deniz** *n* Red Sea; **kızıl saçlı** *n* red-haired, redhead
ızılgerdan [kəzəlgerdan] *n* robin
ızılhaç [kəzəlhatʃ] *n* Red Cross
ızılımsı [kəzələmsə] *adj* **kızılımsı sarı saçlı** *adj* ginger
ızışmak [kəzəʃmak] *v* heat up
ızkardeş [kəzkardeʃ] *n* sister; **üvey kızkardeş** *n* stepsister
ızlık [kəzlək] *n* **kızlık soyadı** *n* maiden name
i [ki] *conj* that
ibar [kibar] *adj* gentle, polite
ibarca [kibardʒa] *adv* gently, politely
kibarlık [kibarlək] *n* politeness
kibirli [kibirli] *adj* stuck-up
kil [kil] *n* clay
kiler [kiler] *n* larder
kilise [kilise] *n* church; **kilise kulesi** *n* steeple; **kilise kulesinin sivri tepesi** *n* spire; **kilisenin dini bölgesi** *n* parish; **Kiliseyi gezebilir miyiz?** Can we visit the church?
kilit [kilit] *n* lock *(door)*; **asma kilit** *n* padlock; **kilidi açmak** *v* unlock; **kilitli dolap** *n* locker; **kilitli iğne** *n* safety pin; **Kilit alabilir miyim?** Can I have a lock?; **Kilit kırılmış** The lock is broken
kilitlemek [kilitlemek] *vt* lock
kilitlmek [kilitlmek] *v* lock out
kilo [kilo] *n* kilo; **aşırı kilolu** *adj* overweight
kilometre [kilometre] *n* kilometre
kilt [kilt] *n* kilt
kim [kim] *pron* who; **Kim arıyor?** Who's calling?; **Kim o?** Who is it?; **Kime şikayet edebilirim?** Who can I complain to?; **Kiminle görüşüyorum?** Who am I talking to?
kime [kime] *adj* whose ▷ *pron* whom
kimi [kimi] *pron* whom
kimin [kimin] *pron* whose
kimlik [kimlik] *n* identification, identity; **kimliği belirsiz** *adj* unidentified; **kimlik belirlemek** *v* identify; **kimlik hırsızlığı** *n* identity theft; **kimlik kartı** *n* badge, identity card, ID card
kimse [kimse] *pron* somebody,

someone; **hiç kimse** *pron* no one, nobody
kimsesiz [kimsesiz] *n* orphan
kimya [kimja] *n* chemistry
kimyasal [kimjasal] *n* chemical
kimyon [kimjon] *n* cumin
kin [kin] *n* grudge; **kin gütmek** *v* spite
kinci [kindʒi] *adj* spiteful
kincilik [kindʒilik] *n* spite
kir [kir] *n* dirt
kira [kira] *n* rent, rental; **kira sözleşmesi** *n* lease; **kiralık araba** *n* rental car; **DVD kiralayabilir miyim?** Do you rent DVDs?
kiracı [kiradʒə] *n* tenant
kiralama [kiralama] *n* hire
kiralamak [kiralamak] *v* hire, lease, rent; **araba kiralama** *n* car hire; **oto kiralama** *n* car rental; **Paten nereden kiralayabiliriz?** Where can we hire skates?
kiralık [kiralək] *n* **kiralık araba** *n* hire car, hired car; **kiralık oda** *n* bedsit
kiraz [kiraz] *n* cherry
kireç [kiretʃ] *n* lime *(compound)*; **kireç taşı** *n* limestone
kiriş [kiriʃ] *n (anatomi)* tendon
kirlenmiş [kirlenmiʃ] *adj* polluted
kirletmek [kirletmek] *v* pollute
kirli [kirli] *adj* dirty, foul, messy; **Çatal bıçak kirli** My cutlery is dirty; **Çarşaflarım kirli** My sheets are dirty
kirlilik [kirlilik] *n* pollution
kirpi [kirpi] *n* hedgehog
kirpik [kirpik] *n* eyelash
kist [kist] *n* cyst
kişi [kiʃi] *n* person; **çift kişilik yatak** *n* double bed; **iki kişilik oc** *n* double room; **kişinin evinin önündeki özel yol** *n* driveway; **tek kişilik oda** *n* single room; **Bi araç ve iki kişi ne kadar?** How much is it for a car with two people?; **Bu akşam için üç kişili bir masa ayırtmak istiyordum** I'd like to book a table for three people for tonight; **Bu akşam saat sekiz için dört kişilik bir masa ayırtmak istiyordum** I'd like to book a table for four peopl for tonight at eight o'clock; **Dört kişilik bir kamper ne kadar?** How much is it for a camper with four people?; **Dört kişilik bir masa lütfen** A table for four people, please; **Kişi başına ne kadar?** How much is it per person?; **Saat yedi buçuğa iki kişilik bir rezervasyon yaptırmak istiyorum** I'd like to make a reservation for half past seven for two people; **Yarın akşam için iki kişilik bir masa ayırtmak istiyordum** I'd like to book a table for two people for tomorrow night
kişilik [kiʃilik] *n* personality
kişisel [kiʃisel] *adj* personal; **kişisel asistan** *n* personal assistant, PA; **kişisel müzik çala** *n* personal stereo; **kişisel olarak** *adv* personally; **kişisel organizatör** *n* personal organiz **Bu benim kişisel kullanımım için** It is for my own personal use
kişniş [kiʃniʃ] *n* coriander
kitap [kitap] *n* book; **ders kitabı**

schoolbook, textbook; **ikinci baskı kitap** *n* paperback; **kitap ayracı** *n* bookmark; **kitap rafı** *n* bookshelf; **referans kitabı** *n* handbook; **yemek kitabı** *n* cookbook, cookery book
tapçı [kitaptʃə] *n* bookshop
tapçık [kitaptʃək] *n* booklet
taplık [kitaplək] *n* bookcase
vi [kivi] *n (kuş)* kiwi
arnet [klarnet] *n* clarinet
asik [klasik] *adj* classic, classical ▷ *n* classic
asör [klasør] *n* ring binder
avye [klavje] *n* keyboard
ima [klima] *n* air conditioner; **Klima çalışmıyor** The air conditioning doesn't work; **Klima var mı?** Does it have air conditioning?; **Odada klima var mı?** Does the room have air conditioning?
inik [klinik] *n* surgery *(doctor's)*
ips [klips] *n* clip
on [klon] *n* clone
onlamak [klonlamak] *v* clone
or [klor] *n* chlorine
üp [klyp] *n* club *(group)*
m/s [kilometrefanje] *abbr* km/h
obay [kobaj] *n* guinea pig *(for experiment)*; **kobay faresi** *n* guinea pig *(rodent)*
oca [kodʒa] *n (eş)* husband; **eski koca** *n* ex-husband
ocaman [kodʒaman] *adj* huge
oç [kotʃ] *n* ram, *(spor)* coach *(trainer)*
oç [kotʃ] *n* **Koç burcu** *n* Aries
od [kod] *n* code; **alan kodu** *n* postcode; **telefon kodu** *n* dialling code; **İngiltere'nin kodu kaç?** What is the dialling code for the UK?
koğuş [kou:ʃ] *n* ward *(hospital room)*; **... hangi koğuşta?** Which ward is... in?
kokain [kokain] *n* cocaine
koklamak [koklamak] *vt* smell
kokmak [kokmak] *vi* smell; **kötü kokmak** *v* stink
kokpit [kokpit] *n* cockpit
kokteyl [koktejl] *n* cocktail; **Kokteyl yapıyor musunuz?** Do you sell cocktails?
koku [koku] *n* aroma, odour, scent, smell; **kokulu otlar** *n* herbs; **pis kokulu** *adj* smelly; **Garip bir koku var** There's a funny smell; **Gaz kokusu alıyorum** I can smell gas
kokuşmuş [kokuʃmuʃ] *adj* vile
kol [kol] *n* arm, handle, lever; **kapı kolu** *n* door handle; **kısa kollu** *adj* short-sleeved; **kol ağzı** *n* sleeve; **kol askısı** *(sağlık)* *n* sling; **kol düğmeleri** *npl* cufflinks; **kol saati** *n* watch; **vites kolu** *n* gear lever, gear stick, gearshift; **Kapının kolu çıktı** The door handle has come off; **Kolu çıktı** The handle has come off; **Kolumu oynatamıyorum** I can't move my arm; **Kolunu incitti** He has hurt his arm
Kola [kola] *n* Coke®
kolay [kolaj] *adj* easy; **kolay gıdıklanan** *adj* ticklish; **En kolay alanlar nereleri?** Which are the easiest runs?
kolaylıkla [kolajləkla] *adv* easily
kolaylıklar [kolajləklar] *npl*

facilities
kolçak [koltʃak] *n* bracelet
kolej [koleʒ] *n* **devlet koleji** *n* public school
koleksiyon [koleksijon] *n* collection
kolektif [kolektif] *adj* collective ▷ *n* collective
kolesterol [kolesterol] *n* cholesterol
kolleksiyoncu [kolleksijondʒu] *n* collector
Kolombiya [kolombija] *adj* Colombian ▷ *n* Colombia
Kolombiyalı [kolombijalə] *n* Colombian
kolsuz [kolsuz] *adj (giysi)* sleeveless
koltuk [koltuk] *n* armchair, easy chair, *(politika)* seat *(constituency)*; **cam kenarı koltuğu** *n* window seat; **koltuk değneği** *n* crutch; **koridor koltuğu** *n* aisle seat; **Çocuk koltuğu var mı?** Do you have a child's seat?; **Bu koltuk boş mu?** Is this seat free?; **Koltuğum koridor tarafında olsun** I'd like an aisle seat; **Koltuğum pencere kenarında olsun** I'd like a window seat; **Sigara içilen bölümde bir koltuk lütfen** I'd like a seat in the smoking area; **Sigara içilmeyen bölümde bir koltuk lütfen** I'd like a non-smoking seat
koltukaltı [koltukaltə] *n* armpit
kolye [kolje] *n* necklace
koma [koma] *n* coma
komedi [komedi] *n* comedy
komedyen [komedjen] *n* comedian
komik [komik] *adj* funny ▷ *n* comi
çok komik *adj* hilarious
komisyon [komisjon] *n* commission; **Komisyon alıyor musunuz?** Do you charge commission?; **Komisyon ne kadar?** What's the commission?
komisyoncu [komisjondʒu] *n* broker
komite [komite] *n* committee
komodin [komodin] *n* bedside table, chest of drawers
kompakt [kompakt] *adj* **kompak disk** *n* compact disc
kompartıman [kompartəman] compartment; **Sigara içilmeyen kompartmanda yer ayırtmak istiyorum** I want to book a seat i a non-smoking compartment
kompleks [kompleks] *n* complex
komplike [komplike] *adj* comple complicated
kompliman [kompliman] *n* compliment
komplo [komplo] *n* conspiracy ▷ plot *(secret plan)*
komşu [komʃu] *n* neighbour
komut [komut] *n* order, commar ▷ *v* **komut vermek** *v* order *(command)*
komünizm [komynizm] *n* communism
konak [konak] *n* mansion
konaklama [konaklama] *n* stopover
konaklamak [konaklamak] *v* **konaklama alanı** *n* service area
konçerto [kontʃerto] **(konçertolar)** *n* concerto

onferans [konferans] *n* conference; **Konferans merkezine lütfen** Please take me to the conference centre
onfeti [konfeti] *npl* confetti
onfor [konfor] *npl* comforts, conveniences; **konfor ve rahatlık** *npl* mod cons
ongo [kongo] *n* Congo
oni [koni] *n* cone
onser [konser] *n* concert; **İyi konserler var mı?** Are there any good concerts on?; **Konser biletlerini nereden alabilirim?** Where can I buy tickets for the concert?; **Konser salonunda bu gece ne var?** What's on tonight at the concert hall?
onserve [konserve] *n* **kutulanmış konserve** *adj* tinned
onsol [konsol] *n* **oyun konsolu** *n* games console
onsolos [konsolos] *n* consul
onsolosluk [konsolosluk] *n* consulate
ontakt [kontakt] *n* **kontakt lens** *npl* contact lenses
ontrabas [kontrabas] *n* double bass
ontrat [kontrat] *n* contract
ontrol [kontrol] *n* control; **doğum kontrol hapı** *n* contraceptive; **doğum kontrolü** *n* birth control, contraception; **kontrol edilemez** *adj* uncontrollable; **kontrol lambası** *n* pilot light; **pasaport kontrol** *n* passport control; **bilet kontrolörü** *n* ticket inspector; **hava trafik kontrolörü** *n* air-traffic controller
kontrplak [kontrplak] *n* plywood
kontuar [kontuar] *n* counter
konu [konu] *n* subject, theme; **konulu eğlence parkı** *n* theme park
konuk [konuk] *n* guest
konukevi [konukevi] *n* guesthouse
konukseverlik [konukseverlik] *n* hospitality
konuşan [konuʃan] *n* **anadilini konuşan** *n* native speaker
konuşkan [konuʃkan] *adj* talkative
konuşlanmış [konuʃlanməʃ] *adj* situated
konuşma [konuʃma] *n* conversation, speech, talk; **abuk sabuk konuşma** *n* rave
konuşmacı [konuʃmadʒə] *n* speaker
konuşmak [konuʃmak] *v* speak ▷ *vi* talk; **biriyle konuşmak** *v* talk to; **... ile konuşmak istiyorum lütfen** I'd like to speak to..., please; **... konuşabiliyorum** I speak...; **Müdürle konuşmak istiyorum lütfen** I'd like to speak to the manager, please
konut [konut] *n* house; **konut kredisi** *n* mortgage; **sosyal konut** *n* council house
konvensiyonel [konvensijonel] *adj (alışılmış)* conventional
konvertibl [konvertipl] *adj* convertible
konvertör [konvertør] *n* **katalitik konvertör** *n* catalytic converter
konvoy [konvoj] *n* convoy

kopmak [kopmak] *vt* snap; **ödü kopmak** *adj* petrified
kopya [kopja] *n (nüsha)* copy *(written text)*, *(taklit)* replica
kopyalamak [kopjalamak] *v* copy
Kore [kore] *adj* Korean ▷ *n* Korea; **Güney Kore** *n* South Korea; **Kuzey Kore** *n* North Korea
Korece [koredʒe] *n (dil)* Korean *(language)*
Koreli [koreli] *n (kişi)* Korean *(person)*
koridor [koridor] *n* aisle, corridor; **koridor koltuğu** *n* aisle seat; **Koltuğum koridor tarafında olsun** I'd like an aisle seat
korkak [korkak] *n* coward
korkakça [korkaktʃa] *adj* cowardly
korkmak [korkmak] *v* fear
korkmuş [korkmuʃ] *adj* afraid, frightened, scared
korku [korku] *n* fear, fright; **kapalı yer korkusu olan** *adj* claustrophobic ▷ *v* **korkarak titremek** *v* shudder; **korku filmi** *n* horror film; **yükseklik korkusu** *n* vertigo
korkuluk [korkuluk] *n* scarecrow
korkunç [korkuntʃ] *adj* appalling, disastrous, dreadful, horrendous, horrible, terrible
korkutmak [korkutmak] *v* frighten, scare; **gözünü korkutmak** *v* intimidate
korkutucu [korkutudʒu] *adj* scary
kornet [kornet] *n* cornet
korno [korno] *n* French horn
koro [koro] *n* choir
korsan [korsan] *n (deniz)* pirate, *(uçak/hava)* hijacker
kort [kort] *n* **tenis kortu** *n* tennis court; **Kort rezervasyonunu nerede yapabilirim?** Where can book a court?; **Tenis kortu kiralamak kaça?** How much is it to hire a tennis court?
koruluk [koruluk] *n* wood *(fores*
koruma [koruma] *n* conservatio protection; **özel koruma** *n* bodyguard; **koruma gözlüğü** *np* goggles
korumak [korumak] *v* defend, guard, protect; **koruma alanı** *n* reserve *(land)*; **koruma altına alma** *n* custody; **sahil koruma görevlisi** *n* coastguard
koruyucu [korujudʒu] *adj* **ekran koruyucusu** *n* screen-saver; **koruyucu güneş kremi** *n* sunblock
Kosova [kosova] *n* Kosovo
Kosta Rika [kostarika] *n* Costa Rica
kostüm [kostym] *n* costume; **ba kostümü** *n* fancy dress
koşer [koʃer] *adj, adv* **Koşer yemeğiniz var mı?** Do you have kosher dishes?
koşma [koʃma] *n* running
koşmak [koʃmak] *vt* run; **dörtna koşmak** *n* gallop; **hızla koşmak** dash, sprint
koşturmak [koʃturmak] *vi* run
koşu [koʃu] *n* run, running; **kısa mesafe hız koşusu** *n* sprint
koşucu [koʃudʒu] *n* runner; **kısa mesafe koşucusu** *n* sprinter
koşul [koʃul] *n* condition
koşullar [koʃullar] *npl* circumstances

oşullu [koʃullu] *adj* conditional
oşulsuz [koʃulsuz] *adj* unconditional
ota [kota] *n* quota
ova [kova] *n* bucket, pail
ova [kova] *n* **Kova burcu** *n* Aquarius
ovalamaca [kovalamadʒa] *n* pursuit
ovboy [kovboj] *n* cowboy; **kovboy filmi** *n* western
ovmak [kovmak] *v* expel
ovuşturma [kovuʃturma] *n* prosecution
oyak [kojak] *n* ravine
oymak [kojmak] *v* lay, put; **geri koymak** *v* put back; **yıldız koymak** *v* star; **yoluna koymak** *v* settle
oyulmak [kojulmak] *v* **yola koyulmak** *v* set off
oyun [kojun] *n* sheep, *(dişi)* ewe; **koyun eti** *n* mutton; **koyun postu** *n* sheepskin
ozalak [kozalak] *n* conifer
ozmetik [kozmetik] *n* **kozmetik cerrahi** *n* cosmetic surgery
öfte [køfte] *n* meatball
ök [køk] *n* root
öknar [køknar] *n* **köknar ağacı** *n* fir (tree)
öle [køle] *n* slave
ömür [kømyr] *n* coal; **kömür ocağı** *n* colliery; **odun kömürü** *n* charcoal
öpek [kjøpek] *n* dog; **İskoç çoban köpeği** *n* collie; **köpek balığı** *n* shark; **köpek kulübesi** *n* kennel; **rehber köpek** *n* guide dog; **yavru köpek** *n* puppy; **Rehber köpeğim var** I have a guide dog
köprü [køpry] *n* bridge; **asma köprü** *n* suspension bridge
köprücük [køprydʒyk] *n* **köprücük kemiği** *n* collarbone
köpük [køpyk] *n* foam; **köpük krema** *n* mousse, whipped cream; **köpüklü banyo** *n* bubble bath; **traş köpüğü** *n* shaving foam
köpüklü [køpykly] *adj* fizzy
kör [kør] *adj* blind, *(bıçak/makas)* blunt; **renk körü** *adj* colour-blind; **Körüm** I'm blind
körfez [kørfez] *n* bay
Körfez [kørfez] *n* **Körfez Ülkeleri** *npl* Gulf States
köri [køri] *n* curry; **köri baharatı** *n* curry powder
köstebek [køstebek] *n (casus)* mole *(infiltrator)*, *(hayvan)* mole *(mammal)*
köşe [køʃe] *n* corner; **çalışma köşesi** *n* work station, workstation; **köşeli parantezler** *npl* brackets; **Köşede** It's on the corner; **Köşeyi dönünce** It's round the corner
kötü [køty] *adj* bad, vicious; **daha kötü/daha kötüsü** *adv* worse; **en kötü** *adj* worst; **kötü bir şekilde** *adv* badly; **kötü kokmak** *v* stink; **kötü muamele etmek** *v* ill-treat; **kötü niyetli** *adj* malicious; **kötüye kullanmak** *v* abuse
kötücül [køtydʒyl] *adj* evil, malignant
kötülemek [køtylemek] *v* deteriorate
kötüleşmek [køtyleʃmek] *v*

worsen
kötülük [køtylyk] *n* vice
kötümser [køtymser] *adj* pessimistic ▷ *n* pessimist
köy [køj] *n* village
kraker [kraker] *n* cracker
kral [kral] *n* king, monarch
kraliçe [kralitʃe] *n* queen
kraliyet [kralijet] *adj* royal ▷ *n* monarchy
krallık [kralləkl] *n* kingdom; **Birleşik Krallık** *(İngiltere) n* United Kingdom
kramp [kramp] *n* spasm
kravat [kravat] *n* tie; **papyon kravat** *n* bow tie
kredi [kredi] *n* credit, loan; **konut kredisi** *n* mortgage; **kredi kartı** *n* credit card; **kredi kartı şifresi** *npl* PIN; **Kredi kartı kabul ediyor musunuz?** Do you take credit cards?; **Kredi kartıma nakit ödeme alabilir miyim?** Can I get a cash advance with my credit card?; **Kredi kartıyla ödeme yapabilir miyim?** Can I pay by credit card?
krek [krek] *n (kokain)* crack *(cocaine)*
krem [krem] *n* cream; **dudak kremi** *n* lip salve; **güneş kremi** *n* suncream; **güneş sonrası krem** *n* after sun lotion; **koruyucu güneş kremi** *n* sunblock; **saç kremi** *n* conditioner; **traş kremi** *n* shaving cream
krema [krema] *n* cream, custard; **köpük krema** *n* mousse, whipped cream; **kremalı pasta** *n* gateau
krematoryum [krematorjum] **(krematoryumlar)** *n* crematorium
krep [krep] *n (yiyecek)* pancake
kreş [kreʃ] *n* crêche, nursery schoo
kriket [kriket] *n* cricket *(game)*
kriko [kriko] *n* jack
kristal [kristal] *n* crystal
kriter [kriter] *n* criterion
kritik [kritik] *adj* critical
kriz [kriz] *n* crisis; **kalp krizi** *n* heart attack; **sinir krizi** *n* nervou breakdown
krom [krom] *n* **krom kaplı** *n* chrome
kronik [kronik] *adj* chronic
kronometre [kronometre] *n* stopwatch
krüsifi [krysifi] *n* crucifix
ksilofon [ksilofon] *n* xylophone
kuaför [kuaføɾ] *n* hairdresser, hairdresser's
kuartet [kuartet] *n* quartet
kucak [kudʒak] *n* lap
kucaklama [kudʒaklama] *n* cuddle, hug
kucaklamak [kudʒaklamak] *v* cuddle ▷ *vt* hug
kuduz [kuduz] *n* rabies
kuğu [ku:u] *n* swan
kukla [kukla] *n* puppet
kulak [kulak] *n* ear; **kulak ağrısı** *n* earache; **kulak çubuğu** *n* cotton bud; **kulak tıkacı** *npl* earplugs; **kulak zarı** *n* eardrum
kulaklık [kulakləkl] *npl* earphones headphones; **Kulaklık var mı?** Does it have headphones?
kule [kule] *n* tower; **kilise kulesi** *n* steeple; **kilise kulesinin sivri tepesi** *n* spire
kullanıcı [kullanədʒə] *n* user;

Internet kullanıcısı *n* Internet user; **kullanıcı dostu** *adj* user-friendly
ullanılmış [kullanəlməʃ] *adj* used
ullanım [kullanəm] *n* use; **son kullanım tarihi** *n* best-before date, expiry date; **tek kullanımlık** *adj* disposable
ullanmak [kullanmak] *v* apply, use; **içkili araba kullanma** *n* drink-driving; **kötüye kullanmak** *v* abuse; **yeniden kullanmak** *v* reuse
ulübe [kulybe] *n* cabin, cottage; **bahçe kulübesi** *n* shed; **köpek kulübesi** *n* kennel; **telefon kulübesi** *n* call box, phonebox
ulüp [kulyp] *n* club; **gece kulübü** *n* nightclub; **İyi bir kulüp biliyor musunuz?** Where is there a good club?
um [kum] *n* grit, sand; **kum havuzu** *n* sandpit; **kum tepesi** *n* sand dune; **kumdan kale** *n* sandcastle
umanda [kumanda] *n, v* **uazaktan kumanda** *n* remote control; **uzaktan kumandalı** *adj* radio-controlled; **Kumanda kilitlendi** The controls have jammed; **Kumandaların nasıl çalıştığını gösterir misiniz?** Can you show me how the controls work?
umar [kumar] *n* gambling ▹ *v* **kumar oynamak** *v* gamble
umarcı [kumardʒə] *n* gambler
umarhane [kumarhane] *n* casino
umaş [kumaʃ] *n* cloth, fabric
kumaşı [kumaʃə] *n* **blucin kumaşı** *n* denim
kumbara [kumbara] *n* piggybank
kumpir [kumpir] **(kumpirler)** *n* baked potato, jacket potato
kumral [kumral] *adj* auburn
kumsal [kumsal] *n* beach; **Buraya yakın sakin bir kumsal var mı?** Is there a quiet beach near here?
kumtaşı [kumtaʃə] *n* sandstone
kundaklama [kundaklama] *n* arson
kunduz [kunduz] *n* beaver
kupa [kupa] *n (kahve)* mug, *(spor)* trophy; **Dünya Kupası** *n* World Cup
kupkuru [kupkuru] *adj* bone dry
kupon [kupon] *n* voucher
kur [kur] *n (para)* currency; **döviz kuru** *n* exchange rate, rate of exchange
kura [kura] *n* draw *(lottery)*
kuraklık [kuraklək] *n* drought
kural [kural] *n* rule; **ahlak kuralları** *npl* morals; **trafik kuralları** *n* Highway Code
kuram [kuram] *n* theory
Kuran [kuran] *n* Koran
kurbağa [kurba:a] *n* frog; **kara kurbağa** *n* toad
kurbağalama [kurba:alama] *n (yüzme)* breaststroke
kurban [kurban] *n (kişi)* victim
kurdele [kurdele] *n* ribbon
kurgu [kurgu] *n* fiction; **bilim kurgu** *n* science fiction
kurmak [kurmak] *v* **iletişim kurmak** *v* communicate; **temas kurmak** *v* contact
kurnaz [kurnaz] *adj* cunning, sly

kurs [kurs] *n* course; **eğitim kursu** *n* training course
kursiyer [kursijer] *n* trainee
kurşun [kurʃun] *n (metal)* lead *(metal)*, *(silah)* bullet; **kurşun kalem** *n* pencil; **kurşunsuz benzin** *n* unleaded petrol
kurşunsuz [kurʃunsuz] *adj* lead-free ▹ *n* unleaded; **...lık kurşunsuz benzin lütfen** ... worth of premium unleaded, please
kurt [kurt] **(kurtlar)** *n* wolf; **kurt gibi aç** *adj* ravenous
kurtarma [kurtarma] *n* rescue
kurtarmak [kurtarmak] *v* rescue, save; **kurtarma aracı** *n* breakdown van
kurtçuk [kurttʃuk] *n* grub
kuru [kuru] *adj* dried, dry; **kız kurusu** *n* spinster; **kuru üzüm** *n* raisin, sultana; **kuru erik** *n* prune; **kuru temizleme** *n* dry-cleaning; **Bunu kuru temizleyiciye vermek istiyorum** I need this dry-cleaned
kurul [kurul] *n* board *(meeting)*
kurulamak [kurulamak] *v* dry; **kurulama bezi** *n* dishcloth; **kurulama havlusu** *n* dish towel
kurum [kurum] *n (enstitü)* institution; **iş bulma kurumu** *n* job centre
kuru temizleyici [kurutemizlejidʒi] *n* dry-cleaner's
kurutmak [kurutmak] *v* dry; **çamaşır kurutma makinesi** *n* spin dryer; **Çamaşırlarımı kurutabileceğim bir yer var mı?** Is there somewhere to dry clothes?
kurutucu [kurutudʒu] *n* dryer
kurye [kurje] *n* courier; **Kuryeyle göndermek istiyorum** I want to send this by courier
kusmak [kusmak] *v* throw up, vomit; **Kusuyor** She has been sic[k]
kusur [kusur] *n* defect, flaw
kuş [kuʃ] *n* bird; **ardıç kuşu** *n* thrush; **balıkçıl kuşu** *n* heron; **guguk kuşu** *n* cuckoo; **kuş gözleme** *n* birdwatching; **kuş gribi** *n* bird flu; **muhabbet kuşu** [*n*] budgerigar; **tavus kuşu** *n* peacock; **yırtıcı kuş** *n* bird of prey
kuşak [kuʃak] *n (jenerasyon)* generation; **burçlar kuşağı** *n* zodiac
kuşet [kuʃet] *n* couchette; **kuşetli vagon** *n* sleeping car; **a bir kuşetli bilet ayırtmak istiyorur[m]** I want to book a sleeper to...; **Kuşetlide yer ayırtabilir miyim[?]** Can I reserve a sleeper?
kuşkonmaz [kuʃkonmaz] *n* asparagus
kuşku [kuʃku] *n* doubt ▹ *v* **kuşku duymak** *v* doubt; **kuşku götürmez bir şekilde** *adv* undoubtedly; **kuşku ve gerilimli bekleyiş** *n* suspense
kuşkulanmak [kuʃkulanmak] *v* suspect
kuşkulu [kuʃkulu] *adj* doubtful, dubious, sceptical, suspicious
kuşüzümü [kuʃyzymy] *n* blackcurrant, currant
kutlama [kutlama] *n* celebration
kutlamak [kutlamak] *v* celebrate[,] congratulate
kutsal [kutsal] *adj* holy, sacred;

Kutsal Cuma *n* Good Friday
kutsamak [kutsamak] *v* bless
kutu [kutu] *n* box; **çöp kutusu** *n* litter bin; **buz kutusu** *n* icebox; **ekmek kutusu** *n* bread bin; **gelen kutusu** *n* inbox; **karton kutu** *n* carton; **kutu açacağı** *n* can-opener, tin-opener; **kutulanmış konserve** *adj* tinned; **şişe geri dönüşüm kutusu** *n* bottle bank; **posta kutusu** *n* letterbox, mailbox, postbox; **sigorta kutusu** *n* fuse box; **teneke kutu** *n* canister; **vites kutusu** *n* gear box
kutulanmış [kutulanməʃ] *adj* canned
kutup [kutup] *adj* polar; **kutup ayısı** *n* polar bear
Kutup [kutup] *n* Pole; **Güney Kutbu** *n* South Pole, the Antarctic, Antarctica; **Kuzey Kutbu** *n* North Pole, the Arctic
Kuveyt [kuvejt] *adj* Kuwaiti ▹ *n* Kuwait
Kuveytli [kuvejtli] *n* Kuwaiti
Kuvvet [kuvvet] *n* strength, power, force; **Hava Kuvvetleri** *n* Air Force
kuvvetli [kuvvetli] *adv* strongly
kuyruk [kujruk] *n (hayvan vb)* tail, *(insan sırası)* queue ▹ *v* **kuyruğa girmek** *v* queue; **kuyruklu yıldız** *n* comet; **Kuyruğun sonu burası mı?** Is this the end of the queue?
kuyu [kuju] *n* well; **petrol kuyusu** *n* oil well
kuyumcu [kujumdʒu] *n* jeweller; **kuyumcu dükkanı** *n* jeweller's
kuzen [kuzen] *n* cousin
kuzey [kuzej] *adj* north, northern ▹ *n* north; **kuzeye doğru** *adj* northbound; **Kuzey Afrika** *adj* North Africa, North African; **Kuzey Afrikalı** *n* North African; **Kuzey Amerika** *adj* North America, North American; **Kuzey Amerikalı** *n* North American; **Kuzey İrlanda** *n* Northern Ireland; **Kuzey Buzul Kuşağı** *n* Arctic Circle; **Kuzey Denizi** *n* North Sea; **Kuzey Kore** *n* North Korea; **Kuzey Kutbu** *n* North Pole, the Arctic; **Kuzey Okyanusu** *n* Arctic Ocean
kuzeybatı [kuzejbatə] *n* northwest
kuzeyde [kuzejde] *adv* north
kuzeydoğu [kuzejdou:] *n* northeast
kuzgunî [kuzguni:] *n* raven
kuzu [kuzu] *n* lamb
Küba [kyba] *adj* Cuban ▹ *n* Cuba
Kübalı [kybalə] *n* Cuban
kübik [kybik] *adj* cubic
küçük [kytʃyk] *adj* minute, small ▹ *n* little, minor; **küçük halı** *n* rug; **küçük Hindistan cevizi** *n* nutmeg; **küçük ilanlar** *npl* small ads; **küçük sandal** *n* dinghy; **yaşça küçük** *adj* junior; **Çok küçük** It's too small; **Bunun bir küçük bedeni var mı?** Do you have this in a smaller size?; **Küçük beden var mı?** Do you have a small?
küf [kyf] *n* mould *(fungus)*
küflü [kyfly] *adj* mouldy
küfretmek [kyfretmek] *v* swear
küfür [kyfyr] *n* curse, swearword

kül [kyl] *n* **yanıp kül olmak** *v* burn down; **Kül tablası alabilir miyim?** May I have an ashtray?
küllük [kyllyk] *n* ashtray
külot [kylot] *npl* briefs, panties, pants, *(kadın)* knickers; **külotlu çorap** *npl* tights
kültür [kyltyr] *n* culture; **genel kültür** *n* general knowledge
kültürel [kyltyrel] *adj* cultural
küp [kyp] *n* cube; **küp buz** *n* ice cube
küpe [kype] *n* earring
kürdan [kyrdan] *n* toothpick; **kürdan gibi** *adj* skinny
kürek [kyrek] *n* oar, shovel, spade; **kısa kürek** *n* paddle; **kürek çekmek** *v* row *(in boat)*; **kürek kemiği** *n* shoulder blade; **kürek sporu** *n* rowing; **kürek teknesi** *n* rowing boat
küresel [kyresel] *adj* global; **küresel ısınma** *n* global warming
küreselleşme [kyresellefme] *n* globalization
kürk [kyrk] *n* fur, *(giysi)* fur coat
kürtaj [kyrtaʒ] *n* abortion
kütle [kytle] *n* mass *(amount)*
kütüphane [kytyphane] *n* library
kütüphaneci [kytyphanedʒi] *n* librarian
küvet [kyvet] *n* bathtub

l

labirent [labirent] *n* maze
laboratuvar [laboratuvar] *n* lab, laboratory; **dil laboratuvarı** *n* language laboratory
lacivert [ladʒivert] *adj* navy-blue
lagün [lagyn] *n* lagoon
lağım [laːəm] *adj* **lağım borusu** *n* sewer
lahana [lahana] *n* cabbage; **Brüksel lahanası** *npl* sprouts; **lahana salatası** *n* coleslaw
lake [lake] *n* lacquer
lale [lalje] *n* tulip
lamba [ljamba] *n* lamp; **ön lamba** *n* headlamp, headlight; **başucu lambası** *n* bedside lamp; **fren lambası** *n* brake light; **kontrol lambası** *n* pilot light; **lamba direği** *n* lamppost; **sis lambası** *n* fog light; **sokak lambası** *n* streetlamp; **spot lambası** *n* spotlight; **yan lambalar** *n*

sidelight; **Lamba çalışmıyor** The lamp is not working
lanet [lanet] *adj* damn
Laos [laos] *n* Laos
larenjit [larenʒit] *n* laryngitis
larva [larva] *n* maggot
lastik [lastik] *n* elastic, rubber, tyre; **iç lastik** *n* inner tube; **lastik çizme** *npl* wellies; **lastik çizmeler** *npl* wellingtons; **lastik bant** *n* elastic band; **lastik eldiven** *npl* rubber gloves; **lastik spor ayakkabısı** *npl* trainers; **Lastiğim indi/Lastiğim patladı** I have a flat tyre; **Lastik patladı** The tyre has burst; **Lastikleri kontrol eder misiniz lütfen?** Can you check the tyres, please?
Latin [ljatin] *n* Latin; **Latin Amerika** Latin America, Latin American
Latviya [ljatvija] *adj* Latvian ▷ *n* Latvia
lav [lav] *n* lava
lavabo [lavabo] *n* sink, washbasin; **Lavabo kirli** The washbasin is dirty
lavanta [lavanta] *n* lavender
lazer [lazer] *n* laser
lazımlık [lazəmlək] *n* potty
leğen [leːen] *n* basin; **leğen kemiği** *n* pelvis
leke [leke] *n* smudge, stain; **leke çıkarıcı** *n* stain remover; **Bu lekeyi çıkarabilir misiniz?** Can you remove this stain?; **Kahve lekesi** This stain is coffee; **Kan lekesi** This stain is blood; **Şarap lekesi** This stain is wine; **Yağ lekesi** This stain is oil
lekelemek [lekelemek] *v* stain
lens [lens] *n* lens; **kontakt lens** *npl* contact lenses; **Lens solüsyonu** cleansing solution for contact lenses; **Lens takıyorum** I wear contact lenses
leopar [leopar] *n* leopard
leotard [leotard] *n* leotard
Letonca [letondʒa] *n (dil)* Latvian *(language)*
Letonyalı [letonjalə] *n (kişi)* Latvian *(person)*
leydi [lejdi] *n* lady
leylak [lejlak] *n* lilac; **leylak renkli** *adj* lilac; **pembemsi leylak rengi** *adj* mauve
lezzet [lezzet] *n* flavour; **lezzet katıcı** *n* flavouring
lezzetli [lezzetli] *adj* delicious, tasteful, tasty
Liberya [liberja] *adj* Liberian ▷ *n* Liberia
Liberyalı [liberjalə] *n* Liberian
Libya [libja] *adj* Libyan ▷ *n* Libya
Libyalı [libjalə] *n* Libyan
lider [lider] *n* leader
lig [lig] *n* league
Lihtenştayn [lihtenʃtajn] *n* Liechtenstein
likör [likør] *n* liqueur; **Likör olarak neleriniz var?** What liqueurs do you have?
liman [liman] *n* harbour, port *(ships)*; **yat limanı** *n* marina
limit [limit] *n* limit; **bagaj limiti** *n* baggage allowance; **Bagaj limiti ne kadar?** What is the baggage allowance?; **Bu yolda hız limiti nedir?** What is the speed limit on this road?

limon [limon] *n* lemon; **limon kabuğu** *n* zest *(lemon-peel)*; **yeşil limon** *n* lime *(fruit)*; **limonlu** with lemon
limonata [limonata] *n* lemonade; **Bir bardak limonata lütfen** A glass of lemonade, please
limonluk [limonluk] *n* conservatory
limuzin [limuzin] *n* limousine
lisans [lisans] *n* licence, certificate; **lisans derecesi** *(edebiyat) abbr* BA
liste [liste] *n* list; **adres listesi** *n* mailing list; **ön eleme listesi** *n* shortlist; **bekleme listesi** *n* waiting list; **fiyat listesi** *n* price list; **liste harici** *adj* unlisted; **şarap listesi** *n* wine list; **Şarap listesi lütfen** The wine list, please
listelemek [listelemek] *n* list
litre [litre] *n* litre
Litvanca [litvandʒa] *n (dil)* Lithuanian *(language)*
Litvanya [litvanja] *adj* Lithuanian ▹ *n* Lithuania
Litvanyalı [litvanjalə] *n (kişi)* Lithuanian *(person)*
lobi [lobi] *n* lobby; **Lobide buluşuruz** I'll meet you in the lobby
logo [logo] *n* logo
lokal [lokal] *n* **lokal anestezi** *n* local anaesthetic
lokanta [lokanta] *n* restaurant; **lokanta müşterisi** *n* diner
lolipop [lolipop] *n* lollipop, lolly
Londra [londra] *n* London
losyon [losjon] *n* lotion; **bronzlaşma losyonu** *n* suntan lotion; **traş losyonu** *n* aftershave; **yüz temizleme losyonu** *n* cleansing lotion
loş [loʃ] *adj* dim
lösemi [løsemi] *n* leukaemia
lunapark [lunapark] *n* funfair
Lübnan [lybnan] *n* Lebanon
Lübnanlı [lybnanlə] *n* Lebanese
lüks [lyks] *adj* luxurious ▹ *n* luxury
Lüksemburg [lyksemburg] *n* Luxembourg
lütfen [lytfen] *excl* please; **Lütfen Arka Sayfaya Bakınız** *abbr* PTO *(please turn over)*; **... koymayın lütfen** I'd like it without..., please; **Adresi yazar mısınız lütfen?** Will you write down the address, please?; **buzlu lütfen** With ice, please; **Binmeme yardım eder misiniz lütfen?** Can you help me get on, please?; **Biraz daha yavaş konuşabilir misiniz lütfen?** Could you speak more slowly, please?; **Burada durun lütfen** Stop here, please; **Burada ineyim lütfen** Please let me off; **Buranın sahibiyle konuşabilir miyim lütfen** Could I speak to the owner, please?; **Daha yüksek sesle konuşabilir misiniz lütfen?** Could you speak louder, please?; **Deneyebilir miyim lütfen?** Can I test it, please?; **Gecikeceğiniz zaman lütfen bize haber verin** Please call us if you'll be late; **Hesabı alalım lütfen** Please bring the bill; **Lütfen bana bir iğne yapın** Please give me an injection; **Lütfen beni bekleyin** Please wait for me; **Lütfen durun** Please stop

the bus; **Menü lütfen** The menu, please; **Sarar mısınız lütfen?** Could you wrap it up for me, please?; **Tekrar eder misiniz lütfen?** Could you repeat that, please?; **Temiz bir kaşık alabilir miyim lütfen?** Could I have a clean spoon, please?; **Tuzu uzatır mısınız lütfen?** Pass the salt, please; **Yanında ekstra... istiyorum lütfen** I'd like it with extra..., please; **Yazabilir misiniz lütfen** Could you write that down, please?

maaş [maaʃ] *n* pay, salary; **emekli maaşı** *n* pension; **yüksek maaşlı** *adj* well-paid
mabed [mabed] *n* shrine
Macar [madʒar] *adj* Hungarian ▷ *n* Hungarian
Macaristan [madʒaristan] *n* Hungary
macera [madʒera] *n* adventure
maceraperest [madʒeraperest] *adj* adventurous
macun [madʒun] *n* paste; **diş macunu** *n* toothpaste
maç [matʃ] *n* match *(sport)*; **futbol maçı** *n* football match; **kendi sahasında maç** *n* home match; **rakip sahada maç** *n* away match; **Futbol maçı görmek isterdim** I'd like to see a football match
Madagaskar [madagaskar] *n* Madagascar
madalya [madalja] *n* medal

madalyon [madaljon] *n* locket, medallion
madam [madam] *n* madam
madde [madde] *n* stuff, substance, *(dizi)* item, *(fizik)* matter, *(yasa vb)* clause; **katkı maddesi** *n* additive, preservative; **patlayıcı madde** *n* explosive; **yiyecek maddeleri** *npl* groceries
maden [maden] *n* mineral; **maden ocağı** *n* mine; **maden suyu** *n* mineral water, sparkling water; **Bir şişe maden suyu** a bottle of mineral water
madenci [madendʒi] *n* miner
madencilik [madendʒilik] *n* mining
madensel [madensel] *adj* mineral
mafsal [mafsal] *n* joint; **mafsal iltihabı** *n* arthritis
magazin [magazin] *n* **online magazin** *n* webzine
mağara [ma:ara] *n* cave
mağaza [ma:aza] *v* large shop; **büyük mağaza** *n* department store
mahalle [mahalle] *n* neighbourhood
mahcup [mahdʒup] *adj* ashamed
mahkeme [mahkeme] *n* court, tribunal
mahkum [mahkum] *n* prisoner ▷ *v* **mahkum etmek** *v* sentence
mahvetmek [mahvetmek] *v* ruin
mahvolmuş [mahvolmuʃ] *adj* devastated
mahzen [mahzen] *n* cellar
makale [makale] *n* article
makara [makara] *n* reel
makarna [makarna] *n* pasta ▷ *npl* macaroni
makas [makas] *npl* scissors, *(tırnak/saç/tel/çalı)* clippers; **tırnak makası** *n* nail scissors
makaslamak [makaslamak] *v* cut up
makine [makine] *n* engine, machine; **çamaşır kurutma makinesi** *n* spin dryer, tumble dryer; **çamaşır makinesi** *n* washing machine; **çim biçme makinesi** *n* lawnmower, mower; **bulaşık makinesi** *n* dishwasher; **cep hesap makinesi** *n* pocket calculator; **dijital fotoğraf makinesi** *n* digital camera; **dikiş makinesi** *n* sewing machine; **ekmek kızartma makinesi** *n* toaster; **fotoğraf makinesi** *n* camera; **fotokopi makinesi** *n* photocopier; **hesap makinesi** *n* calculator; **jetonlu makine** *n* slot machine; **makinede yıkanabilir** *n* machine washable; **makineli tüfek** *n* machine gun; **otomatik satış makinesi** *n* vending machine; **saç kurutma makinesi** *n* hairdryer; **slot makinesi** *n* fruit machine; **traş makinesi** *n* shaver; **Çamaşır makinesi nasıl çalışıyor?** How does the washing machine work?; **Bilet makinası çalışmıyor** The ticket machine isn't working; **Bilet makinası nasıl çalışıyor?** How does the ticket machine work?; **Bilet makinası nerede?** Where is the ticket machine?; **Bu kartı bu makinede kullanabilir miyim?** Can I use my card with this cash

machine?; **Kullanabileceğim bir faks makinesi var mı?** Is there a fax machine I can use?; **Makine kartımı yuttu** The cash machine swallowed my card
maksat [maksat] *n* purpose
maksimum [maksimum] *n* maximum
makul [makul] *adv* reasonably
makyaj [makjaʒ] *n* make-up; **makyaj malzemeleri** *npl* toiletries; **makyaj malzemesi** *npl* cosmetics
mala [mala] *n* trowel
Malawi [malavi] *n* Malawi
Malezya [malezja] *adj* Malaysian ▹ *n* Malaysia
Malezyalı [malezjalə] *n* Malaysian
mali [mali] *adj* financial, fiscal; **mali açıklık** *n* shortfall; **mali destek** *n* sponsorship; **mali destek sağlamak** *v* subsidize; **mali yıl** *n* financial year, fiscal year
malikane [malikane] *n* estate, stately home
mallar [mallar] *npl* goods
malt [malt] *n* **malt viskisi** *n* malt whisky
Malta [malta] *adj* Maltese ▹ *n* Malta; **Malta dili** *(dil) n* Maltese *(language)*
Maltalı [maltalə] *n (kişi)* Maltese *(person)*
malzeme [malzeme] *n* ingredient, material; **makyaj malzemeleri** *npl* toiletries; **makyaj malzemesi** *npl* cosmetics; **malzeme temin etme** *n* supply
mama [mama] *n* **mama önlüğü** *n* bib; **Mama sandalyeniz var mı?** Do you have a high chair?
mamut [mamut] *n* mammoth
manastır [manastər] *n* abbey, convent, monastery; **Manastır halka açık mı?** Is the monastery open to the public?
manav [manav] *n* greengrocer's
manda [manda] *n* buffalo
mandal [mandal] *n* **çamaşır mandalı** *n* clothes peg
mandalina [mandalina] *n* clementine, mandarin *(fruit)*, tangerine
mandıra [mandəra] *n* dairy
manevi [manevi] *adj* spiritual
mangetout [mangetout] *n* mangetout
mango [mango] *n* mango
manikür [manikyr] *n* manicure ▹ *v* **manikür yapmak** *n* manicure
manken [maŋen] *n* **vitrin mankeni** *n* dummy
mantar [mantar] *n (botanik)* mushroom, *(botanik)* toadstool, *(eşya)* cork
mantık [mantək] *n* reason
mantıklı [mantəklə] *adj* logical, reasonable
mantıksız [mantəksəz] *adj* unreasonable
manyak [manjak] *n* madman, maniac
manzara [manzara] *n* landscape, scenery; **güzel manzaralı yer** *n* beauty spot
Maori [maori] *adj* Maori ▹ *n (kişi)* Maori *(person)*; **Maori dili** *(dil) n* Maori *(language)*
marangoz [marangoz] *n* carpenter

marangozluk [marangozluk] *n* carpentry
maraton [maraton] *n* marathon
margarin [margarin] *n* margarine
marka [marka] *n* brand, brand name, *(ticaret)* trademark
marker [marker] *n* highlighter
market [market] *n* **market arabası** *n* shopping trolley
Marksizm [marksizm] *n* Marxism
marmelat [marmelat] *n* marmalade
marş [marʃ] *n* anthem; **milli marş** *n* national anthem
Mart [mart] *n* March
martı [martə] *n* seagull
marul [marul] *n* lettuce
masa [masa] *n* table *(furniture)*; **masa örtüsü** *n* tablecloth; **masa tenisi** *n* table tennis; **servis masası** *n* trolley; **tuvalet masası** *n* dressing table; **Dört kişilik bir masa lütfen** A table for four people, please
masaj [masaʒ] *n* massage
masal [masal] *n* story, tale; **peri masalı** *n* fairytale
masif [masif] *adj* massive
maske [maske] *n* mask
maskeli [maskeli] *adj* masked
masraf [masraf] *n* expense; **işletme masrafları** *npl* overheads
masraflar [masraflar] *npl* expenses
masum [masum] *adj* innocent
maşa [maʃa] *n* **saç maşası** *npl* straighteners
matara [matara] *n* **cep matarası** *n* flask
matbaacı [matbaadʒə] *n* printer *(person)*
matem [matem] *n* mourning
matematik [matematik] *npl* mathematics, maths
matematiksel [matematiksel] *adj* mathematical
matine [matine] *n* matinée; **Sekiz matinesine iki bilet lütfen** two for the eight o'clock showing
matkap [matkap] *n* drill; **pnömatik matkap** *n* pneumatic drill
maun [maun] *n* mahogany
mavi [mavi] *adj* blue
mavna [mavna] *n* barge
maya [maja] *n* yeast
maydanoz [majdanoz] *n* parsley
Mayıs [majəs] *n* May
maymun [majmun] *n* monkey
mayo [majo] *n* bathing suit, swimming costume, swimsuit
mayonez [majonez] *n* mayonnaise
mecburi [medʒburi] *adj* **mecburi yön** *(trafik) n* diversion
meclis [medʒlis] *n (belediye vb)* council; **belediye meclis üyesi** *n* councillor
medeni [medeni] *adj* **medeni hal** *n* marital status
meditasyon [meditasjon] *n* meditation
medya [medja] *npl* media
mega [mega] *adj* mega
mekanik [mekanik] *adj* mechanical
mekanizma [mekanizma] *n* machinery, mechanism
Mekke [mekke] *n* Mecca
Meksika [meksika] *n* Mexico

Meksikalı [meksikalə] *n* Mexican
mektup [mektup] *n* letter *(message)*; **Bu mektubu postalamak istiyorum** I'd like to send this letter
melankoli [melaŋoli] *npl* blues
melas [melas] *n* treacle
melek [melek] *n* angel
melez [melez] *n* mongrel
melodi [melodi] *n* melody, tune
memeli [memeli] *n* mammal
memnun [memnun] *adj* glad, pleased; **kendinden memnun** *adj* smug
memur [memur] *n* official, employee; **Çin'de yüksek memur** *n* mandarin *(official)*; **görevli memur** *(polis/asker)* *n* officer; **gümrük memuru** *n* customs officer; **tasfiye memuru** *n* receiver *(person)*; **trafik memuru** *n* traffic warden
mendil [mendil] *n* handkerchief, hankie; **ıslak bebek mendili** *n* baby wipe; **kağıt mendil** *n* tissue *(anatomy)*, tissue *(paper)*
menenjit [menenʒit] *n* meningitis
menopoz [menopoz] *n* menopause
mensup [mensup] *n* **ordu mensubu** *n (erkek)* serviceman, *(kadın)* servicewoman
menteşe [menteʃe] *n* hinge
menü [meny] *n* menu; **Çocuk menüsü var mı?** Do you have a children's menu?; **Fiks menü alalım** We'll take the set menu; **Fiks menü ne kadar?** How much is the set menu?; **Fiks menünüz var mı?** Do you have a set-price menu?; **Menü lütfen** The menu, please; **Tatlı menüsü lütfen** The dessert menu, please
menzil [menzil] *n* **kısa menzilli silah** *n* shotgun
merak [merak] *n* curiosity ▷ *v* **merak etmek** *v* wonder
meraklı [meraklə] *adj* curious, inquisitive, nosy
mercan [merdʒan] *n* coral
mercanköşk [merdʒaŋøʃk] *n* marjoram, *(yabani)* oregano
mercimek [merdʒimek] *npl* lentils
merdiven [merdiven] *n* staircase; **ayaklı merdiven** *n* stepladder; **merdiven başı** *n* landing; **taşınır merdiven** *n* ladder; **yürüyen merdiven** *n* escalator
merdivenler [merdivenler] *npl* stairs
merhaba [merhaba] *excl* hello!
merhamet [merhamet] *n* mercy
merhem [merhem] *n* ointment
merkez [merkez] *n* centre ▷ *npl* headquarters; **alışveriş merkezi** *n* shopping centre; **çağrı merkezi** *n* call centre; **bahçe merkezi** *n* garden centre; **eğlence merkezi** *n* leisure centre; **genel merkez** *n* HQ; **kent merkezi** *adv* city centre; **kent merkezinde** *adv* downtown; **şehir merkezi** *n* town centre; **merkezi ısıtma** *n* central heating; **yönetim merkezi** *n* head office; **ziyaretçi merkezi** *n* visitor centre; **Kent merkezine lütfen** Please take me to the city centre; **Şehir merkezinden ne kadar uzaktayız?** How far are we from the town centre?; **Şehir**

merkezine en kolay nasıl gidebilirim? What's the best way to get to the city centre?
merkezi [merkezi] *adj* central
mermer [mermer] *n* marble
mesafe [mesafe] *n* distance, space; **kısa mesafe hız koşusu** *n* sprint; **kısa mesafe koşucusu** *n* sprinter
mesai [mesai] *n* work; **fazla mesai** *n* overtime
mesaj [mesaʒ] *n* message, text message; **mesaj atmak** *v* text; **Bana mesaj var mı?** Are there any messages for me?; **Mesaj bırakabilir miyim?** Can I leave a message?; **Sekreterine mesaj bırakabilir miyim?** Can I leave a message with his secretary?
mesele [mesele] *n* issue
meskun [meskun] *adj* residential; **meskun olmayan** *adj* uninhabited
meslek [meslek] *n* occupation *(work)*, profession
meslekdaş [meslekdaʃ] *n* colleague
mesleki [mesleki] *n* vocational
meşe [meʃe] *n* oak; **meşe palamudu** *n* acorn
meşgul [meʃgul] *adj* busy; **meşgul sinyali** *n* busy signal, engaged tone; **Kusura bakmayın, meşgulüm** Sorry, I'm busy
metabolizma [metabolizma] *n* metabolism
metal [metal] *n* metal; **metal çekirdek** *n* pellet
metazori [metazori] *adj* compulsory
Methodist [methodist] *adj* **Methodist mezhebine ait** *n* Methodist
metin [metin] *n* text
metre [metre] *n* metre; **şerit metre** *n* tape measure
metres [metres] *n* mistress
metrik [metrik] *adj* metric
metro [metro] *n* underground, tube; **metro istasyonu** *n* metro station, tube station; **Bir metro haritası lütfen** Could I have a map of the tube, please?; **Buraya en yakın metro istasyonu nerede?/En yakın metro istasyonu nerede?** Where is the nearest tube station?; **En yakın metro istasyonuna nasıl gidebilirim?** How do I get to the nearest tube station?; **Metro haritası var mı?** Do you have a map of the tube?
mevsim [mevsim] *n* season
mevsimlik [mevsimlik] *n* seasonal
mevzuat [mevzuat] *n* legislation
meydan [mejdan] *n* **meydan okuma** *v* challenge
meyve [mejve] *n* fruit *(botany)*, fruit *(collectively)*; **çalı meyvesi** *n* berry; **meyve bahçesi** *n* orchard; **meyve salatası** *n* fruit salad; **meyve suyu** *n* fruit juice, juice; **çarkıfelek meyvası** *n* passion fruit; **meyva kabuğu** *n* peel
mezar [mezar] *n* grave; **mezar taşı** *n* gravestone
mezarlık [mezarlək] *n* cemetery, graveyard
mezgit [mezgit] *n* whiting;

mezgit balığı *n* haddock
mezhep [meshep] *n* sect; **Methodist mezhebine ait** *n* Methodist; **Quaker mezhebinden** *n* Quaker
mezun [mezun] *n* **üniversite mezunu** *n* graduate, undergraduate
mezuniyet [mezunijet] *n* graduation
mıknatıs [məknatəs] *n* magnet
mıknatıslı [məknatəslə] *adj* magnetic
mırıldanmak [mərəldanmak] *v* mutter, *(kedi gibi)* purr
mısır [məsər] *b* maize ▷ *n* *(sebze)* corn; **bebe mısır** *n* sweetcorn; **mısır gevreği** *n* cornflakes; **mısır nişastası** *n* cornflour; **patlamış mısır** *n* popcorn
Mısır [məsər] *adj* Egyptian ▷ *n* *(ülke)* Egypt
Mısırlı [məsərlə] *n* Egyptian
mızrak [məzrak] *n* javelin
mide [mide] *n* stomach; **mide ağrısı** *n* stomachache; **mide bulandırıcı** *adj* sickening; **mide ekşimesi** *n* heartburn
midilli [midilli] *n* pony
midye [midje] *n* mussel
migren [migren] *n* migraine
mikroçip [mikrotʃip] *n* microchip
mikrodalga [mikrodalga] *n* **mikrodalga fırın** *n* microwave oven
mikrofon [mikrofon] *n* microphone, mike; **Mikrofon var mı?** Does it have a microphone?
mikrop [mikrop] *n* germ
mikroskop [mikroskop] *n* microscope
mikser [mikser] *n* blender, liquidizer, mixer
miktar [miktar] *n* amount, quantity; **miktar belirtmek** *v* quantify
mil [mil] *n* mile; **mil ölçer** *n* mileometer; **mil hesabıyla uzaklık** *n* mileage
milenyum [milenjum] *n* millennium
milföy [milføj] *n* **milföy hamuru** *n* puff pastry
milimetre [milimetre] *n* millimetre
milkshake [milkshake] *n* milkshake
millet [millet] *n* nation; **Birleşmiş Milletler** *n* UN, United Nations
milli [milli] *adj* **milli marş** *n* national anthem; **milli park** *n* national park
mil/saat [milsaat] *abbr* mph
milyar [miljar] *n* billion
milyon [miljon] *n* million
milyoner [miljoner] *n* millionaire
mimar [mimar] *n* architect; **iç mimar** *n* interior designer
mimarlık [mimarlək] *n* architecture
mini [mini] *adj* mini; **mini etek** *n* miniskirt
minibar [minibar] *n* minibar
minibüs [minibys] *n* minibus
minimum [minimum] *adj* minimum; **Minimum bağlanma süresi ne kadar?** What's the minimum amount of time?
minyatür [minjatyr] *adj* miniature ▷ *n* miniature

miras [miras] *n* heritage, inheritance; **miras almak** *v* inherit
misafir [misafir] *n* guest, visitor; **davetsiz misafir** *n* intruder
misyoner [misjoner] *n* missionary
miting [miting] *n* rally
mitoloji [mitoloʒi] *n* mythology
miyop [mijop] *adj* near-sighted, short-sighted
mizah [mizah] *n* humour; **mizah dergisi** *n* comic book; **mizah duygusu** *n* sense of humour
MMS [ememes] *n* MMS
mobil [mobil] *n* mobile
mobilya [mobilja] *n* furniture
mobilyalı [mobiljalə] *adj* furnished
moda [moda] *n* fashion; **eski moda** *adj* old-fashioned; **moda akımı** *n* trend; **modası geçmiş** *adj* obsolete; **modaya uygun** *adj* fashionable, trendy; **modaya uymayan** *adj* unfashionable
model [model] *n* model ▷ *v* **modelini yapmak** *v* model; **saç modeli** *n* hairdo, hairstyle
modem [modem] *n* modem
modern [modern] *adj* modern; **modern diller** *npl* modern languages
modernize [modernize] *v* **modernize etmek** *v* modernize
modül [modyl] *n* module
Moğol [moɣol] *adj* Mongolian
Moğolca [moɣoldʒa] *n (dil)* Mongolian *(language)*
Moğolistan [moɣolistan] *n* Mongolia
mola [mola] *n* break; **yemek molası** *n* lunch break; **Ne zaman mola veriyoruz?** When do we stop next?; **Yemek molası ne zaman?** Where do we stop for lunch?
Moldova [moldova] *adj* Moldovan ▷ *n* Moldova
Moldovalı [moldovalə] *n* Moldovan
molekül [molekyl] *n* molecule
Monako [monako] *n* Monaco
Mongolistanlı [mongolistanlə] *n (kişi)* Mongolian *(person)*
moped [moped] *n* moped; **Moped kiralamak istiyorum** I want to hire a moped
mor [mor] *adj* purple
moral [moral] *n* morale
morfin [morfin] *n* morphine
morg [morg] *n* morgue
morina [morina] *n* **morina balığı** *n* cod
Moritanya [moritanja] *n* Mauritania
Morse [morse] *n (alfabe)* Morse
motel [motel] *n* motel
motivasyon [motivasjon] *n* motivation
motor [motor] *n* motor; **arama motoru** *n* search engine; **deniz motoru** *n* motorboat; **motor kapağı** *n* bonnet *(car)*; **motor teknisyeni** *n* motor mechanic; **sürat motoru** *n* speedboat
motorsiklet [motorsiklet] *n* **Motosiklet kiralamak istiyorum** I want to hire a motorbike
motosiklet [motosiklet] *n* motorbike, motorcycle
motosikletçi [motosiklettʃi] *n*

motorcyclist
mozaik [mozaik] *n* mosaic
Mozambik [mozambik] *n* Mozambique
mönü [møny] *n* menu; **fiks mönü** *n* set menu
MP3 [empi:ytʃ] *n* **MP3 çalar** *n* MP3 player
MP4 [empi:dørt] *n* **MP4 çalar** *n* MP4 player
MS [ms] *abbr* AD ▷ *n (hastalık)* MS
muamele [muamele] *n* treatment; **kötü muamele etmek** *v* ill-treat
muazzam [muazzam] *adj* enormous
mucit [mudʒit] *n* inventor
mucize [mudʒize] *n* miracle
muhabbet [muhabbet] *n* **muhabbet kuşu** *n* budgerigar; **muhabbet kuşu** *n* budgie
muhabir [muhabir] *n* correspondent, reporter
muhafazakâr [muhafazaka:r] *adj* conservative
muhakkak [muhakkak] *adv* surely
muhalefet [muhalefet] *n* opposition
muharebe [muharebe] *n* battle; **muharebe zırhlısı** *n* battleship
muhasebeci [muhasebedʒi] *n* accountant
muhasebecilik [muhasebedʒilik] *n* accountancy
muhbir [muhbir] *n* grass *(informer)*
muhteşem [muhteʃem] *adj* superb
muhteviyat [muhtevijat] *n* content ▷ *npl* contents *(list)*
mukavva [mukavva] *n* cardboard, hardboard
muktedir [muktedir] *adj* able, capable
multipl skleroz *n* multiple sclerosis
mum [mum] *n* candle; **mum boya** *n* crayon
mumya [mumja] *n* mummy *(body)*
Musevi [musevi] *n* Jew ▷ *adj* Jewish; **Musevilerin Fısıh Bayramı** *n* Passover
musluk [musluk] *n* tap; **musluk deliği** *n* plughole; **musluk işleri** *n* plumbing
muslukçu [musluktʃu] *n* plumber
muson [muson] *n* monsoon
muşamba [muʃamba] *n* **yer muşambası** *n* lino
mutabık [mutabək] *adj* agreed
mutfak [mutfak] *n* kitchen; **hazır mutfak** *n* fitted kitchen; **mutfak dolabı** *n* dresser; **mutfak havlusu** *n* tea towel; **mutfak robotu** *n* food processor
mutlu [mutlu] *adj* happy; **Mutlu Yıllar!** Happy New Year!
mutluluk [mutluluk] *n* bliss, happiness
mutsuz [mutsuz] *adj* unhappy
muz [muz] *n* banana
mücadele [mydʒadele] *n* struggle
mücevher [mydʒevher] *n* gem, jewel
mücevherat [mydʒevherat] *n* jewellery
müdahale [mydahale] *n* interruption

müdür [mydyr] *n* headteacher, manager, principal, *(kadın)* manageress; **genel müdür** *n* managing director; **müdür yardımcısı** *n* deputy head; **Müdürle konuşmak istiyorum lütfen** I'd like to speak to the manager, please
müflis [myflis] *adj* bankrupt
müfredat [myfredat] *n* curriculum, syllabus
mühendis [myhendis] *n* engineer
mühendislik [myhendislik] *n* engineering
mühlet [myhlet] *n* notice *(termination)*
mühür [myhyr] *n* seal *(mark)*
mühürlemek [myhyrlemek] *v* seal
mükemmel [mykemmel] *adj* excellent, outstanding, perfect; **mükemmel bir şekilde** *adv* perfectly; **Yemek mükemmeldi** The lunch was excellent
mükemmellik [mykemmellik] *n* perfection
mülk [mylk] *n* property; **özel mülk** *n* private property; **devre mülk** *n* timeshare
mülkiyet [mylkijet] *n* possession
münazara [mynazara] *n* discussion
mürekkep [myrekkep] *n* ink
mürettebat [myrettebat] *n* crew; **kabin mürettebatı** *n* cabin crew
müshil [myshil] *n* laxative
müsli [mysli] *n* muesli
Müslüman [myslyman] *adj* Moslem, Muslim ▷ *n* Moslem, Muslim
Müslümanlık [myslymanlək] *n* Islam
müsrüf [mysryf] *v* **müsrüflük etmek** *v* squander
müstakil [mystakil] *adj* self-contained; **müstakil ev** *n* detached house
müstesna [mystesna] *adj* exceptional
müşterek [myʃterek] *adj* common
müşteri [myʃteri] *n* client, customer; **lokanta müşterisi** *n* diner
mütercim [myterdʒim] *n* interpreter
müteşekkir [myteʃekkir] *adj* grateful
müthiş [mythiʃ] *adj* terrific
müttefik [myttefik] *n* ally
müze [myze] *n* museum; **Müze öğleden sonra açık mı?** Is the museum open in the afternoon?; **Müze her gün açık mı?** Is the museum open every day?; **Müze ne zaman açık?** When is the museum open?; **Müze Pazar günleri açık mı?** Is the museum open on Sundays?; **Müze sabahları açık mı?** Is the museum open in the morning?
müzik [myzik] *adj* musical ▷ *n* music; **film müziği** *n* soundtrack; **halk müziği** *n* folk music; **kişisel müzik çalar** *n* personal stereo; **müzik aleti** *n* musical instrument; **müzik seti** *n* music centre; **Canlı müzik dinleyebileceğimiz bir yer var mı?** Where can we hear live music?
müzikal [myzikal] *n* musical

müzisyen [myzisjen] *n* musician, player *(instrumentalist)*; **Yerel müzisyenleri dinleyebileceğimiz bir yer var mı?** Where can we hear local musicians play?
müzmin [myzmin] *adj* obstinate
Myanmar [mjanmar] *n* Myanmar

nabız [nabəz] *n* pulse
nadiren [nadiren] *adv* rarely, scarcely, seldom
nahoş [nahoʃ] *adj* embarrassing
nakış [nakəʃ] *n* embroidery
nakil [nakil] *n* transfer; **kan nakli** *n* blood transfusion
nakit [nakit] *n* cash; **Üzerimde nakit yok** I don't have any cash; **Nakit almak için kartımı kullanabilir miyim?** Can I use my card to get cash?; **Nakit ödemelere indirim yapıyor musunuz?** Do you offer a discount for cash?
nakliye [naklije] *n* freight
nal [nal] *n* **at nalı** *n* horseshoe
namına [namәna] *n* on behalf of
namussuz [namussuz] *adj* bent *(inf: dishonest)*
nane [nane] *n (bitki/şeker)* mint *(herb/sweet)*; **nane şekeri** *n*

peppermint
nankör [naŋør] *adj* ungrateful
nar [nar] *n* pomegranate
nasıl [nasəl] *adj* what ▹ *adv* how; **... merkezine nasıl gidebilirim?** How do I get to the centre of...?; **... na nasıl gidebilirim?** How do I get to...?; **... na nasıl gidebiliriz?** How do we get to...?; **Bilet makinası nasıl çalışıyor?** How does the ticket machine work?; **Bu nasıl çalışıyor?** How does this work?; **Bu yemeği nasıl pişiriyorsunuz?** How do you cook this dish?; **Bunun nasıl yapıldığını biliyor musunuz?** Do you know how to do this?; **Hava yarın nasıl olacak?** What will the weather be like tomorrow?; **Kar nasıl?** What is the snow like?; **Kumandaların nasıl çalıştığını gösterir misiniz?** Can you show me how the controls work?; **Nasıl alacağım?** How should I take it?; **Nasıl okunuyor?** How do you pronounce it?; **Nasıl yazılıyor?** How do you spell it?; **Nasılsınız?** How are you?; **Oraya nasıl gidebilirim?** How do I get there?
nasılsa [nasəlsa] *adv* somehow
NATO [nato] *abbr* NATO
naylon [najlon] *n* nylon; **naylon çorap** *n* stocking; **naylon torba** *n* plastic bag, polythene bag
nazik [nazik] *adj* polite; **Çok naziksiniz** That's very kind of you
ne [ne] *adj* what ▹ *conj* neither ▹ *pron* what; **ne yapacağı belli olmayan** *adj* unpredictable; **... a ne zaman varırız?** What time do we get to...?; **Adınız ne?** What's your name?; **Bu ne demek?** What does this mean?; **Bu nedir?** What is it?; **Bu yemeğin içinde ne var?** What is in this dish?; **Bunun içinde ne var?** What is in this?; **Burada neler yapabiliriz?** What is there to do here?; **Buraya özel ne var?** What is the house speciality?; **Ne giymem gerekiyor?** What should I wear?; **Ne içmek istersiniz?** What would you like to drink?; **Ne işle meşgulsünüz?** What do you do?; **Ne oldu?** What happened?; **Ne zaman kalkıyor?** What time does it leave?; **Otobüs ne zaman geliyor?** What time does the bus arrive?; **Otobüs ne zaman kalkacak?** What time does the bus leave?; **Sandviç olarak ne var?** What kind of sandwiches do you have?
neden [neden] *n* cause *(reason)*
nedime [nedime] *n* bridesmaid
nefes [nefes] *n* breath; **nefes alma** *n* breathing; **nefes almak** *v* breathe, breathe in; **nefes vermek** *v* breathe out
nefis [nefis] *adj* excellent; **Nefisti** That was delicious; **Yemek nefisti** The meal was delicious
nefret [nefret] *n* hatred ▹ *v* **nefret etmek** *v* hate; **nefret etmek** *v* resent
nehir [nehir] *n* river; **Nehirde tekne turu var mı?** Are there any boat trips on the river?; **Nehirde yüzülebilir mi?** Can one swim in the river?

nektarin [nektarin] *n* nectarine
nem [nem] *n* humidity, moisture
nemlendirici [nemlendiridʒi] *n* moisturizer
nemli [nemli] *adj* damp, humid
neon [neon] *n* neon
Nepal [nepal] *n* Nepal
nerede [nerede] *adv* where ▷ *conj* where; **Bunu nerede tamir ettirebilirim?** Where can I get this repaired?; **Duşlar nerede?** Where are the showers?; **Nerede buluşabiliriz?** Where can we meet?; **Nerede buluşalım?** Where shall we meet?; **Nerede kalıyorsunuz?** Where are you staying?; **Nerede oturuyorsunuz?** Where do you live?
nereden [nereden] *pron, conj* **... ın neresindensiniz?** What part of... are you from?
neredeyse [neredejse] *adv* almost
nergiz [nergiz] *n* daffodil
nesne [nesne] *n* object
neşe [neʃe] *n* joy
neşeli [neʃeli] *adj* cheerful, jolly ▷ *n* smiley
net [net] *adj, adv* **net değil** *adj* unclear
netbol [netbol] *n* netball
network [network] *n* **şirketiçi network** *n* intranet
neyse [nejse] *adv* anyway
nice [nidʒe] *adj* **Nice Yıllara!** Happy birthday!
niçin [nitʃin] *adv* why
Nijer [niʒer] *n* Niger
Nijerya [niʒerja] *adj* Nigerian ▷ *n* Nigeria
Nijeryalı [niʒerjalə] *n* Nigerian
Nikaragua [nikaragua] *adj* Nicaraguan ▷ *n* Nicaragua
Nikaragualı [nikaragualə] *n* Nicaraguan
nikotin [nikotin] *n* nicotine
nine [nine] *n* grandma, granny; **ninenin annesi** *n* great-grandmother
ninni [ninni] *n* lullaby
Nisan [nisan] *n* April; **1 Nisan Şakası** *n* April Fools' Day
nişan [niʃan] *n (belirti)* token; **nişan yüzüğü** *n* engagement ring
nişanlı [niʃanlə] *adj* engaged ▷ *n (erkek)* fiancé, *(kadın)* fiancée; **Nişanlıyım** I'm engaged
nişasta [niʃasta] *n* starch; **mısır nişastası** *n* cornflour
nitekim [nitekim] *adv* consequently
nitelemek [nitelemek] *v* qualify
nitelik [nitelik] *n* qualification
nitelikli [nitelikli] *adj* qualified
niteliksiz [niteliksiz] *adj* unskilled
nitrojen [nitroʒen] *n* nitrogen
niyet [nijet] *n* intention; **kötü niyetli** *adj* malicious
niyetlenmek [nijetlenmek] *v* intend to
nizam [nizam] *n* **bitişik nizam ev** *n* semi, semi-detached house
Noel [noel] *n* Christmas, Xmas; **Noel ağacı** *n* Christmas tree; **Noel arifesi** *n* Christmas Eve; **Noel öncesi** *n* advent; **Noel kartı** *n* Christmas card; **Noel şarkısı** *n* carol; **Mutlu Noeller!** Merry Christmas!
nohut [nohut] *n* chickpea

nokta [nokta] *n (gramer)* full stop, *(şekil)* dot, *(yer)* point; **bakış noktası** *n* standpoint, viewpoint; **iki nokta üst üste** *n* colon; **noktalı virgül** *n* semicolon
noktalama [noktalama] *n* punctuation
noodle [noodle] *npl* noodles
normal [normal] *adj* normal; **Normal postayla ne kadar sürer?** How long will it take by normal post?
normalde [normalde] *adv* normally
Norveç [norvetʃ] *adj* Norwegian ▷ *n* Norway
Norveççe [norvetʃtʃe] *adj* Norwegian ▷ *n (dil)* Norwegian *(language)*
Norveçli [norvetʃli] *n (kişi)* Norwegian *(person)*
not [not] *n (mesaj)* note *(message)*; **digital not defteri** *n* e-book; **kısa not** *n* memo; **not almak** *v* jot down, note down; **not defteri** *n* jotter, notebook, notepad; **not kağıdı** *n* notepaper ▷ *v* **not vermek** *v* mark *(grade)*
nota [nota] *n* score *(of music)*, *(müzik)* note *(music)*
nöbet [nøbet] *n* seizure; **öfke nöbeti** *n* tantrum; **gece nöbeti** *n* nightshift; **sara nöbeti** *n* epileptic fit
nöbetçi [nøbettʃi] *n* guard
nörotik [nørotik] *adj* neurotic
numara [numara] *n* number; **bilinmeyen numaralar** *npl* directory enquiries; **cep numarası** *n* mobile number; **hesap numarası** *n* account number; **oda numarası** *n* room number; **referans numarası** *n* reference number; **telefon numarası** *n* phone number; **yanlış numara** *n* wrong number; **... numaralı kapıya gidiniz** Please go to gate...; **Ayakkabı numaram altı** My feet are a size six; **İki yüz iki numaralı odanın anahtarı lütfen** the key for room number two hundred and two; **Üç numaralı pompa lütfen** Pump number three, please; **Beş numaralı kabin nerede?** Where is cabin number five?; **Benim cep numaram...** My mobile number is...; **Bilinmeyen numaralar için hangi numarayı çevireceğim?** What is the number for directory enquiries?; **Ehliyet numaram...** My driving licence number is...; **Faks numarası nedir?** What is the fax number?; **Otuz numaralı vagon nerede?** Where is carriage number thirty?; **Telefon numaranızı alabilir miyim?** Can I have your phone number?; **Telefon numarası nedir?** What's the telephone number?
nüdist [nydist] *n* nudist
nüfus [nyfus] *n* population; **nüfus cüzdanı** *n* birth certificate; **nüfus sayımı** *n* census
nükleer [nykleer] *adj* atomic, nuclear
nükte [nykte] *n* wit
nükteli [nykteli] *adj* humorous

O

o [o] *pron (eşya/hayvan)* it, *(erkek)* he, *(kadın)* she; **o sırada** *adv* meanwhile; **ya o, ya bu** *conj* either *(.. or)*; **Onu tanıyor musunuz?** Do you know him?

obez [obez] *adj* obese

obua [obua] *n* oboe

ocak [odʒak] *n (fırın vb)* cooker; **gazlı ocak** *n* gas cooker; **kömür ocağı** *n* colliery; **maden ocağı** *n* mine; **taş ocağı** *n* quarry

Ocak [odʒak] *n (ay)* January

oda [oda] *n* room; **ameliyat odası** *n* operating theatre; **öğretmen odası** *n* staffroom; **çamaşır odası** *n* utility room; **çift yataklı oda** *n* twin room, twin-bedded room; **çocuk odası** *n* nursery; **bekleme odası** *n* waiting room; **cenazenin gömülmeye ya da yakılmaya hazırlandığı oda** *n* funeral parlour; **iki kişilik oda** *n* double room; **kiralık oda** *n* bedsit; **oda arkadaşı** *n* roommate; **oda görevlisi** *n* chambermaid; **oda numarası** *n* room number; **oda servisi** *n* room service; **oturma odası** *n* living room, sitting room; **sohbet odası** *n* chatroom; **soyunma odası** *n (mağaza)* fitting room, *(spor)* changing room; **tek kişilik oda** *n* single room; **yatak odası** *n* bedroom; **yedek oda** *n* spare room; **Aile odası istiyorum** I'd like to book a family room; **İki kişilik bir oda ayırtmak istiyorum** I want to reserve a double room; **İki kişilik bir oda istiyorum** I'd like to book a double room; **Balkonlu odanız var mı?** Do you have a room with a balcony?; **Başka bir oda istiyorum** I'd like another room; **Bilgisayar odası nerede?** Where is the computer room?; **Bir oda kiralamak istiyorum** I'd like to rent a room; **Bu oda çok küçük** The room is too small; **Oda çok sıcak** The room is too hot; **Oda çok soğuk** The room is too cold; **Oda hesabıma yazın lütfen** Please charge it to my room; **Oda ne kadar?** How much is the room?; **Oda pis** The room is dirty; **Oda servisi var mı?** Is there room service?; **Oda temizlenmemiş** The room isn't clean; **Odada banyo var mı?** Does the room have a private bathroom?; **Odada bir sorun var** There's a problem with the room; **Odada duman kokusu var** My room smells of smoke; **Odada Internet bağlantısı var mı?** Is there an Internet connection in the room?; **Odada kablosuz Internet bağlantısı var mı?** Does the room have wireless Internet access?; **Odada kalorifer var mı?** Does the room have heating?; **Odada klima var mı?** Does the room have air conditioning?; **Odada televizyon var mı?** Does the room have a TV?; **Odada vantilatör var mı?** Does the room have a fan?; **Odamı değiştirebilir miyim?** Can I switch rooms?; **Odamı temizler misiniz lütfen** Can you clean the room, please?; **Odamda böcek var** There are bugs in my room; **Odamda kahvaltı edebilir miyim?** Can I have breakfast in my room?; **Odanız burası** This is your room; **Odanız var mı?** Do you have a room?; **Odayı görebilir miyim?** Can I see the room?; **Odayı kaçta boşaltmam gerek?** When do I have to vacate the room?; **Sessiz bir oda rica ediyorum** I'd like a quiet room; **Sigara içilebilen bir oda rica ediyorum** I'd like a smoking room; **Sigara içilemeyen bir oda rica ediyorum** I'd like a no smoking room; **Soyunma odaları ne tarafta?** Where are the changing rooms?; **Tek kişilik bir oda ayırtmak istiyorum** I want to reserve a single room

odak [odak] *n* focus; **çift odaklı gözlük** *npl* bifocals

odaklanmak [odaklanmak] *v* focus

odun [odun] *n* firewood, log; **odun kömürü** *n* charcoal

ofsayt [ofsajt] *adj* offside

Oğlak [oɣlak] *n* **Oğlak burcu** *n* Capricorn

oğlan [oɣlan] *n* **oğlan çocuğu** *n* boy

oğul [ou:l] *n* son; **üvey oğul** *n* stepson; **vaftiz oğlu** *n* godson; **Oğlum kayıp** My son is missing; **Oğlum kayboldu** My son is lost

oje [oʒe] *n* nail polish; **oje çıkarıcı** *n* nail-polish remover

ok [okej] *n* arrow; **dart oku** *n* dart

OK [okej] *excl* OK!

okey [okej] *adj* okay; **okey!** *excl* okay!

oklava [oklava] *n* rolling pin

oksijen [oksiʒen] *n* oxygen

okşama [okʃama] *n* stroke *(apoplexy)*, stroke *(hit)*

okşamak [okʃamak] *v* stroke

okul [okul] *n* school; **akşam okulu** *n* evening class; **ana okulu** *n* infant school; **dil okulu** *n* language school; **gece okulu** *n* night school; **okul üniforması** *n* school uniform; **okul çantası** *n* schoolbag; **okul çocukları** *n* schoolchildren; **okuldan kaçmak** *v* play truant; **sanat okulu** *n* art school; **yatılı okul** *n* boarding school; **yüksek okul** *n* college; **Burada kayak okulu var mı?** Is there a ski school?; **Okuyorum** I'm still studying

okuma [okuma] *n* reading; **okuma yazması olmayan** *adj*

illiterate
okumak [okumak] *v* read; **dudak okuma** *v* lip-read; **yüksek sesle okumak** *v* read out; **Okuyamıyorum** I can't read it
okunaklı [okunaklə] *adj* legible
okunaksız [okunaksəz] *adj* illegible
okutman [okutman] *n* lecturer
okuyucu [okujudʒu] *n* reader
okyanus [okjanus] *n* ocean; **Hint Okyanusu** *n* Indian Ocean; **Kuzey Okyanusu** *n* Arctic Ocean
Okyanusya [okjanusja] *n* Oceania
olağanüstü [ola:anysty] *adj* extraordinary
olan [olan] *art* **aynı anda olan** *adj* simultaneous
olanaklar [olanaklar] *npl* amenities
olarak [olarak] *conj* **düzenli olarak** *adv* regularly; **doğal olarak** *adv* naturally; **gönüllü olarak** *adv* voluntarily; **otomatik olarak** *adv* automatically; **tam olarak** *adv* exactly
olası [olasə] *adj* likely, possible, probable
olasılık [olasələk] *n* possibility, probability; **olasılık dışı** *adj* unlikely
olasılıkla [olasələkla] *adv* possibly, presumably, probably
olay [olaj] *n* affair, event, incident, occurrence; **önemli olay** *n* highlight
olaylı [olajlə] *adj* eventful
oldukça [olduktʃa] *adv* fairly, rather
olgun [olgun] *adj (kişi)* mature, *(meyve)* ripe; **olgun öğrenci** *n* mature student
olmadıkça [olmadəktʃa] *conj* unless
olmak [olmak] *v* be, become, happen; **ait olmak** *v* belong, belong to; **alabora olmak** *v* capsize; **aynı fikirde olmak** *v* agree; **önemli olmak** *v* matter; **başarısız olmak** *vi* fail; **destek olmak** *v* back up; **doğru olarak** *adv* accurately; **emekli olmak** *v* retire; **gönüllü olmak** *n* volunteer; **sahip olmak** *v* have, own, possess; **sonucu olmak** *v* result in; **teslim olmak** *v* surrender; **var olmak** *v* exist; **yaklaşık olarak** *adv* approximately; **yanıp kül olmak** *v* burn down; **yapmak zorunda olmak** *v* have to; **yok olmak** *v* vanish; **Üye olmak gerekiyor mu?** Do you have to be a member?
olmayan [olmajan] *prep* **dürüst olmayan** *adj* dishonest; **doğru olmayan** *adj* inaccurate; **esnek olmayan** *adj* inflexible; **HIV'li olmayan** *adj* HIV-negative; **pahalı olmayan** *adj* inexpensive; **pratik olmayan** *adj* impractical; **tatmin edici olmayan** *adj* disappointing
olta [olta] *n* fishing rod, fishing tackle; **olta balıkçılığı** *n* angling; **olta balıkçısı** *n* angler
olumlu [olumlu] *adj* positive
olumsuz [olumsuz] *adj* negative ▷ *n* negative
oluşmak [oluʃmak] *v* consist of
oluşturmak [oluʃturmak] *v* make

up
omlet [omlet] *n* omelette
omurga [omurga] *n* backbone
omurilik [omurilik] *n* spinal cord
omuz [omuz] *n* shoulder; **omuz çantası** *n* satchel; **omuz silkmek** *v* shrug; **Omuzumu incittim** I've hurt my shoulder
on [on] *number* ten; **on yıl** *n* decade; **On dakika geciktik** We are ten minutes late; **On yaşında** He is ten years old; **Saat ikiyi on geçiyor** It's ten past two; **Tren on dakika rötarlı** The train is running ten minutes late
ona [ona] *adj (kadın)* her ▷ *pron (erkek)* him, *(kadın)* her
onaltı [onaltə] *number* sixteen
onaltıncı [onaltəndʒə] *adj* sixteenth
onarmak [onarmak] *v* mend, repair
onay [onaj] *n* approval
onaylamak [onajlamak] *v* approve; **başıyla onaylamak** *v* nod
onbaşı [onbaʃə] *n* corporal
on beş [onbeʃ] *num* **On beş Haziran Pazartesi** It's Monday the fifteenth of June
onbeş [onbeʃ] *number* fifteen
onbeşinci [onbeʃindʒi] *adj* fifteenth
onbir [onbir] *number* eleven
onbirinci [onbirindʒi] *adj* eleventh
ondokuz [ondokuz] *number* nineteen
ondokuzuncu [ondokuzundʒu] *adj* nineteenth
ondördüncü [ondørdyndʒy] *adj* fourteenth
ondört [ondørt] *number* fourteen
oniki [oniki] *number* twelve
onikinci [onikindʒi] *adj* twelfth
onlar [onlar] *pron* they
onları [onlarə] *pron* them
onların [onlarən] *adj* their
onlarınki [onlarəŋi] *pron* theirs
onluk [onluk] *adj* decimal
ons [ons] *n* ounce
onsekiz [onsekiz] *number* eighteen
onsekizinci [onsekizindʒi] *adj* eighteenth
onsuz [onsuz] *prep* without
onsuz yapmak [onsuzjapmak] *v* do without
onu [onu] *adj* her ▷ *pron* her, him
onun [onun] *adj* its, *(erkek)* his ▷ *prep* of ▷ *pron (erkek)* his
onuncu [onundʒu] *adj* tenth ▷ *n* tenth
onunki [onuŋi] *pron (kadın)* hers
onur [onur] *n (şeref)* honour ▷ *v* **onur kırmak** *v* insult
onüç [onytʃ] *number* thirteen
onüçüncü [onytʃyndʒy] *adj* thirteenth
onyedi [onjedi] *number* seventeen
onyedinci [onjedindʒi] *adj* seventeenth
opera [opera] *n* opera
operasyon [operasjon] *n* operation *(undertaking)*
operatör [operatør] *n* operator; **tur operatörü** *n* tour operator
oran [oran] *n* proportion, rate, ratio; **faiz oranı** *n* interest rate
oranlamak [oranlamak] *v* rate
orantılı [orantələ] *adj*

proportional
oraya [oraja] *prep* to
ordu [ordu] *n* army; **ordu mensubu** *n (erkek)* serviceman, *(kadın)* servicewoman
org [org] *n* organ *(music)*
organ [organ] *n* organ *(body part)*
organik [organik] *adj* organic
organizasyon [organizasjon] *n* organization
organizatör [organizatør] *n* **kişisel organizatör** *n* personal organizer
organize [organize] *adj* **organize etmek** *v* organize
organizma [organizma] *n* organism
orgazm [orgazm] *n* orgasm
orkestra [orkestra] *n* band *(musical group)*, orchestra; **orkestra şefi** *n* conductor
orkide [orkide] *n* orchid
orman [orman] *n* forest, jungle; **orman tavuğu** *n* grouse *(game bird)*; **yağmur ormanı** *n* rainforest
orta [orta] *adj* intermediate, mid ▹ *n* middle; **orta boy** *adj* medium-sized; **orta sınıf** *adj* middle-class; **orta yaşlı** *adj* middle-aged; **ortaya çıkarmak** *v* disclose; **ortaya çıkmak** *v* show up
Orta [orta] *n* middle; **Orta Afrika Cumhuriyeti** *n* Central African Republic; **Orta Amerika** *n* Central America; **Orta Çağ** *n* Middle Ages; **Orta Doğu** *n* Middle East
ortaçağ [ortatʃa:] *adj* mediaeval
ortak [ortak] *adj* joint; **ortak görüş** *n* communion; **ortak hesap** *n* joint account; **suç ortağı** *n* accomplice
ortalama [ortalama] *adj* average ▹ *n* average
ortaokul [ortaokul] *n* secondary school
oryantal [orjantal] *adj* oriental
ot [ot] *n* grass *(plant)*, *(esrar)* grass *(marijuana)*; **hardal otu** *n* rape *(plant)*; **kokulu otlar** *n* herbs; **süpürge otu** *n* heather; **yabani ot** *n* weed; **yabani ot öldürücü** *n* weedkiller
otel [otel] *n* hotel; **gençlerin kaldığı otel** *n* youth hostel; **Bana bir otelde yer ayırtabilir misiniz?** Can you book me into a hotel?; **Bir otel arıyoruz** We're looking for a hotel; **Bir otel tavsiye edebilir misiniz?** Can you recommend a hotel?; **Bu otele taksi ne kadar?** How much is the taxi fare to this hotel?; **Şu otele en kolay nasıl gidebilirim?** What's the best way to get to this hotel?; **Otelde kalıyorum** I'm staying at a hotel; **Oteli yönetiyor** He runs the hotel; **Otelinizde tekerlekli sandalye girişi var mı?** Is your hotel accessible to wheelchairs?
oto [oto] *n* car; **oto kiralama** *n* car rental; **oto yarışı** *n* motor racing; **oto yıkama** *n* car wash
otobüs [otobys] *n* bus; **hava alanı otobüsü** *n* airport bus; **otobüs bileti** *n* bus ticket; **otobüs durağı** *n* bus stop; **otobüs terminali** *n* bus station; **tur otobüsü** *n* coach *(vehicle)*; **... otobüsü ne kadarda**

bir geliyor? How often are the buses to...?; **... otobüsü ne sıklıkta geliyor?** How frequent are the buses to...?; **... otobüsüne nereden binebilirim?** Where can I get a bus to...?, Where do I catch the bus to...?, Where do I get a bus for...?; **... a bir sonraki otobüs kaçta?** When is the next bus to...?; **... a ilk otobüs kaçta?** When is the first bus to...?; **... a otobüs var mı?** Is there a bus to...?; **... a son otobüs kaçta?** When is the last bus to...?; **Affedersiniz,... a hangi otobüs gidiyor?** Excuse me, which bus goes to...?; **Bu otobüs... a gider mi?** Does this bus go to...?; **Buraya en yakın otobüs durağı nerede?** Where is the nearest bus stop?; **Havaalanına otobüs var mı?** Is there a bus to the airport?; **Kente otobüs var mı?** Is there a bus to the city?; **Nereden otobüs kartı alabilirim?** Where can I buy a bus card?; **Otobüs durağı buraya ne kadar uzakta?** How far is the bus stop?; **Otobüs ne zaman geliyor?** What time does the bus arrive?; **Otobüs ne zaman kalkacak?** What time does the bus leave?; **Otobüs terminali nerede?** Where is the bus station?; **Otobüs terminaline ne kadar uzaktayız?** How far are we from the bus station?; **Plaja otobüs var mı?** Is there a bus to the beach?; **Son otobüs kaçta?** What time is the last bus?; **Tur otobüsü ne zaman kalkıyor?** When is the bus tour of the town?

otomat [otomat] *n* **bilet otomatı** *n* ticket machine

otomatik [otomatik] *adj* automatic; **otomatik ödeme** *n* direct debit; **otomatik olarak** *adv* automatically; **otomatik satış makinesi** *n* vending machine; **Bu araba otomatik mi?** Is it an automatic car?; **Otomatik olsun lütfen** An automatic, please

otopark [otopark] *n* car park; **otopark ödeme cihazı** *n* parking meter; **otopark bileti** *n* parking ticket; **Buralarda bir otopark var mı?** Is there a car park near here?

otostop [otostop] *n* hitchhike; **otostop yapma** *n* hitchhiking

otostopçu [otostoptʃu] *n* hitchhiker

otoyol [otojol] *n* motorway; **Bu otoyol ücretli mi?** Is there a toll on this motorway?; **Otoyola nereden gidebilirim?** How do I get to the motorway?; **Otoyolda trafik yoğun mu?** Is the traffic heavy on the motorway?

oturak [oturak] *n* **Oturağınız var mı?** Do you have a potty?

oturma [oturma] *n* **oturma odası** *n* living room

oturmak [oturmak] *v* occupy, sit down ▷ *vi* sit; **geç saatlere kadar oturmak** *v* stay up; **oturma odası** *n* sitting room; **Nereye oturabilirim** Where can I sit down?; **Oturabileceğim bir yer var mı?** Is there somewhere I can sit down?; **Oturabilir miyim?** Can

I sit here?
oturum [oturum] *n* **oturum açmak** *v* log in, log on; **oturum kapatmak** *v* log off, log out
otuz [otuz] *number* thirty; **Otuz numaralı vagon nerede?** Where is carriage number thirty?
ova [ova] *n* plain
oval [oval] *adj* oval
ovalamak [ovalamak] *v* scrub
oy [oj] *n* vote; **oy birliği** *n* consensus; **oy propagandası yapmak** *v* canvass ▷ *v* **oy vermek** *v* vote
oybirliğiyle [ojbirləəjle] *adj* unanimous
oymak [ojmak] *vt (ağaç)* carve
oynamak [ojnamak] *vt* play *(in sport)*; **kumar oynamak** *v* gamble; **Tenis oynamak istiyoruz** We'd like to play tennis
oynatıcı [ojnatədʒə] *n* **DVD oynatıcı** *n* DVD player
oyuk [ojuk] *adj* hollow
oyun [ojun] *n* game, play; **aile oyunları** *n* board game; **çocuk oyun grubu** *n* playgroup; **bilgisayar oyunu** *n* computer game; **dama oyunu** *npl* draughts; **dart oyunu** *npl* darts; **domino oyunu** *npl* dominoes; **halat çekme oyunu** *n* tug-of-war; **oyun alanı** *n* playground, playing field; **oyun kartı** *n* playing card; **oyun konsolu** *n* games console; **oyun saati** *n* playtime; **oyun salonu** *n* amusement arcade; **oyun yazarı** *n* playwright; **Buralarda çocuk oyun alanı var mı?** Is there a play park near here?; **Oyun oynayabilir miyim?** Can I play video games?
oyunbozan [ojunbozan] *n* spoilsport
oyuncak [ojundʒak] *n* toy; **oyuncak ayı** *n* teddy bear; **oyuncak bebek** *n* doll
oyuncu [ojundʒu] *adj (oyunbaz)* playful ▷ *n (spor)* player *(of sport)*; **kadın oyuncu** *n* actress; **oyuncu kadrosu** *n* cast; **tenis oyuncusu** *n* tennis player
oyunculuk [ojundʒuluk] *n* acting
ozon [ozon] *n* ozone; **ozon tabakası** *n* ozone layer

öd [ød] *n* **ödü kopmak** *adj* petrified
ödeme [ødeme] *n* payment; **ödeme günü geçmiş** *adj* overdue; **banka ödeme emri** *n* standing order
ödemek [ødemek] *vi* pay; **geri ödeme** *n* repayment; **geri ödemek** *v* pay back, repay; **otomatik ödeme** *n* direct debit; **Ayrıca bir şey ödeyecek miyim?** Is there a supplement to pay?; **Şimdi mi ödemem gerekiyor?** Do I pay in advance?; **Şimdi mi ödeyeceğim, sonra mı?** Do I pay now or later?
ödenecek [ødenedʒek] *adj* payable
ödenti [ødenti] *n* income; **hastalık ödentisi** *n* sick pay
ödev [ødev] *n* role; **ev ödevi** *n* homework
ödül [ødyl] *n* award, prize, reward; **ödül töreni** *n* prize-giving
ödüllü [ødylly] *n* prizewinner
ödün [ødyn] *n* compromise; **ödün vermek** *v* compromise
ödünç [ødyntʃ] *n* **ödünç almak** *v* borrow; **ödünç vermek** *v* lend, loan
öfke [øfke] *n* anger; **öfke nöbeti** *n* tantrum; **öfkeden çıldırmış** *adj* furious; **öfkeyle bakmak** *v* glare
öfkeli [øfkeli] *adj* cross
öğle [øːle] *n* midday, noon; **Öğlen** at midday
öğlen [øːlen] *n* midday, noon, at midday; **öğle yemeği** *n* lunch; **öğleden önce** *abbr* a.m.; **öğleden sonra** *abbr* afternoon, p.m.; **öğleden sonra** in the afternoon; **Öğle yemeğinde buluşabilir miyiz?** Can we meet for lunch?; **Öğlen boşum, yemek yiyebilirim** I'm free for lunch; **Müze öğleden sonra açık mı?** Is the museum open in the afternoon?; **Saat öğlen on iki** It's twelve midday; **yarın öğleden sonra** tomorrow afternoon
öğrenci [øːrendʒi] *n* learner, pupil *(learner)*, student; **askeri öğrenci** *n* cadet; **öğrenci indirimi** *n* student discount; **öğrenci sürücü** *n* learner driver; **öğrenci yurdu** *n* hostel; **üniversite sonrası eğitim yapan öğrenci** *n* postgraduate; **erkek öğrenci** *n* schoolboy; **kız öğrenci** *n* schoolgirl; **olgun öğrenci** *n* mature student; **yatılı öğrenci** *n* boarder; **Öğrenci indirimi var mı?** Are there any reductions for

students?; **Öğrenciyim** I'm a student
öğrenmek [øːrenmek] *v* learn
öğretim [øːretim] *n* tuition; **öğretim ücreti** *npl* tuition fees
öğretme [øːretme] *n* teaching
öğretmek [øːretmek] *v* teach
öğretmen [øːretmen] *n* instructor, schoolteacher, teacher; **öğretmen odası** *n* staffroom; **özel öğretmen** *n* tutor; **direksiyon öğretmeni** *n* driving instructor; **yardımcı öğretmen** *n* classroom assistant; **yedek öğretmen** *n* supply teacher
öğün [øːyn] *n* meal
öğüt [øːyt] *n* advice, tip *(suggestion)*
öğütmek [øːytmek] *vt* grind
ökseotu [økseotu] *n* mistletoe
öksürmek [øksyrmek] *vi* cough; **Öksürüyorum** I have a cough
öksürük [øksyryk] *n* cough; **öksürük şurubu** *n* cough mixture; **Öksürüyorum** I have a cough
ölçek [øltʃek] *n* gauge
ölçmek [øltʃmek] *v* gauge, measure
ölçü [øltʃy] *n* scale *(measure)*
ölçüler [øltʃyler] *npl* measurements
ölçüsüz [øltʃysyz] *adj* extortionate; **ölçüsüz içme** *n* binge drinking
öldürmek [øldyrmek] *v* kill
ölmek [ølmek] *v* die
ölü [øly] *adj* dead ▷ *adv* dead
ölüm [øljym] *n* death
ölümcül [ølymdʒyl] *adj* fatal, terminal ▷ *adv* terminally
ön [øn] *adj* front ▷ *n* front; **adının ön harflerini yazmak** *v* initial; **ön ad** *n* first name; **ön adı** *n* Christian name; **ön cam** *n* windscreen; **ön eleme listesi** *n* shortlist; **ön lamba** *n* headlamp, headlight; **ön plan** *n* foreground; **ön yemek** *n* starter; **önüne gelenle yatmak** *v* sleep around; **önden gitmek** *v* go ahead; **öne eğilmek** *v* lean forward; **göz önünde tutarak** *prep* considering; **Öne bakan koltuk olsun lütfen** Facing the front, please; **Hangisi ön kapının anahtarı?** Which is the key for the front door?
önce [øndʒe] *conj* before; **öğleden önce** *abbr* a.m.; **önceden ödenmiş** *adj* prepaid; **önceden rezervasyon** *n* advance booking; **daha önce** *adv* earlier; **daha önceden** *adv* beforehand, previously; **daha önceden olmamış** *adj* unprecedented; **doğum öncesi** *adj* antenatal; **Noel öncesi** *n* advent; **sondan bir önceki** *adj* penultimate; **tarih öncesi** *adj* prehistoric; **yemek öncesi içki** *n* aperitif; **önceki gün** the day before yesterday; **Ayrılmadan önce evi temizlememiz gerekiyor mu?** Do we have to clean the house before we leave?; **saat beşten önce** before five o'clock; **Daha önce bu modelde saç kesmiş miydiniz?** Have you cut my type of hair before?
önceden [øndʒeden] *adv* before

önceki [øndʒeki] *adj* preceding, previous ▷ *adv* formerly
öncelik [øndʒelik] *n* priority; **öncelik belirlemek** *v* put in; **öncelik getirmek** *v* bring forward
öncelikle [øndʒelikle] *adv* firstly
önde [ønde] *adv* ahead
önem [ønem] *n* importance, significance; **önemsiz şey** *n* trifle
önemli [ønemli] *adj* crucial, important, significant, vital; **önemli olay** *n* highlight; **önemli olmak** *v* matter; **çok önemli** *adj* momentous
önemsiz [ønemsiz] *adj* trivial, unimportant
öneri [øneri] *n* proposal, recommendation, suggestion
önermek [ønermek] *v* propose, suggest
öngörmek [øngørmek] *v* foresee, predict
önlem [ønlem] *n* caution, precaution
önleme [ønleme] *n* prevention
önlemek [ønlemek] *v* prevent; **ter önleyici deodorant** *n* antiperspirant
önlük [ønlyk] *n* apron, pinafore; **mama önlüğü** *n* bib
önsezi [ønsezi] *n* intuition
önünde [ønynde] *prep* before
önyargı [ønjargə] *n* prejudice; **önyargılardan arındırma** *n* liberation
önyargılı [ønjargələ] *adj* prejudiced
öpmek [øpmek] *v* kiss
öpücük [øpydʒyk] *n* kiss
ördek [ørdek] *n* duck
örgü [ørgy] *n* knitting; **örgü şişi** *n* knitting needle; **saç örgüsü** *n* pigtail, plait
örmek [ørmek] *vt* knit
örneğin [ørneji:n] *abbr* e.g., i.e.
örnek [ørnek] *adj* model ▷ *n* example, instance, sample
örtmek [ørtmek] *v* cover
örtü [ørty] *n* cover; **bitki örtüsü** *n* vegetation; **masa örtüsü** *n* tablecloth; **yatak örtüsü** *n* bedspread
örümcek [ørymdʒek] *n* spider; **örümcek ağı** *n* cobweb
ötesinde [øtesinde] *prep* beyond
övmek [øvmek] *v* praise
övücü [øvydʒy] *adj* complimentary
öykü [øjky] *n* story; **özyaşam öyküsü** *n* autobiography; **çizgi öykü** *n* comic strip; **kısa öykü** *n* short story; **yaşam öyküsü** *n* biography
öyle [øjle] *adv* so; **öyle ki** *conj* so (that)
öylesine [øjlesine] *adv* so
öyleyse [øjlejse] *adv* then
öz [øz] *adv* **kısa ve öz** *adj* concise
Özbekistan [øzbekistan] *n* Uzbekistan
özdeş [øzdeʃ] *adj* identical
özdisiplin [øzdisiplin] *n* self-discipline
özel [øzel] *adj* private, special; **özel öğretmen** *n* tutor; **özel koruma** *n* bodyguard; **özel mülk** *n* private property; **özel yaşam** *n* privacy; **kişinin evinin önündeki özel yol** *n* driveway; **yayalara özel bölge** pedestrian precinct; **Özel sağlık sigortam var** I have private

health insurance; **Sizinle özel olarak konuşabilir miyim?** Can I speak to you in private?
özelleştirmek [øzelleʃtirmek] *v* privatize
özellik [øzellik] *adj* particular ▷ *n* feature
özellikle [øzellikle] *adv* especially, particularly, specially, specifically
özellikler [øzellikler] *npl* specs
özen [øzen] *n* care, attention; **özenli bir şekilde** *adv* cautiously
özerk [øzerk] *adj* autonomous
özerklik [øzerklik] *n* autonomy
özet [øzet] *n* outline, summary; **hesap özeti** *n* bank statement
özetlemek [øzetlemek] *v* sum up, summarize
özgeçmiş [øzgetʃmiʃ] *n* curriculum vitae
özgü [øzgy] *adj* special, unique to; **Bu şehre özgü bir şey istiyorum** Have you anything typical of this town?; **Bu yöreye özgü bir şey denemek istiyorum lütfen** I'd like to try something local, please; **Bu yöreye özgü bir şey istiyorum** Do you have anything typical of this region?; **Yöreye özgü bir şey ısmarlamak istiyorum** I'd like to order something local
özgün [øzgyn] *adj* authentic, original
özgür [øzgyr] *adj* free *(no restraint)*
özgürlük [øzgyrlyk] *n* freedom
özgüven [øzgyven] *n* confidence *(self-assurance)*
özkontrol [øzkontrol] *n* self-control
özlemek [øzlemek] *v* long
özlü [øzly] *adj* lush
özlük [øzlyk] *n* person, individual; **özlük hakları** *n* civil rights
özsavunma [øssavunma] *n* self-defence
özür [øzyr] *n* alibi, apology, excuse ▷ *v* **özür beyan etmek** *v* excuse
özür dilemek [øzyrdilemek] *v* apologize
özürlü [øzyrly] *adj* disabled, handicapped; **Özürlüler için girişiniz var mı?** Do you provide access for the disabled?; **Özürlüler için indiriminiz var mı?** Is there a reduction for disabled people?; **Özürlüler için kolaylıklarınız nelerdir?** What facilities do you have for disabled people?; **Özürlüler için tuvaletiniz var mı?** Are there any toilets for the disabled?
özürlüler [øzyrlyler] *npl* disabled
özverili [øzverili] *adj* devoted
özyaşam [øzjaʃam] *n* **özyaşam öyküsü** *n* autobiography

P

paha [paha] *n* price, value; **paha biçmek** *v* appreciate
pahalı [pahalə] *adj* dear *(expensive)*, expensive; **hayat pahalılığı** *n* cost of living; **pahalı olmayan** *adj* inexpensive; **pahalı sezon** *n* high season; **Çok pahalı** It's quite expensive; **Benim için çok pahalı** It's too expensive for me
paket [paket] *n* package, packet, parcel; **paket kağıdı** *n* wrapping paper; **paket tatil** *n* package holiday; **paket tur** *n* package tour; **paket yemek** *n* packed lunch; **sımsıkı paketlenmiş** *adj* compact; **Bu paket kaça gider?** How much is it to send this parcel?; **Bu paketi postalamak istiyorum** I'd like to send this parcel
paketleme [paketleme] *n* packaging
paketlemek [paketlemek] *v* wrap up ▷ *vt* pack
paketlenmiş [paketlenmiʃ] *adj* packed
Pakistan [pakistan] *adj* Pakistani ▷ *n* Pakistan
Pakistanlı [pakistanlə] *n* Pakistani
palamut [palamut] *n* **meşe palamudu** *n* acorn
palanga [palanga] *n* tackle
palmiye [palmije] *n* palm *(tree)*
palto [palto] *n* overcoat
palyaço [paljatʃo] *n* clown
pamuk [pamuk] *n* cotton wool, *(bitki)* cotton; **pamuk helva** *n* candyfloss; **pamuklu kalın tişört** *n* sweatshirt
Panama [panama] *n* Panama
pancar [pandʒar] *n* beetroot
panç [pantʃ] *n* punch *(hot drink)*
panda [panda] *n* panda
pandantif [pandantif] *n* pendant
pandispanya [pandispanja] *n* sponge *(cake)*
pandomim [pandomim] *n* pantomime
panik [panik] *n* panic, scare ▷ *v* **paniğe kapılmak** *v* panic
pansiyoner [pansijoner] *n* lodger
panter [panter] *n* panther
pantolon [pantolon] *npl* trousers; **pantolon askıları** *npl* braces
panzehir [panzehir] *n* antidote
papa [papa] *n* pope
papağan [papa:an] *n* parrot
papatya [papatja] *n* daisy
papaz [papaz] *n* **papaz yardımcısı** *n* vicar

papazlık [papazlək] *n* ministry *(religion)*
papyon [papjon] *v* **papyon kravat** *n* bow tie
para [para] *n* money; **fazla para çekme** *n* overdraft; **hesabından çekilen para** *n* debit; **hesabından fazla para çekmiş** *adj* overdrawn; **madeni para** *n* coin; **para iadesi** *n* rebate, refund ▹ *v* **para iadesi yapmak** *v* refund; **Bana acilen para gönderilmesini ayarlayabilir misiniz?** Can you arrange to have some money sent over urgently?; **Hesabımdan para transferi yapmak istiyorum** I would like to transfer some money from my account; **Hiç param yok** I have no money; **Param bitti** I have run out of money; **Paramı geri alabilir miyim?** Can I have my money back?; **Paramı geri istiyorum** I want my money back
para-sailing [parasailing] *n* **Para-sailing için nereye gitmek gerek?** Where can you go para-sailing?
parafin [parafin] *n* paraffin
paragliding [paragliding] *n* **Paragliding için nereye gidebiliriz?** Where can you go paragliding?
paragraf [paragraf] *n* paragraph
Paraguay [paraguaj] *adj* Paraguayan ▹ *n* Paraguay
Paraguaylı [paraguajlə] *n* Paraguayan
paralel [paralel] *adj* parallel
paramedik [paramedik] *n* paramedic
parantez [parantez] *n* **köşeli parantezler** *npl* brackets
parasal [parasal] *adj* monetary; **parasal kaynak** *npl* funds
parascending [parasdʒending] *n* **Parascending yapmak isterdim** I'd like to go parascending
parasetamol [parasetamol] *n* **Parasetamol rica ediyorum** I'd like some paracetamol
paraşüt [paraʃyt] *n* parachute
parça [partʃa] *n* bit, chip *(small piece)*, chunk, part, piece, portion, scrap *(small piece)*, *(müzik)* passage *(musical)*; **iri parça** *n* lump; **kağıt parçası** *n* slip *(paper)*; **yedek parça** *n* spare part
parçalamak [partʃalamak] *vt* smash
pardon [pardon] *part* **Pardon, anlayamadım** Sorry, I didn't catch that; **Pardon, orası benim yerim** Excuse me, that's my seat
parfüm [parfym] *n* perfume
park [park] *n* park; **konulu eğlence parkı** *n* theme park; **milli park** *n* national park; **park etme** *n* parking ▹ *v* **park etmek** *v* park; **yol kenarında geçici park yeri** *n* layby; **Arabamı buraya park edebilir miyim?** Can I park here?; **Arabamı nereye park edebilirim?** Where can I park the car?; **Karavanımızı buraya park edebilir miyiz?** Can we park our caravan here?; **Ne kadarlığına park edebilirim?** How long can I park here?; **Yanımıza park edebilir miyiz?** Can we park by our site?

parka [parka] *n* **su geçirmez parka** *n* cagoule
parkmetre [parkmetre] *n* **Parkmetre bozuk** The parking meter is broken; **Parkmetre için bozuk paranız var mı?** Do you have change for the parking meter?
parkur [parkur] *n* **yarış parkuru** *n* racecourse
parlak [parlak] *adj* bright, shiny; **parlak alev** *n* blaze
parlamak [parlamak] *v* shine ▷ *vi* flash
parlamento [parlamento] *n* parliament
parmak [parmak] *n* finger; **ayak parmağı** *n* toe; **baş parmak** *n* thumb; **işaret parmağı** *n* index finger; **parmak izi** *n* fingerprint; **parmaklarının ucunda yürüme** *n* tiptoe; **parmaksız eldiven** *n* mitten
parmaklık [parmaklək] *n* rail ▷ *npl* railings
parti [parti] *n* *(grup)* party *(group)*, *(sosyal etkinlik)* party *(social gathering)*; **bekarlığa veda partisi** *(erkek)* *n* stag night; **yemekli parti** *n* dinner party
partner [partner] *n* partner; **Bu partnerim** This is my partner; **Partnerim var** I have a partner
pas [pas] *n* *(metal)* rust; **paslanmaz çelik** *n* stainless steel
pasaklı [pasaklə] *adj* sloppy
pasaport [pasaport] *n* passport; **pasaport kontrol** *n* passport control; **İşte pasaportum** Here is my passport; **Çocuk bu pasaportta** The child is on this passport; **Çocuklar bu pasaportta** The children are on this passport; **Pasaportum çalındı** My passport has been stolen; **Pasaportumu kaybettim** I've lost my passport; **Pasaportumu unutmuşum** I've forgotten my passport
pasif [pasif] *adj* passive
Pasifik [pasifik] *n* Pacific
Paskalya [paskalja] *n* Easter; **Paskalya yumurtası** *n* Easter egg
paslı [paslə] *adj* rusty
paso [paso] *n* pass *(permit)*
paspas [paspas] *n* *(ayak silme)* mat, *(yer silme)* mop
paspaslamak [paspaslamak] *v* mop up
pasta [pasta] *n* cake; **kremalı pasta** *n* gateau; **pastanın üzerindeki şekerli süsleme** *n* icing
pastırma [pastərma] *n* **domuz pastırması** *n* bacon
pastörize [pastørize] *adj* pasteurized
patates [patates] **(patatesler)** *n* potato; **patates kızartması** *npl* chips; **patates püresi** *n* mashed potatoes; **patates soyucu** *n* potato peeler
patavatsız [patavatsəz] *adj* tactless
paten [paten] *npl* rollerskates; **buz pateni** *n* ice-skating; **buz pateni sahası** *n* ice rink; **paten alanı** *n* rink, skating rink; **paten yapma** *n* skating ▷ *v* **paten yapmak** *v* skate; **patenle kaymak** *n*

rollerskating
patenler [patenler] *npl* skates
patik [patik] *n* **bale patiği** *npl* ballet shoes
patika [patika] *n* footpath, lane *(driving)*, path; **Patikadan ayrılmayın** Keep to the path
patlak [patlak] *n* puncture
patlama [patlama] *n* blast, explosion; **patlama sesi** *n* bang
patlamak [patlamak] *v* *(delinerek)* burst, *(havaya uçarak)* explode, *(ses çıkararak)* bang
patlayıcı [patlajədʒə] *adj* **patlayıcı madde** *n* explosive
patlıcan [patlədʒan] *n* aubergine
patron [patron] *n* boss; **patronluk taslamak** *v* boss around
pay [paj] *n* share; **boşluk payı** *(tavanda)* *n* headroom
payalamak [pajalamak] *v* tick off
paylaşmak [pajlaʃmak] *v* share, *(iş/masraf)* club together
paylaştırmak [pajlaʃtərmak] *v* share out
pazar [pazar] *n* *(piyasa)* market; **pazar araştırması** *n* market research; **pazar yeri** *n* marketplace
Pazar [pazar] *n* Sunday; **Üç Ekim Pazar** It's Sunday the third of October; **Pazar günü** on Sunday
pazarlama [pazarlama] *n* marketing
pazarlık [pazarlək] *n* bargain; **pazarlık etmek** *v* haggle
Pazartesi [pazartesi] *n* Monday; **Pazartesi'den Çarşamba'ya kadar kalmak istiyorum** I want to stay from Monday till Wednesday; **Pazartesi'nden beri kusuyorum** I've been sick since Monday; **On beş Haziran Pazartesi** It's Monday the fifteenth of June; **Pazartesi günü** on Monday
PC [pi.si:] *n* PC
PDF [pi:di:ef] *n* PDF
peçe [petʃe] *n* veil
peçete [petʃete] *n* napkin; **kağıt peçete** *n* serviette
ped [ped] *n* pad, sanitary towel; **fare pedi** *n* mouse mat
pedal [pedal] *n* pedal; **gaz pedalı** *n* accelerator
pedofil [pedofil] *n* paedophile
pekala [pekala] *adv* fine
Pekin [pekin] *n* Beijing
Pekinez [pekinez] *n* Pekinese
pelikan [pelikan] *n* pelican
pembe [pembe] *adj* pink; **pembe şarap** *n* rosé; **pembemsi leylak rengi** *adj* mauve
penaltı [penaltə] *n* penalty
pencere [pendʒere] *n* window; **pencere camı** *n* window pane; **pencere pervazı** *n* windowsill; **Koltuğum pencere kenarında olsun** I'd like a window seat; **Pencere açılmıyor** The window won't open; **Pencereyi açabilir miyim?** May I open the window?; **Pencereyi açamıyorum** I can't open the window; **Pencereyi kapatabilir miyim?** May I close the window?
pençe [pentʃe] *n* claw, paw
penguen [penguen] *n* penguin
peni [peni] *n* penny
penisilin [penisilin] *n* penicillin;

Penisiline alerjim var I'm allergic to penicillin
pense [pense] *npl* pliers
pentatlon [pentatlon] *n* pentathlon
perakende [perakende] *n* retail; **perakende fiyatı** *n* retail price
perakendeci [perakendedʒi] *n* retailer
perde [perde] *n* curtain, *(ses)* pitch *(sound)*
performans [performans] *n* performance *(functioning)*; **performans göstermek** *v* perform; **sahne performansı** *n* performance *(artistic)*
perhiz [perhiz] *n* diet, fast; **büyük perhizin arife günü** *n* Shrove Tuesday; **Büyük perhizin ilk Çarşambası** *n* Ash Wednesday
peri [peri] *n* fairy; **peri masalı** *n* fairytale
perili [perili] *adj* haunted
perma [perma] *n* perm; **Saçım permalı** My hair is permed
personel [personel] *n* personnel
perspektif [perspektif] *n* perspective
Perşembe [perʃembe] *n* Thursday; **Perşembe günü** on Thursday
Peru [peru] *adj* Peruvian ▷ *n* Peru
peruk [peruk] *n* wig; **yarım peruk** *n* toupee
Perulu [perulu] *n* Peruvian
peş [peʃ] *n, v* **peşine takılmak** *v* pursue
pet [pet] *nf* can
petrol [petrol] *n* **petrol kuyusu** *n* oil well; **petrol platformu** *n* oil rig, rig; **petrol rafinerisi** *n* oil refinery; **petrol sızması** *n* oil slick
peynir [pejnir] *n* cheese; **süzme peynir** *n* cottage cheese
pırasa [pərasa] *n* leek
pırıl pırıl [pərəlpərəl] *adj* brilliant
pijama [piʒama] *npl* pyjamas
piknik [piknik] *n* picnic
piksel [piksel] *n* pixel
pil [pil] *n* battery; **kalp pili** *n* pacemaker; **Bu makineye uygun pil var mı?** Do you have batteries for this camera?; **Pil satıyor musunuz?** Do you have any batteries?
pilot [pilot] *n* pilot
pint [pint] *n (içki)* pint
piramit [piramit] *n* pyramid
pire [pire] *n* flea
pirinç [pirintʃ] *n (metal)* brass, *(yiyecek)* rice; **esmer pirinç** *n* brown rice
pirzola [pirzola] *n* cutlet; **domuz pirzolası** *n* pork chop
pis [pis] *adj* dirty; **pis kokulu** *adj* smelly; **Oda pis** The room is dirty; **Pis** It's dirty
piskopos [piskopos] *n* bishop
pist [pist] *n* **kayak alıştırma pisti** *n* nursery slope; **uçak pisti** *n* runway; **yarış pisti** *n* racetrack
piston [piston] *n* piston
pişirme [piʃirme] *n* cooking
pişirmek [piʃirmek] *v* boil, cook; **fırında pişirme** *n* baking; **fırında pişirmek** *v* bake; **fırında pişirilmiş** *adj* baked
pişmanlık [piʃmanlək] *n* regret
piyade [pijade] *n* infantry
piyango [pijango] *n* lottery
piyanist [pijanist] *n* pianist

piyano [pijano] *n* piano
pizza [pizza] *n* pizza
plaj [plaʒ] *n* beach; **Buralarda iyi bir plaj var mı?** Are there any good beaches near here?; **Plaj ne kadar uzakta?** How far is the beach?; **Plaja gidiyorum** I'm going to the beach; **Plaja otobüs var mı?** Is there a bus to the beach?; **Plajdan ne kadar uzaktayız?** How far are we from the beach?
plaka [plaka] *n (otomobil)* number plate
plaket [plaket] *n* plaque
plan [plan] *n* plan, scheme; **arka plan** *n* background; **ön plan** *n* foreground; **gizli plan** *v* plot *(conspire)*; **şehir planlama** *n* town planning; **sokak planı** *n* street plan
planlama [planlama] *n* planning
planlamak [planlamak] *v* plan
planör [planør] *n* glider; **planörle uçma** *n* gliding
plastik [plastik] *adj* plastic ▷ *n* plastic; **plastik cerrahi** *n* plastic surgery
platform [platform] *n* platform; **petrol platformu** *n* oil rig, rig; **... treni hangi platformdan kalkıyor?** Which platform does the train for... leave from?; **... treninin kalkacağı platform burası mı?** Is this the right platform for the train to...?; **Tren hangi platformdan kalkıyor?** Which platform does the train leave from?
platin [platin] *n* platinum
PlayStation® [plajstation] *n* PlayStation®
plazma [plazma] *n* **plazma ekran** *n* plasma screen; **plazma TV** *n* plasma TV
pnömatik [pnømatik] *adj* **pnömatik matkap** *n* pneumatic drill
podcast [poddʒast] *n* podcast
pohpohlamak [pohpohlamak] *v* flatter
pohpohlanmış [pohpohlanməʃ] *adj* flattered
poker [poker] *n* poker
poliklinik [poliklinik] *n* clinic
polis [polis] *n* police; **erkek polis** *n* policeman; **kadın polis** *n* policewoman; **polis görevlisi** *n* police officer; **polis istasyonu** *n* police station; **Polis çağırın** Call the police; **Polis karakolu nerede?** Where is the police station?; **Polis karakolunu arıyorum** I need to find a police station; **Polise haber vermemiz gerekiyor** We will have to report it to the police; **Sigortam için polise bildirmemiz gerekiyor** I need a police report for my insurance
polisiye [polisije] *n* thriller
politik [politik] *adj* political
politika [politika] *npl* politics
politikacı [politikadʒə] *n* politician
polo [polo] *n* **polo gömlek** *n* polo shirt; **polo yakalı kazak** *n* polo-necked sweater
Polonezce [polonezdʒe] *n (dil)* Polynesian *(language)*

Polonezya [polonezja] *adj* Polynesian; **Polonezya Adaları** *n* Polynesia
Polonezyalı [polonezjalə] *n (kişi)* Polynesian *(person)*
Polonya [polonja] *adj* Polish ▹ *n* Poland
Polonyalı [polonjalə] *n* Polish
pompa [pompa] *n* pump; **bisiklet pompası** *n* bicycle pump; **Bisiklet pompanız var mı?** Do you have a bicycle pump?
pompalamak [pompalamak] *v* pump
popüler [popyler] *adj* popular; **popüler olmayan** *adj* unpopular
popülerlik [popylerlik] *n* popularity
porno [porno] *n* porn
pornografi [pornografi] *n* pornography
pornografik [pornografik] *adj* pornographic
porselen [porselen] *n* china
porsuk [porsuk] *n* badger; **porsuk ağacı** *n* yew
port [port] *n* **port bagaj** *n* luggage rack, roof rack
portakal [portakal] *n* orange; **portakal rengi** *adj* orange; **portakal suyu** *n* orange juice
portatif [portatif] *adj* portable; **portatif karyola** *n* camp bed
portbebe [portbebe] *n* carrycot
Portekiz [portekiz] *adj* Portuguese ▹ *n* Portugal
Portekizce [portekizdʒe] *n (dil)* Portuguese *(language)*
Portekizli [portekizli] *n (kişi)* Portuguese *(person)*
portföy [portføj] *n* portfolio
porto [porto] *n* **porto şarabı** *n* port *(wine)*
Portoriko [portoriko] *n* Puerto Rico
portre [portre] *n* portrait
post [post] *n* fleece; **koyun postu** *n* sheepskin
posta [posta] *n* mail, post *(mail)*; **istenmeyen posta** *n* junk mail; **posta ücreti** *n* postage; **posta damgası** *n* postmark; **posta havalesi** *n* postal order; **posta kutusu** *n* letterbox, mailbox, postbox; **sesli posta** *n* voicemail; **uçak postası** *n* airmail; **Acele posta ile ne kadar zamanda gider?** How long will it take by priority post?; **Normal postayla ne kadar sürer?** How long will it take by normal post?
postacı [postadʒə] **(postacılar)** *n* postman; **kadın postacı** *n* postwoman
postalamak [postalamak] *v* mail, post
postane [postane] *n* post office; **Postane ne zaman açılıyor?** When does the post office open?
poster [poster] *n* poster
potansiyel [potansijel] *adj* potential ▹ *n* potential
pound [pound] *n (İngiliz ağırlık birimi)* pound; **pound sterlin** *(İngiliz para birimi)* *n* pound sterling
pozisyon [pozisjon] *n* position
pratik [pratik] *adj* practical ▹ *n* practice; **pratik olarak** *adv* practically; **pratik olmayan** *adj*

impractical; **pratik yapmak** *v* practise
pratisyen [pratisjen] *n* **pratisyen hekim** *n* GP
prens [prens] *n* prince
prenses [prenses] *n* princess
pres [pres] *n* press, *(spor)* push-up
Presbiteryan [presbiterjan] *adj* Presbyterian ▹ *n* Presbyterian
prestij [prestiʒ] *n* prestige
prezervatif [prezervatif] *n* condom
prim [prim] *n* bonus
priz [priz] *n* socket
profesör [profesør] *n* professor
profesyonel [profesjonel] *adj* professional ▹ *n* professional
profesyonelce [profesjoneldʒe] *adv* professionally
program [program] *n* program, programme, schedule, timetable; **sohbet programı** *n* chat show; **Programa uygun gidiyoruz** We are on schedule; **Programın gerisindeyiz** We are slightly behind schedule
programcı [programdʒə] *n* programmer
programlama [programlama] *n* programming
programlamak [programlamak] *v* program
proje [proʒe] *n* project
projektör [proʒektør] *n* overhead projector, projector; **projektör ışığı** *n* floodlight
propaganda [propaganda] *n* propaganda; **oy propagandası yapmak** *v* canvass
protein [protein] *n* protein
Protestan [protestan] *adj* Protestant ▹ *n* Protestant
protesto [protesto] *n* protest ▹ *v* **protesto etmek** *v* protest
prova [prova] *n* rehearsal
psikiyatrik [psikijatrik] *adj* psychiatric
psikiyatrist [psikijatrist] *n* psychiatrist
psikolog [psikolog] *n* psychologist
psikoloji [psikoloʒi] *n* psychology
psikolojik [psikoloʒik] *adj* psychological
psikoterapi [psikoterapi] *n* psychotherapy
puding [puding] *n* pudding
pudra [pudra] *n* powder; **talk pudrası** *n* talcum powder
pul [pul] *n* stamp, *(balık)* scale *(tiny piece)*; **Pul nereden alabilirim?** Where can I buy stamps?; **Pul satan en yakın yer nerede?** Where is the nearest shop which sells stamps?; **Pul satıyor musunuz?** Do you sell stamps?
pulluk [pulluk] *n* plough
punkçu [puŋtʃu] *n* punk
puro [puro] *n* cigar
puset [puset] *n* pushchair
pusula [pusula] *n* compass
pürüzsüz [pyryssyz] *adj* smooth
püskürtmek [pyskyrtmek] *v* spray

q

Quaker [kuaker] *n* **Quaker mezhebinden** *n* Quaker

r

radar [radar] *n* radar
radyasyon [radjasjon] *n* radiation
radyatör [radjatør] *n* radiator; **Radyatör sızıntı yapıyor** There is a leak in the radiator
radyo [radjo] *n* radio; **dijital radyo** *n* digital radio; **radyo istasyonu** *n* radio station; **Radyoyu açabilir miyim?** Can I switch the radio on?; **Radyoyu kapatabilir miyim?** Can I switch the radio off?
radyoaktif [radjoaktif] *adj* radioactive
raf [raf] **(raflar)** *n* shelf; **kitap rafı** *n* bookshelf; **şömine rafı** *n* mantelpiece
rafineri [rafineri] *n* refinery; **petrol rafinerisi** *n* oil refinery
rağmen [ra:men] *conj* although
rahat [rahat] *adj* comfortable, cosy, laid-back, relaxed
rahatlamış [rahatlaməʃ] *adj*

relieved
rahatlık [rahatlək] *n* peace, comfort; **iç rahatlığı** *n* relief; **konfor ve rahatlık** *npl* mod cons
rahatsız [rahatsəz] *adj* inconvenient, uncomfortable; **rahatsız etmek** *v* disturb
rahatsızlık [rahatsəzlək] *n* inconvenience
rahibe [rahibe] *n* nun
rahip [rahip] *n* priest
raket [raket] *n* racket *(racquet)*, racquet; **tenis raketi** *n* tennis racket; **Raket kiralıyorlar mı?** Do they hire out rackets?; **Raket nereden kiralayabilirim?** Where can I hire a racket?
rakip [rakip] *adj* rival ▷ *n* adversary, rival; **rakip sahada maç** *n* away match
rakun [rakun] *n* racoon
Ramazan [ramazan] *n* Ramadan
rampa [rampa] *n* ramp
randevu [randevu] *n* appointment, engagement, rendezvous;**... ile randevum vardı** I have an appointment with...; **Doktordan randevu alabilir miyim?** Can I have an appointment with the doctor?; **Randevu almak istiyorum** I'd like to make an appointment; **Randevunuz var mıydı?** Do you have an appointment?
ranza [ranza] *n* berth, bunk, bunk beds
rapor [rapor] *n* report ▷ *v* **rapor vermek** *v* report
raptiye [raptije] *n* drawing pin, thumb tack
rastgele [rastgele] *adj* random
rastlantı [rastlantə] *n* coincidence
ravent [ravent] *n* rhubarb
ray [raj] *n* rail
reaktör [reaktør] *n* reactor
reçel [retʃel] *n* jam; **reçel kavanozu** *n* jam jar
reçete [retʃete] *n* prescription; **Bu reçeteyi nerede yaptırabilirim** Where can I get this prescription made up?
reçine [retʃine] *n* resin
red [red] *n* refusal
reddetme [reddetme] *n* refuse
reddetmek [reddetmek] *v* refuse, reject
reddeylemek [reddejlemek] *v* ignore
referans [referans] *n* reference; **referans kitabı** *n* handbook; **referans numarası** *n* reference number
refleks [refleks] *n* reflex
regl [regl] *n* menstruation
rehber [rehber] *n* **rehber köpek** *n* guide dog; **rehberli tur** *n* guided tour; **rehberlik etmek** *v* conduct; **telefon rehberi** *n* telephone directory; **telefon rehberi** *n* directory; **tur rehberi** *n* tour guide; **İngilizce rehberli turunuz var mı?** Is there a guided tour in English?; **Rehber köpeğim var** I have a guide dog; **Rehberli tur kaçta başlıyor?** What time does the guided tour begin?; **Rehberli yürüyüş var mı?** Are there any guided walks?
rehberlik [rehberlik] *n* **Bana rehberlik eder misiniz lütfen**

Can you guide me, please?
rehinci [rehindʒi] *n* pawnbroker
rehine [rehine] *n* hostage
rekabet [rekabet] *n* rivalry; **rekabete açık** *adj* competitive
reklam [reklam] *n* ad, advert, advertisement, commercial; **reklam arası** *n* commercial break; **reklam yapmak** *v* advertise
reklamcılık [reklamdʒələk] *n* advertising
ren [ren] *v* **ren geyiği** *n* reindeer
rende [rende] *n* plane *(tool)*
rendelemek [rendelemek] *v* grate
reng [reng] *n* **vişne çürüğü renginde** *adj* maroon
renk [reŋ] *n* colour; **açık renk** *(ten/saç) adj* fair *(light colour)*; **krem renkli** *adj* cream; **leylak renkli** *adj* lilac; **pembemsi leylak rengi** *adj* mauve; **portakal rengi** *adj* orange; **renk körü** *adj* colour-blind; **renkli televizyon** *n* colour television; **türkuvaz renkli** *adj* turquoise; **Bu makine için renkli film istiyorum** I need a colour film for this camera; **Bu rengi sevmedim** I don't like the colour; **Bu renk olsun** This colour, please; **Bunun başka rengi var mı?** Do you have this in another colour?; **Bunun renkli fotokopisini istiyorum lütfen** I'd like a colour photocopy of this, please; **Renkli film istiyorum lütfen** A colour film, please
renkli [reŋli] *adj* colourful, in colour
resepsiyon [resepsijon] *n* reception
resepsiyonist [resepsijonist] *n* receptionist
resim [resim] *n* painting, picture; **resim çerçevesi** *n* picture frame
resimleme [resimleme] *n (kitabı)* illustration
resmi [resmi] *adj* formal; **resmi olmayan** *adj* unofficial; **resmi tatil günü** *n* public holiday
ressam [ressam] *n* painter
restoran [restoran] *n* restaurant; **İyi bir restoran tavsiye edebilir misiniz?** Can you recommend a good restaurant?
restore [restore] *v* **restore etmek** *v* restore
reşit [reʃit] *n, adj* adult; **reşit olmayan** *adj* underage
revir [revir] *n* infirmary
revizyon [revizjon] *n* check-up, revision
revolver [revolver] *n* revolver
rezene [rezene] *n* fennel
rezervasyon [rezervasjon] *n* booking; **önceden rezervasyon** *n* advance booking; **rezerve etmek** *v* book; **Masa bu akşam saat dokuz için rezerve edildi** The table is booked for nine o'clock this evening; **Rezervasyonumu değiştirebilir miyim?** Can I change my booking?; **Rezervasyonumu iptal ettirmek istiyorum** I want to cancel my booking; **Rezervasyonumu mektupla teyid etmiştim** I confirmed my booking by letter
rıhtım [rəhtəm] *n* jetty, pier

rica [ridʒa] *n* appeal, request ▹ *v* **rica etmek** *v* appeal, request
rimel [rimel] *n* eyeliner, mascara
ringa [ringa] *n* **ringa balığı** *n* herring
risk [risk] *n* risk ▹ *v* **risk almak** *v* risk
riskli [riskli] *adj* risky
ritim [ritim] *n* beat, rhythm
robot [robot] *n* robot; **mutfak robotu** *n* food processor
roket [roket] *n* rocket
rollercoaster [rollerdʒoaster] *n* rollercoaster
rom [rom] *n* rum
roman [roman] *n* novel
romancı [romandʒə] *n* novelist
Romanesk [romanesk] *adj* Romanesque
romantik [romantik] *adj* romantic
Romanya [romanja] *n* Romania
romatizma [romatizma] *n* rheumatism
Romen [romen] *adj* Roman, Romanian
römork [rømork] *n* trailer
röntgen [røntgen] *n* X-ray ▹ *v* **röntgenini çekmek** *v* X-ray
rugbi [rugbi] *n* rugby
ruh [ruh] *n* soul, spirit; **ruh durumu** *n* mood; **ruh hali** *n* temper
ruj [ruʒ] *n* lipstick
rulet [rulet] *n* roulette
Rumen [rumen] *n (kişi)* Romanian *(person)*
Rumence [rumendʒe] *n (dil)* Romanian *(language)*
Rus [rus] *adj* Russian ▹ *n (kişi)* Russian *(person)*
Rusça [rustʃa] *n (dil)* Russian *(language)*
Rusya [rusja] *n* Russia
rüşvet [ryʃvet] *n* bribery ▹ *v* **rüşvet vermek** *v* bribe
rütbe [rytbe] *n* rank *(status)*
rüzgar [ryzgar] *n* wind; **ani rüzgar** *n* gust; **hafif rüzgar** *n* breeze; **şiddetli rüzgar** *n* gale; **rüzgar sörfü** *n* windsurfing; **rüzgara açık** *adj* bleak; **Rüzgar sörfü yapmak istiyorum** I'd like to go windsurfing
rüzgarlı [ryzgarlə] *adj* windy

S

saat [saat] *n (fırın vb)* timer, *(genelde)* clock, *(zaman)* hour; **açılış saatleri** *npl* opening hours; **çalar saat** *n* alarm clock; **çalışma saatleri** *npl* office hours; **çay saati** *n* teatime; **dijital saat** *n* digital watch; **esnek çalışma saati** *n* flexitime; **geç saatlere kadar oturmak** *v* stay up; **iş saatleri dışında** *adv* off-peak; **kapanış saati** *n* closing time; **kol saati** *n* watch; **oyun saati** *n* playtime; **saat başı** *adv* hourly; **saat kayışı** *n* watch strap; **saat yönünde** *adv* clockwise; **saatin aksi yönünde** *adv* anticlockwise; **saatli bomba** *n* time bomb; **sıkışık saat** *npl* peak hours; **sıkışık saatler** *n* rush hour; **yarım saat** *n* half-hour; **ziyaret saatleri** *npl* visiting hours; **Bir saatlik internet bağlantısı kaça?** How much is it to log on for an hour?; **Saati ne kadar?** How much is it per hour?; **Yolculuk iki saat sürüyor** The journey takes two hours; **Ziyaret saatleri nedir?** When are visiting hours?

sabah [sabah] *n* in the morning, morning; **bu sabah** this morning; **Beni yarın sabah yedide uyandırır mısınız?** I'd like an alarm call for tomorrow morning at seven o'clock; **Bu sabahtan beri kusuyorum** I've been sick since this morning; **Müze sabahları açık mı?** Is the museum open in the morning?; **Otobüs sabah kaçta hareket ediyor?** When does the coach leave in the morning?; **yarın sabah** tomorrow morning; **Yarın sabah boşum** I'm free tomorrow morning; **Yarın sabah onda ayrılıyorum** I will be leaving tomorrow morning at ten a.m.

sabahlık [sabahlək] *n* dressing gown

sabır [sabər] *n* patience

sabırlı [sabərlə] *adj* patient

sabırsız [sabərsəz] *adj* impatient

sabırsızlık [sabərsəzlək] *n* impatience

sabırsızlıkla [sabərsəzləkla] *adv* impatiently

sabit [sabit] *adj (değişmez)* constant, *(dengeli)* steady

sabitlemek [sabitlemek] *vt* fix

sabitlenmiş [sabitlenmiʃ] *adj* fixed

sabotaj [sabotaʒ] *n* sabotage; **sabote etmek** *v* sabotage

sabretmek [sabretmek] *v* hang on
sabun [sabun] *n* soap; **sabun tozu** *n* soap powder; **Sabun yok** There is no soap
sabunluk [sabunluk] *n* soap dish
saç [satʃ] *n* hair; **beyaz saçlı** *adj* grey-haired; **kızıl saçlı** *n* red-haired, redhead; **kızılımsı sarı saçlı** *adj* ginger; **saç örgüsü** *n* pigtail, plait; **saç bandı** *n* hairband; **saç fırçası** *n* hairbrush; **saç jölesi** *n* hair gel; **saç kestirme** *n* haircut; **saç kremi** *n* conditioner; **saç kurutma makinesi** *n* hairdryer; **saç maşası** *npl* straighteners; **saç modeli** *n* hairdo, hairstyle; **saç spreyi** *n* hair spray; **saç tokası** *n* hairgrip; **Saç kurutma makinesine ihtiyacım var** I need a hair dryer; **Saçım doğuştan düz** My hair is naturally straight; **Saçım doğuştan kıvırcık** My hair is naturally curly; **Saçım kuru** I have dry hair; **Saçım permalı** My hair is permed; **Saçım röfleli** My hair is highlighted; **Saçım yağlı** I have greasy hair; **Saçıma ne tavsiye edersiniz?** What do you recommend for my hair?; **Saçımı boyar mısınız lütfen?** Can you dye my hair, please?; **Saçımı düzleştirebilir misiniz?** Can you straighten my hair?; **Saçımı yıkar mısınız lütfen?** Can you wash my hair, please?
saçma [satʃma] *adj* absurd ▷ *n* nonsense
saçmalamak [satʃmalamak] *v* rave
sadakat [sadakat] *n* loyalty
sadakatle [sadakatle] *adv* faithfully
sadakatsiz [sadakatsiz] *adj* unfaithful
sade [sade] *adj* plain; **sade çikolata** *n* plain chocolate
sadece [sadedʒe] *adj* mere
sadık [sadək] *adj* faithful
saf [saf] *adj* daft, naive, pure
safari [safari] *n* safari
safir [safir] *n* sapphire
safra [safra] *n* **safra kesesi** *n* gall bladder; **safra kesesi taşı** *n* gallstone
safran [safran] *n* saffron
sağ [sa:] *adj (yan, yön)* right *(not left)*; **sağ elini kullanan** *adj* right-handed; **sağ kanat** *adj* right-wing; **sağdan trafik** *n* right-hand drive; **Sağa dönün** Turn right; **Sağdan ilk sokağa dönün** Take the first turning on your right
sağanak [sa:anak] *n* downpour
sağdıç [sa:dətʃ] *n* best man
sağduyu [sa:duju] *n* common sense, discretion
sağduyulu [sa:dujulu] *adj* sensible
sağır [sa:ər] *adj* deaf; **sağır edici** *adj* deafening; **Sağırım** I'm deaf
sağlam [sa:lam] *adj* sound, tough
sağlamak [sa:lamak] *v* provide; **ürün sağlamak** *v* yield; **geçimini sağlamak** *v* provide for; **mali destek sağlamak** *v* subsidize; **yarar sağlamak** *v* benefit
sağlıcakla [sa:lədʒakla] *excl*

cheerio!
sağlık [sa:lək] *n* health; **sağlık belgesi** *n* medical certificate; **sağlıklı yaşam** *n* keep-fit; **Özel sağlık sigortam var** I have private health insurance; **Sağlık sigortam yok** I don't have health insurance
sağlıklı [sa:ləklə] *adj* healthy
sağlıksız [sa:ləksəz] *adj* unfit, unhealthy
sağmak [sa:mak] *v* milk
saha [saha] *n (spor)* pitch *(sport)*; **buz pateni sahası** *n* ice rink; **golf sahası** *n* golf course; **hava sahası** *n* airspace; **kendi sahasında maç** *n* home match; **rakip sahada maç** *n* away match
sahil [sahil] *n* **sahil koruma görevlisi** *n* coastguard
sahip [sahip] *n* owner; **ev sahibi** *n* host *(entertains)*, landlord; **ev sahibesi** *n* landlady; **hisse sahibi** *n* shareholder; **sahip çıkmak** *v* own up; **sahip olmak** *v* have, own, possess; **toprak sahibi** *n* landowner; **Buranın sahibiyle konuşabilir miyim lütfen** Could I speak to the owner, please?
sahipsiz [sahipsiz] *adj* unattended
sahne [sahne] *n (olay, bölüm)* scene, *(tiyatro mekan)* stage; **sahne performansı** *n* performance *(artistic)*
Sahra [sahra] *n* Sahara
sahte [sahte] *n* fake, forgery
sakal [sakal] *n* beard
sakallı [sakallə] *adj* bearded
sakar [sakar] *adj* clumsy
sakat [sakat] *n* invalid
sakatlık [sakatlək] *n* disability
sakınca [sakəndʒa] *n* **Sakıncası yok** I don't mind; **Sizce sakıncası var mı?** Do you mind?
sakız [sakəz] *n* gum
sakin [sakin] *adj* calm ▷ *n (konut)* inhabitant, *(konut)* resident
sakinleşmek [sakinleʃmek] *v* calm down
sakinleştirici [sakinleʃtiridʒi] *n* tranquillizer
saklamak [saklamak] *v* *(korumak)* reserve ▷ *vi* hide
saklambaç [saklambatʃ] *n* hide-and-seek
saklı [saklə] *adj* hidden
saksafon [saksafon] *n* saxophone
saksağan [saksa:an] *n* magpie
sal [sal] *n* float, raft
salak [salak] *n* idiot
salakça [salaktʃa] *adj* idiotic
salam [salam] *n* salami
salaş [salaʃ] *adj* naff
salata [salata] *n* salad; **karışık salata** *n* mixed salad; **lahana salatası** *n* coleslaw; **meyve salatası** *n* fruit salad; **salata sosu** *n* salad dressing; **sirkeli salata sosu** *n* vinaigrette; **yeşil salata** *n* green salad
salatalık [salatalək] *n* cucumber
saldırgan [saldərgan] *adj* aggressive, offensive
saldırı [saldərə] *n* attack, offence; **terörist saldırı** *n* terrorist attack; **Saldırıya uğradım** I've been attacked
saldırmak [saldərmak] *v* mug ▷ *vt* attack
salgın [salgən] *n* epidemic

Salı [salə] *n* Tuesday; **Salı günü** on Tuesday
salınmak [salənmak] *v* sway
sallamak [sallamak] *v* rock; **el sallamak** *v* wave
sallanan [sallanan] *adj* unsteady
sallanma [sallanma] *n* swing
sallanmak [sallanmak] *vi* swing; **sallanan at** *n* rocking horse; **sallanan sandalye** *n* rocking chair
salon [salon] *n* hall, lounge, saloon; **bowling salonu** *n* bowling alley; **güzellik salonu** *n* beauty salon; **jimnastik salonu** *n* gym; **oyun salonu** *n* amusement arcade; **salon dansı** *n* ballroom dancing; **transit yolcu salonu** *n* transit lounge; **uçuş bekleme salonu** *n* departure lounge; **yemek salonu** *n* dining room; **Konser salonunda bu gece ne var?** What's on tonight at the concert hall?; **Salonda kahve içebilir miyiz?** Could we have coffee in the lounge?
salyangoz [saljangoz] *n* snail
saman [saman] *n* hay, straw; **saman nezlesi** *n* hay fever; **saman yığını** *n* haystack; **saz ve saman çatılı** *adj* thatched
samanlık [samanlək] *n* barn
samimiyetsiz [samimijetsiz] *adj* insincere
sanal [sanal] *adj* virtual; **sanal gerçeklik** *n* virtual reality
sanat [sanat] *n* art; **sanat eseri** *n* work of art; **sanat galerisi** *n* art gallery; **sanat okulu** *n* art school
sanatçı [sanattʃə] *n* artist
sanatsal [sanatsal] *adj* artistic
sanayi [sanaji] *n* industry; **eğlence sanayii** *n* show business; **sanayi sitesi** *n* industrial estate
sandal [sandal] *n* **cankurtaran sandalı** *n* lifeboat
sandalet [sandalet] *n* sandal
sandalye [sandalje] *n* chair *(furniture)*, seat *(furniture)*; **bebe sandalyesi** *n* highchair; **sallanan sandalye** *n* rocking chair; **tekerlekli sandalye** *n* wheelchair; **Bebek sandalyeniz var mı?** Do you have a baby seat?; **Mama sandalyeniz var mı?** Do you have a high chair?
sandık [sandək] *n* chest *(storage)*
sandviç [sandvitʃ] *n* sandwich; **sosisli sandviç** *n* hot dog; **Sandviç olarak ne var?** What kind of sandwiches do you have?
sanık [sanək] *n* accused
San Marino [sanmarino] *n* San Marino
sansasyonel [sansasjonel] *adj* sensational
Santigrat [santigrat] *n* **Santigrat derece** *n* degree centigrade, degree Celsius
santimetre [santimetre] *n* centimetre
santral [santral] *n* switchboard
sap [sap] *n* **kereviz sapı** *n* celery; **saplı tencere** *n* saucepan
sara [sara] *n* epilepsy; **sara nöbeti** *n* epileptic fit
saralı [saralə] *n* epileptic
saray [saraj] *n* palace; **Saray halka açık mı?** Is the palace open to the public?; **Saray ne zaman açık?** When is the palace open?

sardalya [sardalja] *n* sardine
sardunya [sardunja] *n* geranium
sargı [sargə] *n* bandage; **Sargı yapar mısınız?** I'd like a bandage; **Sargılarımı değiştirir misiniz?** I'd like a fresh bandage
sarhoş [sarhoʃ] *adj* drunk ▷ *n* drunk; **dut gibi sarhoş** *adj* pissed *(inf!)*
sarı [sarə] *adj* yellow; **kızılımsı sarı saçlı** *adj* ginger; **sarı şalgam** *n* swede; **yumurta sarısı** *n* egg yolk; **yumurtanın sarısı** *n* yolk
Sarı [sarə] *adj* **Sarı Sayfalar** *npl* Yellow Pages®
sarılık [sarələk] *n* jaundice
sarışın [sarəʃən] *adj* blonde; **Doğma büyüme sarışınım** My hair is naturally blonde
sarkmak [sarkmak] *v* to hang; **dışarıya sarkmak** *v* lean out
sarmak [sarmak] *v* bandage, do up, wrap; **geri sarmak** *v* rewind; **Sarar mısınız lütfen?** Could you wrap it up for me, please?
sarmaşık [sarmaʃək] *n* ivy
sarmısak [sarməsak] *n* garlic; **Bunda sarmısak var mı?** Is there any garlic in it?
sarsılmış [sarsəlməʃ] *adj* shaken
sarsıntı [sarsəntə] *n* concussion
satıcı [satədʒə] **(satıcı kadınlar)** *n* saleswoman, *(erkek)* salesman, dealer, salesperson, supplier, vendor; **uyuşturucu satıcısı** *n* drug dealer
satın [satən] *v* **satın alınmış** *adj* bought; **satın alma** *(şirket) n* buyout; **satın almak** *v* buy
satış [satəʃ] *n* sale; **otomatik satış makinesi** *n* vending machine; **satış elemanı** *n* sales rep, shop assistant; **satış fiyatı** *n* selling price; **son satış tarihi** *n* sell-by date; **telefonla satış** *npl* telesales; **toptan satış** *adj* wholesale
satmak [satmak] *vt* sell; **hepsini satmak** *v* sell out; **perakende satmak** *v* retail
satnav [satnav] *n* sat nav
satranç [satrantʃ] *n* chess
sauna [sauna] *n* sauna
savaş [savaʃ] *n* war; **iç savaş** *n* civil war
savaşmak [savaʃmak] *v* fight
savruk [savruk] *adj* extravagant
savunma [savunma] *n* defence
savunmasız [savunmasəz] *adj* vulnerable
savunucu [savunudʒu] *n* defender
savurmak [savurmak] *v* fling
sayaç [sajatʃ] *n* meter; **Gaz sayacı nerede?** Where is the gas meter?
saydam [sajdam] *adj* transparent
sayfa [sajfa] *n* page; **açılış sayfası** *n* home page; **Lütfen Arka Sayfaya Bakınız** *abbr* PTO; **Sarı Sayfalar** *npl* Yellow Pages®
saygı [sajgə] *n* regard, respect ▷ *v* **saygı duymak** *v* respect
saygıdeğer [sajgəde:er] *adj* reputable, respectable
saygın [sajgən] *adj* prestigious
sayı [sajə] *n* number, *(maç/oyun)* score *(game/match)* ▷ *v* **sayı yapmak** *v* score
sayım [sajəm] *n* **nüfus sayımı** *n* census

sayımlama [sajəmlama] *npl* statistics
sayısız [sajəsəz] *adj* numerous
saymak [sajmak] *v* count
sayvan [sajvan] *n* pavilion
saz [saz] *n* **saz ve saman çatılı** *adj* thatched
sci-fi [sdʒifi] *n* sci-fi
seans [seans] *n* session
sebep [sebep] *n* motive; **bu sebeple** *adv* therefore
sebze [sebze] *n* vegetable; **Sebze de dahil mi?** Are the vegetables included?; **Sebzeleriniz taze mi, dondurulmuş mu?** Are the vegetables fresh or frozen?
seçenek [setʃenek] *n* alternative, option
seçilmiş [setʃilmiʃ] *adj* chosen
seçim [setʃim] *n* choice, election; **genel seçim** *n* general election
seçme [setʃme] *n* selection
seçmek [setʃmek] *v* choose, elect, pick out, select
seçmen [setʃmen] *n* voter; **seçmen bölgesi** *n* constituency, electorate
sedan [sedan] *n* **sedan araba** *n* saloon car
sedye [sedje] *n* stretcher
sefalet [sefalet] *n* misery
sefer [sefer] *n* journey; **bir seferinde** *adv* once; **bir seferlik** *n* one-off; **karşılıklı sefer yapan araç** *n* shuttle
sehpa [sehpa] *n* coffee table
sekiz [sekiz] *number* eight; **Sekiz matinesine iki bilet lütfen** two for the eight o'clock showing
sekizinci [sekizindʒi] *adj* eighth ▷ *n* eighth
sekreter [sekreter] *n* secretary; **Sekreterine mesaj bırakabilir miyim?** Can I leave a message with his secretary?
seksen [seksen] *number* eighty
seksi [seksi] *adj* sexy
seksilik [seksilik] *n* sexuality
sektör [sektør] *n* sector
sel [sel] *n* flood
selam [selam] *excl* hi!
selamlamak [selamlamak] *v* greet, salute
selamlaşma [selamlaʃma] *n* greeting
sele [sele] *n* seat, saddle; **Bu sele rahat değil** The seat is uncomfy; **Sele çok alçak** The seat is too low; **Sele çok yüksek** The seat is too high
selef [selef] *n* predecessor
self-catering [selfdʒatering] *n* self-catering
selfservis [selfservis] *adj* self-service
seloteyp [selotejp] *n* Sellotape®
sembol [sembol] *n* symbol
semer [semer] *n* saddle
sen [sen] *pron* you *(singular)*; **Seni seviyorum** I love you
sendelemek [sendelemek] *v* stagger
sendika [sendika] *n* trade union
sendikacı [sendikadʒə] *n* trade unionist
sendrom [sendrom] *n* **Down sendromu** *n* Down's syndrome
Senegal [senegal] *adj* Senegalese ▷ *n* Senegal
Senegalli [senegalli] *n* Senegalese

senfoni [senfoni] *n* symphony
senin [senin] *adj* your *(singular)*
sent [sent] *n (para birimi)* cent
sepet [sepet] *n* basket; **çöp sepeti** *n* dustbin, wastepaper basket
sepetlemek [sepetlemek] *v* ditch
sera [sera] *n* greenhouse
seramik [seramik] *adj* ceramic
serbest [serbest] *adj* free, independent; **serbest çalışan** *adj* self-employed; **serbest bırakma** *n* release; **serbest bırakmak** *v* release; **Serbest çalışıyorum** I'm self-employed
serçe [sertʃe] *n* sparrow
sergi [sergi] *n* exhibition
sergileme [sergileme] *n* display
sergilemek [sergilemek] *v* display
seri [seri] *n* serial
serin [serin] *adj* cool *(cold)*; **serinletici içecek** *npl* refreshments
sermaye [sermaje] *n* **sermaye devri** *n* turnover
sermek [sermek] *v* **yere sermek** *v* knock out
serpinti [serpinti] *n* spray
sersem [sersem] *n* **Uçak sersemiyim** I'm suffering from jet lag
serseri [serseri] *n* tramp *(beggar)*
sert [sert] *adj* hard *(firm, rigid)*
sertifika [sertifika] *n* certificate
servet [servet] *n* fortune
servis [servis] *n* service; **gizli servis** *n* secret service; **kaza & acil servis** *n* accident & emergency department; **oda servisi** *n* room service; **servis atmak** *n* serve; **servis ücreti** *n* cover charge, service charge; **servis masası** *n* trolley; **servis tabağı** *n* dish *(plate)*; **Çamaşır servisi var mı?** Is there a laundry service?; **Çocuk bakıcı servisiniz var mı?** Is there a child-minding service?; **Oda servisi var mı?** Is there room service?; **Servis berbattı** The service was terrible; **Servis dahil mi?** Is service included?; **Servisten şikayetçiyim** I want to complain about the service; **Tamir servisini çağırabilir misiniz lütfen?** Call the breakdown service, please
ses [ses] *n* sound, voice; **çan sesi** *n* toll; **patlama sesi** *n* bang; **ses kayıt cihazı** *n* recorder *(music)*, tape recorder; **ses sınavı** *n* audition; **sesli posta** *n* voicemail; **yüksek sesle** *adv* aloud, loudly; **yüksek sesle okumak** *v* read out
sessiz [sessiz] *adj* quiet, silent; **Sessiz bir oda rica ediyorum** I'd like a quiet room
sessizce [sessizdʒe] *adv* quietly
sessizlik [sessizlik] *n* silence
sevecen [sevedʒen] *adj* affectionate
sevgi [sevgi] *n* love
sevgili [sevgili] *adj* dear *(loved)*
Sevgili [sevgili] *n* **Sevgililer Günü** *n* Valentine's Day
sevgilim [sevgilim] *n* darling
sevimli [sevimli] *adj* charming, cute
sevinmek [sevinmek] *v* to be pleased; **çok sevinmiş** *adj* thrilled
seviye [sevije] *n* level; **deniz seviyesi** *n* sea level
sevmek [sevmek] *v* like,

love; **... severim** I love ...; **Seni seviyorum** I love you
seyahat [sejahat] *n* journey, travel; **gecelik seyahat çantası** *n* overnight bag; **iş seyahati** *n* business trip; **seyahat acentası** *n* travel agency, travel agent's, *(kişi)* travel agent; **seyahat çeki** *n* traveller's cheque; **seyahat etme** *n* travelling ▹ *v* **seyahat etmek** *vi* travel; **seyahat sigortası** *n* travel insurance; **Seyahat bulantım var** I get travel-sick; **Seyahat sigortam yok** I don't have travel insurance; **Tek başıma seyahat ediyorum** I'm travelling alone
seyis [sejis] *n* groom
sezmek [sezmek] *v* guess
sezon [sezon] *n* season; **pahalı sezon** *n* high season; **sezon dışı/ sezon dışında** *adv* off-season; **ucuz sezon** *n* low season; **yaz sezonu** *n* summertime
sıcak [sədʒak] *adj* hot; **boğucu sıcak** *adj* sweltering; **sıcak su torbası** *n* hot-water bottle; **Çok sıcak** It's very hot; **Çok sıcakladım** I'm too hot; **Biraz fazla sıcak** It's a bit too hot; **Oda çok sıcak** The room is too hot; **Sıcak su yok** There is no hot water
sıcaklık [sədʒaklək] *n* temperature
sıçan [sətʃan] *n* rat
sıçramak [sətʃramak] *v* leap
sıçratmak [sətʃratmak] *v* splash
sıfat [səfat] *adj* adjective
sıfır [səfər] **(sıfırlar)** *n* zero, nil, nought
sığ [səɣ] *adj* shallow; **sığ havuz** *n* paddling pool
sığınak [sɜənak] *n* refuge
sığınma [sɜənma] *n* asylum
sığınmacı [sɜənmadʒə] *n* asylum seeker, refugee
sığır [sɜər] *n* cattle; **sığır eti** *n* beef
sık [sək] *adj* frequent, *(orman)* dense; **sık sorulan sorular** *n* FAQ *(Frequently Asked Question)*
sıkı [səkə] *adj* firm, tight; **eli sıkı** *adj* mean; **sıkı tedbirler almak** *v* crack down on; **sımsıkı kavramak** *v* grip; **sımsıkı paketlenmiş** *adj* compact
sıkıcı [səkədʒə] *adj* boring, drab
sıkılamak [səkəlamak] *v* tighten
sıkılmak [səkəlmak] *v* to get bored; **canı sıkılmış** *adj* bored; **canı sıkkın** *adj* depressed
sıkıntı [səkəntə] *n* nuisance; **can sıkıntısı** *n* boredom
sıkışık [səkəʃək] *adj* **sıkışık saat** *npl* peak hours; **sıkışık saatler** *n* rush hour
sıkışmak [səkəʃmak] *v* squeeze in
sıkışmış [səkəʃməʃ] *adj* jammed
sıklık [səklək] *n* frequency
sıklıkla [səkləkla] *adv* often
sıkmak [səkmak] *v* squeeze; **can sıkmak** *v* bore *(be dull)*
sıla [səla] *n* **sıla acısı çeken** *adj* homesick
sınav [sənav] *n* exam, examination *(medical)*, examination *(school)*; **çetin sınav** *n* ordeal; **deneme sınavı** *adj* mock; **direksiyon sınavı** *n* driving test; **ses sınavı** *n* audition; **sınav görevlisi** *n* examiner; **sınav gözcüsü** *n* invigilator ▹ *v* **sınavı kazanmak** *v* pass *(an exam)*; **yeniden sınava**

girmek *v* resit

sınıf [sənəf] *n* class, classroom; **birinci sınıf** *adj* first-class; **hizmet sınıfı** *n* business class; **ikinci sınıf** *adj* economy class, second class, second-class; **işçi sınıfı** *adj* working-class; **orta sınıf** *adj* middle-class; **sınıf arkadaşı** *n* classmate; **... a birinci sınıf bir gidiş dönüş bilet** a first-class return to...; **Birinci sınıf bir kabin** a first-class cabin; **Birinci sınıf seyahat etmek istiyorum** I would like to travel first class

sınır [sənər] *n* border, boundary, edge, limit, margin, range *(limits)*; **hız sınırı** *n* speed limit; **sınır dışı etmek** *v* deport; **sınır işareti** *n* landmark; **yaş sınırı** *n* age limit

sınırlamak [sənərlamak] *v* restrict

sır [sər] *n* confidence *(secret)*, secret

sıra [səra] *n* order, *(dizi)* row *(line)*, *(okul)* desk, *(oyun)* round *(series)*, *(taksi vb)* rank *(line)*; **sıra evler** *adj* terraced; **taksi sırası** *n* taxi rank

sırada [sərada] *n* while; **o sırada** *adv* meanwhile

sıradağ [sərada:] *n* range *(mountains)*

sıradan [səradan] *adj* ordinary ▷ *n* routine; **sıradan çıkmak** *v* fall out

sıralamak [səralamak] *v* rank

sırasıyla [sərasəjla] *adv* respectively

Sırbistan [sərbistan] *n* Serbia

sırık [sərək] *n* pole; **sırık gibi** *n* lanky; **sırıkla atlama** *n* pole vault

sırılsıklam [sərəlsəklam] *v*

sırılsıklam etmek *v* drench

sırıtış [sərətəʃ] *n* grin

sırıtmak [sərətmak] *v* grin

Sırp [sərp] *adj* Serbian ▷ *n (kişi)* Serbian *(person)*

Sırpça [sərptʃa] *n (dil)* Serbian *(language)*

sırt [sərt] *n* back; **sırt ağrısı** *n* back pain, backache; **sırt çantası** *n* backpack, holdall, rucksack; **sırt çantasıyla dolaşan gezgin** backpacker; **sırt çantasıyla gezme** *n* backpacking; **Sırtım ağrıyor** My back is sore; **Sırtım tutuldu** I've got a bad back; **sırtüstü yüzme** *n* backstroke

sıtma [sətma] *n* malaria

sıvı [səvə] *n* liquid

sıvışmak [səvəʃmak] *v* get away

sızdırmak [səzdərmak] *vi* leak

sızıntı [səzəntə] *n* leak

sızma [səzma] *n* **petrol sızması** *n* oil slick

sibercafe [siberdʒafe] *n* cybercaf[e]

Siberya [siberja] *n* Siberia

sidik [sidik] *v* urine; **sidik torbası** *n* bladder

sifon [sifon] *n* **Tuvaletin sifonu çalışmıyor** The toilet won't flush

sigara [sigara] *n* cigarette, *(argo)* fag; **sigara içen** *n* smoker; **sigara içilmeyen** *adj* non-smoking; **sigara içmek** *v* smoke; **sigara içmeyen** *n* non-smoker

sigorta [sigorta] *n (elektrik)* fuse, *(poliçe)* insurance; **araba sigortası** *n* car insurance; **kaza sigortası** *n* accident insurance; **üçüncü kişi sorumluluk sigortası** *n* third-party insurance

seyahat sigortası *n* travel insurance; **sigorta belgesi** *n* insurance certificate; **sigorta kutusu** *n* fuse box; **sigorta poliçesi** *n* insurance policy; **yaşam sigortası** *n* life insurance; **İşte sigorta bilgilerim** Here are my insurance details; **Bireysel kaza sigortası yaptırmak istiyorum** I'd like to arrange personal accident insurance; **Diş sigortam var mı bilmiyorum?** I don't know if I have dental insurance; **Diş sigortam yok** I don't have dental insurance; **Fiyata tam kapsamlı sigorta dahil mi?** Is fully comprehensive insurance included in the price?; **Sağlık sigortam yok** I don't have health insurance; **Seyahat sigortam yok** I don't have travel insurance; **Sigorta attı** A fuse has blown; **Sigorta belgenizi görebilir miyim lütfen?** Can I see your insurance certificate please?; **Sigorta bilgilerim burada** Here are my insurance details; **Sigorta bilgilerinizi verin lütfen** Give me your insurance details, please; **Sigorta için fiş almam gerekiyor** I need a receipt for the insurance; **Sigortam için polise bildirmemiz gerekiyor** I need a police report for my insurance; **Sigortalıyım** I have insurance; **Sigortanız var mı?** Do you have insurance?; **Sigortayı tamir eder misiniz?** Can you mend a fuse?; **Sigota bunu öder mi?** Will the insurance pay for it?; **Tam kapsamlı sigorta için ne kadar ekstra ödemem gerekiyor?** How much extra is comprehensive insurance cover?

sigortalamak [sigortalamak] *v* insure

sigortalı [sigortalə] *adj* insured

siğil [səəl] *n* wart

sihirbaz [sihirbaz] *n* magician

sihirli [sihirli] *adj* magical

Sikh [sikh] *adj* Sikh ▷ *n* Sikh

siklon [siklon] *n* cyclone

silah [silah] *n* gun, weapon; **kısa menzilli silah** *n* shotgun

silahlı [silahlə] *adj* armed

silecek [siledʒek] *n* **cam sileceği** *n* windscreen wiper; **Cam sileceklerinin deposunu doldurur musunuz lütfen?** Can you top up the windscreen washers?

silikon [silikon] *n* **silikon çip** *n* silicon chip

silindir [silindir] *n* cylinder, roller

silkmek [silkmek] *v* **omuz silkmek** *v* shrug

silmek [silmek] *v* delete, erase, *(silip çıkarmak)* cross out; **silerek temizlemek** *v* wipe; **silip temizlemek** *v* wipe up

simetrik [simetrik] *adj* symmetrical

simit [simit] *n* **cankurtaran simidi** *n* lifebelt

sinagog [sinagog] *n* synagogue; **Sinagog nerede var?** Where is there a synagogue?

sincap [sindʒap] *n* squirrel

sindirim [sindirim] *n* digestion

sindirmek [sindirmek] *v* digest

sinek [sinek] *n* fly
sinema [sinema] *n* cinema; **Bu gece sinemada ne var?** What's on tonight at the cinema?; **Sinemada hangi film oynuyor?** Which film is on at the cinema?; **Sinemada ne oynuyor?** What's on at the cinema?
sinir [sinir] *n (anatomi)* nerve *(anat)*; **sinir bozucu** *adj* annoying, irritating, nerve-racking; **sinir krizi** *n* nervous breakdown; **sinirini bozmak** *v* annoy
sinirli [sinirli] *adj* nervous
sinüs [sinys] *n* sinus
sinyal [sinjal] *n* signal; **meşgul sinyali** *n* busy signal, engaged tone; **sinyal vermek** *v* signal; **telefon sinyali** *n* dialling tone
sipariş [sipariʃ] *n* order; **sipariş formu** *n* order form; **Sipariş verebilir miyim lütfen?** Can I order now, please?
siper [siper] *n* trench
siren [siren] *n* siren
sirk [sirk] *n* circus
sirke [sirke] *n* vinegar; **sirkeli salata sosu** *n* vinaigrette
sis [sis] *n* fog, mist; **sis lambası** *n* fog light
sisli [sisli] *adj* foggy, misty
sistem [sistem] *n* system; **bağışıklık sistemi** *n* immune system; **güneş sistemi** *n* solar system; **GPS sistemi** *n* GPS; **sistem analizcisi** *n* systems analyst; **Kapalı Devre Televizyon Sistemi** *n* CCTV
sistemli [sistemli] *adj* systematic
sistit [sistit] *n* cystitis
sitkom [sitkom] *n* sitcom
sivil [sivil] *adj* civilian ▷ *n* civilian
sivilce [sivildʒe] *n* acne, pimple, zi
sivilceli [sivildʒeli] *adj* spotty
sivrisinek [sivrisinek] *n* mosquit
siyah [sijah] *adj* black; **Siyah beyaz** in black and white
siz [siz] *pron* you *(plural)*, you *(singular polite)*; **Siz döndüğünüzde biz yatmış oluruz** We'll be in bed when you get back; **Siz nasılsınız?** And you **Sizden çok hoşlanıyorum** I like you very much; **Size katılabilir miyim?** Can I join you?; **Sizi yarın arayabilir miyim?** May I call you tomorrow?; **Sizinle özel olarak konuşabilir miyim?** Can I speak to you in private?; **Sizinle çalışmak bir zevkti** It's been a pleasure working with you; **Sizinle nasıl temas kurabilirim** Where can I contact you?; **Sizinle tanışmak bir zevk** It was a pleasure to meet you
sizin [sizin] *adj* your *(plural)*, your *(singular polite)*
sizinki [siziŋi] *pron* yours *(plural)*, yours *(singular)*, yours *(singular polite)*
skandal [skandal] *n* scandal
skateboard [skateboard] *n* skateboard; **skateboard yapma** *n* skateboarding; **Skateboardin yapmak isterdim** I'd like to go skateboarding
skleroz [skleroz] *n* **multipl skleroz** *n* multiple sclerosis
skuter [skuter] *n* scooter
Slovak [slovak] *adj* Slovak ▷ *n (kiş*

Slovak *(person)*
Slovakça [slovaktʃa] *n (dil)* Slovak *(language)*
Slovakya [slovakja] *n* Slovakia
Slovence [slovendʒe] *n (dil)* Slovenian *(language)*
Slovenya [slovenja] *adj* Slovenian ▷ *n* Slovenia
Slovenyalı [slovenjalə] *n (kişi)* Slovenian *(person)*
smokin [smokin] *n* dinner jacket, tuxedo
SMS [esemes] *n* SMS
snooker [snooker] *n* snooker
snowboard [snovboard] *n* **Snowboard kiralamak istiyorum** I want to hire a snowboard; **Snowboarding dersleri veriyor musunuz?** Do you organise snowboarding lessons?
soba [soba] *n* stove
sofistike [sofistike] *adj* sophisticated
soğan [soa:n] *n* onion, *(bitki)* bulb *(plant)*; **Frenk soğanı** *mpl* chives; **taze soğan** *n* spring onion
soğuk [sou:k] *adj* chilly, cold ▷ *n* cold; **Duş soğuk akıyor** The showers are cold; **Et soğuk** The meat is cold; **Oda çok soğuk** The room is too cold; **Soğuk algınlığı için bir şey rica ediyorum** I'd like something for a cold; **Soğuk algınlığım var** I have a cold
soğutmak [sou:tmak] *v* chill
soğutucu [sou:tudʒu] *n* fridge; **soğutucu kayışı** *n* fan belt
sohbet [sohbet] *n* chat ▷ *v* **sohbet etmek** *v* chat; **sohbet odası** *n* chatroom; **sohbet programı** *n* chat show
sokak [sokak] *n* street; **çıkmaz sokak** *n* dead end; **dar sokak** *n* alley; **sokak çalgıcısı** *n* busker; **sokak haritası** *n* street map; **sokak lambası** *n* streetlamp; **sokak planı** *n* street plan; **sokaklarda büyümüş** *adj* streetwise; **yan sokak** *n* side street; **Sağdan ilk sokağa dönün** Take the first turning on your right; **Soldan ikinci sokağa dönün** Take the second turning on your left
sokma [sokma] *n (arı, böcek)* sting
sokmak [sokmak] *v (arı, böcek vb)* sting
sol [sol] *adj* left, left-hand, *(politika)* left-wing ▷ *n* left; **soldan trafik** *n* left-hand drive; **Sola dönün** Turn left; **Soldan ikinci sokağa dönün** Take the second turning on your left
solak [solak] *adj* left-handed
soldaki [soldaki] *adv* left
solist [solist] *n* soloist; **as solist** *n* lead singer
sollamak [sollamak] *v* overtake
solmak [solmak] *v* fade, wilt
solucan [soludʒan] *n* worm
soluk [soluk] *adj* pale
solüsyon [solysjon] *n* **Lens solüsyonu** cleansing solution for contact lenses
som [som] *n* **som balığı** *n* salmon
Somali [somali] *adj* Somali ▷ *n* Somalia
Somalice [somalidʒe] *n* Somali *(language)*

Somalili [somalili] *n (kişi)* Somali *(person)*
somun [somun] **(somunlar)** *n (ekmek)* loaf; **vida somunu** *n* nut *(device)*
son [son] *adj* final, last, ultimate ▷ *n* end, ending, finish; **eninde sonunda** *adv* ultimately; **hafta sonu** *n* weekend; **son derece** *adv* awfully; **son kullanım tarihi** *n* best-before date, expiry date; **son olarak** *adv* lastly; **son satış tarihi** *n* sell-by date; **son teslim tarihi** *n* deadline; **son zamanlarda** *adv* lately, recently; **sondan bir önceki** *adj* penultimate;**... a son otobüs kaçta?** When is the last bus to...?;**... a son tren kaçta?** When is the last train to...?;**... a son vapur kaçta?** When is the last sailing to...?; **En son çıkış kaçta?** When is the last ascent?; **Haziran sonunda** at the end of June; **Kuyruğun sonu burası mı?** Is this the end of the queue?; **Son otobüs kaçta?** What time is the last bus?; **Son teleferik kaçta?** When does the last chair-lift go?; **Son vapur kaçta?** When is the last boat?
sonbahar [sonbahar] *n* autumn
sonda [sonda] *adv* last
sonlandırmak [sonlandərmak] *v* end, finalize
sonra [sonra] *adv* afterwards ▷ *conj* after; **öğleden sonra** *abbr* afternoon, p.m.; **bir sonraki** *adv* next; **daha sonra** *adv* later; **güneş sonrası krem** *n* after sun lotion; **ondan sonra** *conj* then; **bir sonraki hafta** the week after next; **saat sekizden sonra** after eight o'clock
sonsuz [sonsuz] *adj* endless, eternal ▷ *n* eternity, infinitive
sonuç [sonutʃ] *n* conclusion, consequence, outcome, result; **kaza sonucu** *adj* accidental; **sonucu olmak** *v* result in
sonuçlar [sonutʃlar] *npl* repercussions
sonuçta [sonutʃta] *adv* eventuall
sonunda [sonunda] *adv* finally
sopa [sopa] *n (asa)* staff *(stick or rod)*, *(çubuk)* stick, *(silah)* club *(weapon)*; **golf sopası** *n* golf club *(game)*, tee; **sopa çekirgesi** *n* stick insect; **Golf sopaları kiralıyorlar mı?** Do they hire out golf clubs?
soprano [soprano] *n* soprano
sorbet [sorbet] *n* sorbet
sorgulamak [sorgulamak] *v* interrogate, query
sormak [sormak] *v* ask, question
soru [soru] *n* inquiry, query, question; **sık sorulan sorular** *n* FAQ *(Frequently Asked Question*
soru işareti *n* question mark
sorumlu [sorumlu] *adj* accountable, responsible; **bina sorumlusu** *n* janitor
sorumluluk [sorumluluk] *n* responsibility; **üçüncü kişi sorumluluk sigortası** *n* third-party insurance
sorumsuz [sorumsuz] *adj* irresponsible
sorun [sorun] *n* problem; **ufak sorun** *n* hitch; **Bir sorun çıkarsa**

kiminle temas kuracağız? Who do we contact if there are problems?; **Odada bir sorun var** There's a problem with the room; **Sorun değil** No problem
oruşturma [soruʃturma] *n* inquest, investigation
oruşturmak [soruʃturmak] *v* inquire
os [sos] *n* sauce; **domates sosu** *n* tomato sauce; **et sosu** *n* gravy; **salata sosu** *n* salad dressing; **sirkeli salata sosu** *n* vinaigrette; **soya sosu** *n* soy sauce; **terbiye sosu** *n* marinade; **terbiye sosuna yatırmak** *v* marinade
OS [esoes] *n* SOS
osis [sosis] *n* sausage; **sosisli sandviç** *n* hot dog
osyal [sosjal] *adj* sociable, social; **sosyal güvenlik** *n* social security; **sosyal hizmetler** *npl* social services; **sosyal hizmetler görevlisi** *n* social worker
osyalist [sosjalist] *adj* socialist ▷ *n* socialist
osyalizm [sosjalizm] *n* socialism
oy [soj] *n* race; lineage; **soyu tükenmiş** *adj* extinct
oya [soja] *n* soya; **soya sosu** *n* soy sauce
oyadı [sojadə] *n* surname; **kızlık soyadı** *n* maiden name
oygun [sojgun] *n* hold-up, robbery
oyguncu [sojgundʒu] *n* robber
oymak [sojmak] *v* burgle, rob ▷ *vt* *(meyva, deri vb)* peel
oyunmak [sojunmak] *v* strip, undress; **soyunma odası** *n* *(mağaza)* fitting room, *(spor)* changing room
soyut [sojut] *adj* abstract
soyutlanmış [sojutlanməʃ] *adj* isolated
söğüt [sø:yt] *n* willow
sökmek [søkmek] *v* *(parçalarına ayırmak)* take apart, *(vida)* unscrew
sömestr [sømestr] *n* semester
sömürmek [sømyrmek] *v* exploit
sömürü [sømyry] *n* exploitation
söndürmek [søndyrmek] *v* put out, turn off; **bastırarak söndürmek** *v* stub out
söndürücü [søndyrydʒy] *n* *(yangın)* extinguisher; **yangın söndürücü** *n* fire extinguisher
sör [sør] *n* sir
sörf [sørf] *n* surf; **rüzgar sörfü** *n* windsurfing; **sörf tahtası** *n* surfboard; **sörf yapma** *n* surfing; **sörf yapmak** *v* surf; **Sörf için nereye gitmek gerek?** Where can you go surfing?
sörfçü [sørftʃy] *n* surfer
söylemek [søjlemek] *v* say; **açıkça fikrini söylemek** *v* speak up; **şarkı söyleme** *n* singing; **şarkı söylemek** *v* sing; **yalan söylemek** *v* lie
söylenti [søjlenti] *n* rumour
söz [søz] *n* promise; **açık sözlü** *adj* outspoken, straightforward; **söz dinlemek** *v* listen to; **söz dinlememek** *v* disobey; **söz etmek** *v* refer; **söz vermek** *v* promise; **sözünü kesmek** *v* interrupt; **sözünü kesmek** *v* break in (on), disrupt

sözcü [søzdʒy] **(sözcüler)** *n* spokesperson, *(erkek)* spokesman, *(kadın)* spokeswoman
sözcük [søzdʒyk] *n* word; **sözcük dağarcığı** *n* vocabulary; **sözcük grubu** *n* phrase
sözlü [søzly] *adj* oral ▷ *n* oral
sözlük [søzlyk] *n* dictionary; **günlük ifadeler sözlüğü** *n* phrasebook
spagetti [spagetti] *n* spaghetti
spatül [spatyl] *n* spatula
sperm [sperm] *n* sperm
spesifik [spesifik] *adj* specific
spor [spor] *n* sport; **kano sporu** *n* canoeing; **kayma sporu** *n* skiing; **kış sporları** *npl* winter sports; **kürek sporu** *n* rowing; **lastik spor ayakkabısı** *npl* trainers; **spor ayakkabısı** *npl* sneakers; **spor giysisi** *n* sportswear; **yelken sporu** *n* sailing; **Buralarda sport tesisi var mı?** What sports facilities are there?; **Hangi spor gösterisine gidebiliriz?** Which sporting events can we go to?
sporcu [spordʒu] **(sporcular)** *n* *(erkek)* sportsman; **kadın sporcu** *n* sportswoman
sporsever [sporsever] *adj* sporty
spot [spot] *n* **spot lambası** *n* spotlight
stadyum [stadjum] **(stadyumlar)** *n* stadium; **Stadyuma nasıl gidebiliriz?** How do we get to the stadium?
standart [standart] *adj* standard ▷ *n* standard; **yaşam standardı** *n* standard of living; **Standart bir kabin bileti** a standard-class cabin
statüko [statyko] *n* status quo
steno [steno] *n* shorthand
stepne [stepne] *n* spare tyre, spar wheel
stereo [stereo] *n* stereo; **Arabada stereo var mı?** Is there a stereo i the car?; **Stereo var mı?** Does it have a stereo?
steril [steril] *adj* sterile
sterilze [sterilze] *v* **sterilize etmek** *v* sterilize
sterlin [sterlin] *n* sterling; **pound sterlin** *(İngiliz para birimi) n* pound sterling
steroid [steroid] *n* steroid
stil [stil] *n* style
stilist [stilist] *n* stylist
stok [stok] *n* stock
stoklamak [stoklamak] *v* stock
strateji [strateʒi] *n* strategy
stratejik [strateʒik] *adj* strategic
stres [stres] *n* strain, stress
striptizci [striptizdʒi] *n* stripper
stüdyo [stydjo] *n* studio; **stüdyo daire** *n* studio flat
su [su] *n* water; **deniz suyu** *n* sea water; **içme suyu** *n* drinking water; **maden suyu** *n* mineral water; **meyve suyu** *n* fruit juice, juice; **portakal suyu** *n* orange juice; **sığ suda çıplak ayak yürümek** *v* paddle; **sıcak su torbası** *n* hot-water bottle; **su baskınına uğramak** *vi* flood; **su basmak** *vt/vi* flood; **su basması** flooding; **su birikintisi** *n* puddle; **su deposu** *n* reservoir; **su geçirmez** *adj* waterproof; **su**

geçirmez parka *n* cagoule; **su kaplumbağası** *n* turtle; **su kayağı** *n* water-skiing; **su keleri** *m* newt; **su samuru** *n* otter; **su teresi** *n* watercress; **suda boğulmak** *v* drown; **suda pişirilmiş** *(yumurta, balık) adj* poached *(simmered gently)*; **sulu çamur** *n* slush; **sulu kar** *n* sleet; **sulu sepken yağmak** *v* sleet; **Bir bardak su** a glass of water; **Bir şişe maden suyu** a bottle of mineral water, a bottle of sparkling mineral water; **Bir şişe su** a bottle of still mineral water; **Bir sürahi su** a jug of water; **Biraz daha su getirir misiniz?** Please bring more water; **Burada su kayağı yapmak mümkün mü?** Is it possible to go water-skiing here?; **Sıcak su nasıl çalışıyor?** How does the water heater work?; **Sıcak su yok** There is no hot water; **Suyu kontrol eder misiniz lütfen?** Can you check the water, please?; **Suyun derinliği ne kadar?** How deep is the water?

sualtı [sualtə] *adv* underwater

suç [sutʃ] *n* blame, crime; **internet suçu** *n* cybercrime; **suç ortağı** *n* accomplice

suçiçeği [sutʃitʃeji:] *n* chickenpox

suçlama [sutʃlama] *n* accusation, charge *(accusation)*

suçlamak [sutʃlamak] *v* accuse, blame, charge *(accuse)*

suçlu [sutʃlu] *adj* criminal, guilty ▷ *n* criminal

suçluluk [sutʃluluk] *n* guilt

Sudan [sudan] *adj* Sudanese ▷ *n* Sudan

Sudanlı [sudanlə] *n* Sudanese

suit [suit] *n* suite

sulamak [sulamak] *v* water; **bahçe sulama bidonu** *n* watering can

sulandırılmış [sulandərəlməʃ] *adj* diluted

sulandırmak [sulandərmak] *v* dilute

sulh [sulh] *n* peace; **sulh hakimi** *n* magistrate

sulu [sulu] *adj* **sulu hamur** *n* batter; **sulu kabarcık** *n* blister

suluboya [suluboja] *n* watercolour

sunak [sunak] *n* altar

sunma [sunma] *n* presentation

sunucu [sunudʒu] *n (bilişim)* server *(computer)*, *(oyun, film, gösteri)* compere, *(radyo, TV)* presenter; **haber sunucusu** *n* newsreader

surat [surat] *n* face; **suratı asık** *adj* sulky; **suratını asmak** *v* sulk

Suriye [surije] *adj* Syrian ▷ *n* Syria

Suriyeli [surijeli] *n* Syrian

susmak [susmak] *v* shut up

susturucu [susturudʒu] *n* silencer

susuz [susuz] *adj* dehydrated, thirsty; **Susadım** I'm thirsty

susuzluk [susuzluk] *n* thirst

Suudi [suudi] *adj* Saudi ▷ *n* Saudi

Suudi Arabistan [suudiarabistan] *adj* Saudi Arabia, Saudi Arabian

Suudi Arabistanlı [suudiarabistanlə] *n* Saudi Arabian

sübvansiyon [sybvansijon] *n* subsidy

süet [syet] *n* suede
sülün [sylyn] *n* pheasant
sümbül [symbyl] *n* hyacinth
sümüklüböcek [symyklybødʒek] *n* **kabuksuz sümüklüböcek** *n* slug
sünger [synger] *n (banyo)* sponge *(for washing)*
süper [syper] *adj* super
süpermarket [sypermarket] *n* supermarket; **Süpermarket arıyorum** I need to find a supermarket
süprüntü [syprynty] *adj* rubbish
süpürge [sypyrge] *n* broom; **elektrik süpürgesi** *n* Hoover®, vacuum cleaner; **süpürge otu** *n* heather
süpürgelik [sypyrgelik] *n* skirting board
süpürmek [sypyrmek] *v* sweep, *(elektrikli süpürgeyle)* hoover
sürahi [syrahi] *n* carafe, jug; **Bir sürahi beyaz şarap** a carafe of white wine; **Bir sürahi kırmızı şarap** a carafe of red wine; **Bir sürahi su** a jug of water; **Kendi şarabınızdan bir sürahi** a carafe of the house wine
sürat [syrat] *n* speed; **sürat motoru** *n* speedboat
sürdürmek [syrdyrmek] *v* keep up, maintain ▷ *vi* continue
süre [syre] *n* duration; **deneme süresi** *n* trial period; **uzatma süresi** *n* injury time
sürekli [syrekli] *adv* constantly
süresince [syresindʒe] *prep* during
sürgü [syrgy] *n* bolt
sürgün [syrgyn] *n (başka bir yere)* exile
sürmek [syrmek] *v* last, *(otomobil)* drive; **bisiklet sürmek** *v* cycle; **iz sürmek** *v* retrace; **izini sürmek** *v* track down; **tarla sürmek** *vt* plough
sürpriz [syrpriz] *n* surprise
sürtmek [syrtmek] *v* rub
sürü [syry] *n* flock, herd; **sürüden ayrılmış** *n* stray
sürücü [syrydʒy] *n* driver, motorist; **öğrenci sürücü** *n* learner driver; **disk sürücü** *n* disk drive; **sürücü ehliyeti** *n* driving licence; **taksi sürücüsü** *n* taxi driver
sürüklemek [syryklemek] *vt* drag
sürüklenmek [syryklenmek] *vi (sularla)* drift
sürükleyici [syryklejidʒi] *adj* gripping
sürüngen [syryngen] *n* reptile
süs [sys] *n* ornament; **şekerli kek süsü** *n* frosting; **pastanın üzerindeki şekerli süsleme** *n* icing; **toz süsleme şekeri** *n* icing sugar
süslemek [syslemek] *v* decorate; **elişiyle süslemek** *v* embroider
süslenmek [syslenmek] *v* dress up
süt [syt] *n* milk; **bebek sütü** *n* baby milk; **süt ürünleri** *n* dairy products; **sütlü çikolata** *n* milk chocolate; **sütle yapılmış** *n* dairy produce; **sütsüz kahve** *n* black coffee; **UHT süt** *n* UHT milk; **yağı alınmış süt** *n* skimmed milk; **yarım yağlı süt** *n* semi-skimmed milk; **Bu pastörize edilmemiş**

sütten mi yapıldı? Is it made with unpasteurised milk?; **sütü ayrı getirin** with the milk separate; **Süt içer misiniz?** Do you drink milk?; **Taze sütünüz var mı?** Have you got real milk?
sütun [sytun] *n* column, pillar
sütyen [sytjen] *n* bra
süyek [syjek] *n* splint
süzgeç [syzgetʃ] *n* colander
süzmek [syzmek] *v* filter
Swaziland [svaziland] *n* Swaziland

şafak [ʃafak] *n* dawn
şaheser [ʃaheser] *n* masterpiece
şahit [ʃahit] *n* witness; **yalancı şahitlik** *n* perjury; **Yehovanın Şahitleri** *n* Jehovah's Witness
şahmat [ʃahmat] *n* stalemate
şair [ʃair] *n* poet
şaka [ʃaka] *n* joke; **kaba şaka** *n* prank; **şaka yapmak** *v* joke
şal [ʃal] *n* shawl
şalgam [ʃalgam] *n* turnip; **sarı şalgam** *n* swede
şalter [ʃalter] *n* switch; **şalter açmak** *v* switch on
şalvar [ʃalvar] *n* **şalvar biçimi** *adj* baggy
şamandıra [ʃamandəra] *n* buoy
şamata [ʃamata] *n* din
şamdan [ʃamdan] *n* candlestick
şampanya [ʃampanja] *n* champagne
şampiyon [ʃampijon] *n* champion

şampiyona [ʃampijona] *n* championship
şampuan [ʃampuan] *n* shampoo; **Şampuan satıyor musunuz?** Do you sell shampoo?
şans [ʃans] *n* luck
şanslı [ʃanslə] *adj* fortunate, lucky
şanssız [ʃanssəz] *adj* unlucky
şantaj [ʃantaʒ] *n* blackmail; **şantaj yapmak** *n* blackmail
şapel [ʃapel] *n* chapel
şapka [ʃapka] *n* hat
şaplak [ʃaplak] *n*, *v* **şaplak atmak** *v* spank
şarap [ʃarap] *n* wine; **elma şarabı** *n* cider; **ev şarabı** *n* house wine; **kırmızı şarap** *n* red wine; **şarap kadehi** *n* wineglass; **şarap listesi** *n* wine list; **pembe şarap** *n* rosé; **porto şarabı** *n* port *(wine)*; **yemeklik şarap** *n* table wine; **İyi bir beyaz şarap tavsiye edebilir misiniz?** Can you recommend a good white wine?; **İyi bir kırmızı şarap tavsiye edebilir misiniz?** Can you recommend a good red wine?; **İyi bir şarap tavsiye edebilir misiniz?** Can you recommend a good wine?; **İyi bir roze şarap tavsiye edebilir misiniz?** Can you recommend a good rosé wine?; **Bir şişe beyaz şarap** a bottle of white wine; **Bir şişe kırmızı şarap** a bottle of red wine; **Bir şişe kendi şarabınızdan** a bottle of the house wine; **Bir sürahi beyaz şarap** a carafe of white wine; **Bir sürahi kırmızı şarap** a carafe of red wine; **Bu şarap soğutulmamış** This wine is not chilled; **Hiç şarap içmem** I never drink wine; **Kendi şarabınızdan bir sürahi** a carafe of the house wine; **Şarap lekesi** This stain is wine; **Şarap listesi lütfen** The wine list, please; **Şarap soğutulmuş mu?** Is the wine chilled?
şarj [ʃarʒ] *n* charge *(electricity)*; **şarj aleti** *n* charger; **şarj etmek** *(elektrik) v* charge *(electricity)*; **Şarj etmiyor** It's not charging, It's not holding its charge
şarjör [ʃarʒør] *n* magazine *(ammunition)*
şarkı [ʃarkə] *n* song; **çocuk şarkıları** *n* nursery rhyme; **şarkı söyleme** *n* singing; **şarkı söylemek** *v* sing; **Noel şarkısı** *n* carol
şarkıcı [ʃarkədʒə] *n* singer
şarküteri [ʃarkyteri] *n* delicatessen
şart [ʃart] *n* **şartlı tahliye** *n* parole
şaşı [ʃaʃə] *n* **şaşı bakmak** *v* squint
şaşırmış [ʃaʃərməʃ] *adj* astonished bewildered, surprised
şaşırtıcı [ʃaʃərtədʒə] *adj* astonishing, puzzling, surprising; **şaşırtıcı bir şekilde** *adv* surprisingly
şaşırtmak [ʃaʃərtmak] *v* amaze, astonish
şaşkın [ʃaʃkən] *adj* amazed, baffled; **şaşkına dönmüş** *adj* stunned
şayet [ʃajet] *conj* whether
şef [ʃef] *n* chief; **orkestra şefi** *n* conductor
şefkatli [ʃefkatli] *adj* caring

şeftali [ʃeftali] *n* peach
şehir [ʃehir] *n* city, town; **şehir merkezi** *n* town centre; **şehir planlama** *n* town planning; **Bu şehre özgü bir şey istiyorum** Have you anything typical of this town?; **Şehir merkezinden ne kadar uzaktayız?** How far are we from the town centre?; **Şehir merkezine en kolay nasıl gidebilirim?** What's the best way to get to the city centre?
şehit [ʃehit] *n* martyr
şehvet [ʃehvet] *n* lust
şeker [ʃeker] *n* sugar, sweet; **şeker hastalığı** *n* diabetes; **şeker hastası** *n* diabetic; **şekerli kek süsü** *n* frosting; **nane şekeri** *n* peppermint; **pastanın üzerindeki şekerli süsleme** *n* icing; **toz süsleme şekeri** *n* icing sugar
şekersiz [ʃekersiz] *adj* no sugar, sugar-free
şekil [ʃekil] *n* figure, shape; **ağır bir şekilde** *adv* heavily; **özenli bir şekilde** *adv* cautiously; **etkili bir şekilde** *adv* effectively; **kötü bir şekilde** *adv* badly
şelale [ʃelale] *n* waterfall
şempanze [ʃempanze] *n* chimpanzee
şemsiye [ʃemsije] *n* umbrella
şen [ʃen] *adj* happy; **şen şakrak** *adj* merry
şenlik [ʃenlik] *n* festivity; **şenlik ateşi** *n* bonfire
şerefe [ʃerefe] *excl* cheers!
şeri [ʃeri] *n* sherry; **Bir sek şeri lütfen** A dry sherry, please
şerit [ʃerit] *n* strip, stripe, tape; **çift-şeritli yol** *n* dual carriageway; **şerit metre** *n* tape measure; **şeritli yaya geçidi** *n* zebra crossing
şey [ʃej] *n* thing; **önemsiz şey** *n* trifle; **bir şey** *pron* something; **herhangi bir şey** *pron* anything; **hiçbir şey** *n* nothing
şeytan [ʃejtan] *n* devil
şezlong [ʃezlong] *n* deckchair
şık [ʃək] *adj* smart
şımartılmış [ʃəmartəlməʃ] *adj* spoilt
şınav [ʃənav] *n*, *v* **şınav çekmek** *n* press-up
şırınga [ʃərənga] *n* syringe
şiddet [ʃiddet] *n* violence; **şiddet uygulayan** *adj* violent; **şiddetle vurmak** *v* bash; **şiddetli rüzgar** *n* gale
şiddetli [ʃiddetli] *adj* harsh
şifre [ʃifre] *n* code, password; **kredi kartı şifresi** *npl* PIN
Şii [ʃii] *adj* Shiite
şiir [ʃiir] *n* poem, poetry
şikayet [ʃikajet] *n* complaint, grouse *(complaint)*; **Bir şikayette bulunmak istiyorum** I'd like to make a complaint
Şili [ʃili] *adj* Chilean ▷ *n* Chile
Şilili [ʃilili] *n* Chilean
şimdi [ʃiːmdi] *adv* now; **Şimdi kendinizi nasıl hissediyorsunuz?** How are you feeling now?; **Şimdi mi ödeyeceğim, sonra mı?** Do I pay now or later?
şimşek [ʃimʃek] *n* lightning
şirket [ʃirket] *n* company; **şirket arabası** *n* company car; **şirket**

evliliği *n* merger; **şirketiçi network** *n* intranet; **Şirket hakkında bilgi alabilir miyim?** I would like some information about the company; **Şirketimle ilgili bilgiler** Here's some information about my company

şiş [ʃiʃ] *adj* swollen ▷ *n* spit; **örgü şişi** *n* knitting needle; **kebap şişi** *n* skewer; **yangılı ayak şişi** *n* bunion

şişe [ʃiʃe] *n* bottle; **şişe açacağı** *n* bottle-opener; **şişe geri dönüşüm kutusu** *n* bottle bank; **Bir şişe beyaz şarap** a bottle of white wine; **Bir şişe daha getirir misiniz?** Please bring another bottle; **Bir şişe içki deklare etmek istiyorum** I have a bottle of spirits to declare; **Bir şişe kırmızı şarap** a bottle of red wine; **Bir şişe kendi şarabınızdan** a bottle of the house wine; **Bir şişe maden suyu** a bottle of mineral water, a bottle of sparkling mineral water; **Bir şişe su** a bottle of still mineral water

şişirilebilir [ʃiʃirilebilir] *adj* inflatable

şişirmek [ʃiʃirmek] *v* pump up

şişko [ʃiʃko] *adj* gross *(fat)*

şişman [ʃiʃman] *adj* fat

şizofren [ʃizofren] *adj* schizophrenic

şnorkel [ʃnorkel] *n* snorkel; **Şnorkelle dalmak istiyorum** I'd like to go snorkelling

şoför [ʃoføɾ] *n* chauffeur; **kamyon şoförü** *n* lorry driver, truck driver

şok [ʃok] *n* shock; **şok geçirmek** *v* shock

şort [ʃort] *npl* shorts, *(erkek iç çamaşırı)* underpants; **bokser şort** *npl* boxer shorts; **yüzücü şortu** *npl* swimming trunks, trunks

şoven [ʃoven] *n* chauvinist

şömine [ʃømine] *n* fireplace; **şömine rafı** *n* mantelpiece

şöyle [ʃøjle] *adv* thus; **şöyle böyle** *adv* so-so

şu [ʃu] *adj* that; **şu an** *n* present *(time being)*; **şu anda** *adv* currently, presently; **Şu ne kadar?** How much does that cost?

Şubat [ʃubat] *n* February

şunlar [ʃunlar] *adj* those ▷ *pron* those

şunu [ʃunu] *pron* that

şurup [ʃurup] *n* syrup; **öksürük şurubu** *n* cough mixture

t

taahhüt [taahhyt] *n* contract, obligation; **iadeli taahhütlü** *n* recorded delivery; **İadeli taahhütlü ne kadar sürer?** How long will it take by registered post?
tabak [tabak] *n* plate; **fincan tabağı** *n* saucer; **servis tabağı** *n* dish *(plate)*
tabaka [tabaka] *n* layer; **ozon tabakası** *n* ozone layer
taban [taban] *n* **taban tepmek** *n* tramp *(long walk)*; **veri tabanı** *n* database
tabanca [tabandʒa] *n* **kısa kabzalı tabanca** *n* pistol
tabela [tabela] *n* sign; **yol tabelası** *n* signpost
tablo [taplo] *n (grafik)* table *(chart)*; **gösterge tablosu** *n* dashboard
tabu [tabu] *adj* taboo ▷ *n* taboo
tabure [tabure] *n* stool
tabut [tabut] *n* coffin
Tacikistan [tadʒikistan] *n* Tajikistan
taciz [tadʒiz] *n* abuse, harassment; **çocuk tacizi** *n* child abuse
taç [tatʃ] *n* crown; **taç çizgisi** *n* touchline
tahıl [tahəl] *n* **tahıl gevreği** *n* cereal; **tahıl tanesi** *n* grain
Tahiti [tahiti] *n* Tahiti
tahliye [tahlije] *n* evacuation; **şartlı tahliye** *n* parole; **tahliye etmek** *v* vacate
tahmin [tahmin] *n* estimate, guess, *(hava, borsa vb)* forecast; **hava tahmini** *n* weather forecast; **tahmin edilebilir** *adj* predictable; **tahminde bulunmak** *v* estimate; **Hava tahmini nasıl?** What's the weather forecast?
tahribat [tahribat] *n* ruin
tahrip [tahrip] *n* destruction; **tahrip etmek** *n* vandalize
taht [taht] *n* throne
tahta [tahta] *n (ağaç)* wood *(material)*, *(okul)* board *(go aboard)*, *(okul)* board *(wood)*; **ütü tahtası** *n* ironing board; **beyaz yazı tahtası** *n* whiteboard; **ilan tahtası** *n* bulletin board, notice board; **sörf tahtası** *n* surfboard
tahterevalli [tahterevalli] *n* seesaw
takdim [takdim] *n* introduction, presentation; **takdim etmek** *v* present
takılmak [takəlmak] *v* **peşine takılmak** *v* pursue
takılmış [takəlməʃ] *adj* stuck; **Takıldı** It's stuck

takım [takəm] *n* kit; **bando takımı** *n* brass band; **takım elbise** *n* suit; **tamir takımı** *n* repair kit; **yatak takımı** *n* bedclothes, bedding; **Tamir takımı alabilir miyim?** Can I have a repair kit?; **Tamir takımınız var mı?** Do you have a repair kit?
takıntı [takəntə] *n* obsession
takıntılı [takəntələ] *adj* obsessed
takip [takip] *n* chase
taklit [taklit] *n* copy *(reproduction)*, imitation; **taklit etmek** *v* imitate, mimic
takma [takma] *adj* false; **takma ad** *n* alias, nickname, pseudonym; **takma dişler** *npl* dentures
takmak [takmak] **birine takmak** *v* pick on
taksi [taksi] *n* cab, minicab, taxi; **taksi sırası** *n* taxi rank; **taksi sürücüsü** *n* taxi driver; **Bagajımı takside bıraktım** I left my bags in the taxi; **Bana bir taksi gerek** I need a taxi; **Birlikte bir taksi tutabiliriz** We could share a taxi; **Bu otele taksi ne kadar?** How much is the taxi fare to this hotel?; **Havaalanına taksi ne kadar?** How much is the taxi to the airport?; **Kente taksi ne kadar?** How much is the taxi fare into town?; **Nereden taksi bulabilirim?** Where can I get a taxi?; **Taksi durağı nerede?** Where is the taxi stand?; **Valizlerimi taksiye çıkarır mısınız lütfen?** Please take my luggage to a taxi
taksimetre [taksimetre] *n* **Taksimetre bozuk** The meter is broken; **Taksimetrenin gösterdiğinden daha fazla** It's more than on the meter; **Taksimetreniz var mı?** Do you have a meter?
taksit [taksit] *n* instalment
taktik [taktik] *npl* tactics
takunya [takunja] *n* clog
takvim [takvim] *n* calendar
takviye [takvije] *n* reinforcement; **takviye kablosu** *npl* jump leads
talan [talan] *n* **talan olmuş** shambles
talaş [talaʃ] *n* sawdust
talep [talep] *n* claim, demand; **talep etmek** *v* claim, demand
talihsizlik [talihsizlik] *n* misfortune
talimat [talimat] *n* **talimat vermek** *v* instruct
talimatlar [talimatlar] *npl* directions, instructions
talk [talk] *v* **talk pudrası** *n* talcum powder
tam [tam] *adj* exact, precise, sheer, *(bütün)* total; **tam gün** *adv* full-time; **tam olarak** *adv* exactly, fully, precisely
Tamam [tamam] OK!
tamamen [tamamen] *adv* completely, totally
tamir [tamir] *n* repair; **tamir takımı** *n* repair kit; **Bunu nerede tamir ettirebilirim?** Where can I get this repaired?; **Bunu tamir edebilir misiniz?** Can you repair this?; **Saatimi tamir edebilir misiniz?** Can you repair my watch?; **Tamir edebilir misiniz?**

Can you repair it?; **Tamir etmek ne kadar sürer?** How long will it take to repair?; **Tamir ettirmeye değer mi?** Is it worth repairing?; **Tamir kaça malolacak?** How much will the repairs cost?; **Tamir takımı alabilir miyim?** Can I have a repair kit?; **Tamir takımınız var mı?** Do you have a repair kit?

tamirci [tamirdʒi] *n (otomobil)* mechanic; **Tamirci gönderebilir misiniz?** Can you send a mechanic?

tampon [tampon] *n* tampon, *(oto)* bumper

tandem [tandem] *n* **tandem bisiklet** *n* tandem

tane [tane] *n* piece; **kar tanesi** *n* snowflake; **tahıl tanesi** *n* grain

tanı [tanə] *n* diagnosis

tanık [tanək] *n* witness; **Tanıklık eder misiniz?** Can you be a witness for me?

tanım [tanəm] *n* definition

tanımak [tanəmak] *v* know, recognize

tanımlamak [tanəmlamak] *v* define

tanınabilir [tanənabilir] *adj* recognizable

tanınmış [tanənməʃ] *adj* renowned, well-known

tanışmak [tanəʃmak] *vt* meet; **Tanıştığımıza memnun oldum** Pleased to meet you

tanıtım [tanətəm] *n* promotion, publicity; **tanıtımını yapmak** *v* promote

tanıtma [tanətma] *n* introduction; **tanıtma broşürü** *n* prospectus

tanıtmak [tanətmak] *v* introduce

tank [taŋ] *n* tank *(large container)*, *(ordu)* tank *(combat vehicle)*

tanker [taŋer] *n* tanker

tanrı [tanrə] *n* god; **tanrı tanımaz** *n* atheist

tansiyon [tansijon] *n* blood pressure

Tanzanya [tanzanja] *adj* Tanzanian ▷ *n* Tanzania

Tanzanyalı [tanzanjalə] *n* Tanzanian

tapınak [tapənak] *n* temple; **Tapınak halka açık mı?** Is the temple open to the public?; **Tapınak ne zaman açık?** When is the temple open?

tapmak [tapmak] *v* adore

taraf [taraf] *n* side

tarafından [tarafəndan] *prep* by

tarafsız [tarafsəz] *adj* neutral ▷ *n* neutral

taraftar [taraftar] *n* supporter

tarak [tarak] *n* comb; **deniz tarağı** *n* scallop

tarama [tarama] *n (bilgisayar)* scan

taramak [taramak] *v* comb, *(bilgisayar)* scan

tarayıcı [tarajədʒə] *n (internet)* browser, *(scanner)* scanner; **internet tarayıcı** *n* web browser

tarçın [tartʃən] *n* cinnamon

tarhun [tarhun] *n* tarragon

tarım [tarəm] *n* agriculture

tarımsal [tarəmsal] *adj* agricultural

tarif [tarif] *n* account *(report)*, recipe

tarife [tarife] *n* timetable, schedule; **gümrük tarifesi** *n* tariff; **tarifeli uçuş** *n* scheduled flight; **tarifesiz uçuş** *n* charter flight; **Bir tarife alabilir miyim, lütfen?** Can I have a timetable, please?; **Günlük tarifeniz nedir?** What are your rates per day?; **Haftalık tarifeniz nedir?** What are your rates per week?; **Ucuz tarifeli uçuşunuz var mı?** Are there any cheap flights?
tarih [tari:h] *n (geçmiş, ders)* history, *(takvim)* date; **son kullanım tarihi** *n* best-before date, expiry date; **son satış tarihi** *n* sell-by date; **son teslim tarihi** *n* deadline; **tarih öncesi** *adj* prehistoric; **Bugün ayın kaçı?** What is the date?; **Bugünün tarihi nedir?** What is today's date?
tarihçi [tarihtʃi] *n* historian
tarihi [ta:rihi:] *adj* historical
tarla [tarla] *n* field; **tarla sürmek** *vt* plough
tartışma [tartəʃma] *n* argument, row *(argument)*, *(fikir)* debate
tartışmak [tartəʃmak] *v* argue, quarrel, row *(to argue)*, *(fikir)* debate
tartışmalı [tartəʃmalə] *adj* controversial
tartışmasız [tartəʃmasəz] *adj* undisputed
tarz [tarz] *n* style; **Yepyeni bir tarz istiyorum** I want a completely new style
tas [tas] *n* cup
tasalanmak [tasalanmak] *vt* worry
tasarımcı [tasarəmdʒə] *n* designer
tasarlamak [tasarlamak] *v* design, devise
tasavvur [tasavvur] *n* imagination, concept, idea; **tasavvur etmek** *v* fancy, imagine
tasfiye [tasfije] *n* **tasfiye memuru** *n* receiver *(person)*
taslak [taslak] *n* draft
taslamak [taslamak] *v* **patronluk taslamak** *v* boss around
Tasmanya [tasmanja] *n* Tasmania
taş [taʃ] *n* stone; **çakıl taşı** *n* pebble; **kaldırım taşı** *n* kerb; **kireç taşı** *n* limestone; **mezar taşı** *n* gravestone; **safra kesesi taşı** *n* gallstone; **taş ocağı** *n* quarry
taşıma [taʃəma] *n* removal, transport; **toplu taşıma** *n* public transport
taşımak [taʃəmak] *v* bear, transport ▷ *vt* carry
taşınabilir [taʃənabilir] *adj* portable, removable; **taşınabilir ev** *n* mobile home
taşınmak [taʃənmak] *v* move in; **taşınma kamyonu** *n* removal van
taşıt [taʃət] *n* vehicle; **yıllık taşıt testi** *n* MOT
taşıyıcı [taʃəjədʒə] *n* carrier; **taşıyıcı anne** *n* surrogate mother; **taşıyıcı bant** *n* conveyor belt
taşmak [taʃmak] *v* boil over
tat [tat] *n* taste; **tatsız tuzsuz** *adj* tasteless; **Bunun tadı pek iyi değil** It doesn't taste very nice
tatarcık [tatardʒək] *n* midge
tatil [tatil] *n* holiday; **aktivite**

tatili *n* activity holiday; **paket tatil** *n* package holiday; **resmi tatil günü** *n* public holiday; **sömestr tatili** *n* half-term; **tatil evi** *n* holiday home; **tatil yeri** *n* resort; **yaz tatili** *npl* summer holidays; **İyi tatiller!** Enjoy your holiday!; **Burada tatildeyim** I'm here on holiday, I'm on holiday here

tatlandırıcı [tatlandərədʒə] *n* sweetener; **Tatlandırıcınız var mı?** Do you have any sweetener?

tatlı [tatlə] *adj* sweet *(taste)*, *(hoş)* sweet *(pleasing)* ▷ *n* dessert ▷ *npl* afters; **tatlı kaşığı** *n* dessert spoon; **Tatlı menüsü lütfen** The dessert menu, please; **Tatlı rica ediyoruz** We'd like a dessert

tatlılar [tatləlar] *npl* sweets

tatlısu [tatləsu] *adj* **tatlısu balığı** *n* freshwater fish

tatmak [tatmak] *v* taste

tatmin [tatmin] *n* satisfaction; **tatmin edici** *adj* rewarding, satisfactory; **tatmin edici olmayan** *adj* disappointing, unsatisfactory; **tatmin olmuş** *adj* satisfied

tatsız [tatsəz] *adj* grim

tava [tava] *n* pan; **kızartma tavası** *n* frying pan

tavan [tavan] *n* ceiling; **açılır tavan** *n* sunroof; **tavan arası** *n* loft

tavır [tavər] *n* attitude, manner

tavsiye [tavsije] *n* recommendation; **tavsiye etmek** *v* advise, recommend; **Ne tavsiye edersiniz?** What do you recommend?

tavşan [tavʃan] *n* rabbit; **tavşan uykusu** *n* snooze; **yabani tavşan** *n* hare

tavuk, horoz [tavuk, horoz] *n* hen, chicken; **orman tavuğu** *n* grouse *(game bird)*

tavus [tavus] *n* **tavus kuşu** *n* peacock

tay [taj] *n* foal

tayfa [tajfa] *n* crew

Tayland [tajland] *n* Thailand

Taylandca [tajlanddʒa] *n (dil)* Thai *(language)*

Taylandlı [tajlandlə] *n (kişi)* Thai *(person)*

Tayvan [tajvan] *adj* Taiwanese ▷ *n* Taiwan

Tayvanlı [tajvanlə] *n* Taiwanese

taze [taze] *adj* fresh; **taze soğan** *n* spring onion; **Balıklarınız taze mi, dondurulmuş mu?** Is the fish fresh or frozen?; **Sebzeleriniz taze mi, dondurulmuş mu?** Are the vegetables fresh or frozen?; **Taze kahveniz var mı?** Have you got fresh coffee?

tazminat [tazminat] *n* compensation

tebeşir [tebeʃir] *n* chalk

tebrik [tebrik] *interj* **tebrik kartı** *n* greetings card

tebrikler [tebrikler] *npl* congratulations

tecavüz [tedʒavyz] *n (cinsel)* rape *(sexual attack)*; **tecavüz etmek** *v* rape; **Tecavüze uğradım** I've been raped

tecavüzcü [tedʒavyzdʒy] *n* rapist

tedavi [tedavi] *n* cure; **tedavi**

etmek *vt* cure
tedbir [tedbir] *n* measure, step; **sıkı tedbirler almak** *v* crack down on
tedbirli [tedbirli] *adj* cautious
tefsir [tefsir] *n* interpretation; **tefsir etmek** *v* interpret
teğmen [teːmen] *n (subay/polis)* lieutenant
tehdit [tehdit] *n* threat; **tehdit edici** *adj* threatening; **tehdit etmek** *v* threaten
tehlike [tehlike] *n* danger; **tehlike uyarı ışığı** *npl* hazard warning lights; **tehlikeye atmak** *v* endanger; **Çığ tehlikesi var mı?** Is there a danger of avalanches?
tehlikeli [tehlikeli] *adj* dangerous
tek [tek] *adj* only, single; **tek başına** *n* solo; **tek gidiş bileti** *n* one-way ticket; **tek kişilik oda** *n* single room; **tek kullanımlık** *adj* disposable; **tek yatak** *n* single bed; **tek yataklı oda** *n* single; **tek yön bilet** *n* single ticket; **Tek gidiş bilet ne kadar?** How much is a single ticket?; **Tek kişilik bir oda ayırtmak istiyorum** I want to reserve a single room; **Tek kişilik bir oda istiyorum** I'd like to book a single room
tekdüze [tekdyze] *adj* monotonous
tekel [tekel] *n* monopoly
tekerlek [tekerlek] *n* wheel; **üç tekerlekli bisiklet** *n* tricycle; **tekerlekli sandalye** *n* wheelchair; **Tekerlekler kilitleniyor** The wheels lock; **Tekerleklerin havası ne kadar olmalı?** What should the tyre pressure be?
tekil [tekil] *n* singular
tekinsiz [tekinsiz] *adj* uncanny
tekler [tekler] *npl (spor)* singles
teklif [teklif] *n* bid, offer; **teklif etmek** *v* offer
teklifsiz [teklifsiz] *adj* informal
tekme [tekme] *n* kick
tekmelemek [tekmelemek] *vt* kick
tekne [tekne] *n* boat; **balıkçı teknesi** *n* fishing boat; **gemi teknesi** *n* hull; **kürek teknesi** *n* rowing boat
teknik [teknik] *adj* technical ▷ *n* technique; **teknik bilgi** *n* know-how
teknisyen [teknisjen] *n* technician; **motor teknisyeni** *n* motor mechanic
tekno [tekno] *n* techno
teknoloji [teknoloʒi] *n* technology
Teknoloji [teknoloʒi] *n* **Enformasyon Teknolojisi** *n* IT
teknolojik [teknoloʒik] *adj* technological
tekrar [tekrar] *n* repeat; **Tekrar eder misiniz lütfen?** Could you repeat that, please?
tekrarlamak [tekrarlamak] *v* repeat
tekrarlayan [tekrarlajan] *adj* repetitive
tekstil [tekstil] *n* textile
tel [tel] *n* wire; **dikenli tel** *n* barbed wire; **gelin teli** *n* tinsel; **jant teli** *n* spoke; **tel zımba** *n* stapler; **zımba teli** *n* staple *(wire)*
telaffuz [telaffuz] *n* pronunciation; **telaffuz etmek** *v*

pronounce, spell
telafi [telafi] *n* compensation; **telafi etmek** *v* compensate
telaş [telaʃ] *n* rush; **telaş etmek** *vi* rush
telaşla [telaʃla] *adv* hastily
teleferik [teleferik] *n* cable car, chairlift, ski lift
telefon [telefon] *n* phone, telephone; **akıllı telefon** *n* smart phone; **ankesörlü telefon** *n* payphone; **cep telefonu** *n* mobile phone; **fotoğraflı telefon** *n* camera phone; **kapı telefonu** *n* entry phone; **kartlı telefon** *n* cardphone; **telefon etmek** *v* phone; **telefon faturası** *n* phone bill; **telefon görüşmesi** *n* phonecall; **telefon kartı** *n* phonecard, top-up card; **telefon kodu** *n* dialling code; **telefon kulübesi** *n* call box, phonebox; **telefon numarası** *n* phone number; **telefon rehberi** *n* telephone directory; **telefon sinyali** *n* dialling tone; **telefonla aramak** *v* ring up; **telefonla satış** *npl* telesales; **telefonu kapatmak** *v* hang up; **video telefon** *n* videophone; **... a telefon ne kadar?** How much is it to telephone...?; **Acil bir telefon görüşmesi yapmam gerek** I need to make an urgent telephone call; **Bir telefon görüşmesi yapmam gerek** I must make a phone call; **Buradan telefon edebilir miyim?** Can I phone from here?; **Cep telefonumu nerede şarj edebilirim** Where can I charge my mobile phone?; **Nereden telefon edebilirim?** Where can I make a phone call?; **Telefon etmek istiyorum** I want to make a phone call; **Telefon kartı satıyor musunuz?** Do you sell phone cards?; **Telefon numaranızı alabilir miyim?** Can I have your phone number?; **Telefon numarası nedir?** What's the telephone number?; **Telefonla sorunum var** I'm having trouble with the phone; **Telefonunuzu kullanabilir miyim lütfen?** Can I use your phone, please?; **Telefonunuzu kullanabilir miyim?** May I use your phone?; **Uluslararası telefon kartı satıyor musunuz?** Do you sell international phone cards?; **Yirmibeş euroluk telefon kartı rica ediyorum** I'd like a twenty-five euro phone card
telekomünikasyon [telekomynikasjon] *npl* telecommunications
telesekreter [telesekreter] *n* answering machine, answerphone
teleskop [teleskop] *n* telescope
televizyon [televizjon] *n* television, telly; **dijital televizyon** *n* digital television; **renkli televizyon** *n* colour television; **televizyon dizisi** *n* soap opera; **Televizyon nerede?** Where is the television?; **Televizyon odası var mı?** Is there a television lounge?
telgraf [telgraf] *n* telegram; **Bir telgraf çekmek istiyorum** I want

to send a telegram; **Buradan telgraf çekebilir miyim?** Can I send a telegram from here?; **Nereden telgraf çekebilirim?** Where can I send a telegram from?

telif [telif] *n* **telif hakkı** *n* copyright

telsiz [telsiz] *adj* cordless ▷ *n* walkie-talkie

tema [tema] *n* topic

temas [temas] *n* contact; **temas kurmak** *v* contact; **Sizinle nasıl temas kurabilirim?** Where can I contact you?

tembel [tembel] *adj* lazy

temel [temel] *adj* basic, main; **temel ürün** *n* staple *(commodity)*; **temel bilgiler** *npl* basics

temiz [temiz] *adj* clean; **temiz ve tertipli** *adj* neat; **Temiz bir çatal alabilir miyim lütfen?** Could I have a clean fork please?; **Temiz bir bardak alabilir miyim lütfen?** Can I have a clean glass, please?; **Temiz bir kaşık alabilir miyim lütfen?** Could I have a clean spoon, please?

temizleme [temizleme] *n* cleaning

temizlemek [temizlemek] *vt* clean; **kar temizleme aracı** *n* snowplough; **kuru temizleme** *n* dry-cleaning; **silip temizlemek** *v* wipe up; **yüz temizleme losyonu** *n* cleansing lotion

temizleyici [temizlejidʒi] *n* cleanser

temizlik [temizlik] *n* cleanliness; **bahar temizliği** *n* spring-cleaning

temizlikçi [temizliktʃi] *n* cleaner, cleaning lady; **Temizlikçi kaçta geliyor?** When does the cleaner come?

Temmuz [temmuz] *n* July

temsil [temsil] *n* representation; **temsil eden** *adj* representative; **temsil etmek** *v* represent

temsilci [temsildʒi] *n* agent, rep

ten [ten] *n* complexion; **bronzlaşmış ten** *n* tan

tencere [tendʒere] *n* pot; **saplı tencere** *n* saucepan

teneke [teneke] *n* tin; **çöp tenekesi** *n* bin; **teneke kutu** *n* canister

tenis [tenis] *n* tennis; **masa tenisi** *n* table tennis; **tenis kortu** *n* tennis court; **tenis oyuncusu** *n* tennis player; **tenis raketi** *n* tennis racket; **Nerede tenis oynayabilirim?** Where can I play tennis?; **Tenis kortu kiralamak kaça?** How much is it to hire a tennis court?; **Tenis oynamak istiyoruz** We'd like to play tennis

tenkit [teŋit] *n (davranış)* criticism

tenör [tenør] *n* tenor

tente [tente] *n* tarpaulin

tepe [tepe] *n* top, *(coğrafya)* hill; **kilise kulesinin sivri tepesi** *n* spire; **kum tepesi** *n* sand dune; **tepelere tırmanma** *n* hill-walking; **Tepelere yürüyüşe çıkmak isterim** I'd like to go hill walking

tepede [tepede] *adj* top

tepki [tepki] *n* reaction; **tepki göstermek** *v* react

tepmek [tepmek] *v* to kick; **geri tepmek** *v* backfire; **taban**

tepmek *n* tramp *(long walk)*
tepsi [tepsi] *n* tray
ter [ter] *n* sweat; **ter önleyici deodorant** *n* antiperspirant
terapi [terapi] *n* therapy
teras [teras] *n* patio, terrace; **Terasta yiyebilir miyim?** Can I eat on the terrace?
terazi [terazi] *npl* scales
Terazi [terazi] *n* **Terazi burcu** *n* Libra
tercih [terdʒih] *n* preference; **tercih etmek** *v* prefer
tercihen [terdʒihen] *adv* preferably
tercüman [terdʒyman] *n* translator
tercüme [terdʒyme] *n* translation; **tercüme etmek** *v* translate
tere [tere] *n* cress; **su teresi** *n* watercress
tereyağı [tereja:ə] *n* butter
terim [terim] *n* term *(description)*
teriyer [terijer] *n* terrier
terketmek [terketmek] *v* abandon
terleme [terleme] *n* perspiration
terlemek [terlemek] *v* sweat
terli [terli] *adj* sweaty
terlik [terlik] *n* slipper
terminal [terminal] *n* terminal; **otobüs terminali** *n* bus station
termometre [termometre] *n* thermometer
termos [termos] *n* Thermos®
termostat [termostat] *n* thermostat
terörist [terørist] *n* terrorist; **terörist saldırı** *n* terrorist attack
terörizm [terørizm] *n* terrorism
ters [ters] *adj* inverted; **ters tırnak işareti** *npl* inverted commas
tersane [tersane] *n* shipyard
terslik [terslik] *n* mishap
tertip [tertip] *n* arrangement; **temiz ve tertipli** *adj* neat
terzi [terzi] *n* tailor
tesis [tesis] *n* plant *(site/ equipment)*
teslim [teslim] *n* delivery; **son teslim tarihi** *n* deadline; **teslim etmek** *vt* deliver; **teslim olmak** *v* surrender
teslimat [teslimat] *n* delivery
test [test] *n* test; **kan testi** *n* blood test; **Pap smear testi** *n* smear test; **yıllık taşıt testi** *n* MOT
testere [testere] *n* saw
teşekkür [teʃekkyr] *n* **teşekkür ederim** thank you ▷ *v* **teşekkür etmek** *v* thank; **İçmiyorum, sağolun** I'm not drinking, thank you; **İyiyim, teşekkür ederim** Fine, thanks; **Çok teşekkürler** Thank you very much; **Beni davet ettiğiniz için çok teşekkürler** It's very kind of you to invite me; **Bizi davet ettiğiniz için çok teşekkürler** It's very kind of you to invite us
teşekkürler [teʃekkyrler] *excl* thanks!, thank you!
teşvik [teʃvik] *n* incentive
tetanoz [tetanoz] *n* tetanus; **Tetanoz aşısı yaptırmam gerek** I need a tetanus shot
teveccüh [teved͡ʒd͡ʒyh] *n* concern
teyit [tejit] *n* confirmation
teyze [tejze] *n* auntie, aunt *(mother's sister)*

tezahürat [tezahyrat] *n* cheer; **tezahürat yapmak** *v* cheer
tezgah [tezgah] *n* stall
tezgahlar [tezgahlar] *npl* stands
tezgahtar [tezgahtar] *n* sales assistant
Thai [thai] *adj* Thai
tıbbi [təbbi] *adj* medical
tığ [təɣ] *n* **tığ gibi** *adj* slender
tık [tək] *n* click
tıkabasa [təkabasa] *n* **tıkabasa doldurmak** *vi* cram; **tıkabasa dolu** *adj* crammed
tıkaç [təkatʃ] *n* plug; **kulak tıkacı** *npl* earplugs
tıkalı [təkalə] *adj* blocked
tıkamak [təkamak] *v* obstruct
tıkanıklık [təkanəklək] *n* blockage, congestion
tıkanmak [təkanmak] *vi* choke
tıkırdamak [təkərdamak] *v* tick
tıklamak [təklamak] *v* click
tıknaz [təknaz] *adj* plump
tıp [təp] *n* medical
tırmanma [tərmanma] *n (kaya)* rock climbing
tırmanmak [tərmanmak] *v* climb, mount; **tepelere tırmanma** *n* hill-walking; **Tırmanmaya gitmek isterdim** I'd like to go climbing
tırmık [tərmək] *n* rake
tırnak [tərnak] *n* fingernail; **çift tırnak** *npl* quotation marks; **tırnak cilası** *n* nail varnish; **tırnak fırçası** *n* nailbrush; **tırnak makası** *n* nail scissors; **tırnak törpüsü** *n* nailfile; **ters tırnak işareti** *npl* inverted commas
tırtıl [tərtəl] *n* caterpillar
Tibet [tibet] *adj* Tibetan ▷ *n* Tibet
Tibetçe [tibettʃe] *n (dil)* Tibetan *(language)*
Tibetli [tibetli] *n (kişi)* Tibetan *(person)*
ticaret [tidʒaret] *n* business, trade; **ticaret bankası** *n* merchant bank
tifo [tifo] *n* typhoid
tiksinmek [tiksinmek] *v* loathe
tiksinmiş [tiksinmiʃ] *adj* disgusted
tilki [tilki] *n* fox
timsah [timsah] *n* alligator, crocodile
tip [tip] *n* type
tipik [tipik] *adj* typical
tirbuşon [tirbuʃon] *n* corkscrew
tire [tire] *n* hyphen
tişört [tiʃørt] *n* tee-shirt, T-shirt; **pamuklu kalın tişört** *n* sweatshirt
titremek [titremek] *v* shiver, tremble; **korkarak titremek** *v* shudder
tiyatro [tijatro] *n* theatre; **Tiyatroda ne var?** What's on at the theatre?
Togo [togo] *n* Togo
tohum [tohum] *n* seed
toka [toka] *n* clasp; **kemer tokası** *n* buckle; **saç tokası** *n* hairgrip
tokat [tokat] *v* **tokat atmak** *v* smack
tokatlamak [tokatlamak] *v* slap
tokmak [tokmak] *n (kapı, çekmece)* knob
tokyo [tokjo] *n (terlik)* flip-flops
tombola [tombola] *n* bingo
tombul [tombul] *adj* chubby

tomruk [tomruk] *n* log
tomurcuk [tomurdʒuk] *n* blossom
ton [ton] *n (ağırlık)* ton; **çalma tonu** *n* ringtone; **ton balığı** *n* tuna
Tonga [tonga] *n* Tonga
tonik [tonik] *n* tonic; **Ben bir cin tonik alayım lütfen** I'll have a gin and tonic, please
top [top] *n* ball; **badminton topu** *n* shuttlecock; **derli toplu** *(düzenli)* neatly, *(tertipli)* tidy; **havan topu** *n* mortar *(military)*; **kar topu** *n* snowball
topal [topal] *adj* lame
topallamak [topallamak] *v* limp
toparlamak [toparlamak] *v* round up; **toparlayıp kaldırmak** *v* put away
toparlanmak [toparlanmak] *v* get over
toplam [toplam] *n* sum, total
toplamak [toplamak] *v* *(matematik)* add up, *(ortalığı)* clear up, *(ortalığı)* tidy ▷ *vt (çiçek vb)* pick, *(para, pul vb)* collect; **derleyip toplamak** *v* tidy up
toplanmak [toplanmak] *vi* meet ▷ *vt* gather
toplantı [toplantə] *n* meeting; **basın toplantısı** *n* press conference; **danslı toplantı** *n* dancing; **... ile bir toplantı ayarlamak istiyordum** I'd like to arrange a meeting with...
toplu [toplu] *n* **toplu iğne** *n* pin; **toplu taşıma** *n* public transport
topluluk [topluluk] *n* a lot, assembly, community
toplum [toplum] *n* society
toplumbilim [toplumbilim] *n* sociology
toplumcu [toplumdʒu] *adj* communist ▷ *n* communist
toprak [toprak] *n* soil; **toprak kayması** *n* landslide; **toprak sahibi** *n* landowner
toptan [toptan] *n* wholesale
topuk [topuk] *n* heel; **yüksek topuklar** *npl* high heels; **yüksek topuklu** *adj* high-heeled
torba [torba] *n* bag; **alışveriş torbası** *n* carrier bag; **naylon torba** *n* plastic bag, polythene bag; **sıcak su torbası** *n* hot-water bottle; **sidik torbası** *n* bladder; **torba çay** *n* tea bag; **Bir torba daha alabilir miyim lütfen?** Can I have an extra bag, please?; **Torba istemem, sağolun** I don't need a bag, thanks; **Torbanız var mı?** Can I have a bag, please?
torbacık [torbadʒək] *n* sachet
tornavida [tornavida] *n* screwdriver
torpido [torpido] *n* **torpido gözü** *n* glove compartment
torun [torun] *n* grandchild; **erkek torun** *n* grandson; **kız torun** *n* granddaughter
torunlar [torunlar] *npl* grandchildren
tost [tost] *n* toast *(culin)*
toyota [tojota] *n* **Toyota parçaları var mı?** Do you have parts for a Toyota?
toz [toz] *n* dust, powder; **çamaşır tozu** *n* washing powder; **çiçek tozu** *n* pollen; **kabartma tozu** *n* baking powder; **kırmızı toz biber**

n paprika; **sabun tozu** *n* soap powder; **toz almak** *vt* dust; **toz süsleme şekeri** *n* icing sugar; **Çamaşır tozunuz var mı?** Do you have washing powder?
tozlu [tozlu] *adj* dusty
tozluk [tozluk] *npl* leggings
tökezlemek [tøkezlemek] *v* stumble, trip (up)
tören [tøren] *n* ceremony; **ödül töreni** *n* prize-giving; **tören alayı** *n* parade
törpü [tørpy] *n* **tırnak törpüsü** *n* nailfile
törpülemek [tørpylemek] *v* file *(smoothing)*
trabzan [trabzan] *n* banister
trafik [trafik] *n* traffic; **hava trafik kontrolörü** *n* air-traffic controller; **sağdan trafik** *n* right-hand drive; **soldan trafik** *n* left-hand drive; **trafik ışıkları** *npl* traffic lights; **trafik işareti** *n* road sign; **trafik kuralları** *n* Highway Code; **trafik magandalığı** *n* road rage; **trafik memuru** *n* traffic warden; **trafik sıkışıklığı** *n* traffic jam; **Otoyolda trafik yoğun mu?** Is the traffic heavy on the motorway?; **Yoğun trafikten kaçabileceğim bir güzergah var mı?** Is there a route that avoids the traffic?
trajedi [traʒedi] *n* tragedy
trajik [traʒik] *adj* tragic
traktör [traktør] *n* tractor
tramplen [tramplen] *n* diving board, trampoline
tramvay [tramvaj] *n* tram
transfer [transfer] *n* transfer; **Bankamdan para transferi yapmak istiyorum** I would like to transfer some money from my bank in...; **Hesabımdan para transferi yapmak istiyorum** I would like to transfer some money from my account; **Transfer ücreti var mı?** Is there a transfer charge?; **Transfer ne kadar sürer?** How long will it take to transfer?
transistör [transistør] *v* transistor
transit [transit] *n* transit; **transit yolcu salonu** *n* transit lounge
transparan [transparan] *adj* see-through
transvestit [transvestit] *n* transvestite
traş [traʃ] *n* **asker traşı** *n* crew cut, **traş bıçağı** *n* razor, razor blade; **traş köpüğü** *n* shaving foam; **traş kremi** *n* shaving cream; **traş losyonu** *n* aftershave; **traş makinesi** *n* shaver; **traş olmak** *v* shave; **Traş makinem için priz nerede?** Where is the socket for my electric razor?
traşsız [traʃsəz] *adj* unshaven
travmatik [travmatik] *adj* traumatic
tren [tren] *n* train; **her gün işe trenle giden kimse** *n* commuter; **tren abonmanı** *n* railcard; **tren istasyonu** *n* railway station; **... tren saatleri nedir?** What times are the trains to...?; **... treni bu mu?** Is this the train for...?; **... treni hangi platformdan kalkıyor?** Which platform does the train for... leave from?; **... treni hangi sıklıkta**

geliyor? How frequent are the trains to...?; **... treni ne zaman?** What time is the train to ...?; **... trenine nereden binebilirim?** Where can I get a train to ...?; **... treninin kalkacağı platform burası mı?** Is this the right platform for the train to...?; **... a bir sonraki tren kaçta?** When is the next train to ...?; **... a ilk tren kaçta?** When is the first train to ...?; **... a son tren kaçta?** When is the last train to ...?; **Bir sonraki tren lütfen** The next available train, please; **Bu tren... da duruyor mu?** Does the train stop at ...?; **Direk tren mi?** Is it a direct train?; **Tren gecikmeli mı?** Is the train running late?; **Tren hangi platformdan kalkıyor?** Which platform does the train leave from?; **Tren kaçta geliyor?** When is the train due?; **Tren kaçta kalkacak?** What time does the train leave?; **Tren on dakika rötarlı** The train is running ten minutes late; **Tren saatinde mi kalkacak?** Is the train on time?; **Trende restoran var mı?** Is there a buffet car on the train?; **Trende tekerlekli sandalye girişi var mı?** Is the train wheelchair-accessible?; **Trenimi kaçırdım** I've missed my train; **Ucuz tren tarifesi var mı?** Are there any cheap train fares?

Trinidad ve Tobago [trinidadvetobago] *n* Trinidad and Tobago

troley [trolej] *n* **Valizler için troley var mı?** Are there any luggage trolleys?

trolley [trollej] *n* **bagaj trolleyi** *n* luggage trolley

trombon [trombon] *n* trombone

tropik [tropik] *adj* tropical

tsunami [tsunami] *n* tsunami

tuğla [tu:la] *n* brick

tuhaf [tuhaf] *adj* peculiar

tulum [tulum] *n* dungarees ▷ *npl (giysi)* overalls; **uyku tulumu** *n* sleeping bag

Tunus [tunus] *adj* Tunisian ▷ *n* Tunisia

Tunuslu [tunuslu] *n* Tunisian

tur [tur] *n (gezi)* tour; **paket tur** *n* package tour; **rehberli tur** *n* guided tour; **tur operatörü** *n* tour operator; **tur otobüsü** *n* coach *(vehicle)*; **tur rehberi** *n* tour guide; **tura çıkmak** *v* tour; **Kent turunuz var mı?** Are there any sightseeing tours of the town?; **Rehberli tur kaçta başlıyor?** What time does the guided tour begin?; **Tur ne kadar sürüyor?** How long does the tour take?; **Tur otobüsü ne zaman kalkıyor?** When is the bus tour of the town?; **Tur saat... da başlıyor** The tour starts at about...; **Turdan çok zevk aldım** I enjoyed the tour

turba [turba] *n* peat

turist [turist] *n* tourist; **Buraya turist olarak geldim** I'm here as a tourist

turizm [turizm] *n* tourism; **turizm bürosu** *n* tourist office

turna [turna] *n* crane *(bird)*

turnike [turnike] *n* turnstile; **bilet**

turnikesi *n* ticket barrier
turnuva [turnuva] *n* tournament
turp [turp] *n* **kırmızı turp** *n* radish
turta [turta] *n* flan, tart; **elmalı turta** *n* apple pie
tuş [tuʃ] *n (bilgisayar/piyano)* key *(music/computer)*
tuşlamak [tuʃlamak] *v (telefon)* dial
tutarlı [tutarlə] *adj* consistent
tutarsız [tutarsəz] *adj* inconsistent
tutkal [tutkal] *n* glue
tutku [tutku] *n* passion
tutmak [tutmak] *vt* hold, keep; **dışarda tutmak** *v* keep out; **dışında tutmak** *v* exclude; **göz önünde tutarak** *prep* considering; **uçak tutması** *n* airsick
tutuklama [tutuklama] *n* arrest
tutuklamak [tutuklamak] *v* arrest
tutumlu [tutumlu] *adj* thrifty
tutunmak [tutunmak] *v* hold on
tutya [tutja] *n* pewter
tuvalet [tuvalet] *n* lavatory, loo, toilet; **erkekler tuvaleti** *n* gents'; **kadınlar tuvaleti** *n* ladies'; **tuvalet çantası** *n* sponge bag, toilet bag; **tuvalet kağıdı** *n* toilet paper, toilet roll; **tuvalet masası** *n* dressing table; **Özürlüler için tuvaletiniz var mı?** Are there any toilets for the disabled?; **Burada tuvalet var mı?** Is there a toilet on board?; **Tuvalet kağıdı yok** There is no toilet paper; **Tuvaleti kullanabilir miyim?** Can I use the toilet?; **Tuvaletin sifonu çalışmıyor** The toilet won't flush; **Tuvaletler nerede?** Where are the toilets?
tuz [tuz] *n* salt; **tatsız tuzsuz** *adj* tasteless; **tuzlanıp tütsülenmiş ringa balığı** *n* kipper; **tuzlu ve baharatlı** *adj* savoury; **Tuzu uzatır mısınız lütfen?** Pass the salt, please
tuzak [tuzak] *n* ambush, trap
tuzlu [tuzlu] *adj* saltwater, salty
tüberküloz [tyberkyloz] *n* tuberculosis, TB
tüfek [tyfek] *n* rifle; **makineli tüfek** *n* machine gun
tükenmek [tykenmek] *v* **soyu tükenmiş** *adj* extinct
tükenmez [tykenmez] *adj* **tükenmez kalem** *n* Biro®, ballpoint pen
tükenmiş [tykenmiʃ] *adj* exhausted
tüketici [tyketidʒi] *n* consumer
tükürmek [tykyrmek] *v* spit
tükürük [tykyryk] *n* saliva
tül [tyl] *n* net
tümsekli [tymsekli] *adj* bumpy
tünel [tynel] *n* tunnel
tüp [typ] *n* tube; **deney tüpü** *n* test tube; **tüp gaz** *n* camping gas
tür [tyr] *n* kind, species
türbe [tyrbe] *n* tomb
Türk [tyrk] *adj* Turkish ▷ *n* Turk
Türkçe [tyrktʃe] *n* Turkish
Türkiye [tyrkije] *n* Turkey
türkuvaz [tyrkuvaz] *adj* **türkuvaz renkli** *adj* turquoise
tüten [tyten] *n* smoking
tütsü [tytsy] *n* smoke; **tuzlanıp tütsülenmiş ringa balığı** *n* kipper
tütsülenmiş [tytsylenmiʃ] *adj*

smoked
tütün [tytyn] *n* tobacco
tütüncü [tytyndʒy] *n* tobacconist's
tüy [tyj] *n* feather; **tüyler ürpertici** *adj* gruesome
tüyler [tyjler] *n* **diken diken olmuş tüyler** *mpl* goose pimples
TV [tv] *n* TV; **plazma TV** *n* plasma TV

ucuz [udʒuz] *adj* cheap; **ucuz sezon** *n* low season; **Daha ucuz bir şey istiyorum** I want something cheaper; **Daha ucuz bir şeyiniz var mı?** Do you have anything cheaper?; **En ucuz bilet olsun lütfen** I'd like the cheapest option; **Ucuz tarifeli uçuşunuz var mı?** Are there any cheap flights?; **Ucuz tren tarifesi var mı?** Are there any cheap train fares?
uç [utʃ] *n (kalem/dil)* tip *(end of object)*; **aşırı uçta** *n* extremist; **parmaklarının ucunda yürüme** *n* tiptoe; **uç uç böceği** *n* ladybird; **ucu ucuna** *adv* barely
uçak [utʃak] *n* aircraft, plane *(aeroplane)*; **uçak pisti** *n* runway; **uçak postası** *n* airmail; **uçak tutması** *n* jet lag; **uçak tutması** *n* airsick; **Uçağım... da kalkıyor** My

plane leaves at...
uçmak [utʃmak] *vi* fly; **havaya uçmak** *vi* blow; **planörle uçma** *n* gliding; **uçup gitmek** *v* fly away
uçuk [utʃuk] *n (sağlık)* cold sore
uçurmak [utʃurmak] *v* fly, ascend; **havaya uçurmak** *v* blow up
uçurtma [utʃurtma] *n* kite
uçuş [utʃuʃ] *n* flight; **tarifeli uçuş** *n* scheduled flight; **tarifesiz uçuş** *n* charter flight; **uçuş bekleme salonu** *n* departure lounge; **uçuş hostesi** *n* flight attendant; **Uçuşumu değiştirmek istiyorum** I'd like to change my flight; **Uçuşumu iptal ettirmek istiyorum** I'd like to cancel my flight; **Uçuşunuz gecikmeli** The flight has been delayed
U-dönüşü [udønyʃy] *n* U-turn
ufak [ufak] *adj* minor, tiny; **birine ufak bir armağan alma** *n* treat; **ufak karides** *n* shrimp; **ufak sorun** *n* hitch
UFO [ufo] *abbr* UFO
ufuk [ufuk] *n* horizon
Uganda [uganda] *adj* Ugandan ▹ *n* Uganda
Ugandalı [ugandalə] *n* Ugandan
uğraş [u:raʃ] *n* pastime
uğraşmak [u:raʃmak] *v* struggle
uğurlamak [u:urlamak] *v* send off
uğursuz [u:ursuz] *adj* sinister
UHT [uha:te:] *n* **UHT süt** *n* UHT milk
Ukrayna [ukrajna] *adj* Ukrainian ▹ *n* Ukraine
Ukraynaca [ukrajnadʒa] *n (dil)* Ukrainian *(language)*
Ukraynalı [ukrajnalə] *n (kişi)* Ukrainian *(person)*
ulak [ulak] *n* messenger
ulaşmak [ulaʃmak] *vt* reach
ultimatom [ultimatom] *n* ultimatum
ultrason [ultrason] *n* ultrasound
ulumak [ulumak] *v* howl
ulus [ulus] *n* nation, nationality; **çok uluslu** *n* multinational
ulusal [ulusal] *adj* national
ulusalcı [ulusaldʒə] *n* nationalist
ulusalcılık [ulusaldʒələk] *n* nationalism
uluslararası [uluslararasə] *adj* international; **Bir uluslararası telefon kartı lütfen** An international phone card, please; **Buradan uluslararası görüşme yapabilir miyim?** Can I phone internationally from here?; **Nereden uluslararası telefon görüşmesi yapabilirim?** Where can I make an international phone call?
ummak [ummak] *v* expect
Umman [umman] *n* Oman
umulmadık [umulmadək] *adj* unexpected
umursamaz [umursamaz] *adj* casual
umut [umut] *n* hope; **umut etmek** *v* hope
umutla [umutla] *adv* hopefully
umutlu [umutlu] *adj* hopeful
umutsuz [umutsuz] *adj* desperate, hopeless
umutsuzca [umutsuzdʒa] *adv* desperately
umutsuzluk [umutsuzluk] *n*

despair
un [un] *n* flour; **kepekli undan yapılmış** *adj* wholemeal; **un kurabiyesi hamuru** *n* shortcrust pastry
unutmak [unutmak] *v* forget
unutulmaz [unutulmaz] *adj* unforgettable
unutulmuş [unutulmuʃ] *adj* forgotten
ur [ur] *n* tumour
uranyum [uranjum] *n* uranium
URL [ure:le:] *n* URL
Uruguay [uruguaj] *adj* Uruguayan ▷ *n* Uruguay
Uruguaylı [uruguajlə] *n* Uruguayan
uskumru [uskumru] *n* mackerel
usta [usta] *adj* skilful; **usta işi** *adj* ingenious
utanç [utantʃ] *npl* shame; **utanç verici** *adj* disgraceful
utangaç [utangatʃ] *adj* shy
utanmış [utanməʃ] *adj* embarrassed
uyanık [ujanək] *adj* alert, awake
uyanmak [ujanmak] *v* awake, wake up
uyarı [ujarə] *n* warning; **tehlike uyarı ışığı** *npl* hazard warning lights; **uyarı çağrısı** *n* alarm call
uyarlamak [ujarlamak] *n* adapt; **ihtiyaca uyarlanmış** *adj* customized
uyarmak [ujarmak] *v* alert, warn
uydu [ujdu] *n* satellite; **uydu çanak** *n* satellite dish
uydurmak [ujdurmak] *vi* fit ▷ *vt* match; **Olmadı** It doesn't fit me
uyduruk [ujduruk] *adj* fake
uygarlık [ujgarlək] *n* civilization
uygulamak [ujgulamak] *v* carry out
uygulanabilir [ujgulanabilir] *adj* feasible
uygun [ujgun] *adj* appropriate, available, convenient, decent, fit, suitable; **haklı olarak** *adv* rightly; **modaya uygun** *adj* fashionable, trendy; **uygun adım yürümek** *v* march; **uygun olmayan** *adj* unsuitable; **Tekerlekli sandalyeye uygun ulaşım var mı?** Is there wheelchair-friendly transport available to...?
uygunluk [ujgunluk] *n* availability
uyku [ujku] *n* sleep; **tavşan uykusu** *n* snooze; **uyku hapı** *n* sleeping pill; **uyku tulumu** *n* sleeping bag; **uykuda yürüme** *v* sleepwalk; **uykusunu almak** *v* have a lie-in, lie in; **uykuyu uzatmak** *v* snooze; **Uyuyamıyorum** I can't sleep
uykuda [ujkuda] *adj* asleep
uykulu [ujkulu] *adj* drowsy, sleepy
uykusuzluk [ujkusuzluk] *n* insomnia
uyma [ujma] *n* fit
uymak [ujmak] *v* suit ▷ *vi* fit in
uysal [ujsal] *adj* easy-going
uyumak [ujumak] *v* sleep; **Uyuyamıyorum** I can't sleep
uyumlu [ujumlu] *adj* compatible, matching
uyun adım yürüyüş [ujunadəmjyryjyʃ] *n* march
uyuşturucu [ujuʃturudʒu] *n* **uyuşturucu bağımlısı** *n* drug

addict; **uyuşturucu satıcısı** *n* drug dealer
uyuşuk [ujuʃuk] *adj* numb
uyuyakalmak [ujujakalmak] *v* doze off, oversleep, sleep in
uzak [uzak] *adj* distant, far, remote; **uzaktan kumandalı** *adj* radio-controlled; **uzaktan yakından** *adv* remotely; **Banka buraya ne kadar uzakta?** How far is the bank?; **Oldukça uzak** It's quite far; **Plajdan ne kadar uzaktayız?** How far are we from the beach?; **Uzak değil** It's not far; **Uzak mı?** Is it far?; **Uzak Doğu** *n* Far East
uzaklık [uzakløk] *n* distance; **mil hesabıyla uzaklık** *n* mileage
uzakta [uzakta] *adv* away, far
uzatma [uzatma] *n* extension; **uzatma kablosu** *n* extension cable; **uzatma süresi** *n* injury time
uzay [uzaj] *n* space; **uzay aracı** *n* spacecraft
uzman [uzman] *n* expert, specialist; **ayak uzmanı** *n* chiropodist; **doğa bilimleri uzmanı** *n* naturalist
uzmanlaşmak [uzmanlaʃmak] *v* specialize
uzmanlık [uzmanlək] *n* speciality
uzun [uzun] *adj* long; **daha uzun** *adv* longer; **uzun atlama** *n* jump, long jump; **uzun boylu** *adj* tall; **Çok uzun zamandır bekliyoruz** We've been waiting for a very long time
uzunca [uzundʒa] *adv* long
uzunluk [uzunluk] *n* length; **Bu uzunlukta olsun** This length, please
uzun uzadıya [uzunuzadəja] *adv* extensively

ücret [ydʒret] *n* fee, wage; **öğretim ücreti** *npl* tuition fees; **ücreti ödenmemiş** *adj* unpaid; **banka ücretleri** *npl* bank charges; **giriş ücreti** *n* admission charge, entrance fee; **posta ücreti** *n* postage; **servis ücreti** *n* cover charge, service charge; **Yer ayırtmak için ücret ödemek gerekiyor mu?** Is there a booking fee to pay?
ücretli [ydʒretli] *adj* paid; **düşük ücretli** *adj* underpaid
üç [ytʃ] *number* three; **üç boyutlu** *adj* three-dimensional; **üç katı** *adj* treble, triple; **üç tekerlekli bisiklet** *n* tricycle; **Üç çocuğum var** I have three children; **Üç Ekim Pazar** It's Sunday the third of October; **Üç numaralı pompa lütfen** Pump number three, please; **Bu akşam için üç kişilik bir masa ayırtmak istiyordum** I'd like to book a table for three people for tonight; **saat üçte** at three o'clock
üçgen [ytʃgen] *n* triangle
üçüncü [ytʃyndʒy] *adj* third ▷ *n* third; **üçüncü kişi sorumluluk sigortası** *n* third-party insurance; **üçüncü olarak** *adv* thirdly; **Üçüncü Dünya** *n* Third World
üçüzler [ytʃyzler] *npl* triplets
üflemek [yflemek] *v* blow; **üfleme cihazı** *n* Breathalyser®
ülke [ylke] *n* country; **ülke içi** *adj* domestic; **gelişmekte olan ülke** *n* developing country; **Ülkenin haritasını nereden alabilirim?** Where can I buy a map of the country?; **Körfez Ülkeleri** *npl* Gulf States
ümit [ymit] *n* hope, expectation; **ümit veren** *adj* promising
ün [yn] *n* fame, reputation
üniforma [yniforma] *n* uniform; **okul üniforması** *n* school uniform
ünite [ynite] *n* unit
üniversite [yniversite] *n* uni, university; **üniversite mezunu** *n* graduate, undergraduate
ünlem [ynlem] *n* **ünlem işareti** *n* exclamation mark
ünlü [ynly] *adj* famous ▷ *n* celebrity, *(gramer)* vowel
ünsüz [ynsyz] *n (gramer)* consonant
Ürdün [yrdyn] *adj* Jordanian ▷ *n* Jordan
Ürdünlü [yrdynly] *n* Jordanian
üreme [yreme] *n* reproduction
üretici [yretidʒi] *n* manufacturer,

producer
üretim [yretim] *n* production
üretmek [yretmek] *v* manufacture
ürkünç [yrkyntʃ] *adj* frightening
ürkütücü [yrkytydʒy] *adj* alarming, spooky
ürün [yryn] *n* crop, product; **ürün sağlamak** *v* yield; **deniz ürünü** *n* seafood; **kabuklu deniz ürünü** *n* shellfish; **süt ürünleri** *n* dairy products; **temel ürün** *n* staple *(commodity)*
üst [yst] *adj* upper, *(rütbe)* senior ▷ *n (kalite/rütbe)* superior; **üst katta** *adv* upstairs; **üstü açılır araba** *n* convertible; **üstü kapalı yük aracı** *n* van; **üstünü çıkarmak** *v* take off
üste [yste] *n* **üstesinden gelmek** *v* tackle
üstelik [ystelik] *adv* besides
üstün [ystyn] *adj* superior
üstünde [ystynde] *prep* over
üstünlük [ystynlyk] *n* advantage
ütü [yty] *n* **ütü tahtası** *n* ironing board; **Ütüye ihtiyacım var** I need an iron; **Bunu nerede ütületebilirim?** Where can I get this ironed?
ütüleme [ytyleme] *n* ironing
ütülemek [ytylemek] *v* iron
üvey [yvej] *n* **üvey anne** *n* stepmother; **üvey baba** *n* stepfather; **üvey erkek kardeş** *n* stepbrother; **üvey kız evlat** *n* stepdaughter; **üvey kızkardeş** *n* stepsister; **üvey oğul** *n* stepson
üye [yje] *n* member; **belediye meclis üyesi** *n* councillor; **Üye olmak gerekiyor mu?** Do you have to be a member?; **Üye olmam gerekiyor mu?** Do I have to be a member?
üyelik [yjelik] *n* membership; **üyelik kartı** *n* membership card
üzere [yzere] *conj* **Görüşmek üzere** See you soon
üzerinde [yzerinde] *prep* above
üzgün [yzgyn] *adj* sad
üzüm [yzym] *n* grape; **bektaşi üzümü** *n* gooseberry; **kuru üzüm** *n* raisin, sultana; **kırmızı Frenk üzümü** *n* redcurrant

V

vaaz [vaaz] *n* sermon
vade [vade] *prep* **vadesi geçmiş borç** *npl* arrears
vadi [vadi] *n* valley
vaftiz [vaftiz] *n* christening; **vaftiz çocuğu** *n* godchild; **vaftiz kızı** *n* goddaughter; **vaftiz oğlu** *n* godson
vagon [vagon] *n* carriage, *(oto)* estate car; **kuşetli vagon** *n* sleeping car; **yemek vagonu** *n* dining car; **yemekli vagon** *n* buffet car; **Otuz numaralı vagon nerede?** Where is carriage number thirty?
vaha [vaha] **(vahalar)** *n* oasis
vahşi [vahʃi] *adj* brutal; **vahşi doğa** *n* wildlife
vaiz [vaiz] *n* minister *(clergy)*
vaka [vaka] *n* case
vakıflar [vakəflar] *npl* foundations
vakit [vakit] *n* time; **boş vakit** *n* leisure; **hali vakti yerinde** *adj* well-off; **Çok güzel vakit geçiriyoruz** We are having a nice time
vakumlamak [vakumlamak] *v* vacuum
vakumlanmış [vakumlanməʃ] *adj* airtight
valiz [valiz] *n* suitcase; **Valizim hasar görmüş** My suitcase has arrived damaged
vals [vals] *n* waltz; **vals yapmak** *v* waltz
vampir [vampir] *n* vampire
vandal [vandal] *n* vandal
vandalizm [vandalizm] *n* vandalism
vanilya [vanilja] *n* vanilla
vantilatör [vantilatør] *n* fan; **Odada vantilatör var mı?** Does the room have a fan?
vapur [vapur] *n* **... a bir sonraki vapur kaçta?** When is the next sailing to...?; **... a son vapur kaçta?** When is the last sailing to...?; **... a vapur var mı?** Is there a ferry to...?; **İlk vapur kaçta?** When is the first boat?; **Son vapur kaçta?** When is the last boat?; **Vapur kaçta hareket ediyor?** When do we sail?; **Vapur nereden kalkıyor?** Where does the boat leave from?
var [var] *adj* present; **var olmak** *v* exist
varış [varəʃ] *n* arrival
varis [varis] *n* heir, *(kadın)* heiress
varlık [varlək] *n* asset, assets, presence, *(zenginlik)* wealth
varmak [varmak] *v* arrive; **farkına**

varmak *v* notice, realize
varsayım [varsajəm] *n* supposition; **varsayımda bulunmak** *v* speculate
varsaymak [varsajmak] *v* assume, suppose
varsıl [varsəl] *adj* wealthy
vasıta [vasəta] **vasıta ile çarpmak** *vi* crash
vasiyet [vasijet] *n* will *(document)*
vatandaş [vatandaʃ] *n* citizen; **yaşlı vatandaş** *n* senior citizen
vatandaşlık [vatandaʃlək] *n* citizenship
Vatikan [vatikan] *n* Vatican
vazgeçilmez [vazgetʃilmez] *adj* indispensable
vazgeçmek [vazgetʃmek] *v* give up, waive
vazo [vazo] *n* vase
vb [vb] *abbr (kısaltma)* etc
ve [ve] *conj* and
veda [veda] *n* farewell, goodbye; **bekarlığa veda partisi** *(erkek) n* stag night
vegan [vegan] *n* vegan; **Bu yemek veganlara uygun mu?** Is this suitable for vegans?; **Vegan yemeğiniz var mı?** Do you have any vegan dishes?
vejetaryen [veʒetarjen] *adj* vegetarian ▷ *n* vegetarian; **Bu yemek vejetaryenlere uygun mu?** Is this suitable for vegetarians?; **Vejetaryenim** I'm vegetarian; **Buralarda vejetaryen restoranlar var mı?** Are there any vegetarian restaurants here?; **Vejetaryen yemekleriniz var mı?** Do you have any vegetarian dishes?
vekalet [vekalet] **vekalet etmek** *v* substitute
vekaleten [vekaleten] *adj* acting
velet [velet] *n* brat
Venezuela [venezuela] *adj* Venezuelan ▷ *n* Venezuela
Venezuelalı [venezuelalə] *n* Venezuelan
veranda [veranda] *n* porch
vergi [vergi] *n* tax; **gelir vergisi** *n* income tax; **vergi geliri** *n* revenue; **vergi iadesi** *n* tax return; **vergi yükümlüsü** *n* tax payer; **yol vergisi** *n* road tax
veri [veri] *npl* data; **veri tabanı** *n* database
verici [veridʒi] *n* donor; **cesaret verici** *adj* encouraging; **dehşet verici** *adj* horrifying; **endişe veric** *adj* worrying; **heyecan verici** *adj* exciting, thrilling; **keyif verici** *adj* delightful; **utanç verici** *adj* disgraceful
verimlilik [verimlilik] *n* productivity
verimsiz [verimsiz] *adj* infertile
vermek [vermek] *v* hand ▷ *vt* give; **ödün vermek** *v* compromise; **ödünç vermek** *v* lend, loan; **bahşiş vermek** *vt* tip *(reward)*; **bilgi vermek** *v* inform; **ders vermek** *v* lecture; **fiyat vermek** *(açık arttırmada) vi* bid *(at auction)*; **güven vermek** *v* reassure; **güvence vermek** *v* assure; **geri vermek** *v* give back; **hayret verici** *adj* amazing; **hesap vermek** *v* account for; **izin vermek** *n* allow, let, permit; **kara**

vermek *v* decide; **komut vermek** *v* order *(command)*; **nefes vermek** *v* breathe out; **not vermek** *v* mark *(grade)*; **oy vermek** *v* vote; **rapor vermek** *v* report; **rüşvet vermek** *v* bribe; **söz vermek** *v* promise; **talimat vermek** *v* instruct; **tepki vermek** *v* respond; **yanıt vermek** *v* answer; **yanlış hüküm vermek** *v* misjudge; **yetki vermek** *v* authorize; **zarar vermek** *v* damage, harm; **Bahşiş vermek adet midir?** Is it usual to give a tip?
versiyon [versijon] *n* version
vestiyer [vestijer] *n* cloakroom
veteriner [veteriner] *n* vet
veto [veto] *n* veto
veznedar [veznedar] *n* treasurer
vızıldamak [vəzəldamak] *v* hum
vicdan [vidʒdan] *n* conscience; **vicdan azabı** *n* remorse
vicdanlı [vidʒdanlə] *adj* conscientious
vida [vida] *n* screw; **vida somunu** *n* nut *(device)*; **Vida gevşemiş** The screw has come loose
video [video] *n* video; **video kamera** *n* camcorder; **video kamerası** *n* video camera; **video telefon** *n* videophone; **Bu video kamera için teyp alabilir miyim?** Can I have a tape for this video camera, please?
Vietnam [vietnam] *adj* Vietnamese ▷ *n* Vietnam
Vietnamca [vietnamdʒa] *n (dil)* Vietnamese *(language)*
Vietnamlı [vietnamlə] *n (kişi)* Vietnamese *(person)*
villa [villa] *n* villa; **Bir villa kiralamak istiyorum** I'd like to rent a villa
vinç [vintʃ] *n* crane *(for lifting)*
viraj [viraʒ] *n* bend
virgül [virgyl] *n* comma; **noktalı virgül** *n* semicolon
virüs [virys] *n* virus
viski [viski] *n* whisky; **malt viskisi** *n* malt whisky; **bir viski soda** a whisky and soda; **Ben viski alayım** I'll have a whisky
vişne [viʃne] *n* **vişne çürüğü renginde** *adj* maroon
vitamin [vitamin] *n* vitamin
vites [vites] *n* gear; **vites kolu** *n* gear lever, gear stick, gearshift; **vites kutusu** *n* gear box; **Bisiklet vitesli mi?** Does the bike have gears?; **Vites çalışmıyor/Vitesler çalışmıyor** The gears don't work
vitray [vitraj] *n* stained glass
vitrin [vitrin] *n* shop window; **vitrin mankeni** *n* dummy
viyola [vijola] *n* viola
viyolonsel [vijolonsel] *n* cello
vize [vize] *n* visa; **Giriş vizem var** I have an entry visa; **Vizem burada** Here is my visa
vizon [vizon] *n* mink
voleybol [volejbol] *n* volleyball
volkan [volkan] **(volkanlar)** *n* volcano
volt [volt] *n* volt
voltaj [voltaʒ] *n* voltage; **Voltaj ne kadar?** What's the voltage?
votka [votka] *n* vodka
vurgulamak [vurgulamak] *v* emphasize, highlight, stress
vurmak [vurmak] *v* knock, ram,

thump, *(sineklik gibi yassı bir şeyle)* swat ▷ *vt* hit, strike; **ayağını yere vurmak** *v* stamp; **şiddetle vurmak** *v* bash

vurmalı [vurmalə] *n (müzik)* percussion

vuruş [vuruʃ] *n* knock, *(topa sopayla)* bat *(with ball)*; **başlama vuruşu** *n* kick-off; **başlama vuruşu yapmak** *v* kick off; **hafif vuruş** *n* tap

vücut [vydʒut] *n* body; **vücut geliştirme** *n* bodybuilding

waffle [vaffle] *n* waffle

webmaster [vebmaster] *n* webmaster

WiFi [vifi] *n* Wi-Fi

Y

'a [ja] *conj* either... or, or
abancı [jabandʒə] *adj* foreign ▷ *n* alien, foreigner, stranger
'aban gelinciği [jabangelindʒəə] *n* ferret
'abani [jabani] *adj* wild; **yabani havuç** *n* parsnip; **yabani ot** *n* weed; **yabani ot öldürücü** *n* weedkiller; **yabani tavşan** *n* hare
'aban mersini [jabanmersini] *n* blueberry; **kırmızı yaban mersini** *n* cranberry
abanturpu [jabanturpu] *n* horseradish
a da [jada] *adv* alternatively
ağ [ja:] *n* fat, grease, oil; **güneş yağı** *n* suntan oil; **yağ çubuğu** *n* dipstick; **yağı alınmış süt** *n* skimmed milk; **yarım yağlı süt** *n* semi-skimmed milk; **zeytin yağı** *n* olive oil; **Yağ ikaz ışığı yanıyor** The oil warning light won't go off; **Yağ lekesi** This stain is oil
yağlamak [ja:lamak] *v* oil
yağlı [ja:lə] *adj* greasy
yağmak [ja:mak] *v* rain; **dolu yağmak** *v* hail; **kar yağmak** *v* snow; **sulu sepken yağmak** *v* sleet; **yağmur yağmak** *v* rain
yağmur [ja:mur] *n* rain; **asit yağmuru** *n* acid rain; **yağmur ormanı** *n* rainforest; **yağmura dayanıklı** *adj* showerproof; **yağmurlama cihazı** *n* sprinkler; **Sizce yağmur yağacak mı?** Do you think it's going to rain?; **Yağmur yağıyor** It's raining
yağmurlu [ja:murlu] *adj* rainy
yağmurluk [ja:murluk] *n* mac, raincoat
Yahudi [jahudi] *adj* Jewish ▷ *n* Jew
yaka [jaka] *n* collar; **polo yakalı kazak** *n* polo-necked sweater
yakalamak [jakalamak] *v* seize ▷ *vt* catch
yakın [jakən] *adj* close, close by, intimate, near, nearby ▷ *adv* close; **en yakın akraba** *n* next-of-kin; **uzaktan yakından** *adv* remotely; **yakın dost** *n* pal; **Çok yakın** It's very near; **Buraya en yakın metro istasyonu nerede?** Where is the nearest tube station?; **Buraya en yakın otobüs durağı nerede?** Where is the nearest bus stop?; **Buraya yakın bir golf sahası var mı?** Is there a public golf course near here?; **Buraya yakın sakin bir kumsal var mı?** Is there a quiet beach near here?; **En yakın bisiklet tamircisi nerede?** Where is the nearest bike repair

shop?; **En yakın dağ kulübesi nerede?** Where is the nearest mountain hut?; **En yakın dağ kurtarma ekibi nerede?** Where is the nearest mountain rescue service post?; **En yakın eczane nerede?** Where is the nearest chemist?; **En yakın fotoğraf malzemeleri satan dükkan nerede?** Where is the nearest shop which sells photographic equipment?; **En yakın gazete satan dükkan nerede?** Where is the nearest shop which sells newspapers?; **En yakın metro istasyonu nerede?** Where is the nearest tube station?; **En yakın metro istasyonuna nasıl gidebilirim?** How do I get to the nearest tube station?; **Pul satan en yakın yer nerede?** Where is the nearest shop which sells stamps?; **Yakınlarda bir banka var mı?** Is there a bank nearby?

yakından [jakəndan] *adv* closely

yakınında [jakənənda] *adv* around, near

yakınlarda [jakənlarda] *adv* nearby

yakınlık [jakənlək] *n* proximity

yakınmak [jakənmak] *v* complain

yakışıklı [jakəʃəklə] *adj* good-looking, handsome

yakıt [jakət] *n* fuel; **yakıt ikmali yapmak** *v* refuel

yaklaşık [jaklaʃək] *adj* approximate ▷ *adv* about; **yaklaşık olarak** *adv* approximately

yaklaşmak [jaklaʃmak] *v* approach

yakmak [jakmak] *v (ışık)* light ▷ *vi (ateşte)* burn

yalak [jalak] *n* trough

yalamak [jalamak] *v* lick

yalan [jalan] *n* lie; **yalan söylemek** *v* lie

yalancı [jalandʒə] *n* liar; **yalancı şahitlik** *n* perjury

yaldız [jaldəz] *n* **kalay yaldızı** *n* tinfoil

yalı [jalə] *adj* **yalı çapkını** *n* kingfisher

yalıtım [jalətəm] *n* insulation

yalnız [jalnəz] *adj* alone, lonely, lonesome; **yalnız ebeveyn** *n* single parent

yalnızca [jalnəzdʒa] *adv* exclusively, only

yalnızlık [jalnəzlək] *n* loneliness

yama [jama] *n* patch

yamalı [jamalə] *adj* patched

yan [jan] *n (destek)* subsidiary; **ya[n] ayna** *n* wing mirror; **yan etki** *n* side effect; **yan lambalar** *n* sidelight; **yan sokak** *n* side stree[t]; **yana doğru** *adv* sideways; **yanından geçmek** *v* go past

yanak [janak] *n* cheek

yangı [jangə] *n* inflammation

yangın [jangən] *n* fire; **yangın alarmı** *n* fire alarm; **yangın çıkış[ı]** *n* fire escape; **yangın söndürücü** *n* fire extinguisher; **Yangın var!** Fire!

yanıcı [janədʒə] *adj* flammable

yanık [janək] *n* burn; **güneş yanığı** *adj* sunburn, sunburnt

yanılsama [janəlsama] *n* illusion

yanıltıcı [janəltədʒə] *adj*

confusing, misleading
yanıltmak [janəltmak] *v* deceive
yanında [janənda] *prep* beside, next to
yanıt [janət] *n* answer, reply, response; **yanıt vermek** *v* answer; **Yanıtınızı bana mesajla geçer misiniz?** Can you text me your answer?
yanıtlamak [janətlamak] *v* reply
yankesicilik [jaŋesidʒilik] *n* pickpocket
yankı [jaŋə] *n* echo
yanlı [janlə] *adj* biased
yanlış [janləʃ] *adj* incorrect, wrong ▷ *adv* wrong ▷ *n* error; **yanlış alarm** *n* false alarm; **yanlış anlama** *n* misunderstanding; **yanlış anlamak** *v* misunderstand; **yanlış hüküm vermek** *v* misjudge; **yanlış numara** *n* wrong number; **yanlış yere koymak** *v* mislay; **Sanırım yanlış para üstü verdiniz** I think you've given me the wrong change; **Yanlış şerittesiniz** You are in the wrong lane; **Yanlış numara** You have the wrong number
yanlışlıkla [janləʃləkla] *adv* mistakenly
yanmak [janmak] *v* burn; **yanıp kül olmak** *v* burn down
yansıma [jansəma] *n* reflection
yansıtmak [jansətmak] *v* reflect
yansız [jansəz] *adj* impartial, impersonal
yapabilmek [japabilmek] **yapabilir almak** *v* to be able
yapamamak [japamamak] *adj* unable to
yapay [japaj] *adj* artificial, superficial
yapboz [jabboz] *n* jigsaw
yapı [japə] *n* building, construction, structure
yapıcı [japədʒə] *adj* constructive ▷ *n* maker
yapılmış [japəlməʃ] *adj* done; **sütle yapılmış** *n* dairy produce
yapım [japəm] *n* make; **el yapımı** *adj* handmade; **ev yapımı** *adj* home-made; **gemi yapımı** *n* shipbuilding; **yol yapım çalışması** *npl* roadworks
yapışkan [japəʃkan] *adj* sticky
yapışmak [japəʃmak] *vi* stick
yapıştırmak [japəʃtərmak] *v* glue
yapmak [japmak] *v* construct, make ▷ *vt* do; **alıntı yapmak** *v* quote; **ızgara yapmak** *v* grill; **başlama vuruşu yapmak** *v* kick off; **baskı yapmak** *v* lean on, pressure; **baskın yapmak** *v* raid; **blöf yapmak** *v* bluff; **düşük yapmak** *n* miscarriage; **değişiklik yapmak** *v* modify; **dedikodu yapmak** *v* gossip; **diyet yapmak** *v* diet; **ekonomi yapmak** *v* economize; **elle yapmak** *v* handle; **görüşme yapmak** *v* interview; **gösteriş yapmak** *v* show off; **giriş yapmak** *v* check in; **grev yapmak** *vi* strike *(suspend work)*; **hata yapmak** *v* mistake, slip up; **hız yapmak** *v* speeding; **işbirliği yapmak** *v* collaborate; **iniş yapmak** *vi* land; **kaçakçılık yapmak** *v* smuggle; **kamp yapmak** *v* camp; **karalama yapmak** *v* sketch; **karşılıklı**

yapmak *v* exchange; **şaka yapmak** *v* joke; **şantaj yapmak** *n* blackmail; **manikür yapmak** *n* manicure; **modelini yapmak** *v* model; **otostop yapma** *n* hitchhiking; **para iadesi yapmak** *v* refund; **paten yapma** *n* skating; **paten yapmak** *v* skate; **pratik yapmak** *v* practise; **reklam yapmak** *v* advertise; **sayı yapmak** *v* score; **sörf yapma** *n* surfing; **sörf yapmak** *v* surf; **skateboard yapma** *n* skateboarding; **tanıtımını yapmak** *v* promote; **tezahürat yapmak** *v* cheer; **vals yapmak** *v* waltz; **yapmak zorunda olmak** *v* have to; **yatırım yapmak** *v* invest; **yayın yapmak** *v* broadcast; **yeniden yapmak** *v* rebuild, redo; **yorum yapmak** *v* comment

yaprak [japrak] *n* leaf; **defne yaprağı** *n* bay leaf

yapraklar [japraklar] *npl* leaves

yaptırmak [japtərmak] **kayıt yaptırmak** *v* register

yara [jara] *n* injury, scar, sore, wound, *(ülser)* ulcer; **yara bandı** *n* Elastoplast®, plaster *(for wound)*

yaradılış [jaradələʃ] *n* creation

yaralamak [jaralamak] *v* injure, wound

yaralanmış [jaralanməʃ] *adj* injured

yaramaz [jaramaz] *adj (çocuk vb)* mischievous, *(çocuk vb)* naughty

yaramazlık [jaramazlək] *n* mischief

yarar [jarar] *n* benefit; **yarar sağlamak** *v* benefit

yararlı [jararlə] *adj* useful

yararsız [jararsəz] *adj* useless

yarasa [jarasa] *n* bat *(mammal)*

yaratıcı [jaratədʒə] *adj* creative; **gerginlik yaratıcı** *adj* stressful

yaratık [jaratək] *n* creature

yaratmak [jaratmak] *v* create, produce

yarda [jarda] *n* yard *(measurement)*

yardım [jardəm] *n* aid, assistance, favour, help; **ilk yardım** *n* first aid; **ilk yardım çantası** *n* first-aid kit; **yardım derneği** *n* charity; **yardım derneği dükkanı** *n* charity shop; **yardım etmek** *vt* help; **yardım hattı** *n* helpline; **yoksulluk yardımı** *n* dole; **Binmeme yardım eder misiniz lütfen?** Can you help me get on, please?; **Valizleri taşımama yardım eder misiniz lütfen?** Can you help me with my luggage, please?; **Yardım çağırın, çabuk!** Fetch help quickly!; **Yardım edebilir misiniz lütfen?** Can you help me, please?; **Yardıma ihtiyacım var** I need assistance; **Yardımcı olabilir misiniz?** Can you help me?

yardımcı [jardəmdʒə] *adj* associate, helpful; **müdür yardımcısı** *n* deputy head; **papaz yardımcısı** *n* vicar; **yardımcı öğretmen** *n* classroom assistant; **yardımcı olmayan** *adj* unhelpful

yargıç [jargətʃ] *n* judge

yargılamak [jargəlamak] *v* judge

yarı [jarə] *n* **yarı fiyatı/yarı fiyatına** *adv* half-price; **yarı**

yarıya *adv* fifty-fifty, half; **yarı yolda** halfway
yarım [jarəm] *adj* half ▹ *n* half; **yarı final** *n* semifinal; **yarım daire** *n* semicircle; **yarım gün** *adv* part-time; **yarım peruk** *n* toupee; **yarım saat** *n* half-hour; **yarım yağlı süt** *n* semi-skimmed milk
yarımada [jarəmada] *n* peninsula
yarın [ja:rən] *adv* tomorrow; **Sizi yarın arayabilir miyim?** May I call you tomorrow?; **yarın öğleden sonra** tomorrow afternoon; **yarın gece** tomorrow night; **yarın sabah** tomorrow morning; **Yarın açık mı?** Is it open tomorrow?; **Yarın ayrılıyorum** I'm leaving tomorrow; **Yarın bir şeyler yapmak ister misiniz?** Would you like to do something tomorrow?; **Yarın sabah boşum** I'm free tomorrow morning; **Yarın tekrar arayacağım** I'll call back tomorrow
yarış [jarəʃ] *n* race *(contest)*; **at yarışı** *n* horse racing; **oto yarışı** *n* motor racing; **yarış arabası** *n* racing car; **yarış atı** *n* racehorse; **yarış parkuru** *n* racecourse; **yarış pisti** *n* racetrack; **At yarışı görmek isterdim** I'd like to see a horse race
yarışçı [jarəʃtʃə] *n* racer, *(otomobil)* racing driver
yarışma [jarəʃma] *n* competition, contest; **bilgi yarışması** *n* quiz
yarışmacı [jarəʃmadʒə] *n* competitor, contestant, runner
yarışmak [jarəʃmak] *v* compete ▹ *vi* race
yasa [jasa] *n* bill *(legislation)*, law
yasadışı [jasadəʃə] *adj* illegal
yasak [jasak] *adj* forbidden ▹ *n* ban
yasaklamak [jasaklamak] *v* ban, forbid, prohibit
yasaklanmış [jasaklanməʃ] *adj* banned, prohibited
yasal [jasal] *adj* legal
yasalar [jasalar] *n* constitution
yaslamak [jaslamak] *v* lean
yaslanır [jaslanər] *adj* reclining
yastık [jastək] *n* cushion, pillow; **hava yastığı** *n* airbag; **yastık kılıfı** *n* pillowcase
yaş [jaʃ] *n (yıl)* age; **orta yaşlı** *adj* middle-aged; **yaş sınırı** *n* age limit; **yaşça en büyük** *adj* eldest; **yaşça küçük** *adj* junior; **yaşlı vatandaş** *n* senior citizen; **yirmi yaş dişi** *n* wisdom tooth
yaşam [jaʃam] *n* life; **özel yaşam** *n* privacy; **sağlıklı yaşam** *n* keep-fit; **yaşam öyküsü** *n* biography; **yaşam biçimi** *n* lifestyle; **yaşam kavgası** *n* survival; **yaşam sigortası** *n* life insurance; **yaşam standardı** *n* standard of living; **yaşama bakış** *n* outlook
yaşamak [jaʃamak] *v* live; **beraber yaşamak** *v* live together
yaşlı [jaʃlə] *adj* aged, old; **daha yaşlı** *adj* elder
yaşlılar [jaʃləlar] *adj* elderly, geriatric
yaşlılık [jaʃlələk] *n* geriatric
yat [jat] *n (tekne)* yacht; **yat limanı** *n* marina
yatak [jatak] *n* bed, *(döşek)* mattress; **çift kişilik yatak** *n* double bed; **çift yatak** *npl* twin

beds; **çift yataklı oda** *n* twin room, twin-bedded room; **battal boy yatak** *n* king-size bed; **deniz yatağı** *n* Lilo®; **güneşlenme yatağı** *n* sunbed; **tek yatak** *n* single bed; **yatak örtüsü** *n* bedspread; **yatak çarşafı** *n* bed linen; **yatak odası** *n* bedroom; **yatak takımı** *n* bedclothes, bedding; **yatak ve kahvaltı** *n* bed and breakfast; **İki yataklı bir oda rica ediyorum** I'd like a room with twin beds; **Çift yataklı bir oda rica ediyorum** I'd like a room with a double bed; **Tek bir yatak rica ediyorum** I'd like a dorm bed; **Yatak çok rahatsız** The bed is uncomfortable; **Yatakta mı kalmam gerekiyor?** Do I have to stay in bed?

yatakhane [jatakhane] *n* dormitory

yatay [jataj] *adj* horizontal, level

yatık [jatək] *n* **geriye yatık çizgi** *n* backslash

yatırım [jatərəm] *n* investment; **yatırım yapmak** *v* invest

yatırımcı [jatərəmdʒə] *n* investor

yatıştırıcı [jatəʃtərədʒə] *n* sedative

yatmak [jatmak] *v* lie, lie down; **önüne gelenle yatmak** *v* sleep around; **birlikte yatmak** *v* sleep together; **yatma zamanı** *n* bedtime

yavaş [javaʃ] *adj* slow; **yavaş yavaş kaynatmak** *v* simmer; **Bağlantı çok yavaş** The connection seems very slow; **Biraz daha yavaş konuşabilir misiniz lütfen?** Could you speak more slowly, please?

yavaşça [javaʃtʃa] *adv* slowly

yavaşlamak [javaʃlamak] *v* slow down

yavru [javru] *n (aslan/ayı)* cub; **kedi yavrusu** *n* kitten; **yavru köpek** *n* puppy; **yeni doğmuş yavrular** *n* litter *(offspring)*

yay [jaj] *n* bow *(weapon)*, spring *(coil)*

Yay [jaj] *n* **Yay burcu** *n* Sagittarius

yaya [jaja] *n* pedestrian; **ışıklı yaya geçidi** *n* pelican crossing; **şeritli yaya geçidi** *n* zebra crossing; **yaya geçidi** *n* pedestrian crossing; **yayalara ayrılmış** *adj* pedestrianized; **yayalara özel bölge** *n* pedestrian precinct

yaygara [jajgara] *n* fuss

yaygaracı [jajgaradʒə] *adj* fussy

yaygın [jajgən] *adj* widespread; **yaygın bir şekilde** *adv* largely

yayılım [jajələm] *n* spread

yayılmak [jajəlmak] *v* spread out

yayımlama [jajəmlama] *n* publication

yayımlamak [jajəmlamak] *v* publish

yayın [jajən] *n* broadcast; **kablolu yayın** *n* cable television; **yayın yapmak** *v* broadcast

yayınevi [jajənevi] *n* publisher

yayıntı [jajəntə] *n* clutter

yaymak [jajmak] *vt* spread

yaz [jaz] *n (mevsim)* summer; **yaz sezonu** *n* summertime; **yaz tatili** *npl* summer holidays; **yaz boyunca** during the summer;

yazın in summer; **yazdan önce** before summer; **yazdan sonra** after summer
yazar [jazar] **(kadın yazar)** *n* author, writer; **oyun yazarı** *n* playwright; **yazar kasa** *n* till
yazı [jazə] *n* writing; **anma yazısı** *(ölünün ardından) n* obituary; **beyaz yazı tahtası** *n* whiteboard; **el yazısı** *n* handwriting; **kazılmış yazı** *n* inscription; **yazı kağıdı** *n* writing paper
yazıcı [jazədʒə] *n* printer *(machine)*; **CD yazıcı** *n* CD burner; **DVD yazıcı** *n* DVD burner; **Renkli yazıcı var mı?** Is there a colour printer?
yazık [jazək] *n* pity, shame; **ne yazık ki** *adv* unfortunately
yazılım [jazələm] *n* software
yazım [jazəm] *n* spelling; **yazım denetimi** *n* spellchecker
yazın [jazən] in summer
yazışma [jazəʃma] *n* correspondence
yazlık [jazlək] *n* **yazlık iş** *n* holiday job
yazma [jazma] *adv* **okuma yazması olmayan** *adj* illiterate
yazmak [jazmak] *v* write, write down, *(daktilo/bilgisayar)* type; **blog yazmak** *v* blog; **ilaç yazmak** *v* prescribe
yedek [jedek] *adj* spare ▹ *n* backup, reserve *(retention)*, substitute; **yedek öğretmen** *n* supply teacher; **yedek oda** *n* spare room; **yedek parça** *n* spare part; **Yedek çarşaf takımı var mı?** Is there any spare bedding?
yedi [jedi] *number* seven
yedinci [jedindʒi] *adj* seventh ▹ *n* seventh
yeğen [je:en] *n (erkek)* nephew, *(kız)* niece
Yehova [jehova] *n* **Yehovanın Şahitleri** *n* Jehovah's Witness
yelek [jelek] *n* waistcoat; **cankurtaran yeleği** *n* life jacket
yelken [jelken] *n* sail; **yelken sporu** *n* sailing
yelkenli [jelkenli] *n* sailing boat
yemek [jemek] *n* dish *(food)* ▹ *vt* eat; **akşam yemeği** *n* dinner; **ana yemek** *n* main course; **artık yemek** *npl* leftovers; **öğle yemeği** *n* lunch; **ön yemek** *n* starter; **darbe yemek** *vi* strike; **hafif akşam yemeği** *n* supper; **hazır yemek** *n* ready-cooked, takeaway; **paket yemek** *n* packed lunch; **yemek öncesi içki** *n* aperitif; **yemek kitabı** *n* cookbook, cookery book; **yemek molası** *n* lunch break; **yemek salonu** *n* dining room; **yemek vagonu** *n* dining car; **yemek zamanı** *n* dinner time, lunchtime, mealtime; **yemekli parti** *n* dinner party; **yemekli vagon** *n* buffet car; **yemeklik şarap** *n* table wine; **İçinde nişasta olmayan yemeğiniz var mı?** Do you have gluten-free dishes?; **Bir şey yemek ister misiniz?** Would you like something to eat?; **Bu yemeği nasıl pişiriyorsunuz?** How do you cook this dish?; **Bu yemeğin içinde ne var?** What is in this dish?; **Bu yemeğin yanında ne**

veriyorsunuz? How is this dish served?; **Feribotta yemek satan bir yer var mı?** Is there somewhere to eat on the boat?; **Günün yemeği ne?** What is the dish of the day?; **Helal yemeğiniz var mı?** Do you have halal dishes?; **Koşer yemeğiniz var mı?** Do you have kosher dishes?; **Ne yemek istersiniz?** What would you like to eat?; **Vegan yemeğiniz var mı?** Do you have any vegan dishes?; **Vejetaryen yemekleriniz var mı?** Do you have any vegetarian dishes?; **Yöresel bir yemek tavsiye edebilir misiniz?** Can you recommend a local dish?; **Yemek yediniz mi?** Have you eaten?

Yemen [jemen] *n* Yemen

yemin [jemin] *n* oath

yengeç [jengetʃ] *n* crab

Yengeç [jengetʃ] *n* **Yengeç Burcu** *n* Cancer *(horoscope)*

yeni [jeni] *adj* new, recent; **yeni başlayan** *n* beginner; **yeni doğan** *adj* newborn; **yeni doğmuş yavrular** *n* litter *(offspring)*; **yeni gelen** *n* newcomer; **yeni yürümeye başlayan çocuk** *n* toddler; **yeniden çekim** *n* remake; **yeniden badana yapmak** *v* redecorate; **yeniden bir araya gelme** *n* reunion; **yeniden düzenlemek** *v* reorganize; **yeniden ele almak** *vt* reconsider; **yeniden evlenmek / yeniden gösterim** remarry; **yeniden göstermek** *v* replay; **yeniden kullanmak** *v* reuse; **yeniden sınava girmek** *v* resit; **yeniden yapılandırma** *v* restructure; **yeniden yapmak** *v* rebuild, redo; **Yeni bir akü gerekiyor** I need a new battery; **Yepyeni bir tarz istiyorum** I want a completely new style; **Yeni Yıl** *n* New Year

yenilebilir [jenilebilir] *adj* edible

yenilemek [jenilemek] *n* makeover ▹ *v* renew, renovate

yenilenebilir [jenilenebilir] *adj* renewable

yenilgi [jenilgi] *n* defeat; **yenilgiyi kabullenmek** *v* give in

yenilik [jenilik] *n* innovation

yenilikçi [jeniliktʃi] *adj* innovative

yenilmez [jenilmez] *adj* unbeatable

yenilmiş [jenilmiʃ] *n* loser

Yeni Zelanda [jenizelanda] *n* New Zealand; **Yeni Zelandalı** *n* New Zealander

yenmek [jenmek] *v* beat *(outdo)*, conquer, defeat, triumph

yepyeni [jepjeni] *adj* brand-new

yer [jer] *n* floor, ground, location, place, spot, venue; **ayağını yere vurmak** *v* stamp; **başka bir yerde** *adv* elsewhere; **bir yerde** *adv* someplace, somewhere; **doğum yeri** *n* birthplace, place of birth; **güzel manzaralı yer** *n* beauty spot; **gezinti yeri** *n* promenade; **gidilecek yer** *n* destination; **her yerde** *adv* everywhere; **herhangi bir yer** *adv* anywhere; **hiçbir yerde** *adv* nowhere; **kalacak yer** *n* accommodation; **kamp yeri** *n* campsite; **kapalı yer korkusu olan** *adj* claustrophobic; **pazar**

yeri *n* marketplace; **tatil yeri** *n* resort; **yanlış yere koymak** *v* mislay; **yer değiştirme** *n* shift; **yer değiştirmek** *v* shift; **yer muşambası** *n* lino; **yere sermek** *v* knock out; **yerin altında** *adv* underground; **yerini alma** *n* replacement; **yerini almak** *v* replace; **Burada dalınacak en iyi yer neresi?** Where is the best place to dive?; **Gidilecek iyi bir yer biliyor musunuz?** Do you know a good place to go?
yeraltı [jeraltə] *n* **yeraltı harekatı** *n* underground
yerden [jerden] *n* **yerden almak** *v* pick up
yerel [jerel] *adj* local; **Yerel bitkileri ve ağaçları görmek isterdik** We'd like to see local plants and trees; **Yerel müzisyenleri dinleyebileceğimiz bir yer var mı?** Where can we hear local musicians play?; **Yerel yürüyüşler için rehberiniz var mı?** Do you have a guide to local walks?; **Yerel yemeğiniz nedir?** What's the local speciality?; **Yerel yemeğiniz var mı?** Is there a local speciality?
yerfıstığı [jerfəstʒə] *n* peanut
yerine [jerine] *adv* instead ▷ *prep* instead of
yerküre [jerkyre] *n* globe
yerleşmek [jerleʃmek] *v* settle down
yerleştirme [jerleʃtirme] *n* placement
yerleştirmek [jerleʃtirmek] *vt* place
yerli [jerli] *adj* native
yeryüzü [jerjyzy] *n* earth
yeşil [jeʃil] *adj* green *(colour)* ▷ *n* green; **yeşil limon** *n* lime *(fruit)*; **yeşil salata** *n* green salad
Yeşilaycı [jeʃilajdʒə] *adj* teetotal
yetenek [jetenek] *n* ability, talent
yetenekli [jetenekli] *adj* gifted, talented
yeteneksiz [jeteneksiz] *adj* incompetent
yeter [jeter] *adv* **yeter ki** *conj* provided, providing; **Bu kadar yeter, sağolun** That's enough, thank you
yeterli [jeterli] *adj* sufficient
yetersiz [jetersiz] *adj* inadequate, inefficient, insufficient, skimpy; **yetersiz beslenme** *n* malnutrition
yetişkin [jetiʃkin] *n* adult; **yetişkin eğitimi** *n* adult education
yetişmek [jetiʃmek] *v* catch up
yetiştirilme [jetiʃtirilme] *n* upbringing
yetiştirmek [jetiʃtirmek] *v* bring up, *(hayvan)* breed
yetki [jetki] *n* authority; **yetki vermek** *v* authorize
yetkilendirmek [jetkilendirmek] *v* delegate
yetkili [jetkili] *adj* official
yetkin [jetkin] *adj* competent
yetmiş [jetmiʃ] *number* seventy
yığılmak [jɜəlmak] *n* pile-up
yığın [jɜən] *n* heap, pile, stack; **saman yığını** *n* haystack
yıkamak [jəkamak] *v* wash;

bulaşık yıkama *n* washing-up; **bulaşık yıkamak** *v* wash up; **oto yıkama** *n* car wash; **Arabayı yıkamak istiyorum** I would like to wash the car; **Yıkama makinesi nasıl çalışıyor?** How do I use the car wash?

yıkanabilir [jəkanabilir] *adj* **makinede yıkanabilir** *n* machine washable; **Bu yıkanabilir mi?** Is it washable?

yıkıcı [jəkədʒə] *adj* devastating

yıkmak [jəkmak] *v* demolish, pull down

yıl [jəl] *n* year; **akademik yıl** *n* academic year; **artık yıl** *n* leap year; **her yıl** *adv* annually, yearly; **mali yıl** *n* financial year, fiscal year; **on yıl** *n* decade; **yıllık taşıt testi** *n* MOT; **yüzüncü yıl** *n* centenary; **bu yıl** this year; **geçen yıl** last year; **gelecek yıl** next year; **Mutlu Yıllar!** Happy New Year!; **Yeni Yıl** *n* New Year

yılan [jəlan] *n* snake; **çıngıraklı yılan** *n* rattlesnake; **yılan balığı** *n* eel

yıldız [jəldəz] *n (gök)* star *(sky)*, *(kişi)* star *(person)*; **film yıldızı** *n* film star; **kuyruklu yıldız** *n* comet; **yıldız falı** *n* horoscope; **yıldız koymak** *v* star

yıl dönümü [jəldønymy] *n* anniversary

yıllık [jəllək] *adj* annual, yearly

yırtıcı [jərtədʒə] *n* **yırtıcı kuş** *n* bird of prey

yırtık [jərtək] *n* tear *(split)*

yırtmak [jərtmak] *v* rip up, tear, tear up ▷ *vt* rip

yine [jine] *adv* again; **yine de** *adv* yet *(nevertheless)*

yinelenen [jinelenen] *adj* recurring

yirmi [jirmi] *number* twenty; **yirmi yaş dişi** *n* wisdom tooth; **Her yirmi dakikada bir otobüs var** The bus runs every twenty minutes

yirminci [jirmindʒi] *adj* twentieth

yiyecek [jijedʒek] *n* food; **doğal yiyecek** *npl* wholefoods; **yiyecek maddeleri** *npl* groceries; **Yiyecek satıyor musunuz?** Do you have food?

yoga [joga] *n* yoga

yoğun [jou:n] *adj* intense, intensive; **yoğun bakım ünitesi** *n* intensive care unit

yoğunlaşma [jou:nlaʃma] *n* concentration

yoğunlaşmak [jou:nlaʃmak] *v* concentrate

yoğunluk [jou:nluk] *n* density

yoğurt [jou:rt] *n* yoghurt

yok [jok] *adj* absent ▷ *adv* not; **yok etmek** *v* destroy; **yok olmak** *v* vanish

yoklama [joklama] *n* roll call; **kamuoyu yoklaması** *n* opinion poll, poll

yoklamak [joklamak] *v* search, inspect; **elle yoklamak** *v* grope

yokluk [jokluk] *n (devam)* absence, *(eksiklik)* shortage

yoksa [joksa] *conj* otherwise

yoksul [joksul] *adj* hard up, poor

yoksulluk [joksulluk] *n* poverty; **yoksulluk yardımı** *n* dole

yokuş [jokuʃ] *n* slope; **yokuş**

yukarı *adv* uphill

yol [jol] *n* road, way ▷ *npl* means; **çevre yolu** *n* bypass, ring road; **çift-şeritli yol** *n* dual carriageway; **bağlantı yolu** *n* slip road; **bisiklet yolu** *n* cycle path; **bisiklet yolu** *n* cycle lane; **dar yol** *n* lane; **engebeli yol** *n* track; **kestirme yol** *n* shortcut; **yarı yolda** halfway ▷ *v* **yol açmak** *v* cause; **yol çukuru** *n* pothole; **yol göstermek** *vt* lead; **yol haritası** *n* road map; **yol kenarında geçici park yeri** *n* layby; **yol tabelası** *n* signpost; **yol vergisi** *n* road tax; **yol yapım çalışması** *npl* roadworks; **yola çıkmak** *v* go away, start off; **yola koyulmak** *v* set off; **yoluna koymak** *v* settle; **... yol haritası istiyorum** I need a road map of...; **... a gitmek için hangi yoldan gitmem gerek?** Which road do I take for...?; **Bu yolda hız limiti nedir?** What is the speed limit on this road?; **Yol hakkı sizin değildi** It wasn't your right of way; **Yol ne zaman açılır?** When will the road be clear?; **Yol vermedi** She didn't give way; **Yollar buzlu mu?** Are the roads icy?

yolcu [joldʒu] *n* fare, passenger; **büyük yolcu gemisi** *n* liner; **transit yolcu salonu** *n* transit lounge

yolcular [joldʒular] *npl* traveller

yolculuk [joldʒuluk] *n (kısa)* trip, *(otomobil)* drive; **gemiyle yolculuk etmek** *n* sail; **gidiş dönüş yolculuk** *n* round trip; **İyi yolculuklar!** Have a good trip!

yoldaş [joldaʃ] *n* companion

yoluyla [jolujla] *prep* past, via

yorgan [jorgan] *n* duvet, quilt

yorgun [jorgun] *adj* tired; **Biraz yorgunum** I'm a little tired; **Yorgunum** I'm tired

yorucu [jorudʒu] *adj* tiring

yorum [jorum] *n* comment, commentary; **yorum yapmak** *v* comment

yorumcu [jorumdʒu] *n* commentator

yosun [josun] *n* moss, seaweed

yozlaşma [jozlaʃma] *n* corruption

yozlaşmış [jozlaʃməʃ] *adj* corrupt

yön [jøn] *n* direction; **çok yönlü** *n* versatile; **doğu yönünde** *adj* eastbound; **ilgisini başka yöne çekmek** *v* distract; **mecburi yön** *(trafik) n* diversion; **saat yönünde** *adv* clockwise; **saatin aksi yönünde** *adv* anticlockwise; **tek yön bilet** *n* single ticket

yönetici [jønetidʒi] *n* executive

yönetim [jønetim] *n* administration, management, steering; **yönetim merkezi** *n* head office; **yönetimi ele almak** *v* take over

yönetmek [jønetmek] *vt* direct

yönetmelik [jønetmelik] *n* regulation

yöntem [jøntem] *n* method

yöre [jøre] *n* **Bu yöreye özgü bir şey denemek istiyorum lütfen** I'd like to try something local, please; **Bu yöreye özgü bir şey istiyorum** Do you have anything typical of this region?; **Yöreye**

özgü bir şey ısmarlamak istiyorum I'd like to order something local; **Yöresel bir yemek tavsiye edebilir misiniz?** Can you recommend a local dish?

yukarı [jukarə] *adv* up; **yokuş yukarı** *adv* uphill; **yukarıya doğru** *adv* upwards

yukarıya [jukarəja] *adv* up

yulaf [julaf] *npl* oats; **yulaf ezmesi** *n* oatmeal, porridge

yumruk [jumruk] *n* fist, punch *(blow)*

yumruklamak [jumruklamak] *v* punch

yumurta [jumurta] *n* egg; **haşlanmış yumurta** *n* boiled egg; **karıştırılmış yumurta** *npl* scrambled eggs; **Paskalya yumurtası** *n* Easter egg; **yumurta akı** *n* egg white; **yumurta kabı** *n* eggcup; **yumurta sarısı** *n* egg yolk; **yumurtanın sarısı** *n* yolk; **İçinde yumurta olmayan bir yemek yapabilir misiniz?** Could you prepare a meal without eggs?; **Çiğ yumurta yiyemiyorum** I can't eat raw eggs

yumurtalık [jumurtalək] *n (sağlık)* ovary

yumuşak [jumuʃak] *adj* tender ▷ *n* soft

yumuşatıcı [jumuʃatədʒə] *n* **Yumuşatıcı satıyor musunuz?** Do you sell conditioner?; **Yumuşatıcınız var mı?** Do you have softener?

Yunan [junan] *adj* Greek

Yunanca [junandʒa] *n (dil)* Greek *(language)*

Yunanistan [junanistan] *n* Greece

Yunanlı [junanlə] *n (kişi)* Greek *(person)*

yunus [junus] *n* dolphin

yurtdışı [jurddəʃə] *adv* abroad

yurtsever [jurtsever] *adj* patriotic

yusufçuk [jusuftʃuk] *n* dragonfly

yutma [jutma] *n* swallow

yutmak [jutmak] *vt* swallow

yutulmak [jutulmak] *vi* swallow

yuva [juva] *n* nest

yuvar [juvar] *n* **hamur yuvarı** *n* dumpling

yuvarlak [juvarlak] *adj* round; **yuvarlak ekmek** *n* bread roll

yuvarlanma [juvarlanma] *n* roll

yuvarlanmak [juvarlanmak] *vi* roll

yük [jyk] *n* burden, load, pack; **ağır yük taşıma aracı** *n* HGV; **yük arabası** *n* lorry

yükleme [jykleme] *n* shipment

yüklemek [jyklemek] *v* load, *(pil vb)* recharge

yüklenici [jyklenidʒi] *n* contractor

yüksek [jyksek] *adj* high; **Çin'de yüksek memur** *n* mandarin *(official)*; **yüksek atlama** *n* high jump; **yüksek dozda** *n* overdose; **yüksek eğitim** *n* higher education; **yüksek maaşlı** *adj* well-paid; **yüksek okul** *n* college; **yüksek sesle** *adv* aloud, loudly; **yüksek sesle okumak** *v* read out; **yüksek topuklar** *npl* high heels; **yüksek topuklu** *adj* high-heeled; **Sele çok yüksek** The seat is too

high
yükseklik [jykseklik] *n* altitude, height; **yükseklik korkusu** *n* vertigo
yüksekte [jyksekte] *adv* high
yükselmek [jykselmek] *v* go up; **ani yükselme** *n* surge
yükseltici [jykseltidʒi] *n* amplifier
yüküm [jykym] *n* **vergi yükümlüsü** *n* tax payer
yün [jyn] *n* wool
yünlü [jynly] *adj* woollen
yünlüler [jynlyler] *npl* woollens
yürek [jyrek] *n* **iyi yüreklilik** *n* kindness
yüreklendirme [jyreklendirme] *n* encouragement
yüreklendirmek [jyreklendirmek] *v* boost, encourage
yürekli [jyrekli] *adj* courageous
yürüme [jyryme] *n* walking
yürümek [jyrymek] *v* walk; **ayaklarını sürüyerek yürümek** *v* shuffle; **parmaklarının ucunda yürüme** *n* tiptoe; **uygun adım yürümek** *v* march; **uykuda yürüme** *v* sleepwalk; **yürüyen merdiven** *n* escalator
yürürlük [jyryrlyk] *n* **yürürlükten kaldırma** *n* abolition
yürüteç [jyrytetʃ] *n* Zimmer® frame
yürüyüş [jyryjyʃ] *n* hiking, stroll, walk; **yürüyüşe çıkma** *n* hike; **zahmetli yürüyüş** *n* trek; **zahmetli bir yürüyüşe çıkmak** *v* trek; **Civarda ilginç yürüyüş yerleri var mı?** Are there any interesting walks nearby?; **Rehberli yürüyüş var mı?** Are there any guided walks?; **Tepelere yürüyüşe çıkmak isterim** I'd like to go hill walking; **Yürüyüş kaç kilometre?** How many kilometres is the walk?; **Yerel yürüyüşler için rehberiniz var mı?** Do you have a guide to local walks?
yüz [jyz] *adj* facial ▷ *n* face ▷ *number (sayı)* hundred; **yüz bakımı** *n* facial; **yüz havlusu** *n* face cloth ▷ *v* **yüz kızarması** *n* flush; **yüz temizleme losyonu** *n* cleansing lotion; **yüzü kızarmak** *v* flush; **İki yüz... rica ediyorum** I'd like two hundred...; **İki yüz iki numaralı odanın anahtarı lütfen** the key for room number two hundred and two; **Beş yüz... rica ediyorum** I'd like five hundred...; **Yüz... lık... almak istiyorum** I'd like to change one hundred... into...
yüzde [jyzde] *adv* per cent ▷ *n* percentage
yüzdürmek [jyzdyrmek] *vi* float
yüzey [jyzej] *n* surface
yüzgeç [jyzgetʃ] *npl* flippers
yüzkızartıcı [jyzkəzartədʒə] *adj* shocking
yüzme [jyzme] *n* swimming; **Yüzme havuzu nerede?** Where is the public swimming pool?; **Yüzme havuzunuz var mı?** Is there a swimming pool?
yüzmek [jyzmek] *v* bathe ▷ *vt* swim; **sırtüstü yüzme** *n* backstroke; **yüzme havuzu** *n* swimming pool; **Burada güvenle yüzmek mümkün mü?** Is it safe

to swim here?; **Burada yüzülebilir mi?** Can you swim here?; **Nerede yüzebilirim?** Where can I go swimming?; **Yüzme havuzu var mı?** Is there a swimming pool?; **Yüzmeye gidelim** Let's go swimming

yüzücü [jyzydʒy] *n* swimmer; **yüzücü şortu** *npl* swimming trunks, trunks

yüzük [jyzyk] *n* ring, *(nikah)* wedding ring; **nişan yüzüğü** *n* engagement ring

yüzüncü [jyzyndʒy] *num* **yüzüncü yıl** *n* centenary

yüzyıl [jyzjəl] *n* century

Z

zafer [zafer] *n* glory, triumph, victory

zahmet [zahmet] *n* trouble, difficulty; **zahmet etmek** *v* bother; **zahmetli yürüyüş** *n* trek

zahmetli [zahmetli] *adj* demanding

zaman [zaman] *n* time, *(gramer)* tense; **boş zaman** *n* spare time; **en kısa zamanda** *adv* asap; **her zaman** *adv* always; **kısa zamanda** *adv* shortly, soon; **ne zaman/ne zaman ki** *conj* when; **o zamandan beri** *adv* since; **son zamanlarda** *adv* lately, recently; **yatma zamanı** *n* bedtime; **yemek zamanı** *n* dinner time, lunchtime, mealtime; **zaman dilimi** *n* time zone;**... a ne zaman varırız?** What time do we get to...?; **Çok uzun zamandır bekliyoruz** We've been waiting for a very long time;

Gitme zamanı geldi mi? Is it time to go?; **Kenti gezecek kadar zamanımız var mı?** Do we have time to visit the town?; **Ne zaman kalkıyor?** What time does it leave?; **Otobüs ne zaman geliyor?** What time does the bus arrive?; **Otobüs ne zaman kalkacak?** What time does the bus leave?

zamanında [zamanənda] *adj* on time, punctual

zambak [zambak] *n* lily

Zambiya [zambija] *adj* Zambian ▹ *n* Zambia

Zambiyalı [zambijalə] *n* Zambian

zamir [zamir] *n* pronoun

zanaat [zanaat] *n* craft

zanaatkâr [zanaatka:r] *n* craftsman

zanlı [zanlə] *n* culprit, suspect

zaptetmek [zaptetmek] *v* capture

zar [zar] **(zarlar)** *n (kumar)* dice; **kulak zarı** *n* eardrum

zarar [zarar] *n* damage; **zarar vermek** *v* damage, harm; **zararını karşılamak** *v* reimburse

zararlı [zararlə] *adj* harmful

zararsız [zararsəz] *adj* harmless

zarf [zarf] *n* envelope

zarif [zarif] *adj* elegant, graceful

zaten [zaten] *adv* already

zatürre [zatyrre] *n* pneumonia

zayıf [zajəf] *adj (ışık, ses vb)* faint, *(karakter)* weak

zayıflık [zajəflək] *n* weakness

zayiat [zajiat] *n* casualty

zebra [zebra] *n* zebra

zehir [zehir] *n* poison, venom; **böcek zehiri** *n* pesticide; **gıda zehirlenmesi** *n* food poisoning

zehirlemek [zehirlemek] *v* poison; **kan zehirlenmesi** *n* blood poisoning

zehirli [zehirli] *adj* poisonous, toxic

zeka [zekja:] *n* intelligence, wisdom

zeki [zeki] *adj* clever, intelligent

zemin [zemin] *n* ground, earth; **zemin kat** *n* ground floor; **Zemin katta yatak odası var mı?** Do you have any bedrooms on the ground floor?

zencefil [zendʒefil] *n* ginger

zengin [zengin] *adj* rich; **zengin pinti** *n* miser

zevk [zevk] *n* pleasure; **Sizinle tanışmak bir zevk** It was a pleasure to meet you

zevkli [zevkli] *adj* enjoyable

zeytin [zejtin] *n* olive; **zeytin ağacı** *n* olive tree; **zeytin yağı** *n* olive oil

zımba [zəmba] *n, adj* **tel zımba** *n* stapler; **zımba teli** *n* staple *(wire)*

zımbalamak [zəmbalamak] *v* staple

zımpara [zəmpara] *n* sandpaper

zırh [zərh] *n* armour

zırhlı [zərhlə] *adj* **muharebe zırhlısı** *n* battleship

zıt [zət] *n* contrary

zihin [zihin] *n* mind

zihniyet [zihnijet] *n* mentality

zil [zil] *n (kapı, okul)* bell ▹ *npl (müzik)* cymbals; **kapı zili** *n* doorbell

Zimbabwe [zimbabve] *adj* Zimbabwean ▹ *n* Zimbabwe

Zimbabweli [zimbabveli] *n* Zimbabwean
zincir [zindʒir] *n* chain; **Kar zinciri almam gerekiyor mu?** Do I need snow chains?
zindan [zindan] *n* dungeon
zirve [zirve] *n* peak, summit
ziyaret [zijaret] *n* visit; **ziyaret etmek** *v* visit; **ziyaret saatleri** *npl* visiting hours; **Ziyaret saatleri nedir?** When are visiting hours?
ziyaretçi [zijarettʃi] *n* visitor; **ziyaretçi merkezi** *n* visitor centre
zonklamak [zoŋlamak] *v* throb
zoom mercek [zoommerdʒek] *n* **zoom merceği** *n* zoom lens
zor [zor] *adj* hard *(difficult)* ▷ *adv* hard
zorba [zorba] *n* bully; **zorbalık etmek** *v* bully
zorlama [zorlama] *adj* strained
zorlamak [zorlamak] *v* force
zorlayıcı [zorlajədʒə] *adj* challenging, drastic
zorluk [zorluk] *n* complication
zorunlu [zorunlu] *adj* essential
zulüm [zulym] *n* cruelty
züğürt [zy:yrt] *adj* broke
züppe [zyppe] *n* snob
zürafa [zyrafa] *n* giraffe

ENGLISH–TURKISH

İNGILIZCE–TÜRKÇE

a

a [eɪ] *art* bir
abandon [ə'bændən] *v* terketmek
abbey ['æbɪ] *n* manastır
abbreviation [əˌbriːvɪ'eɪʃən] *n* kısaltma
abdomen ['æbdəmən; æb'dəʊ-] *n* karın
abduct [æb'dʌkt] *v* kaçırmak *(birini)*
ability [ə'bɪlɪtɪ] *n* yetenek
able ['eɪbᵊl] *adj* muktedir
abnormal [æb'nɔːməl] *adj* anormal
abolish [ə'bɒlɪʃ] *v* feshetmek
abolition [ˌæbə'lɪʃən] *n* yürürlükten kaldırma
abortion [ə'bɔːʃən] *n* kürtaj
about [ə'baʊt] *adv* yaklaşık ▷ *prep* hakkında; **Do you have any leaflets about...?**... hakkında broşürünüz var mı?
above [ə'bʌv] *prep* üzerinde
abroad [ə'brɔːd] *adv* yurtdışı
abrupt [ə'brʌpt] *adj* ani
abruptly [ə'brʌptlɪ] *adv* aniden
abscess ['æbsɛs; -sɪs] *n* apse; **I have an abscess** Burası apse yaptı
absence ['æbsəns] *n* yokluk *(devam)*
absent ['æbsənt] *adj* yok
absent-minded [ˌæbsən't'maɪndɪd] *adj* dalgın
absolutely [ˌæbsə'luːtlɪ] *adv* kesinlikle
abstract ['æbstrækt] *adj* soyut
absurd [əb'sɜːd] *adj* saçma
Abu Dhabi ['æbuː 'dɑːbɪ] *n* Abu Dabi
abuse [ə'bjuːs] *n* taciz ▷ [ə'bjuːz]*v* kötüye kullanmak; **child abuse** *n* çocuk tacizi
abusive [ə'bjuːsɪv] *adj* hakaretamiz
academic [ˌækə'dɛmɪk] *adj* akademik; **academic year** *n* akademik yıl
academy [ə'kædəmɪ] *n* akademi
accelerate [æk'sɛləˌreɪt] *v* hızlanmak
acceleration [ækˌsɛlə'reɪʃən] *n* hızlanma
accelerator [æk'sɛləˌreɪtə] *n* gaz pedalı
accept [ək'sɛpt] *v* kabul etmek
acceptable [ək'sɛptəbᵊl] *adj* kabul edilebilir
access ['æksɛs] *n* giriş *(geçiş)* ▷ *v* erişmek; **Do you provide access for the disabled?** Özürlüler için girişiniz var mı?
accessible [ək'sɛsəbᵊl] *adj*

erişilebilir
accessory [ək'sɛsərɪ] *n* aksesuar
accident ['æksɪdənt] *n* kaza; **accident & emergency department** *n* kaza & acil servis; **accident insurance** *n* kaza sigortası; **by accident** *adv* kazara; **I'd like to arrange personal accident insurance** Bireysel kaza sigortası yaptırmak istiyorum; **I've had an accident** Kaza geçirdim; **There's been an accident!** Bir kaza oldu!; **What do I do if I have an accident?** Kaza geçirirsem ne yapmam gerekiyor?
accidental [,æksɪ'dɛntᵊl] *adj* kaza sonucu
accidentally [,æksɪ'dɛntəlɪ] *adv* kazara
accommodate [ə'kɒmə,deɪt] *v* barındırmak
accommodation [ə,kɒmə'deɪʃən] *n* kalacak yer
accompany [ə'kʌmpənɪ; ə'kʌmpnɪ] *v* eşlik etmek *(yanında gitmek)*
accomplice [ə'kɒmplɪs; ə'kʌm-] *n* suç ortağı
according [ə'kɔ:dɪŋ] *prep* **according to** *prep* göre
accordingly [ə'kɔ:dɪŋlɪ] *adv* bundan dolayı
accordion [ə'kɔ:dɪən] *n* akordiyon
account [ə'kaʊnt] *n (in bank)* hesap *(banka)*, *(report)* tarif; **account number** *n* hesap numarası; **bank account** *n* banka hesabı; **current account** *n* cari hesap; **joint account** *n* ortak hesap
accountable [ə'kaʊntəbᵊl] *adj* sorumlu
accountancy [ə'kaʊntənsɪ] *n* muhasebecilik
accountant [ə'kaʊntənt] *n* muhasebeci
account for [ə'kaʊnt fɔ:] *v* hesap vermek
accuracy ['ækjʊrəsɪ] *n* doğruluk
accurate ['ækjərɪt] *adj* doğru *(söz, eylem, sonuç)*
accurately ['ækjərɪtlɪ] *adv* doğru olarak
accusation [,ækjʊ'zeɪʃən] *n* suçlama
accuse [ə'kju:z] *v* suçlamak
accused [ə'kju:zd] *n* sanık
ace [eɪs] *n* as *(oyun, spor)*
ache [eɪk] *n* ağrı ▷ *v* ağrımak
achieve [ə'tʃi:v] *v* başarmak
achievement [ə'tʃi:vmənt] *n* başarı
acid ['æsɪd] *n* asit; **acid rain** *n* asit yağmuru
acknowledgement [ək'nɒlɪdʒmənt] *n* ikrar
acne ['æknɪ] *n* sivilce
acorn ['eɪkɔ:n] *n* meşe palamudu
acoustic [ə'ku:stɪk] *adj* akustik
acre ['eɪkə] *n* acre
acrobat ['ækrə,bæt] *n* akrobat
acronym ['ækrənɪm] *n* kısaltma
across [ə'krɒs] *prep* karşıya
act [ækt] *n* hareket ▷ *v* davranmak *(hareket)*
acting ['æktɪŋ] *adj* vekaleten ▷ *n* oyunculuk
action ['ækʃən] *n* eylem
active ['æktɪv] *adj* aktif
activity [æk'tɪvɪtɪ] *n* etkinlik;

activity holiday *n* aktivite tatili; **Do you have activities for children?** Çocuklar için etkinlikleriniz var mı?
actor ['æktə] *n* aktör
actress ['æktrɪs] *n* kadın oyuncu
actual ['æktʃʊəl] *adj* gerçek
actually ['æktʃʊəlɪ] *adv* aslında
acupuncture ['ækjʊˌpʌŋktʃə] *n* akupunktur
ad [æd] *abbr* reklam; **small ads** *npl* küçük ilanlar
AD [eɪ diː] *abbr* MS
adapt [ə'dæpt] *v* uyarlamak
adaptor [ə'dæptə] *n* adaptör
add [æd] *v* eklemek
addict ['ædɪkt] *n* bağımlı; **drug addict** *n* uyuşturucu bağımlısı
addicted [ə'dɪktɪd] *adj* bağımlı
additional [ə'dɪʃənᵊl] *adj* ek
additive ['ædɪtɪv] *n* katkı maddesi
address [ə'drɛs] *n* *(location)* adres, *(speech)* hitap; **address book** *n* adres defteri; **home address** *n* ev adresi; **web address** *n* internet adresi; **My email address is...** E-posta adresim...; **Please send my mail on to this address** Mektuplarımı şu adrese gönderin lütfen; **The website address is...** İnternet adresi...; **What is your email address?** E-posta adresiniz nedir?; **Will you write down the address, please?** Adresi yazar mısınız lütfen?
add up [æd ʌp] *v* toplamak *(matematik)*
adjacent [ə'dʒeɪsᵊnt] *adj* bitişik
adjective ['ædʒɪktɪv] *n* sıfat
adjust [ə'dʒʌst] *v* ayarlamak
adjustable [ə'dʒʌstəbᵊl] *adj* ayarlanabilir
adjustment [ə'dʒʌstmənt] *n* ayarlama
administration [ədˌmɪnɪ'streɪʃən] *n* yönetim
administrative [əd'mɪnɪˌstrətɪv] *adj* idari
admiration [ˌædmə'reɪʃən] *n* hayranlık
admire [əd'maɪə] *v* hayranlık duymak
admission [əd'mɪʃən] *n* kabul; **admission charge** *n* giriş ücreti
admit [əd'mɪt] *v* *(allow in)* içeri almak, *(confess)* kabul etmek *(itiraf)*
admittance [əd'mɪtᵊns] *n* giriş hakkı
adolescence [ˌædə'lɛsəns] *n* ergenlik
adolescent [ˌædə'lɛsᵊnt] *n* ergen
adopt [ə'dɒpt] *v* evlat edinmek
adopted [ə'dɒptɪd] *adj* evlat edinilmiş
adoption [ə'dɒpʃən] *n* evlat edinme
adore [ə'dɔː] *v* tapmak
Adriatic [ˌeɪdrɪ'ætɪk] *adj* Adriyatik
Adriatic Sea [ˌeɪdrɪ'ætɪk siː] *n* Adriyatik Denizi
adult ['ædʌlt; ə'dʌlt] *n* yetişkin; **adult education** *n* yetişkin eğitimi
advance [əd'vɑːns] *n* ilerleme ▷ *v* ilerlemek; **advance booking** *n* önceden rezervasyon
advanced [əd'vɑːnst] *adj* ileri
advantage [əd'vɑːntɪdʒ] *n* üstünlük

advent ['ædvɛnt; -vənt] *n* Noel öncesi
adventure [əd'vɛntʃə] *n* macera
adventurous [əd'vɛntʃərəs] *adj* maceraperest
adverb ['æd,vɜ:b] *n* belirteç
adversary ['ædvəsərı] *n* rakip
advert ['ædvɜ:t] *n* reklam
advertise ['ædvə,taız] *v* reklam yapmak
advertisement [əd'vɜ:tısmənt; -tız-] *n* reklam
advertising ['ædvə,taızıŋ] *n* reklamcılık
advice [əd'vaıs] *n* öğüt
advisable [əd'vaızəbᵊl] *adj* akıllıca
advise [əd'vaız] *v* tavsiye etmek
aerial ['ɛərıəl] *n* anten
aerobics [ɛə'rəʊbıks] *npl* aerobik
aerosol ['ɛərə,sɒl] *n* aerosol
affair [ə'fɛə] *n* olay
affect [ə'fɛkt] *v* etkilemek *(bir sonuç yaratarak)*
affectionate [ə'fɛkʃənıt] *adj* sevecen
afford [ə'fɔ:d] *v* gücü yetmek
affordable [ə'fɔ:dəbᵊl] *adj* keseye uygun
Afghan ['æfgæn; -gən] *adj* Afgan ▷ *n* Afgan
Afghanistan [æf'gænı,stɑ:n; -,stæn] *n* Afganistan
afraid [ə'freıd] *adj* korkmuş
Africa ['æfrıkə] *n* Afrika; **North Africa** *n* Kuzey Afrika; **South Africa** *n* Güney Afrika
African ['æfrıkən] *adj* Afrikalı ▷ *n* Afrikalı; **Central African Republic** *n* Orta Afrika Cumhuriyeti; **North African** *n* Kuzey Afrika, Kuzey Afrikalı; **South African** *n* Güney Afrika, Güney Afrikalı
Afrikaans [,æfrı'kɑ:ns; -'kɑ:nz] *n* Afrikaanca
Afrikaner [afri'kɑ:nə; ,æfrı'kɑ:nə] *n* Afrikaner
after ['ɑ:ftə] *conj* sonra; **after eight o'clock** saat sekizden sonra; **the week after next** bir sonraki hafta
afternoon [,ɑ:ftə'nu:n] *n* öğleden sonra; **in the afternoon** öğleden sonra; **tomorrow afternoon** yarın öğleden sonra
afters ['ɑ:ftəz] *npl* tatlı
aftershave ['ɑ:ftə,ʃeıv] *n* traş losyonu
afterwards ['ɑ:ftəwədz] *adv* sonra
again [ə'gɛn; ə'geın] *adv* yine
against [ə'gɛnst; ə'geınst] *prep* karşı
age [eıdʒ] *n* yaş *(yıl)*; **age limit** *n* yaş sınırı; **Middle Ages** *npl* Orta Çağ
aged ['eıdʒıd] *adj* yaşlı
agency ['eıdʒənsı] *n* ajans; **travel agency** *n* seyahat acentası
agenda [ə'dʒɛndə] *n* gündem
agent ['eıdʒənt] *n* temsilci; **estate agent** *n* emlakçı; **travel agent** *n* seyahat acentası *(kişi)*
aggressive [ə'grɛsıv] *adj* saldırgan
AGM [eı dʒi: ɛm] *abbr* Yıllık Genel cunta
ago [ə'gəʊ] *adv* **a month ago** bir ay önce; **a week ago** bir hafta önce
agony ['ægənı] *n* ıstırap
agree [ə'gri:] *v* aynı fikirde olmak
agreed [ə'gri:d] *adj* mutabık
agreement [ə'gri:mənt] *n*

anlaşma
agricultural ['ægrɪˌkʌltʃərəl] *adj* tarımsal
agriculture ['ægrɪˌkʌltʃə] *n* tarım
ahead [ə'hɛd] *adv* önde
aid [eɪd] *n* yardım; **first aid** *n* ilk yardım; **first-aid kit** *n* ilk yardım çantası; **hearing aid** *n* işitme cihazı
AIDS [eɪdz] *n* AIDS
aim [eɪm] *n* hedef ▹ *v* hedeflemek
air [ɛə] *n* hava; **air hostess** *n* hostes; **air-traffic controller** *n* hava trafik kontrolörü; **Air Force** *n* Hava Kuvvetleri; **Can you check the air, please?** Tekerleklerin havasını kontrol eder misiniz lütfen?; **How long will it take by air?** Hava postası ile ne kadar zamanda gider?
airbag [ɛəbæg] *n* hava yastığı
air-conditioned [ɛəkən'dɪʃənd] *adj* havalandırmalı
air conditioning [ɛə kən'dɪʃənɪŋ] *n* havalandırma
aircraft ['ɛəˌkrɑːft] *n* uçak
airline ['ɛəˌlaɪn] *n* havayolu
airmail ['ɛəˌmeɪl] *n* uçak postası
airport ['ɛəˌpɔːt] *n* hava alanı; **airport bus** *n* hava alanı otobüsü
airsick ['ɛəˌsɪk] *adj* uçak tutması
airspace ['ɛəˌspeɪs] *n* hava sahası
airtight ['ɛəˌtaɪt] *adj* vakumlanmış
aisle [aɪl] *n* koridor; **I'd like an aisle seat** Koltuğum koridor tarafında olsun
alarm [ə'lɑːm] *n* alarm; **alarm call** *n* uyarı çağrısı; **alarm clock** *n* çalar saat; **false alarm** *n* yanlış alarm; **fire alarm** *n* yangın alarmı; **smoke alarm** *n* duman alarmı
alarming [ə'lɑːmɪŋ] *adj* ürkütücü
Albania [æl'beɪnɪə] *n* Arnavutluk
Albanian [æl'beɪnɪən] *adj* Arnavut ▹ *n (language)* Arnavutça *(dil)*, *(person)* Arnavut *(kişi)*
album ['ælbəm] *n* albüm *(müzik, fotoğraf)*; **photo album** *n* fotoğraf albümü
alcohol ['ælkəˌhɒl] *n* alkol; **Does that contain alcohol?** Bunda alkol var mı?
alcohol-free ['ælkəˌhɒlfriː] *adj* alkolsüz
alcoholic [ˌælkə'hɒlɪk] *adj* alkollü ▹ *n* alkolik
alert [ə'lɜːt] *adj* uyanık ▹ *v* uyarmak
Algeria [æl'dʒɪərɪə] *n* Cezayir
Algerian [æl'dʒɪərɪən] *adj* Cezayir ▹ *n* Cezayirli
alias ['eɪlɪəs] *adv* takma ad ▹ *prep* diğer adıyla
alibi ['ælɪˌbaɪ] *n* özür
alien ['eɪljən; 'eɪlɪən] *n* yabancı
alive [ə'laɪv] *adj* canlı *(hayatta)*
all [ɔːl] *adj* bütün *(hepsi)* ▹ *pron* hepsi; **We'd like to see nobody but us all day!** Bütün gün hiç kimseyi değil, sadece kendimizi görmek isterdik!
Allah ['ælə] *n* Allah
allegation [ˌælɪ'geɪʃən] *n* iddia
alleged [ə'lɛdʒd] *adj* iddia edilen
allergic [ə'lɜːdʒɪk] *adj* alerjik
allergy ['ælədʒɪ] *n* alerji; **peanut allergy** *n* fıstık alerjisi
alley ['ælɪ] *n* dar sokak
alliance [ə'laɪəns] *n* ittifak
alligator ['ælɪˌgeɪtə] *n* timsah
allow [ə'laʊ] *v* izin vermek

all right [ɔ:l raɪt] *adv* iyi
ally ['ælaɪ; ə'laɪ] *n* müttefik
almond ['ɑ:mənd] *n* badem
almost ['ɔ:lməʊst] *adv* neredeyse; **It's almost half past two** Saat neredeyse iki buçuk
alone [ə'ləʊn] *adj* yalnız
along [ə'lɒŋ] *prep* boyunca
aloud [ə'laʊd] *adv* yüksek sesle
alphabet ['ælfə,bɛt] *n* alfabe
Alps [ælps] *npl* Alpler
already [ɔ:l'rɛdɪ] *adv* zaten
alright [ɔ:l'raɪt] *adv* **Are you alright?** İyi misiniz?
also ['ɔ:lsəʊ] *adv* dahi *(o da)*
altar ['ɔ:ltə] *n* sunak
alter ['ɔ:ltə] *v* değiştirmek
alternate [ɔ:l'tɜ:nɪt] *adj* karşılıklı
alternative [ɔ:l'tɜ:nətɪv] *adj* alternatif ▷ *n* seçenek
alternatively [ɔ:l'tɜ:nətɪvlɪ] *adv* ya da
although [ɔ:l'ðəʊ] *conj* rağmen
altitude ['æltɪ,tju:d] *n* yükseklik
altogether [,ɔ:ltə'gɛðə; 'ɔ:ltə,gɛðə] *adv* hep birlikte
aluminium [,ælju'mɪnɪəm] *n* alüminyum
always ['ɔ:lweɪz; -wɪz] *adv* her zaman
a.m. [eɪɛm] *abbr* öğleden önce
amateur ['æmətə; -tʃə; -,tjʊə; ,æmə'tɜ:] *n* amatör
amaze [ə'meɪz] *v* şaşırtmak
amazed [ə'meɪzd] *adj* şaşkın
amazing [ə'meɪzɪŋ] *adj* hayret verici
ambassador [æm'bæsədə] *n* büyükelçi
amber ['æmbə] *n* kehribar
ambition [æm'bɪʃən] *n* hırs
ambitious [æm'bɪʃəs] *adj* hırslı
ambulance ['æmbjʊləns] *n* cankurtaran *(tıp)*
ambush ['æmbʊʃ] *n* tuzak
amenities [ə'mi:nɪtɪz] *npl* olanaklar
America [ə'mɛrɪkə] *n* Amerika; **Central America** *n* Orta Amerika; **North America** *n* Kuzey Amerika; **South America** *n* Güney Amerika
American [ə'mɛrɪkən] *adj* Amerikan ▷ *n* Amerikalı; **American football** *n* Amerikan futbolu; **North American** *n* Kuzey Amerika, Kuzey Amerikalı; **South American** *n* Güney Amerika, Güney Amerikalı
ammunition [,æmjʊ'nɪʃən] *n* cephane
among [ə'mʌŋ] *prep* arasında
amount [ə'maʊnt] *n* miktar; **I have the allowed amount of tobacco to declare** İzin verilen miktarda sigara deklare etmek istiyorum
amp [æmp] *n* amper
amplifier ['æmplɪ,faɪə] *n* yükseltici
amuse [ə'mju:z] *v* eğlendirmek *(şakayla)*; **amusement arcade** *n* oyun salonu
an [ɑ:n] *art* bir
anaemic [ə'ni:mɪk] *adj* kansız
anaesthetic [,ænɪs'θɛtɪk] *n* anestetik; **general anaesthetic** *n* genel anestezi; **local anaesthetic** *n* lokal anestezi
analyse ['ænᵊ,laɪz] *v* çözümlemek
analysis [ə'nælɪsɪs] *n* çözümleme

ancestor ['ænsɛstə] *n* ata
anchor ['æŋkə] *n* çapa
anchovy ['æntʃəvɪ] *n* ançuez
ancient ['eɪnʃənt] *adj* eski
and [ænd; ənd; ən] *conj* ve
Andes ['ændi:z] *npl* And Dağları
Andorra [æn'dɔ:rə] *n* Andora
angel ['eɪndʒəl] *n* melek
anger ['æŋgə] *n* öfke
angina [æn'dʒaɪnə] *n* anjin
angle ['æŋgᵊl] *n* açı; **right angle** *n* dik açı
angler ['æŋglə] *n* olta balıkçısı
angling ['æŋglɪŋ] *n* olta balıkçılığı
Angola [æŋ'gəʊlə] *n* Angola
Angolan [æŋ'gəʊlən] *adj* Angola ▷ *n* Angolalı
angry ['æŋgrɪ] *adj* kızgın
animal ['ænɪməl] *n* hayvan
aniseed ['ænɪ,si:d] *n* anason
ankle ['æŋkᵊl] *n* ayak bileği
anniversary [,ænɪ'vɜ:sərɪ] *n* yıl dönümü; **wedding anniversary** *n* evlilik yıldönümü
announce [ə'naʊns] *v* duyurmak
announcement [ə'naʊnsmənt] *n* duyuru
annoy [ə'nɔɪ] *v* sinirini bozmak
annoying [ə'nɔɪɪŋ; an'noying] *adj* sinir bozucu
annual ['ænjʊəl] *adj* yıllık
annually ['ænjʊəlɪ] *adv* her yıl
anonymous [ə'nɒnɪməs] *adj* adsız
anorak ['ænə,ræk] *n* anorak
anorexia [,ænɒ'rɛksɪə] *n* anoreksi
anorexic [,ænɒ'rɛksɪk] *adj* anoreksik
another [ə'nʌðə] *adj* diğer
answer ['ɑ:nsə] *n* yanıt ▷ *v* yanıt vermek
answerphone ['ɑ:nsəfəʊn] *n* telesekreter
ant [ænt] *n* karınca
antagonize [æn'tægə,naɪz] *v* düşmanlığını kazanmak
Antarctic [ænt'ɑ:ktɪk] **the Antarctic** *n* Güney Kutbu
Antarctica [ænt'ɑ:ktɪkə] *n* Güney Kutbu
antelope ['æntɪ,ləʊp] *n* antilop
antenatal [,æntɪ'neɪtᵊl] *adj* doğum öncesi
anthem ['ænθəm] *n* marş
anthropology [,ænθrə'pɒlədʒɪ] *n* insan bilimi
antibiotic [,æntɪbaɪ'ɒtɪk] *n* antibiyotik
antibody ['æntɪ,bɒdɪ] *n* antikor
anticlockwise [,æntɪ'klɒk,waɪz] *adv* saatin aksi yönünde
antidepressant [,æntɪdɪ'prɛsᵊnt] *n* antidepresan
antidote ['æntɪ,dəʊt] *n* panzehir
antifreeze ['æntɪ,fri:z] *n* antifriz
antihistamine [,æntɪ'hɪstə,mi:n; -mɪn] *n* antihistamin
antiperspirant [,æntɪ'pɜ:spərənt] *n* ter önleyici deodorant
antique [æn'ti:k] *n* antika; **antique shop** *n* antikacı dükkanı
antiseptic [,æntɪ'sɛptɪk] *n* antiseptik
antivirus ['æntɪ,vaɪrəs] *n* antivirüs
anxiety [æŋ'zaɪɪtɪ] *n* endişe
any ['ɛnɪ] *pron* her, herhangi
anybody ['ɛnɪ,bɒdɪ; -bədɪ] *pron* herhangi biri
anyhow ['ɛnɪ,haʊ] *adv* her

halükarda
anyone ['ɛnɪˌwʌn; -wən] *pron* herhangi biri
anything ['ɛnɪˌθɪŋ] *pron* herhangi bir şey
anyway ['ɛnɪˌweɪ] *adv* neyse
anywhere ['ɛnɪˌwɛə] *adv* herhangi bir yer
apart [ə'pɑːt] *adv* ayrı
apart from [ə'pɑːt frɒm] *prep* dışında *(ondan ayrı olarak)*
apartment [ə'pɑːtmənt] *n* apartman dairesi; **We're looking for an apartment** Bir apartman dairesi bakıyorduk; **We've booked an apartment in the name of...** ...adına bir apartman dairesi ayırtmıştık
aperitif [ɑːˌpɛrɪ'tiːf] *n* yemek öncesi içki
aperture ['æpətʃə] *n* açıklık *(aralık)*
apologize [ə'pɒləˌdʒaɪz] *v* özür dilemek
apology [ə'pɒlədʒɪ] *n* özür
apostrophe [ə'pɒstrəfɪ] *n* kesme imi
appalling [ə'pɔːlɪŋ] *adj* korkunç
apparatus [ˌæpə'reɪtəs; -'rɑːtəs; 'æpəˌreɪtəs] *n* aygıt
apparent [ə'pærənt; ə'pɛər-] *adj* görünür
apparently [ə'pærəntlɪ; ə'pɛər-] *adv* açıkça
appeal [ə'piːl] *n* rica ▷ *v* rica etmek
appear [ə'pɪə] *v* görünmek
appearance [ə'pɪərəns] *n* görünüş
appendicitis [əˌpɛndɪ'saɪtɪs] *n* apandisit
appetite ['æpɪˌtaɪt] *n* iştah
applaud [ə'plɔːd] *v* alkışlamak
applause [ə'plɔːz] *n* alkış
apple ['æpᵊl] *n* elma; **apple pie** *n* elmalı turta
appliance [ə'plaɪəns] *n* cihaz
applicant ['æplɪkənt] *n* başvurucu
application [ˌæplɪ'keɪʃən] *n* başvuru; **application form** *n* başvuru formu
apply [ə'plaɪ] *v* kullanmak
appoint [ə'pɔɪnt] *v* atamak
appointment [ə'pɔɪntmənt] *n* randevu; **Can I have an appointment with the doctor?** Doktordan randevu alabilir miyim?; **Do you have an appointment?** Randevunuz var mıydı?; **I have an appointment with....** ... ile randevum vardı; **I'd like to make an appointment** Randevu almak istiyorum
appreciate [ə'priːʃɪˌeɪt; -sɪ-] *v* paha biçmek
apprehensive [ˌæprɪ'hɛnsɪv] *adj* endişeli
apprentice [ə'prɛntɪs] *n* çırak
approach [ə'prəʊtʃ] *v* yaklaşmak
appropriate [ə'prəʊprɪɪt] *adj* uygun
approval [ə'pruːvᵊl] *n* onay
approve [ə'pruːv] *v* onaylamak
approximate [ə'prɒksɪmɪt] *adj* yaklaşık
approximately [ə'prɒksɪmɪtlɪ] *adv* yaklaşık olarak
apricot ['eɪprɪˌkɒt] *n* kayısı
April ['eɪprəl] *n* Nisan; **April Fools' Day** *n* 1 Nisan Şakası
apron ['eɪprən] *n* önlük
aquarium [ə'kwɛərɪəm] *n*

akvaryum
Aquarius [ə'kwɛərɪəs] *n* Kova burcu
Arab ['ærəb] *adj* Arap ▹ *n* Arap; **United Arab Emirates** *npl* Birleşik Arap Emirlikleri
Arabic ['ærəbɪk] *adj* Arap ▹ *n* Arapça
arbitration [ˌɑːbɪ'treɪʃən] *n* hakem aracılığıyla çözümleme
arch [ɑːtʃ] *n* kemer
archaeologist [ˌɑːkɪ'ɒlədʒɪst] *n* arkeolog
archaeology [ˌɑːkɪ'ɒlədʒɪ] *n* arkeoloji
archbishop ['ɑːtʃ'bɪʃəp] *n* başpiskopos
architect ['ɑːkɪˌtɛkt] *n* mimar
architecture ['ɑːkɪˌtɛktʃə] *n* mimarlık
archive ['ɑːkaɪv] *n* arşiv
Arctic ['ɑːktɪk] **Arctic Circle** *n* Kuzey Buzul Kuşağı; **Arctic Ocean** *n* Kuzey Okyanusu; **the Arctic** *n* Kuzey Kutbu
area ['ɛərɪə] *n* alan *(ölçü birimi)*; **service area** *n* konaklama alanı
Argentina [ˌɑːdʒən'tiːnə] *n* Arjantin
Argentinian [ˌɑːdʒən'tɪnɪən] *adj* Arjantin ▹ *n (person)* Arjantinli *(kişi)*
argue ['ɑːgjuː] *v* tartışmak
argument ['ɑːgjʊmənt] *n* tartışma
Aries ['ɛəriːz] *n* Koç burcu
arm [ɑːm] *n* kol; **I can't move my arm** Kolumu oynatamıyorum
armchair ['ɑːmˌtʃɛə] *n* koltuk
armed [ɑːmd] *adj* silahlı
Armenia [ɑː'miːnɪə] *n* Ermenistan
Armenian [ɑː'miːnɪən] *adj* Ermeni ▹ *n (language)* Ermenice *(dil)*, *(person)* Ermeni *(kişi)*
armour ['ɑːmə] *n* zırh
armpit ['ɑːmˌpɪt] *n* koltukaltı
army ['ɑːmɪ] *n* ordu
aroma [ə'rəʊmə] *n* koku
aromatherapy [əˌrəʊmə'θɛrəpɪ] *n* aromaterapi
around [ə'raʊnd] *adv* yakınında ▹ *prep* etrafında
arrange [ə'reɪndʒ] *v* düzenlemek *(toplantı)*
arrangement [ə'reɪndʒmənt] *n* düzenleme *(aranjman)*
arrears [ə'rɪəz] *npl* vadesi geçmiş borç
arrest [ə'rɛst] *n* tutuklama ▹ *v* tutuklamak
arrival [ə'raɪvᵊl] *n* varış
arrive [ə'raɪv] *v* varmak
arrogant ['ærəgənt] *adj* kendini beğenmiş
arrow ['ærəʊ] *n* ok
arson ['ɑːsᵊn] *n* kundaklama
art [ɑːt] *n* sanat; **art gallery** *n* sanat galerisi; **art school** *n* sanat okulu; **work of art** *n* sanat eseri
artery ['ɑːtərɪ] *n* atardamar
arthritis [ɑː'θraɪtɪs] *n* mafsal iltihabı
artichoke ['ɑːtɪˌtʃəʊk] *n* enginar
article ['ɑːtɪkᵊl] *n* makale
artificial [ˌɑːtɪ'fɪʃəl] *adj* yapay
artist ['ɑːtɪst] *n* sanatçı
artistic [ɑː'tɪstɪk] *adj* sanatsal
as [əz] *adv* gibi ▹ *conj* iken ▹ *prep* kadar; **How much should I give as a tip?** Ne kadar bahşiş vermem gerek?

asap [eɪsæp] *abbr* en kısa zamanda
ascent [əˈsɛnt] *n* **When is the last ascent?** En son çıkış kaçta?
ashamed [əˈʃeɪmd] *adj* mahcup
ashore [əˈʃɔː] *adv* **Can we go ashore now?** Kıyıya çıkabilir miyiz?
ashtray [ˈæʃˌtreɪ] *n* küllük
Asia [ˈeɪʃə; ˈeɪʒə] *n* Asya
Asian [ˈeɪʃən; ˈeɪʒən] *adj* Asya ▷ *n* Asyalı
Asiatic [ˌeɪʃɪˈætɪk; -zɪ-] *adj* Asyalı
ask [ɑːsk] *v* sormak
ask for [ɑːsk fɔː] *v* aramak
asleep [əˈsliːp] *adj* uykuda
asparagus [əˈspærəgəs] *n* kuşkonmaz
aspect [ˈæspɛkt] *n* bakış açısı
aspirin [ˈæsprɪn] *n* aspirin; **I can't take aspirin** Aspirin alamıyorum; **I'd like some aspirin** Aspirin rica ediyorum
assembly [əˈsɛmblɪ] *n* topluluk
asset [ˈæsɛt] *n* varlık; **assets** *npl* varlık
assignment [əˈsaɪnmənt] *n* görev *(ödev vb)*
assistance [əˈsɪstəns] *n* yardım; **I need assistance** Yardıma ihtiyacım var
assistant [əˈsɪstənt] *n* asistan; **personal assistant** *n* kişisel asistan; **sales assistant** *n* tezgahtar; **shop assistant** *n* satış elemanı
associate [əˈsəʊʃɪɪt] *adj* yardımcı ▷ [əˈsəʊʃɪɪt]*n* iş arkadaşı
association [əˌsəʊsɪˈeɪʃən; -ʃɪ-] *n* birlik *(dernek)*
assortment [əˈsɔːtmənt] *n* çeşit
assume [əˈsjuːm] *v* varsaymak
assure [əˈʃʊə] *v* güvence vermek
asthma [ˈæsmə] *n* astım
astonish [əˈstɒnɪʃ] *v* şaşırtmak
astonished [əˈstɒnɪʃt] *adj* şaşırmış
astonishing [əˈstɒnɪʃɪŋ] *adj* şaşırtıcı
astrology [əˈstrɒlədʒɪ] *n* astroloji
astronaut [ˈæstrəˌnɔːt] *n* astronot
astronomy [əˈstrɒnəmɪ] *n* astronomi
asylum [əˈsaɪləm] *n* sığınma; **asylum seeker** *n* sığınmacı
at [æt] *prep* de, da *(konum)*; **at least** *adv* en azından
atheist [ˈeɪθɪˌɪst] *n* tanrı tanımaz
athlete [ˈæθliːt] *n* atlet
athletic [æθˈlɛtɪk] *adj* atletik
athletics [æθˈlɛtɪks] *npl* atletizm
Atlantic [ətˈlæntɪk] *n* Atlantik
atlas [ˈætləs] *n* atlas
atmosphere [ˈætməsˌfɪə] *n* atmosfer
atom [ˈætəm] *n* atom; **atom bomb** *n* atom bombası
atomic [əˈtɒmɪk] *adj* nükleer
attach [əˈtætʃ] *v* bağlamak
attached [əˈtætʃt] *adj* ekli
attachment [əˈtætʃmənt] *n* ek
attack [əˈtæk] *n* saldırı ▷ *v* saldırmak; **heart attack** *n* kalp krizi; **terrorist attack** *n* terörist saldırı; **I've been attacked** Saldırıya uğradım
attempt [əˈtɛmpt] *n* girişim ▷ *v* kalkışmak
attend [əˈtɛnd] *v* katılmak
attendance [əˈtɛndəns] *n* katılım
attendant [əˈtɛndənt] *n* **flight attendant** *n* uçuş hostesi

attention [ə'tɛnʃən] *n* dikkat
attic ['ætɪk] *n* tavanarası
attitude ['ætɪˌtjuːd] *n* tavır
attorney [ə'tɜːnɪ] *n* avukat
attract [ə'trækt] *v* çekmek
attraction [ə'trækʃən] *n* çekim
attractive [ə'træktɪv] *adj* çekici; **You are very attractive** Çok çekicisiniz
aubergine ['əʊbəˌʒiːn] *n* patlıcan
auburn ['ɔːbᵊn] *adj* kumral
auction ['ɔːkʃən] *n* açık arttırma
audience ['ɔːdɪəns] *n* dinleyiciler
audit ['ɔːdɪt] *n* hesap denetimi ▷ *v* hesapları denetlemek
audition [ɔː'dɪʃən] *n* ses sınavı
auditor ['ɔːdɪtə] *n* denetçi *(maliye)*
August ['ɔːgəst] *n* Ağustos
aunt [ɑːnt] *n (maternal aunt)* teyze
auntie ['ɑːntɪ] *n* teyze
au pair [əʊ 'pɛə; o pɛr] *n* au-pair
austerity [ɒ'stɛrɪtɪ] *n* darlık
Australasia [ˌɒstrə'leɪzɪə] *n* Avustralasya
Australia [ɒ'streɪlɪə] *n* Avustralya
Australian [ɒ'streɪlɪən] *adj* Avustralyalı ▷ *n* Avustralyalı
Austria ['ɒstrɪə] *n* Avusturya
Austrian ['ɒstrɪən] *adj* Avusturya ▷ *n* Avusturyalı
authentic [ɔː'θɛntɪk] *adj* özgün
author, authoress ['ɔːθə, 'ɔːθəˌrɛs] *n* yazar
authorize ['ɔːθəˌraɪz] *v* yetki vermek
autobiography [ˌɔːtəʊbaɪ'ɒgrəfɪ; ˌɔːtəbaɪ-] *n* özyaşam öyküsü
autograph ['ɔːtəˌgrɑːf; -ˌgræf] *n* imza
automatic [ˌɔːtə'mætɪk] *adj* otomatik; **An automatic, please** Otomatik olsun lütfen; **Is it an automatic car?** Bu araba otomatik mi?
automatically [ˌɔːtə'mætɪklɪ] *adv* otomatik olarak
autonomous [ɔː'tɒnəməs] *adj* özerk
autonomy [ɔː'tɒnəmɪ] *n* özerklik
autumn ['ɔːtəm] *n* sonbahar
availability [ə'veɪləbɪlɪtɪ] *n* uygunluk
available [ə'veɪləbᵊl] *adj* uygun
avalanche ['ævəˌlɑːntʃ] *n* çığ
avenue ['ævɪˌnjuː] *n* bulvar
average ['ævərɪdʒ; 'ævrɪdʒ] *adj* ortalama ▷ *n* ortalama
avocado, avocados [ˌævə'kɑːdəʊ, ˌævə'kɑːdəʊs] *n* avokado
avoid [ə'vɔɪd] *v* kaçmak
awake [ə'weɪk] *adj* uyanık ▷ *v* uyanmak
award [ə'wɔːd] *n* ödül
aware [ə'wɛə] *adj* farkında
away [ə'weɪ] *adv* uzakta; **away match** *n* rakip sahada maç
awful ['ɔːfʊl] *adj* berbat; **What awful weather!** Hava çok berbat!
awfully ['ɔːfəlɪ; 'ɔːflɪ] *adv* son derece
awkward ['ɔːkwəd] *adj* beceriksiz
axe [æks] *n* balta
axle ['æksəl] *n* dingil
Azerbaijan [ˌæzəbaɪ'dʒɑːn] *n* Azerbaycan
Azerbaijani [ˌæzəbaɪ'dʒɑːnɪ] *adj* Azerbaycan ▷ *n* Azerbaycanlı

b

B&B [biː ænd biː] *n* Yatak ve Kahvaltı
BA [bɑː] *abbr* lisans derecesi *(edebiyat)*
baby ['beɪbɪ] *n* bebek; **baby milk** *n* bebek sütü; **baby wipe** *n* ıslak bebek mendili; **baby's bottle** *n* biberon; **Are there facilities for parents with babies?** Bebekli aileler için kolaylıklarınız var mı?
babysit ['beɪbɪsɪt] *v* bebek bakmak
babysitter ['beɪbɪsɪtə] *n* bebek bakıcısı
babysitting ['beɪbɪsɪtɪŋ] *n* bebek bakma
bachelor ['bætʃələ; 'bætʃlə] *n* bekar
back [bæk] *adj* arka ▷ *adv* arkada ▷ *n* sırt ▷ *v* geri çekilmek; **back pain** *n* sırt ağrısı; **I've got a bad back** Sırtım tutuldu
backache ['bæk,eɪk] *n* sırt ağrısı
backbone ['bæk,bəʊn] *n* omurga
backfire [,bæk'faɪə] *v* geri tepmek
background ['bæk,graʊnd] *n* arka plan
backing ['bækɪŋ] *n* destekleme
back out [bæk aʊt] *v* geri kalmak
backpack ['bæk,pæk] *n* sırt çantası
backpacker ['bæk,pækə] *n* sırt çantasıyla dolaşan gezgin
backpacking ['bæk,pækɪŋ] *n* sırt çantasıyla gezme
backside [,bæk'saɪd] *n* kıç
backslash ['bæk,slæʃ] *n* geriye yatık çizgi
backstroke ['bæk,strəʊk] *n* sırtüstü yüzme
back up [bæk ʌp] *v* destek olmak
backup [bæk,ʌp] *n* yedek
backwards ['bækwədz] *adv* geriye doğru
bacon ['beɪkən] *n* domuz pastırması
bacteria [bæk'tɪərɪə] *npl* bakteri
bad [bæd] *adj* kötü; **It's a bad line** Çok kötü bir hat
badge [bædʒ] *n* kimlik kartı
badger ['bædʒə] *n* porsuk
badly ['bædlɪ] *adv* kötü bir şekilde
badminton ['bædmɪntən] *n* badminton
bad-tempered [bæd'tɛmpəd] *adj* huysuz
baffled ['bæfᵊld] *adj* şaşkın
bag [bæg] *n* torba; **bum bag** *n* bel çantası; **carrier bag** *n* alışveriş torbası; **overnight bag** *n* gecelik seyahat çantası; **plastic bag** *n* naylon torba; **polythene bag** *n* naylon torba; **shopping bag** *n*

alışveriş çantası; **sleeping bag** *n* uyku tulumu; **tea bag** *n* torba çay; **toilet bag** *n* tuvalet çantası; **Can I have a bag, please?** Torbanız var mı?; **I don't need a bag, thanks** Torba istemem, sağolun
baggage ['bægɪdʒ] *n* bagaj; **baggage allowance** *n* bagaj limiti; **baggage reclaim** *n* bagaj alım; **excess baggage** *n* fazla bagaj; **What is the baggage allowance?** Bagaj limiti ne kadar?
baggy ['bægɪ] *adj* şalvar biçimi
bagpipes ['bæg,paɪps] *npl* gayda
Bahamas [bə'hɑːməz] *npl* Bahama Adaları
Bahrain [bɑː'reɪn] *n* Bahreyn
bail [beɪl] *n* kefalet
bake [beɪk] *v* fırında pişirmek
baked [beɪkt] *adj* fırında pişirilmiş; **baked potato** *n* kumpir
baker ['beɪkə] *n* fırıncı
bakery ['beɪkərɪ] *n* ekmekçi *(fırın)*
baking ['beɪkɪŋ] *n* fırında pişirme; **baking powder** *n* kabartma tozu
balance ['bæləns] *n* denge *(fizik)*; **balance sheet** *n* bilanço; **bank balance** *n* bakiye
balanced ['bælənst] *adj* dengeli
balcony ['bælkənɪ] *n* balkon; **Do you have a room with a balcony?** Balkonlu odanız var mı?
bald [bɔːld] *adj* kel
Balkan ['bɔːlkən] *adj* Balkan
ball [bɔːl] *n (dance)* balo, *(toy)* oyuncak top
ballerina [,bælə'riːnə] *n* balerin
ballet ['bæleɪ; bæ'leɪ] *n* bale; **ballet dancer** *n* balet; **ballet shoes** *npl* bale patiği; **Where can I buy tickets for the ballet?** Baleye nereden bilet alabilirim?
balloon [bə'luːn] *n* balon
bamboo [bæm'buː] *n* bambu
ban [bæn] *n* yasak ▷ *v* yasaklamak
banana [bə'nɑːnə] *n* muz
band [bænd] *n (musical group)* orkestra, *(strip)* bant; **brass band** *n* bando takımı; **elastic band** *n* lastik bant; **rubber band** *n* elastik band
bandage ['bændɪdʒ] *n* bandaj ▷ *v* sarmak
bang [bæŋ] *n* patlama sesi ▷ *v* patlamak *(ses çıkararak)*
Bangladesh [,bɑːŋglə'dɛʃ; ,bæŋ-] *n* Bengaldeş
Bangladeshi [,bɑːŋglə'dɛʃɪ; ,bæŋ-] *adj* Bengaldeş ile ilgili ▷ *n* Bengaldeşli
banister ['bænɪstə] *n* trabzan
banjo ['bændʒəʊ] *n* banço
bank [bæŋk] *n (finance)* banka, *(ridge)* ırmak kıyısı; **bank account** *n* banka hesabı; **bank balance** *n* bakiye; **bank charges** *npl* banka ücretleri; **bank holiday** *n* İngiltere'de bankaların kapalı olduğu tatil günü; **bank statement** *n* hesap özeti; **bottle bank** *n* şişe geri dönüşüm kutusu; **merchant bank** *n* ticaret bankası; **How far is the bank?** Banka buraya ne kadar uzakta?; **I would like to transfer some money from my bank in...** Bankamdan para transferi yapmak istiyorum; **Is the bank open today?** Banka bugün açık mı?; **Is there a bank here?** Burada banka var mı?;

When does the bank close? Banka ne zaman kapanıyor?
banker [ˈbæŋkə] *n* bankacı
banknote [ˈbæŋkˌnəʊt] *n* banknot
bankrupt [ˈbæŋkrʌpt; -rəpt] *adj* müflis
banned [bænd] *adj* yasaklanmış
Baptist [ˈbæptɪst] *n* Baptist
bar [bɑː] *n (alcohol)* bar, *(strip)* çubuk; **snack bar** *n* snack bar; **Where is the bar?** Bar ne tarafta?; **Where is there a nice bar?** İyi bir bar biliyor musunuz?
Barbados [bɑːˈbeɪdəʊs; -dəʊz; -dɒs] *n* Barbados
barbaric [bɑːˈbærɪk] *adj* barbar
barbecue [ˈbɑːbɪˌkjuː] *n* barbekü; **Where is the barbecue area?** Barbekü kısmı nerede?
barber [ˈbɑːbə] *n* berber
bare [bɛə] *adj* çıplak ▹ *v* açığa çıkarmak
barefoot [ˈbɛəˌfʊt] *adj* çıplak ayak ▹ *adv* çıplak ayakla
barely [ˈbɛəlɪ] *adv* ucu ucuna
bargain [ˈbɑːɡɪn] *n* pazarlık
barge [bɑːdʒ] *n* mavna
bark [bɑːk] *v* havlamak
barley [ˈbɑːlɪ] *n* arpa
barmaid [ˈbɑːˌmeɪd] *n* kadın barmen
barman, barmen [ˈbɑːmən, ˈbɑːmɛn] *n* barmen
barn [bɑːn] *n* samanlık
barrel [ˈbærəl] *n* fıçı
barrier [ˈbærɪə] *n* bariyer; **ticket barrier** *n* bilet turnikesi
bartender [ˈbɑːˌtɛndə] *n* barmen
base [beɪs] *n* ana
baseball [ˈbeɪsˌbɔːl] *n* beyzbol; **baseball cap** *n* beyzbol kepi
based [beɪst] *adj* dayanan
basement [ˈbeɪsmənt] *n* bodrum
bash [bæʃ] *n* darbe ▹ *v* şiddetle vurmak
basic [ˈbeɪsɪk] *adj* temel
basically [ˈbeɪsɪklɪ] *adv* aslında
basics [ˈbeɪsɪks] *npl* temel bilgiler
basil [ˈbæzᵊl] *n* fesleğen
basin [ˈbeɪsᵊn] *n* leğen
basis [ˈbeɪsɪs] *n* anafikir
basket [ˈbɑːskɪt] *n* sepet; **wastepaper basket** *n* çöp sepeti
basketball [ˈbɑːskɪtˌbɔːl] *n* basketbol
Basque [bæsk; bɑːsk] *adj* Bask ▹ *n (language)* Bask dili, *(person)* Basklı *(kişi)*
bass [beɪs] *n* bas; **bass drum** *n* bas davul; **double bass** *n* kontrabas
bassoon [bəˈsuːn] *n* fagot
bat [bæt] *n (mammal)* yarasa, *(with ball)* vuruş *(topa sopayla)*
bath [bɑːθ] *n* **bubble bath** *n* köpüklü banyo
bathe [beɪð] *v* yüzmek
bathrobe [ˈbɑːθˌrəʊb] *n* bornoz
bathroom [ˈbɑːθˌruːm; -ˌrʊm] *n* banyo; **Are there support railings in the bathroom?** Banyoda tutunma rayı var mı?; **Does the room have a private bathroom?** Odada banyo var mı?; **The bathroom is flooded** Banyo taşıyor
baths [bɑːθz] *npl* hamam
bathtub [ˈbɑːθˌtʌb] *n* küvet
batter [ˈbætə] *n* sulu hamur
battery [ˈbætərɪ] *n* pil; **Do you have any batteries?** Pil satıyor

musunuz?; **Do you have batteries for this camera?** Bu makineye uygun pil var mı?
attle ['bætᵊl] *n* muharebe
attleship ['bætᵊl,ʃɪp] *n* muharebe zırhlısı
ay [beɪ] *n* körfez; **bay leaf** *n* defne yaprağı
C [bi: si:] *abbr* İÖ
e [bi:; bɪ] *v* olmak
each [bi:tʃ] *n* kumsal
ead [bi:d] *n* boncuk
eak [bi:k] *n* gaga
eam [bi:m] *n* ışın
ean [bi:n] *n* fasulye; **broad bean** *n* bakla *(sebze)*; **coffee bean** *n* kahve çekirdeği; **French beans** *npl* çalı fasulyesi; **runner bean** *n* çalı fasulyesi
eansprout ['bi:nspraʊt] *n* **beansprouts** *npl* fasulye filizi
ear [bɛə] *n* ayı ▹ *v* taşımak; **polar bear** *n* kutup ayısı; **teddy bear** *n* oyuncak ayı
eard [bɪəd] *n* sakal
earded [bɪədɪd] *adj* sakallı
ear up [bɛə ʌp] *v* dayanmak
eat [bi:t] *n* ritim ▹ *v* *(outdo)* yenmek, *(strike)* dövmek
eautiful ['bju:tɪfʊl] *adj* güzel
eautifully ['bju:tɪflɪ] *adv* hoşça
eauty ['bju:tɪ] *n* güzellik; **beauty salon** *n* güzellik salonu; **beauty spot** *n* güzel manzaralı yer
eaver ['bi:və] *n* kunduz
ecause [bɪ'kɒz; -'kəz] *conj* çünkü
ecome [bɪ'kʌm] *v* olmak
ed [bɛd] *n* yatak; **bed and breakfast** *n* yatak ve kahvaltı; **bunk beds** *npl* ranza; **camp bed** *n* portatif karyola; **double bed** *n* çift kişilik yatak; **king-size bed** *n* battal boy yatak; **single bed** *n* tek yatak; **sofa bed** *n* çek-yat; **twin beds** *npl* çift yatak; **Do I have to stay in bed?** Yatakta mı kalmam gerekiyor?; **I'd like a dorm bed** Tek bir yatak rica ediyorum; **The bed is uncomfortable** Yatak çok rahatsız
bedclothes ['bɛd,kləʊðz] *npl* yatak takımı
bedding ['bɛdɪŋ] *n* yatak takımı
bedroom ['bɛd,ru:m; -,rʊm] *n* yatak odası; **Do you have any bedrooms on the ground floor?** Zemin katta yatak odası var mı?
bedsit ['bɛd,sɪt] *n* kiralık oda
bedspread ['bɛd,sprɛd] *n* yatak örtüsü
bedtime ['bɛd,taɪm] *n* yatma zamanı
bee [bi:] *n* arı
beech [bi:tʃ] *n* **beech (tree)** *n* kayın ağacı
beef [bi:f] *n* sığır eti
beefburger ['bi:f,bɜ:gə] *n* hamburger
beer [bɪə] *n* bira; **another beer, please** Bir bira daha lütfen; **A draught beer, please** Bir çekme bira lütfen
beetle ['bi:tᵊl] *n* böcek
beetroot ['bi:t,ru:t] *n* pancar
before [bɪ'fɔ:] *adv* önceden ▹ *conj* önce ▹ *prep* önünde; **before five o'clock** saat beşten önce; **Do we have to clean the house before we leave?** Ayrılmadan önce evi temizlememiz gerekiyor mu?; **the**

day before yesterday önceki gün; **the week before last** bundan bir hafta önce
beforehand [bɪ'fɔːˌhænd] *adv* daha önceden
beg [bɛg] *v* dilenmek
beggar ['bɛgə] *n* dilenci
begin [bɪ'gɪn] *v* başlamak
beginner [bɪ'gɪnə] *n* yeni başlayan
beginning [bɪ'gɪnɪŋ] *n* başlangıç
behave [bɪ'heɪv] *v* davranmak *(tavır)*
behaviour [bɪ'heɪvjə] *n* davranış
behind [bɪ'haɪnd] *adv* arkasında ▷ *n* arka ▷ *prep* arkada; **lag behind** *v* geride kalmak
beige [beɪʒ] *adj* bej
Beijing ['beɪ'dʒɪŋ] *n* Pekin
Belarus ['bɛləˌrʌs; -ˌrʊs] *n* beyaz rusya
Belarussian [ˌbɛləʊ'rʌʃən; ˌbjɛl-] *adj* Belarus ▷ *n (language)* Belarusca, *(person)* Belaruslu
Belgian ['bɛldʒən] *adj* Belçika ▷ *n* Belçikalı
Belgium ['bɛldʒəm] *n* Belçika
belief [bɪ'liːf] *n* inanç
believe [bɪ'liːv] *vi* inandırmak ▷ *vt* inanmak
bell [bɛl] *n* zil *(kapı, okul)*
belly ['bɛlɪ] *n* göbek; **belly button** *n* göbek *(deliği)*
belong [bɪ'lɒŋ] *v* ait olmak; **belong to** *v* ait olmak
belongings [bɪ'lɒŋɪŋz] *npl* eşya
below [bɪ'ləʊ] *adv* altında ▷ *prep* altında
belt [bɛlt] *n* kemer; **conveyor belt** *n* taşıyıcı bant; **money belt** *n* bel çantası; **safety belt** *n* emniyet kemeri
bench [bɛntʃ] *n* bank
bend [bɛnd] *n* viraj ▷ *v* kıvrılmak; **bend down** *v* eğilmek *(kıvrılarak* **bend over** *v* eğilmek *(ayak uçlarına doğru)*
beneath [bɪ'niːθ] *prep* altında
benefit ['bɛnɪfɪt] *n* yarar ▷ *v* yarar sağlamak
bent [bɛnt] *adj (dishonest)* namussuz, *(not straight)* bükülmü
beret ['bɛreɪ] *n* bere *(giyim)*
berry ['bɛrɪ] *n* çalı meyvesi
berth [bɜːθ] *n* ranza
beside [bɪ'saɪd] *prep* yanında
besides [bɪ'saɪdz] *adv* üstelik
best [bɛst] *adj* en iyi ▷ *adv* en iyisi; **best man** *n* sağdıç
bestseller [ˌbɛst'sɛlə] *n* çoksatar
bet [bɛt] *n* bahis ▷ *v* bahse girmek
betray [bɪ'treɪ] *v* ihanet etmek
better ['bɛtə] *adj* daha iyi ▷ *adv* daha iyisi
betting [bɛtɪŋ] *n* bahse girme; **betting shop** *n* bahis bayii
between [bɪ'twiːn] *prep* arasında
bewildered [bɪ'wɪldəd] *adj* şaşırmış
beyond [bɪ'jɒnd] *prep* ötesinde
biased ['baɪəst] *adj* yanlı
bib [bɪb] *n* mama önlüğü
Bible ['baɪbᵊl] *n* İncil
bicarbonate [baɪ'kɑːbənɪt; -ˌneɪt] *n* **bicarbonate of soda** *n* karbonat
bicycle ['baɪsɪkᵊl] *n* bisiklet; **bicycle pump** *n* bisiklet pompası
bid [bɪd] *n* teklif ▷ *v (at auction)* fiya vermek *(açık arttırmada)*
bifocals [baɪ'fəʊkᵊlz] *npl* çift odak

gözlük
ig [bɪg] *adj* büyük; **It's too big** Çok büyük; **The house is quite big** Ev oldukça büyük
igger [bɪgə] *adj* daha büyük; **Do you have a bigger one?** Daha büyük bir odanız var mı?
igheaded ['bɪg,hɛdɪd] *adj* kendini beğenmiş
ike [baɪk] *n* bisiklet; **mountain bike** *n* dağ bisikleti; **Can I keep my bike here?** Bisikletimi buraya bırakabilir miyim?; **Does the bike have brakes?** Bisikletin frenleri var mı?; **Does the bike have gears?** Bisiklet vitesli mi?; **I want to hire a bike** Bisiklet kiralamak istiyorum; **Where can I hire a bike?** Nereden bisiklet kiralayabilirim?; **Where is the nearest bike repair shop?** En yakın bisiklet tamircisi nerede?
ikini [bɪ'ki:nɪ] *n* bikini
ilingual [baɪ'lɪŋgwəl] *adj* iki dilli
ill [bɪl] *n (account)* hesap, *(legislation)* yasa; **phone bill** *n* telefon faturası; **Can I have an itemized bill?** Ayrıntılı hesap alabilir miyim?; **The bill is wrong** Hesapta bir yanlışlık var
illiards ['bɪljədz] *npl* bilardo
illion ['bɪljən] *n* milyar
in [bɪn] *n* çöp tenekesi; **litter bin** *n* çöp kutusu
inding ['baɪndɪŋ] *n* **Can you adjust my bindings, please?** Bağlarımı ayarlar mısınız lütfen?; **Can you tighten my bindings, please?** Bağlarımı sıkılar mısınız lütfen?
bingo ['bɪŋgəʊ] *n* tombola
binoculars [bɪ'nɒkjʊləz; baɪ-] *npl* dürbün
biochemistry [,baɪəʊ'kɛmɪstrɪ] *n* biyokimya
biodegradable [,baɪəʊdɪ'greɪdəbᵊl] *adj* biyo-çözünür
biography [baɪ'ɒgrəfɪ] *n* yaşam öyküsü
biological [,baɪə'lɒdʒɪkᵊl] *adj* biyolojik
biology [baɪ'ɒlədʒɪ] *n* biyoloji
biometric [,baɪəʊ'mɛtrɪk] *adj* biyometrik
birch [bɜ:tʃ] *n* huş ağacı
bird [bɜ:d] *n* kuş; **bird flu** *n* kuş gribi; **bird of prey** *n* yırtıcı kuş
birdwatching [bɜ:dwɒtʃɪŋ] *n* kuş gözleme
Biro® ['baɪrəʊ] *n* tükenmez kalem
birth [bɜ:θ] *n* doğum; **birth certificate** *n* nüfus cüzdanı; **birth control** *n* doğum kontrolü; **place of birth** *n* doğum yeri
birthday ['bɜ:θ,deɪ] *n* doğum günü
birthplace ['bɜ:θ,pleɪs] *n* doğum yeri
biscuit ['bɪskɪt] *n* bisküvi
bishop ['bɪʃəp] *n* piskopos
bit [bɪt] *n* parça
bitch [bɪtʃ] *n* kancık
bite [baɪt] *n* ısırma ▷ *v* ısırmak
bitter ['bɪtə] *adj* acı *(tat)*
black [blæk] *adj* siyah; **black ice** *n* gizli buz; **in black and white** Siyah beyaz
blackberry ['blækbərɪ] *n* böğürtlen
blackbird ['blæk,bɜ:d] *n* karatavuk

blackboard ['blæk,bɔːd] *n* karatahta
blackcurrant [,blæk'kʌrənt] *n* kuşüzümü
blackmail ['blæk,meɪl] *n* şantaj ▷ *v* şantaj yapmak
blackout ['blækaʊt] *n* karartma
bladder ['blædə] *n* sidik torbası; **gall bladder** *n* safra kesesi
blade [bleɪd] *n* bıçak; **razor blade** *n* traş bıçağı; **shoulder blade** *n* kürek kemiği
blame [bleɪm] *n* suç ▷ *v* suçlamak
blank [blæŋk] *adj* boş *(kağıt, zihin)* ▷ *n* boşluk *(yazı, zihin)*; **blank cheque** *n* açık çek
blanket ['blæŋkɪt] *n* battaniye; **electric blanket** *n* elektrikli battaniye; **Please bring me an extra blanket** Bana bir battaniye daha getirir misiniz lütfen?; **We need more blankets** Daha fazla battaniyeye ihtiyacımız var
blast [blɑːst] *n* patlama
blatant ['bleɪtᵊnt] *adj* apaçık
blaze [bleɪz] *n* parlak alev
blazer ['bleɪzə] *n* blazer
bleach [bliːtʃ] *n* ağartıcı
bleached [bliːtʃt] *adj* ağartılmış
bleak [bliːk] *adj* rüzgara açık
bleed [bliːd] *v* kanamak
bleeper ['bliːpə] *n* çağrı cihazı
blender ['blɛndə] *n* mikser
bless [blɛs] *v* kutsamak
blind [blaɪnd] *adj* kör ▷ *n* jaluzi; **Venetian blind** *n* jaluzi; **I'm blind** Körüm
blindfold ['blaɪnd,fəʊld] *n* göz bağı ▷ *v* gözlerini bağlamak
blink [blɪŋk] *v* göz kırpmak
bliss [blɪs] *n* mutluluk
blister ['blɪstə] *n* sulu kabarcık
blizzard ['blɪzəd] *n* kar fırtınası
block [blɒk] *n (buildings)* blok *(bina)*, *(obstruction)* engel, *(solid piece)* blok ▷ *v* bloke etmek
blockage ['blɒkɪdʒ] *n* tıkanıklık
blocked [blɒkt] *adj* tıkalı
blog [blɒg] *n* blog ▷ *v* blog yazmak
bloke [bləʊk] *n* herif
blonde [blɒnd] *adj* sarışın
blood [blʌd] *n* kan; **blood group** *n* kan grubu; **blood poisoning** *n* kan zehirlenmesi; **blood pressure** *n* tansiyon; **blood sports** *n* hayvan dövüşleri; **blood test** *n* kan testi; **blood transfusion** *n* kan nakli; **My blood group is O positive** Kan grubum O pozitif; **This stain is blood** Kan lekesi
bloody ['blʌdɪ] *adj* kanlı
blossom ['blɒsəm] *n* tomurcuk ▷ *v* çiçek açmak
blouse [blaʊz] *n* bluz
blow [bləʊ] *n* esinti ▷ *v* havaya uçmak
blow-dry [bləʊdraɪ] *n* fön
blow up [bləʊ ʌp] *v* havaya uçurmak
blue [bluː] *adj* mavi
blueberry ['bluːbərɪ; -brɪ] *n* yaban mersini
blues [bluːz] *npl* melankoli
bluff [blʌf] *n* blöf ▷ *v* blöf yapmak
blunder ['blʌndə] *n* gaf
blunt [blʌnt] *adj* kör *(bıçak/makas)*
blush [blʌʃ] *v* kızarmak
blusher ['blʌʃə] *n* allık
board [bɔːd] *n (meeting)* kurul,

(wood) tahta *(okul)* ▷ v *(go aboard)* tahta *(okul)*; **board game** *n* aile oyunları; **boarding card** *n* biniş kartı; **boarding pass** *n* biniş kartı; **boarding school** *n* yatılı okul; **bulletin board** *n* ilan tahtası; **diving board** *n* tramplen; **draining board** *n* damlalıklı eviye; **half board** *n* kahvaltı ve akşam yemeği dahil; **ironing board** *n* ütü tahtası; **notice board** *n* ilan tahtası; **skirting board** *n* süpürgelik
boarder ['bɔːdə] *n* yatılı öğrenci
boast [bəʊst] *v* böbürlenmek
boat [bəʊt] *n* tekne; **fishing boat** *n* balıkçı teknesi; **rowing boat** *n* kürek teknesi; **sailing boat** *n* yelkenli; **Are there any boat trips on the river?** Nehirde tekne turu var mı?
body ['bɒdɪ] *n* beden
bodybuilding ['bɒdɪˌbɪldɪŋ] *n* vücut geliştirme
bodyguard ['bɒdɪˌgɑːd] *n* özel koruma
bog [bɒg] *n* bataklık
boil [bɔɪl] *vi* pişirmek ▷ *vt* kaynatmak
boiled [bɔɪld] *adj* kaynamış; **boiled egg** *n* haşlanmış yumurta
boiler ['bɔɪlə] *n* kazan
boiling ['bɔɪlɪŋ] *adj* kaynar
boil over [bɔɪl 'əʊvə] *v* taşmak
Bolivia [bə'lɪvɪə] *n* Bolivya
Bolivian [bə'lɪvɪən] *adj* Bolivya ▷ *n* Bolivyalı
bolt [bəʊlt] *n* sürgü
bomb [bɒm] *n* bomba ▷ *v* bombalamak; **atom bomb** *n* atom bombası
bombing [bɒmɪŋ] *n* bombalama
bond [bɒnd] *n* bağ
bone [bəʊn] *n* kemik; **bone dry** *adj* kupkuru
bonfire ['bɒnˌfaɪə] *n* şenlik ateşi
bonnet ['bɒnɪt] *n* *(car)* motor kapağı
bonus ['bəʊnəs] *n* prim
book [bʊk] *n* kitap ▷ *v* rezerve etmek; **address book** *n* adres defteri
bookcase ['bʊkˌkeɪs] *n* kitaplık
booking ['bʊkɪŋ] *n* rezervasyon; **advance booking** *n* önceden rezervasyon; **booking office** *n* bilet gişesi; **Can I change my booking?** Rezervasyonumu değiştirebilir miyim?; **I want to cancel my booking** Rezervasyonumu iptal ettirmek istiyorum
booklet ['bʊklɪt] *n* kitapçık
bookmark ['bʊkˌmɑːk] *n* kitap ayracı
bookshelf ['bʊkˌʃɛlf] *n* kitap rafı
bookshop ['bʊkˌʃɒp] *n* kitapçı
boost [buːst] *v* yüreklendirmek
boot [buːt] *n* çizme *(ayakkabı)*
booze [buːz] *n* içki
border ['bɔːdə] *n* sınır
bore [bɔː] *v* *(be dull)* can sıkmak, *(drill)* delmek
bored [bɔːd] *adj* canı sıkılmış
boredom ['bɔːdəm] *n* can sıkıntısı
boring ['bɔːrɪŋ] *adj* sıkıcı
born [bɔːn] *adj* doğmuş
borrow ['bɒrəʊ] *v* ödünç almak
Bosnia ['bɒznɪə] *n* Bosna; **Bosnia and Herzegovina** *n* Bosna-

Hersek
Bosnian ['bɒznıən] *adj* Bosna ▷ *n* *(person)* Bosnalı *(kişi)*
boss [bɒs] *n* patron
boss around [bɒs ə'raʊnd] *v* patronluk taslamak
bossy ['bɒsı] *adj* buyurgan
both [bəʊθ] *adj* her iki ▷ *pron* her ikisi de
bother ['bɒðə] *v* zahmet etmek
Botswana [bʊ'tʃwɑ:nə; bʊt'swɑ:nə; bɒt-] *n* Botsvana
bottle ['bɒtᵊl] *n* şişe; **baby's bottle** *n* biberon; **bottle bank** *n* şişe geri dönüşüm kutusu; **hot-water bottle** *n* sıcak su torbası; **a bottle of mineral water** Bir şişe maden suyu; **a bottle of red wine** Bir şişe kırmızı şarap; **Please bring another bottle** Bir şişe daha getirir misiniz?
bottle-opener ['bɒtᵊl'əʊpənə] *n* şişe açacağı
bottom ['bɒtəm] *adj* en alt ▷ *n* dip
bought [bɔ:t] *adj* satın alınmış
bounce [baʊns] *v* avara etmek
bouncer ['baʊnsə] *n* fedai
boundary ['baʊndərı; -drı] *n* sınır
bouquet ['bu:keı] *n* buket
bow *n* [bəʊ] *(weapon)* yay ▷ *v* [baʊ] baş eğmek
bowels ['baʊəlz] *npl* bağırsaklar
bowl [bəʊl] *n* kase
bowling ['bəʊlıŋ] *n* bowling; **bowling alley** *n* bowling salonu; **tenpin bowling** *n* bovling
bow tie [bəʊ] *n* papyon kravat
box [bɒks] *n* boks; **box office** *n* bilet gişesi; **call box** *n* telefon kulübesi; **fuse box** *n* sigorta kutusu; **gear box** *n* vites kutusu
boxer ['bɒksə] *n* boksör; **boxer shorts** *npl* bokser şort
boxing ['bɒksıŋ] *n* boks
boy [bɔı] *n* oğlan çocuğu
boyfriend ['bɔı,frɛnd] *n* erkek arkadaş; **I have a boyfriend** Erke arkadaşım var
bra [brɑ:] *n* sütyen
brace [breıs] *n* *(fastening)* destek *(bağ, kuşak vb)*
bracelet ['breıslıt] *n* kolçak
braces ['breısız] *npl* pantolon askıları
brackets ['brækıts] *npl* köşeli parantezler
brain [breın] *n* beyin
brainy ['breını] *adj* akıllı
brake [breık] *n* fren ▷ *v* frenlemek; **brake light** *n* fren lambası; **Does the bike have back-pedal brakes?** Bisikletin geri frenleri var mı?; **The brakes don't work** Frenler çalışmıyor
bran [bræn] *n* kepek
branch [brɑ:ntʃ] *n* dal *(ağaç vb)*
brand [brænd] *n* marka; **brand name** *n* marka
brand-new [brænd'nju:] *adj* yepyeni
brandy ['brændı] *n* brendi; **I'll have a brandy** Ben brendi alayım
brass [brɑ:s] *n* pirinç *(metal)*; **brass band** *n* bando takımı
brat [bræt] *n* velet
brave [breıv] *adj* cesur
bravery ['breıvərı] *n* cesaret
Brazil [brə'zıl] *n* Brezilya
Brazilian [brə'zıljən] *adj* Brezilya ▷ *n* Brezilyalı

read [brɛd] *n* ekmek; **bread roll** *n* yuvarlak ekmek; **brown bread** *n* esmer ekmek; **Please bring more bread** Biraz daha ekmek getirir misiniz?; **Would you like some bread?** Biraz daha ekmek ister misiniz?

read bin [brɛdbɪn] *n* ekmek kutusu

readcrumbs ['brɛd,krʌmz] *npl* ekmek kırıntısı

reak [breɪk] *n* kırık ▹ *v* kırmak; **lunch break** *n* yemek molası

reak down [breɪk daʊn] *v* bozmak

reakdown ['breɪkdaʊn] *n* arıza; **breakdown truck** *n* çekici; **breakdown van** *n* kurtarma aracı; **nervous breakdown** *n* sinir krizi

reakfast ['brɛkfəst] *n* kahvaltı; **bed and breakfast** *n* yatak ve kahvaltı; **continental breakfast** *n* çörek ve kahve ya da çaydan oluşan kahvaltı; **Can I have breakfast in my room?** Odamda kahvaltı edebilir miyim?; **Is breakfast included?** Kahvaltı dahil mi?; **with breakfast** kahvaltı dahil; **without breakfast** kahvaltı hariç; **What time is breakfast?** Kahvaltı kaçta?; **What would you like for breakfast?** Kahvaltıda ne yemek istersiniz?

break in [breɪk ɪn] *v* terbiye etmek; **break in (on)** *v* sözünü kesmek

break-in [breɪkɪn] *n* hırsızlık

break up [breɪk ʌp] *v* kırmak

breast [brɛst] *n* göğüs

breast-feed ['brɛst,fiːd] *v* emzirmek

breaststroke ['brɛst,strəʊk] *n* kurbağalama *(yüzme)*

breath [brɛθ] *n* nefes

Breathalyser® ['brɛθə,laɪzə] *n* üfleme cihazı

breathe [briːð] *v* nefes almak

breathe in [briːð ɪn] *v* nefes almak

breathe out [briːð aʊt] *v* nefes vermek

breathing ['briːðɪŋ] *n* nefes alma

breed [briːd] *n* cins *(hayvan)* ▹ *v* yetiştirmek *(hayvan)*

breeze [briːz] *n* hafif rüzgar

brewery ['brʊərɪ] *n* bira fabrikası

bribe [braɪb] *v* rüşvet vermek

bribery ['braɪbərɪ; 'bribery] *n* rüşvet

brick [brɪk] *n* tuğla

bricklayer ['brɪk,leɪə] *n* duvarcı

bride [braɪd] *n* gelin *(damadın eşi)*

bridegroom ['braɪd,gruːm; -,grʊm] *n* damat *(gelinin kocası)*

bridesmaid ['braɪdz,meɪd] *n* nedime

bridge [brɪdʒ] *n* köprü; **suspension bridge** *n* asma köprü

brief [briːf] *adj* kısa

briefcase ['briːf,keɪs] *n* evrak çantası

briefing ['briːfɪŋ] *n* brifing

briefly ['briːflɪ] *adv* kısaca

briefs [briːfs] *npl* külot

bright [braɪt] *adj* parlak

brilliant ['brɪljənt] *adj* pırıl pırıl

bring [brɪŋ] *v* getirmek

bring back [brɪŋ bæk] *v* geri getirmek

bring forward [brɪŋ 'fɔːwəd] *v*

öncelik getirmek
bring up [brɪŋ ʌp] *v* yetiştirmek
Britain ['brɪtᵊn] *n* İngiltere
British ['brɪtɪʃ] *adj* İngiliz ▷ *n* İngiliz
broad [brɔːd] *adj* geniş *(yayvan)*
broadband ['brɔːd,bænd] *n* geniş bant
broadcast ['brɔːd,kɑːst] *n* yayın ▷ *v* yayın yapmak
broad-minded [brɔːd'maɪndɪd] *adj* açık fikirli
broccoli ['brɒkəlɪ] *n* brokoli
brochure ['brəʊʃjʊə; -ʃə] *n* broşür
broke [brəʊk] *adj* züğürt
broken ['brəʊkən] *adj* kırık; **broken down** *adj* kırık
broker ['brəʊkə] *n* komisyoncu
bronchitis [brɒŋ'kaɪtɪs] *n* bronşit
bronze [brɒnz] *n* bronz
brooch [brəʊtʃ] *n* broş
broom [bruːm; brʊm] *n* süpürge
broth [brɒθ] *n* et ya da sebze suyuna çorba
brother ['brʌðə] *n* erkek kardeş
brother-in-law ['brʌðə ɪn lɔː] *n* kayın birader
brown [braʊn] *adj* kahverengi; **brown bread** *n* esmer ekmek; **brown rice** *n* esmer pirinç
browse [braʊz] *v* göz atmak
browser ['braʊzə] *n* tarayıcı *(internet)*
bruise [bruːz] *n* bere *(tıp)*
brush [brʌʃ] *n* fırça ▷ *v* fırçalamak
Brussels sprouts ['brʌsᵊlz spraʊts] *npl* Brüksel lahanası
brutal ['bruːtᵊl] *adj* vahşi
bubble ['bʌbᵊl] *n* kabarcık; **bubble bath** *n* köpüklü banyo; **bubble gum** *n* balonlu çiklet
bucket ['bʌkɪt] *n* kova
buckle ['bʌkᵊl] *n* kemer tokası
Buddha ['bʊdə] *n* Buda
Buddhism ['bʊdɪzəm] *n* Budizm
Buddhist ['bʊdɪst] *adj* Budist ▷ *n* Budist
budgerigar ['bʌdʒərɪ,gɑː] *n* muhabbet kuşu
budget ['bʌdʒɪt] *n* bütçe
budgie ['bʌdʒɪ] *n* muhabbet kuşu
buffalo ['bʌfə,ləʊ] *n* manda
buffet ['bʊfeɪ] *n* açık büfe; **buffet car** *n* yemekli vagon
bug [bʌg] *n* böcek; **There are bugs in my room** Odamda böcek var
bugged ['bʌgd] *adj* gizli dinleme cihazı yerleştirilmiş
buggy ['bʌgɪ] *n* at arabası
build [bɪld] *v* inşa etmek
builder ['bɪldə] *n* inşaatçı
building ['bɪldɪŋ] *n* yapı; **building site** *n* inşaat alanı
bulb [bʌlb] *n (electricity)* ampul *(elektrik)*, *(plant)* soğan *(bitki)*
Bulgaria [bʌl'gɛərɪə; bʊl-] *n* Bulgaristan
Bulgarian [bʌl'gɛərɪən; bʊl-] *adj* Bulgar ▷ *n (language)* Bulgarca *(dil)*, *(person)* Bulgar *(kişi)*
bulimia [bjuː'lɪmɪə] *n* bulimia
bull [bʊl] *n* boğa
bulldozer ['bʊl,dəʊzə] *n* buldozer
bullet ['bʊlɪt] *n* kurşun *(silah)*
bully ['bʊlɪ] *n* zorba ▷ *v* zorbalık etmek
bum [bʌm] *n* kıç; **bum bag** *n* bel çantası
bumblebee ['bʌmbᵊl,biː] *n* hezen arısı
bump [bʌmp] *n* çarpma; **bump**

into *v* kazara çarpmak
bumper ['bʌmpə] *n* tampon *(oto)*
bumpy ['bʌmpɪ] *adj* tümsekli
bun [bʌn] *n* çörek
bunch [bʌntʃ] *n* demet
bungalow ['bʌŋgə,ləʊ] *n* bungalov
bungee jumping ['bʌndʒɪ] *n* bungee jumping
bunion ['bʌnjən] *n* yangılı ayak şişi
bunk [bʌŋk] *n* ranza; **bunk beds** *npl* ranza
buoy [bɔɪ; 'buːɪ] *n* şamandıra
burden ['bɜːdᵊn] *n* yük
bureaucracy [bjʊə'rɒkrəsɪ] *n* bürokrasi
bureau de change ['bjʊərəʊ də 'ʃɒnʒ] *n* **bureau de change** *n* döviz bürosu; **I need to find a bureau de change** Döviz bürosu arıyorum; **Is there a bureau de change here?** Burada döviz bürosu var mı?; **When is the bureau de change open?** Döviz bürosu ne zaman açılıyor?
burger ['bɜːgə] *n* burger
burglar ['bɜːglə] *n* hırsız; **burglar alarm** *n* hırsız alarmı
burglary ['bɜːglərɪ] *n* hırsızlık
burgle ['bɜːgᵊl] *v* soymak
Burma ['bɜːmə] *n* Burma
Burmese [bɜː'miːz] *adj* Burma ▷ *n (language)* Burma dili *(dil)*, *(person)* Burmalı *(kişi)*
burn [bɜːn] *n* yanık ▷ *v* yakmak *(ateşte)*
burn down [bɜːn daʊn] *v* yanıp kül olmak
burp [bɜːp] *n* geğirme ▷ *v* geğirmek
burst [bɜːst] *v* patlamak *(delinerek)*
bury ['bɛrɪ] *v* gömmek
bus [bʌs] *n* otobüs; **airport bus** *n* hava alanı otobüsü; **bus station** *n* otobüs terminali; **bus stop** *n* otobüs durağı; **bus ticket** *n* otobüs bileti; **Does this bus go to...?** Bu otobüs... a gider mi?; **Excuse me, which bus goes to...?** Affedersiniz,... a hangi otobüs gidiyor?; **How often are the buses to...?** ... otobüsü ne kadarda bir geliyor?; **Is there a bus to the airport?** Havaalanına otobüs var mı?; **What time does the bus leave?** Otobüs ne zaman kalkacak?; **What time is the last bus?** Son otobüs kaçta?; **When is the next bus to...?** ... a bir sonraki otobüs kaçta?; **Where can I buy a bus card?** Nereden otobüs kartı alabilirim?; **Where can I get a bus to...?** ... otobüsüne nereden binebilirim?; **Where is the bus station?** Otobüs terminali nerede?
bush [bʊʃ] *n (shrub)* çalı, *(thicket)* çalılık
business ['bɪznɪs] *n* ticaret; **business class** *n* hizmet sınıfı; **business trip** *n* iş seyahati; **show business** *n* eğlence sanayii
businessman, businessmen ['bɪznɪs,mæn; -mən, 'bɪznɪs,mɛn] *n* iş adamı
businesswoman, businesswomen ['bɪznɪs,wʊmən, 'bɪznɪs,wɪmɪn] *n* iş kadını
busker ['bʌskə] *n* sokak çalgıcısı
bust [bʌst] *n* göğüs
busy ['bɪzɪ] *adj* meşgul; **busy**

signal *n* meşgul sinyali; **Sorry, I'm busy** Kusura bakmayın, meşgulüm
but [bʌt] *conj* fakat
butcher ['bʊtʃə] *n* kasap
butcher's ['bʊtʃəz] *n* kasap
butter ['bʌtə] *n* tereyağı; **peanut butter** *n* fıstık ezmesi
buttercup ['bʌtə,kʌp] *n* düğün çiçeği
butterfly ['bʌtə,flaɪ] *n* kelebek *(hayvan)*
buttocks ['bʌtəkz] *npl* kalça
button ['bʌtᵊn] *n* düğme *(giysi, elektrik)*; **belly button** *n* göbek *(deliği)*; **Which button do I press?** Hangi düğmeye basacağım?
buy [baɪ] *v* satın almak
buyer ['baɪə] *n* alıcı
buyout ['baɪ,aʊt] *n* satın alma *(şirket)*
by [baɪ] *prep* tarafından
bye [baɪ] *excl* hoşçakal!
bye-bye [baɪbaɪ] *excl* hoşçakal!
bypass ['baɪ,pɑːs] *n* çevre yolu

C

cab [kæb] *n* taksi
cabbage ['kæbɪdʒ] *n* lahana
cabin ['kæbɪn] *n* kabin, kulübe; **cabin crew** *n* kabin mürettebatı; **a first class cabin** Birinci sınıf bir kabin; **a standard class cabin** Standart bir kabin bileti; **Where is cabin number five?** Beş numaralı kabin nerede?
cabinet ['kæbɪnɪt] *n* kabine
cable ['keɪbᵊl] *n* kablo; **cable car** *n* teleferik; **cable television** *n* kablolu yayın
cactus ['kæktəs] *n* kaktüs
cadet [kə'dɛt] *n* askeri öğrenci
café ['kæfeɪ; 'kæfɪ] *n* cafe; **Internet café** *n* internet cafe; **Are there any Internet cafés here?** Buralarda internet cafe var mı?
cafeteria [,kæfɪ'tɪərɪə] *n* kafeterya
caffeine ['kæfiːn; 'kæfɪ,iːn] *n* kafein

cage [keɪdʒ] *n* kafes
cagoule [kə'gu:l] *n* su geçirmez parka
cake [keɪk] *n* kek
calcium ['kælsɪəm] *n* kalsiyum
calculate ['kælkjʊˌleɪt] *v* hesaplamak
calculation [ˌkælkjʊ'leɪʃən] *n* hesaplama
calculator ['kælkjʊˌleɪtə] *n* hesap makinesi; **pocket calculator** *n* cep hesap makinesi
calendar ['kælɪndə] *n* takvim
calf, calves [kɑ:f, kɑ:vz] *n* dana
call [kɔ:l] *n* çağrı ▹ *v* aramak; **alarm call** *n* uyarı çağrısı; **call box** *n* telefon kulübesi; **call centre** *n* çağrı merkezi; **roll call** *n* yoklama
call back [kɔ:l bæk] *v* geri aramak
call for [kɔ:l fɔ:] *v* icap ettirmek
call off [kɔ:l ɒf] *v* iptal etmek
calm [kɑ:m] *adj* sakin
calm down [kɑ:m daʊn] *v* sakinleşmek
calorie ['kælərɪ] *n* kalori
Cambodia [kæm'bəʊdɪə] *n* Kamboçya
Cambodian [kæm'bəʊdɪən] *adj* Kamboçya ▹ *n (person)* Kamboçyalı *(kişi)*
camcorder ['kæmˌkɔ:də] *n* video kamera
camel ['kæməl] *n* deve
camera ['kæmərə; 'kæmrə] *n* fotoğraf makinesi; **camera phone** *n* fotoğraflı telefon; **digital camera** *n* dijital fotoğraf makinesi; **video camera** *n* video kamerası
cameraman, cameramen ['kæmərəˌmæn; 'kæmrə-, 'kæmərəˌmɛn] *n* kameraman
Cameroon [ˌkæmə'ru:n; 'kæməˌru:n] *n* Kamerun
camp [kæmp] *n* kamp ▹ *v* kamp yapmak; **camp bed** *n* portatif karyola
campaign [kæm'peɪn] *n* kampanya
camper ['kæmpə] *n* kampçı, karavan
camping ['kæmpɪŋ] *n* kamping; **camping gas** *n* tüp gaz
campsite ['kæmpˌsaɪt] *n* kamp yeri; **Is there a campsite here?** Buralarda bir kamp yeri var mı?
campus ['kæmpəs] *n* kampüs
can [kæn] *n* pet ▹ *v* yapabilmek; **watering can** *n* bahçe sulama bidonu
Canada ['kænədə] *n* Kanada
Canadian [kə'neɪdɪən] *adj* Kanada ▹ *n* Kanadalı
canal [kə'næl] *n* kanal
Canaries [kə'nɛəri:z] *npl* Kanarya Adaları
canary [kə'nɛərɪ] *n* kanarya
cancel ['kænsᵊl] *v* iptal etmek
cancellation [ˌkænsɪ'leɪʃən] *n* iptal
cancer ['kænsə] *n (illness)* kanser *(hastalık)*
Cancer ['kænsə] *n (horoscope)* Yengeç Burcu
candidate ['kændɪˌdeɪt; -dɪt] *n* aday
candle ['kændᵊl] *n* mum
candlestick ['kændᵊlˌstɪk] *n* şamdan
candyfloss ['kændɪˌflɒs] *n* pamuk

helva
canister ['kænɪstə] *n* teneke kutu
cannabis ['kænəbɪs] *n* esrar *(bitki)*
canned [kænd] *adj* kutulanmış
canoe [kə'nuː] *n* kano
canoeing [kə'nuːɪŋ] *n* kano sporu; **Where can we go canoeing?** Kano sporu nerede yapabiliriz?
can-opener ['kæn'əʊpənə] *n* kutu açacağı
canteen [kæn'tiːn] *n* kantin
canter ['kæntə] *v* eşkin gitmek
canvas ['kænvəs] *n* kaput bezi
canvass ['kænvəs] *v* oy propagandası yapmak
cap [kæp] *n* kep; **baseball cap** *n* beyzbol kepi
capable ['keɪpəbᵊl] *adj* muktedir
capacity [kə'pæsɪtɪ] *n* kapasite
capital ['kæpɪtᵊl] *n* başkent
capitalism ['kæpɪtəˌlɪzəm] *n* kapitalizm
Capricorn ['kæprɪˌkɔːn] *n* Oğlak burcu
capsize [kæp'saɪz] *v* alabora olmak
capsule ['kæpsjuːl] *n* kapsül
captain ['kæptɪn] *n* kaptan
caption ['kæpʃən] *n* başlık
capture ['kæptʃə] *v* zaptetmek
car [kɑː] *n* araba; **buffet car** *n* yemekli vagon; **cable car** *n* teleferik; **car hire** *n* araba kiralama; **car park** *n* otopark; **car rental** *n* oto kiralama; **car wash** *n* oto yıkama; **company car** *n* şirket arabası; **dining car** *n* yemek vagonu; **estate car** *n* vagon *(oto)*; **hired car** *n* kiralık araba; **patrol car** *n* devriye arabası; **racing car** *n* yarış arabası; **rental car** *n* kiralık araba; **saloon car** *n* sedan araba; **sleeping car** *n* kuşetli vagon; **Can you take me by car?** Beni arabayla alabilir misiniz?; **Do I have to return the car here?** Arabayı buraya mı geri getirmem gerekiyor; **I want to hire a car** Araba kiralamak istiyorum; **I've crashed my car** Arabamı çarptım; **My car has been broken into** Arabamı soydular; **When will the car be ready?** Araba ne zaman hazır olur?; **Where can I park the car?** Arabamı nereye park edebilirim?
carafe [kə'ræf; -'rɑːf] *n* sürahi; **a carafe of the house wine** Kendi şarabınızdan bir sürahi
caramel ['kærəməl; -ˌmɛl] *n* karamelâ
carat ['kærət] *n* kırat
caravan ['kærəˌvæn] *n* karavan; **caravan site** *n* karavan kampı; **Can we park our caravan here?** Karavanımızı buraya park edebilir miyiz?; **We'd like a site for a caravan** Karavanımızla kamp edebileceğimiz bir yer arıyoruz
carbohydrate [ˌkɑːbəʊ'haɪdreɪt] *n* karbonhidrat
carbon ['kɑːbᵊn] *n* karbon; **carbon footprint** *n* karbon ayak izi
carburettor [ˌkɑːbjʊ'rɛtə; 'kɑːbjʊˌrɛtə; -bə-] *n* karbüratör
card [kɑːd] *n* kart; **boarding card** *n* biniş kartı; **credit card** *n* kredi kartı; **debit card** *n* banka kartı; **greetings card** *n* tebrik kartı; **ID card** *abbr* kimlik kartı;

membership card *n* üyelik kartı; **playing card** *n* oyun kartı; **report card** *n* karne; **top-up card** *n* telefon kartı; **A memory card for this digital camera, please** Bu dijital kameraya hafıza kartı almak istiyorum lütfen; **Can I have your card?** Kartınızı alabilir miyim?; **Can I use my card to get cash?** Nakit almak için kartımı kullanabilir miyim?; **Do you sell phone cards?** Telefon kartı satıyor musunuz?; **Do you take credit cards?** Kredi kartı kabul ediyor musunuz?; **Do you take debit cards?** Banka kartı kabul ediyor musunuz?; **I need to cancel my card** Kartımı iptal ettirmek istiyorum; **My card has been stolen** Kartım çalındı; **Where can I post these cards?** Bu kartları nereden postalayabilirim?
cardboard ['kɑːdˌbɔːd] *n* mukavva
cardigan ['kɑːdɪgən] *n* hırka
cardphone ['kɑːdfəʊn] *n* kartlı telefon
care [kɛə] *n* bakım *(hasta vb)* ▷ *v* bakmak *(hasta vb)*; **intensive care unit** *n* yoğun bakım ünitesi
career [kə'rɪə] *n* kariyer
careful ['kɛəfʊl] *adj* dikkatli
carefully ['kɛəfʊlɪ] *adv* dikkatli
careless ['kɛəlɪs] *adj* dikkatsiz
caretaker ['kɛəˌteɪkə] *n* bakıcı *(apartman, ev)*
car-ferry ['kɑːfɛrɪ] *n* arabalı feribot
cargo ['kɑːgəʊ] *n* kargo
Caribbean [ˌkærɪ'biːən; kə'rɪbɪən] *adj* Karayip ▷ *n* Karayip denizi
caring ['kɛərɪŋ] *adj* şefkatli
carnation [kɑː'neɪʃən] *n* karanfil *(çiçek)*
carnival ['kɑːnɪvᵊl] *n* karnaval
carol ['kærəl] *n* Noel şarkısı
carpenter ['kɑːpɪntə] *n* marangoz
carpentry ['kɑːpɪntrɪ] *n* marangozluk
carpet ['kɑːpɪt] *n* halı; **fitted carpet** *n* duvardan duvara halı
carriage ['kærɪdʒ] *n* vagon; **Where is carriage number thirty?** Otuz numaralı vagon nerede?
carriageway ['kærɪdʒˌweɪ] *n* **dual carriageway** *n* çift-şeritli yol
carrot ['kærət] *n* havuç
carry ['kærɪ] *v* taşımak
carrycot ['kærɪˌkɒt] *n* portbebe
carry on ['kærɪ ɒn] *v* devam etmek
carry out ['kærɪ aʊt] *v* uygulamak
cart [kɑːt] *n* at arabası
carton ['kɑːtᵊn] *n* karton kutu
cartoon [kɑː'tuːn] *n* karikatür
cartridge ['kɑːtrɪdʒ] *n* fişek *(silah)*
carve [kɑːv] *v* oymak *(ağaç)*
case [keɪs] *n* vaka; **pencil case** *n* kalemlik
cash [kæʃ] *n* nakit; **cash dispenser** *n* bankamatik; **cash register** *n* yazar kasa; **Can I get a cash advance with my credit card?** Kredi kartıma nakit ödeme alabilir miyim?; **Do you offer a discount for cash?** Nakit ödemelere indirim yapıyor musunuz?; **I don't have any cash** Üzerimde nakit yok
cashew ['kæʃuː; kæ'ʃuː] *n* Hint

fıstığı
cashier [kæ'ʃɪə] *n* kasiyer
cashmere ['kæʃmɪə] *n* kaşmir
casino [kə'si:nəʊ] *n* kumarhane
casserole ['kæsə,rəʊl] *n* güveç
cassette [kæ'sɛt] *n* kaset
cast [kɑ:st] *n* oyuncu kadrosu
castle ['kɑ:sᵊl] *n* kale *(şato vb)*
casual ['kæʒjʊəl] *adj* umursamaz
casually ['kæʒjʊəlɪ] *adv* gelişigüzel
casualty ['kæʒjʊəltɪ] *n* zayiat
cat [kæt] *n* kedi
catalogue ['kætə,lɒg] *n* katalog; **I'd like a catalogue** Katalog istiyorum
cataract ['kætə,rækt] *n (eye)* katarakt, *(waterfall)* çağlayan
catarrh [kə'tɑ:] *n* akıntı *(nezle)*
catastrophe [kə'tæstrəfɪ] *n* felaket *(doğal afet)*
catch [kætʃ] *v* yakalamak
catching ['kætʃɪŋ] *adj* bulaşıcı
catch up [kætʃ ʌp] *v* yetişmek
category ['kætɪgərɪ] *n* kategori
catering ['keɪtərɪŋ] *n* catering
caterpillar ['kætə,pɪlə] *n* tırtıl
cathedral [kə'θi:drəl] *n* katedral; **When is the cathedral open?** Katedral ne zaman açık?
Catholic ['kæθəlɪk; 'kæθlɪk] *adj* Katolik ▷ *n* Katolik; **Roman Catholic** *n* Roma Katoliği, Roma Katolik
cattle ['kætᵊl] *npl* davar
Caucasus ['kɔ:kəsəs] *n* Kafkas
cauliflower ['kɒlɪ,flaʊə] *n* karnabahar
cause [kɔ:z] *n (ideals)* amaç, *(reason)* neden ▷ *v* yol açmak
caution ['kɔ:ʃən] *n* önlem
cautious ['kɔ:ʃəs] *adj* tedbirli
cautiously ['kɔ:ʃəslɪ] *adv* özenli bir şekilde
cave [keɪv] *n* mağara
CCTV [si: si: ti: vi:] *abbr* Kapalı Devre Televizyon Sistemi
CD [si: di:] *n* CD; **CD burner** *n* CD yazıcı; **CD player** *n* CD çalar; **Can I make CDs at this computer?** Bu bilgisayarda CD yapabilir miyim?; **When will the CD be ready?** CD ne zaman hazır olur?
CD-ROM [-'rɒm] *n* CD-ROM
ceasefire ['si:s'faɪə] *n* ateşkes
ceiling ['si:lɪŋ] *n* tavan
celebrate ['sɛlɪ,breɪt] *v* kutlamak
celebration ['sɛlɪ,breɪʃən] *n* kutlama
celebrity [sɪ'lɛbrɪtɪ] *n* ünlü
celery ['sɛlərɪ] *n* kereviz sapı
cell [sɛl] *n* hücre
cellar ['sɛlə] *n* mahzen
cello ['tʃɛləʊ] *n* viyolonsel
cement [sɪ'mɛnt] *n* çimento
cemetery ['sɛmɪtrɪ] *n* mezarlık
census ['sɛnsəs] *n* nüfus sayımı
cent [sɛnt] *n* sent *(para birimi)*
centenary [sɛn'ti:nərɪ] *n* yüzüncü yıl
centimetre ['sɛntɪ,mi:tə] *n* santimetre
central ['sɛntrəl] *adj* merkezi; **central heating** *n* merkezi ısıtma **Central America** *n* Orta Amerika
centre ['sɛntə] *n* merkez; **call centre** *n* çağrı merkezi; **city centre** *n* kent merkezi; **job centre** *n* iş bulma kurumu; **leisure centre** *n* eğlence merkezi; **shopping centre** *n* alışveriş

merkezi; **town centre** *n* şehir merkezi; **visitor centre** *n* ziyaretçi merkezi; **How do I get to the centre of...?** ... merkezine nasıl gidebilirim?
century ['sɛntʃərɪ] *n* yüzyıl
CEO [siː iː əʊ] *abbr* CEO
ceramic [sɪ'ræmɪk] *adj* seramik
cereal ['sɪərɪəl] *n* tahıl gevreği
ceremony ['sɛrɪmənɪ] *n* tören
certain ['sɜːtᵊn] *adj* kesin
certainly ['sɜːtᵊnlɪ] *adv* kesinlikle
certainty ['sɜːtᵊntɪ] *n* kesinlik
certificate [sə'tɪfɪkɪt] *n* sertifika; **birth certificate** *n* nüfus cüzdanı; **marriage certificate** *n* evlilik cüzdanı; **medical certificate** *n* sağlık belgesi
Chad [tʃæd] *n* Çad
chain [tʃeɪn] *n* zincir; **Do I need snow chains?** Kar zinciri almam gerekiyor mu?
chair [tʃɛə] *n* *(furniture)* sandalye; **easy chair** *n* koltuk; **rocking chair** *n* sallanan sandalye; **Do you have a high chair?** Mama sandalyeniz var mı?
chairlift ['tʃɛə,lɪft] *n* teleferik; **When does the first chairlift go?** İlk teleferik kaçta?
chairman, chairmen ['tʃɛəmən, 'tʃɛəmɛn] *n* başkan
chalk [tʃɔːk] *n* tebeşir
challenge ['tʃælɪndʒ] *n* meydan okuma ▹ *v* meydan okumak
challenging ['tʃælɪndʒɪŋ] *adj* zorlayıcı
chambermaid ['tʃeɪmbə,meɪd] *n* oda görevlisi
champagne [ʃæm'peɪn] *n* şampanya
champion ['tʃæmpɪən] *n* şampiyon
championship ['tʃæmpɪən,ʃɪp] *n* şampiyona
chance [tʃɑːns] *n* gelişigüzel; **by chance** *adv* kazara
change [tʃeɪndʒ] *n* değişim ▹ *vi* değiştirmek; **changing room** *n* soyunma odası *(spor)*; **I want to change my ticket** Biletimi değiştirmek istiyorum; **I want to change some... into...** ...larımı... la değiştirmek istiyorum; **I'd like to change my flight** Uçuşumu değiştirmek istiyorum
changeable ['tʃeɪndʒəbᵊl] *adj* değiştirilebilir
channel ['tʃænᵊl] *n* kanal
chaos ['keɪɒs] *n* kargaşa
chaotic [keɪ'ɒtɪk] *adj* karmakarışık
chap [tʃæp] *n* ahpap
chapel ['tʃæpᵊl] *n* şapel
chapter ['tʃæptə] *n* bölüm *(kitap)*
character ['kærɪktə] *n* karakter
characteristic [,kærɪktə'rɪstɪk] *n* karakteristik
charcoal ['tʃɑː,kəʊl] *n* odun kömürü
charge [tʃɑːdʒ] *n* *(accusation)* suçlama, *(electricity)* şarj, *(price)* fiyat biçmek ▹ *v* *(accuse)* suçlamak, *(electricity)* şarj etmek *(elektrik)*, *(price)* fiyat biçmek; **admission charge** *n* giriş ücreti; **cover charge** *n* servis ücreti; **service charge** *n* servis ücreti; **Where can I charge my mobile phone?** Cep telefonumu nerede şarj edebilirim
charger ['tʃɑːdʒə] *n* şarj aleti

charity ['tʃærɪtɪ] *n* yardım derneği; **charity shop** *n* yardım derneği dükkanı
charm [tʃɑːm] *n* çekim
charming ['tʃɑːmɪŋ] *adj* sevimli
chart [tʃɑːt] *n* harita; **pie chart** *n* dilimli grafik
chase [tʃeɪs] *n* takip ▹ *v* takip etmek
chat [tʃæt] *n* sohbet ▹ *v* sohbet etmek; **chat show** *n* sohbet programı
chatroom ['tʃætˌruːm; -ˌrʊm] *n* sohbet odası
chauffeur ['ʃəʊfə; ʃəʊ'fɜː] *n* şoför
chauvinist ['ʃəʊvɪˌnɪst] *n* şoven
cheap [tʃiːp] *adj* ucuz; **Do you have anything cheaper?** Daha ucuz bir şeyiniz var mı?; **I'd like the cheapest option** En ucuz bilet olsun lütfen
cheat [tʃiːt] *n* dolandırıcı ▹ *v* dolandırmak
Chechnya ['tʃɛtʃnjə] *n* Çeçenistan
check [tʃɛk] *n* denetim ▹ *v* denetlemek *(kontrol)*
checked [tʃɛkt] *adj* kareli
check in [tʃɛk ɪn] *v* giriş yapmak
check-in [tʃɛkɪn] *n* giriş *(havaalanı)*
check out [tʃɛk aʊt] *v* çıkış yapmak
checkout ['tʃɛkaʊt] *n* çıkış
check-up [tʃɛkʌp] *n* revizyon
cheek [tʃiːk] *n* yanak
cheekbone ['tʃiːkˌbəʊn] *n* elmacık kemiği
cheeky ['tʃiːkɪ] *adj* arsız
cheer [tʃɪə] *n* tezahürat ▹ *v* tezahürat yapmak
cheerful ['tʃɪəfʊl] *adj* neşeli
cheerio [ˌtʃɪərɪ'əʊ] *excl* sağlıcakla!
cheers [tʃɪəz] *excl* şerefe!
cheese [tʃiːz] *n* peynir; **cottage cheese** *n* süzme peynir
chef [ʃɛf] *n* aşçıbaşı
chemical ['kɛmɪkᵊl] *n* kimyasal
chemist ['kɛmɪst] *n* eczacı; **chemist('s)** *n* eczane
chemistry ['kɛmɪstrɪ] *n* kimya
cheque [tʃɛk] *n* çek; **blank cheque** *n* açık çek; **traveller's cheque** *n* seyahat çeki; **Can I change my traveller's cheques here?** Seyahat çeklerimi burada bozdurabilir miyim?; **I want to change these traveller's cheques** Bu seyahat çeklerini bozdurmak istiyorum; **Someone's stolen my traveller's cheques** Biri seyahat çeklerimi çaldı
chequebook ['tʃɛkˌbʊk] *n* çek defteri
cherry ['tʃɛrɪ] *n* kiraz
chess [tʃɛs] *n* satranç
chest [tʃɛst] *n* *(body part)* göğüs, *(storage)* sandık; **chest of drawers** *n* komodin
chestnut ['tʃɛsˌnʌt] *n* kestane
chew [tʃuː] *v* çiğnemek; **chewing gum** *n* çiklet
chick [tʃɪk] *n* civciv
chicken ['tʃɪkɪn] *n* tavuk
chickenpox ['tʃɪkɪnˌpɒks] *n* suçiçeği
chickpea ['tʃɪkˌpiː] *n* nohut
chief [tʃiːf] *adj* baş ▹ *n* şef
child, children [tʃaɪld, 'tʃɪldrən] *n* çocuk; **child abuse** *n* çocuk tacizi; **I need someone to look**

after the children tonight Bu akşam çocuklara bakacak birine ihtiyacım var; **I'd like a child seat for a two-year-old child** İki yaşında bir çocuk için çocuk koltuğu istiyorum; **I'm looking for a present for a child** Bir çocuk için armağan almak istiyordum
childcare ['tʃaɪld,kɛə] *n* çocuk bakımı
childhood ['tʃaɪldhʊd] *n* çocukluk
childish ['tʃaɪldɪʃ] *adj* çocukça
childminder ['tʃaɪld,maɪndə] *n* çocuk bakıcısı
Chile ['tʃɪlɪ] *n* Şili
Chilean ['tʃɪlɪən] *adj* Şili ▷ *n* Şilili
chill [tʃɪl] *v* soğutmak
chilli ['tʃɪlɪ] *n* acı *(biber)*
chilly ['tʃɪlɪ] *adj* soğuk
chimney ['tʃɪmnɪ] *n* baca
chimpanzee [,tʃɪmpæn'ziː] *n* şempanze
chin [tʃɪn] *n* çene
china ['tʃaɪnə] *n* porselen
China ['tʃaɪnə] *n* Çin
Chinese [tʃaɪ'niːz] *adj* Çin ▷ *n* *(language)* Çince *(dil)*, *(person)* Çinli *(kişi)*
chip [tʃɪp] *n* *(electronic)* çip *(elektronik)*, *(small piece)* parça; **silicon chip** *n* silikon çip
chips [tʃɪps] *npl* patates kızartması
chiropodist [kɪ'rɒpədɪst] *n* ayak uzmanı
chisel ['tʃɪzᵊl] *n* keski
chives [tʃaɪvz] *npl* Frenk soğanı
chlorine ['klɔːriːn] *n* klor
chocolate ['tʃɒkəlɪt; 'tʃɒklɪt; -lət] *n* çikolata; **milk chocolate** *n* sütlü çikolata; **plain chocolate** *n* sade çikolata
choice [tʃɔɪs] *n* seçim
choir [kwaɪə] *n* koro
choke [tʃəʊk] *v* tıkanmak
cholesterol [kə'lɛstə,rɒl] *n* kolesterol
choose [tʃuːz] *v* seçmek
chop [tʃɒp] *n* doğrama ▷ *v* doğramak *(et, sebze)*; **pork chop** *n* domuz pirzolası
chopsticks ['tʃɒpstɪks] *npl* Çin çubuğu
chosen ['tʃəʊzᵊn] *adj* seçilmiş
Christ [kraɪst] *n* İsa
christening ['krɪsᵊnɪŋ] *n* vaftiz
Christian ['krɪstʃən] *adj* Hristiyan ▷ *n* Hristiyan; **Christian name** *n* ön adı
Christianity [,krɪstɪ'ænɪtɪ] *n* Hristiyanlık
Christmas ['krɪsməs] *n* Noel; **Christmas card** *n* Noel kartı; **Christmas Eve** *n* Noel arifesi; **Christmas tree** *n* Noel ağacı; **Merry Christmas!** Mutlu Noeller!
chrome [krəʊm] *n* krom kaplı
chronic ['krɒnɪk] *adj* kronik
chrysanthemum [krɪ'sænθəməm] *n* kasımpatı
chubby ['tʃʌbɪ] *adj* tombul
chunk [tʃʌŋk] *n* parça
church [tʃɜːtʃ] *n* kilise; **Can we visit the church?** Kiliseyi gezebilir miyiz?
cider ['saɪdə] *n* elma şarabı
cigar [sɪ'gɑː] *n* puro
cigarette [,sɪgə'rɛt] *n* sigara; **cigarette lighter** *n* çakmak
cinema ['sɪnɪmə] *n* sinema; **What's on at the cinema?**

Sinemada ne oynuyor?
cinnamon ['sınəmən] *n* tarçın
circle ['sɜːkᵊl] *n* daire; **Arctic Circle** *n* Kuzey Buzul Kuşağı
circuit ['sɜːkıt] *n* devre
circular ['sɜːkjʊlə] *adj* dairesel
circulation [ˌsɜːkjʊ'leıʃən] *n* kan dolaşımı
circumstances ['sɜːkəmstənsız] *npl* koşullar
circus ['sɜːkəs] *n* sirk
citizen ['sıtızᵊn] *n* vatandaş; **senior citizen** *n* yaşlı vatandaş
citizenship ['sıtızənˌʃıp] *n* vatandaşlık
city ['sıtı] *n* şehir; **city centre** *n* kent merkezi
civilian [sı'vıljən] *adj* sivil ▹ *n* sivil
civilization [ˌsıvılaı'zeıʃən] *n* uygarlık
claim [kleım] *n* talep ▹ *v* talep etmek; **claim form** *n* istek formu
clap [klæp] *v* alkışlanmak
clarify ['klærıˌfaı] *v* açıklık kazandırmak
clarinet [ˌklærı'nɛt] *n* klarnet
clash [klæʃ] *v* çatışmak
clasp [klɑːsp] *n* toka
class [klɑːs] *n* sınıf; **business class** *n* hizmet sınıfı; **economy class** *n* ikinci sınıf; **second class** *n* ikinci sınıf; **a first-class cabin** Birinci sınıf bir kabin; **a first-class return to...** ... a birinci sınıf bir gidiş dönüş bilet; **I would like to travel first class** Birinci sınıf seyahat etmek istiyorum
classic ['klæsık] *adj* klasik ▹ *n* klasik
classical ['klæsıkᵊl] *adj* klasik
classmate ['klɑːsˌmeıt] *n* sınıf arkadaşı
classroom ['klɑːsˌruːm; -ˌrʊm] *n* sınıf; **classroom assistant** *n* yardımcı öğretmen
clause [klɔːz] *n* madde *(yasa vb)*
claustrophobic [ˌklɔːstrə'fəʊbık; ˌklɒs-] *adj* kapalı yer korkusu olan
claw [klɔː] *n* pençe
clay [kleı] *n* kil
clean [kliːn] *adj* temiz ▹ *v* temizlemek; **Can you clean the room, please?** Odamı temizler misiniz lütfen; **I need this dry-cleaned** Bunu kuru temizleyiciye vermek istiyorum; **I'd like to get these things cleaned** Bunları temizletmek istiyorum; **The room isn't clean** Oda temizlenmemiş; **Where can I get this cleaned?** Bunu nerede temizletebilirim?
cleaner ['kliːnə] *n* temizlikçi; **When does the cleaner come?** Temizlikçi kaçta geliyor?
cleaning ['kliːnıŋ] *n* temizleme; **cleaning lady** *n* temizlikçi
cleanser ['klɛnzə] *n* temizleyici
clear [klıə] *adj* açık *(hava vb)*
clearly ['klıəlı] *adv* açıkça
clear off [klıə ɒf] *v* ayak altından çekilmek
clear up [klıə ʌp] *v* toplamak *(ortalığı)*
clementine ['klɛmənˌtiːn; -ˌtaın] *n* mandalina
clever ['klɛvə] *adj* zeki
click [klık] *n* tık ▹ *v* tıklamak
client ['klaıənt] *n* müşteri
cliff [klıf] *n* kayalık
climate ['klaımıt] *n* iklim; **climate**

change *n* iklim değişikliği
climb [klaɪm] *v* tırmanmak
climber ['klaɪmə] *n* dağcı *(tırmanıcı)*
climbing ['klaɪmɪŋ] *n* dağcılık *(tırmanıcılık)*
clinic ['klɪnɪk] *n* poliklinik
clip [klɪp] *n* klips
clippers ['klɪpəz] *npl* makas *(tırnak/saç/tel/çalı)*
cloakroom ['kləʊk,ruːm; -,rʊm] *n* vestiyer
clock [klɒk] *n* saat *(genelde)*; **alarm clock** *n* çalar saat; **before five o'clock** saat beşten önce; **It's two o'clock** Saat iki
clockwise ['klɒk,waɪz] *adv* saat yönünde
clog [klɒg] *n* takunya
clone [kləʊn] *n* klon ▹ *v* klonlamak
close *adj* [kləʊs] yakın ▹ *adv* [kləʊs] yakın ▹ *v* [kləʊz] kapatmak; **close by** *adj* yakın; **closing time** *n* kapanış saati
closed [kləʊzd] *adj* kapalı
closely [kləʊslɪ] *adv* yakından
closure ['kləʊʒə] *n* kapanış
cloth [klɒθ] *n* kumaş
clothes [kləʊðz] *npl* giysiler; **clothes line** *n* çamaşır ipi; **clothes peg** *n* çamaşır mandalı; **My clothes are damp** Giysilerim ıslak
clothing ['kləʊðɪŋ] *n* giyim
cloud [klaʊd] *n* bulut
cloudy ['klaʊdɪ] *adj* bulutlu; **It's cloudy** Hava bulutlu
clove [kləʊv] *n* karanfil *(baharat)*
clown [klaʊn] *n* palyaço
club [klʌb] *n* *(group)* klüp, *(weapon)* sopa *(silah)*; **golf club** *n* *(stick)* golf sopası, *(society)* golf klübü; **Do they hire out golf clubs?** Golf sopaları kiralıyorlar mı?
club together [klʌb tə'gɛðə] *v* paylaşmak *(iş/masraf)*
clue [kluː] *n* delil
clumsy ['klʌmzɪ] *adj* sakar
clutch [klʌtʃ] *n* debriyaj
clutter ['klʌtə] *n* yayıntı
coach [kəʊtʃ] *n* *(trainer)* koç *(spor)*, *(vehicle)* tur otobüsü
coal [kəʊl] *n* kömür
coarse [kɔːs] *adj* kaba *(kumaş, sakal vb)*
coast [kəʊst] *n* kıyı
coastguard ['kəʊst,gɑːd] *n* sahil koruma görevlisi
coat [kəʊt] *n* kaban; **fur coat** *n* kürk *(giysi)*
coathanger ['kəʊt,hæŋə] *n* elbise askısı
cobweb ['kɒb,wɛb] *n* örümcek ağı
cocaine [kə'keɪn] *n* kokain
cock [kɒk] *n* horoz
cockerel ['kɒkərəl; 'kɒkrəl] *n* horoz
cockpit ['kɒk,pɪt] *n* kokpit
cockroach ['kɒk,rəʊtʃ] *n* hamam böceği
cocktail ['kɒk,teɪl] *n* kokteyl; **Do you sell cocktails?** Kokteyl yapıyor musunuz?
cocoa ['kəʊkəʊ] *n* kakao
coconut ['kəʊkə,nʌt] *n* Hindistan cevizi
cod [kɒd] *n* morina balığı
code [kəʊd] *n* şifre; **dialling code** *n* telefon kodu; **Highway Code** *n* trafik kuralları
coeliac ['siːlɪ,æk] *adj* karın boşluğu

ile ilgili

coffee ['kɒfɪ] *n* kahve; **black coffee** *n* sütsüz kahve; **coffee bean** *n* kahve çekirdeği; **decaffeinated coffee** *n* kafeinsiz kahve; **A white coffee, please** Sütlü kahve lütfen; **Could we have another cup of coffee, please?** Bir fincan kahve daha alabilir miyiz?; **Have you got fresh coffee?** Taze kahveniz var mı?

coffeepot ['kɒfɪˌpɒt] *n* cezve

coffin ['kɒfɪn] *n* tabut

coin [kɔɪn] *n* madeni para

coincide [ˌkəʊɪn'saɪd] *v* çakışmak

coincidence [kəʊ'ɪnsɪdəns] *n* rastlantı

Coke® [kəʊk] *n* Kola

colander ['kɒləndə; 'kʌl-] *n* süzgeç

cold [kəʊld] *adj* soğuk ▷ *n* soğuk; **cold sore** *n* uçuk *(sağlık)*; **I have a cold** Soğuk algınlığım var; **I'd like something for a cold** Soğuk algınlığı için bir şey rica ediyorum; **The food is too cold** Yemek çok soğuk; **The room is too cold** Oda çok soğuk; **Will it be cold tonight?** Bu gece hava soğuk mu olacak?

coleslaw ['kəʊlˌslɔː] *n* lahana salatası

collaborate [kə'læbəˌreɪt] *v* işbirliği yapmak

collapse [kə'læps] *v* çökmek

collar ['kɒlə] *n* yaka

collarbone ['kɒləˌbəʊn] *n* köprücük kemiği

colleague ['kɒliːg] *n* meslekdaş

collect [kə'lɛkt] *v* toplamak *(para, pul vb)*

collection [kə'lɛkʃən] *n* koleksiyon

collective [kə'lɛktɪv] *adj* kolektif ▷ *n* kolektif

collector [kə'lɛktə] *n* kolleksiyoncu; **ticket collector** *n* biletçi

college ['kɒlɪdʒ] *n* yüksek okul

collide [kə'laɪd] *v* çarpışmak

collie ['kɒlɪ] *n* İskoç çoban köpeği

colliery ['kɒljərɪ] *n* kömür ocağı

collision [kə'lɪʒən] *n* çarpışma

Colombia [kə'lɒmbɪə] *n* Kolombiya

Colombian [kə'lɒmbɪən] *adj* Kolombiya ▷ *n* Kolombiyalı

colon ['kəʊlən] *n* iki nokta üst üste

colonel ['kɜːnᵊl] *n* albay

colour ['kʌlə] *n* renk; **A colour film, please** Renkli film istiyorum lütfen; **in colour** Renkli; **I'd like a colour photocopy of this, please** Bunun renkli fotokopisini istiyorum lütfen

colour-blind ['kʌlə'blaɪnd] *adj* renk körü

colourful ['kʌləfʊl] *adj* renkli

colouring ['kʌlərɪŋ] *n* boyama

column ['kɒləm] *n* sütun

coma ['kəʊmə] *n* koma

comb [kəʊm] *n* tarak ▷ *v* taramak

combination [ˌkɒmbɪ'neɪʃən] *n* birleştirme

combine [kəm'baɪn] *v* birleştirmek

come [kʌm] *v* gelmek

come back [kʌm bæk] *v* geri gelmek

comedian [kə'miːdɪən] *n*

komedyen
come down [kʌm daʊn] *v* aşağıya inmek
comedy ['kɒmɪdɪ] *n* komedi
come from [kʌm frəm] *v* gelmek
come in [kʌm ɪn] *v* girmek *(içeriye)*
come off [kʌm ɒf] *v* **The handle has come off** Kolu çıktı
come out [kʌm aʊt] *v* çıkmak
come round [kʌm raʊnd] *v* kendine gelmek
comet ['kɒmɪt] *n* kuyruklu yıldız
come up [kʌm ʌp] *v* gündeme gelmek
comfortable ['kʌmftəbᵊl; 'kʌmfətəbᵊl] *adj* rahat
comic ['kɒmɪk] *n* komik; **comic book** *n* mizah dergisi; **comic strip** *n* çizgi öykü
coming ['kʌmɪŋ] *adj* gelecek
comma ['kɒmə] *n* virgül; **inverted commas** *npl* ters tırnak işareti
command [kə'mɑːnd] *n* emir
comment ['kɒmɛnt] *n* yorum ▷ *v* yorum yapmak
commentary ['kɒməntərɪ; -trɪ] *n* yorum
commentator ['kɒmən,teɪtə] *n* yorumcu
commercial [kə'mɜːʃəl] *n* reklam; **commercial break** *n* reklam arası
commission [kə'mɪʃən] *n* komisyon; **Do you charge commission?** Komisyon alıyor musunuz?; **What's the commission?** Komisyon ne kadar?
commit [kə'mɪt] *v* işlemek
committee [kə'mɪtɪ] *n* komite
common ['kɒmən] *adj* müşterek; **common sense** *n* sağduyu
communicate [kə'mjuːnɪ,keɪt] *v* iletişim kurmak
communication [kə,mjuːnɪ'keɪʃən] *n* iletişim
communion [kə'mjuːnjən] *n* ortak görüş
communism ['kɒmjʊ,nɪzəm] *n* komünizm
communist ['kɒmjʊnɪst] *adj* toplumcu ▷ *n* toplumcu
community [kə'mjuːnɪtɪ] *n* topluluk
commute [kə'mjuːt] *v* her gün işi ile evi arasında gidip gelmek
commuter [kə'mjuːtə] *n* her gün işe trenle giden kimse
compact ['kəm'pækt] *adj* sımsıkı paketlenmiş; **compact disc** *n* kompakt disk
companion [kəm'pænjən] *n* yoldaş
company ['kʌmpənɪ] *n* şirket; **company car** *n* şirket arabası
comparable ['kɒmpərəbᵊl] *adj* kıyaslanabilir
comparatively [kəm'pærətɪvlɪ] *adv* göreceli olarak
compare [kəm'pɛə] *v* kıyaslamak
comparison [kəm'pærɪsᵊn] *n* kıyaslama
compartment [kəm'pɑːtmənt] *n* kompartıman
compass ['kʌmpəs] *n* pusula
compatible [kəm'pætəbᵊl] *adj* uyumlu
compensate ['kɒmpɛn,seɪt] *v* telafi etmek
compensation [,kɒmpɛn'seɪʃən]

n tazminat
compere ['kɒmpɛə] *n* sunucu *(oyun, film, gösteri)*
compete [kəm'pi:t] *v* yarışmak
competent ['kɒmpɪtənt] *adj* yetkin
competition [ˌkɒmpɪ'tɪʃən] *n* yarışma
competitive [kəm'pɛtɪtɪv] *adj* rekabete açık
competitor [kəm'pɛtɪtə] *n* yarışmacı
complain [kəm'pleɪn] *v* yakınmak
complaint [kəm'pleɪnt] *n* şikayet; **I'd like to make a complaint** Bir şikayette bulunmak istiyorum
complementary [ˌkɒmplɪ'mɛntərɪ; -trɪ] *adj* bütünleyici
complete [kəm'pli:t] *adj* bütün
completely [kəm'pli:tlɪ] *adv* tamamen
complex ['kɒmplɛks] *adj* komplike ▹ *n* kompleks
complexion [kəm'plɛkʃən] *n* ten
complicated ['kɒmplɪˌkeɪtɪd] *adj* komplike
complication [ˌkɒmplɪ'keɪʃən] *n* zorluk
compliment *n* ['kɒmplɪmənt] kompliman ▹ *v* ['kɒmplɪˌmɛnt] iltifat etmek
complimentary [ˌkɒmplɪ'mɛntərɪ; -trɪ] *adj* övücü
component [kəm'pəʊnənt] *adj* bileşen ▹ *n* bileşen
composer [kəm'pəʊzə] *n* besteci
composition [ˌkɒmpə'zɪʃən] *n* beste
comprehension [ˌkɒmprɪ'hɛnʃən] *n* anlama
comprehensive [ˌkɒmprɪ'hɛnsɪv] *adj* kapsamlı
compromise ['kɒmprəˌmaɪz] *n* ödün ▹ *v* ödün vermek
compulsory [kəm'pʌlsərɪ] *adj* metazori
computer [kəm'pju:tə] *n* bilgisayar; **computer game** *n* bilgisayar oyunu; **computer science** *n* bilgisayar bilimi; **May I use your computer?** Bilgisayarınızı kullanabilir miyim?; **Where is the computer room?** Bilgisayar odası nerede?
computing [kəm'pju:tɪŋ] *n* bilgisayar çalışması
concentrate ['kɒnsənˌtreɪt] *v* yoğunlaşmak
concentration [ˌkɒnsən'treɪʃən] *n* yoğunlaşma
concern [kən'sɜ:n] *n* teveccüh
concerned [kən'sɜ:nd] *adj* ilgili
concerning [kən'sɜ:nɪŋ] *prep* ilgili
concert ['kɒnsɜ:t; -sət] *n* konser; **Are there any good concerts on?** İyi konserler var mı?; **What's on tonight at the concert hall?** Konser salonunda bu gece ne var?; **Where can I buy tickets for the concert?** Konser biletlerini nereden alabilirim?
concerto, concerti [kən'tʃɛətəʊ, kən'tʃɛətɪ] *n* konçerto
concession [kən'sɛʃən] *n* ayrıcalık
concise [kən'saɪs] *adj* kısa ve öz
conclude [kən'klu:d] *v* son vermek
conclusion [kən'klu:ʒən] *n* sonuç
concrete ['kɒnkri:t] *n* beton

concussion [kən'kʌʃən] *n* sarsıntı
condemn [kən'dɛm] *v* kınamak
condensation [ˌkɒndɛn'seɪʃən] *n* buğu
condition [kən'dɪʃən] *n* koşul
conditional [kən'dɪʃənˀl] *adj* koşullu
conditioner [kən'dɪʃənə] *n* saç kremi
condom ['kɒndɒm; 'kɒndəm] *n* prezervatif
conduct [kən'dʌkt] *v* rehberlik etmek
conductor [kən'dʌktə] *n* orkestra şefi; **bus conductor** *n* biletçi
cone [kəʊn] *n* koni
conference ['kɒnfərəns; -frəns] *n* konferans; **press conference** *n* basın toplantısı; **Please take me to the conference centre** Konferans merkezine lütfen
confess [kən'fɛs] *v* itiraf etmek
confession [kən'fɛʃən] *n* itiraf
confetti [kən'fɛtɪ] *npl* konfeti
confidence ['kɒnfɪdəns] *n* *(secret)* sır, *(self-assurance)* özgüven, *(trust)* güven
confident ['kɒnfɪdənt] *adj* kendine güvenen
confidential [ˌkɒnfɪ'dɛnʃəl] *adj* gizli
confirm [kən'fɜːm] *v* doğrulamak
confirmation [ˌkɒnfə'meɪʃən] *n* teyit
confiscate ['kɒnfɪˌskeɪt] *v* elkoymak
conflict ['kɒnflɪkt] *n* çatışma
confuse [kən'fjuːz] *v* karıştırmak *(fikir)*
confused [kən'fjuːzd] *adj* kafası karışık
confusing [kən'fjuːzɪŋ] *adj* yanıltıcı
confusion [kən'fjuːʒən] *n* karışıklık
congestion [kən'dʒɛstʃən] *n* tıkanıklık
Congo ['kɒŋgəʊ] *n* Kongo
congratulate [kən'grætjʊˌleɪt] *v* kutlamak
congratulations [kənˌgrætjʊ'leɪʃənz] *npl* tebrikler
conifer ['kəʊnɪfə; 'kɒn-] *n* kozalak
conjugation [ˌkɒndʒʊ'geɪʃən] *n* birleşme
conjunction [kən'dʒʌŋkʃən] *n* bağlantı
conjurer ['kʌndʒərə] *n* illüzyonist
connect [kə'nɛkt] *v* bağlamak *(kablo)*
connection [kə'nɛkʃən] *n* bağlantı; **I've missed my connection** Bağlantı uçağımı kaçırdım; **Is there an Internet connection in the room?** Odada internet bağlantısı var mı?; **The connection seems very slow** Bağlantı çok yavaş
conquer ['kɒŋkə] *v* yenmek
conscience ['kɒnʃəns] *n* vicdan
conscientious [ˌkɒnʃɪ'ɛnʃəs] *adj* vicdanlı
conscious ['kɒnʃəs] *adj* bilinçli
consciousness ['kɒnʃəsnɪs] *n* bilinçlilik
consecutive [kən'sɛkjʊtɪv] *adj* ardı ardına
consensus [kən'sɛnsəs] *n* oy birliği
consequence ['kɒnsɪkwəns] *n*

sonuç
consequently ['kɒnsɪkwəntlɪ] *adv* nitekim
conservation [ˌkɒnsə'veɪʃən] *n* koruma
conservative [kən'sɜːvətɪv] *adj* muhafazakâr
conservatory [kən'sɜːvətrɪ] *n* limonluk
consider [kən'sɪdə] *v* hesaba katmak
considerate [kən'sɪdərɪt] *adj* düşünceli *(özenli)*
considering [kən'sɪdərɪŋ] *prep* göz önünde tutarak
consist [kən'sɪst] *v* **consist of** *v* oluşmak
consistent [kən'sɪstənt] *adj* tutarlı
consonant ['kɒnsənənt] *n* ünsüz *(gramer)*
conspiracy [kən'spɪrəsɪ] *n* komplo
constant ['kɒnstənt] *adj* sabit *(değişmez)*
constantly ['kɒnstəntlɪ] *adv* sürekli
constipated ['kɒnstɪˌpeɪtɪd] *adj* kabız; **I'm constipated** Kabızlık çekiyorum
constituency [kən'stɪtjʊənsɪ] *n* seçmen bölgesi
constitution [ˌkɒnstɪ'tjuːʃən] *n* yasalar
construct [kən'strʌkt] *v* yapmak
construction [kən'strʌkʃən] *n* yapı
constructive [kən'strʌktɪv] *adj* yapıcı
consul ['kɒnsᵊl] *n* konsolos
consulate ['kɒnsjʊlɪt] *n* konsolosluk
consult [kən'sʌlt] *v* danışmak
consultant [kən'sʌltᵊnt] *n* *(adviser)* danışman
consumer [kən'sjuːmə] *n* tüketici
contact *n* ['kɒntækt] temas ▹ *v* [kən'tækt] temas kurmak; **contact lenses** *npl* kontakt lens; **Where can I contact you?** Sizinle nasıl temas kurabilirim?; **Who do we contact if there are problems?** Bir sorun çıkarsa kiminle temas kuracağız?
contagious [kən'teɪdʒəs] *adj* bulaşıcı
contain [kən'teɪn] *v* içermek
container [kən'teɪnə] *n* kap
contemporary [kən'tɛmprərɪ] *adj* çağdaş
contempt [kən'tɛmpt] *n* hor görme
content ['kɒntɛnt] *n* muhteviyat; **contents** *(list) npl* muhteviyat
contest ['kɒntɛst] *n* yarışma
contestant [kən'tɛstənt] *n* yarışmacı
context ['kɒntɛkst] *n* içerik
continent ['kɒntɪnənt] *n* kıta
continual [kən'tɪnjʊəl] *adj* daimi
continually [kən'tɪnjʊəlɪ] *adv* daimi
continue [kən'tɪnjuː] *vi* sürdürmek ▹ *vt* devam etmek
continuous [kən'tɪnjʊəs] *adj* kesintisiz
contraception [ˌkɒntrə'sɛpʃən] *n* doğum kontrolü
contraceptive [ˌkɒntrə'sɛptɪv] *n* doğum kontrol hapı

contract ['kɒntrækt] *n* kontrat
contractor ['kɒntræktə; kən'træk-] *n* yüklenici
contradict [ˌkɒntrə'dɪkt] *v* çelişmek
contradiction [ˌkɒntrə'dɪkʃən] *n* çelişki
contrary ['kɒntrərɪ] *n* zıt
contrast ['kɒntrɑːst] *n* karşıtlık
contribute [kən'trɪbjuːt] *v* katkıda bulunmak
contribution [ˌkɒntrɪ'bjuːʃən] *n* katkı
control [kən'trəʊl] *n* kontrol ▷ *v* idare etmek; **birth control** *n* doğum kontrolü; **passport control** *n* pasaport kontrol; **remote control** *n* uazaktan kumanda
controller [kən'trəʊlə] *n* **air-traffic controller** *n* hava trafik kontrolörü
controversial ['kɒntrə'vɜːʃəl] *adj* tartışmalı
convenient [kən'viːnɪənt] *adj* uygun
convent ['kɒnvənt] *n* manastır
conventional [kən'vɛnʃənᵊl] *adj* konvensiyonel *(alışılmış)*
conversation [ˌkɒnvə'seɪʃən] *n* konuşma
convert [kən'vɜːt] *v* değiştirmek *(dönüştürmek)*; **catalytic converter** *n* katalitik konvertör
convertible [kən'vɜːtəbᵊl] *adj* konvertibl ▷ *n* üstü açılır araba
convict [kən'vɪkt] *v* hükümlü
convince [kən'vɪns] *v* inandırmak
convincing [kən'vɪnsɪŋ] *adj* inandırıcı
convoy ['kɒnvɔɪ] *n* konvoy
cook [kʊk] *n* ahçı ▷ *v* pişirmek
cookbook ['kʊkˌbʊk] *n* yemek kitabı
cooker ['kʊkə] *n* ocak *(fırın vb)*; **gas cooker** *n* gazlı ocak
cookery ['kʊkərɪ] *n* aşçılık; **cookery book** *n* yemek kitabı
cooking ['kʊkɪŋ] *n* pişirme
cool [kuːl] *adj (cold)* serin, *(stylish)* havalı
cooperation [kəʊˌɒpə'reɪʃən] *n* işbirliği
cop [kɒp] *n* aynasız
cope [kəʊp] *v* **cope (with)** *v* başa çıkmak
copper ['kɒpə] *n* bakır
copy ['kɒpɪ] *n (reproduction)* taklit, *(written text)* kopya *(nüsha)* ▷ *v* kopyalamak
copyright ['kɒpɪˌraɪt] *n* telif hakkı
coral ['kɒrəl] *n* mercan
cord [kɔːd] *n* **spinal cord** *n* omurilik
cordless ['kɔːdlɪs] *adj* telsiz
corduroy ['kɔːdəˌrɔɪ; ˌkɔːdə'rɔɪ] *n* fitilli kadife
core [kɔː] *n* çekirdekli kısım *(meyve)*
coriander [ˌkɒrɪ'ændə] *n* kişniş
cork [kɔːk] *n* mantar *(eşya)*
corkscrew ['kɔːkˌskruː] *n* tirbuşon
corn [kɔːn] *n* mısır *(sebze)*
corner ['kɔːnə] *n* köşe; **It's on the corner** Köşede; **It's round the corner** Köşeyi dönünce
cornet ['kɔːnɪt] *n* kornet
cornflakes ['kɔːnˌfleɪks] *npl* mısır gevreği
cornflour ['kɔːnˌflaʊə] *n* mısır nişastası

corporal ['kɔ:pərəl; -prəl] *n* onbaşı
corpse [kɔ:ps] *n* ceset
correct [kə'rɛkt] *adj* doğru *(işlem, hareket)* ▹ *v* düzeltmek *(hata, yanlış)*
correction [kə'rɛkʃən] *n* düzelti
correctly [kə'rɛktlı] *adv* doğru olarak
correspondence [,kɒrı'spɒndəns] *n* yazışma
correspondent [,kɒrı'spɒndənt] *n* muhabir
corridor ['kɒrı,dɔ:] *n* koridor
corrupt [kə'rʌpt] *adj* yozlaşmış
corruption [kə'rʌpʃən] *n* yozlaşma
cosmetics [kɒz'mɛtıks] *npl* makyaj malzemesi
cost [kɒst] *n* eder ▹ *v* mal olmak; **cost of living** *n* hayat pahalılığı
Costa Rica ['kɒstə 'ri:kə] *n* Kosta Rika
costume ['kɒstju:m] *n* kostüm; **swimming costume** *n* mayo
cosy ['kəʊzı] *adj* rahat
cot [kɒt] *n* bebek karyolası
cottage ['kɒtıdʒ] *n* kulübe; **cottage cheese** *n* süzme peynir
cotton ['kɒtᵊn] *n* pamuk *(bitki)*; **cotton bud** *n* kulak çubuğu; **cotton wool** *n* pamuk
couch [kaʊtʃ] *n* kanepe
couchette [ku:'ʃɛt] *n* kuşet
cough [kɒf] *n* öksürük ▹ *v* öksürmek; **cough mixture** *n* öksürük şurubu
council ['kaʊnsəl] *n* meclis *(belediye vb)*; **council house** *n* sosyal konut
councillor ['kaʊnsələ] *n* belediye meclis üyesi
count [kaʊnt] *v* saymak
counter ['kaʊntə] *n* kontuar
count on [kaʊnt ɒn] *v* güvenmek
country ['kʌntrı] *n* ülke; **developing country** *n* gelişmekte olan ülke
countryside ['kʌntrı,saıd] *n* kırsal bölge
couple ['kʌpᵊl] *n* çift
courage ['kʌrıdʒ] *n* cesaret
courageous [kə'reıdʒəs] *adj* yürekli
courgette [kʊə'ʒɛt] *n* kabak
courier ['kʊərıə] *n* kurye; **I want to send this by courier** Kuryeyle göndermek istiyorum
course [kɔ:s] *n* kurs; **golf course** *n* golf sahası; **main course** *n* ana yemek; **refresher course** *n* bilgi tazeleme eğitimi; **training course** *n* eğitim kursu
court [kɔ:t] *n* mahkeme; **tennis court** *n* tenis kortu
courtyard ['kɔ:t,jɑ:d] *n* avlu
cousin ['kʌzᵊn] *n* kuzen
cover ['kʌvə] *n* örtü ▹ *v* örtmek; **cover charge** *n* servis ücreti
cow [kaʊ] *n* inek
coward ['kaʊəd] *n* korkak
cowardly ['kaʊədlı] *adj* korkakça
cowboy ['kaʊ,bɔı] *n* kovboy
crab [kræb] *n* yengeç
crack [kræk] *n (cocaine)* krek *(kokain)*, *(fracture)* çatlak ▹ *v* çatlatmak; **crack down on** *v* sıkı tedbirler almak
cracked [krækt] *adj* çatlak
cracker ['krækə] *n* kraker

cradle ['kreɪdᵊl] *n* beşik
craft [krɑːft] *n* zanaat
craftsman ['krɑːftsmən] *n* zanaatkâr
cram [kræm] *v* tıkabasa doldurmak
crammed [kræmd] *adj* tıkabasa dolu
cranberry ['krænbərɪ; -brɪ] *n* kırmızı yaban mersini
crane [kreɪn] *n (bird)* turna, *(for lifting)* vinç
crash [kræʃ] *n* araba kazası ▷ *vi* çarpışmak *(araçla)* ▷ *vt* vasıta ile çarpmak
crawl [krɔːl] *v* emeklemek
crayfish ['kreɪˌfɪʃ] *n* kerevit
crayon ['kreɪən; -ɒn] *n* mum boya
crazy ['kreɪzɪ] *adj* çılgın
cream [kriːm] *adj* krem renkli ▷ *n* krem, krema; **ice cream** *n* dondurma; **shaving cream** *n* traş kremi; **whipped cream** *n* köpük krema
crease [kriːs] *n* kırışıklık
creased [kriːst] *adj* kırışık
create [kriː'eɪt] *v* yaratmak
creation [kriː'eɪʃən] *n* yaradılış
creative [kriː'eɪtɪv] *adj* yaratıcı
creature ['kriːtʃə] *n* yaratık
crêche [krɛʃ] *n* kreş
credentials [krɪ'dɛnʃəlz] *npl* itimatname
credible ['krɛdɪbᵊl] *adj* inandırıcı
credit ['krɛdɪt] *n* kredi; **credit card** *n* kredi kartı; **Can I pay by credit card?** Kredi kartıyla ödeme yapabilir miyim?; **Do you take credit cards?** Kredi kartı kabul ediyor musunuz?
crematorium, crematoria [ˌkrɛmə'tɔːrɪəm, ˌkrɛmə'tɔːrɪə] *n* krematoryum
cress [krɛs] *n* tere
crew [kruː] *n* tayfa; **crew cut** *n* asker traşı
cricket ['krɪkɪt] *n (game)* kriket, *(insect)* cırcır böceği
crime [kraɪm] *n* suç
criminal ['krɪmɪnᵊl] *adj* suçlu ▷ *n* suçlu
crisis ['kraɪsɪs] *n* kriz
crisp [krɪsp] *adj* gevrek *(çıtır çıtır)*
crisps [krɪsps] *npl* cips
crispy ['krɪspɪ] *adj* gevrek
criterion, criteria [kraɪ'tɪərɪən, kraɪ'tɪərɪə] *n* kriter
critic ['krɪtɪk] *n* eleştirmen
critical ['krɪtɪkᵊl] *adj* kritik
criticism ['krɪtɪˌsɪzəm] *n* tenkit *(davranış)*
criticize ['krɪtɪˌsaɪz] *v* eleştirmek
Croatia [krəʊ'eɪʃə] *n* Hırvatistan
Croatian [krəʊ'eɪʃən] *adj* Hırvat ▷ *n (language)* Hırvatça *(dil)*, *(person)* Hırvat *(kişi)*
crochet ['krəʊʃeɪ; -ʃɪ] *v* kroşe yapmak
crockery ['krɒkərɪ] *n* **We need more crockery** Daha fazla tabak çanağa ihtiyacımız var
crocodile ['krɒkəˌdaɪl] *n* timsah
crocus ['krəʊkəs] *n* çiğdem *(çiçek)*
crook [krʊk] *n* düzenbaz, *(swindler)* düzenbaz
crop [krɒp] *n* ürün
cross [krɒs] *adj* öfkeli ▷ *n* çapraz ▷ *v* karşıdan karşıya geçmek; **Red Cross** *n* Kızılhaç
cross-country ['krɒs'kʌntrɪ] *n*

arazide
crossing ['krɒsɪŋ] *n* geçit; **level crossing** *n* hemzemin geçit; **pedestrian crossing** *n* yaya geçidi; **pelican crossing** *n* ışıklı yaya geçidi; **zebra crossing** *n* şeritli yaya geçidi
cross out [krɒs aʊt] *v* silmek *(silip çıkarmak)*
crossroads ['krɒs,rəʊdz] *n* dört yol ağzı
crossword ['krɒs,wɜːd] *n* bulmaca
crouch down [kraʊtʃ daʊn] *v* çömelmek
crow [krəʊ] *n* karga
crowd [kraʊd] *n* kalabalık
crowded [kraʊdɪd] *adj* kalabalık
crown [kraʊn] *n* taç
crucial ['kruːʃəl] *adj* önemli
crucifix ['kruːsɪfɪks] *n* krüsifi
crude [kruːd] *adj* kaba *(iş vb)*
cruel ['kruːəl] *adj* gaddar
cruelty ['kruːəltɪ] *n* zulüm
cruise [kruːz] *n* gemi gezisi
crumb [krʌm] *n* ekmek kırıntısı
crush [krʌʃ] *v* ezmek *(sıkıştırarak)*
crutch [krʌtʃ] *n* koltuk değneği
cry [kraɪ] *n* ağlamak ▷ *v* ağlamak
crystal ['krɪstᵊl] *n* kristal
cub [kʌb] *n* yavru *(aslan/ayı)*
Cuba ['kjuːbə] *n* Küba
Cuban ['kjuːbən] *adj* Küba ▷ *n* Kübalı
cube [kjuːb] *n* küp; **ice cube** *n* küp buz; **stock cube** *n* bulyon
cubic ['kjuːbɪk] *adj* kübik
cuckoo ['kʊkuː] *n* guguk kuşu
cucumber ['kjuː,kʌmbə] *n* salatalık
cuddle ['kʌdᵊl] *n* kucaklama ▷ *v* kucaklamak
cue [kjuː] *n (billiards)* ıstaka
cufflinks ['kʌflɪŋks] *npl* kol düğmeleri
culprit ['kʌlprɪt] *n* zanlı
cultural ['kʌltʃərəl] *adj* kültürel
culture ['kʌltʃə] *n* kültür
cumin ['kʌmɪn] *n* kimyon
cunning ['kʌnɪŋ] *adj* kurnaz
cup [kʌp] *n* tas; **World Cup** *n* Dünya Kupası
cupboard ['kʌbəd] *n* dolap *(mobilya)*
curb [kɜːb] *n* hakimiyet
cure [kjʊə] *n* tedavi ▷ *v* tedavi etmek
curfew ['kɜːfjuː] *n* karartma
curious ['kjʊərɪəs] *adj* meraklı
curl [kɜːl] *n* bukle *(saç)*
curler ['kɜːlə] *n* bigudi
curly ['kɜːlɪ] *adj* kıvırcık; **My hair is naturally curly** Saçım doğuştan kıvırcık
currant ['kʌrənt] *n* kuşüzümü
currency ['kʌrənsɪ] *n* kur *(para)*
current ['kʌrənt] *adj* güncel ▷ *n (electricity)* akım, *(flow)* akış; **current account** *n* cari hesap; **current affairs** *npl* güncel haberler
currently ['kʌrəntlɪ] *adv* şu anda
curriculum [kə'rɪkjʊləm] *n* müfredat; **curriculum vitae** *n* özgeçmiş
curry ['kʌrɪ] *n* köri; **curry powder** *n* köri baharatı
curse [kɜːs] *n* küfür
cursor ['kɜːsə] *n* imleç
curtain ['kɜːtᵊn] *n* perde
cushion ['kʊʃən] *n* yastık

custard ['kʌstəd] *n* krema
custody ['kʌstədɪ] *n* koruma altına alma
custom ['kʌstəm] *n* adet *(gelenek)*
customer ['kʌstəmə] *n* müşteri
customized ['kʌstə,maɪzd] *adj* ihtiyaca uyarlanmış
customs ['kʌstəmz] *npl* gümrük; **customs officer** *n* gümrük memuru
cut [kʌt] *n* kesme ▷ *v* kesmek; **crew cut** *n* asker traşı; **power cut** *n* elektrik kesintisi; **Don't cut too much off** Çok kesmeyin
cutback ['kʌt,bæk] *n* azaltma
cut down [kʌt daʊn] *v* kesmek
cute [kju:t] *adj* sevimli
cutlery ['kʌtlərɪ] *n* çatal, bıçak, kaşık
cutlet ['kʌtlɪt] *n* pirzola
cut off [kʌt ɒf] *v* kesmek
cutting ['kʌtɪŋ] *n* gazete kesiği
cut up [kʌt ʌp] *v* makaslamak
CV [si: vi:] *abbr* CV
cybercafé ['saɪbə,kæfeɪ; -,kæfɪ] *n* sibercafe
cybercrime ['saɪbə,kraɪm] *n* internet suçu
cycle ['saɪkᵊl] *n* *(bike)* bisiklete binme, *(recurring period)* döngü ▷ *v* bisiklet sürmek; **cycle lane** *n* bisiklet yolu; **cycle path** *n* bisiklet yolu
cycling ['saɪklɪŋ] *n* bisiklete binme; **Let's go cycling** Bisiklete binmeye gidelim; **We would like to go cycling** Bisiklete binmek istiyoruz
cyclist ['saɪklɪst] *n* bisikletçi
cyclone ['saɪkləʊn] *n* siklon
cylinder ['sɪlɪndə] *n* silindir
cymbals ['sɪmbᵊlz] *npl* zil *(müzik)*
Cypriot ['sɪprɪət] *adj* Kıbrıs ▷ *n* *(person)* Kıbrıslı *(kişi)*
Cyprus ['saɪprəs] *n* kıbrıs
cyst [sɪst] *n* kist
cystitis [sɪ'staɪtɪs] *n* sistit
Czech [tʃɛk] *adj* Çek ▷ *n* *(language)* Çek dili *(dil)*, *(person)* Çek *(kişi)*; **Czech Republic** *n* Çek Cumhuriyeti

d

dad [dæd] *n* baba
daddy ['dædɪ] *n* babacığım
daffodil ['dæfədɪl] *n* nergiz
daft [dɑːft] *adj* saf
daily ['deɪlɪ] *adj* günlük ▷ *adv* her gün
dairy ['dɛərɪ] *n* mandıra; **dairy produce** *n* sütle yapılmış; **dairy products** *npl* süt ürünleri
daisy ['deɪzɪ] *n* papatya
dam [dæm] *n* baraj
damage ['dæmɪdʒ] *n* zarar ▷ *v* zarar vermek
damaged ['dæmɪdʒd] *adj* **My luggage has been damaged** Bagajım hasar görmüş; **My suitcase has arrived damaged** Valizim hasar görmüş
damn [dæm] *adj* lanet
damp [dæmp] *adj* nemli
dance [dɑːns] *n* dans ▷ *v* dans etmek; **I don't really dance** Dans etmem pek; **I feel like dancing** Dans etmek istiyorum; **Would you like to dance?** Dans etmek ister misiniz?
dancer ['dɑːnsə] *n* dansçı
dancing ['dɑːnsɪŋ] *n* danslı toplantı; **ballroom dancing** *n* salon dansı
dandelion ['dændɪˌlaɪən] *n* kara hindiba
dandruff ['dændrəf] *n* kepek *(saç)*
Dane [deɪn] *n* Danimarkalı
danger ['deɪndʒə] *n* tehlike; **Is there a danger of avalanches?** Çığ tehlikesi var mı?
dangerous ['deɪndʒərəs] *adj* tehlikeli
Danish ['deɪnɪʃ] *adj* Danimarka ▷ *n* *(language)* Danimarka dili *(dil)*
dare [dɛə] *v* cüret etmek
daring ['dɛərɪŋ] *adj* cesur
dark [dɑːk] *adj* karanlık ▷ *n* karanlık; **It's dark** Karanlık
darkness ['dɑːknɪs] *n* karanlık
darling ['dɑːlɪŋ] *n* sevgilim
dart [dɑːt] *n* dart oku
darts [dɑːts] *npl* dart oyunu
dash [dæʃ] *v* hızla koşmak
dashboard ['dæʃˌbɔːd] *n* gösterge tablosu
data ['deɪtə; 'dɑːtə] *npl* veri
database ['deɪtəˌbeɪs] *n* veri tabanı
date [deɪt] *n* tarih *(takvim)*; **best-before date** *n* son kullanım tarihi; **expiry date** *n* son kullanım tarihi; **sell-by date** *n* son satış tarihi; **What is today's date?** Bugünün tarihi nedir?
daughter ['dɔːtə] *n* kız evlat

daughter-in-law ['dɔːtə ɪn lɔː] **(daughters-in-law)** *n* gelin
dawn [dɔːn] *n* şafak
day [deɪ] *n* gün; **day return** *n* günlük bilet; **Valentine's Day** *n* Sevgililer Günü; **Do you run day trips to...?**... a günlük turunuz var mı?; **I want to hire a car for five days** Beş günlüğüne bir araba kiralamak istiyorum; **Is the museum open every day?** Müze her gün açık mı?; **the day after tomorrow** öbür gün; **the day before yesterday** önceki gün; **What a lovely day!** Harika bir gün!; **What are your rates per day?** Günlük tarifeniz nedir?; **What day is it today?** Bugün günlerden ne?; **What is the dish of the day?** Günün yemeği ne?
daytime ['deɪˌtaɪm] *n* gündüz
dead [dɛd] *adj* ölü ▷ *adv* ölü; **dead end** *n* çıkmaz sokak
deadline ['dɛdˌlaɪn] *n* son teslim tarihi
deaf [dɛf] *adj* sağır; **I'm deaf** Sağırım
deafening ['dɛfᵊnɪŋ] *adj* sağır edici
deal [diːl] *n* anlaşma
dealer ['diːlə] *n* satıcı; **drug dealer** *n* uyuşturucu satıcısı
deal with [diːl wɪð] *v* halletmek
dear [dɪə] *adj (expensive)* pahalı, *(loved)* sevgili
death [dɛθ] *n* ölüm
debate [dɪ'beɪt] *n* tartışma *(fikir)* ▷ *v* tartışmak *(fikir)*
debit ['dɛbɪt] *n* hesabından çekilen para ▷ *v* birinin hesabına borç kaydetmek; **debit card** *n* banka kartı; **direct debit** *n* otomatik ödeme
debt [dɛt] *n* borç
decade ['dɛkeɪd; dɪ'keɪd] *n* on yıl
decaffeinated [dɪ'kæfɪˌneɪtɪd] *adj* kafeinsiz; **decaffeinated coffee** *n* kafeinsiz kahve
decay [dɪ'keɪ] *v* çürümek
deceive [dɪ'siːv] *v* yanıltmak
December [dɪ'sɛmbə] *n* Aralık *(ay)*; **on Friday the thirty first of December** Otuz bir Aralık Cuma günü
decent ['diːsᵊnt] *adj* uygun
decide [dɪ'saɪd] *v* karar vermek
decimal ['dɛsɪməl] *adj* onluk
decision [dɪ'sɪʒən] *n* karar
decisive [dɪ'saɪsɪv] *adj* belirleyici
deck [dɛk] *n* güverte; **Can we go out on deck?** Güverteye çıkabilir miyiz?; **How do I get to the car deck?** Araba güvertesine nasıl gidebilirim?
deckchair ['dɛkˌtʃɛə] *n* şezlong
declare [dɪ'klɛə] *v* deklare etmek; **I have a bottle of spirits to declare** Bir şişe içki deklare etmek istiyorum; **I have the allowed amount of alcohol to declare** İzin verilen miktarda içki deklare etmek istiyorum
decorate ['dɛkəˌreɪt] *v* dekore etmek
decorator ['dɛkəˌreɪtə] *n* dekoratör
decrease ['diːkriːs] *n* azalma ▷ [dɪ'kriːs]*v* azalmak
dedicated ['dɛdɪˌkeɪtɪd] *adj* adanmış
dedication [ˌdɛdɪ'keɪʃən] *n* ithaf

deduct [dɪ'dʌkt] *v* çıkarmak *(matematik)*
deep [diːp] *adj* derin
deep-fry [diːpfraɪ] *v* kızartma
deeply ['diːplɪ] *adv* derinden
deer [dɪə] **(***pl* **deer)** geyik
defeat [dɪ'fiːt] *n* yenilgi ▷ *v* yenmek
defect [dɪ'fɛkt] *n* kusur
defence [dɪ'fɛns] *n* savunma
defend [dɪ'fɛnd] *v* korumak
defendant [dɪ'fɛndənt] *n* davalı
defender [dɪ'fɛndə] *n* savunucu
deficit ['dɛfɪsɪt; dɪ'fɪsɪt] *n* açık *(finans)*
define [dɪ'faɪn] *v* tanımlamak
definite ['dɛfɪnɪt] *adj* kesin
definitely ['dɛfɪnɪtlɪ] *adv* kesinlikle
definition [ˌdɛfɪ'nɪʃən] *n* tanım
degree [dɪ'griː] *n* derece *(sıcaklık)*; **degree centigrade** *n* Santigrat derece; **degree Celsius** *n* Santigrat derece; **degree Fahrenheit** *n* Fahrenheit derece
dehydrated [diː'haɪdreɪtɪd] *adj* susuz
de-icer [diː'aɪsə] *n* buz çözücü
delay [dɪ'leɪ] *n* gecikme ▷ *v* gecikmek
delayed [dɪ'leɪd] *adj* gecikmeli; **The flight has been delayed** Uçuşunuz gecikmeli
delegate *n* ['dɛlɪˌɡɪt] delege ▷ *v* ['dɛlɪˌɡeɪt] yetkilendirmek
delete [dɪ'liːt] *v* silmek
deliberate [dɪ'lɪbərɪt] *adj* kasıtlı
deliberately [dɪ'lɪbərətlɪ] *adv* kasıtlı olarak
delicate ['dɛlɪkɪt] *adj* hassas
delicatessen [ˌdɛlɪkə'tɛsᵊn] *n* şarküteri
delicious [dɪ'lɪʃəs] *adj* lezzetli
delight [dɪ'laɪt] *n* haz
delighted [dɪ'laɪtɪd] *adj* hoşnut
delightful [dɪ'laɪtfʊl] *adj* keyif verici
deliver [dɪ'lɪvə] *v* teslim etmek
delivery [dɪ'lɪvərɪ] *n* teslimat; **recorded delivery** *n* iadeli taahhütlü
demand [dɪ'mɑːnd] *n* talep ▷ *v* talep etmek
demanding [dɪ'mɑːndɪŋ] *adj* zahmetli
demo, demos ['dɛməʊ, 'dɛməʊz] *n* demo
democracy [dɪ'mɒkrəsɪ] *n* demokrasi
democratic [ˌdɛmə'krætɪk] *adj* demokratik
demolish [dɪ'mɒlɪʃ] *v* yıkmak
demonstrate ['dɛmənˌstreɪt] *v* bulgularla kanıtlamak
demonstration [ˌdɛmən'streɪʃən] *n* gösteri *(politik)*
demonstrator ['dɛmənˌstreɪtə] *n* gösterici
denim ['dɛnɪm] *n* blucin kumaşı
denims ['dɛnɪmz] *npl* blucin
Denmark ['dɛnmɑːk] *n* Danimarka
dense [dɛns] *adj* sık *(orman)*
density ['dɛnsɪtɪ] *n* yoğunluk
dent [dɛnt] *n* göçük ▷ *v* göçürmek
dental ['dɛntᵊl] *adj* diş; **dental floss** *n* diş ipi; **I don't know if I have dental insurance** Diş sigortam var mı bilmiyorum?
dentist ['dɛntɪst] *n* dişçi; **I need a dentist** Dişçiye ihtiyacım var

dentures ['dɛntʃəz] *npl* takma dişler; **Can you repair my dentures?** Takma dişlerimi onarabilir misiniz?
deny [dɪ'naɪ] *v* inkar etmek
deodorant [di:'əʊdərənt] *n* deodoran
depart [dɪ'pɑ:t] *v* bir yerden hareket etmek
department [dɪ'pɑ:tmənt] *n* bölüm *(idari)*; **accident & emergency department** *n* kaza & acil servis; **department store** *n* büyük mağaza; **Where is the lingerie department?** İç çamaşırları bölümü ne tarafta?
departure [dɪ'pɑ:tʃə] *n* kalkış; **departure lounge** *n* uçuş bekleme salonu
depend [dɪ'pɛnd] *v* güvenine bağlı olmak
deport [dɪ'pɔ:t] *v* sınır dışı etmek
deposit [dɪ'pɒzɪt] *n* depozito
depressed [dɪ'prɛst] *adj* canı sıkkın
depressing [dɪ'prɛsɪŋ] *adj* iç karartıcı
depression [dɪ'prɛʃən] *n* depresyon
depth [dɛpθ] *n* derinlik
descend [dɪ'sɛnd] *v* inmek *(alçalmak)*
describe [dɪ'skraɪb] *v* betimlemek
description [dɪ'skrɪpʃən] *n* betimleme
desert ['dɛzət] *n* çöl; **desert island** *n* ıssız ada
deserve [dɪ'zɜ:v] *v* hak etmek
design [dɪ'zaɪn] *n* dizayn ▷ *v* tasarlamak
designer [dɪ'zaɪnə] *n* tasarımcı; **interior designer** *n* iç mimar
desire [dɪ'zaɪə] *n* arzu ▷ *v* arzu etmek
desk [dɛsk] *n* sıra *(okul)*; **enquiry desk** *n* danışma
despair [dɪ'spɛə] *n* umutsuzluk
desperate ['dɛspərɪt; -prɪt] *adj* umutsuz
desperately ['dɛspərɪtlɪ] *adv* umutsuzca
despise [dɪ'spaɪz] *v* hor görmek
despite [dɪ'spaɪt] *prep* karşın
dessert [dɪ'zɜ:t] *n* tatlı; **dessert spoon** *n* tatlı kaşığı; **The dessert menu, please** Tatlı menüsü lütfen; **We'd like a dessert** Tatlı rica ediyoruz
destination [ˌdɛstɪ'neɪʃən] *n* gidilecek yer
destiny ['dɛstɪnɪ] *n* kader
destroy [dɪ'strɔɪ] *v* yok etmek
destruction [dɪ'strʌkʃən] *n* imha
detail ['di:teɪl] *n* ayrıntı
detailed ['di:teɪld] *adj* ayrıntılı
detective [dɪ'tɛktɪv] *n* dedektif
detention [dɪ'tɛnʃən] *n* gözaltına alma
detergent [dɪ'tɜ:dʒənt] *n* deterjan
deteriorate [dɪ'tɪərɪəˌreɪt] *v* kötülemek
determined [dɪ'tɜ:mɪnd] *adj* kararlı
detour ['di:tʊə] *n* güzergah değiştirme
devaluation [di:ˌvæljuː'eɪʃən] *n* devalüasyon
devastated ['dɛvəˌsteɪtɪd] *adj* mahvolmuş
devastating ['dɛvəˌsteɪtɪŋ] *adj*

yıkıcı
develop [dɪ'vɛləp] *vi* geliştirmek *(büyüme)* ▷ *vt* gelişmek; **developing country** *n* gelişmekte olan ülke
development [dɪ'vɛləpmənt] *n* gelişme *(büyüme)*
device [dɪ'vaɪs] *n* araç
devil ['dɛvᵊl] *n* şeytan
devise [dɪ'vaɪz] *v* tasarlamak
devoted [dɪ'vəʊtɪd] *adj* özverili
diabetes [ˌdaɪə'bi:tɪs; -ti:z] *n* şeker hastalığı
diabetic [ˌdaɪə'bɛtɪk] *adj* diyabetik ▷ *n* şeker hastası
diagnosis [ˌdaɪəg'nəʊsɪs] *n* tanı
diagonal [daɪ'ægənᵊl] *adj* diyagonal
diagram ['daɪəˌgræm] *n* diyagram
dial ['daɪəl; daɪl] *v* tuşlamak *(telefon)*; **dialling code** *n* telefon kodu; **dialling tone** *n* telefon sinyali
dialect ['daɪəˌlɛkt] *n* diyalekt
dialogue ['daɪəˌlɒg] *n* diyalog
diameter [daɪ'æmɪtə] *n* çap
diamond ['daɪəmənd] *n* elmas
diarrhoea [ˌdaɪə'rɪə] *n* ishal
diary ['daɪərɪ] *n* günlük
dice, die [daɪs, daɪ] *npl* zar *(kumar)*
dictation [dɪk'teɪʃən] *n* dikte
dictator [dɪk'teɪtə] *n* diktatör
dictionary ['dɪkʃənərɪ; -ʃənrɪ] *n* sözlük
die [daɪ] *v* ölmek
diesel ['di:zᵊl] *n* dizel; **... worth of diesel, please**...lık dizel lütfen
diet ['daɪət] *n* diyet ▷ *v* diyet yapmak
difference ['dɪfərəns; 'dɪfrəns] *n* fark
different ['dɪfərənt; 'dɪfrənt] *adj* farklı; **I would like something different** Farklı bir şey istiyordum
difficult ['dɪfɪkᵊlt] *adj* güç *(zor)*
difficulty ['dɪfɪkᵊltɪ] *n* güçlük
dig [dɪg] *v* kazmak
digest [dɪ'dʒɛst; daɪ-] *v* sindirmek
digestion [dɪ'dʒɛstʃən; daɪ-] *n* sindirim
digger ['dɪgə] *n* ekskavatör
digital ['dɪdʒɪtᵊl] *adj* dijital; **digital camera** *n* dijital fotoğraf makinesi; **digital radio** *n* dijital radyo; **digital television** *n* dijital televizyon; **digital watch** *n* dijital saat
dignity ['dɪgnɪtɪ] *n* haysiyet
dilemma [dɪ'lɛmə; daɪ-] *n* ikilem
dilute [daɪ'lu:t] *v* sulandırmak
diluted [daɪ'lu:tɪd] *adj* sulandırılmış
dim [dɪm] *adj* loş
dimension [dɪ'mɛnʃən] *n* ebat
diminish [dɪ'mɪnɪʃ] *v* azaltmak
din [dɪn] *n* şamata
diner ['daɪnə] *n* lokanta müşterisi
dinghy ['dɪŋɪ] *n* küçük sandal
dinner ['dɪnə] *n* akşam yemeği; **dinner jacket** *n* smokin; **dinner party** *n* yemekli parti; **dinner time** *n* yemek zamanı; **What time is dinner?** Akşam yemeği kaçta?; **Would you like to go out for dinner?** Benimle akşam yemeğine çıkmak ister misiniz?
dinosaur ['daɪnəˌsɔ:] *n* dinozor
dip [dɪp] *n* *(food/sauce)* ezme *(yiyecek)* ▷ *v* daldırmak

diploma [dɪ'pləʊmə] *n* diploma
diplomat ['dɪplə,mæt] *n* diplomat
diplomatic [,dɪplə'mætɪk] *adj* diplomatik
dipstick ['dɪp,stɪk] *n* yağ çubuğu
direct [dɪ'rɛkt; daɪ-] *adj* kestirme ▹ *v* yönetmek; **direct debit** *n* otomatik ödeme
direction [dɪ'rɛkʃən; daɪ-] *n* yön
directions [dɪ'rɛkʃənz; daɪ-] *npl* talimatlar
directly [dɪ'rɛktlɪ; daɪ-] *adv* doğrudan doğruya
director [dɪ'rɛktə; daɪ-] *n* direktör; **managing director** *n* genel müdür
directory [dɪ'rɛktərɪ; -trɪ; daɪ-] *n* telefon rehberi; **directory enquiries** *npl* bilinmeyen numaralar; **telephone directory** *n* telefon rehberi
dirt [dɜːt] *n* kir
dirty ['dɜːtɪ] *adj* kirli; **My sheets are dirty** Çarşaflarım kirli
disability [,dɪsə'bɪlɪtɪ] *n* sakatlık
disabled [dɪ'seɪbᵊld] *adj* özürlü ▹ *npl* özürlüler
disadvantage [,dɪsəd'vɑːntɪdʒ] *n* dezavantaj
disagree [,dɪsə'griː] *v* görüşe katılmamak
disagreement [,dɪsə'griːmənt] *n* anlaşmazlık
disappear [,dɪsə'pɪə] *v* gözden kaybolmak
disappearance [,dɪsə'pɪərəns] *n* gözden kaybolma
disappoint [,dɪsə'pɔɪnt] *v* hayal kırıklığına uğratmak
disappointed [,dɪsə'pɔɪntɪd] *adj* hayal kırıklığına uğramış
disappointing [,dɪsə'pɔɪntɪŋ] *adj* tatmin edici olmayan
disappointment [,dɪsə'pɔɪntmənt] *n* düş kırıklığı
disaster [dɪ'zɑːstə] *n* felaket
disastrous [dɪ'zɑːstrəs] *adj* korkunç
disc [dɪsk] *n* disk; **compact disc** *n* kompakt disk; **disc jockey** *n* disk jokey; **slipped disc** *n* disk kayması
discharge [dɪs'tʃɑːdʒ] *v* **When will I be discharged?** Ne zaman çıkacağım?
discipline ['dɪsɪplɪn] *n* disiplin
disclose [dɪs'kləʊz] *v* ortaya çıkarmak
disco ['dɪskəʊ] *n* disko
disconnect [,dɪskə'nɛkt] *v* kesilmek *(bağlantı)*
discount ['dɪskaʊnt] *n* indirim; **student discount** *n* öğrenci indirimi; **Do you offer a discount for cash?** Nakit ödemelere indirim yapıyor musunuz?
discourage [dɪs'kʌrɪdʒ] *v* cesaretini kırmak
discover [dɪ'skʌvə] *v* keşfetmek
discretion [dɪ'skrɛʃən] *n* sağduyu
discrimination [dɪ,skrɪmɪ'neɪʃən] *n* ayrımcılık
discuss [dɪ'skʌs] *v* görüşmek
discussion [dɪ'skʌʃən] *n* münazara
disease [dɪ'ziːz] *n* illet; **Alzheimer's disease** *n* Alzheimer hastalığı
disgraceful [dɪs'greɪsfʊl] *adj* utanç verici
disguise [dɪs'gaɪz] *v* kılık

değiştirmek
disgusted [dɪsˈɡʌstɪd] *adj* tiksinmiş
disgusting [dɪsˈɡʌstɪŋ] *adj* iğrenç
dish [dɪʃ] *n (food)* yemek, *(plate)* servis tabağı; **dish towel** *n* kurulama havlusu; **satellite dish** *n* uydu çanak; **soap dish** *n* sabunluk; **Can you recommend a local dish?** Yöresel bir yemek tavsiye edebilir misiniz?; **Do you have any vegetarian dishes?** Vejetaryen yemekleriniz var mı?; **Which dishes have no meat / fish?** İçinde et / balık olmayan ne yemekleriniz var mı?
dishcloth [ˈdɪʃˌklɒθ] *n* kurulama bezi
dishonest [dɪsˈɒnɪst] *adj* dürüst olmayan
dishwasher [ˈdɪʃˌwɒʃə] *n* bulaşık makinesi
disinfectant [ˌdɪsɪnˈfɛktənt] *n* dezenfektan
disk [dɪsk] *n* disk; **disk drive** *n* disk sürücü
diskette [dɪsˈkɛt] *n* disket
dislike [dɪsˈlaɪk] *v* hoşlanmamak
dismal [ˈdɪzməl] *adj* iç karartıcı
dismiss [dɪsˈmɪs] *v* işten çıkarmak
disobedient [ˌdɪsəˈbiːdɪənt] *adj* asi
disobey [ˌdɪsəˈbeɪ] *v* söz dinlememek
dispenser [dɪˈspɛnsə] *n* dağıtıcı; **cash dispenser** *n* bankamatik
display [dɪˈspleɪ] *n* sergileme ▷ *v* sergilemek
disposable [dɪˈspəʊzəbᵊl] *adj* tek kullanımlık
disqualify [dɪsˈkwɒlɪˌfaɪ] *v* diskalifiye etmek
disrupt [dɪsˈrʌpt] *v* sözünü kesmek
dissatisfied [dɪsˈsætɪsˌfaɪd] *adj* hoşnutsuz
dissolve [dɪˈzɒlv] *v* erimek
distance [ˈdɪstəns] *n* uzaklık
distant [ˈdɪstənt] *adj* uzak
distillery [dɪˈstɪlərɪ] *n* damıtımevi
distinction [dɪˈstɪŋkʃən] *n* fark gözetme
distinctive [dɪˈstɪŋktɪv] *adj* belirgin
distinguish [dɪˈstɪŋɡwɪʃ] *v* ayırt etmek
distract [dɪˈstrækt] *v* ilgisini başka yöne çekmek
distribute [dɪˈstrɪbjuːt] *v* dağıtmak
distributor [dɪˈstrɪbjʊtə] *n* distribütör
district [ˈdɪstrɪkt] *n* bölge
disturb [dɪˈstɜːb] *v* rahatsız etmek
ditch [dɪtʃ] *n* hendek ▷ *v* sepetlemek
dive [daɪv] *n* dalış ▷ *v* dalmak *(deniz vb)*; **I'd like to go diving** Dalmak istiyorum
diver [ˈdaɪvə] *n* dalgıç
diversion [daɪˈvɜːʃən] *n* mecburi yön *(trafik)*
divide [dɪˈvaɪd] *v* bölmek
diving [ˈdaɪvɪŋ] *n* dalma *(denize)*; **diving board** *n* tramplen; **scuba diving** *n* tüplü dalış
division [dɪˈvɪʒən] *n* bölme
divorce [dɪˈvɔːs] *n* boşanma ▷ *v* boşanma
divorced [dɪˈvɔːst] *adj* boşanmış

DIY [di: aɪ waɪ] *abbr* kendin-yap
dizzy ['dɪzɪ] *adj* başı dönmüş
DJ [di: dʒeɪ] *abbr* DJ
DNA [di: ɛn eɪ] *n* DNA
do [dʊ] *v* yapmak; **What would you like to do today?** Bugün ne yapmak istersiniz?
dock [dɒk] *n* dok
doctor ['dɒktə] *n* doktor; **Call a doctor!** Bir doktor çağırın; **I need a doctor** Bana bir doktor gerek; **Is there a doctor who speaks English?** İngilizce bilen bir doktor var mı?; **Please call the emergency doctor** Nöbetçi doktoru çağırın lütfen
document ['dɒkjʊmənt] *n* belge; **I want to copy this document** Bu belgenin fotokopisini çektirmek istiyorum
documentary [ˌdɒkjʊ'mɛntərɪ; -trɪ] *n* belgesel
documentation [ˌdɒkjʊmɛn'teɪʃən] *n* belgeleme
documents [ˌdɒkjʊmɛnts] *npl* belgeler
dodge [dɒdʒ] *v* kenara kaçmak
dog [dɒg] *n* köpek; **guide dog** *n* rehber köpek; **hot dog** *n* sosisli sandviç
dole [dəʊl] *n* yoksulluk yardımı
doll [dɒl] *n* oyuncak bebek
dollar ['dɒlə] *n* dolar; **Do you take dollars?** Dolar kabul ediyor musunuz?
dolphin ['dɒlfɪn] *n* yunus
domestic [də'mɛstɪk] *adj* ülke içi
Dominican Republic [də'mɪnɪkən rɪ'pʌblɪk] *n* Dominik Cumhuriyeti
domino ['dɒmɪˌnəʊ] *n* domino
dominoes ['dɒmɪˌnəʊz] *npl* domino oyunu
donate [dəʊ'neɪt] *v* bağışlamak
done [dʌn] *adj* yapılmış
donkey ['dɒŋkɪ] *n* eşek
donor ['dəʊnə] *n* verici
door [dɔː] *n* kapı; **door handle** *n* kapı kolu; **Keep the door locked** Kapınızı kilitleyin; **The door handle has come off** Kapının kolu çıktı; **The door won't close** Kapı kapanmıyor; **The door won't lock** Kapı kilitlenmiyor; **The door won't open** Kapı açılmıyor; **Which is the key for the front door?** Hangisi ön kapının anahtarı?
doorbell ['dɔːˌbɛl] *n* kapı zili
doorman, doormen ['dɔːˌmæn; -mən, 'dɔːˌmɛn] *n* kapıcı
doorstep ['dɔːˌstɛp] *n* kapı eşiği
dorm [dɔːm] *n* **Do you have any single sex dorms?** Yalnızca kadınlar/erkekler için yeriniz var mı?
dormitory ['dɔːmɪtərɪ; -trɪ] *n* yatakhane
dose [dəʊs] *n* doz
dot [dɒt] *n* nokta *(şekil)*
double ['dʌbᵊl] *adj* çift ▷ *v* iki katına çıkmak; **double bass** *n* kontrabas; **double bed** *n* çift kişilik yatak; **double glazing** *n* çift cam; **double room** *n* iki kişilik oda
doubt [daʊt] *n* kuşku ▷ *v* kuşku duymak
doubtful ['daʊtfʊl] *adj* kuşkulu
dough [dəʊ] *n* hamur
doughnut ['dəʊnʌt] *n* donut®

do up [dʊ ʌp] *v* sarmak
dove [dʌv] *n* beyaz güvercin
do without [dʊ wɪˈðaʊt] *v* onsuz yapmak
down [daʊn] *adv* aşağıda
download [ˈdaʊnˌləʊd] *n* indirme *(bilgisayar)* ▹ *v* indirmek *(bilgisayar)*
downpour [ˈdaʊnˌpɔː] *n* sağanak
downstairs [ˈdaʊnˈstɛəz] *adj* alt kat ▹ *adv* alt katta
downtown [ˈdaʊnˈtaʊn] *adv* kent merkezinde
doze [dəʊz] *v* kestirmek
dozen [ˈdʌzᵊn] *n* düzine
doze off [dəʊz ɒf] *v* uyuyakalmak
drab [dræb] *adj* sıkıcı
draft [drɑːft] *n* taslak
drag [dræg] *v* sürüklemek
dragon [ˈdrægən] *n* ejderha
dragonfly [ˈdrægənˌflaɪ] *n* yusufçuk
drain [dreɪn] *n* atık borusu ▹ *v* atık boşaltmak; **draining board** *n* damlalıklı eviye
drainpipe [ˈdreɪnˌpaɪp] *n* atık borusu
drama [ˈdrɑːmə] *n* dram
dramatic [drəˈmætɪk] *adj* dramatik
drastic [ˈdræstɪk] *adj* zorlayıcı
draught [drɑːft] *n* cereyan
draughts [drɑːfts] *npl* dama oyunu
draw [drɔː] *n (lottery)* kura, *(tie)* çekiliş ▹ *v (equal with)* berabere kalmak, *(sketch)* çizmek *(resim)*
drawback [ˈdrɔːˌbæk] *n* engel
drawer [ˈdrɔːə] *n* çekmece
drawers [drɔːz] *n* **chest of drawers** *n* komodin
drawing [ˈdrɔːɪŋ] *n* çizim
drawing pin [ˈdrɔːɪŋ pɪn] *n* **drawing pin** *n* raptiye
dreadful [ˈdrɛdfʊl] *adj* korkunç
dream [driːm] *n* düş *(rüya)* ▹ *v* düş görmek
drench [drɛntʃ] *v* sırılsıklam etmek
dress [drɛs] *n* giysi *(elbise)* ▹ *v* giyinmek; **evening dress** *n* gece elbisesi; **wedding dress** *n* gelinlik; **Is there a dress code?** Giysi kuralı var mı?
dressed [drɛst] *adj* giyinik
dresser [ˈdrɛsə] *n* mutfak dolabı
dressing [ˈdrɛsɪŋ] *n* **salad dressing** *n* salata sosu
dressing gown [ˈdrɛsɪŋ gaʊn] *n* sabahlık
dressing table [ˈdrɛsɪŋ ˈteɪbᵊl] *n* tuvalet masası
dress up [drɛs ʌp] *v* süslenmek
dried [draɪd] *adj* kuru
drift [drɪft] *n* birikinti ▹ *v* sürüklenmek *(sularla)*
drill [drɪl] *n* matkap ▹ *v* delmek *(matkapla)*; **pneumatic drill** *n* pnömatik matkap
drink [drɪŋk] *n* içecek ▹ *v* içmek; **binge drinking** *n* ölçüsüz içme; **drinking water** *n* içme suyu; **soft drink** *n* içecek; **What would you like to drink?** Ne içmek istersiniz?; **Would you like a drink?** Bir şey içmek ister misiniz?
drink-driving [ˈdrɪŋkˈdraɪvɪŋ] *n* içkili araba kullanma
drip [drɪp] *n* damla ▹ *v* damlamak
drive [draɪv] *n* yolculuk *(otomobil)* ▹ *v* sürmek *(otomobil)*; **driving**

instructor *n* direksiyon öğretmeni; **four-wheel drive** *n* dört çekerli; **left-hand drive** *n* soldan trafik; **right-hand drive** *n* sağdan trafik
driver ['draɪvə] *n* sürücü; **learner driver** *n* öğrenci sürücü; **lorry driver** *n* kamyon şoförü; **racing driver** *n* yarışçı *(otomobil)*; **truck driver** *n* kamyon şoförü
driveway ['draɪv,weɪ] *n* kişinin evinin önündeki özel yol
driving lesson ['draɪvɪŋ 'lɛsᵊn] *n* direksiyon dersi
driving licence ['draɪvɪŋ 'laɪsəns] *n* sürücü ehliyeti; **Here is my driving licence** İşte ehliyetim; **I don't have my driving licence on me** Ehliyetim üzerimde değil; **My driving licence number is...** Ehliyet numaram...
driving test ['draɪvɪŋ 'tɛst] *n* direksiyon sınavı
drizzle ['drɪzᵊl] *n* çisenti
drop [drɒp] *n* damla ▷ *v* düşürmek; **eye drops** *npl* göz damlası
drought [draʊt] *n* kuraklık
drown [draʊn] *v* suda boğulmak
drowsy ['draʊzɪ] *adj* uykulu
drug [drʌg] *n* ilaç; **drug addict** *n* uyuşturucu bağımlısı; **drug dealer** *n* uyuşturucu satıcısı
drum [drʌm] *n* davul
drummer ['drʌmə] *n* davulcu
drunk [drʌŋk] *adj* sarhoş ▷ *n* sarhoş
dry [draɪ] *adj* kuru ▷ *v* kurutmak; **bone dry** *adj* kupkuru; **I have dry hair** Saçım kuru
dry-cleaner's ['draɪ'kli:nəz] *n* kuru temizleyici
dry-cleaning ['draɪ'kli:nɪŋ] *n* kuru temizleme
dryer ['draɪə] *n* kurutucu; **spin dryer** *n* çamaşır kurutma makinesi; **tumble dryer** *n* çamaşır kurutma makinesi
dual ['dju:əl] *adj* **dual carriageway** *n* çift-şeritli yol
dubbed [dʌbt] *adj* altyazılı
dubious ['dju:bɪəs] *adj* kuşkulu
duck [dʌk] *n* ördek
due [dju:] *adj* olması beklenen
due to [dju: tʊ] *prep* dolayı
dull [dʌl] *adj* fersiz
dumb [dʌm] *adj* dilsiz
dummy ['dʌmɪ] *n* vitrin mankeni
dump [dʌmp] *n* çöplük ▷ *v* atmak; **rubbish dump** *n* çöp döküm alanı
dumpling ['dʌmplɪŋ] *n* hamur yuvarı
dune [dju:n] *n* **sand dune** *n* kum tepesi
dungarees [,dʌŋgə'ri:z] *npl* tulum
dungeon ['dʌndʒən] *n* zindan
duration [djʊ'reɪʃən] *n* süre
during ['djʊərɪŋ] *prep* süresince
dusk [dʌsk] *n* alacakaranlık
dust [dʌst] *n* toz ▷ *v* toz almak
dustbin ['dʌst,bɪn] *n* çöp sepeti
dustman, dustmen ['dʌstmən, 'dʌstmɛn] *n* çöpçü
dustpan ['dʌst,pæn] *n* faraş
dusty ['dʌstɪ] *adj* tozlu
Dutch [dʌtʃ] *adj* Hollanda'ya ait ▷ *n* Hollandalı
Dutchman, Dutchmen ['dʌtʃmən, 'dʌtʃmɛn] *n* Hollandalı
Dutchwoman, Dutchwomen [,dʌtʃwʊmən, 'dʌtʃ,wɪmɪn] *n*

Hollandalı
duty ['dju:tɪ] *n* görev; **(customs) duty** *n* gümrük
duty-free ['dju:tɪ'fri:] *adj* duty-free ▹ *n* duty-free
duvet ['du:veɪ] *n* yorgan
DVD [di: vi: di:] *n* DVD; **DVD burner** *n* DVD yazıcı; **DVD player** *n* DVD oynatıcı
dwarf, dwarves [dwɔ:f, dwɔ:vz] *n* cüce
dye [daɪ] *n* boya *(giysi)* ▹ *v* boyamak; **Can you dye my hair, please?** Saçımı boyar mısınız lütfen?
dynamic [daɪ'næmɪk] *adj* dinamik
dyslexia [dɪs'lɛksɪə] *n* disleksi
dyslexic [dɪs'lɛksɪk] *adj* disleksik ▹ *n* disleksik

e

each [i:tʃ] *adj* her bir ▹ *pron* her bir
eagle ['i:gᵊl] *n* kartal
ear [ɪə] *n* kulak
earache ['ɪər,eɪk] *n* kulak ağrısı
eardrum ['ɪə,drʌm] *n* kulak zarı
earlier ['ɜ:lɪə] *adv* daha önce
early ['ɜ:lɪ] *adj* erken ▹ *adv* erken; **We arrived early/late** Erken/ geç geldik
earn [ɜ:n] *v* kazanmak
earnings ['ɜ:nɪŋz] *npl* gelir *(aylık kazanç)*
earphones ['ɪə,fəʊnz] *npl* kulaklık
earplugs ['ɪə,plʌgz] *npl* kulak tıkacı
earring ['ɪə,rɪŋ] *n* küpe
earth [ɜ:θ] *n* yeryüzü
earthquake ['ɜ:θ,kweɪk] *n* deprem
easily ['i:zɪlɪ] *adv* kolaylıkla
east [i:st] *adj* doğu ▹ *adv* doğusunda ▹ *n* doğu; **Far East** *n* Uzak Doğu; **Middle East** *n* Orta

Doğu
eastbound ['i:st,baʊnd] *adj* doğu yönünde
Easter ['i:stə] *n* Paskalya; **Easter egg** *n* Paskalya yumurtası
eastern ['i:stən] *adj* doğu
easy ['i:zɪ] *adj* kolay; **easy chair** *n* koltuk
easy-going ['i:zɪ'gəʊɪŋ] *adj* uysal
eat [i:t] *v* yemek; **Have you eaten?** Yemek yediniz mi?; **Is there somewhere to eat on the boat?** Feribotta yemek satan bir yer var mı?; **What would you like to eat?** Ne yemek istersiniz?; **Would you like something to eat?** Bir şey yemek ister misiniz?
e-book ['i:'bʊk] *n* digital not defteri
eccentric [ɪk'sɛntrɪk] *adj* eksantrik
echo ['ɛkəʊ] *n* yankı
ecofriendly ['i:kəʊ,frɛndlɪ] *adj* çevre dostu
ecological [,i:kə'lɒdʒɪkəl] *adj* ekolojik
ecology [ɪ'kɒlədʒɪ] *n* çevrebilim
e-commerce ['i:kɒmɜ:s] *n* e-ticaret
economic [,i:kə'nɒmɪk; ,ɛkə-] *adj* ekonomi
economical [,i:kə'nɒmɪkəl; ,ɛkə-] *adj* ekonomik
economics [,i:kə'nɒmɪks; ,ɛkə-] *npl* ekonomi
economist [ɪ'kɒnəmɪst] *n* ekonomist
economize [ɪ'kɒnə,maɪz] *v* ekonomi yapmak
economy [ɪ'kɒnəmɪ] *n* ekonomi; **economy class** *n* ikinci sınıf
ecstasy ['ɛkstəsɪ] *n* coşku
Ecuador ['ɛkwə,dɔ:] *n* Ekvador
eczema ['ɛksɪmə; ɪg'zi:mə] *n* egzema
edge [ɛdʒ] *n* sınır
edgy ['ɛdʒɪ] *adj* gergin *(sinirli)*
edible ['ɛdɪbəl] *adj* yenilebilir
edition [ɪ'dɪʃən] *n* baskı *(gazete, dergi)*
editor ['ɛdɪtə] *n* editör
educated ['ɛdjʊ,keɪtɪd] *adj* eğitimli
education [,ɛdjʊ'keɪʃən] *n* eğitim *(okul)*; **adult education** *n* yetişkin eğitimi; **higher education** *n* yüksek eğitim
educational [,ɛdjʊ'keɪʃənəl] *adj* eğitimsel
eel [i:l] *n* yılan balığı
effect [ɪ'fɛkt] *n* etki; **side effect** *n* yan etki
effective [ɪ'fɛktɪv] *adj* etkili
effectively [ɪ'fɛktɪvlɪ] *adv* etkili bir şekilde
efficient [ɪ'fɪʃənt] *adj* etkin *(nüfuzlu)*
efficiently [ɪ'fɪʃəntlɪ] *adv* etkili bir biçimde
effort ['ɛfət] *n* çaba
e.g. [i: dʒi:] *abbr* örneğin
egg [ɛg] *n* yumurta; **boiled egg** *n* haşlanmış yumurta; **egg white** *n* yumurta akı; **egg yolk** *n* yumurta sarısı; **Easter egg** *n* Paskalya yumurtası; **scrambled eggs** *npl* karıştırılmış yumurta; **Could you prepare a meal without eggs?** İçinde yumurta olmayan bir yemek yapabilir misiniz?; **I can't eat raw eggs** Çiğ yumurta

yiyemiyorum
eggcup ['ɛg,kʌp] *n* yumurta kabı
Egypt ['i:dʒɪpt] *n* Mısır *(ülke)*
Egyptian [ɪ'dʒɪpʃən] *adj* Mısır ▷ *n* Mısırlı
eight [eɪt] *number* sekiz; **two for the eight o'clock showing** Sekiz matinesine iki bilet lütfen
eighteen ['eɪ'ti:n] *number* onsekiz
eighteenth ['eɪ'ti:nθ] *adj* onsekizinci
eighth [eɪtθ] *adj* sekizinci ▷ *n* sekizinci
eighty ['eɪtɪ] *number* seksen
Eire ['ɛərə] *n* İrlanda
either ['aɪðə; 'i:ðə] *conj (... or)* ya o, ya bu ▷ *pron* biri; **either... or** *conj* ya
elastic [ɪ'læstɪk] *n* lastik; **elastic band** *n* lastik bant
Elastoplast® [ɪ'læstə,plɑ:st] *n* yara bandı
elbow ['ɛlbəʊ] *n* dirsek
elder ['ɛldə] *adj* daha yaşlı
elderly ['ɛldəlɪ] *adj* yaşlılar
eldest ['ɛldɪst] *adj* yaşça en büyük
elect [ɪ'lɛkt] *v* seçmek
election [ɪ'lɛkʃən] *n* seçim; **general election** *n* genel seçim
electorate [ɪ'lɛktərɪt] *n* seçmen bölgesi
electric [ɪ'lɛktrɪk] *adj* elektrikli; **electric blanket** *n* elektrikli battaniye; **electric shock** *n* elektrik çarpması
electrical [ɪ'lɛktrɪkᵊl] *adj* elektrikli
electrician [ɪlɛk'trɪʃən; ˌi:lɛk-] *n* elektrikçi
electricity [ɪlɛk'trɪsɪtɪ; ˌi:lɛk-] *n* elektrik; **Do we have to pay extra for electricity?** Elektrik için ayrıca para ödememiz gerekiyor mu?; **Is the cost of electricity included?** Elektrik ücrete dahil mi?; **There is no electricity** Elektrik yok; **Where is the electricity meter?** Elektrik sayacı nerede?
electronic [ɪlɛk'trɒnɪk; ˌi:lɛk-] *adj* elektronik
electronics [ɪlɛk'trɒnɪks; ˌi:lɛk-] *npl* elektronik bilimi
elegant ['ɛlɪgənt] *adj* zarif
element ['ɛlɪmənt] *n* bileşen
elephant ['ɛlɪfənt] *n* fil
eleven [ɪ'lɛvᵊn] *number* onbir
eleventh [ɪ'lɛvᵊnθ] *adj* onbirinci
eliminate [ɪ'lɪmɪ,neɪt] *v* gidermek
elm [ɛlm] *n* karaağaç
else [ɛls] *adj* diğer
elsewhere [ˌɛls'wɛə] *adv* başka bir yerde
email ['i:meɪl] *n* e-posta ▷ *vt (a person)* e-posta atmak; **email address** *n* e-posta adresi; **Can I have your email?** E-postanızı alabilir miyim?; **Can I send an email?** E-posta gönderebilir miyim?; **Did you get my email?** E-postamı aldınız mı?; **Do you have an email?** E-postanız var mı?; **My email address is...** E-posta adresim...; **What is your email address?** E-posta adresiniz nedir?
embankment [ɪm'bæŋkmənt] *n* bent
embarrassed [ˌɪm'bærəst] *adj* utanmış
embarrassing [ɪm'bærəsɪŋ] *adj*

nahoş
embassy ['ɛmbəsı] *n* elçilik
embroider [ım'brɔıdə] *v* elişiyle süslemek
embroidery [ım'brɔıdərı] *n* nakış
emergency [ı'mɜːdʒənsı] *n* acil durum; **accident & emergency department** *n* kaza & acil servis; **emergency exit** *n* acil çıkış kapısı; **emergency landing** *n* acil iniş
emigrate ['ɛmı,greıt] *v* göç etmek
emotion [ı'məʊʃən] *n* duygu
emotional [ı'məʊʃənᵊl] *adj* duygusal
emperor, empress ['ɛmpərə, 'ɛmprıs] *n* imparator
emphasize ['ɛmfə,saız] *v* vurgulamak
empire ['ɛmpaıə] *n* imparatorluk
employ [ım'plɔı] *v* işe almak
employee [ɛm'plɔıiː; ,ɛmplɔı'iː] *n* işçi
employer [ım'plɔıə] *n* işveren
employment [ım'plɔımənt] *n* işe alma
empty ['ɛmptı] *adj* boş *(mekan)* ▹ *v* boşaltmak
enamel [ı'næməl] *n* emaye
encourage [ın'kʌrıdʒ] *v* yüreklendirmek
encouragement [ın'kʌrıdʒmənt] *n* yüreklendirme
encouraging [ın'kʌrıdʒıŋ] *adj* cesaret verici
encyclopaedia [ɛn,saıkləʊ'piːdıə] *n* ansiklopedi
end [ɛnd] *n* son ▹ *v* sonlandırmak; **dead end** *n* çıkmaz sokak; **at the end of June** Haziran sonunda; **Is this the end of the queue?** Kuyruğun sonu burası mı?
endanger [ın'deındʒə] *v* tehlikeye atmak
ending ['ɛndıŋ] *n* son
endless ['ɛndlıs] *adj* sonsuz
enemy ['ɛnəmı] *n* düşman
energetic [,ɛnə'dʒɛtık] *adj* enerji dolu
energy ['ɛnədʒı] *n* enerji
engaged [ın'geıdʒd] *adj* nişanlı; **engaged tone** *n* meşgul sinyali; **I'm engaged** Nişanlıyım
engagement [ın'geıdʒmənt] *n* randevu; **engagement ring** *n* nişan yüzüğü
engine ['ɛndʒın] *n* makine; **search engine** *n* arama motoru
engineer [,ɛndʒı'nıə] *n* mühendis
engineering [,ɛndʒı'nıərıŋ] *n* mühendislik
England ['ıŋglənd] *n* İngiltere
English ['ıŋglıʃ] *adj* İngiliz ▹ *n* İngilizce; **Do you speak English?** İngilizce biliyor musunuz?; **Does anyone speak English?** İngilizce bilen biri var mı?; **I don't speak English** İngilizce bilmiyorum; **I speak very little English** Çok az İngilizce konuşabiliyorum
Englishman, Englishmen ['ıŋglıʃmən, 'ıŋglıʃmɛn] *n* İngiliz
Englishwoman, Englishwomen ['ıŋglıʃ,wʊmən, 'ıŋglıʃ,wımın] *n* İngiliz kadın
engrave [ın'greıv] *v* kazımak
enjoy [ın'dʒɔı] *v* hoşlanmak
enjoyable [ın'dʒɔıəbᵊl] *adj* zevkli
enlargement [ın'lɑːdʒmənt] *n* büyütme
enormous [ı'nɔːməs] *adj*

muazzam
enough [ɪ'nʌf] *adj* kâfi ▷ *pron* kâfi
enquire [ɪn'kwaɪə] *v* araştırmak
enquiry [ɪn'kwaɪərɪ] *n* araştırma; **enquiry desk** *n* danışma
ensure [ɛn'ʃʊə; -'ʃɔː] *v* garantiye almak
enter ['ɛntə] *v* girmek *(bir yere)*
entertain [,ɛntə'teɪn] *v* eğlendirmek
entertainer [,ɛntə'teɪnə] *n* eğlence düzenleyen
entertaining [,ɛntə'teɪnɪŋ] *adj* eğlendirici
entertainment [,ɛntə'teɪnmənt] *n* eğlence
enthusiasm [ɪn'θjuːzɪ,æzəm] *n* heves
enthusiastic [ɪn,θjuːzɪ'æstɪk] *adj* hevesli
entire [ɪn'taɪə] *adj* bütün *(tamamı)*
entirely [ɪn'taɪəlɪ] *adv* bütünüyle
entrance ['ɛntrəns] *n* giriş *(kapı)*; **entrance fee** *n* giriş ücreti; **Where is the wheelchair-accessible entrance?** Tekerlekli sandalye girişi nerede?
entry ['ɛntrɪ] *n* giriş; **entry phone** *n* kapı telefonu
envelope ['ɛnvə,ləʊp; 'ɒn-] *n* zarf
envious ['ɛnvɪəs] *adj* kıskanç
environment [ɪn'vaɪrənmənt] *n* çevre
environmental [ɪn,vaɪrən'mɛntə,l] *adj* çevresel; **environmentally friendly** *adj* çevre dostu
envy ['ɛnvɪ] *n* haset ▷ *v* hasetlenmek
epidemic [,ɛpɪ'dɛmɪk] *n* salgın
epileptic [,ɛpɪ'lɛptɪk] *n* saralı; **epileptic fit** *n* sara nöbeti
episode ['ɛpɪ,səʊd] *n* bölüm *(dizi)*
equal ['iːkwəl] *adj* eşit ▷ *v* eşitlemek
equality [ɪ'kwɒlɪtɪ] *n* eşitlik *(siyasi)*
equalize ['iːkwə,laɪz] *v* eşitlemek
equation [ɪ'kweɪʒən; -ʃən] *n* eşitlik *(matematik)*
equator [ɪ'kweɪtə] *n* ekvator
Equatorial Guinea [,ɛkwə'tɔːrɪəl 'gɪnɪ] *n* Ekvator Ginesi
equipment [ɪ'kwɪpmənt] *n* donanım
equipped [ɪ'kwɪpt] *adj* donanımlı
equivalent [ɪ'kwɪvələnt] *n* denk *(eşit)*
erase [ɪ'reɪz] *v* silmek
Eritrea [,ɛrɪ'treɪə] *n* Eritre
erotic [ɪ'rɒtɪk] *adj* erotik
error ['ɛrə] *n* yanlış
escalator ['ɛskə,leɪtə] *n* yürüyen merdiven
escape [ɪ'skeɪp] *n* kaçış ▷ *v* kaçmak; **fire escape** *n* yangın çıkışı
escort [ɪs'kɔːt] *v* eşlik etmek *(refakat)*
especially [ɪ'spɛʃəlɪ] *adv* özellikle
espionage ['ɛspɪə,nɑːʒ; ,ɛspɪə'nɑːʒ; 'ɛspɪənɪdʒ] *n* casusluk
essay ['ɛseɪ] *n* deneme
essential [ɪ'sɛnʃəl] *adj* zorunlu
estate [ɪ'steɪt] *n* malikane; **estate agent** *n* emlakçı; **estate car** *n* vagon *(oto)*
estimate *n* ['ɛstɪmɪt] tahmin ▷ *v* ['ɛstɪ,meɪt] tahminde bulunmak
Estonia [ɛ'stəʊnɪə] *n* Estonya

Estonian [ɛ'stəʊnɪən] *adj* Estonya ▹ *n (language)* Estonya dili *(dil)*, *(person)* Estonyalı *(kişi)*
etc [ɪt 'sɛtrə] *abbr* vb *(kısaltma)*
eternal [ɪ'tɜːnᵊl] *adj* sonsuz
eternity [ɪ'tɜːnɪtɪ] *n* sonsuz
ethical ['ɛθɪkᵊl] *adj* ahlaki
Ethiopia [ˌiːθɪ'əʊpɪə] *n* Etyopya
Ethiopian [ˌiːθɪ'əʊpɪən] *adj* Etyopya ▹ *n* Etyopyalı
ethnic ['ɛθnɪk] *adj* etnik
e-ticket ['iː'tɪkɪt] *n* e-bilet
EU [iː juː] *abbr* AB
euro ['jʊərəʊ] *n* avro
Europe ['jʊərəp] *n* Avrupa
European [ˌjʊərə'pɪən] *adj* Avrupa ▹ *n* Avrupalı; **European Union** *n* Avrupa Birliği
evacuate [ɪ'vækjʊˌeɪt] *v* boşaltmak *(bina)*
eve [iːv] *n* arife
even ['iːvᵊn] *adj* düz *(düzgün)* ▹ *adv* hatta
evening ['iːvnɪŋ] *n* akşam; **evening class** *n* akşam okulu; **evening dress** *n* gece elbisesi; **Good evening** İyi akşamlar; **in the evening** akşam; **The table is booked for nine o'clock this evening** Masa bu akşam saat dokuz için rezerve edildi; **What are you doing this evening?** Bu akşam ne yapıyorsunuz?; **What is there to do in the evenings?** Burada akşamları yapılabilecek ne var?
event [ɪ'vɛnt] *n* olay
eventful [ɪ'vɛntfʊl] *adj* olaylı
eventually [ɪ'vɛntʃʊəlɪ] *adv* sonuçta
ever ['ɛvə] *adv* hiç; **Have you ever been to...?...** a hiç gittiniz mi?
every ['ɛvrɪ] *adj* her; **The bus runs every twenty minutes** Her yirmi dakikada bir otobüs var
everybody ['ɛvrɪˌbɒdɪ] *pron* herkes
everyone ['ɛvrɪˌwʌn; -wən] *pron* herkes
everything ['ɛvrɪθɪŋ] *pron* herşey
everywhere ['ɛvrɪˌwɛə] *adv* her yerde
evidence ['ɛvɪdəns] *n* kanıt
evil ['iːvᵊl] *adj* kötücül
evolution [ˌiːvə'luːʃən] *n* evrim
ewe [juː] *n* koyun *(dişi)*
exact [ɪg'zækt] *adj* tam
exactly [ɪg'zæktlɪ] *adv* tam olarak
exaggerate [ɪg'zædʒəˌreɪt] *v* abartmak
exaggeration [ɪg'zædʒəˌreɪʃən] *n* abartı
exam [ɪg'zæm] *n* sınav
examination [ɪgˌzæmɪ'neɪʃən] *n* *(medical)* sınav, *(school)* sınav
examine [ɪg'zæmɪn] *v* incelemek
examiner [ɪg'zæmɪnə] *n* sınav görevlisi
example [ɪg'zɑːmpᵊl] *n* örnek
excellent ['ɛksələnt] *adj* mükemmel; **The lunch was excellent** Yemek mükemmeldi
except [ɪk'sɛpt] *prep* hariç
exception [ɪk'sɛpʃən] *n* dışında *(haricinde)*
exceptional [ɪk'sɛpʃənᵊl] *adj* müstesna
excessive [ɪk'sɛsɪv] *adj* aşırı
exchange [ɪks'tʃeɪndʒ] *v* karşılıklı yapmak; **exchange rate** *n* döviz

kuru; **rate of exchange** *n* döviz kuru; **stock exchange** *n* borsa
excited [ɪk'saɪtɪd] *adj* heyecanlı
exciting [ɪk'saɪtɪŋ] *adj* heyecan verici
exclude [ɪk'sklu:d] *v* dışında tutmak
excluding [ɪk'sklu:dɪŋ] *prep* dışında *(onu hariç tutarak)*
exclusively [ɪk'sklu:sɪvlɪ] *adv* yalnızca
excuse *n* [ɪk'skju:s] özür ▷ *v* [ɪk'skju:z] özür beyan etmek
execute ['ɛksɪˌkju:t] *v* idam etmek
execution [ˌɛksɪ'kju:ʃən] *n* idam
executive [ɪg'zɛkjʊtɪv] *n* yönetici
exercise ['ɛksəˌsaɪz] *n* egzersiz
exhaust [ɪg'zɔ:st] *n* **The exhaust is broken** Egzos patladı
exhausted [ɪg'zɔ:stɪd] *adj* tükenmiş
exhibition [ˌɛksɪ'bɪʃən] *n* sergi
ex-husband [ɛks'hʌzbənd] *n* eski koca
exile ['ɛgzaɪl; 'ɛksaɪl] *n* sürgün *(başka bir yere)*
exist [ɪg'zɪst] *v* var olmak
exit ['ɛgzɪt; 'ɛksɪt] *n* çıkış; **emergency exit** *n* acil çıkış kapısı; **Which exit for...?**... çıkışı nerede?
exotic [ɪg'zɒtɪk] *adj* egzotik
expect [ɪk'spɛkt] *v* ummak
expedition [ˌɛkspɪ'dɪʃən] *n* keşif gezisi
expel [ɪk'spɛl] *v* kovmak
expenditure [ɪk'spɛndɪtʃə] *n* harcamalar
expenses [ɪk'spɛnsɪz] *npl* masraflar
expensive [ɪk'spɛnsɪv] *adj* pahalı; **It's quite expensive** Çok pahalı; **It's too expensive for me** Benim için çok pahalı
experience [ɪk'spɪərɪəns] *n* deneyim; **work experience** *n* iş deneyimi
experienced [ɪk'spɪərɪənst] *adj* deneyimli
experiment [ɪk'spɛrɪmənt] *n* deney
expert ['ɛkspɜ:t] *n* uzman
expire [ɪk'spaɪə] *v* sona erdirme
explain [ɪk'spleɪn] *v* açıklamak
explanation [ˌɛksplə'neɪʃən] *n* açıklama *(izah)*
explode [ɪk'spləʊd] *v* patlamak *(havaya uçarak)*
exploit [ɪk'splɔɪt] *v* sömürmek
exploitation [ˌɛksplɔɪ'teɪʃən] *n* sömürü
explore [ɪk'splɔ:] *v* araştırmak
explorer [ɪk'splɔ:rə] *n* kaşif
explosion [ɪk'spləʊʒən] *n* patlama
explosive [ɪk'spləʊsɪv] *n* patlayıcı madde
export *n* ['ɛkspɔ:t] ihracat ▷ *v* [ɪk'spɔ:t] ihraç etmek
express [ɪk'sprɛs] *v* ifade etmek
expression [ɪk'sprɛʃən] *n* anlatım
extension [ɪk'stɛnʃən] *n* uzatma; **extension cable** *n* uzatma kablosu
extensive [ɪk'stɛnsɪv] *adj* geniş *(ferah, yaygın)*
extensively [ɪk'stɛnsɪvlɪ] *adv* uzun uzadıya
extent [ɪk'stɛnt] *n* boyut
exterior [ɪk'stɪərɪə] *adj* dış *(yapı vb)*
external [ɪk'stɜ:nᵊl] *adj* dış *(harici)*

extinct [ɪk'stɪŋkt] *adj* soyu tükenmiş
extinguisher [ɪk'stɪŋgwɪʃə] *n* söndürücü *(yangın)*
extortionate [ɪk'stɔːʃənɪt] *adj* ölçüsüz
extra ['ɛkstrə] *adj* ilave *(fazladan)* ▷ *adv* ilaveten
extraordinary [ɪk'strɔːdᵊnrɪ; -dᵊnərɪ] *adj* olağanüstü
extravagant [ɪk'strævɪgənt] *adj* savruk
extreme [ɪk'striːm] *adj* aşırı
extremely [ɪk'striːmlɪ] *adv* aşırı derecede
extremism [ɪk'striːmɪzəm] *n* aşırıcılık
extremist [ɪk'striːmɪst] *n* aşırı uçta
ex-wife [ɛks'waɪf] *n* eski karı
eye [aɪ] *n* göz; **eye drops** *npl* göz damlası; **eye shadow** *n* göz farı; **I have something in my eye** Gözüme bir şey kaçtı; **My eyes are sore** Gözlerim yanıyor
eyebrow ['aɪˌbraʊ] *n* kaş
eyelash ['aɪˌlæʃ] *n* kirpik
eyelid ['aɪˌlɪd] *n* göz kapağı
eyeliner ['aɪˌlaɪnə] *n* rimel
eyesight ['aɪˌsaɪt] *n* görme yetisi

f

fabric ['fæbrɪk] *n* kumaş
fabulous ['fæbjʊləs] *adj* inanılmaz
face [feɪs] *n* yüz ▷ *v* bakmak *(karşılıklı)*; **face cloth** *n* yüz havlusu
facial ['feɪʃəl] *adj* yüz ▷ *n* yüz bakımı
facilities [fə'sɪlɪtɪz] *npl* kolaylıklar; **Do you have facilities for children?** Çocuklar için kolaylıklarınız neler?; **What facilities do you have for disabled people?** Özürlüler için kolaylıklarınız nelerdir?
fact [fækt] *n* gerçek *(bilgi)*
factory ['fæktərɪ] *n* fabrika; **I work in a factory** Bir fabrikada çalışıyorum
fade [feɪd] *v* solmak
fag [fæg] *n* sigara *(argo)*
fail [feɪl] *v* başarısız olmak
failure ['feɪljə] *n* başarısızlık

faint [feɪnt] *adj* zayıf *(ışık, ses vb)* ▹ *v* bayılmak
fair [fɛə] *adj (light colour)* açık renk *(ten/saç), (reasonable)* adil ▹ *n* fuar
fairground ['fɛəˌgraʊnd] *n* fuar alanı
fairly ['fɛəlɪ] *adv* oldukça
fairness ['fɛənɪs] *n* dürüstlük
fairy ['fɛərɪ] *n* peri
fairytale ['fɛərɪˌteɪl] *n* peri masalı
faith [feɪθ] *n* inanç
faithful ['feɪθfʊl] *adj* sadık
faithfully ['feɪθfʊlɪ] *adv* sadakatle
fake [feɪk] *adj* uyduruk ▹ *n* sahte
fall [fɔːl] *n* düşüş ▹ *v* düşmek
fall down [fɔːl daʊn] *v* düşmek
fall for [fɔːl fɔː] *v* cazibesine kapılmak
fall out [fɔːl aʊt] *v* sıradan çıkmak
false [fɔːls] *adj* düzmece; **false alarm** *n* yanlış alarm
fame [feɪm] *n* ün
familiar [fə'mɪlɪə] *adj* bildik
family ['fæmɪlɪ; 'fæmlɪ] *n* aile; **I want to reserve a family room** Aile odası ayırtmak istiyorum; **I'd like to book a family room** Aile odası istiyorum; **I'm here with my family** Ailemle geldim
famine ['fæmɪn] *n* kıtlık
famous ['feɪməs] *adj* ünlü
fan [fæn] *n* vantilatör; **fan belt** *n* soğutucu kayışı; **Does the room have a fan?** Odada vantilatör var mı?
fanatic [fə'nætɪk] *n* fanatik
fancy ['fænsɪ] *v* tasavvur etmek; **fancy dress** *n* balo kostümü
fantastic [fæn'tæstɪk] *adj* harika
FAQ [ɛf eɪ kjuː] *abbr* sık sorulan sorular
far [fɑː] *adj* uzak ▹ *adv* uzakta; **Far East** *n* Uzak Doğu; **How far are we from the beach?** Plajdan ne kadar uzaktayız?; **How far are we from the bus station?** Otobüs terminaline ne kadar uzaktayız?; **How far is it?** Ne kadar uzak?; **How far is the bank?** Banka buraya ne kadar uzakta?; **Is it far?** Uzak mı?; **It's not far** Uzak değil; **It's quite far** Oldukça uzak
fare [fɛə] *n* yolcu
farewell [ˌfɛə'wɛl] *excl* elveda!
farm [fɑːm] *n* çiftlik
farmer ['fɑːmə] *n* çiftçi
farmhouse ['fɑːmˌhaʊs] *n* çiftlik evi
farming ['fɑːmɪŋ] *n* çiftçilik
Faroe Islands ['fɛərəʊ 'aɪləndz] *npl* Faroe Adaları
fascinating ['fæsɪˌneɪtɪŋ] *adj* büyüleyici
fashion ['fæʃən] *n* moda
fashionable ['fæʃənəbᵊl] *adj* modaya uygun
fast [fɑːst] *adj* hızlı ▹ *adv* hızlı; **He was driving too fast** Çok hızlı gidiyordu
fat [fæt] *adj* şişman ▹ *n* yağ
fatal ['feɪtᵊl] *adj* ölümcül
fate [feɪt] *n* kader
father ['fɑːðə] *n* baba
father-in-law ['fɑːðə ɪn lɔː] **(fathers-in-law)** *n* kayınpeder
fault [fɔːlt] *n (defect)* hata, *(mistake)* hata; **It wasn't my fault** Hata bende değildi
faulty ['fɔːltɪ] *adj* hatalı
fauna ['fɔːnə] *npl* hayvanat

favour ['feɪvə] *n* yardım
favourite ['feɪvərɪt; 'feɪvrɪt] *adj* gözde ▹ *n* gözde
fax [fæks] *n* faks ▹ *v* fakslamak; **Do you have a fax?** Faksınız var mı?; **How much is it to send a fax?** Faks göndermek ne kadar?; **I want to send a fax** Faks çekmek istiyorum; **Is there a fax machine I can use?** Kullanabileceğim bir faks makinesi var mı?; **Please resend your fax** Faksınızı bir daha gönderin; **There is a problem with your fax** Faksınızda bir sorun var; **What is the fax number?** Faks numarası nedir?
fear [fɪə] *n* korku ▹ *v* korkmak
feasible ['fi:zəbᵊl] *adj* uygulanabilir
feather ['fɛðə] *n* tüy
feature ['fi:tʃə] *n* özellik
February ['fɛbrʊərɪ] *n* Şubat
fed up [fɛd ʌp] *adj* bıkmış
fee [fi:] *n* ücret; **entrance fee** *n* giriş ücreti; **tuition fees** *npl* öğretim ücreti; **Is there a booking fee to pay?** Yer ayırtmak için ücret ödemek gerekiyor mu?
feed [fi:d] *v* beslemek
feedback ['fi:d,bæk] *n* geribildirim
feel [fi:l] *v* hissetmek
feeling ['fi:lɪŋ] *n* his
feet [fi:t] *npl* ayaklar; **My feet are sore** Ayaklarım ağrıyor
felt [fɛlt] *n* keçe
female ['fi:meɪl] *adj* kadın ▹ *n* kadın
feminine ['fɛmɪnɪn] *adj* kadınsı
feminist ['fɛmɪnɪst; 'feminist] *n* feminist
fence [fɛns] *n* çit *(tahta, tel örgü)*
fennel ['fɛnᵊl] *n* rezene
fern [fɜ:n] *n* eğrelti otu
ferret ['fɛrɪt] *n* yaban gelinciği
ferry ['fɛrɪ] *n* feribot; **Where do we catch the ferry to...?**... feribotuna nereden binebiliriz?
fertile ['fɜ:taɪl] *adj* doğurgan
fertilizer ['fɜ:tɪ,laɪzə] *n* gübre
festival ['fɛstɪvᵊl] *n* festival
fetch [fɛtʃ] *v* getirmek
fever ['fi:və] *n* ateş *(sağlık)*; **hay fever** *n* saman nezlesi; **He has a fever** Ateşi çok yüksek
few [fju:] *adj* birkaç ▹ *pron* birkaç
fewer [fju:ə] *adj* daha az *(sayıca)*
fiancé [fɪ'ɒnseɪ] *n* nişanlı *(erkek)*
fiancée [fɪ'ɒnseɪ] *n* nişanlı *(kadın)*
fibre ['faɪbə] *n* fibre
fibreglass ['faɪbə,glɑ:s] *n* cam yünü
fiction ['fɪkʃən] *n* kurgu; **science fiction** *n* bilim kurgu
field [fi:ld] *n* tarla; **playing field** *n* oyun alanı
fierce [fɪəs] *adj* azgın
fifteen ['fɪf'ti:n] *number* onbeş
fifteenth ['fɪf'ti:nθ] *adj* onbeşinci
fifth [fɪfθ] *adj* beşinci
fifty ['fɪftɪ] *number* elli
fifty-fifty ['fɪftɪ'fɪftɪ] *adj* yarı yarıya ▹ *adv* yarı yarıya
fig [fɪg] *n* incir
fight [faɪt] *n* dövüş ▹ *v* savaşmak
fighting [faɪtɪŋ] *n* dövüşme
figure ['fɪgə; 'fɪgjər] *n* şekil
figure out ['fɪgə aʊt] *v* çözmek
Fiji ['fi:dʒi:; fi:'dʒi:] *n* Fiji
file [faɪl] *n (folder)* dosya, *(tool)* eğe ▹ *v (folder)* dosyalamak,

(smoothing) törpülemek
Filipino, Filipina [ˌfɪlɪ'piːnəʊ, ˌfɪlɪ'piːna] *adj* Filipinli ▹ *n* Filipinli
fill [fɪl] *v* doldurmak *(içini)*
fillet ['fɪlɪt] *n* fileto ▹ *v* fileto kesmek
fill in [fɪl ɪn] *v* doldurmak
fill up [fɪl ʌp] *v* doldurmak *(benzin deposu)*
film [fɪlm] *n* film *(fotoğraf vb)*; **film star** *n* film yıldızı; **horror film** *n* korku filmi; **A colour film, please** Renkli film istiyorum lütfen; **Are there any films in English?** İngilizce film var mı?; **Can I film here?** Burada film çekebilir miyim?; **Can you develop this film, please?** Bu filmi banyo edebilir misiniz lütfen?; **The film has jammed** Film takıldı; **When does the film start?** Film kaçta başlıyor; **Where can we go to see a film?** Film görmek için nereye gidebiliriz?; **Which film is on at the cinema?** Sinemada hangi film oynuyor?
filter ['fɪltə] *n* filtre ▹ *v* süzmek
filthy ['fɪlθɪ] *adj* iğrenç
final ['faɪnᵊl] *adj* son ▹ *n* final
finalize ['faɪnəˌlaɪz] *v* sonlandırmak
finally ['faɪnəlɪ] *adv* sonunda
finance [fɪ'næns; 'faɪnæns] *n* finans ▹ *v* finanse etmek
financial [fɪ'nænʃəl; faɪ-] *adj* mali; **financial year** *n* mali yıl
find [faɪnd] *v* bulmak *(aradığı bir şeyi)*
find out [faɪnd aʊt] *v* bulmak *(keşfetmek)*
fine [faɪn] *adj* çok iyi ▹ *adv* pekala ▹ *n* ceza; **How much is the fine?** Ceza ne kadar?; **Where do I pay the fine?** Cezayı nereye yatıracağım?
finger ['fɪŋgə] *n* parmak; **index finger** *n* işaret parmağı
fingernail ['fɪŋgəˌneɪl] *n* tırnak
fingerprint ['fɪŋgəˌprɪnt] *n* parmak izi
finish ['fɪnɪʃ] *n* son ▹ *v* bitmek *(son bulmak)*
finished ['fɪnɪʃt] *adj* hazır
Finland ['fɪnlənd] *n* Finlandiya
Finn ['fɪn] *n* Fin
Finnish ['fɪnɪʃ] *adj* Fin ▹ *n* Finli
fir [fɜː] *n* **fir (tree)** *n* köknar ağacı
fire [faɪə] *n* yangın; **fire alarm** *n* yangın alarmı; **fire brigade** *n* itfaiye; **fire escape** *n* yangın çıkışı; **fire extinguisher** *n* yangın söndürücü; **Fire!** Yangın var!
fireman, firemen ['faɪəmən, 'faɪəmɛn] *n* itfaiyeci
fireplace ['faɪəˌpleɪs] *n* şömine
firewall ['faɪəˌwɔːl] *n* güvenlik duvarı
fireworks ['faɪəˌwɜːks] *npl* havai fişek gösterileri
firm [fɜːm] *adj* sıkı ▹ *n* firma
first [fɜːst] *adj* ilk ▹ *adv* ilkin ▹ *n* ilk; **first aid** *n* ilk yardım; **first name** *n* ön ad; **This is my first trip to...** Bu benim... a ilk gelişim; **When is the first bus to...?**... a ilk otobüs kaçta?
first-class ['fɜːst'klɑːs] *adj* birinci sınıf
firstly ['fɜːstlɪ] *adv* öncelikle
fiscal ['fɪskᵊl] *adj* mali; **fiscal year** *n*

mali yıl
fish [fɪʃ] *n* balık ▷ *v* balık avlamak; **freshwater fish** *n* tatlısu balığı; **Am I allowed to fish here?** Burada balık avlayabilir miyim?; **Can we fish here?** Burada balık avlanabilir mi?; **Could you prepare a meal without fish?** İçinde balık olmayan bir yemek yapabilir misiniz?; **I don't eat fish** Balık yemiyorum; **I'll have the fish** Balık alayım; **Is the fish fresh or frozen?** Balıklarınız taze mi, dondurulmuş mu?; **Is this cooked in fish stock?** Bu yemekte balık suyu var mı?; **What fish dishes do you have?** Balıklardan ne var?; **Where can I go fishing?** Nerede balık tutabilirim?
fisherman, fishermen ['fɪʃəmən, 'fɪʃəmɛn] *n* balıkçı
fishing ['fɪʃɪŋ] *n* balık avlamak; **fishing boat** *n* balıkçı teknesi; **fishing rod** *n* olta; **fishing tackle** *n* olta
fishmonger ['fɪʃˌmʌŋgə] *n* balıkçı *(dükkan)*
fist [fɪst] *n* yumruk
fit [fɪt] *adj* uygun ▷ *n* uyma ▷ *v* uydurmak; **epileptic fit** *n* sara nöbeti; **fitted kitchen** *n* hazır mutfak; **fitted sheet** *n* fitted çarşaf; **fitting room** *n* soyunma odası *(mağaza)*
fit in [fɪt ɪn] *v* uymak
five [faɪv] *number* beş
fix [fɪks] *v* sabitlemek
fixed [fɪkst] *adj* sabitlenmiş
fizzy ['fɪzɪ] *adj* köpüklü
flabby ['flæbɪ] *adj* gevşek *(sarkmış karın vb)*
flag [flæg] *n* bayrak
flame [fleɪm] *n* alev
flamingo [flə'mɪŋgəʊ] *n* flamingo
flammable ['flæməbᵊl] *adj* yanıcı
flan [flæn] *n* turta
flannel ['flænᵊl] *n* fanila
flap [flæp] *v* kanat çırpmak
flash [flæʃ] *n* flaş ▷ *v* parlamak; **The flash is not working** Flaş çalışmıyor
flashlight ['flæʃˌlaɪt] *n* fener
flask [flɑːsk] *n* cep matarası
flat [flæt] *adj* düz *(yassı)* ▷ *n* apartman dairesi; **studio flat** *n* stüdyo daire
flat-screen ['flætˌskriːn] *adj* düz ekran
flatter ['flætə] *v* pohpohlamak
flattered ['flætəd] *adj* pohpohlanmış
flavour ['fleɪvə] *n* lezzet
flavouring ['fleɪvərɪŋ] *n* lezzet katıcı
flaw [flɔː] *n* kusur
flea [fliː] *n* pire; **flea market** *n* bit pazarı
flee [fliː] *v* kaçmak
fleece [fliːs] *n* post
fleet [fliːt] *n* filo
flex [flɛks] *n* kablo
flexible ['flɛksɪbᵊl] *adj* esnek
flexitime ['flɛksɪˌtaɪm] *n* esnek çalışma saati
flight [flaɪt] *n* uçuş; **charter flight** *n* tarifesiz uçuş; **flight attendant** *n* uçuş hostesi; **scheduled flight** *n* tarifeli uçuş; **Are there any cheap flights?** Ucuz tarifeli uçuşunuz var mı?; **I'd like to cancel my**

flight Uçuşumu iptal ettirmek istiyorum; **I'd like to change my flight** Uçuşumu değiştirmek istiyorum; **The flight has been delayed** Uçuşunuz gecikmeli; **Which gate for the flight to...?...** uçağı hangi uçuş kapısında?
fling [flɪŋ] *v* savurmak
flip-flops ['flɪp'flɒpz] *npl* tokyo *(terlik)*
flippers ['flɪpəz] *npl* yüzgeç
flirt [flɜːt] *n* flört ▹ *v* flört etmek
float [fləʊt] *n* sal ▹ *v* yüzdürmek
flock [flɒk] *n* sürü
flood [flʌd] *n* sel ▹ *vi* su baskınına uğramak ▹ *vt/vi* su basmak
flooding ['flʌdɪŋ] *n* su basması
floodlight ['flʌd,laɪt] *n* projektör ışığı
floor [flɔː] *n* yer; **ground floor** *n* zemin kat
flop [flɒp] *n* fiyasko
floppy ['flɒpɪ] *adj* **floppy disk** *n* disket
flora ['flɔːrə] *npl* flora
florist ['flɒrɪst] *n* çiçekçi
flour ['flaʊə] *n* un
flow [fləʊ] *v* akmak
flower ['flaʊə] *n* çiçek ▹ *v* çiçek açmak
flu [fluː] *n* grip; **bird flu** *n* kuş gribi; **I had flu recently** Yakınlarda grip atlattım; **I've got flu** Grip geçiriyorum
fluent ['fluːənt] *adj* akıcı
fluorescent [,flʊə'rɛsᵊnt] *adj* floresan
flush [flʌʃ] *n* yüz kızarması ▹ *v* yüzü kızarmak
flute [fluːt] *n* flüt
fly [flaɪ] *n* sinek ▹ *v* uçmak
fly away [flaɪ ə'weɪ] *v* uçup gitmek
foal [fəʊl] *n* tay
foam [fəʊm] *n* **shaving foam** *n* traş köpüğü
focus ['fəʊkəs] *n* odak ▹ *v* odaklanmak
foetus ['fiːtəs] *n* cenin
fog [fɒg] *n* sis; **fog light** *n* sis lambası
foggy ['fɒgɪ] *adj* sisli
foil [fɔɪl] *n* folyo
fold [fəʊld] *n* kat *(giysi, kağıt vb)* ▹ *v* katlamak
folder ['fəʊldə] *n* dosya
folding [fəʊldɪŋ] *adj* katlanır
folklore ['fəʊk,lɔː] *n* folklor
follow ['fɒləʊ] *v* izlemek
following ['fɒləʊɪŋ] *adj* izleyen
food [fuːd] *n* yiyecek; **food poisoning** *n* gıda zehirlenmesi; **food processor** *n* mutfak robotu; **Do you have food?** Yiyecek satıyor musunuz?
fool [fuːl] *n* ahmak ▹ *v* kandırmak
foot, feet [fʊt, fiːt] *n* ayak; **My feet are a size six** Ayakkabı numaram altı
football ['fʊt,bɔːl] *n* futbol; **American football** *n* Amerikan futbolu; **football match** *n* futbol maçı; **football player** *n* futbolcu; **I'd like to see a football match** Futbol maçı görmek isterdim; **Let's play football** Futbol oynayalım
footballer ['fʊt,bɔːlə] *n* futbolcu
footpath ['fʊt,pɑːθ] *n* patika
footprint ['fʊt,prɪnt] *n* ayakizi

footstep ['fʊtˌstɛp] *n* adım
for [fɔː; fə] *prep* için; **Can I have a tape for this video camera, please?** Bu video kamera için teyp alabilir miyim?; **I want to hire a car for the weekend** Hafta sonu için bir araba kiralamak istiyorum; **I'd like to book a table for four people for tonight at eight o'clock** Bu akşam saat sekiz için dört kişilik bir masa ayırtmak istiyordum; **I'd like two tickets for tonight** Bu akşam için iki bilet almak istiyorum
forbid [fə'bɪd] *v* yasaklamak
forbidden [fə'bɪdᵊn] *adj* yasak
force [fɔːs] *n* güç *(kuvvet)* ▷ *v* zorlamak; **Air Force** *n* Hava Kuvvetleri
forecast ['fɔːˌkɑːst] *n* tahmin *(hava, borsa vb)*; **What's the weather forecast?** Hava tahmini nasıl?
foreground ['fɔːˌgraʊnd] *n* ön plan
forehead ['fɒrɪd; 'fɔːˌhɛd] *n* alın
foreign ['fɒrɪn] *adj* yabancı
foreigner ['fɒrɪnə] *n* yabancı
foresee [fɔː'siː] *v* öngörmek
forest ['fɒrɪst] *n* orman
forever [fɔː'rɛvə; fə-] *adv* ebediyen
forge [fɔːdʒ] *v* demir dövmek
forgery ['fɔːdʒərɪ] *n* sahte
forget [fə'gɛt] *v* unutmak
forgive [fə'gɪv] *v* bağışlamak
forgotten [fə'gɒtᵊn] *adj* unutulmuş
fork [fɔːk] *n* çatal; **Could I have a clean fork please?** Temiz bir çatal alabilir miyim lütfen?
form [fɔːm] *n* form; **application form** *n* başvuru formu; **order form** *n* sipariş formu
formal ['fɔːməl] *adj* resmi
formality [fɔː'mælɪtɪ] *n* formalite
format ['fɔːmæt] *n* format ▷ *v* formatlamak
former ['fɔːmə] *adj* eski *(önceki)*
formerly ['fɔːməlɪ] *adv* önceki
formula ['fɔːmjʊlə] *n* formül
fort [fɔːt] *n* hisar
fortnight ['fɔːtˌnaɪt] *n* iki hafta
fortunate ['fɔːtʃənɪt] *adj* şanslı
fortunately ['fɔːtʃənɪtlɪ] *adv* neyse ki
fortune ['fɔːtʃən] *n* servet
forty ['fɔːtɪ] *number* kırk
forward ['fɔːwəd] *adv* ileriye ▷ *v* iletlemek; **forward slash** *n* eğik çizgi; **lean forward** *v* öne eğilmek
foster ['fɒstə] *v* koruyucu aile olmak; **foster child** *n* koruyucu aile bakımındaki çocuk
foul [faʊl] *adj* kirli ▷ *n* faul
foundations [faʊn'deɪʃənz] *npl* vakıflar
fountain ['faʊntɪn] *n* çeşme; **fountain pen** *n* dolmakalem
four [fɔː] *number* dört
fourteen ['fɔː'tiːn] *number* ondört
fourteenth ['fɔː'tiːnθ] *adj* ondördüncü
fourth [fɔːθ] *adj* dördüncü
fox [fɒks] *n* tilki
fracture ['fræktʃə] *n* kırık
fragile ['frædʒaɪl] *adj* kırılgan
frail [freɪl] *adj* hastalıklı
frame [freɪm] *n* çerçeve; **picture frame** *n* resim çerçevesi; **Zimmer® frame** *n* yürüteç

France [frɑ:ns] *n* Fransa
frankly ['fræŋklɪ] *adv* içtenlikle
frantic ['fræntɪk] *adj* çılgın
fraud [frɔ:d] *n* dolandırıcılık *(sahte para vb)*
freckles ['frɛkᵊlz] *npl* çiller
free [fri:] *adj (no cost)* bedava, *(no restraint)* özgür ▷ *v* özgürlüğünü kavratmak; **free kick** *n* frikik
freedom ['fri:dəm] *n* özgürlük
freelance ['fri:ˌlɑ:ns] *adj* bağımsız ▷ *adv* bağımsız olarak
freeze [fri:z] *v* dondurmak
freezer ['fri:zə] *n* dondurucu *(derin)*
freezing ['fri:zɪŋ] *adj* dondurucu *(çok soğuk)*
freight [freɪt] *n* nakliye
French [frɛntʃ] *adj* Fransız ▷ *n* Fransız; **French beans** *npl* çalı fasulyesi; **French horn** *n* korno
Frenchman, Frenchmen ['frɛntʃmən, 'frɛntʃmɛn] *n* Fransız erkek
Frenchwoman, Frenchwomen ['frɛntʃwʊmən, 'frɛntʃˌwɪmɪn] *n* Fransız kadın
frequency ['fri:kwənsɪ] *n* sıklık
frequent ['fri:kwənt] *adj* sık; **How frequent are the buses to...?...** otobüsü ne sıklıkta geliyor?
fresh [frɛʃ] *adj* taze
freshen up ['frɛʃən ʌp] *v* ferahlamak
fret [frɛt] *v* endişe etmek
Friday ['fraɪdɪ] *n* Cuma; **Good Friday** *n* Kutsal Cuma; **on Friday the thirty first of December** Otuz bir Aralık Cuma günü; **on Friday** Cuma günü
fridge [frɪdʒ] *n* buzdolabı
fried [fraɪd] *adj* kızarmış
friend [frɛnd] *n* arkadaş; **I'm here with my friends** Arkadaşlarımla geldim
friendly ['frɛndlɪ] *adj* dostça
friendship ['frɛndʃɪp] *n* dostluk
fright [fraɪt] *n* korku
frighten ['fraɪtᵊn] *v* korkutmak
frightened ['fraɪtənd] *adj* korkmuş
frightening ['fraɪtᵊnɪŋ] *adj* ürkünç
fringe [frɪndʒ] *n* kahkül
frog [frɒg] *n* kurbağa
from [frɒm; frəm] *prep* den, dan; **How far are we from the beach?** Plajdan ne kadar uzaktayız?
front [frʌnt] *adj* ön ▷ *n* ön
frontier ['frʌntɪə; frʌn'tɪə] *n* cephe
frost [frɒst] *n* don *(hava)*
frosting ['frɒstɪŋ] *n* şekerli kek süsü
frosty ['frɒstɪ] *adj* buzlu
frown [fraʊn] *v* kaşlarını çatmak
frozen ['frəʊzᵊn] *adj* donmuş
fruit [fru:t] *n (botany)* meyve, *(collectively)* meyve; **fruit juice** *n* meyve suyu; **fruit machine** *n* slot makinesi; **fruit salad** *n* meyve salatası; **passion fruit** *n* çarkıfelek meyvası
frustrated [frʌ'streɪtɪd] *adj* engellenmiş
fry [fraɪ] *v* kızartmak; **frying pan** *n* kızartma tavası
fuel [fjʊəl] *n* yakıt
fulfil [fʊl'fɪl] *v* gerçekleştirmek
full [fʊl] *adj* dolu; **full moon** *n* dolunay; **full stop** *n* nokta

(gramer)
full-time ['fʊl,taɪm] *adj* tam gün ▷ *adv* tam gün
fully ['fʊlɪ] *adv* tam olarak
fumes [fjuːmz] *npl* duman *(pis kokulu)*; **exhaust fumes** *npl* egzos gazı
fun [fʌn] *adj* eğlendirici ▷ *n* eğlence
funds [fʌndz] *npl* parasal kaynak
funeral ['fjuːnərəl] *n* cenaze; **funeral parlour** *n* cenazenin gömülmeye ya da yakılmaya hazırlandığı oda
funfair ['fʌn,fɛə] *n* lunapark
funnel ['fʌnᵊl] *n* huni
funny ['fʌnɪ] *adj* komik
fur [fɜː] *n* kürk; **fur coat** *n* kürk *(giysi)*
furious ['fjʊərɪəs] *adj* öfkeden çıldırmış
furnished ['fɜːnɪʃt] *adj* mobilyalı
furniture ['fɜːnɪtʃə] *n* mobilya
further ['fɜːðə] *adj* daha ileri ▷ *adv* daha ileriye; **further education** *n* ileri eğitim
fuse [fjuːz] *n* sigorta *(elektrik)*; **fuse box** *n* sigorta kutusu; **A fuse has blown** Sigorta attı; **Can you mend a fuse?** Sigortayı tamir eder misiniz?
fuss [fʌs] *n* yaygara
fussy ['fʌsɪ] *adj* yaygaracı
future ['fjuːtʃə] *adj* gelecek ▷ *n* gelecek

g

Gabon [gə'bɒn] *n* Gabon
gain [geɪn] *n* kazanç ▷ *v* kazanmak
gale [geɪl] *n* şiddetli rüzgar
gallery ['gælərɪ] *n* galeri; **art gallery** *n* sanat galerisi
gallop ['gæləp] *n* dörtnala gidiş ▷ *v* dörtnala koşmak
gallstone ['gɔːl,stəʊn] *n* safra kesesi taşı
Gambia ['gæmbɪə] *n* Gambiya
gamble ['gæmbᵊl] *v* kumar oynamak
gambler ['gæmblə] *n* kumarcı
gambling ['gæmblɪŋ] *n* kumar
game [geɪm] *n* oyun; **board game** *n* aile oyunları; **games console** *n* oyun konsolu; **Can I play video games?** Oyun oynayabilir miyim?
gang [gæŋ] *n* çete
gangster ['gæŋstə] *n* gangster
gap [gæp] *n* gedik *(yer)*
garage ['gærɑːʒ; -rɪdʒ] *n* garaj;

Which is the key for the garage? Hangisi garaj anahtarı?
garbage ['gɑːbɪdʒ] *n* çöp
garden ['gɑːdᵊn] *n* bahçe; **garden centre** *n* bahçe merkezi; **Can we visit the gardens?** Bahçeleri gezebilir miyiz?
gardener ['gɑːdnə] *n* bahçıvan
gardening ['gɑːdᵊnɪŋ] *n* bahçecilik
garlic ['gɑːlɪk] *n* sarmısak; **Is there any garlic in it?** Bunda sarmısak var mı?
garment ['gɑːmənt] *n* giysi *(kıyafet)*
gas [gæs] *n* gaz; **gas cooker** *n* gazlı ocak; **natural gas** *n* doğal gaz; **I can smell gas** Gaz kokusu alıyorum; **Where is the gas meter?** Gaz sayacı nerede?
gasket ['gæskɪt] *n* conta
gate [geɪt] *n* kapı; **Please go to gate...** ... numaralı kapıya gidiniz; **Which gate for the flight to...?**... uçağı hangi uçuş kapısında?
gateau, gateaux ['gætəʊ, 'gætəʊz] *n* kremalı pasta
gather ['gæðə] *v* toplanmak
gauge [geɪdʒ] *n* ölçek ▷ *v* ölçmek
gaze [geɪz] *v* gözünü dikmek
gear [gɪə] *n (equipment)* vites, *(mechanism)* dişli; **gear lever** *n* vites kolu; **gear stick** *n* vites kolu; **Does the bike have gears?** Bisiklet vitesli mi?; **The gears don't work** Vitesler çalışmıyor
gearbox ['gɪəˌbɒks] *n* vites kutusu
gearshift ['gɪəˌʃɪft] *n* vites kolu
gel [dʒɛl] *n* jöle *(saç)*; **hair gel** *n* saç jölesi
gem [dʒɛm] *n* mücevher
Gemini ['dʒɛmɪˌnaɪ; -ˌniː] *n* İkizler burcu
gender ['dʒɛndə] *n* cinsiyet
gene [dʒiːn] *n* gen
general ['dʒɛnərəl; 'dʒɛnrəl] *adj* genel ▷ *n* genel; **general anaesthetic** *n* genel anestezi; **general election** *n* genel seçim; **general knowledge** *n* genel kültür
generalize ['dʒɛnrəˌlaɪz] *v* genellemek
generally ['dʒɛnrəlɪ] *adv* genellikle
generation [ˌdʒɛnə'reɪʃən] *n* kuşak *(jenerasyon)*
generator ['dʒɛnəˌreɪtə] *n* jeneratör
generosity [ˌdʒɛnə'rɒsɪtɪ] *n* cömertlik
generous ['dʒɛnərəs; 'dʒɛnrəs] *adj* cömert
genetic [dʒɪ'nɛtɪk] *adj* genetik
genetically-modified [dʒɪ'nɛtɪklɪ'mɒdɪˌfaɪd] *adj* genetik olarak değiştirilmiş
genetics [dʒɪ'nɛtɪks] *n* genetik bilimi
genius ['dʒiːnɪəs; -njəs] *n* dahi *(zeki)*
gentle ['dʒɛntᵊl] *adj* kibar
gentleman, gentlemen ['dʒɛntᵊlmən, 'dʒɛntᵊlmɛn] *n* centilmen
gently [dʒɛntlɪ] *adv* kibarca
gents' [dʒɛnts] *n* erkekler tuvaleti; **Where is the gents?** Erkekler tuvaleti nerede?
genuine ['dʒɛnjʊɪn] *adj* gerçek *(mücevher)*
geography [dʒɪ'ɒgrəfɪ] *n* coğrafya

geology [dʒɪ'ɒlədʒɪ] *n* jeoloji
Georgia ['dʒɔːdʒjə] *n (country)* Gürcistan, *(US state)* Georgia *(Amerikan eyaleti)*
Georgian ['dʒɔːdʒjən] *adj* Georgia'ya ait ▷ *n (inhabitant of Georgia)* Gürcü
geranium [dʒɪ'reɪnɪəm] *n* sardunya
gerbil ['dʒɜːbɪl] *n* çöl faresi
geriatric [ˌdʒɛrɪ'ætrɪk] *adj* yaşlılar ▷ *n* yaşlılık
germ [dʒɜːm] *n* mikrop
German ['dʒɜːmən] *adj* Alman ▷ *n (language)* Almanca *(dil)*, *(person)* Alman; **German measles** *n* kızamıkçık
Germany ['dʒɜːmənɪ] *n* Almanya
gesture ['dʒɛstʃə] *n* jest
get [gɛt] *v* almak, *(to a place)* almak
get away [gɛt ə'weɪ] *v* sıvışmak
get back [gɛt bæk] *v* geri getirmek
get in [gɛt ɪn] *v* mekana girmek
get into [gɛt 'ɪntə] *v* girmek
get off [gɛt ɒf] *v* inmek
get on [gɛt ɒn] *v* binmek
get out [gɛt aʊt] *v* çıkmak
get over [gɛt 'əʊvə] *v* toparlanmak
get together [gɛt tə'gɛðə] *v* bir araya gelmek
get up [gɛt ʌp] *v* kalkmak
Ghana ['gɑːnə] *n* Gana
Ghanaian [gɑː'neɪən] *adj* Gana ▷ *n* Ganalı
ghost [gəʊst] *n* hayalet
giant ['dʒaɪənt] *adj* dev gibi ▷ *n* dev
gift [gɪft] *n* armağan; **gift shop** *n* hediye dükkanı; **gift voucher** *n* hediye çeki; **This is a gift for you** Bu armağan sizin için
gifted ['gɪftɪd] *adj* yetenekli
gigantic [dʒaɪ'gæntɪk] *adj* devasa
giggle ['gɪgᵊl] *v* kıkırdamak
gin [dʒɪn] *n* cin *(alkol)*; **I'll have a gin and tonic, please** Ben bir cin tonik alayım lütfen
ginger ['dʒɪndʒə] *adj* kızılımsı sarı saçlı ▷ *n* zencefil
giraffe [dʒɪ'rɑːf; -'ræf] *n* zürafa
girl [gɜːl] *n* kız
girlfriend ['gɜːlˌfrɛnd] *n* kız arkadaş; **I have a girlfriend** Kız arkadaşım var
give [gɪv] *v* vermek
give back [gɪv bæk] *v* geri vermek
give in [gɪv ɪn] *v* yenilgiyi kabullenmek
give out [gɪv aʊt] *v* dağıtmak *(vermek)*
give up [gɪv ʌp] *v* vazgeçmek
glacier ['glæsɪə; 'gleɪs-] *n* buzul
glad [glæd] *adj* memnun
glamorous ['glæmərəs] *adj* göz kamaştırıcı
glance [glɑːns] *n* bakış ▷ *v* gözatmak
gland [glænd] *n* beze
glare [glɛə] *v* öfkeyle bakmak
glaring ['glɛərɪŋ] *adj* bariz
glass [glɑːs] *n* cam, *(vessel)* cam bardak; **magnifying glass** *n* büyüteç; **stained glass** *n* vitray
glasses ['glɑːsɪz] *npl* gözlük; **Can you repair my glasses?** Gözlüklerimi tamir edebilir misiniz?
glazing ['gleɪzɪŋ] *n* **double glazing** *n* çift cam
glider ['glaɪdə] *n* planör
gliding ['glaɪdɪŋ] *n* planörle uçma

global ['glǝʊbᵊl] *adj* küresel; **global warming** *n* küresel ısınma
globalization [ˌglǝʊbᵊlaɪ'zeɪʃǝn] *n* küreselleşme
globe [glǝʊb] *n* yerküre
gloomy ['glu:mɪ] *adj* kasvetli
glorious ['glɔ:rɪǝs] *adj* görkemli
glory ['glɔ:rɪ] *n* zafer
glove [glʌv] *n* eldiven; **glove compartment** *n* torpido gözü; **oven glove** *n* fırın eldiveni; **rubber gloves** *npl* lastik eldiven
glucose ['glu:kǝʊz; -kǝʊs] *n* glükoz
glue [glu:] *n* tutkal ▷ *v* yapıştırmak
gluten ['glu:tᵊn] *n* glüten
GM [dʒi: ɛm] *abbr* GM
go [gǝʊ] *v* gitmek; **I'd like to go home** Eve gitmek istiyorum; **I'm going to...** ... a gitmek istiyorum; **We'd like to go to...** ... a gitmek istiyorduk
go after [gǝʊ 'ɑ:ftǝ] *v* çabalamak
go ahead [gǝʊ ǝ'hɛd] *v* önden gitmek
goal [gǝʊl] *n* gol
goalkeeper ['gǝʊlˌki:pǝ] *n* kaleci
goat [gǝʊt] *n* keçi
go away [gǝʊ ǝ'weɪ] *v* yola çıkmak
go back [gǝʊ bæk] *v* dönmek
go by [gǝʊ baɪ] *v* geçmek
god [gɒd] *n* tanrı
godchild, godchildren ['gɒdˌtʃaɪld, 'gɒdˌtʃɪldrǝn] *n* vaftiz çocuğu
goddaughter ['gɒdˌdɔ:tǝ] *n* vaftiz kızı
godfather ['gɒdˌfɑ:ðǝ] *n* *(baptism)* isim babası *(vaftiz)*, *(criminal leader)* baba *(mafya)*
godmother ['gɒdˌmʌðǝ] *n* isim annesi
go down [gǝʊ daʊn] *v* azalmak
godson ['gɒdˌsʌn] *n* vaftiz oğlu
goggles ['gɒgᵊlz] *npl* koruma gözlüğü
go in [gǝʊ ɪn] *v* girmek *(içeriye)*
gold [gǝʊld] *n* altın *(metal)*
golden ['gǝʊldǝn] *adj* altın *(metal)*
goldfish ['gǝʊldˌfɪʃ] *n* Japon balığı
gold-plated ['gǝʊld'pleɪtɪd] *adj* altın kaplama
golf [gɒlf] *n* golf; **golf club** *n* *(stick)* golf sopası, *(society)* golf klübü; **golf course** *n* golf sahası; **Do they hire out golf clubs?** Golf sopaları kiralıyorlar mı?; **Is there a public golf course near here?** Buraya yakın bir golf sahası var mı?; **Where can I play golf?** Nerede golf oynayabilirim?
gone [gɒn] *adj* geçmiş
good [gʊd] *adj* iyi
goodbye [ˌgʊd'baɪ] *excl* hoşçakal!
good-looking ['gʊd'lʊkɪŋ] *adj* yakışıklı
good-natured ['gʊd'neɪtʃǝd] *adj* iyi huylu
goods [gʊdz] *npl* mallar
go off [gǝʊ ɒf] *v* kapamak
Google® ['gu:gᵊl] *v* Google®
go on [gǝʊ ɒn] *v* devam etmek
goose, geese [gu:s, gi:s] *n* kaz; **goose pimples** *npl* diken diken olmuş tüyler
gooseberry ['gʊzbǝrɪ; -brɪ] *n* bektaşi üzümü
go out [gǝʊ aʊt] *v* dışarı çıkmak
go past [gǝʊ pɑ:st] *v* yanından geçmek

gorgeous ['gɔːdʒəs] *adj* çok güzel
gorilla [gəˈrɪlə] *n* goril
go round [gəʊ raʊnd] *v* idare etmek
gospel ['gɒspᵊl] *n* incil
gossip ['gɒsɪp] *n* dedikodu ▷ *v* dedikodu yapmak
go through [gəʊ θruː] *v* geçirmek
go up [gəʊ ʌp] *v* yükselmek
government ['gʌvənmənt; 'gʌvəmənt] *n* hükümet
gown [gaʊn] *n* **dressing gown** *n* sabahlık
GP [dʒiː piː] *abbr* pratisyen hekim
GPS [dʒiː piː ɛs] *abbr* GPS sistemi
grab [græb] *v* kavramak
graceful ['greɪsfʊl] *adj* zarif
grade [greɪd] *n* derece *(düzey)*
gradual ['grædjʊəl] *adj* derece derece
gradually ['grædjʊəlɪ] *adv* adım adım
graduate ['grædjʊɪt] *n* üniversite mezunu
graduation [ˌgrædjʊ'eɪʃən] *n* mezuniyet
graffiti, graffito [græ'fiːtiː, græ'fiːtəʊ] *npl* grafiti
grain [greɪn] *n* tahıl tanesi
grammar ['græmə] *n* gramer
grammatical [grə'mætɪkᵊl] *adj* gramatik
gramme [græm] *n* gram
grand [grænd] *adj* gösterişli
grandchild ['grænˌtʃaɪld] *n* torun; **grandchildren** *npl* torunlar
granddad ['grænˌdæd] *n* dede
granddaughter ['grænˌdɔːtə] *n* kız torun
grandfather ['grænˌfɑːðə] *n* dede
grandma ['grænˌmɑː] *n* nine
grandmother ['grænˌmʌðə] *n* büyükanne
grandpa ['grænˌpɑː] *n* dede
grandparents ['grænˌpɛərəntz] *npl* büyükanne ve büyükbaba
grandson ['grænsʌn; 'grænd-] *n* erkek torun
granite ['grænɪt] *n* granit
granny ['grænɪ] *n* nine
grant [grɑːnt] *n* fon *(destek)*
grape [greɪp] *n* üzüm
grapefruit ['greɪpˌfruːt] *n* greyfurt
graph [grɑːf; græf] *n* grafik
graphics ['græfɪks] *npl* grafik
grasp [grɑːsp] *v* kavramak
grass [grɑːs] *n* *(informer)* muhbir, *(marijuana)* ot *(esrar)*, *(plant)* ot
grasshopper ['grɑːsˌhɒpə] *n* çekirge
grate [greɪt] *v* rendelemek
grateful ['greɪtfʊl] *adj* müteşekkir
grave [greɪv] *n* mezar
gravel ['grævᵊl] *n* çakıl
gravestone ['greɪvˌstəʊn] *n* mezar taşı
graveyard ['greɪvˌjɑːd] *n* mezarlık
gravy ['greɪvɪ] *n* et sosu
grease [griːs] *n* yağ
greasy ['griːzɪ; -sɪ] *adj* yağlı
great [greɪt] *adj* büyük *(müthiş)*
Great Britain ['greɪt 'brɪtᵊn] *n* İngiltere
great-grandfather ['greɪt'grænˌfɑːðə] *n* dedenin babası
great-grandmother ['greɪt'grænˌmʌðə] *n* ninenin annesi
Greece [griːs] *n* Yunanistan

greedy ['gri:dɪ] *adj* açgözlü
Greek [gri:k] *adj* Yunan ▹ *n* *(language)* Yunanca *(dil)*, *(person)* Yunanlı *(kişi)*
green [gri:n] *adj* *(colour)* yeşil, *(inexperienced)* acemi ▹ *n* yeşil; **green salad** *n* yeşil salata
greengrocer's ['gri:n,grəʊsəz] *n* manav
greenhouse ['gri:n,haʊs] *n* sera
Greenland ['gri:nlənd] *n* Grönland
greet [gri:t] *v* selamlamak
greeting ['gri:tɪŋ] *n* selamlaşma; **greetings card** *n* tebrik kartı
grey [greɪ] *adj* gri
grey-haired [,greɪ'hɛəd] *adj* beyaz saçlı
grid [grɪd] *n* ızgara
grief [gri:f] *n* keder
grill [grɪl] *n* ızgara ▹ *v* ızgara yapmak
grilled [grɪld] *adj* ızgarada
grim [grɪm] *adj* tatsız
grin [grɪn] *n* sırıtış ▹ *v* sırıtmak
grind [graɪnd] *v* öğütmek
grip [grɪp] *v* sımsıkı kavramak
gripping [grɪpɪŋ] *adj* sürükleyici
grit [grɪt] *n* kum
groan [grəʊn] *v* inlemek
grocer ['grəʊsə] *n* bakkal
groceries ['grəʊsərɪz] *npl* yiyecek maddeleri
grocer's ['grəʊsəz] *n* bakkal *(dükkan)*
groom [gru:m; grʊm] *n* seyis, *(bridegroom)* damat *(gelinin kocası)*
grope [grəʊp] *v* elle yoklamak
gross [grəʊs] *adj* *(fat)* şişko, *(income etc.)* hantal
grossly [grəʊslɪ] *adv* kabaca
ground [graʊnd] *n* yer ▹ *v* yere indirmek; **ground floor** *n* zemin kat
group [gru:p] *n* grup; **Are there any reductions for groups?** Grup indirimi var mı?
grouse [graʊs] *n* *(complaint)* şikayet, *(game bird)* orman tavuğu
grow [grəʊ] *vi* büyümek ▹ *vt* bitki yetiştirmek
growl [graʊl] *v* hırlamak
grown-up [grəʊnʌp] *n* erişkin
growth [grəʊθ] *n* büyüme
grow up [grəʊ ʌp] *v* büyümek
grub [grʌb] *n* kurtçuk
grudge [grʌdʒ] *n* kin
gruesome ['gru:səm] *adj* tüyler ürpertici
grumpy ['grʌmpɪ] *adj* huysuz
guarantee [,gærən'ti:] *n* garanti ▹ *v* garanti etmek; **It's still under guarantee** Hala garantisi var
guard [gɑ:d] *n* nöbetçi ▹ *v* korumak; **security guard** *n* güvenlik görevlisi
Guatemala [,gwɑ:tə'mɑ:lə] *n* Guatemala
guess [gɛs] *n* tahmin ▹ *v* sezmek
guest [gɛst] *n* konuk
guesthouse ['gɛst,haʊs] *n* konukevi
guide [gaɪd] *n* rehber *(turizm)* ▹ *v* rehber *(turizm)*; **guide dog** *n* rehber köpek; **guided tour** *n* rehberli tur; **tour guide** *n* tur rehberi; **Can you guide me, please?** Bana rehberlik eder misiniz lütfen; **Do you have a**

guide to local walks? Yerel yürüyüşler için rehberiniz var mı?; **I have a guide dog** Rehber köpeğim var; **Is there a guide who speaks English?** İngilizce konuşan bir rehber var mı?
guidebook ['gaɪdˌbʊk] *n* rehber *(kılavuz)*
guilt [gɪlt] *n* suçluluk
guilty ['gɪltɪ] *adj* suçlu
Guinea ['gɪnɪ] *n* Gine; **guinea pig** *n* *(for experiment)* kobay, *(rodent)* kobay faresi
guitar [gɪ'tɑː] *n* gitar
gum [gʌm] *n* sakız; **chewing gum** *n* çiklet
gun [gʌn] *n* silah; **machine gun** *n* makineli tüfek
gust [gʌst] *n* ani rüzgar
gut [gʌt] *n* bağırsak
guy [gaɪ] *n* adam
Guyana [gaɪ'ænə] *n* Güyan
gym [dʒɪm] *n* jimnastik salonu
gymnast ['dʒɪmnæst] *n* jimnastikçi
gymnastics [dʒɪm'næstɪks] *npl* jimnastik
gynaecologist [ˌgaɪnɪ'kɒlədʒɪst] *n* jinekolog
gypsy ['dʒɪpsɪ] *n* çingene

habit ['hæbɪt] *n* alışkanlık
hack [hæk] *v* doğramak
hacker ['hækə] *n* hacker
haddock ['hædək] *n* mezgit balığı
haemorrhoids ['hɛməˌrɔɪdz] *npl* hemoroid
haggle ['hægᵊl] *v* pazarlık etmek
hail [heɪl] *n* dolu *(hava)* ▷ *v* dolu yağmak
hair [hɛə] *n* saç; **hair gel** *n* saç jölesi; **hair spray** *n* saç spreyi; **Can you dye my hair, please?** Saçımı boyar mısınız lütfen?; **Can you straighten my hair?** Saçımı düzleştirebilir misiniz?; **I have greasy hair** Saçım yağlı; **I need a hair dryer** Saç kurutma makinesine ihtiyacım var; **My hair is naturally straight** Saçım doğuştan düz; **My hair is permed** Saçım permalı; **What do you recommend for my hair?** Saçıma

ne tavsiye edersiniz?
hairband ['hɛə,bænd] *n* saç bandı
hairbrush ['hɛə,brʌʃ] *n* saç fırçası
haircut ['hɛə,kʌt] *n* saç kestirme
hairdo ['hɛə,du:] *n* saç modeli
hairdresser ['hɛə,drɛsə] *n* kuaför
hairdresser's ['hɛə,drɛsəz] *n* kuaför
hairdryer ['hɛə,draɪə] *n* saç kurutma makinesi
hairgrip ['hɛə,grɪp] *n* saç tokası
hairstyle ['hɛə,staɪl] *n* saç modeli
hairy ['hɛərɪ] *adj* kıllı
Haiti ['heɪtɪ; hɑ:'i:tɪ] *n* Haiti
half [hɑ:f] *adj* yarım ▹ *adv* yarı yarıya ▹ *n* yarım; **half board** *n* kahvaltı ve akşam yemeği dahil
half-hour ['hɑ:f,aʊə] *n* yarım saat
half-price ['hɑ:f,praɪs] *adj* yarı fiyatı ▹ *adv* yarı fiyatına
half-term ['hɑ:f,tɜ:m] *n* sömestr tatili
half-time ['hɑ:f,taɪm] *n* devre arası
halfway [,hɑ:f'weɪ] *adv* yarı yolda
hall [hɔ:l] *n* salon; **town hall** *n* belediye binası
hallway ['hɔ:l,weɪ] *n* antre
halt [hɔ:lt] *n* duraksama
ham [hæm] *n* jambon
hamburger ['hæm,bɜ:gə] *n* hamburger
hammer ['hæmə] *n* çekiç
hammock ['hæmək] *n* hamak
hamster ['hæmstə] *n* hamster
hand [hænd] *n* el ▹ *v* vermek; **hand luggage** *n* el bagajı; **Where can I wash my hands?** Ellerimi nerede yıkayabilirim?
handbag ['hænd,bæg] *n* çanta
handball ['hænd,bɔ:l] *n* hentbol
handbook ['hænd,bʊk] *n* referans kitabı
handbrake ['hænd,breɪk] *n* el freni
handcuffs ['hænd,kʌfs] *npl* kelepçe
handicap ['hændɪ,kæp] *n* handikap
handicapped ['hændɪ,kæpt] *adj* özürlü
handkerchief ['hæŋkətʃɪf; -tʃi:f] *n* mendil
handle ['hændᵊl] *n* kol ▹ *v* elle yapmak; **The door handle has come off** Kapının kolu çıktı
handlebars ['hændᵊl,bɑ:z] *npl* gidon
handmade [,hænd'meɪd] *adj* el yapımı; **Is this handmade?** Bu el yapımı mı?
hands-free ['hændz,fri:] *adj* handsfree; **hands-free kit** *n* handsfree set
handsome ['hændsəm] *adj* yakışıklı
handwriting ['hænd,raɪtɪŋ] *n* el yazısı
handy ['hændɪ] *adj* el altında
hang [hæŋ] *vi* asılmak ▹ *vt* asmak
hanger ['hæŋə] *n* askı
hang-gliding ['hæŋ'glaɪdɪŋ] *n* hang-gliding; **I'd like to go hang-gliding** Hang-gliding yapmak isterdim
hang on [hæŋ ɒn] *v* sabretmek
hangover ['hæŋ,əʊvə] *n* akşamdan kalma
hang up [hæŋ ʌp] *v* telefonu kapatmak

hankie ['hæŋkɪ] *n* mendil
happen ['hæpᵊn] *v* olmak
happily ['hæpɪlɪ] *adv* seve seve
happiness ['hæpɪnɪs] *n* mutluluk
happy ['hæpɪ] *adj* mutlu; **Happy New Year!** Mutlu Yıllar!
harassment ['hærəsmənt] *n* taciz
harbour ['hɑːbə] *n* liman
hard [hɑːd] *adj (difficult)* zor, *(firm, rigid)* sert ▷ *adv* zor; **hard disk** *n* bilgisayar hafızası; **hard shoulder** *n* dönemeç
hardboard ['hɑːd,bɔːd] *n* mukavva
hardly ['hɑːdlɪ] *adv* güçlükle
hard up [hɑːd ʌp] *adj* yoksul
hardware ['hɑːd,wɛə] *n* hırdavat
hare [hɛə] *n* yabani tavşan
harm [hɑːm] *v* zarar vermek
harmful ['hɑːmfʊl] *adj* zararlı
harmless ['hɑːmlɪs] *adj* zararsız
harp [hɑːp] *n* harp *(müzik)*
harsh [hɑːʃ] *adj* şiddetli
harvest ['hɑːvɪst] *n* hasat ▷ *v* hasat kaldırmak
hastily [heɪstɪlɪ] *adv* telaşla
hat [hæt] *n* şapka
hatchback ['hætʃ,bæk] *n* hatchback
hate [heɪt] *v* nefret etmek
hatred ['heɪtrɪd] *n* nefret
haunted ['hɔːntɪd] *adj* perili
have [hæv] *v* sahip olmak
have to [hæv tʊ] *v* yapmak zorunda olmak
hawthorn ['hɔː,θɔːn] *n* akdiken
hay [heɪ] *n* saman; **hay fever** *n* saman nezlesi
haystack ['heɪ,stæk] *n* saman yığını
hazelnut ['heɪzᵊl,nʌt] *n* fındık
he [hiː] *pron* o *(erkek)*
head [hɛd] *n (body part)* baş *(vücut)*, *(principal)* baş *(yönetim)* ▷ *v* başı çekmek; **deputy head** *n* müdür yardımcısı; **head office** *n* yönetim merkezi
headache ['hɛd,eɪk] *n* baş ağrısı; **I'd like something for a headache** Baş ağrısı için bir şey rica ediyorum
headlamp ['hɛd,læmp] *n* ön lamba
headlight ['hɛd,laɪt] *n* ön lamba
headline ['hɛd,laɪn] *n* başlık *(haber)*
headphones ['hɛd,fəʊnz] *npl* kulaklık; **Does it have headphones?** Kulaklık var mı?
headquarters [,hɛd'kwɔːtəz] *npl* merkez
headroom ['hɛd,rʊm; -,ruːm] *n* boşluk payı *(tavanda)*
headscarf, headscarves ['hɛd,skɑːf, 'hɛd,skɑːvz] *n* eşarp
headteacher ['hɛd,tiːtʃə] *n* müdür
heal [hiːl] *v* iyileşmek
health [hɛlθ] *n* sağlık; **I don't have health insurance** Sağlık sigortam yok; **I have private health insurance** Özel sağlık sigortam var
healthy ['hɛlθɪ] *adj* sağlıklı
heap [hiːp] *n* yığın
hear [hɪə] *v* işitmek
hearing ['hɪərɪŋ] *n* işitme; **hearing aid** *n* işitme cihazı
heart [hɑːt] *n* kalp; **heart attack** *n* kalp krizi; **I have a heart condition** Kalp hastasıyım

heartbroken ['hɑːtˌbrəʊkən] *adj* kalbi kırık
heartburn ['hɑːtˌbɜːn] *n* mide ekşimesi
heat [hiːt] *n* ısı ▷ *v* ısıtmak
heater ['hiːtə] *n* ısıtıcı
heather ['hɛðə] *n* süpürge otu
heating ['hiːtɪŋ] *n* ısıtma; **central heating** *n* merkezi ısıtma
heat up [hiːt ʌp] *v* kızışmak
heaven ['hɛvᵊn] *n* cennet
heavily ['hɛvɪlɪ] *adv* ağır bir şekilde
heavy ['hɛvɪ] *adj* ağır; **This is too heavy** Bu çok ağır
hedge [hɛdʒ] *n* çit *(çalılık)*
hedgehog ['hɛdʒˌhɒg] *n* kirpi
heel [hiːl] *n* topuk; **high heels** *npl* yüksek topuklar
height [haɪt] *n* yükseklik
heir [ɛə] *n* varis
heiress ['ɛərɪs] *n* varis *(kadın)*
helicopter ['hɛlɪˌkɒptə] *n* helikopter
hell [hɛl] *n* cehennem
hello [hɛ'ləʊ] *excl* merhaba!
helmet ['hɛlmɪt] *n* kask *(motosiklet)*; **Can I have a helmet?** Kask alabilir miyim?
help [hɛlp] *n* yardım ▷ *v* yardım etmek; **Can you help me?** Yardımcı olabilir misiniz?; **Fetch help quickly!** Yardım çağırın, çabuk!
helpful ['hɛlpfʊl] *adj* yardımcı
helpline ['hɛlpˌlaɪn] *n* yardım hattı
hen [hɛn] *n* tavuk; **hen night** *n* kına gecesi
hepatitis [ˌhɛpə'taɪtɪs] *n* karaciğer iltihabı
her [hɜː; hə; ə] *pron* onu, ona *(kadın)*
herbs [hɜːbz] *npl* kokulu otlar
herd [hɜːd] *n* sürü
here [hɪə] *adv* burada
hereditary [hɪ'rɛdɪtərɪ; -trɪ] *adj* kalıtsal
heritage ['hɛrɪtɪdʒ] *n* miras
hernia ['hɜːnɪə] *n* fıtık
hero ['hɪərəʊ] *n* kahraman
heroin ['hɛrəʊɪn] *n* eroin
heroine ['hɛrəʊɪn] *n* kadın kahraman
heron ['hɛrən] *n* balıkçıl kuşu
herring ['hɛrɪŋ] *n* ringa balığı
hers [hɜːz] *pron* onunki *(kadın)*
herself [hə'sɛlf] *pron* kendisi *(kadın)*
hesitate ['hɛzɪˌteɪt] *v* duraksamak
heterosexual [ˌhɛtərəʊ'sɛksjʊəl] *adj* heteroseksüel
HGV [eɪtʃ dʒiː viː] *abbr* ağır yük taşıma aracı
hi [haɪ] *excl* selam!
hiccups ['hɪkʌps] *npl* hıçkırık
hidden ['hɪdᵊn] *adj* saklı
hide [haɪd] *vi* saklamak
hide-and-seek [ˌhaɪdænd'siːk] *n* saklambaç
hideous ['hɪdɪəs] *adj* itici
hifi ['haɪ'faɪ] *n* hi-fi
high [haɪ] *adj* yüksek ▷ *adv* yüksekte; **high heels** *npl* yüksek topuklar; **high jump** *n* yüksek atlama; **high season** *n* pahalı sezon; **How high is it?** Yüksekliği ne kadar?
highchair ['haɪˌtʃɛə] *n* bebe sandalyesi
high-heeled ['haɪˌhiːld] *adj* yüksek topuklu

highlight ['haɪ,laɪt] *n* önemli olay ▷ *v* vurgulamak
highlighter ['haɪ,laɪtə] *n* marker
high-rise ['haɪ,raɪz] *n* gökdelen
hijack ['haɪ,dʒæk] *v* gaspetmek
hijacker ['haɪ,dʒækə] *n* korsan *(uçak/hava)*
hike [haɪk] *n* yürüyüşe çıkma
hiking [haɪkɪŋ] *n* yürüyüş
hilarious [hɪ'lɛərɪəs] *adj* çok komik
hill [hɪl] *n* tepe *(coğrafya)*; **I'd like to go hill walking** Tepelere yürüyüşe çıkmak isterim
hill-walking ['hɪl,wɔːkɪŋ] *n* tepelere tırmanma
him [hɪm; ɪm] *pron* onu, ona *(erkek)*
himself [hɪm'sɛlf; ɪm'sɛlf] *pron* kendisi *(erkek)*
Hindu ['hɪnduː; hɪn'duː] *adj* Hindu ▷ *n* Hindu
Hinduism ['hɪndʊ,ɪzəm] *n* Hinduizm
hinge [hɪndʒ] *n* menteşe
hint [hɪnt] *n* ima ▷ *v* imada bulunmak
hip [hɪp] *n* kalça
hippie ['hɪpɪ] *n* hippi
hippo ['hɪpəʊ] *n* hipopotam
hippopotamus, hippopotami [,hɪpə'pɒtəməs, ,hɪpə'pɒtəmaɪ] *n* hipopotam
hire ['haɪə] *n* kiralama ▷ *v* kiralamak; **car hire** *n* araba kiralama; **hire car** *n* kiralık araba; **How much is it to hire a tennis court?** Tenis kortu kiralamak kaça?; **I want to hire a bike** Bisiklet kiralamak istiyorum; **I want to hire a car for five days** Beş günlüğüne bir araba kiralamak istiyorum; **I'd like to hire...** ... kiralamak istiyorum
his [hɪz; ɪz] *adj* onun *(erkek)* ▷ *pron* onun *(erkek)*
historian [hɪ'stɔːrɪən] *n* tarihçi
historical [hɪ'stɒrɪkᵊl] *adj* tarihi
history ['hɪstərɪ; 'hɪstrɪ] *n* tarih *(geçmiş, ders)*
hit [hɪt] *n* çarpma ▷ *v* vurmak
hitch [hɪtʃ] *n* ufak sorun
hitchhike ['hɪtʃ,haɪk] *v* otostop
hitchhiker ['hɪtʃ,haɪkə] *n* otostopçu
hitchhiking ['hɪtʃ,haɪkɪŋ] *n* otostop yapma
HIV-negative [eɪtʃ aɪ viː 'nɛgətɪv] *adj* HIV'li olmayan
HIV-positive [eɪtʃ aɪ viː 'pɒzɪtɪv] *adj* HIV'li
hobby ['hɒbɪ] *n* hobi
hockey ['hɒkɪ] *n* hokey; **ice hockey** *n* buz hokeyi
hold [həʊld] *v* tutmak
holdall ['həʊld,ɔːl] *n* sırt çantası
hold on [həʊld ɒn] *v* tutunmak
hold up [həʊld ʌp] *v* kaldırmak
hold-up [həʊldʌp] *n* soygun
hole [həʊl] *n* delik *(çorap, duvar vb)*; **I have a hole in my shoe** Ayakkabımda delik var
holiday ['hɒlɪ,deɪ; -dɪ] *n* tatil; **activity holiday** *n* aktivite tatili; **bank holiday** *n* İngiltere'de bankaların kapalı olduğu tatil günü; **holiday home** *n* tatil evi; **holiday job** *n* yazlık iş; **package holiday** *n* paket tatil; **public holiday** *n* resmi tatil günü; **Enjoy**

your holiday! İyi tatiller!; **I'm here on holiday** Burada tatildeyim
Holland [ˈhɒlənd] *n* Hollanda
hollow [ˈhɒləʊ] *adj* oyuk
holly [ˈhɒlɪ] *n* çoban püskülü
holy [ˈhəʊlɪ] *adj* kutsal
home [həʊm] *adv* evde ▹ *n* ev; **home address** *n* ev adresi; **home match** *n* kendi sahasında maç; **home page** *n* açılış sayfası; **mobile home** *n* taşınabilir ev; **nursing home** *n* huzurevi *(yaşlılar için)*; **stately home** *n* malikane; **I'd like to go home** Eve gitmek istiyorum; **Please come home by 11p.m.** Akşam saat on bire kadar evde olun lütfen; **When do you go home?** Eve ne zaman gideceksiniz?; **Would you like to phone home?** Evi aramak ister misiniz?
homeland [ˈhəʊmˌlænd] *n* anavatan
homeless [ˈhəʊmlɪs] *adj* evsiz
home-made [ˈhəʊmˈmeɪd] *adj* ev yapımı
homeopathic [ˌhəʊmɪˈɒpæθɪk] *adj* homeopatik
homeopathy [ˌhəʊmɪˈɒpəθɪ] *n* homeopati
homesick [ˈhəʊmˌsɪk] *adj* sıla acısı çeken
homework [ˈhəʊmˌwɜːk] *n* ev ödevi
Honduras [hɒnˈdjʊərəs] *n* Honduras
honest [ˈɒnɪst] *adj* dürüst
honestly [ˈɒnɪstlɪ] *adv* dürüstçe
honesty [ˈɒnɪstɪ] *n* dürüstlük
honey [ˈhʌnɪ] *n* bal
honeymoon [ˈhʌnɪˌmuːn] *n* balayı; **We are on our honeymoon** Balayındayız
honeysuckle [ˈhʌnɪˌsʌkəl] *n* hanımeli
honour [ˈɒnə] *n* onur *(şeref)*
hood [hʊd] *n* kapüşon
hook [hʊk] *n* kanca
hooray [huːˈreɪ] *excl* hurra!
Hoover® [ˈhuːvə] *n* elektrik süpürgesi; **hoover** *v* süpürmek *(elektrikli süpürgeyle)*
hope [həʊp] *n* umut ▹ *v* umut etmek
hopeful [ˈhəʊpfʊl] *adj* umutlu
hopefully [ˈhəʊpfʊlɪ] *adv* umutla
hopeless [ˈhəʊplɪs] *adj* umutsuz
horizon [həˈraɪzən] *n* ufuk
horizontal [ˌhɒrɪˈzɒntəl] *adj* yatay
hormone [ˈhɔːməʊn] *n* hormon
horn [hɔːn] *n* boynuz; **French horn** *n* korno
horoscope [ˈhɒrəˌskəʊp] *n* yıldız falı
horrendous [hɒˈrɛndəs] *adj* korkunç
horrible [ˈhɒrəbəl] *adj* korkunç
horrifying [ˈhɒrɪˌfaɪɪŋ] *adj* dehşet verici
horror [ˈhɒrə] *n* dehşet; **horror film** *n* korku filmi
horse [hɔːs] *n* at *(hayvan)*; **horse racing** *n* at yarışı; **horse riding** *n* binicilik; **rocking horse** *n* sallanan at; **Can we go horse riding?** Ata binebilir miyiz?; **I'd like to see a horse race** At yarışı görmek isterdim; **Let's go horse riding** Ata binmeye gidelim

horseradish ['hɔːsˌrædɪʃ] *n* yabanturpu
horseshoe ['hɔːsˌʃuː] *n* at nalı
hose [həʊz] *n* hortum
hosepipe ['həʊzˌpaɪp] *n* hortum
hospital ['hɒspɪtᵊl] *n* hastane; **maternity hospital** *n* doğum hastanesi; **mental hospital** *n* akıl hastanesi; **How do I get to the hospital?** Hastaneye nasıl gidebilirim?; **I work in a hospital** Hastanede çalışıyorum; **We must get him to hospital** Hastaneye götürmemiz gerek; **Where is the hospital?** Hastane nerede?; **Will he have to go to hospital?** Hastaneye gitmesi gerekiyor mu?
hospitality [ˌhɒspɪ'tælɪtɪ] *n* konukseverlik
host [həʊst] *n (entertains)* ev sahibi, *(multitude)* kalabalık
hostage ['hɒstɪdʒ] *n* rehine
hostel ['hɒstᵊl] *n* öğrenci yurdu
hostess ['həʊstɪs] *n* **air hostess** *n* hostes
hostile ['hɒstaɪl] *adj* düşmanca
hot [hɒt] *adj* sıcak; **hot dog** *n* sosisli sandviç; **I'm too hot** Çok sıcakladım; **It's very hot** Çok sıcak; **The food is too hot** Yemek çok sıcak; **The room is too hot** Oda çok sıcak
hotel [həʊ'tɛl] *n* otel; **Can you book me into a hotel?** Bana bir otelde yer ayırtabilir misiniz?; **Can you recommend a hotel?** Bir otel tavsiye edebilir misiniz?; **He runs the hotel** Oteli yönetiyor; **I'm staying at a hotel** Otelde kalıyorum; **Is your hotel accessible to wheelchairs?** Otelinizde tekerlekli sandalye girişi var mı?; **We're looking for a hotel** Bir otel arıyoruz; **What's the best way to get to this hotel?** Şu otele en kolay nasıl gidebilirim?
hour [aʊə] *n* saat *(zaman)*; **office hours** *npl* çalışma saatleri; **opening hours** *npl* açılış saatleri; **peak hours** *npl* sıkışık saat; **rush hour** *n* sıkışık saatler; **visiting hours** *npl* ziyaret saatleri; **How much is it per hour?** Saati ne kadar?; **The journey takes two hours** Yolculuk iki saat sürüyor; **When are visiting hours?** Ziyaret saatleri nedir?
hourly ['aʊəlɪ] *adj* saat başı ▷ *adv* saat başı
house [haʊs] *n* ev; **council house** *n* sosyal konut; **detached house** *n* müstakil ev; **semi-detached house** *n* bitişik nizam ev; **Do we have to clean the house before we leave?** Ayrılmadan önce evi temizlememiz gerekiyor mu?
household ['haʊsˌhəʊld] *n* hane halkı
housewife, housewives ['haʊsˌwaɪf, 'haʊsˌwaɪvz] *n* evkadını
housework ['haʊsˌwɜːk] *n* ev işi
hovercraft ['hɒvəˌkrɑːft] *n* hoverkraft
how [haʊ] *adv* nasıl; **Do you know how to do this?** Bunun nasıl yapıldığını biliyor musunuz?; **How are you?** Nasılsınız?; **How do I get to...?**... na nasıl gidebilirim?; **How**

does this work? Bu nasıl çalışıyor?
however [haʊ'ɛvə] *adv* ancak
howl [haʊl] *v* ulumak
HQ [eɪtʃ kju:] *abbr* genel merkez
hubcap ['hʌb,kæp] *n* jant kapağı
hug [hʌg] *n* kucaklama ▷ *v* kucaklamak
huge [hju:dʒ] *adj* kocaman
hull [hʌl] *n* gemi teknesi
hum [hʌm] *v* vızıldamak
human ['hju:mən] *adj* insan; **human being** *n* insanoğlu; **human rights** *npl* insan hakları
humanitarian [hju:,mænɪ'tɛərɪən] *adj* hümanist
humble ['hʌmbᵊl] *adj* alçak gönüllü
humid ['hju:mɪd] *adj* nemli
humidity [hju:'mɪdɪtɪ] *n* nem
humorous ['hju:mərəs] *adj* nükteli
humour ['hju:mə] *n* mizah; **sense of humour** *n* mizah duygusu
hundred ['hʌndrəd] *number* yüz *(sayı)*; **I'd like five hundred...** Beş yüz... rica ediyorum; **the key for room number two hundred and two** İki yüz iki numaralı odanın anahtarı lütfen
Hungarian [hʌŋ'gɛərɪən] *adj* Macar ▷ *n* Macar
Hungary ['hʌŋgərɪ] *n* Macaristan
hunger ['hʌŋgə] *n* açlık
hungry ['hʌŋgrɪ] *adj* aç *(karın)*; **I'm hungry** Açım; **I'm not hungry** Aç değilim
hunt [hʌnt] *n* avlamak ▷ *v* avlamak
hunter ['hʌntə] *n* avcı
hunting ['hʌntɪŋ] *n* av
hurdle ['hɜ:dᵊl] *n* engel
hurricane ['hʌrɪkᵊn; -keɪn] *n* kasırga
hurry ['hʌrɪ] *n* acele ▷ *v* acele etmek; **I'm in a hurry** Acelem var
hurry up ['hʌrɪ ʌp] *v* acele etmek
hurt [hɜ:t] *adj* incinmiş ▷ *v* incitmek
husband ['hʌzbənd] *n* koca *(eş)*
hut [hʌt] *n* baraka
hyacinth ['haɪəsɪnθ] *n* sümbül
hydrogen ['haɪdrɪdʒən] *n* hidrojen
hygiene ['haɪdʒi:n] *n* hijyen
hymn [hɪm] *n* ilahi
hypermarket ['haɪpə,mɑ:kɪt] *n* hipermarket
hyphen ['haɪfᵊn] *n* tire

I [aɪ] *pron* ben *(kişi)*
ice [aɪs] *n* buz; **black ice** *n* gizli buz; **ice cube** *n* küp buz; **ice hockey** *n* buz hokeyi; **ice lolly** *n* çubuk buz; **ice rink** *n* buz pateni sahası; **With ice, please** buzlu lütfen
iceberg ['aɪsbɜːg] *n* buzdağı
icebox ['aɪsˌbɒks] *n* buz kutusu
ice cream ['aɪs 'kriːm] *n* **ice cream** *n* dondurma; **I'd like an ice cream** Ben dondurma alayım
Iceland ['aɪslənd] *n* İzlanda
Icelandic [aɪs'lændɪk] *adj* İzlanda ▷ *n* İzlandalı
ice-skating ['aɪsˌskeɪtɪŋ] *n* buz pateni
icing ['aɪsɪŋ] *n* pastanın üzerindeki şekerli süsleme; **icing sugar** *n* toz süsleme şekeri
icon ['aɪkɒn] *n* ikon
icy ['aɪsɪ] *adj* buzlu; **Are the roads icy?** Yollar buzlu mu?
idea [aɪ'dɪə] *n* fikir *(düşünce)*
ideal [aɪ'dɪəl] *adj* ideal
ideally [aɪ'dɪəlɪ] *adv* en iyi şekilde
identical [aɪ'dɛntɪkᵊl] *adj* özdeş
identification [aɪˌdɛntɪfɪ'keɪʃən] *n* kimlik
identify [aɪ'dɛntɪˌfaɪ] *v* kimlik belirlemek
identity [aɪ'dɛntɪtɪ] *n* kimlik; **identity card** *n* kimlik kartı; **identity theft** *n* kimlik hırsızlığı
ideology [ˌaɪdɪ'ɒlədʒɪ] *n* ideoloji
idiot ['ɪdɪət] *n* salak
idiotic [ˌɪdɪ'ɒtɪk] *adj* salakça
idle ['aɪdᵊl] *adj* boş *(insan)*
i.e. [aɪ iː] *abbr* örneğin
if [ɪf] *conj* eğer
ignition [ɪg'nɪʃən] *n* ateşleme
ignorance ['ɪgnərəns] *n* cehalet
ignorant ['ɪgnərənt] *adj* cahil
ignore [ɪg'nɔː] *v* reddeylemek
ill [ɪl] *adj* hasta; **My child is ill** Çocuğum hasta
illegal [ɪ'liːgᵊl] *adj* yasadışı
illegible [ɪ'lɛdʒɪbᵊl] *adj* okunaksız
illiterate [ɪ'lɪtərɪt] *adj* okuma yazması olmayan
illness ['ɪlnɪs] *n* hastalık
ill-treat [ɪl'triːt] *v* kötü muamele etmek
illusion [ɪ'luːʒən] *n* yanılsama
illustration [ˌɪlə'streɪʃən] *n* resimleme *(kitabı)*
image ['ɪmɪdʒ] *n* imge
imaginary [ɪ'mædʒɪnərɪ; -dʒɪnrɪ] *adj* hayali
imagination [ɪˌmædʒɪ'neɪʃən] *n* hayal
imagine [ɪ'mædʒɪn] *v* tasavvur etmek

imitate ['ɪmɪˌteɪt] *v* taklit etmek
imitation [ˌɪmɪ'teɪʃən] *n* taklit
immature [ˌɪmə'tjʊə; -'tʃʊə] *adj* gelişmemiş
immediate [ɪ'mi:dɪət] *adj* acil
immediately [ɪ'mi:dɪətlɪ] *adv* anında
immigrant ['ɪmɪgrənt] *n* göçmen
immigration [ˌɪmɪ'greɪʃən] *n* göçme
immoral [ɪ'mɒrəl] *adj* ahlak dışı
impact ['ɪmpækt] *n* etki *(sonuç)*
impartial [ɪm'pɑ:ʃəl] *adj* yansız
impatience [ɪm'peɪʃəns] *n* sabırsızlık
impatient [ɪm'peɪʃənt] *adj* sabırsız
impatiently [ɪm'peɪʃəntlɪ] *adv* sabırsızlıkla
impersonal [ɪm'pɜ:sənᵊl] *adj* yansız
import *n* ['ɪmpɔ:t] ithal ▷ *v* [ɪm'pɔ:t] ithal etmek
importance [ɪm'pɔ:tᵊns] *n* önem
important [ɪm'pɔ:tᵊnt] *adj* önemli
impossible [ɪm'pɒsəbᵊl] *adj* imkansız
impractical [ɪm'præktɪkᵊl] *adj* pratik olmayan
impress [ɪm'prɛs] *v* etkilemek *(iz bırakmak)*
impressed [ɪm'prɛst] *adj* etkilenmiş
impression [ɪm'prɛʃən] *n* izlenim
impressive [ɪm'prɛsɪv] *adj* etkileyici
improve [ɪm'pru:v] *v* geliştirmek
improvement [ɪm'pru:vmənt] *n* gelişme *(iyileşme)*
in [ɪn] *prep* içinde
inaccurate [ɪn'ækjʊrɪt] *adj* doğru olmayan
inadequate [ɪn'ædɪkwɪt] *adj* yetersiz
inadvertently [ˌɪnəd'vɜ:tᵊntlɪ] *adv* kasıtsız olarak
inbox ['ɪnbɒks] *n* gelen kutusu
incentive [ɪn'sɛntɪv] *n* teşvik
inch [ɪntʃ] *n* inç
incident ['ɪnsɪdənt] *n* olay
include [ɪn'klu:d] *v* dahil etmek
included [ɪn'klu:dɪd] *adj* dahil; **Is breakfast included?** Kahvaltı dahil mi?; **Is fully comprehensive insurance included in the price?** Fiyata tam kapsamlı sigorta dahil mi?; **Is service included?** Servis dahil mi?; **Is the cost of electricity included?** Elektrik ücrete dahil mi?; **Is VAT included?** KDV dahil mi?; **What is included in the price?** Fiyata neler dahil?
including [ɪn'klu:dɪŋ] *prep* dahil
inclusive [ɪn'klu:sɪv] *adj* kapsamlı
income ['ɪnkʌm; 'ɪnkəm] *n* gelir *(maaş)*; **income tax** *n* gelir vergisi
incompetent [ɪn'kɒmpɪtənt] *adj* yeteneksiz
incomplete [ˌɪnkəm'pli:t] *adj* eksik
inconsistent [ˌɪnkən'sɪstənt] *adj* tutarsız
inconvenience [ˌɪnkən'vi:njəns; -'vi:nɪəns] *n* rahatsızlık
inconvenient [ˌɪnkən'vi:njənt; -'vi:nɪənt] *adj* rahatsız
incorrect [ˌɪnkə'rɛkt] *adj* yanlış
increase ['ɪnkri:s] *n* artış ▷ [ɪn'kri:s] *v* artmak
increasingly [ɪn'kri:sɪŋlɪ] *adv* gitgide artarak

incredible [ɪn'krɛdəbᵊl] *adj* inanılmaz
indecisive [ˌɪndɪ'saɪsɪv] *adj* kararsız
indeed [ɪn'di:d] *adv* gerçekten
independence [ˌɪndɪ'pɛndəns] *n* bağımsızlık
independent [ˌɪndɪ'pɛndənt] *adj* bağımsız
index ['ɪndɛks] *n (list)* indeks, *(numerical scale)* dizin *(sayısal)*; **index finger** *n* işaret parmağı
India ['ɪndɪə] *n* Hindistan
Indian ['ɪndɪən] *adj* Hint ▹ *n* Hintli; **Indian Ocean** *n* Hint Okyanusu
indicate ['ɪndɪˌkeɪt] *v* işaretlemek
indicator ['ɪndɪˌkeɪtə] *n* gösterge
indigestion [ˌɪndɪ'dʒɛstʃən] *n* hazımsızlık
indirect [ˌɪndɪ'rɛkt] *adj* dolaylı
indispensable [ˌɪndɪ'spɛnsəbᵊl] *adj* vazgeçilmez
individual [ˌɪndɪ'vɪdjʊəl] *adj* birey
Indonesia [ˌɪndəʊ'ni:zɪə] *n* Endonezya
Indonesian [ˌɪndəʊ'ni:zɪən] *adj* Endonezya ▹ *n (person)* Endonezyalı
indoor ['ɪnˌdɔ:] *adj* kapalı alan
indoors [ˌɪn'dɔ:z] *adv* içeride
industrial [ɪn'dʌstrɪəl] *adj* endüstriyel; **industrial estate** *n* sanayi sitesi
industry ['ɪndəstrɪ] *n* endüstri
inefficient [ˌɪnɪ'fɪʃənt] *adj* yetersiz
inevitable [ɪn'ɛvɪtəbᵊl] *adj* kaçınılmaz
inexpensive [ˌɪnɪk'spɛnsɪv] *adj* pahalı olmayan
inexperienced [ˌɪnɪk'spɪərɪənst] *adj* deneyimsiz
infantry ['ɪnfəntrɪ] *n* piyade
infection [ɪn'fɛkʃən] *n* enfeksiyon
infectious [ɪn'fɛkʃəs] *adj* bulaşıcı; **Is it infectious?** Bulaşıcı mı?
inferior [ɪn'fɪərɪə] *adj* aşağı *(durum)* ▹ *n* ast
infertile [ɪn'fɜ:taɪl] *adj* verimsiz
infinitive [ɪn'fɪnɪtɪv] *n* sonsuz
infirmary [ɪn'fɜ:mərɪ] *n* revir
inflamed [ɪn'fleɪmd] *adj* kızgın
inflammation [ˌɪnflə'meɪʃən] *n* yangı
inflatable [ɪn'fleɪtəbᵊl] *adj* şişirilebilir
inflation [ɪn'fleɪʃən] *n* enflasyon
inflexible [ɪn'flɛksəbᵊl] *adj* esnek olmayan
influence ['ɪnflʊəns] *n* etki *(nüfuz)* ▹ *v* etkilemek
influenza [ˌɪnflʊ'ɛnzə] *n* grip
inform [ɪn'fɔ:m] *v* bilgi vermek
informal [ɪn'fɔ:məl] *adj* teklifsiz
information [ˌɪnfə'meɪʃən] *n* bilgi; **information office** *n* enformasyon bürosu; **Here's some information about my company** Şirketimle ilgili bilgiler; **I'd like some information about...** ... hakkında bilgi istiyordum
informative [ɪn'fɔ:mətɪv] *adj* bilgilendirici
infrastructure ['ɪnfrəˌstrʌktʃə] *n* altyapı
infuriating [ɪn'fjʊərɪeɪtɪŋ] *adj* çileden çıkaran
ingenious [ɪn'dʒi:njəs; -nɪəs] *adj* usta işi
ingredient [ɪn'gri:dɪənt] *n*

malzeme
inhabitant [ɪnˈhæbɪtənt] *n* sakin *(konut)*
inhaler [ɪnˈheɪlə] *n* inhalasyon cihazı
inherit [ɪnˈhɛrɪt] *v* miras almak
inheritance [ɪnˈhɛrɪtəns] *n* miras
inhibition [ˌɪnɪˈbɪʃən; ˌɪnhɪ-] *n* ketlenme
initial [ɪˈnɪʃəl] *adj* başlangıç *(ilk)* ▷ *v* adının ön harflerini yazmak
initially [ɪˈnɪʃəlɪ] *adv* başlangıçta
initials [ɪˈnɪʃəlz] *npl* adın baş harfleri
initiative [ɪˈnɪʃɪətɪv] *n* girişim *(inisiyatif)*
inject [ɪnˈdʒɛkt] *v* enjekte etmek
injection [ɪnˈdʒɛkʃən] *n* enjeksiyon
injure [ˈɪndʒə] *v* yaralamak
injured [ˈɪndʒəd] *adj* yaralanmış
injury [ˈɪndʒərɪ] *n* yara; **injury time** *n* uzatma süresi
injustice [ɪnˈdʒʌstɪs] *n* adaletsizlik
ink [ɪŋk] *n* mürekkep
in-laws [ɪnlɔːz] *npl* eşinin ailesi
inmate [ˈɪnˌmeɪt] *n* hükümlü
inn [ɪn] *n* han
inner [ˈɪnə] *adj* iç; **inner tube** *n* iç lastik
innocent [ˈɪnəsənt] *adj* masum
innovation [ˌɪnəˈveɪʃən] *n* yenilik
innovative [ˈɪnəˌveɪtɪv] *adj* yenilikçi
inquest [ˈɪnˌkwɛst] *n* soruşturma
inquire [ɪnˈkwaɪə] *v* soruşturmak
inquiry [ɪnˈkwaɪərɪ] *n* soru; **inquiries office** *n* danışma bürosu
inquisitive [ɪnˈkwɪzɪtɪv] *adj* meraklı
insane [ɪnˈseɪn] *adj* deli
inscription [ɪnˈskrɪpʃən] *n* kazılmış yazı
insect [ˈɪnsɛkt] *n* böcek; **insect repellent** *n* böcek ilacı; **stick insect** *n* sopa çekirgesi; **Do you have insect repellent?** Böcek ilacınız var mı?
insecure [ˌɪnsɪˈkjʊə] *adj* güvensiz
insensitive [ɪnˈsɛnsɪtɪv] *adj* duyarsız
inside *adv* [ˌɪnˈsaɪd] içeride ▷ *n* [ˈɪnˈsaɪd] içerisi ▷ *prep* içeride
insincere [ˌɪnsɪnˈsɪə] *adj* samimiyetsiz
insist [ɪnˈsɪst] *v* ısrar etmek
insomnia [ɪnˈsɒmnɪə] *n* uykusuzluk
inspect [ɪnˈspɛkt] *v* denetlemek *(teftiş)*
inspector [ɪnˈspɛktə] *n* denetçi *(müfettiş)*; **ticket inspector** *n* bilet kontrolörü
instability [ˌɪnstəˈbɪlɪtɪ] *n* dengesizlik
instalment [ɪnˈstɔːlmənt] *n* taksit
instance [ˈɪnstəns] *n* örnek
instant [ˈɪnstənt] *adj* derhal
instantly [ˈɪnstəntlɪ] *adv* derhal
instead [ɪnˈstɛd] *adv* yerine; **instead of** *prep* yerine
instinct [ˈɪnstɪŋkt] *n* içgüdü
institute [ˈɪnstɪˌtjuːt] *n* enstitü
institution [ˌɪnstɪˈtjuːʃən] *n* kurum *(enstitü)*
instruct [ɪnˈstrʌkt] *v* talimat vermek
instructions [ɪnˈstrʌkʃənz] *npl* talimatlar
instructor [ɪnˈstrʌktə] *n* öğretmen; **driving instructor** *n*

direksiyon öğretmeni
instrument [ˈɪnstrəmənt] *n* alet; **musical instrument** *n* müzik aleti
insufficient [ˌɪnsəˈfɪʃənt] *adj* yetersiz
insulation [ˌɪnsjʊˈleɪʃən] *n* yalıtım
insulin [ˈɪnsjʊlɪn] *n* ensülin
insult *n* [ˈɪnsʌlt] hakaret ▹ *v* [ɪnˈsʌlt] onur kırmak
insurance [ɪnˈʃʊərəns; -ˈʃɔː-] *n* sigorta *(poliçe)*; **accident insurance** *n* kaza sigortası; **car insurance** *n* araba sigortası; **insurance certificate** *n* sigorta belgesi; **insurance policy** *n* sigorta poliçesi; **life insurance** *n* yaşam sigortası; **third-party insurance** *n* üçüncü kişi sorumluluk sigortası; **travel insurance** *n* seyahat sigortası; **Can I see your insurance certificate please?** Sigorta belgenizi görebilir miyim lütfen?; **Do you have insurance?** Sigortanız var mı?; **Give me your insurance details, please** Sigorta bilgilerinizi verin lütfen; **Here are my insurance details** İşte sigorta bilgilerim; **How much extra is comprehensive insurance cover?** Tam kapsamlı sigorta için ne kadar ekstra ödemem gerekiyor?; **I don't have dental insurance** Diş sigortam yok; **I don't have health insurance** Sağlık sigortam yok; **I have insurance** Sigortalıyım; **I'd like to arrange personal accident insurance** Bireysel kaza sigortası yaptırmak istiyorum; **Is fully comprehensive insurance included in the price?** Fiyata tam kapsamlı sigorta dahil mi?
insure [ɪnˈʃʊə; -ˈʃɔː] *v* sigortalamak
insured [ɪnˈʃʊəd; -ˈʃɔːd] *adj* sigortalı
intact [ɪnˈtækt] *adj* bütün *(bölünmemiş)*
intellectual [ˌɪntɪˈlɛktʃʊəl] *adj* entellektüel ▹ *n* entellektüel
intelligence [ɪnˈtɛlɪdʒəns] *n* zeka
intelligent [ɪnˈtɛlɪdʒənt] *adj* zeki
intend [ɪnˈtɛnd] *v* **intend to** *v* niyetlenmek
intense [ɪnˈtɛns] *adj* yoğun
intensive [ɪnˈtɛnsɪv] *adj* yoğun; **intensive care unit** *n* yoğun bakım ünitesi
intention [ɪnˈtɛnʃən] *n* niyet
intentional [ɪnˈtɛnʃənᵊl] *adj* kasıtlı
intercom [ˈɪntəˌkɒm] *n* interkom
interest [ˈɪntrɪst; -tərɪst] *n* *(curiosity)* ilgi *(merak)*, *(income)* faiz ▹ *v* ilgilenmek; **interest rate** *n* faiz oranı
interested [ˈɪntrɪstɪd; -tərɪs-] *adj* ilgili
interesting [ˈɪntrɪstɪŋ; -tərɪs-] *adj* ilgi çekici
interior [ɪnˈtɪərɪə] *n* iç; **interior designer** *n* iç mimar
intermediate [ˌɪntəˈmiːdɪɪt] *adj* orta
internal [ɪnˈtɜːnᵊl] *adj* iç *(organ vb)*
international [ˌɪntəˈnæʃənᵊl] *adj* uluslararası; **Where can I make an international phone call?** Nereden uluslararası telefon görüşmesi yapabilirim?

Internet ['ɪntəˌnɛt] *n* internet; **Internet café** *n* internet cafe; **Internet user** *n* internet kullanıcısı; **Are there any Internet cafés here?** Buralarda internet cafe var mı?; **Does the room have wireless Internet access?** Odada kablosuz internet bağlantısı var mı?; **Is there an Internet connection in the room?** Odada internet bağlantısı var mı?

interpret [ɪn'tɜːprɪt] *v* tefsir etmek

interpreter [ɪn'tɜːprɪtə] *n* mütercim

interrogate [ɪn'tɛrəˌgeɪt] *v* sorgulamak

interrupt [ˌɪntə'rʌpt] *v* sözünü kesmek

interruption [ˌɪntə'rʌpʃən] *n* müdahale

interval ['ɪntəvəl] *n* ara *(konser, tiyatro)*

interview ['ɪntəˌvjuː] *n* görüşme ▹ *v* görüşme yapmak

interviewer ['ɪntəˌvjuːə] *n* görüşmeci

intimate ['ɪntɪmɪt] *adj* yakın

intimidate [ɪn'tɪmɪˌdeɪt] *v* gözünü korkutmak

into ['ɪntuː; 'ɪntə] *prep* içeri; **bump into** *v* kazara çarpmak

intolerant [ɪn'tɒlərənt] *adj* hoşgörüsüz

intranet ['ɪntrəˌnɛt] *n* şirketiçi network

introduce [ˌɪntrə'djuːs] *v* tanıtmak

introduction [ˌɪntrə'dʌkʃən] *n* tanıtma

intruder [ɪn'truːdə] *n* davetsiz misafir

intuition [ˌɪntjʊ'ɪʃən] *n* önsezi

invade [ɪn'veɪd] *v* akın etmek

invalid ['ɪnvəˌliːd] *n* sakat

invent [ɪn'vɛnt] *v* icat etmek

invention [ɪn'vɛnʃən] *n* icat

inventor [ɪn'vɛntə] *n* mucit

inventory ['ɪnvəntərɪ; -trɪ] *n* envanter

invest [ɪn'vɛst] *v* yatırım yapmak

investigation [ɪnˌvɛstɪ'geɪʃən] *n* soruşturma

investment [ɪn'vɛstmənt] *n* yatırım

investor [ɪn'vɛstə] *n* yatırımcı

invigilator [ɪn'vɪdʒɪˌleɪtə] *n* sınav gözcüsü

invisible [ɪn'vɪzəbᵊl] *adj* görünmez

invitation [ˌɪnvɪ'teɪʃən] *n* davet

invite [ɪn'vaɪt] *v* davet etmek

invoice ['ɪnvɔɪs] *n* fatura ▹ *v* faturalamak

involve [ɪn'vɒlv] *v* dahil etmek

iPod® ['aɪˌpɒd] *n* iPod®

IQ [aɪ kjuː] *abbr* IQ

Iran [ɪ'rɑːn] *n* İran

Iranian [ɪ'reɪnɪən] *adj* İran ▹ *n* *(person)* İranlı *(kişi)*

Iraq [ɪ'rɑːk] *n* Irak

Iraqi [ɪ'rɑːkɪ] *adj* Irak ▹ *n* Iraklı

Ireland ['aɪələnd] *n* İrlanda; **Northern Ireland** *n* Kuzey İrlanda

iris ['aɪrɪs] *n* iris

Irish ['aɪrɪʃ] *adj* İrlanda ▹ *n* İrlandalı

Irishman, Irishmen ['aɪrɪʃmən, 'aɪrɪʃmɛn] *n* İrlandalı *(erkek)*

Irishwoman, Irishwomen ['aɪrɪʃwʊmən, 'aɪrɪʃwɪmɪn] *n*

İrlandalı *(kadın)*
iron ['aɪən] *n* demir ▹ *v* ütülemek
ironic [aɪ'rɒnɪk] *adj* alaycı
ironing ['aɪənɪŋ] *n* ütüleme; **ironing board** *n* ütü tahtası
ironmonger's ['aɪən,mʌŋgəz] *n* demirci dükkanı
irony ['aɪrənɪ] *n* ince alay
irregular [ɪ'rɛgjʊlə] *adj* düzensiz
irrelevant [ɪ'rɛləvənt] *adj* alakasız
irresponsible [,ɪrɪ'spɒnsəbᵊl] *adj* sorumsuz
irritable ['ɪrɪtəbᵊl] *adj* çabuk kızan
irritating ['ɪrɪ,teɪtɪŋ] *adj* sinir bozucu
Islam ['ɪzlɑːm] *n* Müslümanlık
Islamic ['ɪzləmɪk] *adj* İslami
island ['aɪlənd] *n* ada; **desert island** *n* ıssız ada
isolated ['aɪsə,leɪtɪd] *adj* soyutlanmış
ISP [aɪ ɛs piː] *abbr* ISP
Israel ['ɪzreɪəl; -rɪəl] *n* İsrail
Israeli [ɪz'reɪlɪ] *adj* İsrail ▹ *n* İsrailli
issue ['ɪʃjuː] *n* mesele ▹ *v* kamuoyuna açıklamak
it [ɪt] *pron* o *(eşya/hayvan)*; **I can't read it** Okuyamıyorum; **Is it safe for children?** Çocuklara verilebilir mi?; **It hurts** Acıyor; **It won't turn on** Açılmıyor; **It's ten to two** Saat ikiye on var
IT [aɪ tiː] *abbr* Enformasyon Teknolojisi
Italian [ɪ'tæljən] *adj* İtalyan ▹ *n* *(language)* İtalyanca *(dil)*, *(person)* İtalyan *(kişi)*
Italy ['ɪtəlɪ] *n* İtalya
itch [ɪtʃ] *v* kaşınmak
itchy [ɪtʃɪ] *adj* kaşıntılı
item ['aɪtəm] *n* madde *(dizi)*
itinerary [aɪ'tɪnərərɪ; ɪ-] *n* güzergah
its [ɪts] *adj* onun
itself [ɪt'sɛlf] *pron* kendisi
ivory ['aɪvərɪ; -vrɪ] *n* fildişi
ivy ['aɪvɪ] *n* sarmaşık

jab [dʒæb] *n* aşı *(tıp)*
jack [dʒæk] *n* kriko
jacket ['dʒækɪt] *n* ceket; **dinner jacket** *n* smokin; **jacket potato** *n* kumpir; **life jacket** *n* cankurtaran yeleği
jackpot ['dʒæk,pɒt] *n* jackpot
jail [dʒeɪl] *n* hapishane ▷ *v* hapse atmak
jam [dʒæm] *n* reçel; **jam jar** *n* reçel kavanozu; **traffic jam** *n* trafik sıkışıklığı
Jamaican [dʒə'meɪkən] *adj* Jamaika ▷ *n* Jamaikalı
jammed [dʒæmd] *adj* sıkışmış
janitor ['dʒænɪtə] *n* bina sorumlusu
January ['dʒænjʊərɪ] *n* Ocak *(ay)*
Japan [dʒə'pæn] *n* Japonya
Japanese [,dʒæpə'ni:z] *adj* Japon ▷ *n (language)* Japonca *(dil)*, *(person)* Japon *(kişi)*
jar [dʒɑ:] *n* kavanoz; **jam jar** *n* reçel kavanozu
jaundice ['dʒɔ:ndɪs] *n* sarılık
javelin ['dʒævlɪn] *n* mızrak
jaw [dʒɔ:] *n* çene
jazz [dʒæz] *n* caz
jealous ['dʒɛləs] *adj* kıskanç
jeans [dʒi:nz] *npl* blucin
jelly ['dʒɛlɪ] *n* jöle *(tatlı)*
jellyfish ['dʒɛlɪ,fɪʃ] *n* deniz anası; **Are there jellyfish here?** Burada deniz anası var mı?
jersey ['dʒɜ:zɪ] *n* kazak
Jesus ['dʒi:zəs] *n* İsa
jet [dʒɛt] *n* jet; **jet lag** *n* uçak tutması; **jumbo jet** *n* jumbo jet
jetty ['dʒɛtɪ] *n* rıhtım
Jew [dʒu:] *n* Yahudi
jewel ['dʒu:əl] *n* mücevher
jeweller ['dʒu:ələ] *n* kuyumcu
jeweller's ['dʒu:ələz] *n* kuyumcu dükkanı
jewellery ['dʒu:əlrɪ] *n* mücevherat
Jewish ['dʒu:ɪʃ] *adj* Yahudi
jigsaw ['dʒɪg,sɔ:] *n* yapboz
job [dʒɒb] *n* iş; **job centre** *n* iş bulma kurumu
jobless ['dʒɒblɪs] *adj* işşiz
jockey ['dʒɒkɪ] *n* jokey
jog [dʒɒg] *v* jogging yapmak
jogging ['dʒɒgɪŋ] *n* jogging
join [dʒɔɪn] *v* birleştirmek, katılmak
joiner ['dʒɔɪnə] *n* doğramacı
joint [dʒɔɪnt] *adj* ortak ▷ *n (junction)* bağlantı, *(meat)* kemikli et; **joint account** *n* ortak hesap
joke [dʒəʊk] *n* şaka ▷ *v* şaka yapmak
jolly ['dʒɒlɪ] *adj* neşeli
Jordan ['dʒɔ:dⁿn] *n* Ürdün

Jordanian [dʒɔːˈdeɪnɪən] *adj* Ürdün ▷ *n* Ürdünlü
jot down [dʒɒt daʊn] *v* not almak
jotter [ˈdʒɒtə] *n* not defteri
journalism [ˈdʒɜːnᵊˌlɪzəm] *n* gazetecilik
journalist [ˈdʒɜːnᵊlɪst] *n* gazeteci
journey [ˈdʒɜːnɪ] *n* seyahat
joy [dʒɔɪ] *n* neşe
joystick [ˈdʒɔɪˌstɪk] *n* joystick
judge [dʒʌdʒ] *n* yargıç ▷ *v* yargılamak
judo [ˈdʒuːdəʊ] *n* judo
jug [dʒʌg] *n* sürahi; **a jug of water** Bir sürahi su
juggler [ˈdʒʌglə] *n* hokkabaz
juice [dʒuːs] *n* meyve suyu; **orange juice** *n* portakal suyu
July [dʒuːˈlaɪ; dʒə-; dʒʊ-] *n* Temmuz
jump [dʒʌmp] *n* uzun atlama ▷ *v* atlamak; **high jump** *n* yüksek atlama; **jump leads** *npl* takviye kablosu; **long jump** *n* uzun atlama
jumper [ˈdʒʌmpə] *n* kazak
jumping [ˈdʒʌmpɪŋ] *n* **show-jumping** *n* engel atlama
junction [ˈdʒʌŋkʃən] *n* kavşak; **Go right at the next junction** Bir sonraki kavşaktan sağa dönün
June [dʒuːn] *n* Haziran; **at the beginning of June** Haziran başında; **at the end of June** Haziran sonunda; **for the whole of June** bütün Haziran boyunca; **It's Monday the fifteenth of June** On beş Haziran Pazartesi
jungle [ˈdʒʌŋgᵊl] *n* orman
junior [ˈdʒuːnjə] *adj* yaşça küçük
junk [dʒʌŋk] *n* pılı pırtı; **junk mail** *n* istenmeyen posta
jury [ˈdʒʊərɪ] *n* jüri
just [dʒəst] *adv* henüz
justice [ˈdʒʌstɪs] *n* adalet
justify [ˈdʒʌstɪˌfaɪ] *v* haklılığını göstermek

k

kangaroo [ˌkæŋɡəˈruː] *n* kanguru
karaoke [ˌkɑːrəˈəʊkɪ] *n* karaoke
karate [kəˈrɑːtɪ] *n* karate
Kazakhstan [ˌkɑːzɑːkˈstæn; -ˈstɑːn] *n* Kazakistan
kebab [kəˈbæb] *n* kebap
keen [kiːn] *adj* istekli
keep [kiːp] *v* bırakmak, tutmak
keep-fit [ˈkiːpˌfɪt] *n* sağlıklı yaşam
keep out [kiːp aʊt] *v* dışarda tutmak
keep up [kiːp ʌp] *v* sürdürmek; **keep up with** *v* uygun adım yürümek
kennel [ˈkɛnᵊl] *n* köpek kulübesi
Kenya [ˈkɛnjə; ˈkiːnjə] *n* Kenya
Kenyan [ˈkɛnjən; ˈkiːnjən] *adj* Kenya ▷ *n* Kenyalı
kerb [kɜːb] *n* kaldırım taşı
kerosene [ˈkɛrəˌsiːn] *n* gazyağı
ketchup [ˈkɛtʃəp] *n* ketçap
kettle [ˈkɛtᵊl] *n* çaydanlık
key [kiː] *n (for lock)* anahtar *(kilit)*, *(music/computer)* tuş *(bilgisayar/piyano)*; **car keys** *npl* araba anahtarları; **Can I have a key?** Anahtar alabilir miyim?; **I left the keys in the car** Anahtarları arabada bıraktım; **I'm having trouble with the key** Anahtarla sorunum var; **I've forgotten the key** Anahtarımı unuttum; **the key for room number two hundred and two** İki yüz iki numaralı odanın anahtarı lütfen; **The key doesn't work** Anahtar uymuyor; **We need a second key** Yedek bir anahtar istiyoruz; **What's this key for?** Bu anahtar nerenin?; **Where do we get the key...?** Anahtarı nereden alacağız?; **Where do we hand in the key when we're leaving?** Ayrılırken anahtarı nereye bırakacağız?; **Which is the key for the back door?** Hangisi arka kapının anahtarı?; **Which is the key for this door?** Bu kapının anahtarı hangisi?
keyboard [ˈkiːˌbɔːd] *n* klavye
keyring [ˈkiːˌrɪŋ] *n* anahtarlık
kick [kɪk] *n* tekme ▷ *v* tekmelemek
kick off [kɪk ɒf] *v* başlama vuruşu yapmak
kick-off [kɪkɒf] *n* başlama vuruşu
kid [kɪd] *n* çocuk ▷ *v* dalga geçmek
kidnap [ˈkɪdnæp] *v* kaçırmak *(adam)*
kidney [ˈkɪdnɪ] *n* böbrek
kill [kɪl] *v* öldürmek
killer [ˈkɪlə] *n* katil
kilo [ˈkiːləʊ] *n* kilo

kilometre [kɪˈlɒmɪtə; ˈkɪləˌmiːtə] *n* kilometre
kilt [kɪlt] *n* kilt
kind [kaɪnd] *adj* iyi kalpli ▷ *n* tür
kindly [ˈkaɪndlɪ] *adv* iyilikle
kindness [ˈkaɪndnɪs] *n* iyi yüreklilik
king [kɪŋ] *n* kral
kingdom [ˈkɪŋdəm] *n* krallık
kingfisher [ˈkɪŋˌfɪʃə] *n* yalı çapkını
kiosk [ˈkiːɒsk] *n* büfe *(dükkan)*
kipper [ˈkɪpə] *n* tuzlanıp tütsülenmiş ringa balığı
kiss [kɪs] *n* öpücük ▷ *v* öpmek
kit [kɪt] *n* takım; **hands-free kit** *n* handsfree set; **repair kit** *n* tamir takımı; **Can I have a repair kit?** Tamir takımı alabilir miyim?
kitchen [ˈkɪtʃɪn] *n* mutfak; **fitted kitchen** *n* hazır mutfak
kite [kaɪt] *n* uçurtma
kitten [ˈkɪtᵊn] *n* kedi yavrusu
kiwi [ˈkiːwiː] *n* kivi *(kuş)*
knee [niː] *n* diz
kneecap [ˈniːˌkæp] *n* dizkapağı
kneel [niːl] *v* diz çökmek
kneel down [niːl daʊn] *v* diz çökmek
knickers [ˈnɪkəz] *npl* külot *(kadın)*
knife [naɪf] *n* bıçak
knit [nɪt] *v* örmek
knitting [ˈnɪtɪŋ] *n* örgü; **knitting needle** *n* örgü şişi
knob [nɒb] *n* tokmak *(kapı, çekmece)*
knock [nɒk] *n* vuruş ▷ *v* vurmak, *(on the door etc.)* kapıyı çalmak
knock down [nɒk daʊn] *v* devirmek *(düşürmek)*
knock out [nɒk aʊt] *v* yere sermek
knot [nɒt] *n* düğüm
know [nəʊ] *v* bilmek, tanımak
know-all [ˈnəʊɔːl] *n* bilgiç
know-how [ˈnəʊˌhaʊ] *n* teknik bilgi
knowledge [ˈnɒlɪdʒ] *n* bilgi
knowledgeable [ˈnɒlɪdʒəbᵊl] *adj* bilgili
known [nəʊn] *adj* bilinen
Koran [kɔːˈrɑːn] *n* Kuran
Korea [kəˈriːə] *n* Kore; **North Korea** *n* Kuzey Kore; **South Korea** *n* Güney Kore
Korean [kəˈriːən] *adj* Kore ▷ *n (language)* Korece *(dil)*, *(person)* Koreli *(kişi)*
kosher [ˈkəʊʃə] *adj* kaşer
Kosovo [ˈkɔsɔvɔ; ˈkɒsəvəʊ] *n* Kosova
Kuwait [kʊˈweɪt] *n* Kuveyt
Kuwaiti [kʊˈweɪtɪ] *adj* Kuveyt ▷ *n* Kuveytli
Kyrgyzstan [ˈkɪəgɪzˌstɑːn; -ˌstæn] *n* Kırgızistan

lab [læb] *n* laboratuvar
label ['leɪbᵊl] *n* etiket *(fiyat vb)*
laboratory [lə'bɒrətərɪ; -trɪ; 'læbrə,tɔːrɪ] *n* laboratuvar; **language laboratory** *n* dil laboratuvarı
labour ['leɪbə] *n* emek
labourer ['leɪbərə] *n* işçi
lace [leɪs] *n* dantel
lack [læk] *n* eksiklik
lacquer ['lækə] *n* lake
lad [læd] *n* delikanlı
ladder ['lædə] *n* taşınır merdiven
ladies ['leɪdɪz] *n* **ladies'** *n* kadınlar tuvaleti; **Where is the ladies?** Bayanlar tuvaleti nerede?
ladle ['leɪdᵊl] *n* kepçe *(mutfak)*
lady ['leɪdɪ] *n* leydi
ladybird ['leɪdɪ,bɜːd] *n* uç uç böceği
lager ['lɑːgə] *n* hafif bira
lagoon [lə'guːn] *n* lagün
laid-back ['leɪdbæk] *adj* rahat
lake [leɪk] *n* göl
lamb [læm] *n* kuzu
lame [leɪm] *adj* topal
lamp [læmp] *n* lamba; **bedside lamp** *n* başucu lambası; **The lamp is not working** Lamba çalışmıyor
lamppost ['læmp,pəʊst] *n* lamba direği
lampshade ['læmp,ʃeɪd] *n* abajur
land [lænd] *n* kara *(coğrafya)* ▷ *v* iniş yapmak
landing ['lændɪŋ] *n* merdiven başı
landlady ['lænd,leɪdɪ] *n* ev sahibesi
landlord ['lænd,lɔːd] *n* ev sahibi
landmark ['lænd,mɑːk] *n* sınır işareti
landowner ['lænd,əʊnə] *n* toprak sahibi
landscape ['lænd,skeɪp] *n* manzara
landslide ['lænd,slaɪd] *n* toprak kayması
lane [leɪn] *n* dar yol, *(driving)* patika; **cycle lane** *n* bisiklet yolu
language ['læŋgwɪdʒ] *n* dil *(lisan)*; **language laboratory** *n* dil laboratuvarı; **language school** *n* dil okulu; **sign language** *n* işaret dili; **What languages do you speak?** Hangi dilleri konuşabiliyorsunuz?
lanky ['læŋkɪ] *adj* sırık gibi
Laos [laʊz; laʊs] *n* Laos
lap [læp] *n* kucak
laptop ['læp,tɒp] *n* dizüstü bilgisayarı; **Can I use my own laptop here?** Burada dizüstü bilgisayarımı kullanabilir miyim?

larder ['lɑːdə] *n* kiler
large [lɑːdʒ] *adj* büyük *(iri)*; **Do you have a large?** Büyük beden var mı?; **Do you have an extra large?** Ekstra büyük beden var mı?
largely ['lɑːdʒlı] *adv* yaygın bir şekilde
laryngitis [ˌlærın'dʒaıtıs] *n* larenjit
laser ['leızə] *n* lazer
lass [læs] *n* genç kız
last [lɑːst] *adj* son ▷ *adv* sonda ▷ *v* sürmek; **When does the last chair-lift go?** Son teleferik kaçta?; **When is the last bus to...?**... a son otobüs kaçta?
lastly ['lɑːstlı] *adv* son olarak
late [leıt] *adj (dead)* eski *(ölmüş)*, *(delayed)* gecikmeli ▷ *adv* geç; **Is the train running late?** Tren gecikmeli mı?; **It's too late** Çok geç
lately ['leıtlı] *adv* son zamanlarda
later ['leıtə] *adv* daha sonra; **Can you try again later?** Daha sonra tekrar arayabilir misiniz; **Shall I come back later?** Daha sonra tekrar geleyim mi?
Latin ['lætın] *n* Latin
Latin America ['lætın ə'mɛrıkə] *n* Latin Amerika
Latin American ['lætın ə'mɛrıkən] *adj* Latin Amerika
latitude ['lætıˌtjuːd] *n* enlem
Latvia ['lætvıə] *n* Latviya
Latvian ['lætvıən] *adj* Latviya ▷ *n (language)* Letonca *(dil)*, *(person)* Letonyalı *(kişi)*
laugh [lɑːf] *n* gülüş ▷ *v* kahkahayla gülmek
laughter ['lɑːftə] *n* kahkaha
launch [lɔːntʃ] *v* başlatmak, denize indirmek
Launderette® [ˌlɔːndə'rɛt; lɔːn'drɛt] *n* çamaşırhane; **Is there a launderette near here?** Buralarda bir çamaşırhane var mı?
laundry ['lɔːndrı] *n* çamaşır
lava ['lɑːvə] *n* lav
lavatory ['lævətərı; -trı] *n* tuvalet
lavender ['lævəndə] *n* lavanta
law [lɔː] *n* yasa; **law school** *n* hukuk fakültesi
lawn [lɔːn] *n* çim alan
lawnmower ['lɔːnˌmaʊə] *n* çim biçme makinesi
lawyer ['lɔːjə; 'lɔıə] *n* avukat
laxative ['læksətıv] *n* müshil
lay [leı] *v* koymak
layby ['leıˌbaı] *n* yol kenarında geçici park yeri
layer ['leıə] *n* katman; **ozone layer** *n* ozon tabakası
lay off [leı ɒf] *v* işten çıkarmak
layout ['leıˌaʊt] *n* düzenleme *(masa vb)*
lazy ['leızı] *adj* tembel
lead[1] [liːd] *n (in play/film)* başrol *(oyun/film)*, *(position)* ana ▷ *v* yol göstermek; **jump leads** *npl* takviye kablosu; **lead singer** *n* as solist
lead[2] [lɛd] *n (metal)* kurşun *(metal)*
leader ['liːdə] *n* lider
lead-free [ˌlɛd'friː] *adj* kurşunsuz
leaf [liːf] *n* yaprak; **bay leaf** *n* defne yaprağı
leaflet ['liːflıt] *n* broşür; **Do you have a leaflet in English?** İngilizce broşürünüz var mı?; **Do**

you have any leaflets about...?... hakkında broşürünüz var mı?; **Do you have any leaflets?** Broşürünüz var mı?
league [li:g] *n* lig
leak [li:k] *n* sızıntı ▷ *v* sızdırmak; **There is a leak in the radiator** Radyatör sızıntı yapıyor
lean [li:n] *v* yaslamak; **lean forward** *v* öne eğilmek
lean on [li:n ɒn] *v* baskı yapmak
lean out [li:n aʊt] *v* dışarıya sarkmak
leap [li:p] *v* sıçramak; **leap year** *n* artık yıl
learn [lɜ:n] *v* öğrenmek
learner ['lɜ:nə] *n* öğrenci; **learner driver** *n* öğrenci sürücü
lease [li:s] *n* kira sözleşmesi ▷ *v* kiralamak
least [li:st] *adj* en az; **at least** *adv* en azından
leather ['lɛðə] *n* deri *(hayvan, giysi vb)*
leave [li:v] *n* izin *(işten izne ayrılmak)* ▷ *v* ayrılmak, biryerden ayrılmak; **maternity leave** *n* doğum izni; **paternity leave** *n* babalık izni; **sick leave** *n* hastalık izni
leave out [li:v aʊt] *v* çıkarmak
leaves [li:vz] *npl* yapraklar
Lebanese [ˌlɛbə'ni:z] *adj* Lübnan'a ait ▷ *n* Lübnanlı
Lebanon ['lɛbənən] *n* Lübnan
lecture ['lɛktʃə] *n* ders ▷ *v* ders vermek
lecturer ['lɛktʃərə] *n* okutman
leek [li:k] *n* pırasa
left [lɛft] *adj* sol ▷ *adv* soldaki ▷ *n* sol; **Go left at the next junction** Bir sonraki kavşaktan sola dönün; **Turn left** Sola dönün
left-hand [ˌleft'hænd] *adj* sol; **left-hand drive** *n* soldan trafik
left-handed [ˌleft'hændɪd] *adj* solak
left-luggage [ˌleft'lʌgɪdʒ] *n* emanet bagaj; **left-luggage locker** *n* bagaj emanet dolabı; **left-luggage office** *n* emanet bagaj bürosu
leftovers ['lɛftˌəʊvəz] *npl* artık yemek
left-wing [ˌleftˌwɪŋ] *adj* sol *(politika)*
leg [lɛg] *n* bacak
legal ['li:gᵊl] *adj* yasal
legend ['lɛdʒənd] *n* efsane
leggings ['lɛgɪŋz] *npl* tozluk
legible ['lɛdʒəbᵊl] *adj* okunaklı
legislation [ˌlɛdʒɪs'leɪʃən] *n* mevzuat
leisure ['lɛʒə; 'li:ʒər] *n* boş vakit; **leisure centre** *n* eğlence merkezi
lemon ['lɛmən] *n* limon; **with lemon** limonlu
lemonade [ˌlɛmə'neɪd] *n* limonata
lend [lɛnd] *v* ödünç vermek
length [lɛŋkθ; lɛŋθ] *n* uzunluk
lens [lɛnz] *n* lens; **contact lenses** *npl* kontakt lens; **zoom lens** *n* zoom merceği; **cleansing solution for contact lenses** Lens solüsyonu; **I wear contact lenses** Lens takıyorum
Lent [lɛnt] *n* 40 günlük Paskalya dönemi
lentils ['lɛntɪlz] *npl* mercimek
Leo ['li:əʊ] *n* Aslan burcu

leopard ['lɛpəd] *n* leopar
leotard ['lɪəˌtɑːd] *n* leotard
less [lɛs] *adv* daha az *(miktar olarak)* ▹ *pron* daha az
lesson ['lɛsᵊn] *n* ders *(sınıf)*; **driving lesson** *n* direksiyon dersi; **Can we take lessons?** Ders alabilir miyiz?; **Do you give lessons?** Ders veriyor musunuz?; **Do you organise skiing lessons?** Kayak dersleri veriyor musunuz?; **Do you organise snowboarding lessons?** Snowboarding dersleri veriyor musunuz?
let [lɛt] *v* izin vermek
let down [lɛt daʊn] *v* hayal kırıklığına uğratmak
let in [lɛt ɪn] *v* içeriye almak
letter ['lɛtə] *n (a, b, c)* harf, *(message)* mektup
letterbox ['lɛtəˌbɒks] *n* posta kutusu
lettuce ['lɛtɪs] *n* marul
leukaemia [luː'kiːmɪə] *n* lösemi
level ['lɛvᵊl] *adj* yatay ▹ *n* düzey; **level crossing** *n* hemzemin geçit; **sea level** *n* deniz seviyesi
lever ['liːvə] *n* kol
liar ['laɪə] *n* yalancı
liberal ['lɪbərəl; 'lɪbrəl] *adj* açık görüşlü
liberation [ˌlɪbə'reɪʃən] *n* önyargılardan arındırma
Liberia [laɪ'bɪərɪə] *n* Liberya
Liberian [laɪ'bɪərɪən] *adj* Liberya ▹ *n* Liberyalı
Libra ['liːbrə] *n* Terazi burcu
librarian [laɪ'brɛərɪən] *n* kütüphaneci
library ['laɪbrərɪ] *n* kütüphane
Libya ['lɪbɪə] *n* Libya
Libyan ['lɪbɪən] *adj* Libya ▹ *n* Libyalı
lice [laɪs] *npl* bit *(saç)*
licence ['laɪsəns] *n* ehliyet; **driving licence** *n* sürücü ehliyeti; **I don't have my driving licence on me** Ehliyetim üzerimde değil; **My driving licence number is...** Ehliyet numaram...
lick [lɪk] *v* yalamak
lid [lɪd] *n* kapak
lie [laɪ] *n* yalan ▹ *v* yalan söylemek, yatmak
Liechtenstein ['lɪktənˌstaɪn; 'lɪçtənʃtain] *n* Lihtenştayn
lie down [laɪ daʊn] *v* yatmak
lie in [laɪ ɪn] *v* uykusunu almak
lie-in [laɪɪn] *n* **have a lie-in** *v* uykusunu almak
lieutenant [lɛf'tɛnənt; luː'tɛnənt] *n* teğmen *(subay/polis)*
life [laɪf] *n* yaşam; **life insurance** *n* yaşam sigortası; **life jacket** *n* cankurtaran yeleği
lifebelt ['laɪfˌbɛlt] *n* cankurtaran simidi
lifeboat ['laɪfˌbəʊt] *n* cankurtaran sandalı
lifeguard ['laɪfˌgɑːd] *n* cankurtaran *(sahil)*; **Get the lifeguard!** Cankurtaran çağırın!; **Is there a lifeguard?** Cankurtaran var mı?
life-saving ['laɪfˌseɪvɪŋ] *adj* can kurtaran
lifestyle ['laɪfˌstaɪl] *n* yaşam biçimi
lift [lɪft] *n (free ride)* birini arabayla evine bırakma, *(up/down)* kaldırma/indirme ▹ *v* kaldırmak

(yukarıya); **ski lift** *n* teleferik
light [laɪt] *adj (not dark)* açık *(renk)*, *(not heavy)* hafif ▷ *n* ışık ▷ *v* yakmak *(ışık)*; **brake light** *n* fren lambası; **hazard warning lights** *npl* tehlike uyarı ışığı; **light bulb** *n* ampul; **pilot light** *n* kontrol lambası; **traffic lights** *npl* trafik ışıkları
lighter ['laɪtə] *n* çakmak
lighthouse ['laɪt,haʊs] *n* deniz feneri
lighting ['laɪtɪŋ] *n* ışıklandırma
lightning ['laɪtnɪŋ] *n* şimşek
like [laɪk] *prep* gibi ▷ *v* sevmek
likely ['laɪklɪ] *adj* olası
lilac ['laɪlək] *adj* leylak renkli ▷ *n* leylak
Lilo® ['laɪləʊ] *n* deniz yatağı
lily ['lɪlɪ] *n* zambak; **lily of the valley** *n* inci çiçeği
lime [laɪm] *n (compound)* kireç, *(fruit)* yeşil limon
limestone ['laɪm,stəʊn] *n* kireç taşı
limit ['lɪmɪt] *n* sınır; **age limit** *n* yaş sınırı; **speed limit** *n* hız sınırı
limousine ['lɪmə,zi:n; ,lɪmə'zi:n] *n* limuzin
limp [lɪmp] *v* topallamak
line [laɪn] *n* çizgi; **washing line** *n* çamaşır ipi
linen ['lɪnɪn] *n* keten *(kumaş)*; **bed linen** *n* yatak çarşafı
liner ['laɪnə] *n* büyük yolcu gemisi
lingerie ['lænʒərɪ] *n* iç çamaşırı
linguist ['lɪŋgwɪst] *n* dilbilimci
linguistic [lɪŋ'gwɪstɪk] *adj* dilbilim
lining ['laɪnɪŋ] *n* astar *(kumaş)*
link [lɪŋk] *n* halka *(zincir)*; **link (up)** *v* birleştirmek *(parçaları)*
lino ['laɪnəʊ] *n* yer muşambası
lion ['laɪən] *n* aslan
lioness ['laɪənɪs] *n* aslan *(dişi)*
lip [lɪp] *n* dudak; **lip salve** *n* dudak kremi
lip-read ['lɪp,ri:d] *v* dudak okuma
lipstick ['lɪp,stɪk] *n* ruj
liqueur [lɪ'kjʊə; likœr] *n* likör; **What liqueurs do you have?** Likör olarak neleriniz var?
liquid ['lɪkwɪd] *n* sıvı; **washing-up liquid** *n* bulaşık deterjanı
liquidizer ['lɪkwɪ,daɪzə] *n* mikser
list [lɪst] *n* liste ▷ *v* listelemek; **mailing list** *n* adres listesi; **price list** *n* fiyat listesi; **waiting list** *n* bekleme listesi; **wine list** *n* şarap listesi; **The wine list, please** Şarap listesi lütfen
listen ['lɪsᵊn] *v* dinlemek; **listen to** *v* söz dinlemek
listener ['lɪsnə] *n* dinleyici
literally ['lɪtərəlɪ] *adv* harfi harfine
literature ['lɪtərɪtʃə; 'lɪtrɪ-] *n* edebiyat
Lithuania [,lɪθjʊ'eɪnɪə] *n* Litvanya
Lithuanian [,lɪθjʊ'eɪnɪən] *adj* Litvanya ▷ *n (language)* Litvanca *(dil)*, *(person)* Litvanyalı *(kişi)*
litre ['li:tə] *n* litre
litter ['lɪtə] *n (offspring)* yeni doğmuş yavrular, *(rubbish)* çöp; **litter bin** *n* çöp kutusu
little ['lɪtᵊl] *adj* küçük
live¹ [lɪv] *v* yaşamak
live² [laɪv] *adj* canlı *(yaşayan)*; **Where can we hear live music?** Canlı müzik dinleyebileceğimiz bir yer var mı?
lively ['laɪvlɪ] *adj* enerjik

live on [lɪv ɒn] *v* geçinmek
liver ['lɪvə] *n* karaciğer
live together [lɪv] *v* beraber yaşamak
living ['lɪvɪŋ] *n* canlı *(yaşayan)*; **cost of living** *n* hayat pahalılığı; **living room** *n* oturma odası; **standard of living** *n* yaşam standardı
lizard ['lɪzəd] *n* kertenkele
load [ləʊd] *n* yük ▷ *v* yüklemek
loaf, loaves [ləʊf, ləʊvz] *n* somun *(ekmek)*
loan [ləʊn] *n* kredi ▷ *v* ödünç vermek
loathe [ləʊð] *v* tiksinmek
lobby ['lɒbɪ] *n* **I'll meet you in the lobby** Lobide buluşuruz
lobster ['lɒbstə] *n* istakoz
local ['ləʊkᵊl] *adj* yerel; **local anaesthetic** *n* lokal anestezi; **We'd like to see local plants and trees** Yerel bitkileri ve ağaçları görmek isterdik; **What's the local speciality?** Yerel yemeğiniz nedir?
location [ləʊ'keɪʃən] *n* yer; **My location is...** Yerim tam olarak...
lock [lɒk] *n* *(door)* kilit, *(hair)* bukle *(saç)* ▷ *v* kilitlemek; **Can I have a lock?** Kilit alabilir miyim?; **The door won't lock** Kapı kilitlenmiyor; **The lock is broken** Kilit kırılmış; **The wheels lock** Tekerlekler kilitleniyor
locker ['lɒkə] *n* kilitli dolap; **left-luggage locker** *n* bagaj emanet dolabı
locket ['lɒkɪt] *n* madalyon
lock out [lɒk aʊt] *v* kilitlmek
locksmith ['lɒk,smɪθ] *n* çilingir
lodger ['lɒdʒə] *n* pansiyoner
loft [lɒft] *n* tavan arası
log [lɒg] *n* tomruk
logical ['lɒdʒɪkᵊl] *adj* mantıklı
log in [lɒg ɪn] *v* oturum açmak
logo ['ləʊgəʊ; 'lɒg-] *n* logo
log off [lɒg ɒf] *v* oturum kapatmak
log on [lɒg ɒn] *v* oturum açmak
log out [lɒg aʊt] *v* oturum kapatmak
lollipop ['lɒlɪ,pɒp] *n* lolipop
lolly ['lɒlɪ] *n* lolipop
London ['lʌndən] *n* Londra
loneliness ['ləʊnlɪnɪs] *n* yalnızlık
lonely ['ləʊnlɪ] *adj* yalnız
lonesome ['ləʊnsəm] *adj* yalnız
long [lɒŋ] *adj* uzun ▷ *adv* uzunca ▷ *v* özlemek; **long jump** *n* uzun atlama
longer [lɒŋə] *adv* daha uzun
longitude ['lɒndʒɪ,tju:d; 'lɒŋg-] *n* boylam
loo [lu:] *n* tuvalet
look [lʊk] *n* bakış ▷ *v* gözünü dikmek; **look at** *v* gözünü dikmek
look after [lʊk ɑ:ftə] *v* bakmak
look for [lʊk fɔ:] *v* aramak
look round [lʊk raʊnd] *v* bakınmak
look up [lʊk ʌp] *v* aramak
loose [lu:s] *adj* gevşek *(düğüm vb)*
lorry ['lɒrɪ] *n* yük arabası; **lorry driver** *n* kamyon şoförü
lose [lu:z] *vi* kaybolmak ▷ *vt* kaybetmek
loser ['lu:zə] *n* yenilmiş
loss [lɒs] *n* kayıp
lost [lɒst] *adj* kayıp; **lost-property office** *n* kayıp eşya bürosu
lost-and-found ['lɒstænd'faʊnd]

n kaybolup bulunmuş
lot [lɒt] *n* **a lot** *n* topluluk
lotion ['ləʊʃən] *n* losyon; **after sun lotion** *n* güneş sonrası krem; **cleansing lotion** *n* yüz temizleme losyonu; **suntan lotion** *n* bronzlaşma losyonu
lottery ['lɒtərɪ] *n* piyango
loud [laʊd] *adj* gürültülü; **It's too loud** Çok gürültülü
loudly [laʊdlɪ] *adv* yüksek sesle
loudspeaker [ˌlaʊd'spiːkə] *n* hoparlör
lounge [laʊndʒ] *n* salon; **departure lounge** *n* uçuş bekleme salonu; **transit lounge** *n* transit yolcu salonu; **Could we have coffee in the lounge?** Salonda kahve içebilir miyiz?
lousy ['laʊzɪ] *adj* alçak
love [lʌv] *n* sevgi/aşk ▹ *v* sevmek
lovely ['lʌvlɪ] *adj* hoş
lover ['lʌvə] *n* aşık
low [ləʊ] *adj* aşağı *(konum)* ▹ *adv* aşağı *(konum)*; **low season** *n* ucuz sezon
low-alcohol ['ləʊˌælkəˌhɒl] *adj* düşük alkollü
lower ['ləʊə] *adj* daha aşağı ▹ *v* düşürmek
low-fat ['ləʊˌfæt] *adj* az-yağlı
loyalty ['lɔɪəltɪ] *n* sadakat
luck [lʌk] *n* şans
luckily ['lʌkɪlɪ] *adv* neyse ki
lucky ['lʌkɪ] *adj* şanslı
lucrative ['luːkrətɪv] *adj* kazançlı
luggage ['lʌgɪdʒ] *n* bagaj; **hand luggage** *n* el bagajı; **luggage rack** *n* port bagaj; **luggage trolley** *n* bagaj trolleyi; **Can I insure my luggage?** Bagajımı sigorta ettirebilir miyim?; **My luggage has been damaged** Bagajım hasar görmüş; **My luggage has been lost** Bagajım kaybolmuş; **My luggage hasn't arrived** Bagajım çıkmadı; **Where do I check in my luggage?** Bagajlarımı nerede check-in yaptırabilirim; **Where is the luggage for the flight from...?** ... uçağının bagajları nerede?
lukewarm [ˌluːk'wɔːm] *adj* ılık
lullaby ['lʌləˌbaɪ] *n* ninni
lump [lʌmp] *n* iri parça
lunatic ['luː'nætɪk] *n* kaçık
lunch [lʌntʃ] *n* öğle yemeği; **lunch break** *n* yemek molası; **packed lunch** *n* paket yemek
lunchtime ['lʌntʃˌtaɪm] *n* yemek zamanı
lung [lʌŋ] *n* akciğer
lush [lʌʃ] *adj* özlü
lust [lʌst] *n* şehvet
Luxembourg ['lʌksəmˌbɜːg] *n* Lüksemburg
luxurious [lʌg'zjʊərɪəs] *adj* lüks
luxury ['lʌkʃərɪ] *n* lüks
lyrics ['lɪrɪks] *npl* güfte

mac [mæk] *abbr* yağmurluk
macaroni [ˌmækəˈrəʊnɪ] *npl* makarna
machine [məˈʃiːn] *n* makine; **answering machine** *n* telesekreter; **machine gun** *n* makineli tüfek; **machine washable** *adj* makinede yıkanabilir; **sewing machine** *n* dikiş makinesi; **slot machine** *n* jetonlu makine; **ticket machine** *n* bilet otomatı; **vending machine** *n* otomatik satış makinesi; **washing machine** *n* çamaşır makinesi; **Can I use my card with this cash machine?** Bu kartı bu makinede kullanabilir miyim?; **How does the washing machine work?** Çamaşır makinesi nasıl çalışıyor?; **Is there a fax machine I can use?** Kullanabileceğim bir faks makinesi var mı?; **The cash machine swallowed my card** Makine kartımı yuttu; **Where are the washing machines?** Çamaşır makineleri nerede?
machinery [məˈʃiːnərɪ] *n* mekanizma
mackerel [ˈmækrəl] *n* uskumru
mad [mæd] *adj (angry)* çılgın, *(insane)* kaçık
Madagascar [ˌmædəˈgæskə] *n* Madagaskar
madam [ˈmædəm] *n* madam
madly [ˈmædlɪ] *adv* çılgınca
madman [ˈmædmən] *n* manyak
madness [ˈmædnɪs] *n* çılgınlık
magazine [ˌmægəˈziːn] *n (ammunition)* şarjör, *(periodical)* dergi; **Where can I buy a magazine?** Dergi nereden alabilirim?
maggot [ˈmægət] *n* larva
magic [ˈmædʒɪk] *adj* büyülü ▷ *n* büyü
magical [ˈmædʒɪkəl] *adj* sihirli
magician [məˈdʒɪʃən] *n* sihirbaz
magistrate [ˈmædʒɪˌstreɪt; -strɪt] *n* sulh hakimi
magnet [ˈmægnɪt] *n* mıknatıs
magnetic [mægˈnɛtɪk] *adj* mıknatıslı
magnificent [mægˈnɪfɪsᵊnt] *adj* harika
magpie [ˈmægˌpaɪ] *n* saksağan
mahogany [məˈhɒgənɪ] *n* maun
maid [meɪd] *n* hizmetçi kadın
maiden [ˈmeɪdᵊn] *n* **maiden name** *n* kızlık soyadı
mail [meɪl] *n* posta ▷ *v* postalamak; **junk mail** *n* istenmeyen posta
mailbox [ˈmeɪlˌbɒks] *n* posta

kutusu
mailing list ['meɪlɪŋ 'lɪst] *n* **mailing list** *n* adres listesi
main [meɪn] *adj* temel; **main course** *n* ana yemek; **main road** *n* anayol
mainland ['meɪnlənd] *n* anakara
mainly ['meɪnlɪ] *adv* başlıca
maintain [meɪn'teɪn] *v* sürdürmek
maintenance ['meɪntɪnəns] *n* bakım *(araba vb)*
maize [meɪz] *n* mısır
majesty ['mædʒɪstɪ] *n* görkem
major ['meɪdʒə] *adj* büyük
majority [mə'dʒɒrɪtɪ] *n* büyük çoğunluk
make [meɪk] *v* yapmak
makeover ['meɪk,əʊvə] *n* yenilemek
maker ['meɪkə] *n* yapıcı
make up [meɪk ʌp] *v* oluşturmak
make-up [meɪkʌp] *n* makyaj
malaria [mə'lɛərɪə] *n* sıtma
Malawi [mə'lɑːwɪ] *n* Malawi
Malaysia [mə'leɪzɪə] *n* Malezya
Malaysian [mə'leɪzɪən] *adj* Malezya ▹ *n* Malezyalı
male [meɪl] *adj* erkek ▹ *n* erkek
malicious [mə'lɪʃəs] *adj* kötü niyetli
malignant [mə'lɪgnənt] *adj* kötücül
malnutrition [,mælnjuː'trɪʃən] *n* yetersiz beslenme
Malta ['mɔːltə] *n* Malta
Maltese [mɔːl'tiːz] *adj* Malta ▹ *n* *(language)* Malta dili *(dil)*, *(person)* Maltalı *(kişi)*
mammal ['mæməl] *n* memeli
mammoth ['mæməθ] *adj* devasa ▹ *n* mamut
man, men [mæn, mɛn] *n* erkek; **best man** *n* sağdıç
manage ['mænɪdʒ] *v* becermek
manageable ['mænɪdʒəbᵊl] *adj* üstesinden gelinebilir
management ['mænɪdʒmənt] *n* yönetim
manager ['mænɪdʒə] *n* müdür; **I'd like to speak to the manager, please** Müdürle konuşmak istiyorum lütfen
manageress [,mænɪdʒə'rɛs; 'mænɪdʒə,rɛs] *n* müdür *(kadın)*
mandarin ['mændərɪn] *n* *(fruit)* mandalina, *(official)* Çin'de yüksek memur
mangetout ['mɑ̃ʒ'tuː] *n* mangetout
mango ['mæŋgəʊ] *n* mango
mania ['meɪnɪə] *n* çılgınlık
maniac ['meɪnɪ,æk] *n* manyak
manicure ['mænɪ,kjʊə] *n* manikür ▹ *v* manikür yapmak
manipulate [mə'nɪpjʊ,leɪt] *v* idare etmek
mankind [,mæn'kaɪnd] *n* insanlık
man-made ['mæn,meɪd] *adj* insan yapısı
manner ['mænə] *n* tavır
manners ['mænəz] *npl* görgü
manpower ['mæn,paʊə] *n* insan gücü
mansion ['mænʃən] *n* konak
mantelpiece ['mæntᵊl,piːs] *n* şömine rafı
manual ['mænjʊəl] *n* kullanım kılavuzu
manufacture [,mænjʊ'fæktʃə] *v*

üretmek
manufacturer [ˌmænjʊ'fæktʃərə] *n* üretici
manure [mə'njʊə] *n* gübre
manuscript ['mænjʊˌskrɪpt] *n* elyazması
many ['mɛnɪ] *adj* çok ▹ *pron* çok
Maori ['maʊrɪ] *adj* Maori ▹ *n* *(language)* Maori dili *(dil)*, *(person)* Maori *(kişi)*
map [mæp] *n* harita; **road map** *n* yol haritası; **street map** *n* sokak haritası; **Can I have a map?** Harita alabilir miyim?; **Can you show me where it is on the map?** Haritada yerini gösterebilir misiniz?; **Do you have a map of the ski runs?** Kayak güzergahlarının haritası var mı?; **Do you have a map of the tube?** Metro haritası var mı?; **Have you got a map of...?** ... haritası var mı?; **I need a road map of...** ... yol haritası istiyorum; **Is there a cycle map of this area?** Bu bölgenin bisiklet haritası var mı?; **Where can I buy a map of the area?** Bölgenin haritasını nereden alabilirim?
maple ['meɪpᵊl] *n* akçaağaç
marathon ['mærəθən] *n* maraton
marble ['mɑ:bᵊl] *n* mermer
march [mɑ:tʃ] *n* uyun adım yürüyüş ▹ *v* uygun adım yürümek
March [mɑ:tʃ] *n* Mart
mare [mɛə] *n* kısrak
margarine [ˌmɑ:dʒə'ri:n; ˌmɑ:gə-] *n* margarin
margin ['mɑ:dʒɪn] *n* sınır
marigold ['mærɪˌgəʊld] *n* kadife çiçeği
marijuana [ˌmærɪ'hwɑ:nə] *n* Hint keneviri *(yaprakları esrar olarak kullanılır)*
marina [mə'ri:nə] *n* yat limanı
marinade *n* [ˌmærɪ'neɪd] terbiye sosu ▹ *v* ['mærɪˌneɪd] terbiye sosuna yatırmak
marital ['mærɪtᵊl] *adj* **marital status** *n* medeni hal
maritime ['mærɪˌtaɪm] *adj* denizcilikle ilgili
marjoram ['mɑ:dʒərəm] *n* mercanköşk
mark [mɑ:k] *n* işaret ▹ *v* *(grade)* not vermek, *(make sign)* işaretlemek; **exclamation mark** *n* ünlem işareti; **question mark** *n* soru işareti; **quotation marks** *npl* çift tırnak
market ['mɑ:kɪt] *n* pazar *(piyasa)*; **market research** *n* pazar araştırması; **stock market** *n* borsa; **When is the market on?** Hangi günler pazar kuruluyor?
marketing ['mɑ:kɪtɪŋ] *n* pazarlama
marketplace ['mɑ:kɪtˌpleɪs] *n* pazar yeri
marmalade ['mɑ:məˌleɪd] *n* marmelat
maroon [mə'ru:n] *adj* vişne çürüğü renginde
marriage ['mærɪdʒ] *n* evlilik; **marriage certificate** *n* evlilik cüzdanı
married ['mærɪd] *adj* evli; **I'm married** Evliyim
marrow ['mærəʊ] *n* ilik *(anatomi)*
marry ['mærɪ] *v* evlenmek
marsh [mɑ:ʃ] *n* bataklık

martyr ['mɑːtə] *n* şehit
marvellous ['mɑːvᵊləs] *adj* harika
Marxism ['mɑːksɪzəm] *n* Marksizm
marzipan ['mɑːzɪˌpæn] *n* badem ezmesi
mascara [mæ'skɑːrə] *n* rimel
masculine ['mæskjʊlɪn] *adj* erkeksi
mask [mɑːsk] *n* maske
masked [mɑːskt] *adj* maskeli
mass [mæs] *n (amount)* kütle, *(church)* ayin *(kilise)*; **When is mass?** Ayin ne zaman?
massacre ['mæsəkə] *n* katliam
massage ['mæsɑːʒ; -sɑːdʒ] *n* masaj
massive ['mæsɪv] *adj* masif
mast [mɑːst] *n* direk *(kale, gemi)*
master ['mɑːstə] *n* bey ▹ *v* üstesinden gelmek
masterpiece ['mɑːstəˌpiːs] *n* şaheser
mat [mæt] *n* paspas *(ayak silme)*; **mouse mat** *n* fare pedi
match [mætʃ] *n (partnership)* denk *(uygun)*, *(sport)* maç ▹ *v* uydurmak; **away match** *n* rakip sahada maç; **home match** *n* kendi sahasında maç; **I'd like to see a football match** Futbol maçı görmek isterdim
matching [mætʃɪŋ] *adj* uyumlu
mate [meɪt] *n* ahbap
material [mə'tɪərɪəl] *n* malzeme
maternal [mə'tɜːnᵊl] *adj* annelik
mathematical [ˌmæθə'mætɪkᵊl; ˌmæθ'mæt-] *adj* matematiksel
mathematics [ˌmæθə'mætɪks; ˌmæθ'mæt-] *npl* matematik
maths [mæθs] *npl* matematik
matter ['mætə] *n* madde *(fizik)* ▹ *v* önemli olmak
mattress ['mætrɪs] *n* yatak *(döşek)*
mature [mə'tjʊə; -'tʃʊə] *adj* olgun *(kişi)*; **mature student** *n* olgun öğrenci
Mauritania [ˌmɒrɪ'teɪnɪə] *n* Moritanya
Mauritius [mə'rɪʃəs] *n* Mauritius Adası
mauve [məʊv] *adj* pembemsi leylak rengi
maximum ['mæksɪməm] *adj* en fazla ▹ *n* maksimum
May [meɪ] *n* Mayıs
maybe ['meɪˌbiː] *adv* belki
mayonnaise [ˌmeɪə'neɪz] *n* mayonez
mayor, mayoress [mɛə, 'mɛərɪs] *n* belediye başkanı
maze [meɪz] *n* labirent
me [miː] *pron* ben *(kişi)*
meadow ['mɛdəʊ] *n* çayır
meal [miːl] *n* öğün
mealtime ['miːlˌtaɪm] *n* yemek zamanı
mean [miːn] *adj* eli sıkı ▹ *v* kastetmek
meaning ['miːnɪŋ] *n* anlam
means [miːnz] *npl* yol
meantime ['miːnˌtaɪm] *adv* bu arada
meanwhile ['miːnˌwaɪl] *adv* o sırada
measles ['miːzəlz] *npl* kızamık; **German measles** *n* kızamıkçık; **I had measles recently** Yakınlarda kızamık geçirdim

measure ['mɛʒə] *v* ölçmek; **tape measure** *n* şerit metre
measurements ['mɛʒəmənts] *npl* ölçüler
meat [miːt] *n* et *(yiyecek)*; **red meat** *n* kırmızı et; **Do you eat meat?** Et yiyor musunuz?; **I don't eat meat** Et yemiyorum; **I don't eat red meat** Kırmızı et yemiyorum; **I don't like meat** Et sevmem; **The meat is cold** Et soğuk; **This meat is off** Et bozulmuş
meatball ['miːtˌbɔːl] *n* köfte
Mecca ['mɛkə] *n* Mekke
mechanic [mɪ'kænɪk] *n* tamirci *(otomobil)*; **Can you send a mechanic?** Tamirci gönderebilir misiniz?
mechanical [mɪ'kænɪkᵊl] *adj* mekanik
mechanism ['mɛkəˌnɪzəm] *n* mekanizma
medal ['mɛdᵊl] *n* madalya
medallion [mɪ'dæljən] *n* madalyon
media ['miːdɪə] *npl* medya
mediaeval [ˌmɛdɪ'iːvᵊl] *adj* ortaçağ
medical ['mɛdɪkᵊl] *adj* tıbbi ▷ *n* tıp; **medical certificate** *n* sağlık belgesi
medication [ˌmɛdɪ'keɪʃən] *n* **I'm on this medication** Bu ilacı kullanıyorum
medicine ['mɛdɪsɪn; 'mɛdsɪn] *n* ilaç
meditation [ˌmɛdɪ'teɪʃən] *n* meditasyon
Mediterranean [ˌmɛdɪtə'reɪnɪən] *adj* Akdeniz ▷ *n* Akdeniz
medium ['miːdɪəm] *adj (between extremes)* ılımlı
medium-sized ['miːdɪəmˌsaɪzd] *adj* orta boy
meet [miːt] *vi* toplanmak ▷ *vt* tanışmak; **It was a pleasure to meet you** Sizinle tanışmak bir zevk
meeting ['miːtɪŋ] *n* buluşma
meet up [miːt ʌp] *v* buluşmak
mega ['mɛgə] *adj* mega
melody ['mɛlədɪ] *n* melodi
melon ['mɛlən] *n* kavun
melt [mɛlt] *vi* eritmek
member ['mɛmbə] *n* üye
membership ['mɛmbəˌʃɪp] *n* üyelik; **membership card** *n* üyelik kartı
memento [mɪ'mɛntəʊ] *n* hatıra
memo ['mɛməʊ; 'miːməʊ] *n* kısa not
memorial [mɪ'mɔːrɪəl] *n* anıt
memorize ['mɛməˌraɪz] *v* ezberlemek
memory ['mɛmərɪ] *n* bellek; **memory card** *n* hafıza kartı
mend [mɛnd] *v* onarmak
meningitis [ˌmɛnɪn'dʒaɪtɪs] *n* menenjit
menopause ['mɛnəʊˌpɔːz] *n* menopoz
menstruation [ˌmɛnstrʊ'eɪʃən] *n* regl
mental ['mɛntᵊl] *adj* akıl; **mental hospital** *n* akıl hastanesi
mentality [mɛn'tælɪtɪ] *n* zihniyet
mention ['mɛnʃən] *v* bahsetmek
menu ['mɛnjuː] *n* mönü; **set**

menu *n* fiks mönü
mercury ['mɜːkjʊrɪ] *n* cıva
mercy ['mɜːsɪ] *n* merhamet
mere [mɪə] *adj* sadece
merge [mɜːdʒ] *v* kaynaştırmak
merger ['mɜːdʒə] *n* şirket evliliği
meringue [mə'ræŋ] *n* beze *(tatlı)*
mermaid ['mɜːˌmeɪd] *n* deniz kızı
merry ['mɛrɪ] *adj* şen şakrak
merry-go-round ['mɛrɪgəʊ'raʊnd] *n* atlıkarınca
mess [mɛs] *n* dağınıklık
mess about [mɛs ə'baʊt] *v* boş durmak
message ['mɛsɪdʒ] *n* mesaj; **text message** *n* mesaj; **Are there any messages for me?** Bana mesaj var mı?; **Can I leave a message with his secretary?** Sekreterine mesaj bırakabilir miyim?; **Can I leave a message?** Mesaj bırakabilir miyim?
messenger ['mɛsɪndʒə] *n* ulak
mess up [mɛs ʌp] *v* berbat etmek
messy ['mɛsɪ] *adj* kirli
metabolism [mɪ'tæbəˌlɪzəm] *n* metabolizma
metal ['mɛtᵊl] *n* metal
meteorite ['miːtɪəˌraɪt] *n* göktaşı
meter ['miːtə] *n* sayaç; **parking meter** *n* otopark ödeme cihazı
method ['mɛθəd] *n* yöntem
Methodist ['mɛθədɪst] *adj* Methodist mezhebine ait
metre ['miːtə] *n* metre
metric ['mɛtrɪk] *adj* metrik
Mexican ['mɛksɪkən] *adj* Meksika'ya ait ▷ *n* Meksikalı
Mexico ['mɛksɪˌkəʊ] *n* Meksika
microchip ['maɪkrəʊˌtʃɪp] *n* mikroçip
microphone ['maɪkrəˌfəʊn] *n* mikrofon; **Does it have a microphone?** Mikrofon var mı?
microscope ['maɪkrəˌskəʊp] *n* mikroskop
mid [mɪd] *adj* orta
midday ['mɪd'deɪ] *n* öğle; **It's twelve midday** Saat öğlen on iki
middle ['mɪdᵊl] *n* orta; **Middle Ages** *npl* Orta Çağ; **Middle East** *n* Orta Doğu
middle-aged ['mɪdᵊlˌeɪdʒɪd] *adj* orta yaşlı
middle-class ['mɪdᵊlˌklɑːs] *adj* orta sınıf
midge [mɪdʒ] *n* tatarcık
midnight ['mɪdˌnaɪt] *n* geceyarısı; **at midnight** Geceyarısı
midwife, midwives ['mɪdˌwaɪf, 'mɪdˌwaɪvz] *n* ebe
migraine ['miːgreɪn; 'maɪ-] *n* migren
migrant ['maɪgrənt] *adj* göçmen ▷ *n* göçmen
migration [maɪ'greɪʃən] *n* göç
mike [maɪk] *n* mikrofon
mild [maɪld] *adj* ılımlı
mile [maɪl] *n* mil
mileage ['maɪlɪdʒ] *n* mil hesabıyla uzaklık
mileometer [maɪ'lɒmɪtə] *n* mil ölçer
military ['mɪlɪtərɪ; -trɪ] *adj* askeri
milk [mɪlk] *n* süt ▷ *v* sağmak; **baby milk** *n* bebek sütü; **milk chocolate** *n* sütlü çikolata; **semi-skimmed milk** *n* yarım yağlı süt; **skimmed milk** *n* yağı alınmış süt; **UHT milk** *n* UHT süt; **Do you**

drink milk? Süt içer misiniz?; **Have you got real milk?** Taze sütünüz var mı?; **Is it made with unpasteurised milk?** Bu pastörize edilmemiş sütten mi yapıldı?; **with the milk separate** sütü ayrı getirin
milkshake ['mɪlk,ʃeɪk] *n* milkshake
mill [mɪl] *n* değirmen
millennium [mɪ'lɛnɪəm] *n* milenyum
millimetre ['mɪlɪ,miːtə] *n* milimetre
million ['mɪljən] *n* milyon
millionaire [,mɪljə'nɛə] *n* milyoner
mimic ['mɪmɪk] *v* taklit etmek
mince [mɪns] *v* kıyma
mind [maɪnd] *n* zihin ▷ *v* aldırmak
mine [maɪn] *n* maden ocağı ▷ *pron* benim
miner ['maɪnə] *n* madenci
mineral ['mɪnərəl; 'mɪnrəl] *adj* madensel ▷ *n* maden; **mineral water** *n* maden suyu; **a bottle of sparkling mineral water** Bir şişe maden suyu
miniature ['mɪnɪtʃə] *adj* minyatür ▷ *n* minyatür
minibar ['mɪnɪ,bɑː] *n* minibar
minibus ['mɪnɪ,bʌs] *n* minibüs
minicab ['mɪnɪ,kæb] *n* taksi
minimal ['mɪnɪməl] *adj* en düşük
minimize ['mɪnɪ,maɪz] *v* en aza indirgemek
minimum ['mɪnɪməm] *adj* en az ▷ *n* en az
mining ['maɪnɪŋ] *n* madencilik
miniskirt ['mɪnɪ,skɜːt] *n* mini etek
minister ['mɪnɪstə] *n* *(clergy)* vaiz, *(government)* bakan *(hükümet)*; **prime minister** *n* başbakan
ministry ['mɪnɪstrɪ] *n* *(government)* bakanlık, *(religion)* papazlık
mink [mɪŋk] *n* vizon
minor ['maɪnə] *adj* ufak ▷ *n* küçük
minority [maɪ'nɒrɪtɪ; mɪ-] *n* azınlık
mint [mɪnt] *n* *(coins)* darphane, *(herb/sweet)* nane *(bitki/şeker)*
minus ['maɪnəs] *prep* eksi
minute *adj* [maɪ'njuːt] küçük ▷ *n* ['mɪnɪt] dakika; **Could you watch my bag for a minute, please?** Bir dakikalığına çantama göz kulak olur musunuz lütfen?; **We are ten minutes late** On dakika geciktik
miracle ['mɪrəkᵊl] *n* mucize
mirror ['mɪrə] *n* ayna; **rear-view mirror** *n* arka ayna; **wing mirror** *n* yan ayna
misbehave [,mɪsbɪ'heɪv] *v* yaramazlık yapmak
miscarriage [mɪs'kærɪdʒ] *n* düşük yapmak
miscellaneous [,mɪsə'leɪnɪəs] *adj* çeşitli
mischief ['mɪstʃɪf] *n* yaramazlık
mischievous ['mɪstʃɪvəs] *adj* yaramaz *(çocuk vb)*
miser ['maɪzə] *n* zengin pinti
miserable ['mɪzərəbᵊl; 'mɪzrə-] *adj* kepaze
misery ['mɪzərɪ] *n* sefalet
misfortune [mɪs'fɔːtʃən] *n* talihsizlik
mishap ['mɪshæp] *n* terslik
misjudge [,mɪs'dʒʌdʒ] *v* yanlış

hüküm vermek
mislay [mɪsˈleɪ] *v* yanlış yere koymak
misleading [mɪsˈliːdɪŋ] *adj* yanıltıcı
misprint [ˈmɪsˌprɪnt] *n* baskı hatası
miss [mɪs] *v* kaçırmak *(treni, otobüsü)*
Miss [mɪs] *n* Bayan *(evlenmemiş kadınlara hitap şekli)*
missile [ˈmɪsaɪl] *n* füze
missing [ˈmɪsɪŋ] *adj* kayıp; **My child is missing** Çocuğum kayıp
missionary [ˈmɪʃənərɪ] *n* misyoner
mist [mɪst] *n* sis
mistake [mɪˈsteɪk] *n* hata ▹ *v* hata yapmak
mistaken [mɪˈsteɪkən] *adj* hatalı
mistakenly [mɪˈsteɪkənlɪ] *adv* yanlışlıkla
mistletoe [ˈmɪsᵊlˌtəʊ] *n* ökseotu
mistress [ˈmɪstrɪs] *n* metres
misty [ˈmɪstɪ] *adj* sisli
misunderstand [ˌmɪsʌndəˈstænd] *v* yanlış anlamak
misunderstanding [ˌmɪsʌndəˈstændɪŋ] *n* yanlış anlama; **There's been a misunderstanding** Bir yanlış anlama var
mitten [ˈmɪtᵊn] *n* parmaksız eldiven
mix [mɪks] *n* karışık *(şeker/çiçek)* ▹ *v* karıştırmak *(nesne)*
mixed [mɪkst] *adj* karışık; **mixed salad** *n* karışık salata
mixer [ˈmɪksə] *n* mikser
mixture [ˈmɪkstʃə] *n* karışım
mix up [mɪks ʌp] *v* karıştırmak *(salata, baharat vb)*
mix-up [mɪksʌp] *n* karışıklık
MMS [ɛm ɛm ɛs] *abbr* MMS
moan [məʊn] *v* inlemek
moat [məʊt] *n* hendek
mobile [ˈməʊbaɪl] *adj* mobil; **mobile home** *n* taşınabilir ev; **mobile number** *n* cep numarası; **mobile phone** *n* cep telefonu
mock [mɒk] *adj* deneme sınavı ▹ *v* alay etmek
mod cons [ˈmɒd kɒnz] *npl* konfor ve rahatlık
model [ˈmɒdᵊl] *adj* örnek ▹ *n* model ▹ *v* modelini yapmak
modem [ˈməʊdɛm] *n* modem
moderate [ˈmɒdərɪt] *adj* ılımlı
moderation [ˌmɒdəˈreɪʃən] *n* ılımlılık
modern [ˈmɒdən] *adj* modern; **modern languages** *npl* modern diller
modernize [ˈmɒdəˌnaɪz] *v* modernize etmek
modest [ˈmɒdɪst] *adj* alçak gönüllü
modification [ˌmɒdɪfɪˈkeɪʃən] *n* değişiklik
modify [ˈmɒdɪˌfaɪ] *v* değişiklik yapmak
module [ˈmɒdjuːl] *n* modül
moist [mɔɪst] *adj* ıslak
moisture [ˈmɔɪstʃə] *n* nem
moisturizer [ˈmɔɪstʃəˌraɪzə] *n* nemlendirici
Moldova [mɒlˈdəʊvə] *n* Moldova
Moldovan [mɒlˈdəʊvən] *adj* Moldova ▹ *n* Moldovalı

mole [məʊl] *n (infiltrator)* köstebek *(casus), (mammal)* köstebek *(hayvan), (skin)* ben *(cilt)*
molecule ['mɒlɪˌkjuːl] *n* molekül
moment ['məʊmənt] *n* an
momentarily ['məʊməntərəlɪ; -trɪlɪ] *adv* bir anlığına
momentary ['məʊməntərɪ; -trɪ] *adj* bir anlık
momentous [məʊ'mɛntəs] *adj* çok önemli
Monaco ['mɒnəˌkəʊ; mə'nɑːkəʊ; mɔnako] *n* Monako
monarch ['mɒnək] *n* kral
monarchy ['mɒnəkɪ] *n* kraliyet
monastery ['mɒnəstərɪ; -strɪ] *n* manastır; **Is the monastery open to the public?** Manastır halka açık mı?
Monday ['mʌndɪ] *n* Pazartesi; **It's Monday the fifteenth of June** On beş Haziran Pazartesi; **on Monday** Pazartesi günü
monetary ['mʌnɪtərɪ; -trɪ] *adj* parasal
money ['mʌnɪ] *n* para; **money belt** *n* bel çantası; **pocket money** *n* cep harçlığı; **Can I have my money back?** Paramı geri alabilir miyim?; **Can you arrange to have some money sent over urgently?** Bana acilen para gönderilmesini ayarlayabilir misiniz?; **I have no money** Hiç param yok; **I have run out of money** Param bitti; **I would like to transfer some money from my account** Hesabımdan para transferi yapmak istiyorum
Mongolia [mɒŋ'gəʊlɪə] *n* Moğolistan
Mongolian [mɒŋ'gəʊlɪən] *adj* Moğol ▷ *n (language)* Moğolca *(dil), (person)* Mongolistanlı *(kişi)*
mongrel ['mʌŋgrəl] *n* melez
monitor ['mɒnɪtə] *n* gözcü
monk [mʌŋk] *n* keşiş
monkey ['mʌŋkɪ] *n* maymun
monopoly [mə'nɒpəlɪ] *n* tekel
monotonous [mə'nɒtənəs] *adj* tekdüze
monsoon [mɒn'suːn] *n* muson
monster ['mɒnstə] *n* canavar
month [mʌnθ] *n* ay *(zaman)*; **a month ago** bir ay önce; **in a month's time** bir ay sonra
monthly ['mʌnθlɪ] *adj* aylık *(zaman)*
monument ['mɒnjʊmənt] *n* anıt
mood [muːd] *n* ruh durumu
moody ['muːdɪ] *adj* bedbin
moon [muːn] *n* ay *(uydu)*; **full moon** *n* dolunay
moor [mʊə; mɔː] *n* bozkır ▷ *v* bağlamak *(tekne)*
mop [mɒp] *n* paspas *(yer silme)*
moped ['məʊpɛd] *n* moped; **I want to hire a moped** Moped kiralamak istiyorum
mop up [mɒp ʌp] *v* paspaslamak
moral ['mɒrəl] *adj* ahlaki ▷ *n* ders *(ahlaki)*
morale [mɒ'rɑːl] *n* moral
morals ['mɒrəlz] *npl* ahlak kuralları
more [mɔː] *adj* daha fazla ▷ *adv* daha ▷ *pron* fazla; **Could you speak more slowly, please?** Biraz daha yavaş konuşabilir misiniz lütfen?; **Please bring**

more bread Biraz daha ekmek getirir misiniz?; **We need more blankets** Daha fazla battaniyeye ihtiyacımız var
morgue [mɔːg] *n* morg
morning ['mɔːnɪŋ] *n* sabah; **morning sickness** *n* hamilelik bulantısı; **in the morning** sabah; **I will be leaving tomorrow morning at ten a.m.** Yarın sabah onda ayrılıyorum; **I've been sick since this morning** Bu sabahtan beri kusuyorum; **Is the museum open in the morning?** Müze sabahları açık mı?; **this morning** bu sabah; **tomorrow morning** yarın sabah
Moroccan [məˈrɒkən] *adj* Fas ▷ *n* Faslı
Morocco [məˈrɒkəʊ] *n* Fas
morphine ['mɔːfiːn] *n* morfin
Morse [mɔːs] *n* Morse *(alfabe)*
mortar ['mɔːtə] *n* *(military)* havan topu, *(plaster)* harç
mortgage ['mɔːgɪdʒ] *n* konut kredisi ▷ *v* ipotek etmek
mosaic [məˈzeɪɪk] *n* mozaik
Moslem ['mɒzləm] *adj* Müslüman ▷ *n* Müslüman
mosque [mɒsk] *n* cami; **Where is there a mosque?** Cami nerede var?
mosquito [məˈskiːtəʊ] *n* sivrisinek
moss [mɒs] *n* yosun
most [məʊst] *adj* en çok ▷ *adv* *(superlative)* en çok ▷ *n* *(majority)* çok
mostly ['məʊstlɪ] *adv* çoğunlukla
MOT [ɛm əʊ tiː] *abbr* yıllık taşıt testi
motel [məʊˈtɛl] *n* motel
moth [mɒθ] *n* güve
mother ['mʌðə] *n* anne; **mother tongue** *n* anadil; **surrogate mother** *n* taşıyıcı anne
mother-in-law ['mʌðə ɪn lɔː] **(mothers-in-law)** *n* kayınvalide
motionless ['məʊʃənlɪs] *adj* hareketsiz
motivated ['məʊtɪˌveɪtɪd] *adj* motive olmuş
motivation [ˌməʊtɪˈveɪʃən] *n* motivasyon
motive ['məʊtɪv] *n* sebep
motor ['məʊtə] *n* motor; **motor mechanic** *n* motor teknisyeni; **motor racing** *n* oto yarışı
motorbike ['məʊtəˌbaɪk] *n* motosiklet; **I want to hire a motorbike** Motosiklet kiralamak istiyorum
motorboat ['məʊtəˌbəʊt] *n* deniz motoru
motorcycle ['məʊtəˌsaɪkᵊl] *n* motosiklet
motorcyclist ['məʊtəˌsaɪklɪst] *n* motosikletçi
motorist ['məʊtərɪst] *n* sürücü
motorway ['məʊtəˌweɪ] *n* otoyol; **How do I get to the motorway?** Otoyola nereden gidebilirim?; **Is there a toll on this motorway?** Bu otoyol ücretli mi?
mould [məʊld] *n* *(fungus)* küf, *(shape)* kalıp *(pasta, jöle, briket vb)*
mouldy ['məʊldɪ] *adj* küflü
mount [maʊnt] *v* tırmanmak
mountain ['maʊntɪn] *n* dağ; **mountain bike** *n* dağ bisikleti; **Where is the nearest mountain**

rescue service post? En yakın dağ kurtarma ekibi nerede?
mountaineer [ˌmaʊntɪˈnɪə] *n* dağcı
mountaineering [ˌmaʊntɪˈnɪərɪŋ] *n* dağcılık
mountainous [ˈmaʊntɪnəs] *adj* dağlık
mount up [maʊnt ʌp] *v* birikmek
mourning [ˈmɔːnɪŋ] *n* matem
mouse, mice [maʊs, maɪs] *n* fare; **mouse mat** *n* fare pedi
mousse [muːs] *n* köpük krema
moustache [məˈstɑːʃ] *n* bıyık
mouth [maʊθ] *n* ağız; **mouth organ** *n* armonika
mouthwash [ˈmaʊθˌwɒʃ] *n* gargara
move [muːv] *n* hareket ▹ *vi* kımıldamak ▹ *vt* kımıldatmak
move back [muːv bæk] *v* geri gitmek
move forward [muːv fɔːwəd] *v* ileri gitmek
move in [muːv ɪn] *v* taşınmak
movement [ˈmuːvmənt] *n* hareket
movie [ˈmuːvɪ] *n* film *(sinema)*
moving [ˈmuːvɪŋ] *adj* dokunaklı *(sahne, film)*
mow [məʊ] *v* biçmek
mower [ˈmaʊə] *n* çim biçme makinesi
Mozambique [ˌməʊzəmˈbiːk] *n* Mozambik
mph [maɪlz pə aʊə] *abbr* mil/saat
Mr [ˈmɪstə] *n* Bay
Mrs [ˈmɪsɪz] *n* Bayan *(hanım)*
Ms [mɪz; məs] *n* Bayan *(evli olup olmadığını belirtmeyenler için)*
MS [mɪz; məs] *abbr* MS *(hastalık)*
much [mʌtʃ] *adj* fazla ▹ *adv* fazla, *(graded)* çokça; **There's too much... in it** Çok fazla... koymuşsunuz
mud [mʌd] *n* çamur
muddle [ˈmʌdᵊl] *n* kargaşa
muddy [ˈmʌdɪ] *adj* çamurlu
mudguard [ˈmʌdˌɡɑːd] *n* çamurluk
muesli [ˈmjuːzlɪ] *n* müsli
muffler [ˈmʌflə] *n* atkı *(giysi)*
mug [mʌɡ] *n* kupa *(kahve)* ▹ *v* saldırmak
mugger [ˈmʌɡə] *n* kapkaççı
mugging [mʌɡɪŋ] *n* kapkaççılık
mule [mjuːl] *n* katır
multinational [ˌmʌltɪˈnæʃənᵊl] *adj* çok uluslu ▹ *n* çok uluslu
multiple [ˈmʌltɪpᵊl] *adj* **multiple sclerosis** *n* multipl skleroz
multiplication [ˌmʌltɪplɪˈkeɪʃən] *n* çarpma işlemi
multiply [ˈmʌltɪˌplaɪ] *v* çarpmak *(matematik)*
mum [mʌm] *n* anne
mummy [ˈmʌmɪ] *n (body)* mumya, *(mother)* annecim
mumps [mʌmps] *n* kabakulak
murder [ˈmɜːdə] *n* cinayet ▹ *v* katletmek
murderer [ˈmɜːdərə] *n* katil
muscle [ˈmʌsᵊl] *n* kas
muscular [ˈmʌskjʊlə] *adj* kas
museum [mjuːˈzɪəm] *n* müze; **Is the museum open every day?** Müze her gün açık mı?; **When is the museum open?** Müze ne zaman açık?
mushroom [ˈmʌʃruːm; -rʊm] *n*

mantar *(botanik)*
music ['mju:zɪk] *n* müzik; **folk music** *n* halk müziği; **music centre** *n* müzik seti; **Where can we hear live music?** Canlı müzik dinleyebileceğimiz bir yer var mı?
musical ['mju:zɪkᵊl] *adj* müzik ▹ *n* müzikal; **musical instrument** *n* müzik aleti
musician [mju:'zɪʃən] *n* müzisyen; **Where can we hear local musicians play?** Yerel müzisyenleri dinleyebileceğimiz bir yer var mı?
Muslim ['mʊzlɪm; 'mʌz-] *adj* Müslüman ▹ *n* Müslüman
mussel ['mʌsᵊl] *n* midye
must [mʌst] *v* gereğinde olmak
mustard ['mʌstəd] *n* hardal
mutter ['mʌtə] *v* mırıldanmak
mutton ['mʌtᵊn] *n* koyun eti
mutual ['mju:tʃʊəl] *adj* karşılıklı
my [maɪ] *pron* benim
Myanmar ['maɪænmɑ:; 'mjænmɑ:] *n* Myanmar
myself [maɪ'sɛlf] *pron* kendim
mysterious [mɪ'stɪərɪəs] *adj* gizemli
mystery ['mɪstərɪ] *n* gizem
myth [mɪθ] *n* efsane
mythology [mɪ'θɒlədʒɪ] *n* mitoloji

naff [næf] *adj* salaş
nag [næg] *v* dırdır etmek
nail [neɪl] *n* çivi; **nail polish** *n* oje; **nail scissors** *npl* tırnak makası; **nail varnish** *n* tırnak cilası; **nail-polish remover** *n* oje çıkarıcı
nailbrush ['neɪl,brʌʃ] *n* tırnak fırçası
nailfile ['neɪl,faɪl] *n* tırnak törpüsü
naive [nɑ:'i:v; naɪ'i:v] *adj* saf
naked ['neɪkɪd] *adj* çıplak
name [neɪm] *n* ad *(kişi)*; **brand name** *n* marka; **first name** *n* ön ad; **maiden name** *n* kızlık soyadı; **I booked a room in the name of...** ... adına yer ayırtmıştım; **My name is...** Benim adım...; **What's your name?** Adınız ne?
nanny ['nænɪ] *n* çocuk bakıcısı
nap [næp] *n* kestirme *(uyku)*
napkin ['næpkɪn] *n* peçete
nappy ['næpɪ] *n* bebek bezi

narrow ['nærəʊ] *adj* dar
narrow-minded ['nærəʊ'maɪndɪd] *adj* dar görüşlü
nasty ['nɑːstɪ] *adj* berbat
nation ['neɪʃən] *n* ulus; **United Nations** *n* Birleşmiş Milletler
national ['næʃənᵊl] *adj* ulusal; **national anthem** *n* milli marş; **national park** *n* milli park
nationalism ['næʃənəˌlɪzəm; 'næʃnə-] *n* ulusalcılık
nationalist ['næʃənəlɪst] *n* ulusalcı
nationality [ˌnæʃə'nælɪtɪ] *n* ulus
nationalize ['næʃənəˌlaɪz; 'næʃnə-] *v* kamulaştırmak
native ['neɪtɪv] *adj* yerli; **native speaker** *n* anadilini konuşan
NATO ['neɪtəʊ] *abbr* NATO
natural ['nætʃrəl; -tʃərəl] *adj* doğal; **natural gas** *n* doğal gaz; **natural resources** *npl* doğal kaynaklar
naturalist ['nætʃrəlɪst; -tʃərəl-] *n* doğa bilimleri uzmanı
naturally ['nætʃrəlɪ; -tʃərə-] *adv* doğal olarak
nature ['neɪtʃə] *n* doğa
naughty ['nɔːtɪ] *adj* yaramaz *(çocuk vb)*
nausea ['nɔːzɪə; -sɪə] *n* bulantı
naval ['neɪvᵊl] *adj* deniz *(askeri)*
navel ['neɪvᵊl] *n* göbek
navy ['neɪvɪ] *n* donanma *(deniz)*
navy-blue ['neɪvɪ'bluː] *adj* lacivert
NB [ɛn biː] *abbr (notabene)* dikkatinize
near [nɪə] *adj* yakın ▹ *adv* yakınında ▹ *prep* bitişiğinde; **How do I get to the nearest tube station?** En yakın metro istasyonuna nasıl gidebilirim?; **It's very near** Çok yakın; **Where is the nearest bus stop?** Buraya en yakın otobüs durağı nerede?
nearby *adj* ['nɪəˌbaɪ] yakın ▹ *adv* [ˌnɪə'baɪ] yakınlarda; **Is there a bank nearby?** Yakınlarda bir banka var mı?
nearly ['nɪəlɪ] *adv* hemen hemen
near-sighted [ˌnɪə'saɪtɪd] *adj* miyop
neat [niːt] *adj* temiz ve tertipli
neatly [niːtlɪ] *adv* derli toplu *(düzenli)*
necessarily ['nɛsɪsərɪlɪ; ˌnɛsɪ'sɛrɪlɪ] *adv* kaçınılmaz bir şekilde
necessary ['nɛsɪsərɪ] *adj* gerekli
necessity [nɪ'sɛsɪtɪ] *n* gereklilik
neck [nɛk] *n* boyun
necklace ['nɛklɪs] *n* kolye
nectarine ['nɛktərɪn] *n* nektarin
need [niːd] *n* ihtiyaç ▹ *v* gerek duymak
needle ['niːdᵊl] *n* iğne; **knitting needle** *n* örgü şişi
negative ['nɛgətɪv] *adj* olumsuz ▹ *n* olumsuz
neglect [nɪ'glɛkt] *n* ihmal ▹ *v* ihmal etmek
neglected [nɪ'glɛktɪd] *adj* ihmal edilmiş
negligee ['nɛglɪˌʒeɪ] *n* gecelik *(hafif)*
negotiate [nɪ'gəʊʃɪˌeɪt] *v* görüşmek
negotiations [nɪˌgəʊʃɪ'eɪʃənz] *npl* görüşmeler
negotiator [nɪ'gəʊʃɪˌeɪtə] *n*

görüşmeci
neighbour ['neɪbə] *n* komşu
neighbourhood ['neɪbə,hʊd] *n* mahalle
neither ['naɪðə; 'ni:ðə] *adv* hiçbiri ▹ *conj* ne ▹ *pron* hiçbir
neon ['ni:ɒn] *n* neon
Nepal [nɪ'pɔ:l] *n* Nepal
nephew ['nɛvju:; 'nɛf-] *n* yeğen *(erkek)*
nerve [nɜ:v] *n (boldness)* cüret, *(anat)* sinir *(anatomi)*
nerve-racking ['nɜ:v'rækɪŋ] *adj* sinir bozucu
nervous ['nɜ:vəs] *adj* sinirli; **nervous breakdown** *n* sinir krizi
nest [nɛst] *n* yuva
net [nɛt] *n* tül
Net [nɛt] *n* İnternet
netball ['nɛt,bɔ:l] *n* netbol
Netherlands ['nɛðələndz] *npl* Hollanda
nettle ['nɛtᵊl] *n* ısırgan
network ['nɛt,wɜ:k] *n* ağ *(bilişim)*
neurotic [njʊ'rɒtɪk] *adj* nörotik
neutral ['nju:trəl] *adj* tarafsız ▹ *n* tarafsız
never ['nɛvə] *adv* asla
nevertheless [,nɛvəðə'lɛs] *adv* bununla birlikte
new [nju:] *adj* yeni; **New Year** *n* Yeni Yıl; **New Zealand** *n* Yeni Zelanda; **New Zealander** *n* Yeni Zelandalı
newborn ['nju:,bɔ:n] *adj* yeni doğan
newcomer ['nju:,kʌmə] *n* yeni gelen
news [nju:z] *npl* haberler; **When is the news?** Haberler kaçta?
newsagent ['nju:z,eɪdʒənt] *n* gazete bayii
newspaper ['nju:z,peɪpə] *n* gazete; **Do you have newspapers?** Gazete satıyor musunuz?; **I would like a newspaper** Gazete almak istiyorum; **Where can I buy a newspaper?** Gazete nereden alabilirim?; **Where is the nearest shop which sells newspapers?** En yakın gazete satan dükkan nerede?
newsreader ['nju:z,ri:də] *n* haber sunucusu
newt [nju:t] *n* su keleri
next [nɛkst] *adj* gelecek ▹ *adv* bir sonraki; **next to** *prep* yanında; **the week after next** bir sonraki hafta; **What is the next stop?** Bir sonraki durak neresi?; **When is the next bus to...?**... a bir sonraki otobüs kaçta?
next-of-kin ['nɛkstɒv'kɪn] *n* en yakın akraba
Nicaragua [,nɪkə'rægjʊə; nika'raɣwa] *n* Nikaragua
Nicaraguan [,nɪkə'rægjʊən; -gwən] *adj* Nikaragua ▹ *n* Nikaragualı
nice [naɪs] *adj* hoş
nickname ['nɪk,neɪm] *n* takma ad
nicotine ['nɪkə,ti:n] *n* nikotin
niece [ni:s] *n* yeğen *(kız)*
Niger ['naɪ'dʒɪər] *n* Nijer
Nigeria [naɪ'dʒɪərɪə] *n* Nijerya
Nigerian [naɪ'dʒɪərɪən] *adj* Nijerya ▹ *n* Nijeryalı
night [naɪt] *n* gece; **hen night** *n* kına gecesi; **night school** *n* gece

okulu; **stag night** *n* bekarlığa veda partisi *(erkek)*; **at night** gece; **Good night** İyi geceler; **How much is it per night?** Odanın geceliği ne kadar?; **I want to stay an extra night** Bir gece daha kalmak istiyorum; **I'd like to stay for two nights** İki gece kalmak istiyorum; **last night** dün gece; **tomorrow night** yarın gece
nightclub ['naɪt,klʌb] *n* gece kulübü
nightdress ['naɪt,drɛs] *n* gecelik
nightie ['naɪtɪ] *n* gecelik
nightlife ['naɪt,laɪf] *n* gece hayatı
nightmare ['naɪt,mɛə] *n* karabasan
nightshift ['naɪt,ʃɪft] *n* gece nöbeti
nil [nɪl] *n* sıfır
nine [naɪn] *number* dokuz
nineteen [,naɪn'tiːn] *number* ondokuz
nineteenth [,naɪn'tiːnθ] *adj* ondokuzuncu
ninety ['naɪntɪ] *number* doksan
ninth [naɪnθ] *adj* dokuzuncu ▹ *n* dokuzda bir
nitrogen ['naɪtrədʒən] *n* nitrojen
no [nəʊ] *pron* hiç; **no!** *excl* hayır; **no one** *pron* hiç kimse; **I have no money** Hiç param yok
nobody ['nəʊbədɪ] *pron* hiç kimse; **We'd like to see nobody but us all day!** Bütün gün hiç kimseyi değil, sadece kendimizi görmek isterdik!
nod [nɒd] *v* başıyla onaylamak
noise [nɔɪz] *n* gürültü; **I can't sleep for the noise** Gürültüden uyuyamıyorum
noisy ['nɔɪzɪ] *adj* gürültülü; **It's noisy** Çok gürültülü; **The room is too noisy** Bu oda çok gürültülü
nominate ['nɒmɪ,neɪt] *v* aday göstermek
nomination [,nɒmɪ'neɪʃən] *n* adaylık
none [nʌn] *pron* hiçbiri
nonsense ['nɒnsəns] *n* saçma
non-smoker [nɒn'sməʊkə] *n* sigara içmeyen
non-smoking [nɒn'sməʊkɪŋ] *adj* sigara içilmeyen; **I want to book a seat in a non-smoking compartment** Sigara içilmeyen kompartmanda yer ayırtmak istiyorum
non-stop ['nɒn'stɒp] *adv* hiç durmadan
noodles ['nuːdᵊlz] *npl* noodle
noon [nuːn] *n* öğle
nor [nɔː; nə] *conj* ne de
normal ['nɔːmᵊl] *adj* normal; **How long will it take by normal post?** Normal postayla ne kadar sürer?
normally ['nɔːməlɪ] *adv* normalde
north [nɔːθ] *adj* kuzey ▹ *adv* kuzeyde ▹ *n* kuzey; **North Africa** *n* Kuzey Afrika; **North African** *n* Kuzey Afrika, Kuzey Afrikalı; **North America** *n* Kuzey Amerika; **North American** *n* Kuzey Amerika, Kuzey Amerikalı; **North Korea** *n* Kuzey Kore; **North Pole** *n* Kuzey Kutbu; **North Sea** *n* Kuzey Denizi
northbound ['nɔːθ,baʊnd] *adj* kuzeye doğru
northeast [,nɔːθ'iːst; ,nɔːr'iːst] *n*

kuzeydoğu
northern ['nɔːðən] *adj* kuzey; **Northern Ireland** *n* Kuzey İrlanda
northwest [ˌnɔːθ'wɛst; ˌnɔː'wɛst] *n* kuzeybatı
Norway ['nɔːˌweɪ] *n* Norveç
Norwegian [nɔː'wiːdʒən] *adj* Norveç ▷ *n (language)* Norveççe *(dil), (person)* Norveçli *(kişi)*
nose [nəʊz] *n* burun
nosebleed ['nəʊzˌbliːd] *n* burun kanaması
nostril ['nɒstrɪl] *n* burun deliği
nosy ['nəʊzɪ] *adj* meraklı
not [nɒt] *adv* yok
note [nəʊt] *n (banknote)* banknot, *(message)* not *(mesaj), (music)* nota *(müzik)*; **sick note** *n* hasta belgesi
notebook ['nəʊtˌbʊk] *n* not defteri
note down [nəʊt daʊn] *v* not almak
notepad ['nəʊtˌpæd] *n* not defteri
notepaper ['nəʊtˌpeɪpə] *n* not kağıdı
nothing ['nʌθɪŋ] *pron* hiçbir şey
notice ['nəʊtɪs] *n (note)* farkına varma, *(termination)* mühlet ▷ *v* farkına varmak; **notice board** *n* ilan tahtası
noticeable ['nəʊtɪsəbᵊl] *adj* dikkat çeken
notify ['nəʊtɪˌfaɪ] *v* bildirimde bulunmak
nought [nɔːt] *n* sıfır
noun [naʊn] *n* ad *(gramer)*
novel ['nɒvᵊl] *n* roman
novelist ['nɒvəlɪst] *n* romancı
November [nəʊ'vɛmbə] *n* Kasım *(ay)*
now [naʊ] *adv* şimdi
nowadays ['naʊəˌdeɪz] *adv* bugünlerde
nowhere ['nəʊˌwɛə] *adv* hiçbir yerde
nuclear ['njuːklɪə] *adj* nükleer
nude [njuːd] *adj* çıplak ▷ *n* çıplak
nudist ['njuːdɪst] *n* nüdist
nuisance ['njuːsəns] *n* sıkıntı
numb [nʌm] *adj* uyuşuk
number ['nʌmbə] *n* sayı; **account number** *n* hesap numarası; **mobile number** *n* cep numarası; **number plate** *n* plaka *(otomobil)*; **phone number** *n* telefon numarası; **reference number** *n* referans numarası; **room number** *n* oda numarası; **wrong number** *n* yanlış numara
numerous ['njuːmərəs] *adj* sayısız
nun [nʌn] *n* rahibe
nurse [nɜːs] *n* hemşire; **I'd like to speak to a nurse** Hemşireyle konuşmak istiyorum
nursery ['nɜːsrɪ] *n* çocuk odası; **nursery rhyme** *n* çocuk şarkıları; **nursery school** *n* kreş
nursing home ['nɜːsɪŋ həʊm] *n* **nursing home** *n* huzurevi *(yaşlılar için)*
nut [nʌt] *n (device)* vida somunu, *(food)* fındık fıstık; **nut allergy** *n* fıstık alerjisi; **Could you prepare a meal without nuts?** İçinde fındık fıstık olmayan bir yemek yapabilir misiniz?
nutmeg ['nʌtmɛg] *n* küçük Hindistan cevizi
nutrient ['njuːtrɪənt] *n* besleyici

(gıda)
nutrition [nju:'trɪʃən] *n* beslenme
nutritious [nju:'trɪʃəs] *adj* besleyici
nutter ['nʌtə] *n* kaçık
nylon ['naɪlɒn] *n* naylon

oak [əʊk] *n* meşe
oar [ɔ:] *n* kürek
oasis, oases [əʊ'eɪsɪs, əʊ'eɪsi:z] *n* vaha
oath [əʊθ] *n* yemin
oatmeal ['əʊt,mi:l] *n* yulaf ezmesi
oats [əʊts] *npl* yulaf
obedient [ə'bi:dɪənt] *adj* itaatkar
obese [əʊ'bi:s] *adj* obez
obey [ə'beɪ] *v* boyun eğmek
obituary [ə'bɪtjʊərɪ] *n* anma yazısı *(ölünün ardından)*
object ['ɒbdʒɪkt] *n* nesne
objection [əb'dʒɛkʃən] *n* itiraz
objective [əb'dʒɛktɪv] *n* amaç
oblong ['ɒb,lɒŋ] *adj* dikdörtgen şeklinde
obnoxious [əb'nɒkʃəs] *adj* iğrenç
oboe ['əʊbəʊ] *n* obua
obscene [əb'si:n] *adj* açık saçık
observant [əb'zɜ:vənt] *adj* gözlemci

observatory [əb'zɜːvətərɪ; -trɪ] *n* gözlemevi
observe [əb'zɜːv] *v* gözlemlemek
observer [əb'zɜːvə] *n* gözlemci
obsessed [əb'sɛst] *adj* takıntılı
obsession [əb'sɛʃən] *n* takıntı
obsolete ['ɒbsə,liːt; ,ɒbsə'liːt] *adj* modası geçmiş
obstacle ['ɒbstəkᵊl] *n* engel
obstinate ['ɒbstɪnɪt] *adj* müzmin
obstruct [əb'strʌkt] *v* tıkamak
obtain [əb'teɪn] *v* elde etmek
obvious ['ɒbvɪəs] *adj* açık *(kavram)*
obviously ['ɒbvɪəslɪ] *adv* açıkçası
occasion [ə'keɪʒən] *n* fırsat *(durum)*
occasional [ə'keɪʒənᵊl] *adj* arasıra
occasionally [ə'keɪʒənəlɪ] *adv* arada sırada
occupation [,ɒkjʊ'peɪʃən] *n* *(invasion)* işgal, *(work)* meslek
occupy ['ɒkjʊ,paɪ] *v* oturmak
occur [ə'kɜː] *v* meydana gelmek
occurrence [ə'kʌrəns] *n* olay
ocean ['əʊʃən] *n* okyanus; **Arctic Ocean** *n* Kuzey Okyanusu; **Indian Ocean** *n* Hint Okyanusu
Oceania [,əʊʃɪ'ɑːnɪə] *n* Okyanusya
o'clock [ə'klɒk] *adv* **after eight o'clock** saat sekizden sonra; **at three o'clock** saat üçte; **I'd like to book a table for four people for tonight at eight o'clock** Bu akşam saat sekiz için dört kişilik bir masa ayırtmak istiyordum; **It's one o'clock** Saat bir; **It's six o'clock** Saat altı
October [ɒk'təʊbə] *n* Ekim *(ay)*; **It's Sunday the third of October** Üç Ekim Pazar
octopus ['ɒktəpəs] *n* ahtapot
odd [ɒd] *adj* acaip
odour ['əʊdə] *n* koku
of [ɒv; əv] *prep* onun
off [ɒf] *adv* kapalı ▹ *prep* den, dan; **time off** *n* izin *(işten alınan)*
offence [ə'fɛns] *n* saldırı
offend [ə'fɛnd] *v* gücendirmek
offensive [ə'fɛnsɪv] *adj* saldırgan
offer ['ɒfə] *n* teklif ▹ *v* teklif etmek; **special offer** *n* indirimli fiyatla sunulan eşya
office ['ɒfɪs] *n* büro; **booking office** *n* bilet gişesi; **box office** *n* bilet gişesi; **head office** *n* yönetim merkezi; **information office** *n* enformasyon bürosu; **left-luggage office** *n* emanet bagaj bürosu; **lost-property office** *n* kayıp eşya bürosu; **office hours** *npl* çalışma saatleri; **post office** *n* postane; **registry office** *n* evlendirme dairesi; **ticket office** *n* bilet gişesi; **tourist office** *n* turizm bürosu; **Do you have a press office?** Basın büronuz var mı?; **How do I get to your office?** Büronuza nasıl gelebilirim?; **I work in an office** Bir büroda çalışıyorum
officer ['ɒfɪsə] *n* görevli memur *(polis/asker)*; **customs officer** *n* gümrük memuru; **police officer** *n* polis görevlisi; **prison officer** *n* hapishane görevlisi
official [ə'fɪʃəl] *adj* yetkili
off-licence ['ɒf,laɪsəns] *n* içki satan dükkan
off-peak ['ɒf,piːk] *adv* iş saatleri

dışında
off-season ['ɒf,siːzᵊn] *adj* sezon dışı ▷ *adv* sezon dışında
offside ['ɒf'saɪd] *adj* ofsayt
often ['ɒfᵊn; 'ɒftᵊn] *adv* sıklıkla
oil [ɔɪl] *n* yağ ▷ *v* yağlamak; **olive oil** *n* zeytin yağı; **The oil warning light won't go off** Yağ ikaz ışığı yanıyor; **This stain is oil** Yağ lekesi
oil refinery [ɔɪl rɪ'faɪnərɪ] *n* petrol rafinerisi
oil rig [ɔɪl rɪg] *n* petrol platformu
oil slick [ɔɪl slɪk] *n* petrol sızması
oil well [ɔɪl wɛl] *n* petrol kuyusu
ointment ['ɔɪntmənt] *n* merhem
OK [,əʊ'keɪ] *excl* OK!
okay [,əʊ'keɪ] *adj* okey; **okay!** *excl* okey!
old [əʊld] *adj* yaşlı; **old-age pensioner** *n* emekli
old-fashioned ['əʊld'fæʃənd] *adj* eski moda
olive ['ɒlɪv] *n* zeytin; **olive oil** *n* zeytin yağı; **olive tree** *n* zeytin ağacı
Oman [əʊ'mɑːn] *n* Umman
omelette ['ɒmlɪt] *n* omlet
on [ɒn] *adv* açık ▷ *prep* de, da; **on behalf of** *n* namına; **on time** *adj* zamanında; **I don't have my driving licence on me** Ehliyetim üzerimde değil; **I'm here on holiday** Burada tatildeyim; **I'm on a diet** Rejimdeyim; **It's on the corner** Köşede; **Take the first turning on your right** Sağdan ilk sokağa dönün; **The drinks are on me** İçkiler benden; **What's on tonight at the cinema?** Bu gece sinemada ne var?; **Which film is on at the cinema?** Sinemada hangi film oynuyor?
once [wʌns] *adv* bir seferinde
one [wʌn] *number* bir ▷ *pron* bir; **no one** *pron* hiç kimse
one-off [wʌnɒf] *n* bir seferlik
onion ['ʌnjən] *n* soğan; **spring onion** *n* taze soğan
online ['ɒn,laɪn] *adj* çevirimiçi ▷ *adv* hatta *(bilgisayar)*
onlooker ['ɒn,lʊkə] *n* izleyici
only ['əʊnlɪ] *adj* tek ▷ *adv* yalnızca
open ['əʊpᵊn] *adj* açık *(kapı, pencere vb)* ▷ *v* açmak *(kapı vb)*; **opening hours** *npl* açılış saatleri; **Are you open?** Açık mısınız?; **Is it open today?** Bugün açık mı?; **Is the castle open to the public?** Kale halka açık mı?; **Is the museum open in the afternoon?** Müze öğleden sonra açık mı?
opera ['ɒpərə] *n* opera; **soap opera** *n* televizyon dizisi; **What's on tonight at the opera?** Bu gece operada ne var?
operate ['ɒpə,reɪt] *v (to function)* işlemek, *(to perform surgery)* ameliyat etmek
operating theatre ['ɒpə,reɪtɪŋ 'θɪətə] *n* ameliyat odası
operation [,ɒpə'reɪʃən] *n (surgery)* ameliyat *(tıp)*, *(undertaking)* operasyon
operator ['ɒpə,reɪtə] *n* operatör
opinion [ə'pɪnjən] *n* fikir *(bir konuda)*; **opinion poll** *n* kamuoyu yoklaması; **public opinion** *n* kamuoyu
opponent [ə'pəʊnənt] *n* karşıt

opportunity [ˌɒpəˈtjuːnɪtɪ] *n* fırsat *(olanak)*
oppose [əˈpəʊz] *v* karşı çıkmak
opposed [əˈpəʊzd] *adj* karşı
opposing [əˈpəʊzɪŋ] *adj* karşı çıkan
opposite [ˈɒpəzɪt; -sɪt] *adj* karşıt ▷ *adv* karşılıklı ▷ *prep* karşısında
opposition [ˌɒpəˈzɪʃən] *n* muhalefet
optician [ɒpˈtɪʃən] *n* gözlükçü
optimism [ˈɒptɪˌmɪzəm] *n* iyimserlik
optimist [ˈɒptɪˌmɪst] *n* iyimser
optimistic [ɒptɪˈmɪstɪk] *adj* iyimser
option [ˈɒpʃən] *n* seçenek
optional [ˈɒpʃənᵊl] *adj* isteğe bağlı
opt out [ɒpt aʊt] *v* çekilmek
or [ɔː] *conj* ya; **either... or** *conj* ya
oral [ˈɔːrəl; ˈɒrəl] *adj* sözlü ▷ *n* sözlü
orange [ˈɒrɪndʒ] *adj* portakal rengi ▷ *n* portakal; **orange juice** *n* portakal suyu
orchard [ˈɔːtʃəd] *n* meyve bahçesi
orchestra [ˈɔːkɪstrə] *n* orkestra
orchid [ˈɔːkɪd] *n* orkide
ordeal [ɔːˈdiːl] *n* çetin sınav
order [ˈɔːdə] *n* emir, sıra ▷ *v* *(command)* komut vermek, *(request)* ısmarlamak; **order form** *n* sipariş formu; **postal order** *n* posta havalesi; **standing order** *n* banka ödeme emri; **I'd like to order something local** Yöreye özgü bir şey ısmarlamak istiyorum
ordinary [ˈɔːdᵊnrɪ] *adj* sıradan
oregano [ˌɒrɪˈɡɑːnəʊ] *n* mercanköşk *(yabani)*
organ [ˈɔːɡən] *n* *(body part)* organ, *(music)* org; **mouth organ** *n* armonika
organic [ɔːˈɡænɪk] *adj* organik
organism [ˈɔːɡəˌnɪzəm] *n* organizma
organization [ˌɔːɡənaɪˈzeɪʃən] *n* organizasyon
organize [ˈɔːɡəˌnaɪz] *v* organize etmek
organizer [ˈɔːɡəˌnaɪzə] *n* **personal organizer** *n* kişisel organizatör
orgasm [ˈɔːɡæzəm] *n* orgazm
Orient [ˈɔːrɪənt] *n* Doğu
oriental [ˌɔːrɪˈɛntᵊl] *adj* oryantal
origin [ˈɒrɪdʒɪn] *n* kaynak *(çıkış noktası)*
original [əˈrɪdʒɪnᵊl] *adj* özgün
originally [əˈrɪdʒɪnəlɪ] *adv* başlangıç olarak
ornament [ˈɔːnəmənt] *n* süs
orphan [ˈɔːfən] *n* kimsesiz
ostrich [ˈɒstrɪtʃ] *n* devekuşu
other [ˈʌðə] *adj* diğer
otherwise [ˈʌðəˌwaɪz] *adv* başka türlü ▷ *conj* yoksa
otter [ˈɒtə] *n* su samuru
ounce [aʊns] *n* ons
our [aʊə] *adj* bizim
ours [aʊəz] *pron* bizimki
ourselves [aʊəˈsɛlvz] *pron* biz *(kendimiz)*
out [aʊt] *adj* dış *(iç karşıtı)* ▷ *adv* dışarıda; **He's out** Dışarıda
outbreak [ˈaʊtˌbreɪk] *n* ayaklanma
outcome [ˈaʊtˌkʌm] *n* sonuç
outdoor [ˈaʊtˈdɔː] *adj* açık hava; **What outdoor activities are there?** Açık hava sporu olarak ne yapabilirim?
outdoors [ˌaʊtˈdɔːz] *adv* açık

havada
outfit ['aʊtˌfɪt] *n* kılık
outgoing ['aʊtˌgəʊɪŋ] *adj* dışa dönük
outing ['aʊtɪŋ] *n* dışarı çıkmak
outline ['aʊtˌlaɪn] *n* özet
outlook ['aʊtˌlʊk] *n* yaşama bakış
out-of-date ['aʊtɒv'deɪt] *adj* günü geçmiş
out-of-doors ['aʊtɒv'dɔːz] *adv* açık havada
outrageous [aʊt'reɪdʒəs] *adj* dehşet verici
outset ['aʊtˌsɛt] *n* başlangıç *(çıkış)*
outside *adj* ['aʊtˌsaɪd] dışarı ▹ *adv* [ˌaʊt'saɪd] dışarıda ▹ *n* ['aʊt'saɪd] dışarısı ▹ *prep* dışında; **I want to make an outside call, can I have a line?** Dışarıyı aramak istiyorum, hat bağlar mısınız?
outsize ['aʊtˌsaɪz] *adj* bedenine göre büyük
outskirts ['aʊtˌskɜːts] *npl* eteklerinde
outspoken [ˌaʊt'spəʊkən] *adj* açık sözlü
outstanding [ˌaʊt'stændɪŋ] *adj* mükemmel
oval ['əʊvᵊl] *adj* oval
ovary ['əʊvərɪ] *n* yumurtalık *(sağlık)*
oven ['ʌvᵊn] *n* fırın; **microwave oven** *n* mikrodalga fırın; **oven glove** *n* fırın eldiveni
ovenproof ['ʌvᵊnˌpruːf] *adj* ateşe dayanıklı
over ['əʊvə] *adj* bitmiş ▹ *prep* üstünde
overall [ˌəʊvər'ɔːl] *adv* kapsamlı
overalls [ˌəʊvə'ɔːlz] *npl* tulum
(giysi)
overcast ['əʊvəˌkɑːst] *adj* bulutlu
overcharge [ˌəʊvə'tʃɑːdʒ] *v* fazla fiyat istemek
overcoat ['əʊvəˌkəʊt] *n* palto
overcome [ˌəʊvə'kʌm] *v* üstesinden gelmek
overdone [ˌəʊvə'dʌn] *adj* çok pişmiş
overdose ['əʊvəˌdəʊs] *n* yüksek dozda
overdraft ['əʊvəˌdrɑːft] *n* fazla para çekme
overdrawn [ˌəʊvə'drɔːn] *adj* hesabından fazla para çekmiş
overdue [ˌəʊvə'djuː] *adj* ödeme günü geçmiş
overestimate [ˌəʊvər'ɛstɪˌmeɪt] *v* gözünde büyütmek
overheads ['əʊvəˌhɛdz] *npl* işletme masrafları
overlook [ˌəʊvə'lʊk] *v* gözden kaçırmak
overrule [ˌəʊvə'ruːl] *v* kararı bozmak
overseas [ˌəʊvə'siːz] *adv* denizaşırı
oversight ['əʊvəˌsaɪt] *n* *(mistake)* hata, *(supervision)* gözetim
oversleep [ˌəʊvə'sliːp] *v* uyuyakalmak
overtake [ˌəʊvə'teɪk] *v* sollamak
overtime ['əʊvəˌtaɪm] *n* fazla mesai
overweight [ˌəʊvə'weɪt] *adj* aşırı kilolu
owe [əʊ] *v* borçlu olmak
owing to ['əʊɪŋ tuː] *prep* için
owl [aʊl] *n* baykuş
own [əʊn] *adj* kendi ▹ *v* sahip olmak

owner ['əʊnə] *n* sahip
own up [əʊn ʌp] *v* sahip çıkmak
oxygen ['ɒksɪdʒən] *n* oksijen
oyster ['ɔɪstə] *n* istridye
ozone ['əʊzəʊn; əʊ'zəʊn] *n* ozon; **ozone layer** *n* ozon tabakası

PA [pi: eɪ] *abbr* kişisel asistan
pace [peɪs] *n* adım
pacemaker ['peɪs,meɪkə] *n* kalp pili
Pacific [pə'sɪfɪk] *n* Pasifik
pack [pæk] *n* yük ▹ *v* paketlemek
package ['pækɪdʒ] *n* paket; **package holiday** *n* paket tatil; **package tour** *n* paket tur
packaging ['pækɪdʒɪŋ] *n* paketleme
packed [pækt] *adj* paketlenmiş; **packed lunch** *n* paket yemek
packet ['pækɪt] *n* paket
pad [pæd] *n* ped
paddle ['pædᵊl] *n* kısa kürek ▹ *v* sığ suda çıplak ayak yürümek
padlock ['pæd,lɒk] *n* asma kilit
paedophile ['pi:dəʊ,faɪl] *n* pedofil
page [peɪdʒ] *n* sayfa ▹ *v* anons etmek; **home page** *n* açılış sayfası; **Yellow Pages®** *npl* Sarı Sayfalar

pager ['peɪdʒə] *n* çağrı cihazı
paid [peɪd] *adj* ücretli
pail [peɪl] *n* kova
pain [peɪn] *n* acı; **back pain** *n* sırt ağrısı; **It hurts here** Burası acıyor
painful ['peɪnfʊl] *adj* acılı
painkiller ['peɪn,kɪlə] *n* ağrı kesici
paint [peɪnt] *n* boya *(yapı)* ▷ *v* boyamak
paintbrush ['peɪnt,brʌʃ] *n* boya fırçası
painter ['peɪntə] *n* ressam
painting ['peɪntɪŋ] *n* resim
pair [pɛə] *n* çift
Pakistan [,pɑːkɪ'stɑːn] *n* Pakistan
Pakistani [,pɑːkɪ'stɑːnɪ] *adj* Pakistan ▷ *n* Pakistanlı
pal [pæl] *n* yakın dost
palace ['pælɪs] *n* saray; **Is the palace open to the public?** Saray halka açık mı?; **When is the palace open?** Saray ne zaman açık?
pale [peɪl] *adj* soluk
Palestine ['pælɪ,staɪn] *n* Filistin
Palestinian [,pælɪ'stɪnɪən] *adj* Filistin ▷ *n* Filistinli
palm [pɑːm] *n (part of hand)* avuçiçi, *(tree)* palmiye
pamphlet ['pæmflɪt] *n* broşür
pan [pæn] *n* tava; **frying pan** *n* kızartma tavası
Panama [,pænə'mɑː; 'pænə,mɑː] *n* Panama
pancake ['pæn,keɪk] *n* krep *(yiyecek)*
panda ['pændə] *n* panda
panic ['pænɪk] *n* panik ▷ *v* paniğe kapılmak
panther ['pænθə] *n* panter
panties ['pæntɪz] *npl* külot
pantomime ['pæntə,maɪm] *n* pandomim
pants [pænts] *npl* külot
paper ['peɪpə] *n* kağıt; **paper round** *n* gazete dağıtım; **scrap paper** *n* karalama kağıdı; **toilet paper** *n* tuvalet kağıdı; **tracing paper** *n* aydınger kağıdı; **wrapping paper** *n* paket kağıdı; **writing paper** *n* yazı kağıdı
paperback ['peɪpə,bæk] *n* ikinci baskı kitap
paperclip ['peɪpə,klɪp] *n* ataş
paperweight ['peɪpə,weɪt] *n* kağıt ağırlığı
paperwork ['peɪpə,wɜːk] *n* evrak işi
paprika ['pæprɪkə; pæ'priː-] *n* kırmızı toz biber
paracetamol [,pærə'siːtə,mɒl; -'sɛtə-] *n* **I'd like some paracetamol** Parasetamol rica ediyorum
parachute ['pærə,ʃuːt] *n* paraşüt
parade [pə'reɪd] *n* tören alayı
paradise ['pærə,daɪs] *n* cennet
paraffin ['pærəfɪn] *n* parafin
paragraph ['pærə,grɑːf; -,græf] *n* paragraf
Paraguay ['pærə,gwaɪ] *n* Paraguay
Paraguayan [,pærə'gwaɪən] *adj* Paraguay ▷ *n* Paraguaylı
parallel ['pærə,lɛl] *adj* paralel
paralysed ['pærə,laɪzd] *adj* felçli
paramedic [,pærə'medɪk] *n* paramedik
parcel ['pɑːsᵊl] *n* paket; **How much is it to send this parcel?**

Bu paket kaça gider?; **I'd like to send this parcel** Bu paketi postalamak istiyorum
pardon ['pɑːdᵊn] *n* bağışlama
parent ['pɛərənt] *n* ebeveyn; **parents** *npl* ebeveynler; **single parent** *n* yalnız ebeveyn
parish ['pærɪʃ] *n* kilisenin dini bölgesi
park [pɑːk] *n* park ▹ *v* park etmek; **car park** *n* otopark; **national park** *n* milli park; **theme park** *n* konulu eğlence parkı; **Can I park here?** Arabamı buraya park edebilir miyim?; **Can we park our caravan here?** Karavanımızı buraya park edebilir miyiz?; **How long can I park here?** Ne kadarlığına park edebilirim?; **Is there a car park near here?** Buralarda bir otopark var mı?; **Where can I park the car?** Arabamı nereye park edebilirim?
parking [pɑːkɪŋ] *n* park etme; **parking meter** *n* otopark ödeme cihazı; **parking ticket** *n* otopark bileti
parliament ['pɑːləmənt] *n* parlamento
parole [pə'rəʊl] *n* şartlı tahliye
parrot ['pærət] *n* papağan
parsley ['pɑːslɪ] *n* maydanoz
parsnip ['pɑːsnɪp] *n* yabani havuç
part [pɑːt] *n* parça; **spare part** *n* yedek parça; **Do you have parts for a Toyota?** Toyota parçaları var mı?
partial ['pɑːʃəl] *adj* kısmi
participate [pɑː'tɪsɪˌpeɪt] *v* katılmak
particular [pə'tɪkjʊlə] *adj* özellik
particularly [pə'tɪkjʊləlɪ] *adv* özellikle
parting ['pɑːtɪŋ] *n* ayrılış
partly ['pɑːtlɪ] *adv* kısmen
partner ['pɑːtnə] *n* partner; **I have a partner** Partnerim var; **This is my partner** Bu partnerim
partridge ['pɑːtrɪdʒ] *n* keklik
part-time ['pɑːtˌtaɪm] *adj* yarım gün ▹ *adv* yarım gün
part with [pɑːt wɪð] *v* ayırılmak
party ['pɑːtɪ] *n (group)* parti *(grup)*, *(social gathering)* parti *(sosyal etkinlik)* ▹ *v* partiye katılmak; **dinner party** *n* yemekli parti; **search party** *n* arama ekibi
pass [pɑːs] *n (in mountains)* geçit *(dağ)*, *(meets standard)* geçer *(standartlara uygun)*, *(permit)* paso ▹ *v (an exam)* sınavı kazanmak ▹ *vi* geçilmek ▹ *vt* geçmek; **boarding pass** *n* biniş kartı; **ski pass** *n* kayak izni
passage ['pæsɪdʒ] *n (musical)* parça *(müzik)*, *(route)* geçit
passenger ['pæsɪndʒə] *n* yolcu
passion ['pæʃən] *n* tutku; **passion fruit** *n* çarkıfelek meyvası
passive ['pæsɪv] *adj* pasif
pass out [pɑːs aʊt] *v* bayılmak
Passover ['pɑːsˌəʊvə] *n* Musevilerin Fısıh Bayramı
passport ['pɑːspɔːt] *n* pasaport; **passport control** *n* pasaport kontrol; **Here is my passport** İşte pasaportum; **I've forgotten my passport** Pasaportumu unutmuşum; **I've lost my passport** Pasaportumu

kaybettim; **My passport has been stolen** Pasaportum çalındı; **Please give me my passport back** Pasaportumu alabilir miyim?; **The children are on this passport** Çocuklar bu pasaportta

password ['pɑːsˌwɜːd] *n* şifre

past [pɑːst] *adj* geçmiş ▷ *n* geçmiş ▷ *prep* yoluyla

pasta ['pæstə] *n* makarna; **I'd like pasta as a starter** Başlangıç olarak makarna alayım

paste [peɪst] *n* macun

pasteurized ['pæstəˌraɪzd] *adj* pastörize

pastime ['pɑːsˌtaɪm] *n* uğraş

pastry ['peɪstrɪ] *n* hamur; **puff pastry** *n* milföy hamuru; **shortcrust pastry** *n* un kurabiyesi hamuru

patch [pætʃ] *n* yama

patched [pætʃt] *adj* yamalı

path [pɑːθ] *n* patika; **cycle path** *n* bisiklet yolu; **Keep to the path** Patikadan ayrılmayın

pathetic [pə'θɛtɪk] *adj* acınası

patience ['peɪʃəns] *n* sabır

patient ['peɪʃənt] *adj* sabırlı ▷ *n* hasta

patio ['pætɪˌəʊ] *n* teras

patriotic ['pætrɪəˌtɪk] *adj* yurtsever

patrol [pə'trəʊl] *n* devriye; **patrol car** *n* devriye arabası

pattern ['pætᵊn] *n* kalıp *(dikiş)*

pause [pɔːz] *n* duraklama

pavement ['peɪvmənt] *n* kaldırım

pavilion [pə'vɪljən] *n* sayvan

paw [pɔː] *n* pençe

pawnbroker ['pɔːnˌbrəʊkə] *n* rehinci

pay [peɪ] *n* maaş ▷ *v* ödemek; **sick pay** *n* hastalık ödentisi

payable ['peɪəbᵊl] *adj* ödenecek

pay back [peɪ bæk] *v* geri ödemek

payment ['peɪmənt] *n* ödeme

payphone ['peɪˌfəʊn] *n* ankesörlü telefon

PC [piː siː] *n* PC

PDF [piː diː ɛf] *n* PDF

peace [piːs] *n* barış

peaceful ['piːsfʊl] *adj* barışçıl

peach [piːtʃ] *n* şeftali

peacock ['piːˌkɒk] *n* tavus kuşu

peak [piːk] *n* zirve; **peak hours** *npl* sıkışık saat

peanut ['piːˌnʌt] *n* yerfıstığı; **peanut allergy** *n* fıstık alerjisi; **peanut butter** *n* fıstık ezmesi

pear [pɛə] *n* armut

pearl [pɜːl] *n* inci

peas [piːs] *npl* bezelye

peat [piːt] *n* turba

pebble ['pɛbᵊl] *n* çakıl taşı

peculiar [pɪ'kjuːlɪə] *adj* tuhaf

pedal ['pɛdᵊl] *n* pedal

pedestrian [pɪ'dɛstrɪən] *n* yaya; **pedestrian crossing** *n* yaya geçidi; **pedestrian precinct** *n* yayalara özel bölge

pedestrianized [pɪ'dɛstrɪəˌnaɪzd] *adj* yayalara ayrılmış

pedigree ['pɛdɪˌgriː] *adj* cins

peel [piːl] *n* meyva kabuğu ▷ *v* soymak *(meyva, deri vb)*

peg [pɛg] *n* kanca

Pekinese [ˌpiːkɪŋ'iːz] *n* Pekinez

pelican ['pɛlɪkən] *n* pelikan; **pelican crossing** *n* ışıklı yaya geçidi

pellet ['pɛlɪt] *n* metal çekirdek
pelvis ['pɛlvɪs] *n* leğen kemiği
pen [pɛn] *n* kalem; **ballpoint pen** *n* Tükenmez kalem; **felt-tip pen** *n* keçe kalem; **fountain pen** *n* dolmakalem; **Do you have a pen I could borrow?** Kaleminiz var mı?
penalize ['piːnəˌlaɪz] *v* cezalandırmak
penalty ['pɛnᵊltɪ] *n* penaltı
pencil ['pɛnsᵊl] *n* kurşun kalem; **pencil case** *n* kalemlik; **pencil sharpener** *n* kalem açacağı
pendant ['pɛndənt] *n* pandantif
penfriend ['pɛnˌfrɛnd] *n* kalem arkadaşı
penguin ['pɛŋgwɪn] *n* penguen
penicillin [ˌpɛnɪ'sɪlɪn] *n* penisilin
peninsula [pɪ'nɪnsjʊlə] *n* yarımada
penknife ['pɛnˌnaɪf] *n* çakı
penny ['pɛnɪ] *n* peni
pension ['pɛnʃən] *n* emekli maaşı
pensioner ['pɛnʃənə] *n* emekli; **old-age pensioner** *n* emekli
pentathlon [pɛn'tæθlən] *n* pentatlon
penultimate [pɪ'nʌltɪmɪt] *adj* sondan bir önceki
people ['piːpᵊl] *npl* insanlar
pepper ['pɛpə] *n* biber
peppermill ['pɛpəˌmɪl] *n* biberlik
peppermint ['pɛpəˌmɪnt] *n* nane şekeri
per [pɜː; pə] *prep* başına; **per cent** *adv* yüzde; **How much is it per person?** Kişi başına ne kadar?
percentage [pə'sɛntɪdʒ] *n* yüzde
percussion [pə'kʌʃən] *n* vurmalı *(müzik)*
perfect ['pɜːfɪkt] *adj* mükemmel
perfection [pə'fɛkʃən] *n* mükemmellik
perfectly ['pɜːfɪktlɪ] *adv* mükemmel bir şekilde
perform [pə'fɔːm] *v* performans göstermek
performance [pə'fɔːməns] *n* *(artistic)* sahne performansı, *(functioning)* performans
perfume ['pɜːfjuːm] *n* parfüm
perhaps [pə'hæps; præps] *adv* belki
period ['pɪərɪəd] *n* dönem; **trial period** *n* deneme süresi
perjury ['pɜːdʒərɪ] *n* yalancı şahitlik
perm [pɜːm] *n* perma
permanent ['pɜːmənənt] *adj* kalıcı
permanently ['pɜːmənəntlɪ] *adv* kalıcı bir şekilde
permission [pə'mɪʃən] *n* izin *(birine bir şey yapmak için verilen)*
permit *n* ['pɜːmɪt] izin ▷ *v* [pə'mɪt] izin vermek; **work permit** *n* çalışma izni; **Do you need a fishing permit?** Avlanma izin belgesi gerekiyor mu?
persecute ['pɜːsɪˌkjuːt] *v* eziyet etmek
persevere [ˌpɜːsɪ'vɪə] *v* azmetmek
Persian ['pɜːʃən] *adj* İranlı
persistent [pə'sɪstənt] *adj* ısrarlı
person ['pɜːsᵊn] *n* kişi; **How much is it per person?** Kişi başına ne kadar?
personal ['pɜːsənᵊl] *adj* kişisel; **personal assistant** *n* kişisel asistan; **personal organizer** *n*

kişisel organizatör; **personal stereo** *n* kişisel müzik çalar
personality [ˌpɜːsəˈnælɪtɪ] *n* kişilik
personally [ˈpɜːsənəlɪ] *adv* kişisel olarak
personnel [ˌpɜːsəˈnɛl] *n* personel
perspective [pəˈspɛktɪv] *n* perspektif
perspiration [ˌpɜːspəˈreɪʃən] *n* terleme
persuade [pəˈsweɪd] *v* ikna etme
persuasive [pəˈsweɪsɪv] *adj* ikna edici
Peru [pəˈruː] *n* Peru
Peruvian [pəˈruːvɪən] *adj* Peru ▹ *n* Perulu
pessimist [ˈpɛsɪˌmɪst] *n* kötümser
pessimistic [ˈpɛsɪˌmɪstɪk] *adj* kötümser
pest [pɛst] *n* baş belası
pester [ˈpɛstə] *v* musallat olmak
pesticide [ˈpɛstɪˌsaɪd] *n* böcek zehiri
pet [pɛt] *n* ev hayvanı
petition [pɪˈtɪʃən] *n* dilekçe
petrified [ˈpɛtrɪˌfaɪd] *adj* ödü kopmak
petrol [ˈpɛtrəl] *n* benzin; **petrol station** *n* benzin istasyonu; **petrol tank** *n* benzin deposu; **unleaded petrol** *n* kurşunsuz benzin; **I've run out of petrol** Benzinim bitti; **Is there a petrol station near here?** Buraya en yakın benzin istasyonu nerede?; **The petrol has run out** Benzin bitti
pewter [ˈpjuːtə] *n* tutya
pharmacist [ˈfɑːməsɪst] *n* eczacı
pharmacy [ˈfɑːməsɪ] *n* eczane; **Which pharmacy provides emergency service?** Hangi eczane nöbetçi?
PhD [piː eɪtʃ diː] *n* doktora
pheasant [ˈfɛzᵊnt] *n* sülün
philosophy [fɪˈlɒsəfɪ] *n* felsefe
phobia [ˈfəʊbɪə] *n* fobi
phone [fəʊn] *n* telefon ▹ *v* telefon etmek; **camera phone** *n* fotoğraflı telefon; **entry phone** *n* kapı telefonu; **mobile phone** *n* cep telefonu; **phone back** *v* geri aramak; **phone bill** *n* telefon faturası; **phone number** *n* telefon numarası; **smart phone** *n* akıllı telefon; **Can I have your phone number?** Telefon numaranızı alabilir miyim?; **Can I phone from here?** Buradan telefon edebilir miyim?; **Can I use your phone, please?** Telefonunuzu kullanabilir miyim lütfen?; **Do you sell international phone cards?** Uluslararası telefon kartı satıyor musunuz?; **I must make a phone call** Bir telefon görüşmesi yapmam gerek; **I want to make a phone call** Telefon etmek istiyorum; **I'd like a twenty-five euro phone card** Yirmibeş euroluk telefon kartı rica ediyorum; **I'd like some coins for the phone, please** Telefon için bozuk para rica ediyorum; **I'm having trouble with the phone** Telefonla sorunum var; **May I use your phone?** Telefonunuzu kullanabilir miyim?; **Where can I charge my mobile phone?** Cep

telefonumu nerede şarj edebilirim; **Where can I make a phone call?** Nereden telefon edebilirim?
phonebook ['fəʊn,bʊk] *n* telefon rehberi
phonebox ['fəʊn,bɒks] *n* telefon kulübesi
phonecall ['fəʊn,kɔːl] *n* telefon görüşmesi
phonecard ['fəʊn,kɑːd] *n* telefon kartı; **A phonecard, please** Bir telefon kartı lütfen; **Where can I buy a phonecard?** Nereden telefon kartı alabilirim?
photo ['fəʊtəʊ] *n* fotoğraf; **photo album** *n* fotoğraf albümü; **Can I download photos to here?** Fotoğraf inidirebilir miyim?; **Can you put these photos on CD, please?** Bu fotoğrafları CD'ye yükleybilir misiniz lütfen?; **How much do the photos cost?** Fotoğraflar kaça malolur?; **I'd like the photos glossy** Fotoğrafları parlak kağıda basın lütfen; **I'd like the photos matt** Fotoğrafları mat kağıda basın lütfen; **When will the photos be ready?** Fotoğraflar ne zaman hazır olur?
photocopier ['fəʊtəʊ,kɒpɪə] *n* fotokopi makinesi
photocopy ['fəʊtəʊ,kɒpɪ] *n* fotokopi ▷ *v* fotokopisini çekmek; **I'd like a photocopy of this, please** Bunun fotokopisini istiyorum lütfen; **Where can I get some photocopying done?** Nerede fotokopi çektirebilirim?
photograph ['fəʊtə,grɑːf; -,græf] *n* fotoğraf ▷ *v* fotoğrafını çekmek
photographer [fə'tɒgrəfə] *n* fotoğrafçı
photography [fə'tɒgrəfɪ] *n* fotoğrafçılık
phrase [freɪz] *n* sözcük grubu
phrasebook ['freɪz,bʊk] *n* günlük ifadeler sözlüğü
physical ['fɪzɪkᵊl] *adj* fiziksel ▷ *n* fizik *(görünüş)*
physicist ['fɪzɪsɪst] *n* fizikçi
physics ['fɪzɪks] *npl* fizik
physiotherapist [,fɪzɪəʊ'θɛrəpɪst] *n* fizyoterapist
physiotherapy [,fɪzɪəʊ'θɛrəpɪ] *n* fizyoterapi
pianist ['pɪənɪst] *n* piyanist
piano [pɪ'ænəʊ] *n* piyano
pick [pɪk] *n* kazma ▷ *v* toplamak *(çiçek vb)*
pick on [pɪk ɒn] *v* birine takmak
pick out [pɪk aʊt] *v* seçmek
pickpocket ['pɪk,pɒkɪt] *n* yankesicilik
pick up [pɪk ʌp] *v* yerden almak
picnic ['pɪknɪk] *n* piknik
picture ['pɪktʃə] *n* resim; **picture frame** *n* resim çerçevesi
picturesque [,pɪktʃə'rɛsk] *adj* resmedilmeye değer
pie [paɪ] *n* börek; **apple pie** *n* elmalı turta; **pie chart** *n* dilimli grafik
piece [piːs] *n* parça
pier [pɪə] *n* rıhtım
pierce [pɪəs] *v* delmek
pierced [pɪəst] *adj* delik *(kulak vb)*
piercing ['pɪəsɪŋ] *n* delici
pig [pɪg] *n* domuz; **guinea pig** *n* *(for experiment)* kobay, *(rodent)* kobay faresi
pigeon ['pɪdʒɪn] *n* güvercin

piggybank ['pɪɡɪˌbæŋk] *n* kumbara
pigtail ['pɪɡˌteɪl] *n* saç örgüsü
pile [paɪl] *n* yığın
piles [paɪlz] *npl* basur
pile-up [paɪlʌp] *n* yığılmak
pilgrim ['pɪlɡrɪm] *n* hacı
pilgrimage ['pɪlɡrɪmɪdʒ] *n* hac
pill [pɪl] *n* hap; **sleeping pill** *n* uyku hapı; **I'm not on the pill** Doğum kontrol hapı kullanmıyorum; **I'm on the pill** Doğum kontrol hapı kullanıyorum
pillar ['pɪlə] *n* sütun
pillow ['pɪləʊ] *n* yastık
pillowcase ['pɪləʊˌkeɪs] *n* yastık kılıfı
pilot ['paɪlət] *n* pilot; **pilot light** *n* kontrol lambası
pimple ['pɪmpᵊl] *n* sivilce
pin [pɪn] *n* toplu iğne; **drawing pin** *n* raptiye; **rolling pin** *n* oklava; **safety pin** *n* kilitli iğne
PIN [pɪn] *npl* kredi kartı şifresi
pinafore ['pɪnəˌfɔː] *n* önlük
pinch [pɪntʃ] *v* çimdiklemek
pine [paɪn] *n* çam
pineapple ['paɪnˌæpᵊl] *n* ananas
pink [pɪŋk] *adj* pembe
pint [paɪnt] *n* pint *(içki)*
pip [pɪp] *n* çekirdek
pipe [paɪp] *n* boru; **exhaust pipe** *n* egzos borusu
pipeline ['paɪpˌlaɪn] *n* boru hattı
pirate ['paɪrɪt] *n* korsan *(deniz)*
Pisces ['paɪsiːz; 'pɪ-] *n* Balık burcu
pistol ['pɪstᵊl] *n* kısa kabzalı tabanca
piston ['pɪstən] *n* piston
pitch [pɪtʃ] *n (sound)* perde *(ses)*, *(sport)* saha *(spor)* ▷ *v* fırlatmak
pity ['pɪtɪ] *n* acıma *(duygu)* ▷ *v* acımak
pixel ['pɪksᵊl] *n* piksel
pizza ['piːtsə] *n* pizza
place [pleɪs] *n* yer ▷ *v* yerleştirmek; **place of birth** *n* doğum yeri; **Do you know a good place to go?** Gidilecek iyi bir yer biliyor musunuz?; **Where is the best place to dive?** Burada dalınacak en iyi yer neresi?
placement ['pleɪsmənt] *n* yerleştirme
plain [pleɪn] *adj* düz *(desensiz, süssüz)* ▷ *n* ova; **plain chocolate** *n* sade çikolata
plait [plæt] *n* saç örgüsü
plan [plæn] *n* plan ▷ *v* planlamak; **street plan** *n* sokak planı
plane [pleɪn] *n (aeroplane)* uçak, *(surface)* düzlem, *(tool)* rende
planet ['plænɪt] *n* gezegen
planning [plænɪŋ] *n* planlama
plant [plɑːnt] *n (site/equipment)* tesis, *(vegetable organism)* bitki ▷ *v* dikmek *(bitki)*; **plant pot** *n* çiçek saksısı; **pot plant** *n* saksı çiçeği; **We'd like to see local plants and trees** Yerel bitkileri ve ağaçları görmek isterdik
plaque [plæk; plɑːk] *n* plaket
plaster ['plɑːstə] *n (for wall)* badana, *(for wound)* yara bandı; **I'd like some plasters** Yara bandı rica ediyorum
plastic ['plæstɪk; 'plɑːs-] *adj* plastik ▷ *n* plastik; **plastic bag** *n* naylon torba; **plastic surgery** *n* plastik cerrahi

plate [pleɪt] *n* tabak; **number plate** *n* plaka *(otomobil)*
platform ['plætfɔːm] *n* platform; **Is this the right platform for the train to...?** ... treninin kalkacağı platform burası mı?; **Which platform does the train leave from?** Tren hangi platformdan kalkıyor?
platinum ['plætɪnəm] *n* platin
play [pleɪ] *n* oyun ▹ *v* *(in sport)* oynamak, *(music)* çalmak; **play truant** *v* okuldan kaçmak; **playing card** *n* oyun kartı; **playing field** *n* oyun alanı; **Can I play video games?** Oyun oynayabilir miyim?; **We'd like to play tennis** Tenis oynamak istiyoruz; **Where can we go to see a play?** Tiyatro oyunu görmek için nereye gidebiliriz?
player ['pleɪə] *n* *(instrumentalist)* müzisyen, *(of sport)* oyuncu *(spor)*; **CD player** *n* CD çalar; **MP3 player** *n* MP3 çalar; **MP4 player** *n* MP4 çalar
playful ['pleɪfʊl] *adj* oyuncu *(oyunbaz)*
playground ['pleɪˌgraʊnd] *n* oyun alanı
playgroup ['pleɪˌgruːp] *n* çocuk oyun grubu
PlayStation® ['pleɪˌsteɪʃən] *n* PlayStation®
playtime ['pleɪˌtaɪm] *n* oyun saati
playwright ['pleɪˌraɪt] *n* oyun yazarı
pleasant ['plɛzᵊnt] *adj* hoş
please [pliːz] *excl* lütfen
pleased [pliːzd] *adj* memnun; **Pleased to meet you** Tanıştığımıza memnun oldum
pleasure ['plɛʒə] *n* zevk; **It was a pleasure to meet you** Sizinle tanışmak bir zevk; **It's been a pleasure working with you** Sizinle çalışmak bir zevkti
plenty ['plɛntɪ] *n* çok
pliers ['plaɪəz] *npl* pense
plot [plɒt] *n* *(piece of land)* arsa, *(secret plan)* komplo ▹ *v* *(conspire)* gizli plan
plough [plaʊ] *n* pulluk ▹ *v* tarla sürmek
plug [plʌg] *n* tıkaç; **spark plug** *n* buji
plughole ['plʌgˌhəʊl] *n* musluk deliği
plug in [plʌg ɪn] *v* elektriğe bağlamak
plum [plʌm] *n* erik
plumber ['plʌmə] *n* muslukçu
plumbing ['plʌmɪŋ] *n* musluk işleri
plump [plʌmp] *adj* tıknaz
plunge [plʌndʒ] *v* hızla atlamak
plural ['plʊərəl] *n* çoğul
plus [plʌs] *prep* ayrıca
plywood ['plaɪˌwʊd] *n* kontrplak
p.m. [piː ɛm] *abbr* öğleden sonra
pneumonia [njuː'məʊnɪə] *n* zatürre
poached [pəʊtʃt] *adj* *(caught illegally)* kaçak avlanmış, *(simmered gently)* suda pişirilmiş *(yumurta, balık)*
pocket ['pɒkɪt] *n* cep; **pocket calculator** *n* cep hesap makinesi; **pocket money** *n* cep harçlığı
podcast ['pɒdˌkɑːst] *n* podcast

poem ['pəʊɪm] *n* şiir
poet ['pəʊɪt] *n* şair
poetry ['pəʊɪtrɪ] *n* şiir
point [pɔɪnt] *n* nokta *(yer)* ▷ *v* göstermek
pointless ['pɔɪntlɪs] *adj* anlamsız
point out [pɔɪnt aʊt] *v* dikkatini çekmek
poison ['pɔɪzᵊn] *n* zehir ▷ *v* zehirlemek
poisonous ['pɔɪzənəs] *adj* zehirli
poke [pəʊk] *v* dürtmek
poker ['pəʊkə] *n* poker
Poland ['pəʊlənd] *n* Polonya
polar ['pəʊlə] *adj* kutup; **polar bear** *n* kutup ayısı
pole [pəʊl] *n* direk, direk *(elektrik, telgraf)*; **North Pole** *n* Kuzey Kutbu; **pole vault** *n* sırıkla atlama; **South Pole** *n* Güney Kutbu; **tent pole** *n* çadır direği
Pole [pəʊl] *n* Kutup
police [pə'liːs] *n* polis; **police officer** *n* polis görevlisi; **police station** *n* polis istasyonu; **Call the police** Polis çağırın; **I need a police report for my insurance** Sigortam için polise bildirmemiz gerekiyor; **We will have to report it to the police** Polise haber vermemiz gerekiyor; **Where is the police station?** Polis karakolu nerede?
policeman, policemen [pə'liːsmən, pə'liːsmɛn] *n* erkek polis
policewoman, policewomen [pə'liːswʊmən, pə'liːswɪmɪn] *n* kadın polis
policy ['pɒlɪsɪ] *n* **insurance policy** *n* sigorta poliçesi
polio ['pəʊlɪəʊ] *n* çocuk felci
polish ['pɒlɪʃ] *n* cila ▷ *v* cilalamak; **nail polish** *n* oje; **shoe polish** *n* ayakkabı cilası
Polish ['pəʊlɪʃ] *adj* Polonya ▷ *n* Polonyalı
polite [pə'laɪt] *adj* kibar
politely [pə'laɪtlɪ] *adv* kibarca
politeness [pə'laɪtnɪs] *n* kibarlık
political [pə'lɪtɪkᵊl] *adj* politik
politician [ˌpɒlɪ'tɪʃən] *n* politikacı
politics ['pɒlɪtɪks] *npl* politika
poll [pəʊl] *n* kamuoyu yoklaması; **opinion poll** *n* kamuoyu yoklaması
pollen ['pɒlən] *n* çiçek tozu
pollute [pə'luːt] *v* kirletmek
polluted [pə'luːtɪd] *adj* kirlenmiş
pollution [pə'luːʃən] *n* kirlilik
Polynesia [ˌpɒlɪ'niːʒə; -ʒɪə] *n* Polonezya Adaları
Polynesian [ˌpɒlɪ'niːʒən; -ʒɪən] *adj* Polonezya ▷ *n (language)* Polonezce *(dil)*, *(person)* Polonezyalı *(kişi)*
pomegranate ['pɒmɪˌgrænɪt; 'pɒmˌgrænɪt] *n* nar
pond [pɒnd] *n* gölcük
pony ['pəʊnɪ] *n* midilli; **pony trekking** *n* midilliyle gezme
ponytail ['pəʊnɪˌteɪl] *n* atkuyruğu
poodle ['puːdᵊl] *n* kaniş
pool [puːl] *n (resources)* fon *(mali birikim)*, *(water)* havuz; **paddling pool** *n* sığ havuz; **swimming pool** *n* yüzme havuzu; **Is it an outdoor pool?** Açık yüzme havuzu mu?; **Is the pool heated?** Havuz ısıtılmış mı?; **Is there a children's pool?**

Çocuk havuzu var mı?; **Is there a paddling pool for the children?** Çocuklar için yüzme havuzu var mı?; **Is there a swimming pool?** Yüzme havuzu var mı?, Yüzme havuzunuz var mı?
poor [pʊə; pɔː] *adj* yoksul
poorly ['pʊəlɪ; 'pɔː-] *adj* acemice
popcorn ['pɒpˌkɔːn] *n* patlamış mısır
pope [pəʊp] *n* papa
poplar ['pɒplə] *n* kavak
poppy ['pɒpɪ] *n* gelincik *(çiçek)*
popular ['pɒpjʊlə] *adj* popüler
popularity ['pɒpjʊlærɪtɪ] *n* popülerlik
population [ˌpɒpjʊ'leɪʃən] *n* nüfus
pop-up [pɒpʌp] *n* ortaya çıkmak
porch [pɔːtʃ] *n* veranda
pork [pɔːk] *n* domuz eti; **pork chop** *n* domuz pirzolası; **I don't eat pork** Domuz eti yemiyorum
porn [pɔːn] *n (informal)* porno
pornographic [pɔː'nɒgræfɪk] *adj* pornografik
pornography [pɔː'nɒgrəfɪ] *n* pornografi
porridge ['pɒrɪdʒ] *n* yulaf ezmesi
port [pɔːt] *n (ships)* liman, *(wine)* porto şarabı
portable ['pɔːtəbᵊl] *adj* taşınabilir
porter ['pɔːtə] *n* hamal
portfolio [pɔːt'fəʊlɪəʊ] *n* portföy
portion ['pɔːʃən] *n* parça
portrait ['pɔːtrɪt; -treɪt] *n* portre
Portugal ['pɔːtjʊgᵊl] *n* Portekiz
Portuguese [ˌpɔːtjʊ'giːz] *adj* Portekiz ▷ *n (language)* Portekizce *(dil)*, *(person)* Portekizli *(kişi)*
position [pə'zɪʃən] *n* pozisyon
positive ['pɒzɪtɪv] *adj* olumlu
possess [pə'zɛs] *v* sahip olmak
possession [pə'zɛʃən] *n* mülkiyet
possibility [ˌpɒsɪ'bɪlɪtɪ] *n* olasılık
possible ['pɒsɪbᵊl] *adj* olası
possibly ['pɒsɪblɪ] *adv* olasılıkla
post [pəʊst] *n (mail)* posta, *(position)* görev *(pozisyon)*, *(stake)* direk *(çit)* ▷ *v* postalamak; **post office** *n* postane; **When does the post office open?** Postane ne zaman açılıyor?; **Where can I post these cards?** Bu kartları nereden postalayabilirim?
postage ['pəʊstɪdʒ] *n* posta ücreti
postbox ['pəʊstˌbɒks] *n* posta kutusu
postcard ['pəʊstˌkɑːd] *n* kartpostal; **Can I have stamps for four postcards to...** Bu dört kartpostal için pul alacaktım... a gidecek; **Do you have any postcards?** Kartpostal satıyor musunuz?; **I'm looking for postcards** Kartpostal bakıyordum; **Where can I buy some postcards?** Nereden kartpostal alabilirim?
postcode ['pəʊstˌkəʊd] *n* alan kodu
poster ['pəʊstə] *n* poster
postgraduate [pəʊst'grædjʊɪt] *n* üniversite sonrası eğitim yapan öğrenci
postman, postmen ['pəʊstmən, 'pəʊstmɛn] *n* postacı
postmark ['pəʊstˌmɑːk] *n* posta damgası
postpone [pəʊst'pəʊn; pə'spəʊn] *v* ertelemek

postwoman, postwomen ['pəʊstwʊmən, 'pəʊstwɪmɪn] *n* kadın postacı
pot [pɒt] *n* tencere; **plant pot** *n* çiçek saksısı; **pot plant** *n* saksı çiçeği
potato, potatoes [pə'teɪtəʊ, pə'teɪtəʊz] *n* patates; **baked potato** *n* kumpir; **jacket potato** *n* kumpir; **mashed potatoes** *npl* patates püresi; **potato peeler** *n* patates soyucu
potential [pə'tɛnʃəl] *adj* potansiyel ▹ *n* potansiyel
pothole ['pɒt,həʊl] *n* yol çukuru
pottery ['pɒtərɪ] *n* çanak çömlek
potty ['pɒtɪ] *n* lazımlık
pound [paʊnd] *n* pound *(İngiliz ağırlık birimi)*; **pound sterling** *n* pound sterlin *(İngiliz para birimi)*
pour [pɔː] *v* akmak
poverty ['pɒvətɪ] *n* yoksulluk
powder ['paʊdə] *n* toz; **baking powder** *n* kabartma tozu; **soap powder** *n* sabun tozu; **talcum powder** *n* talk pudrası; **washing powder** *n* çamaşır tozu; **Do you have washing powder?** Çamaşır tozunuz var mı?
power ['paʊə] *n* güç *(erk)*; **power cut** *n* elektrik kesintisi; **solar power** *n* güneş enerjisi
powerful ['paʊəfʊl] *adj* güçlü
practical ['præktɪkᵊl] *adj* pratik
practically ['præktɪkəlɪ; -klɪ] *adv* pratik olarak
practice ['præktɪs] *n* pratik
practise ['præktɪs] *v* pratik yapmak
praise [preɪz] *v* övmek
pram [præm] *n* bebek arabası
prank [præŋk] *n* kaba şaka
prawn [prɔːn] *n* karides
pray [preɪ] *v* dua etmek
prayer [prɛə] *n* dua
precaution [prɪ'kɔːʃən] *n* önlem
preceding [prɪ'siːdɪŋ] *adj* önceki
precinct ['priːsɪŋkt] *n* bölge *(kent)*; **pedestrian precinct** *n* yayalara özel bölge
precious ['prɛʃəs] *adj* değerli
precise [prɪ'saɪs] *adj* tam
precisely [prɪ'saɪslɪ] *adv* tam olarak
predecessor ['priːdɪ,sɛsə] *n* selef
predict [prɪ'dɪkt] *v* öngörmek
predictable [prɪ'dɪktəbᵊl] *adj* tahmin edilebilir
prefect ['priːfɛkt] *n* başkan *(okul)*
prefer [prɪ'fɜː] *v* tercih etmek
preferably ['prɛfərəblɪ; 'prɛfrəblɪ] *adv* tercihen
preference ['prɛfərəns; 'prɛfrəns] *n* tercih
pregnancy ['prɛgnənsɪ] *n* gebelik
pregnant ['prɛgnənt] *adj* gebe
prehistoric [,priːhɪ'stɒrɪk] *adj* tarih öncesi
prejudice ['prɛdʒʊdɪs] *n* önyargı
prejudiced ['prɛdʒʊdɪst] *adj* önyargılı
premature [,prɛmə'tjʊə; 'prɛmə,tjʊə] *adj* erken
premiere ['prɛmɪ,ɛə; 'prɛmɪə] *n* gala
premises ['prɛmɪsɪz] *npl* bina ve etrafındaki arazi
premonition [,prɛmə'nɪʃən] *n* kehanet
preoccupied [priː'ɒkjʊ,paɪd] *adj*

kafasını takmış
prepaid [pri:'peɪd] *adj* önceden ödenmiş
preparation [,prɛpə'reɪʃən] *n* hazırlık
prepare [prɪ'pɛə] *v* hazırlama
prepared [prɪ'pɛəd] *adj* hazırlanmış
Presbyterian [,prɛzbɪ'tɪərɪən] *adj* Presbiteryan ▹ *n* Presbiteryan
prescribe [prɪ'skraɪb] *v* ilaç yazmak
prescription [prɪ'skrɪpʃən] *n* reçete; **Where can I get this prescription made up?** Bu reçeteyi nerede yaptırabilirim
presence ['prɛzəns] *n* varlık
present *adj* ['prɛznt] var ▹ *n* ['prɛznt] *(gift)* armağan, *(time being)* şu an ▹ *v* [prɪ'zɛnt] takdim etmek; **I'm looking for a present for my husband** Eşime bir armağan almak istiyordum
presentation [,prɛzən'teɪʃən] *n* sunma
presenter [prɪ'zɛntə] *n* sunucu *(radyo, TV)*
presently ['prɛzəntlɪ] *adv* şu anda
preservative [prɪ'zɜ:vətɪv] *n* katkı maddesi
president ['prɛzɪdənt] *n* başkan *(şirket)*
press [prɛs] *n* pres ▹ *v* bastırmak; **press conference** *n* basın toplantısı
press-up [prɛsʌp] *n* şınav çekmek
pressure ['prɛʃə] *n* basınç ▹ *v* baskı yapmak; **blood pressure** *n* tansiyon
prestige [prɛ'sti:ʒ] *n* prestij
prestigious [prɛ'stɪdʒəs] *adj* saygın
presumably [prɪ'zju:məblɪ] *adv* olasılıkla
presume [prɪ'zju:m] *v* farzetmek
pretend [prɪ'tɛnd] *v* yapar gibi görünmek
pretext ['pri:tɛkst] *n* bahane
prettily ['prɪtɪlɪ] *adv* hoş bir şekilde
pretty ['prɪtɪ] *adj* hoş ▹ *adv* bayağı *(oldukça)*
prevent [prɪ'vɛnt] *v* önlemek
prevention [prɪ'vɛnʃən] *n* önleme
previous ['pri:vɪəs] *adj* önceki
previously ['pri:vɪəslɪ] *adv* daha önceden
prey [preɪ] *n* ev
price [praɪs] *n* fiyat; **price list** *n* fiyat listesi; **retail price** *n* perakende fiyatı; **selling price** *n* satış fiyatı; **Does the price include boots?** Fiyata botlar da dahil mi?; **Please write down the price** Fiyatı yazar mısınız?; **What is included in the price?** Fiyata neler dahil?
prick [prɪk] *v* delmek *(iğneyle)*
pride [praɪd] *n* gurur
priest [pri:st] *n* rahip
primarily ['praɪmərəlɪ] *adv* başlıca
primary ['praɪmərɪ] *adj* ilk; **primary school** *n* ilkokul
primitive ['prɪmɪtɪv] *adj* ilkel
primrose ['prɪm,rəʊz] *n* çuha çiçeği
prince [prɪns] *n* prens
princess [prɪn'sɛs] *n* prenses
principal ['prɪnsɪpᵊl] *adj* baş *(tepede)* ▹ *n* müdür

principle ['prɪnsɪpᵊl] *n* ilke
print [prɪnt] *n* baskı *(matbaa)* ▷ *v* basmak *(matbaa)*
printer ['prɪntə] *n (machine)* yazıcı, *(person)* matbaacı; **Is there a colour printer?** Renkli yazıcı var mı?
printout ['prɪntaʊt] *n* çıktı *(bilgisayar)*
priority [praɪ'ɒrɪtɪ] *n* öncelik
prison ['prɪzᵊn] *n* hapishane; **prison officer** *n* hapishane görevlisi
prisoner ['prɪzənə] *n* mahkum
privacy ['praɪvəsɪ; 'prɪvəsɪ] *n* özel yaşam
private ['praɪvɪt] *adj* özel; **private property** *n* özel mülk; **Can I speak to you in private?** Sizinle özel olarak konuşabilir miyim?
privatize ['praɪvɪˌtaɪz] *v* özelleştirmek
privilege ['prɪvɪlɪdʒ] *n* ayrıcalık
prize [praɪz] *n* ödül
prize-giving ['praɪzˌgɪvɪŋ] *n* ödül töreni
prizewinner ['praɪzˌwɪnə] *n* ödüllü
probability [ˌprɒbə'bɪlɪtɪ] *n* olasılık
probable ['prɒbəbᵊl] *adj* olası
probably ['prɒbəblɪ] *adv* olasılıkla
problem ['prɒbləm] *n* sorun; **No problem** Sorun değil; **There's a problem with the room** Odada bir sorun var; **Who do we contact if there are problems?** Bir sorun çıkarsa kiminle temas kuracağız?
proceedings [prə'si:dɪŋz] *npl* dava
proceeds ['prəʊsi:dz] *npl* gelir *(toplanan para)*
process ['prəʊsɛs] *n* işlem
procession [prə'sɛʃən] *n* alay *(tören/gelin)*
produce [prə'dju:s] *v* yaratmak
producer [prə'dju:sə] *n* üretici
product ['prɒdʌkt] *n* ürün
production [prə'dʌkʃən] *n* üretim
productivity [ˌprɒdʌk'tɪvɪtɪ] *n* verimlilik
profession [prə'fɛʃən] *n* meslek
professional [prə'fɛʃənᵊl] *adj* profesyonel ▷ *n* profesyonel
professionally [prə'fɛʃənəlɪ] *adv* profesyonelce
professor [prə'fɛsə] *n* profesör
profit ['prɒfɪt] *n* kazanç
profitable ['prɒfɪtəbᵊl] *adj* kazançlı
program ['prəʊgræm] *n* program ▷ *v* programlamak
programme ['prəʊgræm] *n* program
programmer ['prəʊgræmə] *n* programcı
programming ['prəʊgræmɪŋ] *n* programlama
progress ['prəʊgrɛs] *n* ilerleme
prohibit [prə'hɪbɪt] *v* yasaklamak
prohibited [prə'hɪbɪtɪd] *adj* yasaklanmış
project ['prɒdʒɛkt] *n* proje
projector [prə'dʒɛktə] *n* projektör; **overhead projector** *n* projektör
promenade [ˌprɒmə'nɑ:d] *n* gezinti yeri
promise ['prɒmɪs] *n* söz ▷ *v* söz vermek
promising ['prɒmɪsɪŋ] *adj* ümit

veren
promote [prə'məʊt] *v* tanıtımını yapmak
promotion [prə'məʊʃən] *n* tanıtım
prompt [prɒmpt] *adj* çabuk
promptly [prɒmptlɪ] *adv* çabucak
pronoun ['prəʊ,naʊn] *n* zamir
pronounce [prə'naʊns] *v* telaffuz etmek
pronunciation [prə,nʌnsɪ'eɪʃən] *n* telaffuz
proof [pru:f] *n (evidence)* kanıt, *(for checking)* deneme baskısı
propaganda [,prɒpə'gændə] *n* propaganda
proper ['prɒpə] *adj* doğru dürüst
properly ['prɒpəlɪ] *adv* doğru dürüst; **This isn't cooked properly** Bu doğru dürüst pişmemiş; **This part doesn't work properly** Bu kısım doğru dürüst çalışmıyor
property ['prɒpətɪ] *n* mülk; **private property** *n* özel mülk
proportion [prə'pɔ:ʃən] *n* oran
proportional [prə'pɔ:ʃənᵊl] *adj* orantılı
proposal [prə'pəʊzᵊl] *n* öneri
propose [prə'pəʊz] *v* önermek
prosecute ['prɒsɪ,kju:t] *v* kovuşturma açmak
prospect ['prɒspɛkt] *n* gelecek beklentisi
prospectus [prə'spɛktəs] *n* tanıtma broşürü
prosperity [prɒ'spɛrɪtɪ] *n* gönenç
prostitute ['prɒstɪ,tju:t] *n* fahişe
protect [prə'tɛkt] *v* korumak
protection [prə'tɛkʃən] *n* koruma
protein ['prəʊti:n] *n* protein
protest *n* ['prəʊtɛst] protesto ▷ *v* [prə'tɛst] protesto etmek
Protestant ['prɒtɪstənt] *adj* Protestan ▷ *n* Protestan
proud [praʊd] *adj* gururlu
prove [pru:v] *v* kanıtlamak
proverb ['prɒvɜ:b] *n* atasözü
provide [prə'vaɪd] *v* sağlamak; **provide for** *v* geçimini sağlamak
provided [prə'vaɪdɪd] *conj* yeter ki
providing [prə'vaɪdɪŋ] *conj* yeter ki
provisional [prə'vɪʒənᵊl] *adj* geçici *(bir süreliğine)*
proximity [prɒk'sɪmɪtɪ] *n* yakınlık
prune [pru:n] *n* kuru erik
pry [praɪ] *v* gözetlemek
pseudonym ['sju:də,nɪm] *n* takma ad
psychiatric [,saɪkɪ'ætrɪk] *adj* psikiyatrik
psychiatrist [saɪ'kaɪətrɪst] *n* psikiyatrist
psychological [,saɪkə'lɒdʒɪkᵊl] *adj* psikolojik
psychologist [saɪ'kɒlədʒɪst] *n* psikolog
psychology [saɪ'kɒlədʒɪ] *n* psikoloji
psychotherapy [,saɪkəʊ'θɛrəpɪ] *n* psikoterapi
PTO [pi: ti: əʊ] *abbr* Lütfen Arka Sayfaya Bakınız
pub [pʌb] *n* birahane
public ['pʌblɪk] *adj* halk ▷ *n* halk; **public holiday** *n* resmi tatil günü; **public opinion** *n* kamuoyu; **public relations** *npl* halkla ilişkiler; **public school** *n* devlet

koleji; **public transport** *n* toplu taşıma; **Is the castle open to the public?** Kale halka açık mı?
publican ['pʌblɪkən] *n* bar işletmecisi
publication [ˌpʌblɪ'keɪʃən] *n* yayımlama
publish ['pʌblɪʃ] *v* yayımlamak
publisher ['pʌblɪʃə] *n* yayınevi
pudding ['pʊdɪŋ] *n* puding
puddle ['pʌdᵊl] *n* su birikintisi
Puerto Rico ['pwɜːtəʊ 'riːkəʊ; 'pwɛə-] *n* Portoriko
pull [pʊl] *v* çekmek
pull down [pʊl daʊn] *v* yıkmak
pull out [pʊl aʊt] *vi* kenara çekmek *(araç)*
pullover ['pʊlˌəʊvə] *n* kazak
pull up [pʊl ʌp] *v* kenara çekmek *(araç)*
pulse [pʌls] *n* nabız
pulses [pʌlsɪz] *npl* bakliyat
pump [pʌmp] *n* pompa ▷ *v* pompalamak; **bicycle pump** *n* bisiklet pompası; **Do you have a pump?** Bisiklet pompanız var mı?; **Pump number three, please** Üç numaralı pompa lütfen
pumpkin ['pʌmpkɪn] *n* balkabağı
pump up [pʌmp ʌp] *v* şişirmek
punch [pʌntʃ] *n (blow)* yumruk; *(hot drink)* panç ▷ *v* yumruklamak
punctual ['pʌŋktjʊəl] *adj* zamanında
punctuation [ˌpʌŋktjʊ'eɪʃən] *n* noktalama
puncture ['pʌŋktʃə] *n* patlak
punish ['pʌnɪʃ] *v* cezalandırmak
punishment ['pʌnɪʃmənt] *n* ceza; **capital punishment** *n* idam cezası; **corporal punishment** *n* dayak cezası
punk [pʌŋk] *n* punkçu
pupil ['pjuːpᵊl] *n (eye)* gözbebeği, *(learner)* öğrenci
puppet ['pʌpɪt] *n* kukla
puppy ['pʌpɪ] *n* yavru köpek
purchase ['pɜːtʃɪs] *v* satın almak
pure [pjʊə] *adj* saf
purple ['pɜːpᵊl] *adj* mor
purpose ['pɜːpəs] *n* maksat
purr [pɜː] *v* mırıldanmak *(kedi gibi)*
purse [pɜːs] *n* cüzdan *(kadın)*
pursue [pə'sjuː] *v* peşine takılmak
pursuit [pə'sjuːt] *n* kovalamaca
pus [pʌs] *n* irin
push [pʊʃ] *v* ittirmek
pushchair ['pʊʃˌtʃɛə] *n* puset
push-up [pʊʃʌp] *n* pres *(spor)*
put [pʊt] *v* koymak; **I would like to put my jewellery in the safe** Mücevherlerimi kasaya koymak istiyorum
put aside [pʊt ə'saɪd] *v* biriktirmek
put away [pʊt ə'weɪ] *v* toparlayıp kaldırmak
put back [pʊt bæk] *v* geri koymak
put forward [pʊt fɔːwəd] *v* ileriye almak
put in [pʊt ɪn] *v* öncelik belirlemek
put off [pʊt ɒf] *v* ertelemek
put up [pʊt ʌp] *v* dikmek
puzzle ['pʌzᵊl] *n* bilmece
puzzled ['pʌzᵊld] *adj* kafası karışmış
puzzling ['pʌzlɪŋ] *adj* şaşırtıcı
pyjamas [pə'dʒɑːməz] *npl* pijama
pylon ['paɪlən] *n* elektrik direği
pyramid ['pɪrəmɪd] *n* piramit

q

Qatar [kæ'tɑː] *n* Katar
quail [kweɪl] *n* bıldırcın
quaint [kweɪnt] *adj* eski ve hoş
Quaker ['kweɪkə] *n* Quaker mezhebinden
qualification [ˌkwɒlɪfɪ'keɪʃən] *n* nitelik
qualified ['kwɒlɪˌfaɪd] *adj* nitelikli
qualify ['kwɒlɪˌfaɪ] *v* nitelemek
quality ['kwɒlɪtɪ] *n* kalite
quantify ['kwɒntɪˌfaɪ] *v* miktar belirtmek
quantity ['kwɒntɪtɪ] *n* miktar
quarantine ['kwɒrənˌtiːn] *n* karantina
quarrel ['kwɒrəl] *n* kavga ▷ *v* tartışmak
quarry ['kwɒrɪ] *n* taş ocağı
quarter ['kwɔːtə] *n* çeyrek; **quarter final** *n* çeyrek final; **It's quarter past two** Saat ikiyi çeyrek geçiyor; **It's quarter to two** Saat ikiye çeyrek var
quartet [kwɔː'tɛt] *n* kuartet
quay [kiː] *n* iskele *(deniz)*
queen [kwiːn] *n* kraliçe
query ['kwɪərɪ] *n* soru ▷ *v* sorgulamak
question ['kwɛstʃən] *n* soru ▷ *v* sormak; **question mark** *n* soru işareti
questionnaire [ˌkwɛstʃə'nɛə; ˌkɛs-] *n* anket
queue [kjuː] *n* kuyruk *(insan sırası)* ▷ *v* kuyruğa girmek
quick [kwɪk] *adj* çabuk
quickly [kwɪklɪ] *adv* çabukça
quiet ['kwaɪət] *adj* sessiz; **I'd like a quiet room** Sessiz bir oda rica ediyorum
quietly ['kwaɪətlɪ] *adv* sessizce
quilt [kwɪlt] *n* yorgan
quit [kwɪt] *v* bırakmak
quite [kwaɪt] *adv* büsbütün, bütünüyle
quiz, quizzes [kwɪz, 'kwɪzɪz] *n* bilgi yarışması
quota ['kwəʊtə] *n* kota
quotation [kwəʊ'teɪʃən] *n* alıntı; **quotation marks** *npl* çift tırnak
quote [kwəʊt] *n* alıntı ▷ *v* alıntı yapmak

r

rabbi ['ræbaɪ] *n* haham
rabbit ['ræbɪt] *n* tavşan
rabies ['reɪbi:z] *n* kuduz
race [reɪs] *n (contest)* yarış, *(origin)* ırk ▷ *v* yarışmak; **I'd like to see a horse race** At yarışı görmek isterdim
racecourse ['reɪs,kɔ:s] *n* yarış parkuru
racehorse ['reɪs,hɔ:s] *n* yarış atı
racer ['reɪsə] *n* yarışçı
racetrack ['reɪs,træk] *n* yarış pisti
racial ['reɪʃəl] *adj* ırkla ilgili
racing ['reɪsɪŋ] *n* **horse racing** *n* at yarışı; **motor racing** *n* oto yarışı; **racing car** *n* yarış arabası; **racing driver** *n* yarışçı *(otomobil)*
racism ['reɪsɪzəm] *n* ırkçılık
racist ['reɪsɪst] *adj* ırkçı ▷ *n* ırkçı
rack [ræk] *n* askılık; **luggage rack** *n* port bagaj
racket ['rækɪt] *n (racquet)* raket; **tennis racket** *n* tenis raketi; **Where can I hire a racket?** Raket nereden kiralayabilirim?
racoon [rə'ku:n] *n* rakun
racquet ['rækɪt] *n* raket
radar ['reɪdɑ:] *n* radar
radiation [,reɪdɪ'eɪʃən] *n* radyasyon
radiator ['reɪdɪ,eɪtə] *n* radyatör; **There is a leak in the radiator** Radyatör sızıntı yapıyor
radio ['reɪdɪəʊ] *n* radyo; **digital radio** *n* dijital radyo; **radio station** *n* radyo istasyonu; **Can I switch the radio off?** Radyoyu kapatabilir miyim?; **Can I switch the radio on?** Radyoyu açabilir miyim?
radioactive [,reɪdɪəʊ'æktɪv] *adj* radyoaktif
radio-controlled ['reɪdɪəʊ'kən'trəʊld] *adj* uzaktan kumandalı
radish ['rædɪʃ] *n* kırmızı turp
raffle ['ræfᵊl] *n* çekiliş
raft [rɑ:ft] *n* sal
rag [ræg] *n* çaput
rage [reɪdʒ] *n* hiddet; **road rage** *n* trafik magandalığı
raid [reɪd] *n* baskın ▷ *v* baskın yapmak
rail [reɪl] *n* parmaklık, ray
railcard ['reɪl,kɑ:d] *n* tren abonmanı
railings ['reɪlɪŋz] *npl* parmaklık
railway ['reɪl,weɪ] *n* demiryolu; **railway station** *n* tren istasyonu
rain [reɪn] *n* yağmur ▷ *v* yağmur yağmak; **acid rain** *n* asit yağmuru; **Do you think it's going to rain?**

Sizce yağmur yağacak mı?; **It's raining** Yağmur yağıyor
rainbow ['reɪn,bəʊ] *n* gökkuşağı
raincoat ['reɪn,kəʊt] *n* yağmurluk
rainforest ['reɪn,fɒrɪst] *n* yağmur ormanı
rainy ['reɪnɪ] *adj* yağmurlu
raise [reɪz] *v* kabartmak
raisin ['reɪzᵊn] *n* kuru üzüm
rake [reɪk] *n* tırmık
rally ['rælɪ] *n* miting
ram [ræm] *n* koç ▷ *v* vurmak
Ramadan [,ræmə'dɑːn] *n* Ramazan
rambler ['ræmblə] *n* avare
ramp [ræmp] *n* rampa
random ['rændəm] *adj* rastgele
range [reɪndʒ] *n* *(limits)* sınır, *(mountains)* sıradağ ▷ *v* çeşitlilik göstermek
rank [ræŋk] *n* *(line)* sıra *(taksi vb)*, *(status)* rütbe ▷ *v* sıralamak
ransom ['rænsəm] *n* fidye
rape [reɪp] *n* *(plant)* hardal otu, *(sexual attack)* tecavüz *(cinsel)* ▷ *v* tecavüz etmek; **I've been raped** Tecavüze uğradım
rapids ['ræpɪdz] *npl* çağlayanlar
rapist ['reɪpɪst] *n* tecavüzcü
rare [rɛə] *adj* *(uncommon)* az görülür, *(undercooked)* az pişmiş
rarely ['rɛəlɪ] *adv* nadiren
rash [ræʃ] *n* kızarıklık
raspberry ['rɑːzbərɪ; -brɪ] *n* ahududu
rat [ræt] *n* sıçan
rate [reɪt] *n* oran ▷ *v* oranlamak; **interest rate** *n* faiz oranı; **rate of exchange** *n* döviz kuru
rather ['rɑːðə] *adv* oldukça
ratio ['reɪʃɪ,əʊ] *n* oran
rational ['ræʃənᵊl] *adj* akıllıca
rattle ['rætᵊl] *n* çıngırak
rattlesnake ['rætᵊl,sneɪk] *n* çıngıraklı yılan
rave [reɪv] *n* abuk sabuk konuşma ▷ *v* saçmalamak
raven ['reɪvᵊn] *n* kuzgunî
ravenous ['rævənəs] *adj* kurt gibi aç
ravine [rə'viːn] *n* koyak
raw [rɔː] *adj* çiğ *(pişmemiş)*
razor ['reɪzə] *n* traş bıçağı; **razor blade** *n* traş bıçağı
reach [riːtʃ] *v* ulaşmak
react [rɪ'ækt] *v* tepki göstermek
reaction [rɪ'ækʃən] *n* tepki
reactor [rɪ'æktə] *n* reaktör
read [riːd] *v* okumak
reader ['riːdə] *n* okuyucu
readily ['rɛdɪlɪ] *adv* hazır bir şekilde
reading ['riːdɪŋ] *n* okuma
read out [riːd] *v* yüksek sesle okumak
ready ['rɛdɪ] *adj* hazır; **Are you ready?** Hazır mısınız?; **I'm not ready** Hazır değilim; **I'm ready** Hazırım; **When will it be ready?** Ne zaman hazır olur?; **When will the car be ready?** Araba ne zaman hazır olur?
ready-cooked ['rɛdɪ'kʊkt] *adj* hazır yemek
real ['rɪəl] *adj* gerçek *(durum)*
realistic [,rɪə'lɪstɪk] *adj* gerçekçi
reality [rɪ'ælɪtɪ] *n* gerçeklik; **reality TV** *n* biri bizi gözetliyor; **virtual reality** *n* sanal gerçeklik
realize ['rɪə,laɪz] *v* farkına varmak

really ['rɪəlɪ] *adv* gerçekten
rear [rɪə] *adj* arka ▷ *n* arka; **rear-view mirror** *n* arka ayna
reason ['riːzᵊn] *n* mantık
reasonable ['riːzənəbᵊl] *adj* mantıklı
reasonably ['riːzənəblɪ] *adv* makul
reassure [ˌriːə'ʃʊə] *v* güven vermek
reassuring [ˌriːə'ʃʊəɪŋ] *adj* güven verici
rebate ['riːbeɪt] *n* para iadesi
rebellious [rɪ'bɛljəs] *adj* isyankar
rebuild [riː'bɪld] *v* yeniden yapmak
receipt [rɪ'siːt] *n* fiş; **I need a receipt for the insurance** Sigorta için fiş almam gerekiyor; **I need a receipt, please** Fiş istiyorum lütfen
receive [rɪ'siːv] *v* almak
receiver [rɪ'siːvə] *n (electronic)* alıcı, *(person)* tasfiye memuru
recent ['riːsᵊnt] *adj* yeni
recently ['riːsəntlɪ] *adv* son zamanlarda
reception [rɪ'sɛpʃən] *n* resepsiyon
receptionist [rɪ'sɛpʃənɪst] *n* resepsiyonist
recession [rɪ'sɛʃən] *n* durgunluk *(piyasa)*
recharge [riː'tʃɑːdʒ] *v* yüklemek *(pil vb)*
recipe ['rɛsɪpɪ] *n* tarif
recipient [rɪ'sɪpɪənt] *n* alıcı *(kişi)*
reckon ['rɛkən] *v* hesaba katmak
reclining [rɪ'klaɪnɪŋ] *adj* yaslanır
recognizable ['rɛkəgˌnaɪzəbᵊl] *adj* tanınabilir
recognize ['rɛkəgˌnaɪz] *v* tanımak
recommend [ˌrɛkə'mɛnd] *v* tavsiye etmek
recommendation [ˌrɛkəmɛn'deɪʃən] *n* öneri
reconsider [ˌriːkən'sɪdə] *v* yeniden ele almak
record *n* ['rɛkɔːd] kayıt ▷ *v* [rɪ'kɔːd] kaydetmek
recorder [rɪ'kɔːdə] *n (music)* ses kayıt cihazı, *(scribe)* kayıt aleti
recording [rɪ'kɔːdɪŋ] *n* kayıt
recover [rɪ'kʌvə] *v* iyileşmek
recovery [rɪ'kʌvərɪ] *n* iyileşme
recruitment [rɪ'kruːtmənt] *n* eleman alma
rectangle ['rɛkˌtæŋgᵊl] *n* dikdörtgen
rectangular [rɛk'tæŋgjʊlə] *adj* dikdörtgen biçiminde
rectify ['rɛktɪˌfaɪ] *v* düzeltmek *(hatalı bir davranış)*
recurring [rɪ'kʌrɪŋ] *adj* yinelenen
recycle [riː'saɪkᵊl] *v* geri dönüştürmek
recycling [riː'saɪklɪŋ] *n* geri dönüştürmek
red [rɛd] *adj* kırmızı; **red meat** *n* kırmızı et; **red wine** *n* kırmızı şarap; **Red Cross** *n* Kızılhaç; **Red Sea** *n* Kızıl Deniz; **a bottle of red wine** Bir şişe kırmızı şarap; **I don't eat red meat** Kırmızı et yemiyorum
redcurrant ['rɛd'kʌrənt] *n* kırmızı Frenk üzümü
redecorate [riː'dɛkəˌreɪt] *v* yeniden badana yapmak
red-haired ['rɛdˌhɛəd] *adj* kızıl saçlı
redhead ['rɛdˌhɛd] *n* kızıl saçlı
redo [riː'duː] *v* yeniden yapmak

reduce [rɪ'dju:s] *v* azaltmak
reduction [rɪ'dʌkʃən] *n* indirim; **Are there any reductions for children?** Çocuklara indirim var mı?; **Are there any reductions for groups?** Grup indirimi var mı?; **Are there any reductions for senior citizens?** Yaşlılara indirim var mı?; **Is there a reduction for disabled people?** Özürlüler için indiriminiz var mı?; **Is there a reduction with this pass?** Bu kartla indirim alabilir miyim?
redundancy [rɪ'dʌndənsɪ] *n* işten çıkarma *(ihtiyaç fazlası olarak)*
redundant [rɪ'dʌndənt] *adj* işten çıkarılmış *(ihtiyaç fazlası olarak)*
reed [ri:d] *n* kamış
reel [ri:l; rɪəl] *n* makara
refer [rɪ'fɜ:] *v* söz etmek
referee [ˌrɛfə'ri:] *n* hakem
reference ['rɛfərəns; 'rɛfrəns] *n* gönderme *(kaynak)*; **reference number** *n* referans numarası
refill [ri:'fɪl] *v* doldurmaya devam etmek
refinery [rɪ'faɪnərɪ] *n* rafineri; **oil refinery** *n* petrol rafinerisi
reflect [rɪ'flɛkt] *v* yansıtmak
reflection [rɪ'flɛkʃən] *n* yansıma
reflex ['ri:flɛks] *n* refleks
refreshing [rɪ'frɛʃɪŋ] *adj* iç ferahlatıcı
refreshments [rɪ'frɛʃmənts] *npl* serinletici içecek
refrigerator [rɪ'frɪdʒəˌreɪtə] *n* buzdolabı
refuel [ri:'fju:əl] *v* yakıt ikmali yapmak
refuge ['rɛfju:dʒ] *n* sığınak
refugee [ˌrɛfjʊ'dʒi:] *n* sığınmacı
refund *n* ['ri:ˌfʌnd] para iadesi ▷ *v* [rɪ'fʌnd] para iadesi yapmak
refusal [rɪ'fju:zᵊl] *n* red
refuse¹ [rɪ'fju:z] *v* reddetmek
refuse² ['rɛfju:s] *n* reddetme
regain [rɪ'geɪn] *v* kendine gelmek
regard [rɪ'gɑ:d] *n* saygı ▷ *v* değerlendirmek
regarding [rɪ'gɑ:dɪŋ] *prep* ilgili olarak
regiment ['rɛdʒɪmənt] *n* alay *(askeri)*
region ['ri:dʒən] *n* bölge; **Where can I buy a map of the region?** Bu bölgenin haritasını nereden alabilirim?
regional ['ri:dʒənᵊl] *adj* bölgesel
register ['rɛdʒɪstə] *n* kayıt ▷ *v* kayıt yaptırmak; **cash register** *n* yazar kasa
registered ['rɛdʒɪstəd] *adj* kayıtlı
registration [ˌrɛdʒɪ'streɪʃən] *n* kayıt
regret [rɪ'grɛt] *n* pişmanlık ▷ *v* hayıflanmak
regular ['rɛgjʊlə] *adj* düzenli
regularly ['rɛgjʊləlɪ] *adv* düzenli olarak
regulation [ˌrɛgjʊ'leɪʃən] *n* düzeltme, yönetmelik
rehearsal [rɪ'hɜ:sᵊl] *n* prova
rehearse [rɪ'hɜ:s] *v* denemek
reimburse [ˌri:ɪm'bɜ:s] *v* zararını karşılamak
reindeer ['reɪnˌdɪə] *n* ren geyiği
reins [reɪnz] *npl* dizgin *(at)*
reject [rɪ'dʒɛkt] *v* reddetmek
relapse ['ri:ˌlæps] *n* eski haline dönmek

related [rɪ'leɪtɪd] *adj* akraba
relation [rɪ'leɪʃən] *n* ilişki; **public relations** *npl* halkla ilişkiler
relationship [rɪ'leɪʃənʃɪp] *n* ilişki
relative ['rɛlətɪv] *n* göreceli
relatively ['rɛlətɪvlɪ] *adv* göreceli olarak
relax [rɪ'læks] *v* gevşemek
relaxation [ˌriːlæk'seɪʃən] *n* gevşeme
relaxed [rɪ'lækst] *adj* rahat
relaxing [rɪ'læksɪŋ] *adj* gevşetici
relay ['riːleɪ] *n* eski grubun yerini alan yeni grup
release [rɪ'liːs] *n* serbest bırakma ▷ *v* serbest bırakmak
relegate ['rɛlɪˌgeɪt] *v* daha önemsiz bir göreve kaydırmak
relevant ['rɛlɪvənt] *adj* ilişkin
reliable [rɪ'laɪəbᵊl] *adj* güvenilir
relief [rɪ'liːf] *n* iç rahatlığı
relieve [rɪ'liːv] *v* dindirmek *(acı)*
relieved [rɪ'liːvd] *adj* rahatlamış
religion [rɪ'lɪdʒən] *n* din
religious [rɪ'lɪdʒəs] *adj* dini
reluctant [rɪ'lʌktənt] *adj* gönülsüz
reluctantly [rɪ'lʌktəntlɪ] *adv* gönülsüzce
rely [rɪ'laɪ] *v* **rely on** *v* güvenmek
remain [rɪ'meɪn] *v* kalmak
remaining [rɪ'meɪnɪŋ] *adj* kalan
remains [rɪ'meɪnz] *npl* kalıntı
remake ['riːˌmeɪk] *n* yeniden çekim
remark [rɪ'mɑːk] *n* görüş *(fikir)*
remarkable [rɪ'mɑːkəbᵊl] *adj* dikkate değer
remarkably [rɪ'mɑːkəblɪ] *adv* dikkat çekecek derecede
remarry [riː'mærɪ] *v* yeniden evlenmek
remedy ['rɛmɪdɪ] *n* ilaç
remember [rɪ'mɛmbə] *v* hatırlamak
remind [rɪ'maɪnd] *v* hatırlatmak
reminder [rɪ'maɪndə] *n* hatırlatıcı
remorse [rɪ'mɔːs] *n* vicdan azabı
remote [rɪ'məʊt] *adj* uzak; **remote control** *n* uazaktan kumanda
remotely [rɪ'məʊtlɪ] *adv* uzaktan yakından
removable [rɪ'muːvəbᵊl] *adj* taşınabilir
removal [rɪ'muːvᵊl] *n* taşıma; **removal van** *n* taşınma kamyonu
remove [rɪ'muːv] *v* kaldırmak
remover [rɪ'muːvə] *n* **nail-polish remover** *n* oje çıkarıcı
rendezvous ['rɒndɪˌvuː] *n* randevu
renew [rɪ'njuː] *v* yenilemek
renewable [rɪ'njuːəbᵊl] *adj* yenilenebilir
renovate ['rɛnəˌveɪt] *v* yenilemek
renowned [rɪ'naʊnd] *adj* tanınmış
rent [rɛnt] *n* kira ▷ *v* kiralamak; **Do you rent DVDs?** DVD kiralayabilir miyim?; **I'd like to rent a room** Bir oda kiralamak istiyorum
rental ['rɛntᵊl] *n* kira; **car rental** *n* oto kiralama; **rental car** *n* kiralık araba
reorganize [riː'ɔːgəˌnaɪz] *v* yeniden düzenlemek
rep [rɛp] *n* temsilci
repair [rɪ'pɛə] *n* tamir ▷ *v* onarmak; **repair kit** *n* tamir takımı; **Can you repair it?** Tamir edebilir misiniz?; **Can you repair my watch?**

Saatimi tamir edebilir misiniz?; **Can you repair this?** Bunu tamir edebilir misiniz?; **Do you have a repair kit?** Tamir takımınız var mı?; **How long will it take to repair?** Tamir etmek ne kadar sürer?; **How much will the repairs cost?** Tamir kaça malolacak?; **Where can I get this repaired?** Bunu nerede tamir ettirebilirim?; **Where is the nearest bike repair shop?** En yakın bisiklet tamircisi nerede?
repay [rɪ'peɪ] *v* geri ödemek
repayment [rɪ'peɪmənt] *n* geri ödeme
repeat [rɪ'pi:t] *n* tekrar ▷ *v* tekrarlamak; **Could you repeat that, please?** Tekrar eder misiniz lütfen?
repeatedly [rɪ'pi:tɪdlɪ] *adv* defalarca
repellent [rɪ'pɛlənt] *adj* itici; **insect repellent** *n* böcek ilacı
repercussions [ˌri:pə'kʌʃənz] *npl* sonuçlar
repetitive [rɪ'pɛtɪtɪv] *adj* tekrarlayan
replace [rɪ'pleɪs] *v* yerini almak
replacement [rɪ'pleɪsmənt] *n* yerini alma
replay *n* ['ri:ˌpleɪ] yeniden gösterim ▷ *v* [ri:'pleɪ] yeniden göstermek
replica ['rɛplɪkə] *n* kopya *(taklit)*
reply [rɪ'plaɪ] *n* yanıt ▷ *v* yanıtlamak
report [rɪ'pɔ:t] *n* rapor ▷ *v* rapor vermek; **report card** *n* karne
reporter [rɪ'pɔ:tə] *n* muhabir
represent [ˌrɛprɪ'zɛnt] *v* temsil etmek
representative [ˌrɛprɪ'zɛntətɪv] *adj* temsil eden
reproduction [ˌri:prə'dʌkʃən] *n* üreme
reptile ['rɛptaɪl] *n* sürüngen
republic [rɪ'pʌblɪk] *n* cumhuriyet
repulsive [rɪ'pʌlsɪv] *adj* iğrenç
reputable ['rɛpjʊtəbᵊl] *adj* saygıdeğer
reputation [ˌrɛpjʊ'teɪʃən] *n* ün
request [rɪ'kwɛst] *n* rica ▷ *v* rica etmek
require [rɪ'kwaɪə] *v* gerektirmek
requirement [rɪ'kwaɪəmənt] *n* gereksinim
rescue ['rɛskju:] *n* kurtarma ▷ *v* kurtarmak; **Where is the nearest mountain rescue service post?** En yakın dağ kurtarma ekibi nerede?
research [rɪ'sɜ:tʃ; 'ri:sɜ:tʃ] *n* araştırma; **market research** *n* pazar araştırması
resemblance [rɪ'zɛmbləns] *n* benzerlik
resemble [rɪ'zɛmbᵊl] *v* benzetmek
resent [rɪ'zɛnt] *v* nefret etmek
resentful [rɪ'zɛntfʊl] *adj* içerlemiş
reservation [ˌrɛzə'veɪʃən] *n* itiraz
reserve [rɪ'zɜ:v] *n (land)* koruma alanı, *(retention)* yedek ▷ *v* saklamak *(korumak)*
reserved [rɪ'zɜ:vd] *adj* ayrılmış
reservoir ['rɛzəˌvwɑ:] *n* su deposu
resident ['rɛzɪdənt] *n* sakin *(konut)*
residential [ˌrɛzɪ'dɛnʃəl] *adj* meskun

resign [rɪ'zaɪn] *v* istifa etmek
resin ['rɛzɪn] *n* reçine
resist [rɪ'zɪst] *v* direnmek
resistance [rɪ'zɪstəns] *n* direnme
resit [riː'sɪt] *v* yeniden sınava girmek
resolution [ˌrɛzə'luːʃən] *n* kararlılık
resort [rɪ'zɔːt] *n* tatil yeri; **resort to** *v* başvurmak
resource [rɪ'zɔːs; -'sɔːs] *n* kaynak *(destek)*; **natural resources** *npl* doğal kaynaklar
respect [rɪ'spɛkt] *n* saygı ▷ *v* saygı duymak
respectable [rɪ'spɛktəbᵊl] *adj* saygıdeğer
respectively [rɪ'spɛktɪvlɪ] *adv* sırasıyla
respond [rɪ'spɒnd] *v* tepki vermek
response [rɪ'spɒns] *n* yanıt
responsibility [rɪˌspɒnsə'bɪlɪtɪ] *n* sorumluluk
responsible [rɪ'spɒnsəbᵊl] *adj* sorumlu
rest [rɛst] *n* dinlenme ▷ *v* dinlenmek; **the rest** *n* dinlenme
restaurant ['rɛstəˌrɒŋ; 'rɛstrɒŋ; -rɒnt] *n* restoran; **Are there any vegetarian restaurants here?** Buralarda vejetaryen restoranlar var mı?
restful ['rɛstfʊl] *adj* dinlendirici
restless ['rɛstlɪs] *adj* huzursuz
restore [rɪ'stɔː] *v* restore etmek
restrict [rɪ'strɪkt] *v* sınırlamak
restructure [riː'strʌktʃə] *v* yeniden yapılandırma
result [rɪ'zʌlt] *n* sonuç; **result in** *v* sonucu olmak
resume [rɪ'zjuːm] *v* devam etmek
retail ['riːteɪl] *n* perakende ▷ *v* perakende satmak; **retail price** *n* perakende fiyatı
retailer ['riːteɪlə] *n* perakendeci
retire [rɪ'taɪə] *v* emekli olmak
retired [rɪ'taɪəd] *adj* emekli; **I'm retired** Emekliyim
retirement [rɪ'taɪəmənt] *n* emeklilik
retrace [rɪ'treɪs] *v* iz sürmek
return [rɪ'tɜːn] *n (coming back)* geri dönüş, *(yield)* getiri ▷ *vi* geri döndürmek ▷ *vt* geri dönmek; **day return** *n* günlük bilet; **return ticket** *n* gidiş-dönüş bilet; **tax return** *n* vergi iadesi
reunion [riː'juːnjən] *n* yeniden bir araya gelme
reuse [riː'juːz] *v* yeniden kullanmak
reveal [rɪ'viːl] *v* ifşa etmek
revenge [rɪ'vɛndʒ] *n* intikam
revenue ['rɛvɪˌnjuː] *n* vergi geliri
reverse [rɪ'vɜːs] *n* geri dönme ▷ *v* geri dönmek
review [rɪ'vjuː] *n* eleştiri *(kitap, film vb)*
revise [rɪ'vaɪz] *v* gözden geçirmek *(yeniden)*
revision [rɪ'vɪʒən] *n* revizyon
revive [rɪ'vaɪv] *v* canlandırmak
revolting [rɪ'vəʊltɪŋ] *adj* iğrenç
revolution [ˌrɛvə'luːʃən] *n* devrim
revolutionary [ˌrɛvə'luːʃənərɪ] *adj* devrimci
revolver [rɪ'vɒlvə] *n* revolver
reward [rɪ'wɔːd] *n* ödül
rewarding [rɪ'wɔːdɪŋ] *adj* tatmin edici

rewind [riːˈwaɪnd] *v* geri sarmak
rheumatism [ˈruːməˌtɪzəm] *n* romatizma
rhubarb [ˈruːbɑːb] *n* ravent
rhyme [raɪm] *n* **nursery rhyme** *n* çocuk şarkıları
rhythm [ˈrɪðəm] *n* ritim
rib [rɪb] *n* kaburga
ribbon [ˈrɪbᵊn] *n* kurdele
rice [raɪs] *n* pirinç *(yiyecek)*; **brown rice** *n* esmer pirinç
rich [rɪtʃ] *adj* zengin
ride [raɪd] *n* gezinti *(at/araba/bisiklet)* ▷ *v* binmek *(hayvana)*
rider [ˈraɪdə] *n* binici
ridiculous [rɪˈdɪkjʊləs] *adj* gülünç
riding [ˈraɪdɪŋ] *n* ata binme; **horse riding** *n* binicilik
rifle [ˈraɪfᵊl] *n* tüfek
rig [rɪg] *n* petrol platformu; **oil rig** *n* petrol platformu
right [raɪt] *adj* *(correct)* doğru *(işlem, hareket)*, *(not left)* sağ *(yan, yön)* ▷ *adv* doğru olarak ▷ *n* hak; **civil rights** *npl* özlük hakları; **human rights** *npl* insan hakları; **right angle** *n* dik açı; **right of way** *n* geçiş hakkı; **Go right at the next junction** Bir sonraki kavşaktan sağa dönün; **It wasn't your right of way** Yol hakkı sizin değildi; **Turn right** Sağa dönün
right-hand [ˈraɪtˌhænd] *adj* sağ taraf; **right-hand drive** *n* sağdan trafik
right-handed [ˈraɪtˌhændɪd] *adj* sağ elini kullanan
rightly [ˈraɪtlɪ] *adv* haklı olarak
right-wing [ˈraɪtˌwɪŋ] *adj* sağ kanat
rim [rɪm] *n* ağız *(çaydanlık vb)*
ring [rɪŋ] *n* yüzük ▷ *v* çalmak *(zil/çan)*; **engagement ring** *n* nişan yüzüğü; **ring binder** *n* klasör; **ring road** *n* çevre yolu; **wedding ring** *n* yüzük *(nikah)*
ring back [rɪŋ bæk] *v* geri aramak
ringtone [ˈrɪŋˌtəʊn] *n* çalma tonu
ring up [rɪŋ ʌp] *v* telefonla aramak
rink [rɪŋk] *n* paten alanı; **ice rink** *n* buz pateni sahası; **skating rink** *n* paten alanı
rinse [rɪns] *n* durulama ▷ *v* durulamak
riot [ˈraɪət] *n* ayaklanma ▷ *v* başkaldırmak
rip [rɪp] *v* yırtmak
ripe [raɪp] *adj* olgun *(mevye)*
rip off [rɪp ɒf] *v* kazıklamak
rip-off [rɪpɒf] *n* kazık *(pahalı)*
rip up [rɪp ʌp] *v* yırtmak
rise [raɪz] *n* doğrulma ▷ *v* doğrulmak
risk [rɪsk] *n* risk ▷ *vt* risk almak
risky [ˈrɪskɪ] *adj* riskli
ritual [ˈrɪtjʊəl] *adj* ayinsel ▷ *n* ayin *(tören)*
rival [ˈraɪvᵊl] *adj* rakip ▷ *n* rakip
rivalry [ˈraɪvəlrɪ] *n* rekabet
river [ˈrɪvə] *n* nehir; **Can one swim in the river?** Nehirde yüzülebilir mi?
road [rəʊd] *n* yol; **main road** *n* anayol; **ring road** *n* çevre yolu; **road map** *n* yol haritası; **road rage** *n* trafik magandalığı; **road sign** *n* trafik işareti; **road tax** *n* yol vergisi; **slip road** *n* bağlantı yolu; **Are the roads icy?** Yollar buzlu mu?; **Do you have a road map of**

this area? Bu bölgenin karayolları haritası var mı?; **I need a road map of...** ... yol haritası istiyorum; **Is the road to... snowed up?** ... yolunda kar var mı?; **What is the speed limit on this road?** Bu yolda hız limiti nedir?; **When will the road be clear?** Yol ne zaman açılır?; **Which road do I take for...?** ... a gitmek için hangi yoldan gitmem gerek?
roadblock ['rəʊd,blɒk] *n* çevirme *(trafik)*
roadworks ['rəʊd,wɜːks] *npl* yol yapım çalışması
roast [rəʊst] *adj* kavrulmuş
rob [rɒb] *v* soymak
robber [rɒbə] *n* soyguncu
robbery ['rɒbərɪ] *n* soygun
robin ['rɒbɪn] *n* kızılgerdan
robot ['rəʊbɒt] *n* robot
rock [rɒk] *n* kaya ▷ *v* sallamak; **rock climbing** *n* tırmanma *(kaya)*
rocket ['rɒkɪt] *n* roket
rod [rɒd] *n* çubuk *(demir)*
rodent ['rəʊdᵊnt] *n* kemirgen
role [rəʊl] *n* ödev
roll [rəʊl] *n* yuvarlanma ▷ *v* yuvarlanmak; **bread roll** *n* yuvarlak ekmek; **roll call** *n* yoklama
roller ['rəʊlə] *n* silindir
rollercoaster ['rəʊlə,kəʊstə] *n* rollercoaster
rollerskates ['rəʊlə,skeɪts] *npl* paten
rollerskating ['rəʊlə,skeɪtɪŋ] *n* patenle kaymak
Roman ['rəʊmən] *adj* Romen; **Roman Catholic** *n* Roma Katoliği, Roma Katolik
romance ['rəʊmæns] *n* aşk ilişkisi
Romanesque [,rəʊmə'nɛsk] *adj* Romanesk
Romania [rəʊ'meɪnɪə] *n* Romanya
Romanian [rəʊ'meɪnɪən] *adj* Romen ▷ *n (language)* Rumence *(dil)*, *(person)* Rumen *(kişi)*
romantic [rəʊ'mæntɪk] *adj* romantik
roof [ruːf] *n* çatı
roof rack ['ruːf,ræk] *n* port bagaj
room [ruːm; rʊm] *n* oda; **changing room** *n* soyunma odası *(spor)*; **dining room** *n* yemek salonu; **double room** *n* iki kişilik oda; **fitting room** *n* soyunma odası *(mağaza)*; **living room** *n* oturma odası; **room number** *n* oda numarası; **room service** *n* oda servisi; **single room** *n* tek kişilik oda; **sitting room** *n* oturma odası; **spare room** *n* yedek oda; **twin room** *n* çift yataklı oda; **twin-bedded room** *n* çift yataklı oda; **utility room** *n* çamaşır odası; **waiting room** *n* bekleme odası; **Can I see the room?** Odayı görebilir miyim?; **Can I switch rooms?** Odamı değiştirebilir miyim?; **Can you clean the room, please?** Odamı temizler misiniz lütfen; **Do you have a room for tonight?** Bu gece için odanız var mı?; **Does the room have air conditioning?** Odada klima var mı?; **How much is the room?** Oda ne kadar?; **I need a room with wheelchair access** Tekerlekli

sandalye girişi olan bir oda istiyorum; **I want to reserve a double room** İki kişilik bir oda ayırtmak istiyorum; **I want to reserve a single room** Tek kişilik bir oda ayırtmak istiyorum; **I'd like a no smoking room** Sigara içilemeyen bir oda rica ediyorum; **I'd like a room with a view of the sea** Deniz manzaralı bir oda rica ediyorum; **I'd like to rent a room** Bir oda kiralamak istiyorum; **Please charge it to my room** Oda hesabıma yazın lütfen; **The room is dirty** Oda pis; **The room is too cold** Oda çok soğuk; **There's a problem with the room** Odada bir sorun var

roommate ['ru:m,meɪt; 'rʊm-] *n* oda arkadaşı

root [ru:t] *n* kök

rope [rəʊp] *n* ip

rope in [rəʊp ɪn] *v* inandırmak

rose [rəʊz] *n* gül

rosé ['rəʊzeɪ] *n* pembe şarap

rosemary ['rəʊzmərɪ] *n* biberiye

rot [rɒt] *v* çürümek

rotten ['rɒtᵊn] *adj* çürümüş

rough [rʌf] *adj* kaba *(aceleyle yapılmış)*

roughly ['rʌflɪ] *adv* kabaca

roulette [ru:'lɛt] *n* rulet

round [raʊnd] *adj* yuvarlak ▷ *n (circle)* halka *(çember)*, *(series)* sıra *(oyun)* ▷ *prep* etrafını; **paper round** *n* gazete dağıtım; **round trip** *n* gidiş dönüş yolculuk; **Whose round is it?** İçki sırası kimde?

roundabout ['raʊndə,baʊt] *n* döner kavşak

round up [raʊnd ʌp] *v* toparlamak

route [ru:t] *n* güzergah; **Is there a route that avoids the traffic?** Yoğun trafikten kaçabileceğim bir güzergah var mı?

routine [ru:'ti:n] *n* sıradan

row¹ [rəʊ] *n (line)* sıra *(dizi)* ▷ *v (in boat)* kürek çekmek; **Where can we go rowing?** Kürek çekmek için nereye gidebiliriz?

row² [raʊ] *n (argument)* tartışma ▷ *v (to argue)* tartışmak

rowing [rəʊɪŋ] *n* kürek sporu; **rowing boat** *n* kürek teknesi

royal ['rɔɪəl] *adj* kraliyet

rub [rʌb] *v* sürtmek

rubber ['rʌbə] *n* lastik; **rubber band** *n* elastik band; **rubber gloves** *npl* lastik eldiven

rubbish ['rʌbɪʃ] *adj* süprüntü ▷ *n* çöp; **rubbish dump** *n* çöp döküm alanı

rucksack ['rʌk,sæk] *n* sırt çantası

rude [ru:d] *adj* kaba *(davranış)*

rug [rʌg] *n* küçük halı

rugby ['rʌgbɪ] *n* rugbi

ruin ['ru:ɪn] *n* tahribat ▷ *v* mahvetmek

rule [ru:l] *n* kural

rule out [ru:l aʊt] *v* hesaba katmamak

ruler ['ru:lə] *n (commander)* hükümdar, *(measure)* cetvel

rum [rʌm] *n* rom

rumour ['ru:mə] *n* söylenti

run [rʌn] *n* koşu ▷ *vi* koşturmak ▷ *vt* koşmak

run away [rʌn ə'weɪ] *v* kaçmak *(uzaklara)*

runner ['rʌnə] *n* yarışmacı; **runner bean** *n* çalı fasulyesi
runner-up ['rʌnəʌp] *n* ikinci *(yarışma)*
running ['rʌnɪŋ] *n* koşma, koşu
run out of [rʌn aʊt ɒv] *v* bitmek *(tükenmek)*
run over [rʌn 'əʊvə] *v* ezmek *(arabayla)*
runway ['rʌn,weɪ] *n* uçak pisti
rural ['rʊərəl] *adj* kırsal
rush [rʌʃ] *n* telaş ▹ *v* telaş etmek; **rush hour** *n* sıkışık saatler
rusk [rʌsk] *n* bebe bisküvisi
Russia ['rʌʃə] *n* Rusya
Russian ['rʌʃən] *adj* Rus ▹ *n* *(language)* Rusça *(dil)*, *(person)* Rus *(kişi)*
rust [rʌst] *n* pas *(metal)*
rusty ['rʌstɪ] *adj* paslı
ruthless ['ruːθlɪs] *adj* acımasız
rye [raɪ] *n* çavdar

S

Sabbath ['sæbəθ] *n* dinlenme günü *(Yahudiler için Cumartesi, Hristiyanlar için Pazar)*
sabotage ['sæbə,tɑːʒ] *n* sabotaj ▹ *v* sabote etmek
sachet ['sæʃeɪ] *n* torbacık
sack [sæk] *n* *(container)* çuval, *(dismissal)* işten atma ▹ *v* işten atmak
sacred ['seɪkrɪd] *adj* kutsal
sacrifice ['sækrɪ,faɪs] *n* feda etmek
sad [sæd] *adj* üzgün
saddle ['sædᵊl] *n* semer
saddlebag ['sædᵊl,bæg] *n* heybe
sadly [sædlɪ] *adv* acıklı bir şekilde
safari [sə'fɑːrɪ] *n* safari
safe [seɪf] *adj* güvenli ▹ *n* kasa; **I have some things in the safe** Kasada eşyalarım vardı; **I would like to put my jewellery in the safe** Mücevherlerimi kasaya

koymak istiyorum; **Put that in the safe, please** Bunu kasaya koyun lütfen
safety ['seɪftɪ] *n* güvenlik; **safety belt** *n* emniyet kemeri; **safety pin** *n* kilitli iğne
saffron ['sæfrən] *n* safran
Sagittarius [ˌsædʒɪ'tɛərɪəs] *n* Yay burcu
Sahara [sə'hɑːrə] *n* Sahra
sail [seɪl] *n* yelken ▷ *v* gemiyle yolculuk etmek
sailing ['seɪlɪŋ] *n* yelken sporu; **sailing boat** *n* yelkenli
sailor ['seɪlə] *n* bahriyeli
saint [seɪnt; sənt] *n* aziz
salad ['sæləd] *n* salata; **mixed salad** *n* karışık salata; **salad dressing** *n* salata sosu
salami [sə'lɑːmɪ] *n* salam
salary ['sælərɪ] *n* maaş
sale [seɪl] *n* satış; **sales assistant** *n* tezgahtar; **sales rep** *n* satış elemanı
salesman, salesmen ['seɪlzmən, 'seɪlzmɛn] *n* satıcı *(erkek)*
salesperson ['seɪlzpɜːsᵊn] *n* satıcı
saleswoman, saleswomen ['seɪlzwʊmən, 'seɪlzwɪmɪn] *n* satıcı
saliva [sə'laɪvə] *n* tükürük
salmon ['sæmən] *n* som balığı
salon ['sælɒn] *n* **beauty salon** *n* güzellik salonu
saloon [sə'luːn] *n* salon; **saloon car** *n* sedan araba
salt [sɔːlt] *n* tuz; **Pass the salt, please** Tuzu uzatır mısınız lütfen?
saltwater ['sɔːltˌwɔːtə] *adj* tuzlu
salty ['sɔːltɪ] *adj* tuzlu; **The food is too salty** Yemek çok tuzlu
salute [sə'luːt] *v* selamlamak
salve [sælv] *n* **lip salve** *n* dudak kremi
same [seɪm] *adj* aynı; **I'll have the same** Bana da aynısından
sample ['sɑːmpᵊl] *n* örnek
sand [sænd] *n* kum; **sand dune** *n* kum tepesi
sandal ['sændᵊl] *n* sandalet
sandcastle [sændkɑːsᵊl] *n* kumdan kale
sandpaper ['sændˌpeɪpə] *n* zımpara
sandpit ['sændˌpɪt] *n* kum havuzu
sandstone ['sændˌstəʊn] *n* kumtaşı
sandwich ['sænwɪdʒ; -wɪtʃ] *n* sandviç; **What kind of sandwiches do you have?** Sandviç olarak ne var?
San Marino [ˌsæn mə'riːnəʊ] *n* San Marino
sapphire ['sæfaɪə] *n* safir
sarcastic [sɑː'kæstɪk] *adj* alaycı
sardine [sɑː'diːn] *n* sardalya
satchel ['sætʃəl] *n* omuz çantası
satellite ['sætᵊˌlaɪt] *n* uydu; **satellite dish** *n* uydu çanak
satisfaction [ˌsætɪs'fækʃən] *n* tatmin
satisfactory [ˌsætɪs'fæktərɪ; -trɪ] *adj* tatmin edici
satisfied ['sætɪsˌfaɪd] *adj* tatmin olmuş
sat nav ['sæt næv] *n* satnav
Saturday ['sætədɪ] *n* Cumartesi; **every Saturday** her Cumartesi; **last Saturday** geçen Cumartesi;

next Saturday önümüzdeki Cumartesi; **on Saturday** Cumartesi günü; **on Saturdays** Cumartesileri; **this Saturday** bu Cumartesi
sauce [sɔːs] *n* sos; **soy sauce** *n* soya sosu; **tomato sauce** *n* domates sosu
saucepan ['sɔːspən] *n* saplı tencere
saucer ['sɔːsə] *n* fincan tabağı
Saudi ['sɔːdɪ; 'saʊ-] *adj* Suudi ▷ *n* Suudi
Saudi Arabia ['sɔːdɪ; 'saʊ-] *n* Suudi Arabistan
Saudi Arabian ['sɔːdɪ ə'reɪbɪən] *adj* Suudi Arabistan ▷ *n* Suudi Arabistanlı
sauna ['sɔːnə] *n* sauna
sausage ['sɒsɪdʒ] *n* sosis
save [seɪv] *v* kurtarmak
save up [seɪv ʌp] *v* biriktirmek
savings ['seɪvɪŋz] *npl* birikim
savoury ['seɪvərɪ] *adj* tuzlu ve baharatlı
saw [sɔː] *n* testere
sawdust ['sɔːˌdʌst] *n* talaş
saxophone ['sæksəˌfəʊn] *n* saksafon
say [seɪ] *v* söylemek
saying ['seɪɪŋ] *n* deyim
scaffolding ['skæfəldɪŋ] *n* iskele *(inşaat)*
scale [skeɪl] *n (measure)* ölçü, *(tiny piece)* pul *(balık)*
scales [skeɪlz] *npl* terazi
scallop ['skɒləp; 'skæl-] *n* deniz tarağı
scam [skæm] *n* dolandırıcılık *(hileli iş)*
scampi ['skæmpɪ] *npl* büyük karides
scan [skæn] *n* tarama *(bilgisayar)* ▷ *v* taramak *(bilgisayar)*
scandal ['skændᵊl] *n* skandal
Scandinavia [ˌskændɪ'neɪvɪə] *n* İskandinavya
Scandinavian [ˌskændɪ'neɪvɪən] *adj* İskandinav
scanner ['skænə] *n* tarayıcı *(scanner)*
scar [skɑː] *n* yara
scarce [skɛəs] *adj* kıt
scarcely ['skɛəslɪ] *adv* nadiren
scare [skɛə] *n* panik ▷ *v* korkutmak
scarecrow ['skɛəˌkrəʊ] *n* korkuluk
scared [skɛəd] *adj* korkmuş
scarf, scarves [skɑːf, skɑːvz] *n* eşarp
scarlet ['skɑːlɪt] *adj* kan kırmızısı
scary ['skɛərɪ] *adj* korkutucu
scene [siːn] *n* sahne *(olay, bölüm)*
scenery ['siːnərɪ] *n* manzara
scent [sɛnt] *n* koku
sceptical ['skɛptɪkᵊl] *adj* kuşkulu
schedule ['ʃɛdjuːl; 'skɛdʒʊəl] *n* program; **We are on schedule** Programa uygun gidiyoruz; **We are slightly behind schedule** Programın gerisindeyiz
scheme [skiːm] *n* plan
schizophrenic [ˌskɪtsəʊ'frɛnɪk] *adj* şizofren
scholarship ['skɒləʃɪp] *n* burs
school [skuːl] *n* okul; **art school** *n* sanat okulu; **boarding school** *n* yatılı okul; **elementary school** *n* ilkokul; **infant school** *n* ana okulu; **language school** *n* dil okulu; **law school** *n* hukuk fakültesi; **night**

school *n* gece okulu; **nursery school** *n* kreş; **primary school** *n* ilkokul; **public school** *n* devlet koleji; **school uniform** *n* okul üniforması; **secondary school** *n* ortaokul
schoolbag ['sku:l,bæg] *n* okul çantası
schoolbook ['sku:l,bʊk] *n* ders kitabı
schoolboy ['sku:l,bɔɪ] *n* erkek öğrenci
schoolchildren ['sku:l,tʃɪldrən] *n* okul çocukları
schoolgirl ['sku:l,gɜ:l] *n* kız öğrenci
schoolteacher ['sku:l,ti:tʃə] *n* öğretmen
science ['saɪəns] *n* bilim; **science fiction** *n* bilim kurgu
scientific [,saɪən'tɪfɪk] *adj* bilimsel
scientist ['saɪəntɪst] *n* bilim adamı
scifi ['saɪ,faɪ] *n* sci-fi
scissors ['sɪzəz] *npl* makas; **nail scissors** *npl* tırnak makası
sclerosis [sklɪə'rəʊsɪs] *n* **multiple sclerosis** *n* multipl skleroz
scoff [skɒf] *v* alay etmek
scold [skəʊld] *v* azarlamak
scooter ['sku:tə] *n* skuter
score [skɔ:] *n* *(game/match)* sayı *(maç/oyun)*, *(of music)* nota ▹ *v* sayı yapmak
Scorpio ['skɔ:pɪ,əʊ] *n* Akrep burcu
scorpion ['skɔ:pɪən] *n* akrep
Scot [skɒt] *n* İskoç
Scotland ['skɒtlənd] *n* İskoçya
Scots [skɒts] *adj* İskoç
Scotsman, Scotsmen ['skɒtsmən, 'skɒtsmɛn] *n* İskoç *(erkek)*
Scotswoman, Scotswomen ['skɒts,wʊmən, 'skɒts,wɪmɪn] *n* İskoç
Scottish ['skɒtɪʃ] *adj* İskoç
scout [skaʊt] *n* izci
scrap [skræp] *n* *(dispute)* kavga, *(small piece)* parça ▹ *v* atmak; **scrap paper** *n* karalama kağıdı
scrapbook ['skræp,bʊk] *n* karalama defteri
scratch [skrætʃ] *n* çizme *(boyasını vb)* ▹ *v* çizmek *(arabanın boyasını vb)*
scream [skri:m] *n* çığlık ▹ *v* çığlık atmak
screen [skri:n] *n* ekran; **plasma screen** *n* plazma ekran
screen-saver ['skri:nseɪvər] *n* ekran koruyucusu
screw [skru:] *n* vida; **The screw has come loose** Vida gevşemiş
screwdriver ['skru:,draɪvə] *n* tornavida
scribble ['skrɪbᵊl] *v* karalamak
scrub [skrʌb] *v* ovalamak
sculptor ['skʌlptə] *n* heykeltraş
sculpture ['skʌlptʃə] *n* heykel
sea [si:] *n* deniz *(coğrafya)*; **North Sea** *n* Kuzey Denizi; **Red Sea** *n* Kızıl Deniz; **sea level** *n* deniz seviyesi; **sea water** *n* deniz suyu; **Is the sea rough today?** Bugün deniz dalgalı mı?
seafood ['si:,fu:d] *n* deniz ürünü
seagull ['si:,gʌl] *n* martı
seal [si:l] *n* *(animal)* fok, *(mark)* mühür ▹ *v* mühürlemek
seam [si:m] *n* dikiş *(giysinin)*
seaman, seamen ['si:mən,

'si:mɛn] *n* denizci
search [sɜ:tʃ] *n* arama ▷ *v* aramak; **search engine** *n* arama motoru; **search party** *n* arama ekibi
seashore ['si:ˌʃɔ:] *n* deniz kıyısı *(sahil)*
seasick ['si:ˌsɪk] *adj* deniz tutmuş
seaside ['si:ˌsaɪd] *n* deniz kıyısı
season ['si:zᵊn] *n* mevsim; **high season** *n* pahalı sezon; **low season** *n* ucuz sezon; **season ticket** *n* abonman kartı
seasonal ['si:zənᵊl] *adj* mevsimlik
seasoning ['si:zənɪŋ] *n* çeşni
seat [si:t] *n (constituency)* koltuk *(politika)*, *(furniture)* sandalye; **aisle seat** *n* koridor koltuğu; **window seat** *n* cam kenarı koltuğu; **Do you have a baby seat?** Bebek sandalyeniz var mı?; **I'd like a non-smoking seat** Sigara içilmeyen bölümde bir koltuk lütfen; **I'd like a seat in the smoking area** Sigara içilen bölümde bir koltuk lütfen; **Is this seat free?** Bu koltuk boş mu?
seatbelt ['si:tˌbɛlt] *n* emniyet kemeri
seaweed ['si:ˌwi:d] *n* yosun
second ['sɛkənd] *adj* ikinci ▷ *n* ikinci; **second class** *n* ikinci sınıf
second-class ['sɛkəndˌklɑ:s] *adj* ikinci sınıf
secondhand ['sɛkəndˌhænd] *adj* ikinci el
secondly ['sɛkəndlɪ] *adv* ikinci olarak
second-rate ['sɛkəndˌreɪt] *adj* ikinci kalite
secret ['si:krɪt] *adj* gizli ▷ *n* sır; **secret service** *n* gizli servis
secretary ['sɛkrətrɪ] *n* sekreter
secretly ['si:krɪtlɪ] *adv* gizlice
sect [sɛkt] *n* mezhep
section ['sɛkʃən] *n* bölüm *(bina, konum)*
sector ['sɛktə] *n* sektör
secure [sɪ'kjʊə] *adj* güvenli
security [sɪ'kjʊərɪtɪ] *n* güvenlik; **security guard** *n* güvenlik görevlisi; **social security** *n* sosyal güvenlik
sedative ['sɛdətɪv] *n* yatıştırıcı
see [si:] *v* görmek; **Where can we go to see a film?** Film görmek için nereye gidebiliriz?
seed [si:d] *n* tohum
seek [si:k] *v* aramak
seem [si:m] *v* görünmek
seesaw ['si:ˌsɔ:] *n* tahterevalli
see-through ['si:ˌθru:] *adj* transparan
seize [si:z] *v* yakalamak
seizure ['si:ʒə] *n* nöbet
seldom ['sɛldəm] *adv* nadiren
select [sɪ'lɛkt] *v* seçmek
selection [sɪ'lɛkʃən] *n* seçme
self-assured ['sɛlfə'ʃʊəd] *adj* kendine güvenen
self-catering ['sɛlfˌkeɪtərɪŋ] *n* self-catering
self-centred ['sɛlfˌsɛntəd] *adj* bencil
self-conscious ['sɛlfˌkɒnʃəs] *adj* içine kapanık
self-contained ['sɛlfˌkən'teɪnd] *adj* müstakil
self-control ['sɛlfˌkən'trəʊl] *n* özkontrol
self-defence ['sɛlfˌdɪ'fɛns] *n*

özsavunma
self-discipline ['sɛlf,dɪsɪplɪn] *n* özdisiplin
self-employed ['sɛlɪm'plɔɪd] *adj* serbest çalışan
selfish ['sɛlfɪʃ] *adj* bencil
self-service ['sɛlf,sɜːvɪs] *adj* selfservis
sell [sɛl] *v* satmak; **sell-by date** *n* son satış tarihi; **selling price** *n* satış fiyatı
sell off [sɛl ɒf] *v* elden çıkarmak
Sellotape® ['sɛlə,teɪp] *n* seloteyp
sell out [sɛl aʊt] *v* hepsini satmak
semester [sɪ'mɛstə] *n* sömestr
semi ['sɛmɪ] *n* bitişik nizam ev
semicircle ['sɛmɪ,sɜːkᵊl] *n* yarım daire
semicolon [,sɛmɪ'kəʊlən] *n* noktalı virgül
semifinal [,sɛmɪ'faɪnᵊl] *n* yarı final
send [sɛnd] *v* göndermek; **I want to send this by courier** Kuryeyle göndermek istiyorum
send back [sɛnd bæk] *v* geri göndermek
sender ['sɛndə] *n* gönderen
send off [sɛnd ɒf] *v* uğurlamak
send out [sɛnd aʊt] *v* göndermek
Senegal [,sɛnɪ'gɔːl] *n* Senegal
Senegalese [,sɛnɪgə'liːz] *adj* Senegal ▹ *n* Senegalli
senior ['siːnjə] *adj* üst *(rütbe)*; **senior citizen** *n* yaşlı vatandaş
sensational [sɛn'seɪʃənᵊl] *adj* sansasyonel
sense [sɛns] *n* duyu; **sense of humour** *n* mizah duygusu
senseless ['sɛnslɪs] *adj* amaçsız
sensible ['sɛnsɪbᵊl] *adj* sağduyulu
sensitive ['sɛnsɪtɪv] *adj* duyarlı
sensuous ['sɛnsjʊəs] *adj* duyarlı *(tensel)*
sentence ['sɛntəns] *n* *(punishment)* ceza, *(words)* cümle ▹ *v* mahkum etmek
sentimental [,sɛntɪ'mɛntᵊl] *adj* duygusal
separate *adj* ['sɛpərɪt] ayrı ▹ *v* ['sɛpə,reɪt] ayırmak; **with the milk separate** sütü ayrı getirin
separately ['sɛpərətlɪ] *adv* ayrı olarak
separation [,sɛpə'reɪʃən] *n* ayrılma
September [sɛp'tɛmbə] *n* Eylül
sequel ['siːkwəl] *n* devamı
sequence ['siːkwəns] *n* dizi
Serbia ['sɜːbɪə] *n* Sırbistan
Serbian ['sɜːbɪən] *adj* Sırp ▹ *n* *(language)* Sırpça *(dil)*, *(person)* Sırp *(kişi)*
sergeant ['sɑːdʒənt] *n* çavuş
serial ['sɪərɪəl] *n* seri
series ['sɪəriːz; -rɪz] *n* dizi
serious ['sɪərɪəs] *adj* ciddi; **Is it serious?** Ciddi bir şey mi?
seriously ['sɪərɪəslɪ] *adv* ciddiyetle
sermon ['sɜːmən] *n* vaaz
servant ['sɜːvᵊnt] *n* hizmetçi; **civil servant** *n* hükümet görevlisi
serve [sɜːv] *n* servis atmak ▹ *v* hizmet etmek
server ['sɜːvə] *n* *(computer)* sunucu *(bilişim)*, *(person)* hizmet eden
service ['sɜːvɪs] *n* servis ▹ *v* hizmet etmek; **room service** *n* oda servisi; **secret service** *n* gizli servis; **service area** *n* konaklama alanı; **service charge** *n* servis

ücreti; **service station** *n* benzin istasyonu; **social services** *npl* sosyal hizmetler; **Call the breakdown service, please** Tamir servisini çağırabilir misiniz lütfen?; **I want to complain about the service** Servisten şikayetçiyim; **Is service included?** Servis dahil mi?; **Is there a child-minding service?** Çocuk bakıcı servisiniz var mı?; **Is there room service?** Oda servisi var mı?; **The service was terrible** Servis berbattı
serviceman, servicemen ['sɜːvɪsˌmæn; -mən, 'sɜːvɪsˌmɛn] *n* ordu mensubu *(erkek)*
servicewoman, servicewomen ['sɜːvɪsˌwʊmən, 'sɜːvɪsˌwɪmɪn] *n* ordu mensubu *(kadın)*
serviette [ˌsɜːvɪ'ɛt] *n* kağıt peçete
session ['sɛʃən] *n* seans
set [sɛt] *n* ayarlama ▷ *v* ayarlamak
setback ['sɛtbæk] *n* engel
set off [sɛt ɒf] *v* yola koyulmak
set out [sɛt aʊt] *v* düzenlemek *(masa, eşya vb)*
settee [sɛ'tiː] *n* divan
settle ['sɛtᵊl] *v* yoluna koymak
settle down ['sɛtᵊl daʊn] *v* yerleşmek
seven ['sɛvᵊn] *number* yedi
seventeen ['sɛvᵊn'tiːn] *number* onyedi
seventeenth ['sɛvᵊn'tiːnθ] *adj* onyedinci
seventh ['sɛvᵊnθ] *adj* yedinci ▷ *n* yedinci
seventy ['sɛvᵊntɪ] *number* yetmiş
several ['sɛvrəl] *adj* birkaç ▷ *pron* birkaç
sew [səʊ] *v* dikmek
sewer ['suːə] *n* lağım borusu
sewing ['səʊɪŋ] *n* dikiş *(eylem)*; **sewing machine** *n* dikiş makinesi
sew up [səʊ ʌp] *v* dikmek *(onarmak)*
sex [sɛks] *n* cinsiyet *(seks)*
sexism ['sɛksɪzəm] *n* cinsiyet ayrımcılığı
sexist ['sɛksɪst] *adj* cinsiyet ayrımcılığı yapan
sexual ['sɛksjʊəl] *adj* cinsel; **sexual intercourse** *n* cinsel birleşim
sexuality [ˌsɛksjʊ'ælɪtɪ] *n* seksilik
sexy ['sɛksɪ] *adj* seksi
shabby ['ʃæbɪ] *adj* eski püskü
shade [ʃeɪd] *n* gölge *(tente, ağaç altı)*
shadow ['ʃædəʊ] *n* gölge *(birinin ya da bir şeyin)*; **eye shadow** *n* göz farı
shake [ʃeɪk] *vi* çalkalanmak ▷ *vt* çalkalamak
shaken ['ʃeɪkən] *adj* sarsılmış
shaky ['ʃeɪkɪ] *adj* bitkin
shallow ['ʃæləʊ] *adj* sığ
shambles ['ʃæmbᵊlz] *npl* talan olmuş
shame [ʃeɪm] *n* utanç
shampoo [ʃæm'puː] *n* şampuan
shape [ʃeɪp] *n* şekil
share [ʃɛə] *n* pay ▷ *v* paylaşmak
shareholder ['ʃɛəˌhəʊldə] *n* hisse sahibi
share out [ʃɛə aʊt] *v* paylaştırmak
shark [ʃɑːk] *n* köpek balığı
sharp [ʃɑːp] *adj* keskin

shave [ʃeɪv] *v* traş olmak; **shaving cream** *n* traş kremi; **shaving foam** *n* traş köpüğü
shaver ['ʃeɪvə] *n* traş makinesi
shawl [ʃɔ:l] *n* şal
she [ʃi:] *pron* o *(kadın)*
shed [ʃɛd] *n* bahçe kulübesi
sheep [ʃi:p] *n* koyun
sheepdog ['ʃi:p,dɒg] *n* çoban köğeği
sheepskin ['ʃi:p,skɪn] *n* koyun postu
sheer [ʃɪə] *adj* tam
sheet [ʃi:t] *n* çarşaf; **balance sheet** *n* bilanço; **fitted sheet** *n* fitted çarşaf; **We need more sheets** Daha fazla çarşafa ihtiyacımız var
shelf, shelves [ʃɛlf, ʃɛlvz] *n* raf
shell [ʃɛl] *n* kabuk; **shell suit** *n* eşofman
shellfish ['ʃɛl,fɪʃ] *n* kabuklu deniz ürünü
shelter ['ʃɛltə] *n* barınak
shepherd ['ʃɛpəd] *n* çoban
sherry ['ʃɛrɪ] *n* şeri
shield [ʃi:ld] *n* kalkan
shift [ʃɪft] *n* yer değiştirme ▷ *v* yer değiştirmek
shifty ['ʃɪftɪ] *adj* kaypak
Shiite ['ʃi:aɪt] *adj* Şii
shin [ʃɪn] *n* kaval kemiği
shine [ʃaɪn] *v* parlamak
shiny ['ʃaɪnɪ] *adj* parlak
ship [ʃɪp] *n* gemi
shipbuilding ['ʃɪp,bɪldɪŋ] *n* gemi yapımı
shipment ['ʃɪpmənt] *n* yükleme
shipwreck ['ʃɪp,rɛk] *n* deniz kazası
shipwrecked ['ʃɪp,rɛkt] *adj* deniz kazası geçirmiş
shipyard ['ʃɪp,jɑ:d] *n* tersane
shirt [ʃɜ:t] *n* gömlek; **polo shirt** *n* polo gömlek
shiver ['ʃɪvə] *v* titremek
shock [ʃɒk] *n* şok ▷ *v* şok geçirmek; **electric shock** *n* elektrik çarpması
shocking ['ʃɒkɪŋ] *adj* yüzkızartıcı
shoe [ʃu:] *n* ayakkabı; **shoe polish** *n* ayakkabı cilası; **shoe shop** *n* ayakkabıcı; **Can you re-heel these shoes?** Ayakkabılarımın topuklarını değiştirebilir misiniz?; **Can you repair these shoes?** Bu ayakkabıları tamir edebilir misiniz?; **I have a hole in my shoe** Ayakkabımda delik var; **Which floor are shoes on?** Ayakkabılar hangi katta?
shoelace ['ʃu:,leɪs] *n* ayakkabı bağı
shoot [ʃu:t] *v* ateş etmek
shooting ['ʃu:tɪŋ] *n* ateş etme
shop [ʃɒp] *n* dükkan/mağaza; **antique shop** *n* antikacı dükkanı; **gift shop** *n* hediye dükkanı; **shop assistant** *n* satış elemanı; **shop window** *n* vitrin
shopkeeper ['ʃɒp,ki:pə] *n* bakkal
shoplifting ['ʃɒp,lɪftɪŋ] *n* aşırma *(dükkanda)*
shopping ['ʃɒpɪŋ] *n* alışveriş; **shopping bag** *n* alışveriş çantası; **shopping centre** *n* alışveriş merkezi; **shopping trolley** *n* market arabası
shore [ʃɔ:] *n* kıyı
short [ʃɔ:t] *adj* kısa; **short story** *n* kısa öykü
shortage ['ʃɔ:tɪdʒ] *n* yokluk *(eksiklik)*
shortcoming ['ʃɔ:t,kʌmɪŋ] *n*

eksiklik
shortcut ['ʃɔ:t,kʌt] *n* kestirme yol
shortfall ['ʃɔ:t,fɔ:l] *n* mali açıklık
shorthand ['ʃɔ:t,hænd] *n* steno
shortlist ['ʃɔ:t,lɪst] *n* ön eleme listesi
shortly ['ʃɔ:tlɪ] *adv* kısa zamanda
shorts [ʃɔ:ts] *npl* şort
short-sighted ['ʃɔ:t'saɪtɪd] *adj* miyop
short-sleeved ['ʃɔ:t,sli:vd] *adj* kısa kollu
shot [ʃɒt] *n* ateş
shotgun ['ʃɒt,gʌn] *n* kısa menzilli silah
shoulder ['ʃəʊldə] *n* omuz; **hard shoulder** *n* dönemeç; **shoulder blade** *n* kürek kemiği; **I've hurt my shoulder** Omuzumu incittim
shout [ʃaʊt] *n* bağırtı ▷ *v* bağırmak
shovel ['ʃʌvᵊl] *n* kürek
show [ʃəʊ] *n* gösteri *(eğlence)* ▷ *v* göstermek; **show business** *n* eğlence sanayii; **Where can we go to see a show?** Gösteri için nereye gidebiliriz?
shower ['ʃaʊə] *n* duş; **shower cap** *n* duş başlığı; **shower gel** *n* duş jeli; **Are there showers?** Burada duş var mı?; **The shower doesn't work** Duş çalışmıyor; **The shower is dirty** Duş kirli; **The showers are cold** Duş soğuk akıyor; **Where are the showers?** Duşlar nerede?
showerproof ['ʃaʊə,pru:f] *adj* yağmura dayanıklı
showing ['ʃəʊɪŋ] *n* gösterim *(film vb)*
show off [ʃəʊ ɒf] *v* gösteriş yapmak
show-off [ʃəʊɒf] *n* gösteriş
show up [ʃəʊ ʌp] *v* ortaya çıkmak
shriek [ʃri:k] *v* feryat etmek
shrimp [ʃrɪmp] *n* ufak karides
shrine [ʃraɪn] *n* mabed
shrink [ʃrɪŋk] *v* kısalmak
shrub [ʃrʌb] *n* çalı
shrug [ʃrʌg] *v* omuz silkmek
shrunk [ʃrʌŋk] *adj* kısalmış
shudder ['ʃʌdə] *v* korkarak titremek
shuffle ['ʃʌfᵊl] *v* ayaklarını sürüyerek yürümek
shut [ʃʌt] *v* kapatmak
shut down [ʃʌt daʊn] *v* kapatmak
shutters ['ʃʌtəz] *n* kepenk
shuttle ['ʃʌtᵊl] *n* karşılıklı sefer yapan araç
shuttlecock ['ʃʌtᵊl,kɒk] *n* badminton topu
shut up [ʃʌt ʌp] *v* susmak
shy [ʃaɪ] *adj* utangaç
Siberia [saɪ'bɪərɪə] *n* Siberya
siblings ['sɪblɪŋz] *npl* kardeşler
sick [sɪk] *adj* hasta; **sick leave** *n* hastalık izni; **sick note** *n* hasta belgesi; **sick pay** *n* hastalık ödentisi
sickening ['sɪkənɪŋ] *adj* mide bulandırıcı
sickness ['sɪknɪs] *n* hastalık; **morning sickness** *n* hamilelik bulantısı; **travel sickness** *n* araba tutması
side [saɪd] *n* taraf; **side effect** *n* yan etki; **side street** *n* yan sokak
sideboard ['saɪd,bɔ:d] *n* büfe *(mobilya)*
sidelight ['saɪd,laɪt] *n* yan lambalar

sideways ['saɪd,weɪz] *adv* yana doğru
sieve [sɪv] *n* elek
sigh [saɪ] *n* iç çekme ▷ *v* iç geçirmek
sight [saɪt] *n* görüş *(göz)*
sightseeing ['saɪt,siːɪŋ] *n* gezip görme
sign [saɪn] *n* işaret ▷ *v* işaret etmek; **road sign** *n* trafik işareti; **sign language** *n* işaret dili; **I can't find the at sign** at işaretini bulamıyorum
signal ['sɪgnᵊl] *n* işaret ▷ *v* sinyal vermek; **busy signal** *n* meşgul sinyali
signature ['sɪgnɪtʃə] *n* imza
significance [sɪg'nɪfɪkəns] *n* önem
significant [sɪg'nɪfɪkənt] *adj* önemli
sign on [saɪn ɒn] *v* kaydolmak
signpost ['saɪn,pəʊst] *n* yol tabelası
Sikh [siːk] *adj* Sikh ▷ *n* Sikh
silence ['saɪləns] *n* sessizlik
silencer ['saɪlənsə] *n* susturucu
silent ['saɪlənt] *adj* sessiz
silk [sɪlk] *n* ipek
silly ['sɪlɪ] *adj* aptalca
silver ['sɪlvə] *n* gümüş
similar ['sɪmɪlə] *adj* benzer
similarity ['sɪmɪ'lærɪtɪ] *n* benzerlik
simmer ['sɪmə] *v* yavaş yavaş kaynatmak
simple ['sɪmpᵊl] *adj* basit
simplify ['sɪmplɪ,faɪ] *v* basitleştirmek
simply ['sɪmplɪ] *adv* basitçe
simultaneous [,sɪməl'teɪnɪəs; ,saɪməl'teɪnɪəs] *adj* aynı anda olan
simultaneously [,sɪməl'teɪnɪəslɪ] *adv* aynı anda
sin [sɪn] *n* günah
since [sɪns] *adv* o zamandan beri ▷ *conj* den beri; **I've been sick since Monday** Pazartesi'nden beri kusuyorum
sincere [sɪn'sɪə] *adj* içten
sincerely [sɪn'sɪəlɪ] *adv* içtenlikle
sing [sɪŋ] *v* şarkı söylemek
singer ['sɪŋə] *n* şarkıcı; **lead singer** *n* as solist
singing ['sɪŋɪŋ] *n* şarkı söyleme
single ['sɪŋgᵊl] *adj* tek ▷ *n* tek yataklı oda; **single bed** *n* tek yatak; **single parent** *n* yalnız ebeveyn; **single room** *n* tek kişilik oda; **single ticket** *n* tek yön bilet; **How much is a single ticket?** Tek gidiş bilet ne kadar?; **I want to reserve a single room** Tek kişilik bir oda ayırtmak istiyorum
singles ['sɪŋgᵊlz] *npl* tekler *(spor)*
singular ['sɪŋgjʊlə] *n* tekil
sinister ['sɪnɪstə] *adj* uğursuz
sink [sɪŋk] *n* lavabo ▷ *v* batmak
sinus ['saɪnəs] *n* sinüs
sir [sɜː] *n* sör
siren ['saɪərən] *n* siren
sister ['sɪstə] *n* kızkardeş
sister-in-law ['sɪstə ɪn lɔː] *n* elti
sit [sɪt] *v* oturmak
sitcom ['sɪt,kɒm] *n* sitkom
sit down [sɪt daʊn] *v* oturmak
site [saɪt] *n* alan *(yer)*; **building site** *n* inşaat alanı; **caravan site** *n* karavan kampı
situated ['sɪtjʊ,eɪtɪd] *adj* konuşlanmış

situation [ˌsɪtjʊ'eɪʃən] *n* durum
six [sɪks] *number* altı; **It's six o'clock** Saat altı
sixteen ['sɪks'tiːn] *number* onaltı
sixteenth ['sɪks'tiːnθ] *adj* onaltıncı
sixth [sɪksθ] *adj* altıncı
sixty ['sɪkstɪ] *number* altmış
size [saɪz] *n* boyut
skate [skeɪt] *v* paten yapmak
skateboard ['skeɪtˌbɔːd] *n* skateboard; **I'd like to go skateboarding** Skateboarding yapmak isterdim
skateboarding ['skeɪtˌbɔːdɪŋ] *n* skateboard yapma
skates [skeɪts] *npl* patenler
skating ['skeɪtɪŋ] *n* paten yapma; **skating rink** *n* paten alanı
skeleton ['skɛlɪtən] *n* iskelet
sketch [skɛtʃ] *n* karalama ▷ *v* karalama yapmak
skewer ['skjʊə] *n* kebap şişi
ski [skiː] *n* kayak ▷ *v* kayak yapmak; **ski lift** *n* teleferik; **ski pass** *n* kayak izni; **Can we hire skis here?** Burada kayak kiralayabilir miyiz?; **Do you have a map of the ski runs?** Kayak güzergahlarının haritası var mı?; **How much is a ski pass?** Kayak kartı ne kadar?; **I want to hire ski poles** Kayak sopası kiralamak istiyorum; **I want to hire skis** Kayak kiralamak istiyorum; **I'd like a ski pass for a day** Bir günlük kayak kartı almak istiyorum; **Is there a ski school?** Burada kayak okulu var mı?; **Where can I buy a ski pass?** Kayak kartı nereden alabilirim?
skid [skɪd] *v* kaymak
skier ['skiːə] *n* kayakçı
skiing ['skiːɪŋ] *n* kayma sporu
skilful ['skɪlfʊl] *adj* becerikli
skill [skɪl] *n* beceri
skilled [skɪld] *adj* becerikli
skimpy ['skɪmpɪ] *adj* yetersiz
skin [skɪn] *n* cilt
skinhead ['skɪnˌhɛd] *n* dazlak kafa
skinny ['skɪnɪ] *adj* kürdan gibi
skin-tight ['skɪn'taɪt] *adj* daracık
skip [skɪp] *v* atlamak
skirt [skɜːt] *n* etek *(giysi)*
skive [skaɪv] *v* kaytarmak
skull [skʌl] *n* kafatası
sky [skaɪ] *n* gök
skyscraper ['skaɪˌskreɪpə] *n* gökdelen
slack [slæk] *adj* gevşek *(tavır)*
slam [slæm] *v* çarparak kapatmak
slang [slæŋ] *n* argo
slap [slæp] *v* tokatlamak
slash [slæʃ] *n* **forward slash** *n* eğik çizgi
slate [sleɪt] *n* arduvaz
slave [sleɪv] *n* köle ▷ *v* köle gibi çalışmak
sledge [slɛdʒ] *n* kızak; **Where can we go sledging?** Kızak kaymak için nereye gitmemiz gerek?
sledging ['slɛdʒɪŋ] *n* kızak kaymak
sleep [sliːp] *n* uyku ▷ *v* uyumak; **sleeping bag** *n* uyku tulumu; **sleeping car** *n* kuşetli vagon; **sleeping pill** *n* uyku hapı
sleep around [sliːp ə'raʊnd] *v* önüne gelenle yatmak
sleep in [sliːp ɪn] *v* uyuyakalmak
sleep together [sliːp tə'gɛðə] *v*

birlikte yatmak
sleepwalk ['sli:p,wɔ:k] *v* uykuda yürüme
sleepy ['sli:pɪ] *adj* uykulu
sleet [sli:t] *n* sulu kar ▹ *v* sulu sepken yağmak
sleeve [sli:v] *n* kol ağzı
sleeveless ['sli:vlɪs] *adj* kolsuz *(giysi)*
slender ['slɛndə] *adj* tığ gibi
slice [slaɪs] *n* dilim ▹ *v* dilimlemek
slick [slɪk] *n* **oil slick** *n* petrol sızması
slide [slaɪd] *n* kayma ▹ *v* kaymak
slight [slaɪt] *adj* az
slightly ['slaɪtlɪ] *adv* azıcık
slim [slɪm] *adj* ince *(vücut vb)*
sling [slɪŋ] *n* kol askısı *(sağlık)*
slip [slɪp] *n (mistake)* hata, *(paper)* kağıt parçası, *(underwear)* iç gömleği ▹ *v* kaymak; **slip road** *n* bağlantı yolu; **slipped disc** *n* disk kayması
slipper ['slɪpə] *n* terlik
slippery ['slɪpərɪ; -prɪ] *adj* kaygan
slip up [slɪp ʌp] *v* hata yapmak
slip-up [slɪpʌp] *n* hata
slope [sləʊp] *n* yokuş; **nursery slope** *n* kayak alıştırma pisti
sloppy ['slɒpɪ] *adj* pasaklı
slot [slɒt] *n* boşluk *(konum)*; **slot machine** *n* jetonlu makine
Slovak ['sləʊvæk] *adj* Slovak ▹ *n (language)* Slovakça *(dil)*, *(person)* Slovak *(kişi)*
Slovakia [sləʊ'vækɪə] *n* Slovakya
Slovenia [sləʊ'vi:nɪə] *n* Slovenya
Slovenian [sləʊ'vi:nɪən] *adj* Slovenya ▹ *n (language)* Slovence *(dil)*, *(person)* Slovenyalı *(kişi)*
slow [sləʊ] *adj* yavaş; **The connection seems very slow** Bağlantı çok yavaş
slow down [sləʊ daʊn] *v* yavaşlamak
slowly [sləʊlɪ] *adv* yavaşça
slug [slʌg] *n* kabuksuz sümüklüböcek
slum [slʌm] *n* gecekondu
slush [slʌʃ] *n* sulu çamur
sly [slaɪ] *adj* kurnaz
smack [smæk] *v* tokat atmak
small [smɔ:l] *adj* küçük; **small ads** *npl* küçük ilanlar; **Do you have a small?** Küçük beden var mı?; **Do you have this in a smaller size?** Bunun bir küçük bedeni var mı?; **It's too small** Çok küçük; **The room is too small** Bu oda çok küçük
smart [smɑ:t] *adj* şık; **smart phone** *n* akıllı telefon
smash [smæʃ] *v* parçalamak
smashing ['smæʃɪŋ] *adj* harika
smell [smɛl] *n* koku ▹ *vi* kokmak ▹ *vt* koklamak; **I can smell gas** Gaz kokusu alıyorum; **My room smells of smoke** Odada duman kokusu var; **There's a funny smell** Garip bir koku var
smelly ['smɛlɪ] *adj* pis kokulu
smile [smaɪl] *n* gülümseme ▹ *v* gülümsemek
smiley ['smaɪlɪ] *n* neşeli
smoke [sməʊk] *n* duman ▹ *v* sigara içmek; **smoke alarm** *n* duman alarmı; **My room smells of smoke** Odada duman kokusu var
smoked ['sməʊkt] *adj* tütsülenmiş
smoker ['sməʊkə] *n* sigara içen

smoking ['sməʊkɪŋ] *n* tüten
smooth [smu:ð] *adj* pürüzsüz
SMS [ɛs ɛm ɛs] *n* SMS
smudge [smʌdʒ] *n* leke
smug [smʌg] *adj* kendinden memnun
smuggle ['smʌgᵊl] *v* kaçakçılık yapmak
smuggler ['smʌglə] *n* kaçakçı
smuggling ['smʌglɪŋ] *n* kaçakçılık
snack [snæk] *n* atıştırma; **snack bar** *n* snack bar
snail [sneɪl] *n* salyangoz
snake [sneɪk] *n* yılan
snap [snæp] *v* kopmak
snapshot ['snæp,ʃɒt] *n* enstantane
snarl [snɑ:l] *v* hırlamak
snatch [snætʃ] *v* kapmak
sneakers ['sni:kəz] *npl* spor ayakkabısı
sneeze [sni:z] *v* hapşırmak
sniff [snɪf] *v* burnunu çekmek
snigger ['snɪgə] *v* kıs kıs gülmek
snob [snɒb] *n* züppe
snooker ['snu:kə] *n* snooker
snooze [snu:z] *n* tavşan uykusu ▷ *v* uykuyu uzatmak
snore [snɔ:] *v* horlamak
snorkel ['snɔ:kᵊl] *n* şnorkel
snow [snəʊ] *n* kar ▷ *v* kar yağmak; **Do I need snow chains?** Kar zinciri almam gerekiyor mu?; **Do you think it will snow?** Kar yağacak mı dersiniz?; **It's snowing** Kar yağıyor; **The snow is very heavy** Kar çok şiddetli; **What are the snow conditions?** Kar durumu nasıl?; **What is the snow like?** Kar nasıl?
snowball ['snəʊ,bɔ:l] *n* kar topu
snowboard ['snəʊ,bɔ:d] *n* **I want to hire a snowboard** Snowboard kiralamak istiyorum
snowflake ['snəʊ,fleɪk] *n* kar tanesi
snowman ['snəʊ,mæn] *n* kardan adam
snowplough ['snəʊ,plaʊ] *n* kar temizleme aracı
snowstorm ['snəʊ,stɔ:m] *n* kar fırtınası
so [səʊ] *adv* öyle, öylesine; **so (that)** *conj* öyle ki
soak [səʊk] *v* ıslatmak
soaked [səʊkt] *adj* ıslak
soap [səʊp] *n* sabun; **soap dish** *n* sabunluk; **soap opera** *n* televizyon dizisi; **soap powder** *n* sabun tozu; **There is no soap** Sabun yok
sob [sɒb] *v* hıçkırarak ağlamak
sober ['səʊbə] *adj* ayık
sociable ['səʊʃəbᵊl] *adj* sosyal
social ['səʊʃəl] *adj* sosyal; **social security** *n* sosyal güvenlik; **social services** *npl* sosyal hizmetler; **social worker** *n* sosyal hizmetler görevlisi
socialism ['səʊʃə,lɪzəm] *n* sosyalizm
socialist ['səʊʃəlɪst] *adj* sosyalist ▷ *n* sosyalist
society [sə'saɪətɪ] *n* toplum
sociology [,səʊsɪ'ɒlədʒɪ] *n* toplumbilim
sock [sɒk] *n* çorap
socket ['sɒkɪt] *n* priz; **Where is the socket for my electric razor?** Traş makinem için priz nerede?

sofa ['səʊfə] *n* kanepe *(koltuk)*; **sofa bed** *n* çek-yat
soft [sɒft] *adj* yumuşak; **soft drink** *n* içecek
softener ['sɒfᵊnə] *n* yumuşatıcı
software ['sɒft,wɛə] *n* yazılım
soggy ['sɒgɪ] *adj* ıslak
soil [sɔɪl] *n* toprak
solar ['səʊlə] *adj* güneş; **solar power** *n* güneş enerjisi; **solar system** *n* güneş sistemi
soldier ['səʊldʒə] *n* asker
sold out [səʊld aʊt] *adj* satılıp tükenmiş
solicitor [sə'lɪsɪtə] *n* hukuk danışmanı
solid ['sɒlɪd] *adj* katı *(maddenin hali)*
solo ['səʊləʊ] *n* tek başına
soloist ['səʊləʊɪst] *n* solist
soluble ['sɒljʊbᵊl] *adj* çözünür
solution [sə'lu:ʃən] *n* çözüm
solve [sɒlv] *v* çözmek
solvent ['sɒlvənt] *n* çözücü
Somali [səʊ'mɑ:lɪ] *adj* Somali ▷ *n (language)* Somalice, *(person)* Somalili *(kişi)*
Somalia [səʊ'mɑ:lɪə] *n* Somali
some [sʌm; səm] *adj* herhangi ▷ *pron* bazı, biraz; **Could you lend me some money?** Bana biraz borç verebilir misiniz?
somebody ['sʌmbədɪ] *pron* birisi
somehow ['sʌm,haʊ] *adv* nasılsa
someone ['sʌm,wʌn; -wən] *pron* birisi
someplace ['sʌm,pleɪs] *adv* bir yerde
something ['sʌmθɪŋ] *pron* bir şey; **I'd like to order something local** Yöreye özgü bir şey ısmarlamak istiyorum; **Would you like something to eat?** Bir şey yemek ister misiniz?; **Would you like to do something tomorrow?** Yarın bir şeyler yapmak ister misiniz?
sometime ['sʌm,taɪm] *adv* bir ara
sometimes ['sʌm,taɪmz] *adv* bazen
somewhere ['sʌm,wɛə] *adv* bir yerde
son [sʌn] *n* oğul
song [sɒŋ] *n* şarkı
son-in-law [sʌn ɪn lɔ:] **(sons-in-law)** *n* damat *(kızının kocası)*
soon [su:n] *adv* kısa zamanda; **as soon as possible** en kısa zamanda
sooner ['su:nə] *adv* daha erken
soot [sʊt] *n* kurum *(is)*
sophisticated [sə'fɪstɪ,keɪtɪd] *adj* sofistike
soppy ['sɒpɪ] *adj* aşırı duygusal
soprano [sə'prɑ:nəʊ] *n* soprano
sorbet ['sɔ:beɪ; -bɪt] *n* sorbet
sorcerer ['sɔ:sərə] *n* büyücü
sore [sɔ:] *adj* ağrılı ▷ *n* yara; **cold sore** *n* uçuk *(sağlık)*
sorry ['sɒrɪ] *interj* **sorry!** *excl* affedersiniz!; **I'm sorry** Özür dilerim; **I'm sorry to trouble you** Rahatsız ettiğim için özür dilerim; **I'm very sorry, I didn't know the regulations** Özür dilerim, kuralları bilmiyordum; **Sorry we're late** Geciktiğimiz için özür dileriz; **Sorry, I didn't catch that** Pardon, anlayamadım; **Sorry, I'm not interested** Kusura bakmayın,

ilgilenmiyorum
sort [sɔ:t] *n* çeşit
sort out [sɔ:t aʊt] *v* halletmek
SOS [ɛs əʊ ɛs] *n* SOS
so-so [səʊsəʊ] *adv* şöyle böyle
soul [səʊl] *n* ruh
sound [saʊnd] *adj* sağlam ▷ *n* ses
soundtrack ['saʊnd,træk] *n* film müziği
soup [su:p] *n* çorba; **What is the soup of the day?** Günün çorbası ne?
sour ['saʊə] *adj* ekşi
south [saʊθ] *adj* güney ▷ *adv* güneyde ▷ *n* güney; **South Africa** *n* Güney Afrika; **South African** *n* Güney Afrika, Güney Afrikalı; **South America** *n* Güney Amerika; **South American** *n* Güney Amerika, Güney Amerikalı; **South Korea** *n* Güney Kore; **South Pole** *n* Güney Kutbu
southbound ['saʊθ,baʊnd] *adj* güneye giden
southeast [,saʊθ'i:st; ,saʊ'i:st] *n* güneydoğu
southern ['sʌðən] *adj* güney
southwest [,saʊθ'wɛst; ,saʊ'wɛst] *n* güneybatı
souvenir [,su:və'nɪə; 'su:və,nɪə] *n* anmalık
soya ['sɔɪə] *n* soya
spa [spɑ:] *n* ılıca
space [speɪs] *n* boşluk *(mekan)*
spacecraft ['speɪs,krɑ:ft] *n* uzay aracı
spade [speɪd] *n* kürek
spaghetti [spə'gɛtɪ] *n* spagetti
Spain [speɪn] *n* İspanya
spam [spæm] *n* istenmeyen e-mail
Spaniard ['spænjəd] *n* İspanyol
spaniel ['spænjəl] *n* cocker spaniel
Spanish ['spænɪʃ] *adj* İspanyol ▷ *n* İspanyol
spank [spæŋk] *v* şaplak atmak
spanner ['spænə] *n* İngiliz anahtarı
spare [spɛə] *adj* yedek ▷ *v* hayatını bağışlamak; **spare part** *n* yedek parça; **spare room** *n* yedek oda; **spare time** *n* boş zaman; **spare tyre** *n* stepne; **spare wheel** *n* stepne; **Is there any spare bedding?** Yedek çarşaf takımı var mı?
spark [spɑ:k] *n* kıvılcım; **spark plug** *n* buji
sparrow ['spærəʊ] *n* serçe
spasm ['spæzəm] *n* kramp
spatula ['spætjʊlə] *n* spatül
speak [spi:k] *v* konuşmak; **I'd like to speak to..., please**... ile konuşmak istiyorum lütfen; **I'd like to speak to a doctor** Doktorla konuşmak istiyorum lütfen; **I'd like to speak to the manager, please** Müdürle konuşmak istiyorum lütfen
speaker ['spi:kə] *n* konuşmacı; **native speaker** *n* anadilini konuşan
speak up [spi:k ʌp] *v* açıkça fikrini söylemek
special ['spɛʃəl] *adj* özel; **special offer** *n* indirimli fiyatla sunulan eşya
specialist ['spɛʃəlɪst] *n* uzman
speciality [,spɛʃɪ'ælɪtɪ] *n* uzmanlık
specialize ['spɛʃə,laɪz] *v* uzmanlaşmak

specially ['spɛʃəlɪ] *adv* özellikle
species ['spiːʃiːz; 'spiːʃɪˌiːz] *n* tür
specific [spɪ'sɪfɪk] *adj* spesifik
specifically [spɪ'sɪfɪklɪ] *adv* özellikle
specify ['spɛsɪˌfaɪ] *v* belirtmek
specs [spɛks] *npl* özellikler
spectacles ['spɛktəkᵊlz] *npl* gözlük
spectacular [spɛk'tækjʊlə] *adj* görülmeye değer
spectator [spɛk'teɪtə] *n* izleyici
speculate ['spɛkjʊˌleɪt] *v* varsayımda bulunmak
speech [spiːtʃ] *n* konuşma
speechless ['spiːtʃlɪs] *adj* nutku tutulmuş
speed [spiːd] *n* hız; **speed limit** *n* hız sınırı; **What is the speed limit on this road?** Bu yolda hız limiti nedir?
speedboat ['spiːdˌbəʊt] *n* sürat motoru
speeding ['spiːdɪŋ] *n* hız yapmak
speedometer [spɪ'dɒmɪtə] *n* hızölçer
speed up [spiːd ʌp] *v* hızlanmak
spell [spɛl] *n (magic)* büyü, *(time)* dönem *(belirli bir süre)* ▷ *v* telaffuz etmek
spellchecker ['spɛlˌtʃɛkə] *n* yazım denetimi
spelling ['spɛlɪŋ] *n* heceleme
spend [spɛnd] *v* harcamak
sperm [spɜːm] *n* sperm
spice [spaɪs] *n* baharat
spicy ['spaɪsɪ] *adj* acılı
spider ['spaɪdə] *n* örümcek
spill [spɪl] *v* dökmek
spinach ['spɪnɪdʒ; -ɪtʃ] *n* ıspanak
spine [spaɪn] *n* belkemiği
spinster ['spɪnstə] *n* kız kurusu
spire [spaɪə] *n* kilise kulesinin sivri tepesi
spirit ['spɪrɪt] *n* ruh
spirits ['spɪrɪts] *npl* alkollü içki
spiritual ['spɪrɪtjʊəl] *adj* manevi
spit [spɪt] *n* şiş ▷ *v* tükürmek
spite [spaɪt] *n* kincilik ▷ *v* kin gütmek
spiteful ['spaɪtfʊl] *adj* kinci
splash [splæʃ] *v* sıçratmak
splendid ['splɛndɪd] *adj* görkemli
splint [splɪnt] *n* süyek
splinter ['splɪntə] *n* kıymık
split [splɪt] *v* ayırmak
split up [splɪt ʌp] *v* ayrılmak
spoil [spɔɪl] *v* berbat etmek
spoilsport ['spɔɪlˌspɔːt] *n* oyunbozan
spoilt [spɔɪlt] *adj* şımartılmış
spoke [spəʊk] *n* jant teli
spokesman, spokesmen ['spəʊksmən, 'spəʊksmɛn] *n* sözcü *(erkek)*
spokesperson ['spəʊksˌpɜrsən] *n* sözcü
spokeswoman, spokeswomen ['spəʊksˌwʊmən, 'spəʊksˌwɪmɪn] *n* sözcü *(kadın)*
sponge [spʌndʒ] *n (cake)* pandispanya, *(for washing)* sünger *(banyo)*; **sponge bag** *n* tuvalet çantası
sponsor ['spɒnsə] *n* finansör ▷ *v* finanse etmek
sponsorship ['spɒnsəʃɪp] *n* mali destek
spontaneous [spɒn'teɪnɪəs] *adj* kendiliğinden

spooky ['spu:kɪ] *adj* ürkütücü
spoon [spu:n] *n* kaşık; **Could I have a clean spoon, please?** Temiz bir kaşık alabilir miyim lütfen?
spoonful ['spu:n,fʊl] *n* bir kaşık dolusu
sport [spɔ:t] *n* spor; **winter sports** *npl* kış sporları; **What sports facilities are there?** Buralarda sport tesisi var mı?; **Which sporting events can we go to?** Hangi spor gösterisine gidebiliriz?
sportsman, sportsmen ['spɔ:tsmən, 'spɔ:tsmɛn] *n* sporcu *(erkek)*
sportswear ['spɔ:ts,wɛə] *n* spor giysisi
sportswoman, sportswomen ['spɔ:ts,wʊmən, 'spɔ:ts,wɪmɪn] *n* kadın sporcu
sporty ['spɔ:tɪ] *adj* sporsever
spot [spɒt] *n (blemish)* akne, *(place)* yer ▷ *v* dikkat etmek
spotless ['spɒtlɪs] *adj* pırıl pırıl
spotlight ['spɒt,laɪt] *n* spot lambası
spotty ['spɒtɪ] *adj* sivilceli
spouse [spaʊs] *n* eş *(karıkoca)*
sprain [spreɪn] *n* burkulma ▷ *v* burkmak *(bilek)*
spray [spreɪ] *n* serpinti ▷ *v* püskürtmek; **hair spray** *n* saç spreyi
spread [sprɛd] *n* yayılım ▷ *v* yaymak
spread out [sprɛd aʊt] *v* yayılmak
spreadsheet ['sprɛd,ʃi:t] *n* hesap çizelgesi
spring [sprɪŋ] *n (coil)* yay, *(season)* ilkbahar; **spring onion** *n* taze soğan
spring-cleaning ['sprɪŋ,kli:nɪŋ] *n* bahar temizliği
springtime ['sprɪŋ,taɪm] *n* bahar
sprinkler ['sprɪŋklə; 'sprinkler] *n* yağmurlama cihazı
sprint [sprɪnt] *n* kısa mesafe hız koşusu ▷ *v* hızla koşmak
sprinter ['sprɪntə] *n* kısa mesafe koşucusu
spy [spaɪ] *n* casus ▷ *v* casusluk etmek
spying ['spaɪɪŋ] *n* casusluk
squabble ['skwɒbᵊl] *v* ağız dalaşı
squander ['skwɒndə] *v* müsrüflük etmek
square [skwɛə] *adj* kare ▷ *n* kare
squash [skwɒʃ] *n* ezme ▷ *v* ezmek
squeak [skwi:k] *v* cıyaklamak
squeeze [skwi:z] *v* sıkmak
squeeze in [skwi:z ɪn] *v* sıkışmak
squid [skwɪd] *n* kalamar
squint [skwɪnt] *v* şaşı bakmak
squirrel ['skwɪrəl; 'skwɜ:rəl; 'skwʌr-] *n* sincap
Sri Lanka [,sri: 'læŋkə] *n* Sri Lanka
stab [stæb] *v* bıçaklamak
stability [stə'bɪlɪtɪ] *n* denge *(durum)*
stable ['steɪbᵊl] *adj* dengede ▷ *n* ahır
stack [stæk] *n* yığın
stadium, stadia ['steɪdɪəm, 'steɪdɪə] *n* stadyum; **How do we get to the stadium?** Stadyuma nasıl gidebiliriz?
staff [stɑ:f] *n (stick or rod)* sopa *(asa)*, *(workers)* eleman
staffroom ['stɑ:f,ru:m] *n*

öğretmen odası
stage [steɪdʒ] *n* sahne *(tiyatro mekan)*
stagger ['stægə] *v* sendelemek
stain [steɪn] *n* leke ▷ *v* lekelemek; **stain remover** *n* leke çıkarıcı; **Can you remove this stain?** Bu lekeyi çıkarabilir misiniz?; **This stain is coffee** Kahve lekesi; **This stain is wine** Şarap lekesi
staircase ['stɛəˌkeɪs] *n* merdiven
stairs [stɛəz] *npl* merdivenler
stale [steɪl] *adj* bayat
stalemate ['steɪlˌmeɪt] *n* şahmat
stall [stɔːl] *n* tezgah
stamina ['stæmɪnə] *n* dayanıklılık
stammer ['stæmə] *v* kekelemek
stamp [stæmp] *n* pul ▷ *v* ayağını yere vurmak; **Can I have stamps for four postcards to...** Bu dört kartpostal için pul alacaktım... a gidecek; **Do you sell stamps?** Pul satıyor musunuz?; **Where can I buy stamps?** Pul nereden alabilirim?; **Where is the nearest shop which sells stamps?** Pul satan en yakın yer nerede?
stand [stænd] *v* ayakta durmak
standard ['stændəd] *adj* standart ▷ *n* standart; **standard of living** *n* yaşam standardı
stand for [stænd fɔː] *v* anlamına gelmek
stand out [stænd aʊt] *v* kendini göstermek
standpoint ['stændˌpɔɪnt] *n* bakış noktası
stands ['stændz] *npl* tezgahlar
stand up [stænd ʌp] *v* ayağa kalkmak
staple ['steɪpᵊl] *n (commodity)* temel ürün, *(wire)* zımba teli ▷ *v* zımbalamak
stapler ['steɪplə] *n* tel zımba
star [stɑː] *n (person)* yıldız *(kişi)*, *(sky)* yıldız *(gök)* ▷ *v* yıldız koymak; **film star** *n* film yıldızı
starch [stɑːtʃ] *n* nişasta
stare [stɛə] *v* boşluğa bakmak
stark [stɑːk] *adj* katı *(durum)*
start [stɑːt] *n* başlangıç *(iş, yarış vb)* ▷ *vi* başlatmak ▷ *vt* başlamak
starter ['stɑːtə] *n* ön yemek
startle ['stɑːtᵊl] *v* irkilmek
start off [stɑːt ɒf] *v* yola çıkmak
starve [stɑːv] *v* açlık çekmek
state [steɪt] *n* durum *(ruhsal)* ▷ *v* ifade etmek; **Gulf States** *npl* Körfez Ülkeleri
statement ['steɪtmənt] *n* açıklama *(beyan)*; **bank statement** *n* hesap özeti
station ['steɪʃən] *n* istasyon; **bus station** *n* otobüs terminali; **metro station** *n* metro istasyonu; **petrol station** *n* benzin istasyonu; **police station** *n* polis istasyonu; **radio station** *n* radyo istasyonu; **railway station** *n* tren istasyonu; **service station** *n* benzin istasyonu; **tube station** *n* metro istasyonu; **Is there a petrol station near here?** Buraya en yakın benzin istasyonu nerede?; **Where is the nearest tube station?** Buraya en yakın metro istasyonu nerede?
stationer's ['steɪʃənəz] *n* kırtasiyeci
stationery ['steɪʃənərɪ] *n* kırtasiye

statistics [stə'tıstıks] *npl* sayımlama
statue ['stætju:] *n* heykel
status ['steıtəs] *n* **marital status** *n* medeni hal
status quo ['steıtəs kwəʊ] *n* statüko
stay [steı] *n* kalış ▷ *v* kalmak; **I want to stay an extra night** Bir gece daha kalmak istiyorum; **I want to stay from Monday till Wednesday** Pazartesi'den Çarşamba'ya kadar kalmak istiyorum; **I'd like to stay for two nights** İki gece kalmak istiyorum
stay in [steı ın] *v* evde kalmak
stay up [steı ʌp] *v* geç saatlere kadar oturmak
steady ['stɛdı] *adj* sabit *(dengeli)*
steak [steık] *n* biftek; **rump steak** *n* biftek
steal [sti:l] *v* çalmak
steam [sti:m] *n* buhar
steel [sti:l] *n* çelik; **stainless steel** *n* paslanmaz çelik
steep [sti:p] *adj* dik *(yokuş vb)*; **Is it very steep?** Yokuş çok mu dik?
steeple ['sti:pᵊl] *n* kilise kulesi
steering ['stıəıŋ] *n* yönetim; **steering wheel** *n* direksiyon
step [stɛp] *n* adım
stepbrother ['stɛp,brʌðə] *n* üvey erkek kardeş
stepdaughter ['stɛp,dɔ:tə] *n* üvey kız evlat
stepfather ['stɛp,fɑ:ðə] *n* üvey baba
stepladder ['stɛp,lædə] *n* ayaklı merdiven
stepmother ['stɛp,mʌðə] *n* üvey anne
stepsister ['stɛp,sıstə] *n* üvey kızkardeş
stepson ['stɛp,sʌn] *n* üvey oğul
stereo ['stɛrıəʊ; 'stıər-] *n* stereo; **personal stereo** *n* kişisel müzik çalar; **Is there a stereo in the car?** Arabada stereo var mı?
stereotype ['stɛrıə,taıp; 'stıər-] *n* basmakalıp
sterile ['stɛraıl] *adj* steril
sterilize ['stɛrı,laız] *v* sterilize etmek
sterling ['stɜ:lıŋ] *n* sterlin
steroid ['stıərɔıd; 'stɛr-] *n* steroid
stew [stju:] *n* güveç
steward ['stjʊəd] *n* hostes
stick [stık] *n* sopa *(çubuk)* ▷ *v* yapışmak; **stick insect** *n* sopa çekirgesi; **walking stick** *n* baston
sticker ['stıkə] *n* etiket *(defter vb)*
stick out [stık aʊt] *v* çıkarmak
sticky ['stıkı] *adj* yapışkan
stiff [stıf] *adj* katı *(kumaş vb)*
stifling ['staıflıŋ] *adj* boğucu
still [stıl] *adj* durgun ▷ *adv* hala
sting [stıŋ] *n* sokma *(arı, böcek)* ▷ *v* sokmak *(arı, böcek vb)*
stingy ['stındʒı] *adj* ısırıcı
stink [stıŋk] *n* leş gibi kokma ▷ *v* kötü kokmak
stir [stɜ:] *v* karıştırmak *(çorba vb)*
stitch [stıtʃ] *n* dikiş *(tıp, nakış vb)* ▷ *v* dikmek *(tıp, nakış vb)*
stock [stɒk] *n* stok ▷ *v* stoklamak; **stock cube** *n* bulyon; **stock exchange** *n* borsa; **stock market** *n* borsa
stockbroker ['stɒk,brəʊkə] *n* borsacı

stockholder ['stɒk,həʊldə] *n* hissedar
stocking ['stɒkɪŋ] *n* naylon çorap
stock up [stɒk ʌp] *v* **stock up on** *v* depoyu doldurmak
stomach ['stʌmək] *n* mide
stomachache ['stʌmək,eɪk] *n* mide ağrısı
stone [stəʊn] *n* taş
stool [stu:l] *n* tabure
stop [stɒp] *n* durdurma ▹ *vi* durdurmak ▹ *vt* bırakmak; **bus stop** *n* otobüs durağı; **full stop** *n* nokta *(gramer)*
stopover ['stɒp,əʊvə] *n* konaklama
stopwatch ['stɒp,wɒtʃ] *n* kronometre
storage ['stɔ:rɪdʒ] *n* depo
store [stɔ:] *n* depo ▹ *v* depolamak; **department store** *n* büyük mağaza
storm [stɔ:m] *n* fırtına; **Do you think there will be a storm?** Fırtına çıkabilir mi?
stormy ['stɔ:mɪ] *adj* fırtınalı
story ['stɔ:rɪ] *n* öykü; **short story** *n* kısa öykü
stove [stəʊv] *n* soba
straight [streɪt] *adj* doğru *(çizgi)*; **straight on** *adv* dosdoğru
straighteners ['streɪtᵊnəz] *npl* saç maşası
straightforward [,streɪt'fɔ:wəd] *adj* açık sözlü
strain [streɪn] *n* stres ▹ *v* psikolojik anlamda germek
strained [streɪnd] *adj* zorlama
stranded ['strændɪd] *adj* kısılıp kalmak
strange [streɪndʒ] *adj* garip
stranger ['streɪndʒə] *n* yabancı
strangle ['stræŋgᵊl] *v* boğazlamak
strap [stræp] *n* kayış; **watch strap** *n* saat kayışı
strategic [strə'ti:dʒɪk] *adj* stratejik
strategy ['strætɪdʒɪ] *n* strateji
straw [strɔ:] *n* saman
strawberry ['strɔ:bərɪ; -brɪ] *n* çilek
stray [streɪ] *n* sürüden ayrılmış
stream [stri:m] *n* dere
street [stri:t] *n* cadde; **street map** *n* sokak haritası; **street plan** *n* sokak planı
streetlamp ['stri:t,læmp] *n* sokak lambası
streetwise ['stri:t,waɪz] *adj* sokaklarda büyümüş
strength [strɛŋθ] *n* güç *(kuvvet)*
strengthen ['strɛŋθən] *v* güçlendirmek
stress [strɛs] *n* stres ▹ *v* vurgulamak
stressed ['strɛst] *adj* gerilmiş
stressful ['strɛsfʊl] *adj* gerginlik yaratıcı
stretch [strɛtʃ] *v* esnetmek
stretcher ['strɛtʃə] *n* sedye
stretchy ['strɛtʃɪ] *adj* esnek *(materyal)*
strict [strɪkt] *adj* katı *(kural vb)*
strictly [strɪktlɪ] *adv* katı bir şekilde
strike [straɪk] *n* grev ▹ *vi* darbe yemek, *(suspend work)* grev yapmak ▹ *vt* vurmak; **because of a strike** grev vardı, o yüzden
striker ['straɪkə] *n* grevci
striking ['straɪkɪŋ] *adj* çarpıcı

string [strɪŋ] *n* ip
strip [strɪp] *n* şerit ▷ *v* soyunmak
stripe [straɪp] *n* şerit
striped [straɪpt] *adj* çizgili
stripper ['strɪpə] *n* striptizci
stripy ['straɪpɪ] *adj* çizgili
stroke [strəʊk] *n* *(apoplexy)* okşama, *(hit)* okşama ▷ *v* okşamak
stroll [strəʊl] *n* yürüyüş
strong [strɒŋ] *adj* güçlü
strongly [strɒŋlɪ] *adv* kuvvetli
structure ['strʌktʃə] *n* yapı
struggle ['strʌgᵊl] *v* uğraşmak
stub [stʌb] *n* izmarit *(sigara)*
stubborn ['stʌbᵊn] *adj* inatçı
stub out [stʌb aʊt] *v* bastırarak söndürmek
stuck [stʌk] *adj* takılmış
stuck-up [stʌkʌp] *adj* kibirli
stud [stʌd] *n* kabara
student ['stju:dᵊnt] *n* öğrenci; **student discount** *n* öğrenci indirimi
studio ['stju:dɪˌəʊ] *n* stüdyo; **studio flat** *n* stüdyo daire
study ['stʌdɪ] *v* çalışmak
stuff [stʌf] *n* madde
stuffy ['stʌfɪ] *adj* havasız
stumble ['stʌmbᵊl] *v* tökezlemek
stunned [stʌnd] *adj* şaşkına dönmüş
stunning ['stʌnɪŋ] *adj* göz kamaştırıcı
stunt [stʌnt] *n* dublör
stuntman, stuntmen ['stʌntmən, 'stʌntmɛn] *n* dublör
stupid ['stju:pɪd] *adj* aptal
stutter ['stʌtə] *v* kekelemek
style [staɪl] *n* stil
styling ['staɪlɪŋ] *n* **Do you sell styling products?** Saç bakım ürünleri satıyor musunuz?
stylist ['staɪlɪst] *n* stilist
subject ['sʌbdʒɪkt] *n* konu
submarine ['sʌbməˌri:n; ˌsʌbmə'ri:n] *n* denizaltı
subscription [səb'skrɪpʃən] *n* abonelik
subsidiary [səb'sɪdɪərɪ] *n* yan *(destek)*
subsidize ['sʌbsɪˌdaɪz] *v* mali destek sağlamak
subsidy ['sʌbsɪdɪ] *n* sübvansiyon
substance ['sʌbstəns] *n* madde
substitute ['sʌbstɪˌtju:t] *n* yedek ▷ *v* vekalet etmek
subtitled ['sʌbˌtaɪtᵊld] *adj* altyazılı
subtitles ['sʌbˌtaɪtᵊlz] *npl* altyazı
subtle ['sʌtᵊl] *adj* belli belirsiz
subtract [səb'trækt] *v* çıkarma işlemi
suburb ['sʌbɜ:b] *n* banliyö
suburban [sə'bɜ:bᵊn] *adj* banliyö
subway ['sʌbˌweɪ] *n* altgeçit
succeed [sək'si:d] *v* başarmak
success [sək'sɛs] *n* başarı
successful [sək'sɛsfʊl] *adj* başarılı
successfully [sək'sɛsfʊlɪ] *adv* başarıyla
successive [sək'sɛsɪv] *adj* ardıl
successor [sək'sɛsə] *n* halef
such [sʌtʃ] *adj* böyle ▷ *adv* böylesine
suck [sʌk] *v* emmek
Sudan [su:'dɑ:n; -'dæn] *n* Sudan
Sudanese [ˌsu:dᵊ'ni:z] *adj* Sudan ▷ *n* Sudanlı
sudden ['sʌdᵊn] *adj* ani
suddenly ['sʌdᵊnlɪ] *adv* aniden
sue [sju:; su:] *v* dava etmek
suede [sweɪd] *n* süet

suffer ['sʌfə] *v* acı çekmek
sufficient [sə'fɪʃənt] *adj* yeterli
suffocate ['sʌfə,keɪt] *v* boğmak
sugar ['ʃʊgə] *n* şeker; **icing sugar** *n* toz süsleme şekeri; **no sugar** şekersiz
sugar-free ['ʃʊgəfri:] *adj* şekersiz
suggest [sə'dʒɛst; səg'dʒɛst] *v* önermek
suggestion [sə'dʒɛstʃən] *n* öneri
suicide ['su:ɪ,saɪd; 'sju:-] *n* intihar; **suicide bomber** *n* intihar bombacısı
suit [su:t; sju:t] *n* takım elbise ▷ *v* uymak; **bathing suit** *n* mayo; **shell suit** *n* eşofman
suitable ['su:təbᵊl; 'sju:t-] *adj* uygun
suitcase ['su:t,keɪs; 'sju:t-] *n* valiz
suite [swi:t] *n* suit
sulk [sʌlk] *v* suratını asmak
sulky ['sʌlkɪ] *adj* suratı asık
sultana [sʌl'tɑ:nə] *n* kuru üzüm
sum [sʌm] *n* toplam
summarize ['sʌmə,raɪz] *v* özetlemek
summary ['sʌmərɪ] *n* özet
summer ['sʌmə] *n* yaz *(mevsim)*; **summer holidays** *npl* yaz tatili; **after summer** yazdan sonra; **during the summer** yaz boyunca; **in summer** yazın
summertime ['sʌmə,taɪm] *n* yaz sezonu
summit ['sʌmɪt] *n* zirve
sum up [sʌm ʌp] *v* özetlemek
sun [sʌn] *n* güneş
sunbathe ['sʌn,beɪð] *v* güneşte yanmak
sunbed ['sʌn,bɛd] *n* güneşlenme yatağı
sunblock ['sʌn,blɒk] *n* koruyucu güneş kremi
sunburn ['sʌn,bɜ:n] *n* güneş yanığı
sunburnt ['sʌn,bɜ:nt] *adj* güneş yanığı; **I am sunburnt** Güneş yanığım var
suncream ['sʌn,kri:m] *n* güneş kremi
Sunday ['sʌndɪ] *n* Pazar; **Is the museum open on Sundays?** Müze Pazar günleri açık mı?; **on Sunday** Pazar günü
sunflower ['sʌn,flaʊə] *n* ayçiçeği
sunglasses ['sʌn,glɑ:sɪz] *npl* güneş gözlüğü
sunlight ['sʌnlaɪt] *n* gün ışığı
sunny ['sʌnɪ] *adj* güneşli; **It's sunny** Hava güneşli
sunrise ['sʌn,raɪz] *n* gün doğuşu
sunroof ['sʌn,ru:f] *n* açılır tavan
sunscreen ['sʌn,skri:n] *n* güneşlik
sunset ['sʌn,sɛt] *n* gün batımı
sunshine ['sʌn,ʃaɪn] *n* gün ışığı
sunstroke ['sʌn,strəʊk] *n* güneş çarpması
suntan ['sʌn,tæn] *n* bronzlaşma; **suntan lotion** *n* bronzlaşma losyonu; **suntan oil** *n* güneş yağı
super ['su:pə] *adj* süper
superb [sʊ'pɜ:b; sjʊ-] *adj* muhteşem
superficial [,su:pə'fɪʃəl] *adj* yapay
superior [su:'pɪərɪə] *adj* üstün ▷ *n* üst *(kalite/rütbe)*
supermarket ['su:pə,mɑ:kɪt] *n* süpermarket; **I need to find a supermarket** Süpermarket arıyorum
supernatural [,su:pə'nætʃrəl;

-'nætʃərəl] *adj* doğaüstü
superstitious [ˌsuːpəˈstɪʃəs] *adj* batıl inançları olan
supervise ['suːpəˌvaɪz] *v* denetlemek
supervisor ['suːpəˌvaɪzə] *n* amir *(iş)*
supper ['sʌpə] *n* hafif akşam yemeği
supplement ['sʌplɪmənt] *n* ilave *(ek)*
supplier [sə'plaɪə] *n* satıcı
supplies [sə'plaɪz] *npl* erzak
supply [sə'plaɪ] *n* malzeme temin etme ▹ *v* temin etmek; **supply teacher** *n* yedek öğretmen
support [sə'pɔːt] *n* destek *(manevi)* ▹ *v* desteklemek
supporter [sə'pɔːtə] *n* taraftar
suppose [sə'pəʊz] *v* varsaymak
supposedly [sə'pəʊzɪdlɪ] *adv* varsayalım ki
supposing [sə'pəʊzɪŋ] *conj* diyelim ki
surcharge ['sɜːˌtʃɑːdʒ] *n* fazla fiyat isteme
sure [ʃʊə; ʃɔː] *adj* emin
surely ['ʃʊəlɪ; 'ʃɔː-] *adv* muhakkak
surf [sɜːf] *n* sörf ▹ *v* sörf yapmak; **Where can you go surfing?** Sörf için nereye gitmek gerek?
surface ['sɜːfɪs] *n* yüzey
surfboard ['sɜːfˌbɔːd] *n* sörf tahtası
surfer ['sɜːfə] *n* sörfçü
surfing ['sɜːfɪŋ] *n* sörf yapma
surge [sɜːdʒ] *n* ani yükselme
surgeon ['sɜːdʒən] *n* cerrah
surgery ['sɜːdʒərɪ] *n* *(doctor's)* klinik, *(operation)* ameliyat; **cosmetic surgery** *n* kozmetik cerrahi; **plastic surgery** *n* plastik cerrahi
surname ['sɜːˌneɪm] *n* soyadı
surplus ['sɜːpləs] *adj* fazla ▹ *n* fazlalık
surprise [sə'praɪz] *n* sürpriz
surprised [sə'praɪzd] *adj* şaşırmış
surprising [sə'praɪzɪŋ] *adj* şaşırtıcı
surprisingly [sə'praɪzɪŋlɪ] *adv* şaşırtıcı bir şekilde
surrender [sə'rɛndə] *v* teslim olmak
surround [sə'raʊnd] *v* çevrelemek
surroundings [sə'raʊndɪŋz] *npl* çevre
survey ['sɜːveɪ] *n* inceleme
surveyor [sɜː'veɪə] *n* denetçi
survival [sə'vaɪvᵊl] *n* yaşam kavgası
survive [sə'vaɪv] *v* hayatta kalmak
survivor [sə'vaɪvə] *n* hayatta kalan
suspect *n* ['sʌspɛkt] zanlı ▹ *v* [sə'spɛkt] kuşkulanmak
suspend [sə'spɛnd] *v* askıya almak
suspenders [sə'spɛndəz] *npl* jartiyer
suspense [sə'spɛns] *n* kuşku ve gerilimli bekleyiş
suspension [sə'spɛnʃən] *n* askıya alma; **suspension bridge** *n* asma köprü
suspicious [sə'spɪʃəs] *adj* kuşkulu
swallow ['swɒləʊ] *n* yutma ▹ *vi* yutulmak ▹ *vt* yutmak
swamp [swɒmp] *n* bataklık
swan [swɒn] *n* kuğu
swap [swɒp] *v* değiştirmek
swat [swɒt] *v* vurmak *(sineklik gibi*

yassı bir şeyle)
sway [sweɪ] *v* salınmak
Swaziland ['swɑːzɪˌlænd] *n* Swaziland
swear [swɛə] *v* küfretmek
swearword ['swɛəˌwɜːd] *n* küfür
sweat [swɛt] *n* ter ▹ *v* terlemek
sweater ['swɛtə] *n* kazak; **polo-necked sweater** *n* polo yakalı kazak
sweatshirt ['swɛtˌʃɜːt] *n* pamuklu kalın tişört
sweaty ['swɛtɪ] *adj* terli
swede [swiːd] *n* sarı şalgam
Swede [swiːd] *n* İsveçli
Sweden ['swiːdᵊn] *n* İsveç
Swedish ['swiːdɪʃ] *adj* İsveç ▹ *n* İsveçli
sweep [swiːp] *v* süpürmek
sweet [swiːt] *adj (pleasing)* tatlı *(hoş), (taste)* tatlı ▹ *n* şeker
sweetcorn ['swiːtˌkɔːn] *n* bebe mısır
sweetener ['swiːtᵊnə] *n* tatlandırıcı; **Do you have any sweetener?** Tatlandırıcınız var mı?
sweets ['swiːtz] *npl* tatlılar
sweltering ['swɛltərɪŋ] *adj* boğucu sıcak
swerve [swɜːv] *v* direksiyonu kırmak
swim [swɪm] *v* yüzmek
swimmer ['swɪmə] *n* yüzücü
swimming ['swɪmɪŋ] *n* yüzme; **swimming costume** *n* mayo; **swimming pool** *n* yüzme havuzu; **swimming trunks** *npl* yüzücü şortu; **Is there a swimming pool?** Yüzme havuzu var mı?; **Where is the public swimming pool?** Yüzme havuzu nerede?
swimsuit ['swɪmˌsuːt; -ˌsjuːt] *n* mayo
swing [swɪŋ] *n* sallanma ▹ *v* sallanmak
Swiss [swɪs] *adj* İsviçre ▹ *n* İsviçreli
switch [swɪtʃ] *n* elektrik düğmesi ▹ *v* elektrik düğmesini çevirmek
switchboard ['swɪtʃˌbɔːd] *n* santral
switch off [swɪtʃ ɒf] *v* elektriği kapamak
switch on [swɪtʃ ɒn] *v* şalter açmak
Switzerland ['swɪtsələnd] *n* İsviçre
swollen ['swəʊlən] *adj* şiş
sword [sɔːd] *n* kılıç
swordfish ['sɔːdˌfɪʃ] *n* kılıç balığı
swot [swɒt] *v* ineklemek
syllable ['sɪləbᵊl] *n* hece
syllabus ['sɪləbəs] *n* müfredat
symbol ['sɪmbᵊl] *n* sembol
symmetrical [sɪ'mɛtrɪkᵊl] *adj* simetrik
sympathetic [ˌsɪmpə'θɛtɪk] *adj* anlayışlı
sympathize ['sɪmpəˌθaɪz] *v* halden anlamak
sympathy ['sɪmpəθɪ] *n* halden anlama
symphony ['sɪmfənɪ] *n* senfoni
symptom ['sɪmptəm] *n* belirti *(hastalık)*
synagogue ['sɪnəˌgɒg] *n* sinagog; **Where is there a synagogue?** Sinagog nerede var?
syndrome ['sɪndrəʊm] *n* **Down's syndrome** *n* Down sendromu

Syria ['sɪrɪə] *n* Suriye
Syrian ['sɪrɪən] *adj* Suriye ▷ *n* Suriyeli
syringe ['sɪrɪndʒ; sɪ'rɪndʒ] *n* şırınga
syrup ['sɪrəp] *n* şurup
system ['sɪstəm] *n* sistem; **immune system** *n* bağışıklık sistemi; **solar system** *n* güneş sistemi; **systems analyst** *n* sistem analizcisi
systematic [ˌsɪstɪ'mætɪk] *adj* sistemli

t

table ['teɪbᵊl] *n (chart)* tablo *(grafik)*, *(furniture)* masa; **bedside table** *n* komodin; **coffee table** *n* sehpa; **dressing table** *n* tuvalet masası; **table tennis** *n* masa tenisi; **table wine** *n* yemeklik şarap; **A table for four people, please** Dört kişilik bir masa lütfen; **I'd like to book a table for three people for tonight** Bu akşam için üç kişilik bir masa ayırtmak istiyordum; **I'd like to book a table for two people for tomorrow night** Yarın akşam için iki kişilik bir masa ayırtmak istiyordum; **The table is booked for nine o'clock this evening** Masa bu akşam saat dokuz için rezerve edildi
tablecloth ['teɪbᵊlˌklɒθ] *n* masa örtüsü
tablespoon ['teɪbᵊlˌspuːn] *n* çorba

kaşığı
tablet ['tæblɪt] *n* hap
taboo [tə'bu:] *adj* tabu ▷ *n* tabu
tackle ['tækᵊl; 'teɪkᵊl] *n* palanga ▷ *v* üstesinden gelmek; **fishing tackle** *n* olta
tact [tækt] *n* incelik
tactful ['tæktfʊl] *adj* incelikli
tactics ['tæktɪks] *npl* taktik
tactless ['tæktlɪs] *adj* patavatsız
tadpole ['tæd,pəʊl] *n* iribaş
tag [tæg] *n* etiket *(bilişim)*
Tahiti [tə'hi:tɪ] *n* Tahiti
tail [teɪl] *n* kuyruk *(hayvan vb)*
tailor ['teɪlə] *n* terzi
Taiwan ['taɪ'wɑ:n] *n* Tayvan
Taiwanese [,taɪwɑ:'ni:z] *adj* Tayvan ▷ *n* Tayvanlı
Tajikistan [tɑ:,dʒɪkɪ'stɑ:n; -stæn] *n* Tacikistan
take [teɪk] *v* almak, *(time)* almak
take after [teɪk 'ɑ:ftə] *v* benzemek
take apart [teɪk ə'pɑ:t] *v* sökmek *(parçalarına ayırmak)*
take away [teɪk ə'weɪ] *v* çıkarmak
takeaway ['teɪkə,weɪ] *n* hazır yemek
take back [teɪk bæk] *v* geri almak
take off [teɪk ɒf] *v* üstünü çıkarmak
takeoff ['teɪk,ɒf] *n* kalkış *(uçak)*
take over [teɪk 'əʊvə] *v* yönetimi ele almak
takeover ['teɪk,əʊvə] *n* devralma
takings ['teɪkɪŋz] *npl* hasılat
tale [teɪl] *n* hikaye
talent ['tælənt] *n* yetenek
talented ['tæləntɪd] *adj* yetenekli
talk [tɔ:k] *n* konuşma ▷ *v* konuşmak; **talk to** *v* biriyle konuşmak
talkative ['tɔ:kətɪv] *adj* konuşkan
tall [tɔ:l] *adj* uzun boylu
tame [teɪm] *adj* evcil
tampon ['tæmpɒn] *n* tampon
tan [tæn] *n* bronzlaşmış ten
tandem ['tændəm] *n* tandem bisiklet
tangerine [,tændʒə'ri:n] *n* mandalina
tank [tæŋk] *n* *(combat vehicle)* tank *(ordu)*, *(large container)* tank; **petrol tank** *n* benzin deposu; **septic tank** *n* foseptik çukuru
tanker ['tæŋkə] *n* tanker
tanned [tænd] *adj* güneşte yanmış
tantrum ['tæntrəm] *n* öfke nöbeti
Tanzania [,tænzə'nɪə] *n* Tanzanya
Tanzanian [,tænzə'nɪən] *adj* Tanzanya ▷ *n* Tanzanyalı
tap [tæp] *n* hafif vuruş
tap-dancing ['tæp,dɑ:nsɪŋ] *n* step dansı
tape [teɪp] *n* şerit ▷ *v* kaydetmek; **tape measure** *n* şerit metre; **tape recorder** *n* ses kayıt cihazı
target ['tɑ:gɪt] *n* hedef
tariff ['tærɪf] *n* gümrük tarifesi
tarmac ['tɑ:mæk] *n* asfalt
tarpaulin [tɑ:'pɔ:lɪn] *n* tente
tarragon ['tærəgən] *n* tarhun
tart [tɑ:t] *n* turta
tartan ['tɑ:tᵊn] *adj* ekose
task [tɑ:sk] *n* görev
Tasmania [tæz'meɪnɪə] *n* Tasmanya
taste [teɪst] *n* tat ▷ *v* tatmak
tasteful ['teɪstfʊl] *adj* lezzetli
tasteless ['teɪstlɪs] *adj* tatsız

tuzsuz
tasty ['teɪstɪ] *adj* lezzetli
tattoo [tæ'tu:] *n* dövme
Taurus ['tɔ:rəs] *n* Boğa burcu
tax [tæks] *n* vergi; **income tax** *n* gelir vergisi; **road tax** *n* yol vergisi; **tax payer** *n* vergi yükümlüsü; **tax return** *n* vergi iadesi
taxi ['tæksɪ] *n* taksi; **taxi driver** *n* taksi sürücüsü; **taxi rank** *n* taksi sırası; **How much is the taxi fare into town?** Kente taksi ne kadar?; **I left my bags in the taxi** Bagajımı takside bıraktım; **I need a taxi** Bana bir taksi gerek; **Where can I get a taxi?** Nereden taksi bulabilirim?; **Where is the taxi stand?** Taksi durağı nerede?
TB [ti: bi:] *n* tüberküloz
tea [ti:] *n* çay; **herbal tea** *n* bitki çayı; **tea bag** *n* torba çay; **tea towel** *n* mutfak havlusu; **A tea, please** Bir çay lütfen; **Could we have another cup of tea, please?** Bir çay daha alabilir miyiz?
teach [ti:tʃ] *v* öğretmek
teacher ['ti:tʃə] *n* öğretmen; **supply teacher** *n* yedek öğretmen
teaching ['ti:tʃɪŋ] *n* öğretme
teacup ['ti:ˌkʌp] *n* çay fincanı
team [ti:m] *n* ekip
teapot ['ti:ˌpɒt] *n* çaydanlık
tear[1] [tɪə] *n (from eye)* gözyaşı
tear[2] [tɛə] *n (split)* yırtık ▷ *v* yırtmak; **tear up** *v* yırtmak
teargas ['tɪəˌgæs] *n* gözyaşı bombası
tease [ti:z] *v* kızdırmak
teaspoon ['ti:ˌspu:n] *n* çay kaşığı
teatime ['ti:ˌtaɪm] *n* çay saati
technical ['tɛknɪkᵊl] *adj* teknik
technician [tɛk'nɪʃən] *n* teknisyen
technique [tɛk'ni:k] *n* teknik
techno ['tɛknəʊ] *n* tekno
technological [tɛk'nɒlədʒɪkᵊl] *adj* teknolojik
technology [tɛk'nɒlədʒɪ] *n* teknoloji
tee [ti:] *n* golf sopası
teenager ['ti:nˌeɪdʒə] *n* ergen
teens [ti:nz] *npl* ergenler
tee-shirt ['ti:ˌʃɜ:t] *n* tişört
teethe [ti:ð] *v* diş çıkarmak
teetotal [ti:'təʊtᵊl] *adj* Yeşilaycı
telecommunications [ˌtɛlɪkəˌmju:nɪ'keɪʃənz] *npl* telekomünikasyon
telegram ['tɛlɪˌgræm] *n* telgraf; **Can I send a telegram from here?** Buradan telgraf çekebilir miyim?
telephone ['tɛlɪˌfəʊn] *n* telefon; **telephone directory** *n* telefon rehberi; **How much is it to telephone...?**... a telefon ne kadar?; **I need to make an urgent telephone call** Acil bir telefon görüşmesi yapmam gerek; **What's the telephone number?** Telefon numarası nedir?
telesales ['tɛlɪˌseɪlz] *npl* telefonla satış
telescope ['tɛlɪˌskəʊp] *n* teleskop
television ['tɛlɪˌvɪʒən] *n* televizyon; **cable television** *n* kablolu yayın; **colour television** *n* renkli televizyon; **digital television** *n* dijital televizyon;

Where is the television? Televizyon nerede?
tell [tɛl] *v* anlatmak
teller ['tɛlə] *n* anlatıcı
tell off [tɛl ɒf] *v* azarlamak
telly ['tɛlɪ] *n* televizyon
temp [tɛmp] *n* geçici görevli
temper ['tɛmpə] *n* ruh hali
temperature ['tɛmprɪtʃə] *n* sıcaklık
temple ['tɛmpᵊl] *n* tapınak; **Is the temple open to the public?** Tapınak halka açık mı?; **When is the temple open?** Tapınak ne zaman açık?
temporary ['tɛmpərərɪ; 'tɛmprərɪ] *adj* geçici
tempt [tɛmpt] *v* kışkırtmak
temptation [tɛmp'teɪʃən] *n* ayartma
tempting ['tɛmptɪŋ] *adj* baştan çıkarıcı
ten [tɛn] *number* on; **It's ten o'clock** Saat on
tenant ['tɛnənt] *n* kiracı
tend [tɛnd] *v* eğilim göstermek
tendency ['tɛndənsɪ] *n* eğilim
tender ['tɛndə] *adj* yumuşak
tendon ['tɛndən] *n* kiriş *(anatomi)*
tennis ['tɛnɪs] *n* tenis; **table tennis** *n* masa tenisi; **tennis player** *n* tenis oyuncusu; **tennis racket** *n* tenis raketi; **How much is it to hire a tennis court?** Tenis kortu kiralamak kaça?; **Where can I play tennis?** Nerede tenis oynayabilirim?
tenor ['tɛnə] *n* tenör
tense [tɛns] *adj* gergin *(huzursuz)* ▹ *n* zaman *(gramer)*
tension ['tɛnʃən] *n* gerginlik
tent [tɛnt] *n* çadır; **tent peg** *n* çadır kazığı; **tent pole** *n* çadır direği; **We'd like a site for a tent** Bir çadır yeri istiyoruz
tenth [tɛnθ] *adj* onuncu ▹ *n* onuncu
term [tɜːm] *n (description)* terim, *(division of year)* dönem *(akademik dönem)*
terminal ['tɜːmɪnᵊl] *adj* ölümcül ▹ *n* terminal
terminally ['tɜːmɪnᵊlɪ] *adv* ölümcül
terrace ['tɛrəs] *n* teras; **Can I eat on the terrace?** Terasta yiyebilir miyim?
terraced ['tɛrəst] *adj* sıra evler
terrible ['tɛrəbᵊl] *adj* korkunç
terribly ['tɛrəblɪ] *adv* aşırı derecede
terrier ['tɛrɪə] *n* teriyer
terrific [tə'rɪfɪk] *adj* müthiş
terrified ['tɛrɪˌfaɪd] *adj* aşırı derecede korkmuş
terrify ['tɛrɪˌfaɪ] *v* dehşete düşürmek
territory ['tɛrɪtərɪ; -trɪ] *n* bölge *(arazi)*
terrorism ['tɛrəˌrɪzəm] *n* terörizm
terrorist ['tɛrərɪst] *n* terörist; **terrorist attack** *n* terörist saldırı
test [tɛst] *n* test ▹ *v* denemek; **driving test** *n* direksiyon sınavı; **smear test** *n* Pap smear testi; **test tube** *n* deney tüpü
testicle ['tɛstɪkᵊl] *n* haya *(anatomi)*
tetanus ['tɛtənəs] *n* tetanoz; **I need a tetanus shot** Tetanoz

aşısı yaptırmam gerek
text [tɛkst] *n* metin ▹ *v* mesaj atmak; **text message** *n* mesaj
textbook ['tɛkst,bʊk] *n* ders kitabı
textile ['tɛkstaɪl] *n* tekstil
Thai [taɪ] *adj* Thai ▹ *n (language)* Taylandca *(dil)*, *(person)* Taylandlı *(kişi)*
Thailand ['taɪ,lænd] *n* Tayland
than [ðæn; ðən] *conj* den, dan; **It's more than on the meter** Taksimetrenin gösterdiğinden daha fazla
thank [θæŋk] *v* teşekkür etmek
thanks [θæŋks] *excl* teşekkürler!
that [ðæt; ðət] *adj* şu, bu ▹ *conj* ki ▹ *pron* şu, bu, şunu; **Does that contain alcohol?** Bunda alkol var mı?
thatched [θætʃt] *adj* saz ve saman çatılı
thaw [θɔː] *v* eritmek
the [ðə] *def art* bu, şu, o
theatre ['θɪətə] *n* tiyatro; **operating theatre** *n* ameliyat odası; **What's on at the theatre?** Tiyatroda ne var?
theft [θɛft] *n* hırsızlık; **identity theft** *n* kimlik hırsızlığı
their [ðɛə] *pron* onların
theirs [ðɛəz] *pron* onlarınki
them [ðɛm; ðəm] *pron* onları
theme [θiːm] *n* konu; **theme park** *n* konulu eğlence parkı
themselves [ðəm'sɛlvz] *pron* kendileri
then [ðɛn] *adv* öyleyse ▹ *conj* ondan sonra
theology [θɪ'ɒlədʒɪ] *n* din bilimi
theory ['θɪərɪ] *n* kuram
therapy ['θɛrəpɪ] *n* terapi
there [ðɛə] *adv* orada; **It's over there** Orada
therefore ['ðɛə,fɔː] *adv* bu sebeple
thermometer [θə'mɒmɪtə] *n* termometre
Thermos® ['θɜːməs] *n* termos
thermostat ['θɜːmə,stæt] *n* termostat
these [ðiːz] *adj* bunların ▹ *pron* bunlar
they [ðeɪ] *pron* onlar
thick [θɪk] *adj* kalın
thickness ['θɪknɪs] *n* kalınlık
thief [θiːf] *n* hırsız
thigh [θaɪ] *n* but
thin [θɪn] *adj* ince
thing [θɪŋ] *n* şey
think [θɪŋk] *v* düşünmek
third [θɜːd] *adj* üçüncü ▹ *n* üçüncü; **third-party insurance** *n* üçüncü kişi sorumluluk sigortası; **Third World** *n* Üçüncü Dünya
thirdly [θɜːdlɪ] *adv* üçüncü olarak
thirst [θɜːst] *n* susuzluk
thirsty ['θɜːstɪ] *adj* susuz
thirteen ['θɜː'tiːn] *number* onüç
thirteenth ['θɜː'tiːnθ] *adj* onüçüncü
thirty ['θɜːtɪ] *number* otuz
this [ðɪs] *adj* bu ▹ *pron* bu; **I'll have this** Bunu alayım; **This is your room** Odanız burası; **What is in this?** Bunun içinde ne var?
thistle ['θɪsᵊl] *n* deve dikeni
thorn [θɔːn] *n* diken
thorough ['θʌrə] *adj* baştanbaşa
thoroughly ['θʌrəlɪ] *adv* derinlemesine
those [ðəʊz] *adj* şunlar ▹ *pron*

şunlar
though [ðəʊ] *adv* gerçi ▷ *conj* her ne kadar
thought [θɔːt] *n* düşünce
thoughtful ['θɔːtfʊl] *adj* düşünceli
thoughtless ['θɔːtlɪs] *adj* düşüncesiz
thousand ['θaʊzənd] *number* bin *(sayı)*
thousandth ['θaʊzənθ] *adj* bininci ▷ *n* bininci
thread [θrɛd] *n* iplik
threat [θrɛt] *n* tehdit
threaten ['θrɛtᵊn] *v* tehdit etmek
threatening ['θrɛtᵊnɪŋ] *adj* tehdit edici
three [θriː] *number* üç; **It's three o'clock** Saat üç
three-dimensional [ˌθriːdɪ'mɛnʃənᵊl] *adj* üç boyutlu
thrifty ['θrɪftɪ] *adj* tutumlu
thrill [θrɪl] *n* heyecan
thrilled [θrɪld] *adj* çok sevinmiş
thriller ['θrɪlə] *n* polisiye
thrilling ['θrɪlɪŋ] *adj* heyecan verici
throat [θrəʊt] *n* boğaz
throb [θrɒb] *v* zonklamak
throne [θrəʊn] *n* taht
through [θruː] *prep* içinden
throughout [θruː'aʊt] *prep* baştan başa
throw [θrəʊ] *v* atmak
throw away [θrəʊ ə'weɪ] *v* atmak
throw out [θrəʊ aʊt] *v* atmak
throw up [θrəʊ ʌp] *v* kusmak
thrush [θrʌʃ] *n* ardıç kuşu
thug [θʌg] *n* eşkiya
thumb [θʌm] *n* baş parmak
thumb tack ['θʌmˌtæk] *n* raptiye
thump [θʌmp] *v* vurmak
thunder ['θʌndə] *n* gök gürültüsü
thunderstorm ['θʌndəˌstɔːm] *n* gök gürültülü fırtına
thundery ['θʌndərɪ] *adj* gök gürültülü
Thursday ['θɜːzdɪ] *n* Perşembe; **on Thursday** Perşembe günü
thyme [taɪm] *n* kekik
Tibet [tɪ'bɛt] *n* Tibet
Tibetan [tɪ'bɛtᵊn] *adj* Tibet ▷ *n (language)* Tibetçe *(dil)*, *(person)* Tibetli *(kişi)*
tick [tɪk] *n* im ▷ *v* tıkırdamak
ticket ['tɪkɪt] *n* bilet; **bus ticket** *n* otobüs bileti; **one-way ticket** *n* tek gidiş bileti; **parking ticket** *n* otopark bileti; **return ticket** *n* gidiş-dönüş bilet; **season ticket** *n* abonman kartı; **single ticket** *n* tek yön bilet; **stand-by ticket** *n* beklemede bilet; **ticket barrier** *n* bilet turnikesi; **ticket collector** *n* biletçi; **ticket inspector** *n* bilet kontrolörü; **ticket machine** *n* bilet otomatı; **ticket office** *n* bilet gişesi; **a child's ticket** Bir çocuk bileti; **Can I buy the tickets here?** Biletleri buradan alabilir miyim?; **Can you book the tickets for us?** Biletleri siz ayırtır mısınız lütfen?; **Do I need to buy a car-parking ticket?** Bilet almam gerekiyor mu?; **Do you have multi-journey tickets?** Birkaç seyahati içeren bilet satıyor musunuz?; **How much are the tickets?** Biletler ne kadar?; **How much is a return ticket?** Gidiş dönüş bilet ne kadar?; **I want to upgrade my ticket** Biletimi birinci sınıfa

çevirmek istiyorum; **I'd like two tickets for next Friday** Cuma günü için iki bilet almak istiyorum; **I'd like two tickets, please** İki bilet, lütfen; **I've lost my ticket** Biletimi kaybettim; **two return tickets to...** ... a gidiş dönüş iki bilet; **The ticket machine isn't working** Bilet makinası çalışmıyor; **Two tickets for tonight, please** Bu akşam için iki bilet lütfen; **Where can I buy tickets for the concert?** Konser biletlerini nereden alabilirim?; **Where can I get tickets?** Nereden bilet alabilirim?; **Where is the ticket machine?** Bilet makinası nerede?

tickle ['tɪkᵊl] *v* gıdıklamak

ticklish ['tɪklɪʃ] *adj* kolay gıdıklanan

tick off [tɪk ɒf] *v* payalamak

tide [taɪd] *n* gelgit

tidy ['taɪdɪ] *adj* derli toplu *(tertipli)* ▷ *v* toplamak *(ortalığı)*

tidy up ['taɪdɪ ʌp] *v* derleyip toplamak

tie [taɪ] *n* kravat ▷ *v* bağlamak; **bow tie** *n* papyon kravat

tie up [taɪ ʌp] *v* birini bağlamak

tiger ['taɪgə] *n* kaplan

tight [taɪt] *adj* sıkı

tighten ['taɪtᵊn] *v* sıkılamak

tights [taɪts] *npl* külotlu çorap

tile [taɪl] *n* fayans

tiled ['taɪld] *adj* fayans döşeli

till [tɪl] *conj* ...'e kadar *(zaman)* ▷ *prep* ...e kadar *(yer)* ▷ *n* yazar kasa

timber ['tɪmbə] *n* kereste

time [taɪm] *n* zaman; **closing time** *n* kapanış saati; **dinner time** *n* yemek zamanı; **on time** *adj* zamanında; **spare time** *n* boş zaman; **time off** *n* izin *(işten alınan)*; **time zone** *n* zaman dilimi; **By what time?** En geç ne zaman?; **Is it time to go?** Gitme zamanı geldi mi?; **We've been waiting for a very long time** Çok uzun zamandır bekliyoruz; **What time do we get to...?** ... a ne zaman varırız?; **What time does it leave?** Ne zaman kalkıyor?; **What time does the bus arrive?** Otobüs ne zaman geliyor?; **What time does the bus leave?** Otobüs ne zaman kalkacak?; **What time is the train to...?** ... treni ne zaman?

time bomb ['taɪm,bɒm] *n* saatli bomba

timer ['taɪmə] *n* saat *(fırın vb)*

timeshare ['taɪm,ʃɛə] *n* devre mülk

timetable ['taɪm,teɪbᵊl] *n* program

tin [tɪn] *n* teneke; **tin-opener** *n* kutu açacağı

tinfoil ['tɪn,fɔɪl] *n* kalay yaldızı

tinned [tɪnd] *adj* kutulanmış konserve

tinsel ['tɪnsəl] *n* gelin teli

tinted ['tɪntɪd] *adj* boyalı

tiny ['taɪnɪ] *adj* ufak

tip [tɪp] *n (end of object)* uç *(kalem/ dil)*, *(reward)* bahşiş, *(suggestion)* öğüt ▷ *v (incline)* devirmek *(dökmek)*, *(reward)* bahşiş vermek; **How much should I give as a tip?** Ne kadar bahşiş vermem gerek?; **Is it usual to give a tip?** Bahşiş vermek adet midir?

tipsy ['tɪpsɪ] *adj* çakırkeyif
tiptoe ['tɪp,təʊ] *n* parmaklarının ucunda yürüme
tired ['taɪəd] *adj* yorgun; **I'm tired** Yorgunum
tiring ['taɪəɪŋ] *adj* yorucu
tissue ['tɪsjuː; 'tɪʃuː] *n (anatomy)* kağıt mendil, *(paper)* kağıt mendil
title ['taɪtᵊl] *n* başlık *(kitap, albüm vb)*
to [tuː; tʊ; tə] *prep* oraya, orada
toad [təʊd] *n* kara kurbağa
toadstool ['təʊd,stuːl] *n* mantar *(botanik)*
toast [təʊst] *n (culin)* tost, *(tribute)* kadeh kaldırmak
toaster ['təʊstə] *n* ekmek kızartma makinesi
tobacco [tə'bækəʊ] *n* tütün
tobacconist's [tə'bækənɪsts] *n* tütüncü
tobogganing [tə'bɒgənɪŋ] *n* kızak kayma
today [tə'deɪ] *adv* bugün; **What day is it today?** Bugün günlerden ne?; **What is today's date?** Bugünün tarihi nedir?
toddler ['tɒdlə] *n* yeni yürümeye başlayan çocuk
toe [təʊ] *n* ayak parmağı
toffee ['tɒfɪ] *n* karamela
together [tə'gɛðə] *adv* birlikte; **All together, please** Hepsini birlikte yazın lütfen
Togo ['təʊgəʊ] *n* Togo
toilet ['tɔɪlɪt] *n* tuvalet; **toilet bag** *n* tuvalet çantası; **toilet paper** *n* tuvalet kağıdı; **toilet roll** *n* tuvalet kağıdı; **Are there any toilets for the disabled?** Özürlüler için tuvaletiniz var mı?; **Can I use the toilet?** Tuvaleti kullanabilir miyim?; **Is there a toilet on board?** Otobüste tuvalet var mı?; **The toilet won't flush** Tuvaletin sifonu çalışmıyor; **There is no toilet paper** Tuvalet kağıdı yok; **Where are the toilets?** Tuvaletler nerede?
toiletries ['tɔɪlɪtriːs] *npl* makyaj malzemeleri
token ['təʊkən] *n* nişan *(belirti)*
tolerant ['tɒlərənt] *adj* hoşgörülü
toll [təʊl] *n* çan sesi
tomato, tomatoes [tə'mɑːtəʊ, tə'mɑːtəʊz] *n* domates; **tomato sauce** *n* domates sosu
tomb [tuːm] *n* türbe
tomboy ['tɒm,bɔɪ] *n* erkek Fatma
tomorrow [tə'mɒrəʊ] *adv* yarın; **Is it open tomorrow?** Yarın açık mı?; **tomorrow morning** yarın sabah
ton [tʌn] *n* ton *(ağırlık)*
tone [təʊn] *n* **dialling tone** *n* telefon sinyali; **engaged tone** *n* meşgul sinyali
Tonga ['tɒŋgə] *n* Tonga
tongue [tʌŋ] *n* dil *(anatomi)*; **mother tongue** *n* anadil
tonic ['tɒnɪk] *n* tonik
tonight [tə'naɪt] *adv* bu gece; **What's on tonight at the cinema?** Bu gece sinemada ne var?
tonsillitis [,tɒnsɪ'laɪtɪs] *n* bademcik iltihabı
tonsils ['tɒnsəlz] *npl* bademcikler
too [tuː] *adv* -de, -da *(kıyaslama)*, de, da *(kıyaslama)*

tool [tuːl] *n* araç *(mekanik)*
tooth, teeth ['tuːθ, tiːθ] *n* diş; **wisdom tooth** *n* yirmi yaş dişi; **I've broken a tooth** Dişim kırıldı; **This tooth hurts** Bu dişim ağrıyor
toothache ['tuːθˌeɪk] *n* diş ağrısı
toothbrush ['tuːθˌbrʌʃ] *n* diş fırçası
toothpaste ['tuːθˌpeɪst] *n* diş macunu
toothpick ['tuːθˌpɪk] *n* kürdan
top [tɒp] *adj* tepede ▷ *n* tepe
topic ['tɒpɪk] *n* tema
topical ['tɒpɪkᵊl] *adj* güncel *(haber vb)*
top-secret ['tɒp'siːkrɪt] *adj* çok gizli
top up [tɒp ʌp] *v* doldurmak
torch [tɔːtʃ] *n* el feneri
tornado [tɔː'neɪdəʊ] *n* kasırga
tortoise ['tɔːtəs] *n* kaplumbağa
torture ['tɔːtʃə] *n* işkence ▷ *v* işkence etmek
toss [tɒs] *v* atmak
total ['təʊtᵊl] *adj* tam *(bütün)* ▷ *n* toplam
totally ['təʊtᵊlɪ] *adv* tamamen
touch [tʌtʃ] *v* dokunmak
touchdown ['tʌtʃˌdaʊn] *n* gol *(Amerikan futbolunda)*
touched [tʌtʃt] *adj* duygulanmış
touching ['tʌtʃɪŋ] *adj* dokunaklı *(konuşma)*
touchline ['tʌtʃˌlaɪn] *n* taç çizgisi
touchpad ['tʌtʃˌpæd] *n* akıllı dokunuş
touchy ['tʌtʃɪ] *adj* hassas
tough [tʌf] *adj* sağlam
toupee ['tuːpeɪ] *n* yarım peruk
tour [tʊə] *n* tur *(gezi)* ▷ *v* tura çıkmak; **guided tour** *n* rehberli tur; **package tour** *n* paket tur; **tour guide** *n* tur rehberi; **tour operator** *n* tur operatörü; **Are there any sightseeing tours of the town?** Kent turunuz var mı?; **How long does the tour take?** Tur ne kadar sürüyor?; **I enjoyed the tour** Turdan çok zevk aldım; **Is there a guided tour in English?** İngilizce rehberli turunuz var mı?; **What time does the guided tour begin?** Rehberli tur kaçta başlıyor?; **When is the bus tour of the town?** Tur otobüsü ne zaman kalkıyor?
tourism ['tʊərɪzəm] *n* turizm
tourist ['tʊərɪst] *n* turist; **tourist office** *n* turizm bürosu; **I'm here as a tourist** Buraya turist olarak geldim
tournament ['tʊənəmənt; 'tɔː-; 'tɜː-] *n* turnuva
towards [tə'wɔːdz; tɔːdz] *prep* ...e doğru *(yön)*
tow away [təʊ ə'weɪ] *v* arabayı çekmek
towel ['taʊəl] *n* havlu; **bath towel** *n* banyo havlusu; **dish towel** *n* kurulama havlusu; **sanitary towel** *n* ped; **tea towel** *n* mutfak havlusu; **Could you lend me a towel?** Bana bir havlu verebilir misiniz?; **Please bring me more towels** Birkaç tane daha havlu getirir misiniz lütfen?
tower ['taʊə] *n* kule
town [taʊn] *n* şehir; **town centre** *n* şehir merkezi; **town hall** *n* belediye binası; **town planning** *n*

şehir planlama
toxic ['tɒksɪk] *adj* zehirli
toy [tɔɪ] *n* oyuncak
trace [treɪs] *n* belirti
tracing paper ['treɪsɪŋ 'peɪpə] *n* **tracing paper** *n* aydınger kağıdı
track [træk] *n* engebeli yol
track down [træk daʊn] *v* izini sürmek
tracksuit ['træk,su:t; -,sju:t] *n* antreman giysisi
tractor ['træktə] *n* traktör
trade [treɪd] *n* ticaret; **trade union** *n* sendika; **trade unionist** *n* sendikacı
trademark ['treɪd,mɑ:k] *n* marka *(ticaret)*
tradition [trə'dɪʃən] *n* gelenek
traditional [trə'dɪʃənᵊl] *adj* geleneksel *(töre)*
traffic ['træfɪk] *n* trafik; **traffic jam** *n* trafik sıkışıklığı; **traffic lights** *npl* trafik ışıkları; **traffic warden** *n* trafik memuru; **Is the traffic heavy on the motorway?** Otoyolda trafik yoğun mu?
tragedy ['trædʒɪdɪ] *n* trajedi
tragic ['trædʒɪk] *adj* trajik
trailer ['treɪlə] *n* römork
train [treɪn] *n* tren ▷ *v* eğitmek; **Does the train stop at...?** Bu tren... da duruyor mu?; **How frequent are the trains to...?** ... treni hangi sıklıkta geliyor?; **I've missed my train** Trenimi kaçırdım; **Is the train wheelchair-accessible?** Trende tekerlekli sandalye girişi var mı?; **Is this the train for...?** ... treni bu mu?; **The next available train, please** Bir sonraki tren lütfen; **What time does the train arrive in...?** Tren... a kaçta varıyor?; **What time does the train leave?** Tren kaçta kalkacak?; **What times are the trains to...?** ... tren saatleri nedir?; **When is the first train to...?** ... a ilk tren kaçta?; **When is the last train to...?** ... a son tren kaçta?; **When is the next train to...?** ... a bir sonraki tren kaçta?; **When is the train due?** Tren kaçta geliyor?; **Where can I get a train to...?** ... trenine nereden binebilirim?; **Which platform does the train leave from?** Tren hangi platformdan kalkıyor?
trained [treɪnd] *adj* eğitilmiş
trainee [treɪ'ni:] *n* kursiyer
trainer ['treɪnə] *n* eğitmen *(spor vb)*
trainers ['treɪnəz] *npl* lastik spor ayakkabısı
training ['treɪnɪŋ] *n* eğitim *(kurs)*; **training course** *n* eğitim kursu
tram [træm] *n* tramvay
tramp [træmp] *n (beggar)* serseri, *(long walk)* taban tepmek
trampoline ['træmpəlɪn; -,li:n] *n* tramplen
tranquillizer ['træŋkwɪ,laɪzə] *n* sakinleştirici
transaction [træn'zækʃən] *n* işlem
transcript ['trænskrɪpt] *n* belge *(döküm)*
transfer *n* ['trænsfɜ:] transfer ▷ *v* [træns'fɜ:] transfer; **How long will it take to transfer?** Transfer

ne kadar sürer?; **I would like to transfer some money from my account** Hesabımdan para transferi yapmak istiyorum; **Is there a transfer charge?** Transfer ücreti var mı?
transform [træns'fɔːm] *v* dönüştürmek
transfusion [træns'fjuːʒən] *n* kan aktarımı; **blood transfusion** *n* kan nakli
transistor [træn'zɪstə] *n* transistör
transit ['trænsɪt; 'trænz-] *n* transit; **transit lounge** *n* transit yolcu salonu
transition [træn'zɪʃən] *n* geçiş
translate [træns'leɪt; trænz-] *v* tercüme etmek
translation [træns'leɪʃən; trænz-] *n* tercüme
translator [træns'leɪtə; trænz-] *n* tercüman
transparent [træns'pærənt; -'pɛər-] *adj* saydam
transplant ['træns,plɑːnt] *n* aktarım *(doku/organ)*
transport *n* ['træns,pɔːt] taşıma ▹ *v* [træns'pɔːt] taşımak; **public transport** *n* toplu taşıma
transvestite [trænz'vɛstaɪt] *n* transvestit
trap [træp] *n* tuzak
trash [træʃ] *n* çöp
traumatic ['trɔːmə,tɪk] *adj* travmatik
travel ['trævᵊl] *n* seyahat ▹ *v* seyahat etmek; **travel agency** *n* seyahat acentası; **travel agent's** *n* seyahat acentası; **travel sickness** *n* araba tutması; **I don't have travel insurance** Seyahat sigortam yok; **I get travel-sick** Seyahat bulantım var; **I'm travelling alone** Tek başıma seyahat ediyorum
traveller ['trævələ; 'trævlə] *n* yolcular; **traveller's cheque** *n* seyahat çeki
travelling ['trævᵊlɪŋ] *n* seyahat etme
tray [treɪ] *n* tepsi
treacle ['triːkᵊl] *n* melas
tread [trɛd] *v* adımlamak
treasure ['trɛʒə] *n* define
treasurer ['trɛʒərə] *n* veznedar
treat [triːt] *n* birine ufak bir armağan alma ▹ *v* davranmak *(muamele)*
treatment ['triːtmənt] *n* muamele
treaty ['triːtɪ] *n* anlaşma *(tarih)*
treble ['trɛbᵊl] *v* üç katı
tree [triː] *n* ağaç
trek [trɛk] *n* zahmetli yürüyüş ▹ *v* zahmetli bir yürüyüşe çıkmak
trekking ['trɛkɪŋ] *n* **I'd like to go pony trekking** Ata binmek istiyorum
tremble ['trɛmbᵊl] *v* titremek
tremendous [trɪ'mɛndəs] *adj* çok büyük
trench [trɛntʃ] *n* siper
trend [trɛnd] *n* moda akımı
trendy ['trɛndɪ] *adj* modaya uygun
trial ['traɪəl] *n* duruşma; **trial period** *n* deneme süresi
triangle ['traɪ,æŋgᵊl] *n* üçgen
tribe [traɪb] *n* kabile
tribunal [traɪ'bjuːnᵊl; trɪ-] *n*

mahkeme
trick [trɪk] *n* dolap *(hile)* ▷ *v* kandırmak
tricky ['trɪkɪ] *adj* dolambaçlı
tricycle ['traɪsɪkᵊl] *n* üç tekerlekli bisiklet
trifle ['traɪfᵊl] *n* önemsiz şey
trim [trɪm] *v* kesip düzeltmek
Trinidad and Tobago ['trɪnɪˌdæd ænd təˈbeɪgəʊ] *n* Trinidad ve Tobago
trip [trɪp] *n* yolculuk *(kısa)*; **business trip** *n* iş seyahati; **round trip** *n* gidiş dönüş yolculuk; **trip (up)** *v* tökezlemek; **Have a good trip!** İyi yolculuklar!
triple ['trɪpᵊl] *adj* üç katı
triplets ['trɪplɪts] *npl* üçüzler
triumph ['traɪəmf] *n* zafer ▷ *v* yenmek
trivial ['trɪvɪəl] *adj* önemsiz
trolley ['trɒlɪ] *n* servis masası; **luggage trolley** *n* bagaj trolleyi; **shopping trolley** *n* market arabası
trombone [trɒmˈbəʊn] *n* trombon
troops ['tru:ps] *npl* birlikler *(askeri)*
trophy ['trəʊfɪ] *n* kupa *(spor)*
tropical ['trɒpɪkᵊl] *adj* tropik
trot [trɒt] *v* tırıs gitmek
trouble ['trʌbᵊl] *n* güçlük
troublemaker ['trʌbᵊlˌmeɪkə] *n* güçlük çıkaran
trough [trɒf] *n* yalak
trousers ['traʊzəz] *npl* pantolon
trout [traʊt] *n* alabalık
trowel ['traʊəl] *n* mala
truant ['tru:ənt] *n* **play truant** *v* okuldan kaçmak
truce [tru:s] *n* ateşkes
truck [trʌk] *n* kamyon; **breakdown truck** *n* çekici; **truck driver** *n* kamyon şoförü
true [tru:] *adj* gerçek *(söz)*
truly ['tru:lɪ] *adv* gerçekten
trumpet ['trʌmpɪt] *n* borazan
trunk [trʌŋk] *n* ağaç gövdesi; **swimming trunks** *npl* yüzücü şortu
trunks [trʌŋks] *npl* yüzücü şortu
trust [trʌst] *n* güven ▷ *v* güvenmek
trusting ['trʌstɪŋ] *adj* güvenen
truth [tru:θ] *n* gerçek *(doğruluk)*
truthful ['tru:θfʊl] *adj* dürüst
try [traɪ] *n* çaba ▷ *v* çabalamak
try on [traɪ ɒn] *v* denemek *(giysi)*
try out [traɪ aʊt] *v* denemek
T-shirt ['ti:ˌʃɜ:t] *n* tişört
tsunami [tsʊˈnæmɪ] *n* tsunami
tube [tju:b] *n* tüp; **inner tube** *n* iç lastik; **test tube** *n* deney tüpü; **tube station** *n* metro istasyonu
tuberculosis [tjʊˌbɜ:kjʊˈləʊsɪs] *n* tüberküloz
Tuesday ['tju:zdɪ] *n* Salı; **Shrove Tuesday** *n* büyük perhizin arife günü; **on Tuesday** Salı günü
tug-of-war ['tʌgɒv'wɔ:] *n* halat çekme oyunu
tuition [tju:ˈɪʃən] *n* öğretim; **tuition fees** *npl* öğretim ücreti
tulip ['tju:lɪp] *n* lale
tummy ['tʌmɪ] *n* karın
tumour ['tju:mə] *n* ur
tuna ['tju:nə] *n* ton balığı
tune [tju:n] *n* melodi
Tunisia [tju:ˈnɪzɪə; -ˈnɪsɪə] *n* Tunus
Tunisian [tju:ˈnɪzɪən; -ˈnɪsɪən]

adj Tunus ▷ *n* Tunuslu
tunnel ['tʌnᵊl] *n* tünel
turbulence ['tɜːbjʊləns] *n* çalkantı
Turk [tɜːk] *n* Türk
turkey ['tɜːkɪ] *n* hindi
Turkey ['tɜːkɪ] *n* Türkiye
Turkish ['tɜːkɪʃ] *adj* Türk ▷ *n* Türkçe
turn [tɜːn] *n* dönme ▷ *v* dönmek
turn around [tɜːn ə'raʊnd] *v* arkaya dönmek
turn back [tɜːn bæk] *v* geri dönmek
turn down [tɜːn daʊn] *v* geri çevirmek
turning ['tɜːnɪŋ] *n* kıvrım
turnip ['tɜːnɪp] *n* şalgam
turn off [tɜːn ɒf] *v* kapatmak
turn on [tɜːn ɒn] *v* açmak
turn out [tɜːn aʊt] *v* ışığı söndürmek
turnover ['tɜːnˌəʊvə] *n* sermaye devri
turn round [tɜːn raʊnd] *v* arkaya dönmek
turnstile ['tɜːnˌstaɪl] *n* turnike
turn up [tɜːn ʌp] *v* boy göstermek
turquoise ['tɜːkwɔɪz; -kwɑːz] *adj* türkuvaz renkli
turtle ['tɜːtᵊl] *n* su kaplumbağası
tutor ['tjuːtə] *n* özel öğretmen
tutorial [tjuː'tɔːrɪəl] *n* ders *(özel)*
tuxedo [tʌk'siːdəʊ] *n* smokin
TV [tiː viː] *n* TV; **plasma TV** *n* plazma TV; **reality TV** *n* biri bizi gözetliyor
tweezers ['twiːzəz] *npl* cımbız
twelfth [twɛlfθ] *adj* onikinci
twelve [twɛlv] *number* oniki
twentieth ['twɛntɪɪθ] *adj* yirminci
twenty ['twɛntɪ] *number* yirmi
twice [twaɪs] *adv* iki kere
twin [twɪn] *n* ikiz; **twin beds** *npl* çift yatak; **twin room** *n* çift yataklı oda; **twin-bedded room** *n* çift yataklı oda
twinned ['twɪnd] *adj* kardeş *(şehir)*
twist [twɪst] *v* bükmek
twit [twɪt] *n* avanak
two [tuː] *num* iki
type [taɪp] *n* tip ▷ *v* yazmak *(daktilo/bilgisayar)*
typewriter ['taɪpˌraɪtə] *n* daktilo
typhoid ['taɪfɔɪd] *n* tifo
typical ['tɪpɪkᵊl] *adj* tipik
typist ['taɪpɪst] *n* daktilograf
tyre ['taɪə] *n* lastik; **spare tyre** *n* stepne; **Can you check the tyres, please?** Lastikleri kontrol eder misiniz lütfen?; **The tyre has burst** Lastik patladı

U

UFO ['ju:fəʊ] *abbr* UFO
Uganda [ju:'gændə] *n* Uganda
Ugandan [ju:'gændən] *adj* Uganda ▹ *n* Ugandalı
ugh [ʊx; ʊh; ʌh] *excl* ığğ
ugly ['ʌglɪ] *adj* çirkin
UK [ju: keɪ] *n* birleşik krallık
Ukraine [ju:'kreɪn] *n* Ukrayna
Ukrainian [ju:'kreɪnɪən] *adj* Ukrayna ▹ *n (language)* Ukraynaca *(dil), (person)* Ukraynalı *(kişi)*
ulcer ['ʌlsə] *n* yara *(ülser)*
Ulster ['ʌlstə] *n* Kuzey İrlanda
ultimate ['ʌltɪmɪt] *adj* son
ultimately ['ʌltɪmɪtlɪ] *adv* eninde sonunda
ultimatum [ˌʌltɪ'meɪtəm] *n* ultimatom
ultrasound ['ʌltrəˌsaʊnd] *n* ultrason
umbrella [ʌm'brɛlə] *n* şemsiye
umpire ['ʌmpaɪə] *n* hakem
UN [ju: ɛn] *abbr* Birleşmiş Milletler
unable [ʌn'eɪbᵊl] *adj* **unable to** *adj* yapamamak
unacceptable [ˌʌnək'sɛptəbᵊl] *adj* kabul edilemez
unanimous [ju:'nænɪməs] *adj* oybirliğiyle
unattended [ˌʌnə'tɛndɪd] *adj* sahipsiz
unavoidable [ˌʌnə'vɔɪdəbᵊl] *adj* kaçınılmaz
unbearable [ʌn'bɛərəbᵊl] *adj* dayanılmaz
unbeatable [ʌn'bi:təbᵊl] *adj* yenilmez
unbelievable [ˌʌnbɪ'li:vəbᵊl] *adj* inanılmaz
unbreakable [ʌn'breɪkəbᵊl] *adj* kırılmaz
uncanny [ʌn'kænɪ] *adj* tekinsiz
uncertain [ʌn'sɜ:tᵊn] *adj* belirsiz
uncertainty [ʌn'sɜ:tᵊntɪ] *n* belirsizlik
unchanged [ʌn'tʃeɪndʒd] *adj* değişmemiş
uncivilized [ʌn'sɪvɪˌlaɪzd] *adj* ilkel
uncle ['ʌŋkᵊl] *n* amca
unclear [ʌn'klɪə] *adj* net değil
uncomfortable [ʌn'kʌmftəbᵊl] *adj* rahatsız
unconditional [ˌʌnkən'dɪʃənᵊl] *adj* koşulsuz
unconscious [ʌn'kɒnʃəs] *adj* bilinçsiz
uncontrollable [ˌʌnkən'trəʊləbᵊl] *adj* kontrol edilemez
unconventional [ˌʌnkən'vɛnʃənᵊl] *adj* göreneklere uymayan
undecided [ˌʌndɪ'saɪdɪd] *adj*

kararsız
undeniable [ˌʌndɪˈnaɪəbᵊl] *adj* inkar edilemez
under [ˈʌndə] *prep* altında
underage [ˌʌndərˈeɪdʒ] *adj* reşit olmayan
underestimate [ˌʌndərɛstɪˈmeɪt] *v* hafife almak
undergo [ˌʌndəˈgəʊ] *v* geçmek *(deneyim/ameliyat)*
undergraduate [ˌʌndəˈgrædjʊɪt] *n* üniversite mezunu
underground [ˈʌndəˌgraʊnd] *adj* yerin altında ▷ *n* yeraltı harekatı
underline [ˌʌndəˈlaɪn] *v* altını çizmek
underneath [ˌʌndəˈniːθ] *adv* altında ▷ *prep* altında
underpaid [ˌʌndəˈpeɪd] *adj* düşük ücretli
underpants [ˈʌndəˌpænts] *npl* şort *(erkek iç çamaşırı)*
underpass [ˈʌndəˌpɑːs] *n* alt geçit
underskirt [ˈʌndəˌskɜːt] *n* jüpon
understand [ˌʌndəˈstænd] *v* anlamak
understandable [ˌʌndəˈstændəbᵊl] *adj* anlaşılır
understanding [ˌʌndəˈstændɪŋ] *adj* anlayış
undertaker [ˈʌndəˌteɪkə] *n* cenaze kaldırıcısı
underwater [ˈʌndəˈwɔːtə] *adv* sualtı
underwear [ˈʌndəˌwɛə] *n* iç çamaşırı
undisputed [ˌʌndɪˈspjuːtɪd] *adj* tartışmasız
undo [ʌnˈduː] *v* açmak *(paket, fermuar vb)*
undoubtedly [ʌnˈdaʊtɪdlɪ] *adv* kuşku götürmez bir şekilde
undress [ʌnˈdrɛs] *v* soyunmak
unemployed [ˌʌnɪmˈplɔɪd] *adj* işsiz
unemployment [ˌʌnɪmˈplɔɪmənt] *n* işsizlik
unexpected [ˌʌnɪkˈspɛktɪd] *adj* umulmadık
unexpectedly [ˌʌnɪkˈspɛktɪdlɪ] *adv* umulmadık bir şekilde
unfair [ʌnˈfɛə] *adj* haksız
unfaithful [ʌnˈfeɪθfʊl] *adj* sadakatsiz
unfamiliar [ˌʌnfəˈmɪljə] *adj* aşina olmayan
unfashionable [ʌnˈfæʃənəbᵊl] *adj* modaya uymayan
unfavourable [ʌnˈfeɪvərəbᵊl; -ˈfeɪvrə-] *adj* elverişsiz
unfit [ʌnˈfɪt] *adj* sağlıksız
unforgettable [ˌʌnfəˈgɛtəbᵊl] *adj* unutulmaz
unfortunately [ʌnˈfɔːtʃənɪtlɪ] *adv* ne yazık ki
unfriendly [ʌnˈfrɛndlɪ] *adj* düşmanca
ungrateful [ʌnˈgreɪtfʊl] *adj* nankör
unhappy [ʌnˈhæpɪ] *adj* mutsuz
unhealthy [ʌnˈhɛlθɪ] *adj* sağlıksız
unhelpful [ʌnˈhɛlpfʊl] *adj* yardımcı olmayan
uni [ˈjuːnɪ] *n* üniversite
unidentified [ˌʌnaɪˈdɛntɪˌfaɪd] *adj* kimliği belirsiz
uniform [ˈjuːnɪˌfɔːm] *n* üniforma; **school uniform** *n* okul üniforması
unimportant [ˌʌnɪmˈpɔːtᵊnt] *adj* önemsiz

uninhabited [ˌʌnɪnˈhæbɪtɪd] *adj* meskun olmayan
unintentional [ˌʌnɪnˈtɛnʃənᵊl] *adj* kasıtsız
union [ˈjuːnjən] *n* birlik; **European Union** *n* Avrupa Birliği; **trade union** *n* sendika
unique [juːˈniːk] *adj* eşsiz
unit [ˈjuːnɪt] *n* ünite
unite [juːˈnaɪt] *v* birleştirmek *(kişileri)*
United Kingdom [juːˈnaɪtɪd ˈkɪŋdəm] *n* Birleşik Krallık *(İngiltere)*
United States [juːˈnaɪtɪd steɪts] *n* Birleşik Devletler *(Amerika)*
universe [ˈjuːnɪˌvɜːs] *n* evren
university [ˌjuːnɪˈvɜːsɪtɪ] *n* üniversite
unknown [ʌnˈnəʊn] *adj* bilinmez
unleaded [ʌnˈlɛdɪd] *n* kurşunsuz; **unleaded petrol** *n* kurşunsuz benzin; **... worth of premium unleaded, please** ...lık kurşunsuz benzin lütfen
unless [ʌnˈlɛs] *conj* olmadıkça
unlike [ʌnˈlaɪk] *prep* farklı olarak
unlikely [ʌnˈlaɪklɪ] *adj* olasılık dışı
unlisted [ʌnˈlɪstɪd] *adj* liste harici
unload [ʌnˈləʊd] *v* boşaltmak *(yük)*
unlock [ʌnˈlɒk] *v* kilidi açmak
unlucky [ʌnˈlʌkɪ] *adj* şanssız
unmarried [ʌnˈmærɪd] *adj* evlenmemiş
unnecessary [ʌnˈnɛsɪsərɪ; -ɪsrɪ] *adj* gereksiz
unofficial [ˌʌnəˈfɪʃəl] *adj* resmi olmayan
unpack [ʌnˈpæk] *v* boşaltmak
unpaid [ʌnˈpeɪd] *adj* ücreti ödenmemiş
unpleasant [ʌnˈplɛzᵊnt] *adj* hoş olmayan
unplug [ʌnˈplʌg] *v* fişten çekmek
unpopular [ʌnˈpɒpjʊlə] *adj* popüler olmayan
unprecedented [ʌnˈprɛsɪˌdɛntɪd] *adj* daha önceden olmamış
unpredictable [ˌʌnprɪˈdɪktəbᵊl] *adj* ne yapacağı belli olmayan
unreal [ʌnˈrɪəl] *adj* gerçek dışı
unrealistic [ˌʌnrɪəˈlɪstɪk] *adj* gerçeklerle bağdaşmayan
unreasonable [ʌnˈriːznəbᵊl] *adj* mantıksız
unreliable [ˌʌnrɪˈlaɪəbᵊl] *adj* güvenilmez
unroll [ʌnˈrəʊl] *v* açmak *(rulo/sargı)*
unsatisfactory [ˌʌnsætɪsˈfæktərɪ; -trɪ] *adj* tatmin edici olmayan
unscrew [ʌnˈskruː] *v* sökmek *(vida)*
unshaven [ʌnˈʃeɪvᵊn] *adj* traşsız
unskilled [ʌnˈskɪld] *adj* niteliksiz
unstable [ʌnˈsteɪbᵊl] *adj* dengesiz
unsteady [ʌnˈstɛdɪ] *adj* sallanan
unsuccessful [ˌʌnsəkˈsɛsfʊl] *adj* başarısız
unsuitable [ʌnˈsuːtəbᵊl; ʌnˈsjuːt-] *adj* uygun olmayan
unsure [ʌnˈʃʊə] *adj* emin olmayan
untidy [ʌnˈtaɪdɪ] *adj* dağınık
untie [ʌnˈtaɪ] *v* çözmek *(bağcık)*
until [ʌnˈtɪl] *conj* kadar *(zaman, olay vb)* ▷ *prep* kadar *(yer)*
unusual [ʌnˈjuːʒʊəl] *adj* alışılmadık

unwell [ʌn'wɛl] *adj* iyi değil
unwind [ʌn'waɪnd] *v* açmak *(sargı)*
unwise [ʌn'waɪz] *adj* akıllıca olmayan
unwrap [ʌn'ræp] *v* açmak *(paket)*
unzip [ʌn'zɪp] *v* fermuarı açmak
up [ʌp] *adv* yukarıya
upbringing ['ʌp,brɪŋɪŋ] *n* yetiştirilme
update *n* ['ʌp,deɪt] güncellemek ▷ *v* [ʌp'deɪt] güncellemek
uphill ['ʌp'hɪl] *adv* yokuş yukarı
upper ['ʌpə] *adj* üst
upright ['ʌp,raɪt] *adv* dik
upset *adj* [ʌp'sɛt] keyfi kaçık ▷ *v* [ʌp'sɛt] keyfini kaçırmak
upside down ['ʌp,saɪd daʊn] *adv* baş aşağı
upstairs ['ʌp'stɛəz] *adv* üst katta
uptight [ʌp'taɪt] *adj* gergin *(sinirleri yay gibi)*
up-to-date [ʌptʊdeɪt] *adj* güncel *(yenilenmiş)*
upwards ['ʌpwədz] *adv* yukarıya doğru
uranium [jʊ'reɪnɪəm] *n* uranyum
urgency ['ɜːdʒənsɪ] *n* ivedilik
urgent ['ɜːdʒənt] *adj* ivedi
urine ['jʊərɪn] *n* idrar
URL [juː ɑː ɛl] *n* URL
Uruguay ['jʊərə,gwaɪ] *n* Uruguay
Uruguayan [,jʊərə'gwaɪən] *adj* Uruguay ▷ *n* Uruguaylı
us [ʌs] *pron* biz; **Please call us if you'll be late** Gecikeceğiniz zaman lütfen bize haber verin
US [juː ɛs] *n* Birleşik Devletler
USA [juː ɛs eɪ] *n* ABD
use *n* [juːs] kullanım ▷ *v* [juːz] kullanmak; **It is for my own personal use** Bu benim kişisel kullanımım için
used [juːzd] *adj* kullanılmış
useful ['juːsfʊl] *adj* yararlı
useless ['juːslɪs] *adj* yararsız
user ['juːzə] *n* kullanıcı; **Internet user** *n* internet kullanıcısı
user-friendly ['juːzə,frɛndlɪ] *adj* kullanıcı dostu
use up [juːz ʌp] *v* harcamak
usual ['juːʒʊəl] *adj* alışılagelmiş
usually ['juːʒʊəlɪ] *adv* genellikle
U-turn ['juː,tɜːn] *n* U-dönüşü
Uzbekistan [,ʌzbɛkɪ'stɑːn] *n* Özbekistan

V

vacancy ['veɪkənsɪ] *n* açık iş
vacant ['veɪkənt] *adj* boş *(daire, ev, sandalye)*
vacate [və'keɪt] *v* tahliye etmek
vaccinate ['væksɪˌneɪt] *v* aşılamak
vaccination [ˌvæksɪ'neɪʃən] *n* aşı *(tıp)*; **I need a vaccination** Aşı yaptırmam gerek
vacuum ['vækjʊəm] *v* vakumlamak; **vacuum cleaner** *n* elektrik süpürgesi
vague [veɪg] *adj* belirsiz
vain [veɪn] *adj* kendini beğenmiş
valid ['vælɪd] *adj* geçerli
valley ['vælɪ] *n* vadi
valuable ['væljʊəbᵊl] *adj* değerli
valuables ['væljʊəbᵊlz] *npl* değerli eşyalar; **I'd like to put my valuables in the safe** Değerli eşyalarımı kasaya koymak istiyorum; **Where can I leave my valuables?** Değerli eşyalarımı nereye bırakabilirim?
value ['vælju:] *n* değer
vampire ['væmpaɪə] *n* vampir
van [væn] *n* üstü kapalı yük aracı; **breakdown van** *n* kurtarma aracı; **removal van** *n* taşınma kamyonu
vandal ['vændᵊl] *n* vandal
vandalism ['vændəˌlɪzəm] *n* vandalizm
vandalize ['vændəˌlaɪz] *v* tahrip etmek
vanilla [və'nɪlə] *n* vanilya
vanish ['vænɪʃ] *v* yok olmak
variable ['vɛərɪəbᵊl] *adj* değişken
varied ['vɛərɪd] *adj* çeşitli
variety [və'raɪɪtɪ] *n* çeşit
various ['vɛərɪəs] *adj* çeşitli
varnish ['vɑ:nɪʃ] *n* cila *(vernik)* ▹ *v* cilalamak; **nail varnish** *n* tırnak cilası
vary ['vɛərɪ] *v* çeşitlilik göstermek
vase [vɑ:z] *n* vazo
VAT [væt] *abbr* KDV; **Is VAT included?** KDV dahil mi?
Vatican ['vætɪkən] *n* Vatikan
vault [vɔ:lt] *n* **pole vault** *n* sırıkla atlama
veal [vi:l] *n* dana eti
vegan ['vi:gən] *n* vegan; **Do you have any vegan dishes?** Vegan yemeğiniz var mı?
vegetable ['vɛdʒtəbᵊl] *n* sebze; **Are the vegetables fresh or frozen?** Sebzeleriniz taze mi, dondurulmuş mu?; **Are the vegetables included?** Sebze de dahil mi?
vegetarian [ˌvɛdʒɪ'tɛərɪən] *adj* vejetaryen ▹ *n* vejetaryen; **Do you**

have any vegetarian dishes? Vejetaryen yemekleriniz var mı?; **I'm vegetarian** Vejetaryenim
vegetation [ˌvɛdʒɪ'teɪʃən] *n* bitki örtüsü
vehicle ['viːɪkᵊl] *n* araç *(otomobil)*
veil [veɪl] *n* peçe
vein [veɪn] *n* damar
Velcro® ['vɛlkrəʊ] *n* cırt bant
velvet ['vɛlvɪt] *n* kadife
vendor ['vɛndɔː] *n* satıcı
Venezuela [ˌvɛnɪ'zweɪlə] *n* Venezuela
Venezuelan [ˌvɛnɪ'zweɪlən] *adj* Venezuela ▷ *n* Venezuelalı
venison ['vɛnɪzᵊn; -sᵊn] *n* geyik eti
venom ['vɛnəm] *n* zehir
ventilation [ˌvɛntɪ'leɪʃən] *n* havalandırma
venue ['vɛnjuː] *n* yer
verb [vɜːb] *n* fiil
verdict ['vɜːdɪkt] *n* jüri kararı
versatile ['vɜːsəˌtaɪl] *adj* çok yönlü
version ['vɜːʃən; -ʒən] *n* versiyon
versus ['vɜːsəs] *prep* karşı
vertical ['vɜːtɪkᵊl] *adj* dikey
vertigo ['vɜːtɪˌgəʊ] *n* yükseklik korkusu
very ['vɛrɪ] *adv* çok; **It's very kind of you to invite us** Bizi davet ettiğiniz için çok teşekkürler
vest [vɛst] *n* atlet
vet [vɛt] *n* veteriner
veteran ['vɛtərən; 'vɛtrən] *adj* emektar ▷ *n* emektar
veto ['viːtəʊ] *n* veto
via ['vaɪə] *prep* yoluyla
vicar ['vɪkə] *n* papaz yardımcısı
vice [vaɪs] *n* kötülük
vice versa ['vaɪsɪ 'vɜːsə] *adv* ya da aksine
vicinity [vɪ'sɪnɪtɪ] *n* çevre
vicious ['vɪʃəs] *adj* kötü
victim ['vɪktɪm] *n* kurban *(kişi)*
victory ['vɪktərɪ] *n* zafer
video ['vɪdɪˌəʊ] *n* video; **video camera** *n* video kamerası
videophone ['vɪdɪəˌfəʊn] *n* video telefon
Vietnam [ˌvjɛt'næm] *n* Vietnam
Vietnamese [ˌvjɛtnə'miːz] *adj* Vietnam ▷ *n (language)* Vietnamca *(dil)*, *(person)* Vietnamlı *(kişi)*
view [vjuː] *n* görüş
viewer ['vjuːə] *n* izleyici
viewpoint ['vjuːˌpɔɪnt] *n* bakış noktası
vile [vaɪl] *adj* kokuşmuş
villa ['vɪlə] *n* villa; **I'd like to rent a villa** Bir villa kiralamak istiyorum
village ['vɪlɪdʒ] *n* köy
villain ['vɪlən] *n* hain *(kötü)*
vinaigrette [ˌvɪneɪ'grɛt] *n* sirkeli salata sosu
vine [vaɪn] *n* asma *(bitki)*
vinegar ['vɪnɪgə] *n* sirke
vineyard ['vɪnjəd] *n* bağ *(üzüm)*
viola [vɪ'əʊlə] *n* viyola
violence ['vaɪələns] *n* şiddet
violent ['vaɪələnt] *adj* şiddet uygulayan
violin [ˌvaɪə'lɪn] *n* keman
violinist [ˌvaɪə'lɪnɪst] *n* kemancı
virgin ['vɜːdʒɪn] *n* bakire
Virgo ['vɜːgəʊ] *n* Başak burcu
virtual ['vɜːtʃʊəl] *adj* sanal; **virtual reality** *n* sanal gerçeklik
virus ['vaɪrəs] *n* virüs
visa ['viːzə] *n* vize; **Here is my visa** Vizem burada; **I have an entry**

visa Giriş vizem var
visibility [ˌvɪzɪˈbɪlɪtɪ] *n* görüş *(göz)*
visible [ˈvɪzɪbᵊl] *adj* görünür
visit [ˈvɪzɪt] *n* ziyaret ▹ *v* ziyaret etmek; **visiting hours** *npl* ziyaret saatleri
visitor [ˈvɪzɪtə] *n* ziyaretçi; **visitor centre** *n* ziyaretçi merkezi
visual [ˈvɪʒʊəl; -zjʊ-] *adj* görsel
visualize [ˈvɪʒʊəˌlaɪz; -zjʊ-] *v* gözünde canlandırmak
vital [ˈvaɪtᵊl] *adj* önemli
vitamin [ˈvɪtəmɪn; ˈvaɪ-] *n* vitamin
vivid [ˈvɪvɪd] *adj* canlı *(parlak)*
vocabulary [vəˈkæbjʊlərɪ] *n* sözcük dağarcığı
vocational [vəʊˈkeɪʃənᵊl] *adj* mesleki
vodka [ˈvɒdkə] *n* votka
voice [vɔɪs] *n* ses
voicemail [ˈvɔɪsˌmeɪl] *n* sesli posta
void [vɔɪd] *adj* geçersiz ▹ *n* boşluk *(uzay, geometri)*
volcano, volcanoes [vɒlˈkeɪnəʊ, vɒlˈkeɪnəʊz] *n* volkan
volleyball [ˈvɒlɪˌbɔːl] *n* voleybol
volt [vəʊlt] *n* volt
voltage [ˈvəʊltɪdʒ] *n* voltaj; **What's the voltage?** Voltaj ne kadar?
volume [ˈvɒljuːm] *n* hacim
voluntarily [ˈvɒləntərɪlɪ] *adv* gönüllü olarak
voluntary [ˈvɒləntərɪ; -trɪ] *adj* gönüllü
volunteer [ˌvɒlənˈtɪə] *n* gönüllü olmak ▹ *v* gönüllü olmak
vomit [ˈvɒmɪt] *v* kusmak
vote [vəʊt] *n* oy ▹ *v* oy vermek
voucher [ˈvaʊtʃə] *n* kupon; **gift voucher** *n* hediye çeki
vowel [ˈvaʊəl] *n* ünlü *(gramer)*
vulgar [ˈvʌlgə] *adj* kaba *(insan)*
vulnerable [ˈvʌlnərəbᵊl] *adj* savunmasız
vulture [ˈvʌltʃə] *n* akbaba

wafer ['weɪfə] *n* gofret
waffle ['wɒfᵊl] *n* waffle ▹ *v* gevelemek
wage [weɪdʒ] *n* ücret
waist [weɪst] *n* bel
waistcoat ['weɪsˌkəʊt] *n* yelek
wait [weɪt] *v* beklemek; **wait for** *v* beklemek; **waiting list** *n* bekleme listesi; **waiting room** *n* bekleme odası
waiter ['weɪtə] *n* garson
waitress ['weɪtrɪs] *n* kadın garson
wait up [weɪt ʌp] *v* yatmayıp beklemek
waive [weɪv] *v* vazgeçmek
wake up [weɪk ʌp] *v* uyanmak
Wales [weɪlz] *n* Galler
walk [wɔːk] *n* yürüyüş ▹ *v* yürümek; **Are there any guided walks?** Rehberli yürüyüş var mı?; **Do you have a guide to local walks?** Yerel yürüyüşler için rehberiniz var mı?; **How many kilometres is the walk?** Yürüyüş kaç kilometre?
walkie-talkie [ˌwɔːkɪ'tɔːkɪ] *n* telsiz
walking ['wɔːkɪŋ] *n* yürüme; **walking stick** *n* baston
walkway ['wɔːkˌweɪ] *n* yaya yolu
wall [wɔːl] *n* duvar
wallet ['wɒlɪt] *n* cüzdan *(erkek)*; **I've lost my wallet** Cüzdanımı kaybettim; **My wallet has been stolen** Cüzdanım çalındı
wallpaper ['wɔːlˌpeɪpə] *n* duvar kağıdı
walnut ['wɔːlˌnʌt] *n* ceviz
walrus ['wɔːlrəs; 'wɒl-] *n* deniz aygırı
waltz [wɔːls] *n* vals ▹ *v* vals yapmak
wander ['wɒndə] *v* dolaşmak
want [wɒnt] *v* istemek
war [wɔː] *n* savaş; **civil war** *n* iç savaş
ward [wɔːd] *n* *(area)* bölge *(seçim)*, *(hospital room)* koğuş; **Which ward is... in?**... hangi koğuşta?
warden ['wɔːdᵊn] *n* bekçi; **traffic warden** *n* trafik memuru
wardrobe ['wɔːdrəʊb] *n* gardrop
warehouse ['wɛəˌhaʊs] *n* depo
warm [wɔːm] *adj* ılık
warm up [wɔːm ʌp] *v* ısıtmak
warn [wɔːn] *v* uyarmak
warning ['wɔːnɪŋ] *n* uyarı; **hazard warning lights** *npl* tehlike uyarı ışığı
warranty ['wɒrəntɪ] *n* garanti; **The car is still under warranty** Arabanın garantisi var
wart [wɔːt] *n* siğil
wash [wɒʃ] *v* yıkamak; **car wash** *n*

oto yıkama; **I would like to wash the car** Arabayı yıkamak istiyorum
washable ['wɒʃəbᵊl] *adj* **machine washable** *adj* makinede yıkanabilir; **Is it washable?** Bu yıkanabilir mi?
washbasin ['wɒʃˌbeɪsᵊn] *n* lavabo; **The washbasin is dirty** Lavabo kirli
washing ['wɒʃɪŋ] *n* çamaşır; **washing line** *n* çamaşır ipi; **washing machine** *n* çamaşır makinesi; **washing powder** *n* çamaşır tozu
washing-up ['wɒʃɪŋʌp] *n* bulaşık yıkama; **washing-up liquid** *n* bulaşık deterjanı
wash up [wɒʃ ʌp] *v* bulaşık yıkamak
wasp [wɒsp] *n* eşekarısı
waste [weɪst] *n* israf ▹ *v* israf etmek
watch [wɒtʃ] *n* kol saati ▹ *v* gözetlemek; **digital watch** *n* dijital saat
watch out [wɒtʃ aʊt] *v* dikkat etmek
water ['wɔːtə] *n* su ▹ *v* sulamak; **drinking water** *n* içme suyu; **mineral water** *n* maden suyu; **sea water** *n* deniz suyu; **sparkling water** *n* maden suyu; **watering can** *n* bahçe sulama bidonu; **a glass of water** Bir bardak su; **Can you check the water, please?** Suyu kontrol eder misiniz lütfen?; **How deep is the water?** Suyun derinliği ne kadar?; **Is hot water included in the price?** Fiyata sıcak su dahil mi?; **Please bring more water** Biraz daha su getirir misiniz?; **There is no hot water** Sıcak su yok
watercolour ['wɔːtəˌkʌlə] *n* suluboya
watercress ['wɔːtəˌkrɛs] *n* su teresi
waterfall ['wɔːtəˌfɔːl] *n* şelale
watermelon ['wɔːtəˌmɛlən] *n* karpuz
waterproof ['wɔːtəˌpruːf] *adj* su geçirmez
water-skiing ['wɔːtəˌskiːɪŋ] *n* su kayağı; **Is it possible to go water-skiing here?** Burada su kayağı yapmak mümkün mü?
wave [weɪv] *n* dalga ▹ *v* el sallamak
wavelength ['weɪvˌlɛŋθ] *n* dalgaboyu
wavy ['weɪvɪ] *adj* dalgalı
wax [wæks] *n* balmumu
way [weɪ] *n* yol; **right of way** *n* geçiş hakkı; **It wasn't your right of way** Yol hakkı sizin değildi; **She didn't give way** Yol vermedi
way in [weɪ ɪn] *n* giriş *(yer, nokta)*
way out [weɪ aʊt] *n* çıkış
we [wiː] *pron* biz
weak [wiːk] *adj* zayıf *(karakter)*
weakness ['wiːknɪs] *n* zayıflık
wealth [wɛlθ] *n* varlık *(zenginlik)*
wealthy ['wɛlθɪ] *adj* varsıl
weapon ['wɛpən] *n* silah
wear [wɛə] *v* giymek
weasel ['wiːzᵊl] *n* gelincik *(hayvan)*
weather ['wɛðə] *n* hava *(meteoroloji)*; **weather forecast** *n* hava tahmini; **Is the weather going to change?** Hava

değişecek mi?; **What awful weather!** Hava çok berbat!; **What will the weather be like tomorrow?** Hava yarın nasıl olacak?
web [wɛb] *n* ağ; **web address** *n* internet adresi; **web browser** *n* internet tarayıcı
webcam ['wɛb,kæm] *n* internet kamerası
webmaster ['wɛb,mɑːstə] *n* webmaster
website ['wɛb,saɪt] *n* internet sitesi
webzine ['wɛb,ziːn] *n* online magazin
wedding ['wɛdɪŋ] *n* düğün; **wedding anniversary** *n* evlilik yıldönümü; **wedding dress** *n* gelinlik; **wedding ring** *n* yüzük *(nikah)*; **We are here for a wedding** Buraya bir düğüne geldik
Wednesday ['wɛnzdɪ] *n* Çarşamba; **Ash Wednesday** *n* Büyük perhizin ilk Çarşambası; **on Wednesday** Çarşamba günü
weed [wiːd] *n* yabani ot
weedkiller ['wiːd,kɪlə] *n* yabani ot öldürücü
week [wiːk] *n* hafta; **a week ago** bir hafta önce; **How much is it for a week?** Bir haftalığı ne kadar?; **last week** geçen hafta; **next week** gelecek hafta
weekday ['wiːk,deɪ] *n* hafta içi
weekend [,wiːk'ɛnd] *n* hafta sonu; **I want to hire a car for the weekend** Hafta sonu için bir araba kiralamak istiyorum
weep [wiːp] *v* ağlamak
weigh [weɪ] *v* çekmek *(ağırlık)*
weight [weɪt] *n* ağırlık
weightlifter ['weɪt,lɪftə] *n* halterci
weightlifting ['weɪt,lɪftɪŋ] *n* ağırlık kaldırma
weird [wɪəd] *adj* acaip
welcome ['wɛlkəm] *n* karşılama ▷ *v* karşılamak; **welcome!** *excl* hoşgeldiniz!
well [wɛl] *adj* afiyette ▷ *adv* iyi ▷ *n* kuyu; **oil well** *n* petrol kuyusu; **well done!** *excl* aferin!; **He's not well** Hiç iyi değil
well-behaved ['wɛl'bɪ'heɪvd] *adj* iyi yetiştirilmiş
wellies ['wɛlɪz] *npl* lastik çizme
wellingtons ['wɛlɪŋtənz] *npl* lastik çizmeler
well-known ['wɛl'nəʊn] *adj* tanınmış
well-off ['wɛl'ɒf] *adj* hali vakti yerinde
well-paid ['wɛl'peɪd] *adj* yüksek maaşlı
Welsh [wɛlʃ] *adj* Gal ▷ *n* Galli
west [wɛst] *adj* batı ▷ *adv* batıda ▷ *n* batı; **West Indian** *n* Batı Hint Adaları; **West Indies** *npl* Batı Hint Adaları
westbound ['wɛst,baʊnd] *adj* batıya doğru
western ['wɛstən] *adj* batı ▷ *n* kovboy filmi
wet [wɛt] *adj* ıslak
wetsuit ['wɛt,suːt] *n* balıkadam kıyafeti
whale [weɪl] *n* balina
what [wɒt; wət] *adj* ne, nasıl ▷ *pron* ne, nasıl; **What do you do?**

Ne işle meşgulsünüz?; **What is it?** Bu nedir?

wheat [wiːt] *n* buğday; **wheat intolerance** *n* buğday alerjisi

wheel [wiːl] *n* tekerlek; **spare wheel** *n* stepne; **steering wheel** *n* direksiyon

wheelbarrow ['wiːlˌbærəʊ] *n* el arabası

wheelchair ['wiːlˌtʃɛə] *n* tekerlekli sandalye; **Can you visit... in a wheelchair?**... a tekerlekli sandalyeyle gidilebilir mi?; **Do you have a lift for wheelchairs?** Tekerlekli sandalyeler için asansör var mı?; **Do you have wheelchairs?** Tekerlekli sandalyeniz var mı?; **I need a room with wheelchair access** Tekerlekli sandalye girişi olan bir oda istiyorum; **I use a wheelchair** Tekerlekli sandalyedeyim; **Is there wheelchair-friendly transport available to...?** Tekerlekli sandalyeye uygun ulaşım var mı?; **Is your hotel accessible to wheelchairs?** Otelinizde tekerlekli sandalye girişi var mı?; **Where is the nearest repair shop for wheelchairs?** Tekerlekli sandalye tamiri için en yakın dükkan nerede?; **Where is the wheelchair-accessible entrance?** Tekerlekli sandalye girişi nerede?

when [wɛn] *adv* ne zaman ki ▹ *conj* ne zaman; **When does it begin?** Ne zaman başlıyor?; **When does it finish?** Ne zaman bitiyor?

where [wɛə] *adv* nerede ▹ *conj* nerede; **Can you show me where we are on the map?** Nerede olduğumuzu haritada gösterebilir misiniz?; **Where are we?** Neredeyiz?; **Where are you staying?** Nerede kalıyorsunuz?; **Where can we meet?** Nerede buluşabiliriz?; **Where is...?**... nerede?; **Where is the gents?** Erkekler tuvaleti nerede?

whether ['wɛðə] *conj* şayet

which [wɪtʃ] *pron* hangi; **Which is the key for this door?** Bu kapının anahtarı hangisi?

while [waɪls] *conj* iken ▹ *n* sırada

whip [wɪp] *n* kırbaç; **whipped cream** *n* köpük krema

whisk [wɪsk] *n* çırpıcı

whiskers ['wɪskəz] *npl* bıyık

whisky ['wɪskɪ] *n* viski; **malt whisky** *n* malt viskisi; **a whisky and soda** bir viski soda; **I'll have a whisky** Ben viski alayım

whisper ['wɪspə] *v* fısıldamak

whistle ['wɪsᵊl] *n* ıslık ▹ *v* ıslık çalmak

white [waɪt] *adj* beyaz; **egg white** *n* yumurta akı; **a carafe of white wine** Bir sürahi beyaz şarap

whiteboard ['waɪtˌbɔːd] *n* beyaz yazı tahtası

whitewash ['waɪtˌwɒʃ] *v* badanalamak

whiting ['waɪtɪŋ] *n* mezgit

who [huː] *pron* kim; **Who am I talking to?** Kiminle görüşüyorum?; **Who is it?** Kim o?; **Who's calling?** Kim arıyor?

whole [həʊl] *adj* bütün *(tüm)* ▹ *n* bütün *(tamamı)*; **for the whole of**

June bütün Haziran boyunca
wholefoods ['həʊl,fu:dz] *npl* doğal yiyecek
wholemeal ['həʊl,mi:l] *adj* kepekli undan yapılmış
wholesale ['həʊl,seɪl] *adj* toptan satış ▷ *n* toptan
whom [hu:m] *pron* kime, kimi
whose [hu:z] *adj* kime ▷ *pron* kimin
why [waɪ] *adv* niçin
wicked ['wɪkɪd] *adj* hain *(cadı vb)*
wide [waɪd] *adj* geniş *(yayvan)* ▷ *adv* ferah *(geniş)*
widespread ['waɪd,sprɛd] *adj* yaygın
widow ['wɪdəʊ] *n* dul *(kocası/karısı ölmüş)*; **I'm widowed** Dulum
widower ['wɪdəʊə] *n* dul *(kocası/karısı ölmüş)*
width [wɪdθ] *n* genişlik
wife, wives [waɪf, waɪvz] *n* karı *(eş)*
Wi-Fi [waɪ faɪ] *n* WiFi
wig [wɪg] *n* peruk
wild [waɪld] *adj* yabani
wildlife ['waɪld,laɪf] *n* vahşi doğa
will [wɪl] *n (document)* vasiyet, *(motivation)* irade
willing ['wɪlɪŋ] *adj* istekli
willingly ['wɪlɪŋlɪ] *adv* seve seve
willow ['wɪləʊ] *n* söğüt
willpower ['wɪl,paʊə] *n* irade
wilt [wɪlt] *v* solmak
win [wɪn] *v* kazanmak
wind[1] [wɪnd] *n* rüzgar ▷ *vt (with a blow etc.)* esmek *(rüzgar)*
wind[2] [waɪnd] *v (coil around)* esmek *(rüzgar)*
windmill ['wɪnd,mɪl; 'wɪn,mɪl] *n* değirmen
window ['wɪndəʊ] *n* pencere; **shop window** *n* vitrin; **window pane** *n* pencere camı; **window seat** *n* cam kenarı koltuğu; **I can't open the window** Pencereyi açamıyorum; **I'd like a window seat** Koltuğum pencere kenarında olsun; **May I close the window?** Pencereyi kapatabilir miyim?; **May I open the window?** Pencereyi açabilir miyim?
windowsill ['wɪndəʊ,sɪl] *n* pencere pervazı
windscreen ['wɪnd,skri:n] *n* ön cam; **windscreen wiper** *n* cam sileceği
windsurfing ['wɪnd,sɜ:fɪŋ] *n* rüzgar sörfü
windy ['wɪndɪ] *adj* rüzgarlı
wine [waɪn] *n* şarap; **house wine** *n* ev şarabı; **red wine** *n* kırmızı şarap; **table wine** *n* yemeklik şarap; **wine list** *n* şarap listesi; **a bottle of white wine** Bir şişe beyaz şarap; **Can you recommend a good wine?** İyi bir şarap tavsiye edebilir misiniz?; **This wine is not chilled** Bu şarap soğutulmamış
wineglass ['waɪn,glɑ:s] *n* şarap kadehi
wing [wɪŋ] *n* kanat; **wing mirror** *n* yan ayna
wink [wɪŋk] *v* göz kırpmak
winner ['wɪnə] *n* kazanma
winning ['wɪnɪŋ] *adj* kazanan
winter ['wɪntə] *n* kış; **winter sports** *npl* kış sporları
wipe [waɪp] *v* silerek temizlemek; **baby wipe** *n* ıslak bebek mendili

wipe up [waɪp ʌp] *v* silip temizlemek
wire [waɪə] *n* tel; **barbed wire** *n* dikenli tel
wisdom ['wɪzdəm] *n* zeka; **wisdom tooth** *n* yirmi yaş dişi
wise [waɪz] *adj* akıllı
wish [wɪʃ] *n* dilek ▹ *v* dilemek
wit [wɪt] *n* nükte
witch [wɪtʃ] *n* cadı
with [wɪð; wɪθ] *prep* ile
withdraw [wɪð'drɔː] *v* çekmek
withdrawal [wɪð'drɔːəl] *n* çekme
within [wɪ'ðɪn] *prep (space)* içinde, *(term)* içine
without [wɪ'ðaʊt] *prep* onsuz
witness ['wɪtnɪs] *n* tanık; **Jehovah's Witness** *n* Yehovanın Şahitleri; **Can you be a witness for me?** Tanıklık eder misiniz?
witty ['wɪtɪ] *adj* esprili
wolf, wolves [wʊlf, wʊlvz] *n* kurt
woman, women ['wʊmən, 'wɪmɪn] *n* kadın
wonder ['wʌndə] *v* merak etmek
wonderful ['wʌndəfʊl] *adj* harika
wood [wʊd] *n (forest)* koruluk, *(material)* tahta *(ağaç)*
wooden ['wʊdᵊn] *adj* ağaç/tahta
woodwind ['wʊd,wɪnd] *n* ağaç üflemeli *(çalgı)*
woodwork ['wʊd,wɜːk] *n* ağaç işleri
wool [wʊl] *n* yün; **cotton wool** *n* pamuk
woollen ['wʊlən] *adj* yünlü
woollens ['wʊlənz] *npl* yünlüler
word [wɜːd] *n* sözcük
work [wɜːk] *n* iş ▹ *v* çalışmak; **work experience** *n* iş deneyimi; **work of art** *n* sanat eseri; **work permit** *n* çalışma izni; **work station** *n* çalışma köşesi; **I'm here for work** Buraya iş için geldim
worker ['wɜːkə] *n* işçi; **social worker** *n* sosyal hizmetler görevlisi
workforce ['wɜːk,fɔːs] *n* işgücü
working-class ['wɜːkɪŋklɑːs] *adj* işçi sınıfı
workman, workmen ['wɜːkmən, 'wɜːkmɛn] *n* işçi
work out [wɜːk aʊt] *v* çözmek
workplace ['wɜːk,pleɪs] *n* işyeri
workshop ['wɜːk,ʃɒp] *n* atölye
workspace ['wɜːk,speɪs] *n* çalışma alanı
workstation ['wɜːk,steɪʃən] *n* çalışma köşesi
world [wɜːld] *n* dünya; **Third World** *n* Üçüncü Dünya; **World Cup** *n* Dünya Kupası
worm [wɜːm] *n* solucan
worn [wɔːn] *adj* eskimiş
worried ['wʌrɪd] *adj* endişeli
worry ['wʌrɪ] *v* tasalanmak
worrying ['wʌrɪɪŋ] *adj* endişe verici
worse [wɜːs] *adj* daha kötü ▹ *adv* daha kötüsü
worsen ['wɜːsᵊn] *v* kötüleşmek
worship ['wɜːʃɪp] *v* ibadet etmek
worst [wɜːst] *adj* en kötü
worth [wɜːθ] *n* değer; **Is it worth repairing?** Tamir ettirmeye değer mi?
worthless ['wɜːθlɪs] *adj* değersiz
wound [wuːnd] *n* yara ▹ *v* yaralamak
wrap [ræp] *v* sarmak; **wrapping**

paper *n* paket kağıdı
wrap up [ræp ʌp] *v* paketlemek
wreck [rɛk] *n* enkaz ▷ *v* berbat etmek
wreckage ['rɛkɪdʒ] *n* enkaz
wren [rɛn] *n* çalıkuşu
wrench [rɛntʃ] *n* burma ▷ *v* burmak
wrestler ['rɛslə] *n* güreşçi
wrestling ['rɛslɪŋ] *n* güreş
wrinkle ['rɪŋkᵊl] *n* kırışık
wrinkled ['rɪŋkᵊld] *adj* kırışmış
wrist [rɪst] *n* bilek
write [raɪt] *v* yazmak
write down [raɪt daʊn] *v* yazmak
writer ['raɪtə] *n* yazar
writing ['raɪtɪŋ] *n* yazı; **writing paper** *n* yazı kağıdı
wrong [rɒŋ] *adj* yanlış ▷ *adv* yanlış; **wrong number** *n* yanlış numara; **I think you've given me the wrong change** Sanırım yanlış para üstü verdiniz; **The bill is wrong** Hesapta bir yanlışlık var; **You have the wrong number** Yanlış numara

Xmas ['ɛksməs; 'krɪsməs] *n* Noel
X-ray [ɛksreɪ] *n* röntgen ▷ *v* röntgenini çekmek
xylophone ['zaɪləˌfəʊn] *n* ksilofon

Y

yacht [jɒt] *n* yat *(tekne)*
yard [jɑːd] *n* *(enclosure)* avlu, *(measurement)* yarda
yawn [jɔːn] *v* esnemek
year [jɪə] *n* yıl; **academic year** *n* akademik yıl; **financial year** *n* mali yıl; **leap year** *n* artık yıl; **New Year** *n* Yeni Yıl; **Happy New Year!** Mutlu Yıllar!; **last year** geçen yıl; **next year** gelecek yıl; **this year** bu yıl
yearly ['jɪəlɪ] *adj* yıllık ▹ *adv* her yıl
yeast [jiːst] *n* maya
yell [jɛl] *v* bağırmak
yellow ['jɛləʊ] *adj* sarı; **Yellow Pages®** *npl* Sarı Sayfalar
Yemen ['jɛmən] *n* Yemen
yes [jɛs] *excl* evet
yesterday ['jɛstədɪ; -ˌdeɪ] *adv* dün
yet [jɛt] *adv* *(interrogative)* artık, *(with negative)* henüz ▹ *conj* *(nevertheless)* yine de
yew [juː] *n* porsuk ağacı
yield [jiːld] *v* ürün sağlamak
yoga ['jəʊɡə] *n* yoga
yoghurt ['jəʊɡət; 'jɒɡ-] *n* yoğurt
yolk [jəʊk] *n* yumurtanın sarısı
you [juː; jʊ] *pron* *(plural)* siz, *(singular polite)* siz, *(singular)* sen
young [jʌŋ] *adj* genç
younger [jʌŋə] *adj* daha genç
youngest [jʌŋɪst] *adj* en genç
your [jɔː; jʊə; jə] *adj* *(plural)* sizin, *(singular polite)* sizin, *(singular)* senin
yours [jɔːz; jʊəz] *pron* *(plural)* sizinki, *(singular polite)* sizinki, *(singular)* sizinki
yourself [jɔː'sɛlf; jʊə-] *pron* kendin, *(intensifier)* kendin, *(polite)* kendin
yourselves [jɔː'sɛlvz] *pron* *(intensifier)* kendiniz, *(polite)* kendiniz, *(reflexive)* kendiniz
youth [juːθ] *n* gençlik; **youth club** *n* gençlik klubü; **youth hostel** *n* gençlerin kaldığı otel

Z

ambia ['zæmbɪə] *n* Zambiya
ambian ['zæmbɪən] *adj* Zambiya ▹ *n* Zambiyalı
ebra ['zi:brə; 'zɛbrə] *n* zebra; **zebra crossing** *n* şeritli yaya geçidi
ero, zeroes ['zɪərəʊ, 'zɪərəʊz] *n* sıfır
est [zɛst] *n (excitement)* haz, *(lemon-peel)* limon kabuğu
imbabwe [zɪm'bɑ:bwɪ; -weɪ] *n* Zimbabwe
imbabwean [zɪm'bɑ:bwɪən; -weɪən] *adj* Zimbabwe ▹ *n* Zimbabweli
inc [zɪŋk] *n* çinko
ip [zɪp] *n* fermuar; **zip (up)** *v* kapatmak *(fermuar)*
it [zɪt] *n* sivilce
odiac ['zəʊdɪ,æk] *n* burçlar kuşağı
one [zəʊn] *n* bölge *(savaş, kuraklık)*; **time zone** *n* zaman dilimi
zoo [zu:] *n* hayvanat bahçesi
zoology [zəʊ'ɒlədʒɪ; zu:-] *n* hayvanbilim
zoom [zu:m] *n* **zoom lens** *n* zoom merceği
zucchini [tsu:'ki:nɪ; zu:-] *n* kabak